R. LARRY TODD

Carefully scratch off the silver coating with a coin to see your personal redemption code.

This code can be used only once and cannot be shared!

If the code has been scratched off when you receive it, the code may not be valid. Once the code has been scratched off, this access card cannot be returned to the publisher. You may buy access at **www.oup.com/dashboard**.

The code on this card is valid for 2 years from the date of first purchase. Complete terms and conditions are available at **register.dashboard.oup.com**.

Access length: 6 months from redemption of the code.

Directions for registering your **Dashboard Student Account**

Visit **www.oup.com/dashboard** and click the link to redeem your access code.

Select your textbook from the list of available Dashboard courses.

Follow the on-screen instructions to identify your specific course section.

Enter your personal redemption code when prompted on the checkout screen.

Once you complete registration, you are automatically enrolled in your Dashboard course.

For assistance with code redemption or registration for Dashboard, please contact customer support at **dashboard.support@oup.com.**

DISCOVERING *Music*

DISCOVERING *Music*

R. LARRY TODD
Duke University

NEW YORK OXFORD
Oxford University Press

Oxford University Press is a department of the University of Oxford. It furthers the University's objective of excellence in research, scholarship, and education by publishing worldwide. Oxford is a registered trade mark of Oxford University Press in the UK and certain other countries.

Published in the United States of America by Oxford University Press
198 Madison Avenue, New York, NY 10016, United States of America.

For titles covered by Section 112 of the US Higher Education Opportunity Act, please visit www.oup.com/us/he for the latest information about pricing and alternate formats.

Library of Congress Cataloging-in-Publication Data

Names: Todd, R. Larry.
Title: Discovering music / R. Larry Todd.
Description: Oxford ; New York : Oxford University Press, [2017]
Identifiers: LCCN 2016053944 | ISBN 9780190255107 (pbk.)
Subjects: LCSH: Music appreciation.
Classification: LCC MT90 .T54 2017 | DDC 780—dc23 LC record available at
https://lccn.loc.gov/2016053944

Printing Number: 9 8 7 6 5 4 3 2 1
Printed by LSC Communications, Inc.

For my students, past, present, and future

Brief Contents

Contents

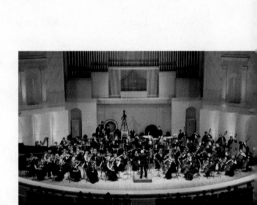

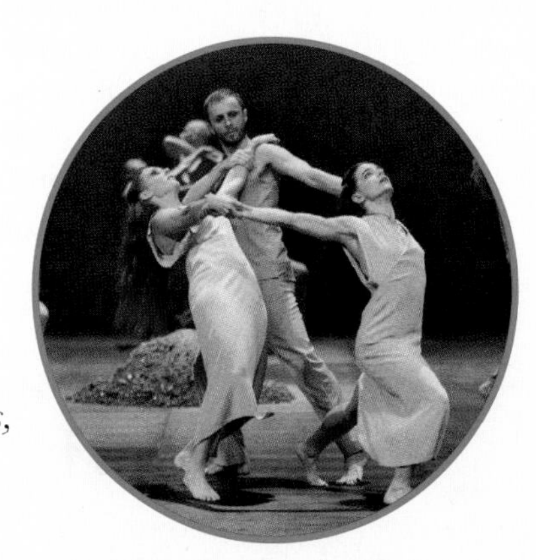

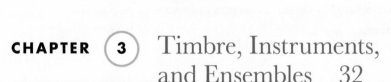

CHAPTER 40 Late Nineteenth-Century Music 380

CHAPTER 43 Neoclassicism 452

CHAPTER 44 National Styles 467

CHAPTER 45 American Music: Beginnings to Aaron Copland 477

A Letter from R. Larry Todd

Dear Student:

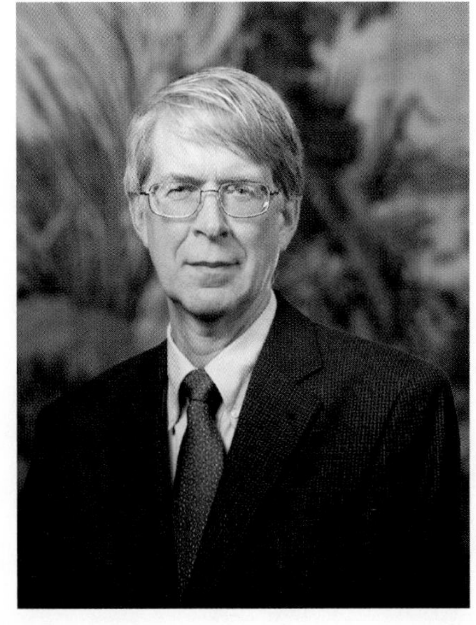

As a music professor, historian, and lifelong pianist, I have a deep-seated love of classical music. But for many of you, I'm sure, classical music is largely an unfamiliar world.

My goals in teaching Music Appreciation are simple: To inspire you to listen to, understand, and enjoy a greater variety of music than they previously have experienced. **I want your lives to be enriched—like mine has been—by the music of our greatest composers and performers.**

I realize that simply introducing classical music and directing you to listen is not enough. It helps first to understand the value of acquiring listening skills. It is essential to pose the question, "Why should I listen?" Providing some answers is, I hope, an important step in inspiring you to want to learn more.

The next step is how to listen. In my text, I have adopted an approach that takes you from recognizing broad patterns and key ideas to deeper levels of understanding. I call these visually engaging charts of each highlighted piece "Listening Maps." In each case, they summarize a few strategic points of entry into the music to build your appreciation and to promote further discovery. I believe these **Listening Maps are easier to understand at a glance than the standard Listening Guides found in other texts.** The Listening Maps are simply structured and color-coded, and they include important details often lacking in Listening Guides.

My mission in writing this book is to give you the tools you need to build lifelong listening skills; to share with you my own appreciation for musical styles; and to trace the amazing narrative of classical musical traditions in all their richness and diversity. As you explore the book, its Listening Maps, and the accompanying audio and visual content I have created, I hope you will find that this complete package offers something new and compelling for you.

R. Larry Todd

Preface

Discovering Music presents an overview of primarily Western music for introductory courses in music appreciation. In colleges and universities today, students taking this course often have a wide variety of musical backgrounds and preparation. Some students have few or no musical skills, while others already have the ability to read and play music to differing degrees, and still others enroll in the course with more advanced levels of musical knowledge. A considerable challenge for the instructor—and the textbook writer—is to strike a suitable level of instruction that meets the varying needs of this diverse group. *Discovering Music* is designed for students with little to no musical backgrounds, yet it has much to offer even to students with musical training. In short, it will help all students get the most out of their listening experience.

Approach

This book discusses eighty works drawn from the history of music, starting in the Middle Ages and continuing through present times. The highlighted works range from the chant *Viderunt omnes*, dating from the fifth century, to the Russian composer Sofia Gubaidulina's Violin Concerto from 2007, and so trace a span of over 1,500 years. Most of the selections are familiar compositions that have long been considered masterpieces and standard repertoire of the Western classical tradition. How they connect with one another is a remarkable, ever-changing narrative that constantly engages our musical imaginations. Fixtures in the concert hall, these compositions represent snapshots of the rich historical flow of music. In these moments, we can explore why a particular composer and composition speak to us, resonate with us, and ultimately move us.

Relating this vast stretch of time to our present-day preoccupations and needs is not an easy task. How do we explain to students why a remote piece of chant from the Middle Ages, a complex, brainy fugue of J. S. Bach, or a challenging modernist experiment from the twentieth century is relevant to their lives? The answer, perhaps, is to recognize that where we are today is unavoidably a reflection of history writ large. All of this music *is* connected, though we do not often see (or take the time to see) how it is bound together. There is, too, the issue of how different generations value music from different historical periods. Bach's music fell into neglect after his death in 1750, and its revival was a long process that took much of the nineteenth and twentieth centuries. In the 1990s, the music of the seer-like Hildegard of Bingen from the distant twelfth century, largely unknown and forgotten, was rediscovered and suddenly found favor. Today's students are seemingly further and further removed from the Western classical tradition, but that does not mean that the music is mute, or that it can no longer speak to them.

Music that has established a foothold in time remains relevant to our postmodern world in powerful ways. There is something universal about Monteverdi's treatment of the Orpheus myth in *Orfeo*, Beethoven's iconic Fifth Symphony, or

Stravinsky's *Rite of Spring*. Even though these works come down to us from utterly different historical times, we can still connect with them meaningfully.

At the outset, music appreciation students need to develop certain basic skills in how to listen, but they also need to consider why to listen. This book begins by reviewing fundamentals of Western music before launching its historical survey. Then, as each new composition is introduced, the text offers guidance on both *how* and *why* to listen. Here I have adopted a strategy that aims to demystify the experience of listening to unfamiliar music. The reasons for why to listen vary considerably. They can range, for example, from considering how music can mirror a text, to analyzing the shifting dynamics of a soloist versus a group of musicians. We might listen to examine how music can present dramatic conflict and resolve it, or how music can satisfy our contrasting needs for structure and spontaneity. The Western classical tradition operates not only in the purely musical realm but also in the realm of ideas. Sometimes these ideas are encoded in texts, but often not; sometimes they are mirrored clearly in the music (for example, the idea of spring in Vivaldi's *Four Seasons* and Stravinsky's *Rite of Spring*), and sometimes they are just roughly sketched or suggested.

Features

Discovering Music offers the depth, breadth, and context that students need, in a concise format that is visually appealing. Written to inspire students to connect intellectually and emotionally with music from the Western canon and beyond, the text is supported by a suite of online ancillaries, including interactive listening maps, videos and animations, an instructor's manual, a computerized test bank, and an interactive e-book.

- Visual **Listening Maps** help students follow along and engage with each piece. They include four main components:
    - **Opening table** of basic information, clearly identifying form, meter, tempo, and scoring and providing a brief overview
    - **"Why to Listen"** description, explaining the special significance of the piece
    - **"First Listen"** chart, color coded to show the basic structure of the piece at a glance, with timings
    - **"A Deeper Listen"** chart, showing more detail, also with timings and color coded to match "First Listen." Some entries include numbered annotations that call out particular points in the music and tie in with the narrative of the main text.
- **Making Connections boxes** highlight intriguing historical and cultural links with the music discussed, deepening the listening context.
- **Check Your Knowledge questions** at the end of each chapter help students test their comprehension of key concepts as they read.
- **Part Overviews with Timelines** introduce the text's parts, previewing the following chapters and providing cultural context.
- **Part Summaries** conclude each part, providing lists of key terms and composers and a bulleted recap.

- **Women composers** are well represented throughout the text, with examples drawn from Hildegard of Bingen, Fanny Mendelssohn Hensel, Clara Schumann, Amy Beach, Bessie Smith, Ellen Taaffe Zwilich, and Sofia Gubaidulina.
- **Musical Journey interludes** between parts broaden the coverage to introduce world music, helping place Western music in the larger context of non-Western cultures.

Marginal links indicate that related videos and other material are available online at OUP's Dashboard site.

Organization

Discovering Music begins by considering the basic elements of Western music, divided into easy-to-follow categories, including pitch, rhythm and meter, texture, dynamics, instruments and timbre, and form. A short chapter then sketches the principal historical periods and their musical styles. The first part ends with a chapter titled "How to Listen," which introduces John Philip Sousa's march "The Stars and Stripes Forever" and applies the concepts presented in the preceding chapters.

In Part II, the text begins its historical survey with the Middle Ages, followed in turn by the Renaissance, Baroque, Classical, Romantic, and Modern Era sections. Positioned within the narrative of Western music are six fermata-like interludes, carefully chosen and prepared by Andrew Shahriari of Kent State University, that remind us that Western music is of course part of a larger narrative of world music. These interludes feature the same type of Listening Maps found in the rest of the book, enabling students to make connections and distinctions among musical traditions.

Each historical part begins with a part opener and timeline, designed to introduce students to musical and cultural highlights from each period. The chapters within each part then offer a mixture of history and musical style, focusing on principal composers and their innovations. The selected works have been chosen to enhance students' understanding of the musical past, and its relevance to us today.

Discovering Music is the product of many years of teaching, playing, and listening to this music. It provides just one approach that speaks to our need for music, relating broad aesthetic concepts to the experience of listening to great compositions from across the centuries. When all is said and done, this book can only offer selected entry points into a rich musical tradition that remains inexhaustible.

Dashboard

The complete Discovering Music program delivers everything that instructors and students need to succeed in Music Appreciation.

Dashboard for *Discovering Music* delivers streaming audio, video, digital listening maps, auto-graded assessment material, an interactive eBook, and more in a simple, intuitive, and mobile-friendly format. Marginal icons in the text direct students to related content on Dashboard. A built-in color-coded gradebook allows instructors to track student progress in real time.

Dashboard for *Discovering Music* includes:

- **Interactive eBook** with embedded audio and video
- Streaming audio for all key pieces discussed in the text
- **Digital Listening Maps** that animate the First Listen segment of the in-text Listening Maps
- **Author videos** featuring R. Larry Todd explaining and demonstrating key concepts
- **Instrument videos hosted by members of the Boston Symphony Orchestra, created specifically for Dashboard**
- **Early instrument demonstrations** from the Peabody Conservatory
- **Opera performance videos**
- **Auto-graded assessments and activities**

A Dashboard access card is included with all new copies of the softcover and loose leaf text. Students may also purchase access separately at your campus bookstore or online with a credit card at www.oup.com/dashboard.

A full set of instructor resources on the Ancillary Resource Center (ARC) makes course prep easier. Resources include a computerized test bank, PowerPoint lecture outlines, and a detailed Instructor's Manual. After obtaining your access code from your Oxford representative, follow this link to access this material: https://arc2.oup-arc.com/

Contact your Oxford University Press representative or call 800.280.0280 for additional information on accessing these resources.

Acknowledgments

In the course of writing this textbook, I have acquired considerable debts; to acknowledge them here is a particularly pleasant task. First, to my editors at Oxford University Press I owe my heartiest thanks—to Richard Carlin for his vision of and support for this book, and to Lauren Mine for her many suggestions that improved it considerably, and for efficiently finding solutions for the more intractable aspects of the production process. Peter Chambers contributed several ideas that improved the prose, and Michele Laseau and Renata De Oliviera created attractive designs and layouts for the book, while Marianne Paul, the production editor, oversaw assembling all the various parts of the whole. I am indebted to Andrew Shahriari of Kent State University for writing several world-music interludes, and for eloquently reminding us that the Western tradition remains part of a much broader, global perspective. Several former students, including Angela Mace, Kirsten Rutschmann, Sidney Richardson, and Katharina Uhde, have worked beyond the call to prepare and polish musical examples. To the many colleagues listed below who have offered much needed feedback about the text, including its listening diagrams, illustrations, and much else, my best thanks. And to my duo partners Nancy Green and Katharina Uhde, my deepest gratitude for their collaboration in the videos, and to Michael Stipe for recording and producing them. I am always in debt to my dear friend Paul Green Jr. for the use of his impeccable Steinway D and to the wise Socrates, and I would be remiss if I did not single out Gretchen Hoag and Rick Nelson at Duke University, Katharina Uhde and Joseph Bognar at Valparaiso University for assistance with the video projects, and Wiley Ross and Doug Linn for audio engineering. Finally, to my wife, Karin, my love and thanks yet again for tolerating the vagaries of an author and his prose. Her unflagging support was critical to completing this project.

List of Reviewers:

Kelley Alig, *East Central University (OK)*
Scott Bacon, *Drexel University*
Michael Barta, *Southern Illinois University—Carbondale*
Charles Bates, *Ohio Northern University*
Will Benson, *Cleveland State CC*
Michael Boyle, *Oklahoma City CC*
Angela Mace Christian, *Colorado State University*
Alfred W. Cochran, *Kansas State University*
Seth Coluzzi, *Brandeis University*
John Michael Cooper, *Southwestern University*
Robert Culbertson, *Lamar University*
Vicki Curry, *James Madison University*
Chris Dickey, *Washington State University*
Dr. Dawn M. Farmer, *Saint Mary's College*
Brian Gillentine, *Itawamba CC*
Howard Goldstein, *Auburn University*
Graham G. Hunt, *The University of Texas at Arlington*
Yoshi Ishikawa, *Univ. of Colorado, Boulder*
Heather Killmeyer, *East Tennessee State University*
Emil Koester, *Riverside CC—Norco*
Paul Konye, *Siena College*
Thomas Labe, *Cameron University*
Ben Leggett, *Southwest Tennessee CC*
Jason Lester, *Wharton County Junior College*
Timothy Maynard, *Lone Star College—Montgomery*
Christina MacDonald, *Florida State University*

Scott Meredith, *University of Wyoming*
Jeff Meyer, *Concordia College*
Michael Monroe, *Gordon College*
Sheryl Murphy-Manley, *Sam Houston State University*
Alana Nelson, *Northern Illinois University*
Jocelyn Nelson, *East Carolina University*
Christopher Nigrelli, *Lenoir-Rhyne University*
Lynn Payette, *National Park Community College*
Katrina Phillips, *Alabama State University*
Emily Pollock, *Massachusetts Institute of Technology*
Gary Pritchard, *Cerritos College*
Mary Procopio, *Mott Community College*
Laura M. Pruett, *Merrimack College*
James Schlefer, *NYC College of Technology*
Jed Smart, *Southern Union State CC (AL)*
Cecelia Smith, *South Texas College*
Rebecca Sorley, *U of Indianapolis*
Michael Staron, *Triton College*
Michael Strasser, *Baldwin Wallace University*
Eric Strother, *Anderson University*
Micah Volz, *Central Michigan University*
Marvin Williams, *Kingsborough CC*
Dr. Jacob Womack, *Concord University*
Beverlie Yocum, *Leigh Carbon CC*
Allen Zurcher, *Gannon University*

DISCOVERING *Music*

PART

The Elements of Music

My idea is that there is music in the air, music all around us, the world is full of it and you simply take as much as you require. —SIR EDWARD ELGAR

Music is all around us, but we must learn how to listen. The swooping, curving steel exterior of the Walt Disney Concert Hall in Los Angeles captures the excitement of listening to great music.

Listening to music, whether absorbing it passively or dwelling on it actively, involves receiving a stream of information that stimulates and challenges the brain. Consider the famous four notes that open Beethoven's Fifth Symphony, readily available online. You will instantly recognize the burst of three rapid notes followed by a fourth, prolonged note that stops the music in its tracks. What information do those notes communicate?

Quite a lot, it turns out. These auditory signals simultaneously identify details such as:

- the height of the pitches,
- how long they last (their durations),
- which instruments are playing them, and
- how loud they are.

We may not consciously worry about these details when we hear the opening of Beethoven's symphony or any other piece of music. But they combine to create a powerful overall effect. If we can begin to appreciate how different aspects of music work and interact, we can enhance the pleasure of listening.

That is the goal of the first part of this book, organized into six chapters. In Chapters 1 and 2, we will introduce the basic concepts of:

- *pitch* and how it is notated, along with melody and key;
- *rhythm* (which concerns durations of pitches);
- *texture* in music (how musical fabrics can be created in different ways); and
- *dynamics* (the relative intensity of sound).

Chapters 3 and 4 discuss common instruments and introduce the idea of form in Western music. Chapter 5 takes up the concept of classical music and briefly reviews the main stylistic periods we will encounter, from the Middle Ages to the present. Chapter 6 gives us an opportunity to sharpen our listening skills by applying some of the concepts from Chapters 1 through 5 to a well-known piece of American music. But first we will start by exploring the elementary musical sounds known as pitches and the concepts of melody and key.

Autograph manuscript of Beethoven's Fifth Symphony.

CHAPTER

1 Pitch, Melody, and Key

Speaking broadly, we can define music as sounds heard over time in succession. We might further specify that these sounds are organized in some way.

Try this experiment. Start a timer on your phone, and over ten minutes, note every sound that you hear and what time it begins and ends. When you are finished, you will have created a "score" for a musical performance consisting of a series of sounds in a specific timed progression. The more precisely you note the times, the more accurate the score will be. Of course, there are more properties of a sound than merely its beginning and ending. We also need to consider whether a sound is high or low, loud or soft, sharp or smooth, grating or soothing—not to mention other elements that come into play. In addition, a sound may change in quality over time: it may start out rough but then become smoother, or vice versa. The more you refine your "score," the more accurately you will be able to reproduce the sound events later.

Over the centuries, musicians and those who study music have grappled with the need to develop both a language to describe musical sounds and a system to notate music in time. In this chapter, we will begin with the basic concepts of **pitch**—how high or low a musical sound is—and how to notate it.

Pitch

All musical instruments produce sounds by setting a vibrating medium in motion. For pianos and violins, the medium is strings; for organs and flutes, it is columns of air; for drums, it is stretched membranes; and for the human voice, it is vocal cords. **Frequencies** are the rates of vibrations produced. To the human ear, audible frequencies range from about 20 to 20,000 vibrations per second.

A musical sound projects first and foremost a **fundamental pitch**, determined by the length of the vibrating column of string or other material. The longer the column, the lower the pitch. The longest organ pipes or piano strings produce their lowest fundamental pitches; the shortest organ pipes or piano strings produce their highest fundamental pitches. In the case of a drum, the overall size (or area) of the vibrating membrane will determine the fundamental pitch.

The shorter the bars on this marimba, the higher the pitch.

A vibrating medium also emits considerably fainter sounds known as **partials**, **harmonics**, or **overtones**.

A musical pitch is actually a blend of the fundamental pitch and these fainter sounds. If the fundamental is obscured, such as when two sticks are struck or rubbed together, we hear the sound as non-pitched noise. But when a flutist blows into a flute, for example, causing vibrations in a column of air, we hear the resulting sounds as musical pitches.

A pitch is thus a blend of many vibrations generated through a medium such as a taut string or a column of air. Figure 1.1 shows a string fixed at two points. When the string is plucked, the entire length vibrates to produce both the fundamental pitch and the fainter pitches known as partials. These partials are generated by periodic vibrations that activate portions of the string: one-half, one-third, one-fourth, and so on. Several partials—vibrating along with the fundamental, in halves, thirds, and quarters—combine to create the composite pitch.

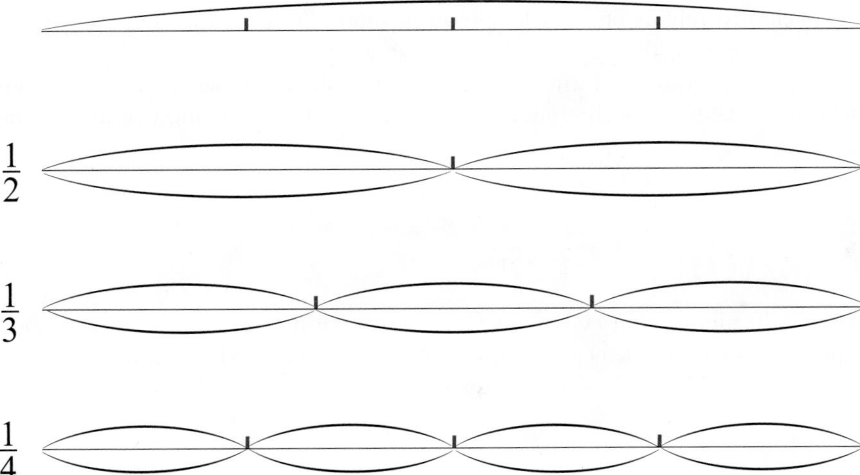

FIG. 1.1 Representation of a fundamental pitch and its partials.

Different instruments or voices sound differently because each produces a unique combination of fundamental pitches and partials. A **tone**, or musical sound that is "pure," is one that has no partials; while this doesn't exist in nature, you can hear such tones by using a music synthesizer. Pure tones lack the richness that partials give. On the other end of the spectrum, we define **noise** as sound that is so rich in overlapping partials that the fundamental pitch is obscured.

Listening to music, we sense that certain pitches are higher or lower than others and that some are close together while others are farther apart. If you sing the opening of "The Star-Spangled Banner," for example, you can easily recognize that the pitch for the word "say" is considerably lower than the pitch for "see." You will also notice that the pitches for "by the dawn's" are clustered together, while those for "say can you see" are separated by wider gaps. We can make a simple diagram showing these relationships:

Oh, say, can you see, by the dawn's

As this example shows, the anthem begins with a dramatic drop in pitch, followed by a steady climb until the word "by," then a gradual descent to the word "dawn's."

When we hum a tune, we are aware of its general shape: whether it ascends or descends, centers on a few pitches in a narrow range, or actively leaps about. With training, musicians can refine their sense of pitch, and some can accurately identify pitches by relying on their long-term memory. Only a few—about one in ten thousand—possess this special ability, known as "perfect pitch." But for everyone, music is a succession of distinct sounds. Distinguishing the height of these sounds helps us make sense of the music and, ultimately, derive the most pleasure from listening.

Notating Pitch

Around the ninth century CE, early forms of **notation**, a system of written symbols representing musical elements, appeared. Not until centuries later, however, did the five-line **staff** (Fig. 1.2) became common.

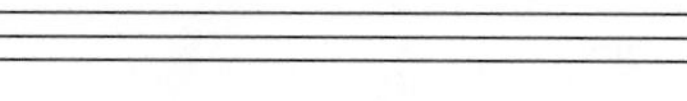

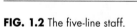

FIG. 1.2 The five-line staff.

The five lines and four spaces of the modern staff accommodate nine pitches, represented by oval-shaped symbols known as **notes** (see Fig. 1.3). Notes can be positioned either on the lines or in the spaces, and higher positions represent higher pitches. Extensions of the staff, called **ledger lines** (short horizontal lines placed

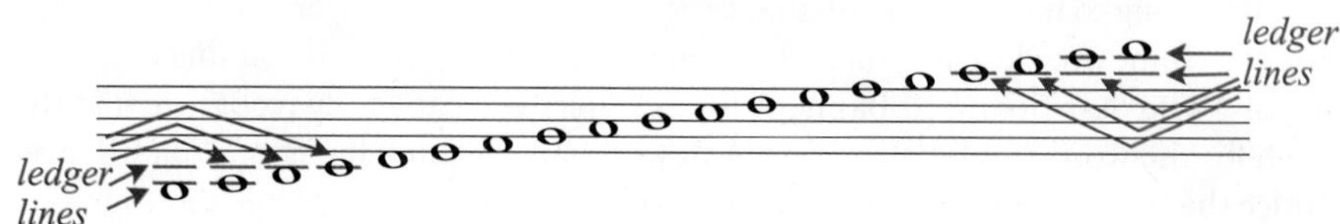

FIG. 1.3 Note positions on the staff.

MAKING CONNECTIONS *The Physics of Sound: The Octave*

The ancient Greeks were among the first to discover a unique property of the octave. As we have already discussed, if you pluck a length of string, you will hear a fundamental pitch, representing the full vibration of the string from end to end. If you then divide the string in half and pluck it, you will hear the same pitch, but it will be an octave higher. You could continue halving the string, and each new length would produce the next higher octave.

For example, a string vibrating end to end 440 times a second produces the pitch A above "middle" C on the piano keyboard. Divided in half, that string would vibrate 880 times per second (twice as fast) and produce the A an octave above. If you were to double the original string in length, the vibration rate would be 220 per second, and you would hear the A an octave *below* the original A.

The ancient Greek poet Sappho with a lyre.

below or above the staff), can accommodate pitches outside this range. Notes are read from left to right.

We use seven letters of the alphabet to identify pitches: A, B, C, D, E, F, and G (in ascending order). After G, the cycle begins again. A complete series of eight pitches—such as A, B, C, D, E, F, G, and A again; or C, D, E, F, G, A, B, and C again—spans a distance known as an **octave**. Octaves are a convenient way to measure the ranges of musical instruments. For example, the piano has a range of a little more than seven octaves; the flute, on the other hand, is limited to about three octaves.

CLEFS

A sign known as a **clef** appears at the beginning of a staff to help identify pitches. Different instruments use different clefs, but two are the most common:

The **treble clef** (𝄞) specifies higher pitches

The **bass clef** (𝄢) specifies lower pitches

Instruments that have a high range (for instance, the flute, trumpet, or violin) are notated using the treble clef, and instruments with a low range (trombone, tuba, or string bass) use the bass clef. The piano, because of its extended range of eighty-eight keys, spans the bass and treble registers, so piano music normally shows notes using both clefs, on separate staves that are bracketed together (Fig. 1.4).

FIG. 1.4 Treble and bass clefs in piano music.

A quick look at a piano keyboard helps illustrate which pitches appear on the two clefs. By convention, the treble clef establishes that the second line of the staff is for the pitch G above middle C on the piano (see Fig. 1.5). **Middle C** is the fortieth of the eighty-eight keys and is notated on the first ledger line below the treble staff or on the first above the bass staff. The bass clef establishes the fourth line from the bottom of the staff as the pitch F below middle C.

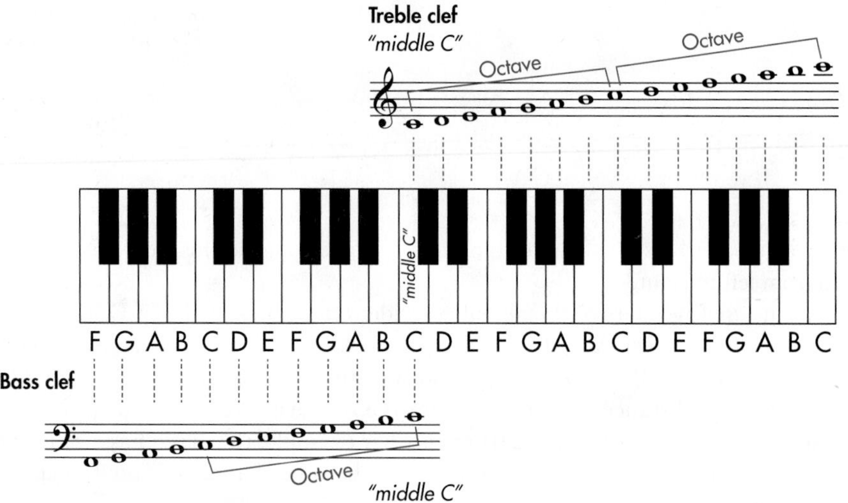

FIG. 1.5 Pitches on the treble and bass clefs.

SHARPS, FLATS, AND NATURALS

In addition to the seven basic pitches represented by the letters A through G, Western music uses other pitches that lie between. The most common are five pitches produced by the black keys on the piano, for a total of twelve different pitches. These keys are located between the white keys (with the exceptions of E and F, and B and C, which have no black keys between them). A **sharp** (♯) is slightly higher than a basic pitch, and a **flat** (♭) is slightly lower than a basic pitch.

Depending on the context, different names apply to the black keys and the pitches they produce. As an example, consider the black key between middle C and D, indicated in Figure 1.6: it could be labeled either C♯ or D♭. A **natural sign** (♮) cancels a preceding flat or sharp, so that in our example, D♮ is the same as D.

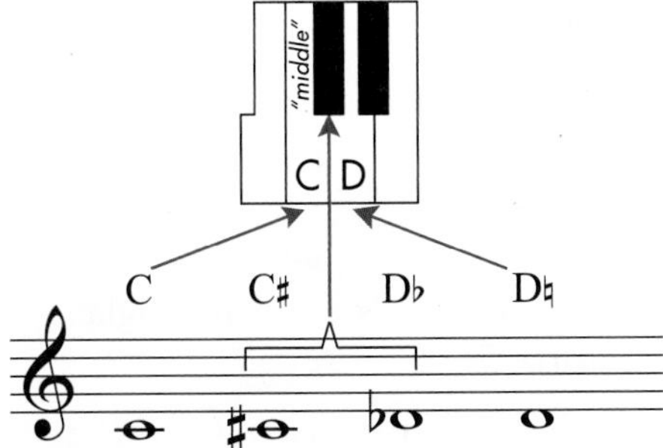

FIG. 1.6 C♯ or D♭.

Often, the same sharped or flatted notes remain valid throughout a large part of a composition, if not its entirety. In these cases, a **key signature** immediately after the clefs at the beginning of the staves indicates the relevant sharps or flats. Some examples of key signatures are shown in Figure 1.7.

FIG. 1.7 Key signature examples.

An **accidental** is a sharp, flat, or natural that indicates a momentary departure from the key signature by raising or lowering a note. In notation, all accidentals appear immediately *before* the notes they modify.

Melody

By themselves, individual pitches are not especially memorable. But if we string together a succession of several pitches into a particular shape, a distinctive **melody**, or musically satisfying series, appears. Let's return to "The Star-Spangled Banner" and reconsider its opening text, arranged here to approximate the shape of the melody:

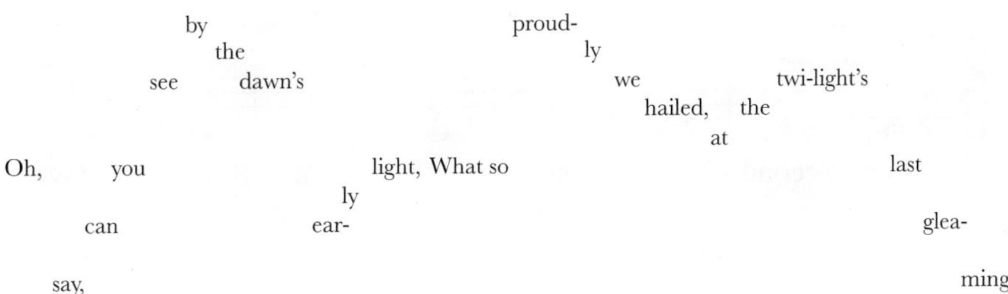

Now, here are the text and melody in musical notation:

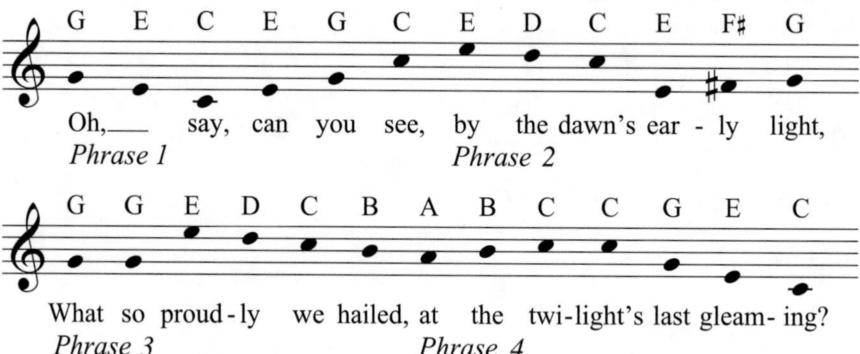

The notated version takes up less space on the page and gives the information about each pitch in a more direct way. The original diagram is more open to interpretation, as the exact pitches of each note are not shown.

PHRASES AND INTERVALS

As anyone who has sung "The Star-Spangled Banner" knows, it consists of several melodic portions, or **phrases**. Each one, marked by the punctuation in the text, has its own mixture of descending and ascending pitches. Occasionally, a phrase ends with a pause, known as a **cadence**, which gives a sense of momentary rest or, at the end of the melody, conclusion. In our excerpt, the music comes to a cadence at the end of the phrase "at the twilight's last gleaming."

Each phrase in a melody consists of several pitches. The distance between any two pitches is known as an **interval**. Some intervals are relatively small; in fact, some move smoothly by step between neighboring pitches, as in "by the dawn's." Other intervals are larger and entail leaps between pitches, as in "Oh, say, can you see."

The number of steps between consecutive pitches determines the size of an interval. Thus, two adjacent pitches form the interval of a second. By gradually increasing the distance between two pitches, we may generate intervals of a second, third, fourth, fifth, sixth, seventh, and finally, octave (*not* an eighth). When two musicians play or sing the exact same pitch, the interval is known as a **unison**.

Figure 1.8 gives a summary of the basic interval types.

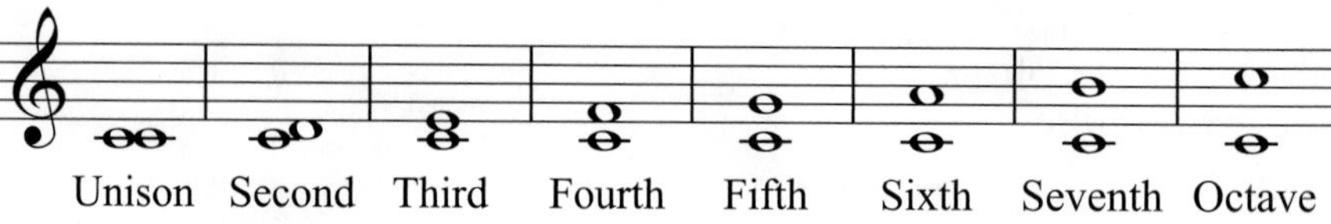

FIG. 1.8 Basic interval types.

Typically, melodies use a variety of intervals that mix **conjunct motion** (by step) and **disjunct motion** (by leap). In "The Star-Spangled Banner," we encounter examples of both conjunct and disjunct intervals. "By the" is a conjunct descending second (one step down); disjunct intervals include thirds (descending: "Oh, __"; ascending: "say, can"), an ascending fourth ("you see"), and a descending sixth ("dawn's ear-").

CONSONANCE AND DISSONANCE

To Western ears, some intervals have a harsh quality and are thus called **dissonances**. A common example is the interval of the second; its jangling, dissonant qualities are particularly evident if two adjacent pitches, say C and D, are played simultaneously.

Of the larger intervals, thirds and sixths (e.g., C-E and C-A) have a more rounded, pleasant quality and are thus considered **consonances**.

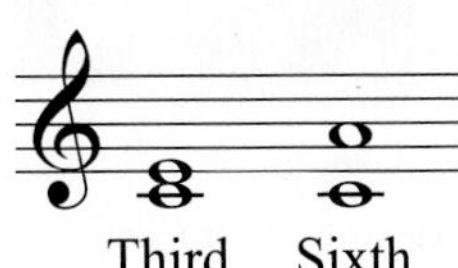

Some common fourths and fifths, for example, C-F, C-G, have a hollow, stable quality and are also considered consonant.

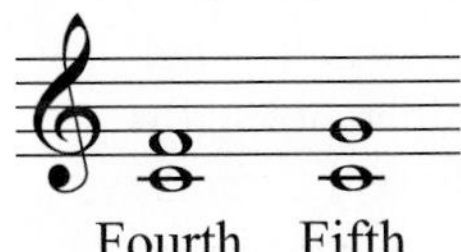

Sevenths, for example C-B, have an angular, unstable quality and are dissonant.

Another interval type, the consonant octave, forms a special category because its pitches duplicate each other and seem to blend together. (When male and female voices sing the same melody, they naturally duplicate, or double, one another in octaves.)

How did we come to accept certain intervals as consonant and others as dissonant? The answer involves the acoustical properties of pitches, the neurology of how we hear them, and some ideas dating back to the ancient Greeks (see Making Connections below). Other cultures may perceive these intervals differently. For now, we'll underscore simply that consonance and dissonance are fundamental to most music.

From infancy we are conditioned to associate dissonance with stress and tension, and consonance with relaxation and resolution. Dissonance can create a sense

MAKING CONNECTIONS *The Ancient Greeks and Consonances*

Pythagoras experimenting with musical pitches.

The ancient Greeks were among the first to study musical pitches. Pythagoras, a sixth-century BCE philosopher-mathematician, is credited with discovering the basic ratio that underlies the common octave. Two fixed strings, columns of air, or other sounding media in a 2:1 ratio produce two pitches one octave apart. Similarly, the ratio 3:2 produces a fifth, and 4:3 produces a fourth.

The Greeks used these basic formulas to represent basic intervals, which they described as consonant and reflecting the mathematical harmony of the universe. Some early philosophers believed that the movement of the planets emitted inaudible musical sounds, also drawn from these special interval relationships. This idea, known as the *music of the spheres*, was prevalent among astronomers and musicians for centuries.

Pythagoras was highly esteemed in the West. He was often depicted plucking strings of different lengths, playing flutes or bells of different sizes, or weighing hammers of different sizes representing simple mathematical ratios. When struck on an anvil, the hammers produced the desired consonant intervals.

of disorder or, if prolonged, chaos; consonance, on the other hand, can create a sense of order and agreement. Most Western music is built on consonant musical intervals, into which dissonances are introduced to provide variety. Until the twentieth century, classical composers generally observed routine rules about how to use dissonances. Typically, a dissonance moved to a consonance, creating first a sense of tension and then relaxation. By increasing the number of dissonances in a piece, composers could powerfully affect listeners' response to their music.

Key

Regardless of how they use consonant and dissonant intervals, Western composers typically construct their melodies around prominently recurring pitches. Usually a melody develops from a central or basic pitch known as the **tonic**. By isolating the basic pitch and then building an ascending series of pitches in an octave, we can generate a **scale**, which determines the **key** of the particular melody. For example, if the central pitch is C, we say that the melody is in the key of C, and use a scale beginning on C to generate the most prominent pitches in the melody. If the central pitch of the melody is F, then that melody is in the key of F, and so on.

THE MAJOR AND MINOR SCALES

The vast majority of Western music depends on one of two scales, the **major scale** or **minor scale**, in use since about the sixteenth century. Major and minor scales have eight pitches each, and these scales can be generated by any of the twelve pitches Western composers commonly use. That means that there are twelve major scales, and twelve minor scales, for a total of twenty-four. To understand the difference between major and minor, we will look briefly at a C-major and a C-minor scale.

Fig. 1.9 shows a major scale based on C—that is, a C-major scale.

FIG. 1.9 C-major scale.

Watch Larry Todd demonstrate the major and minor scales.

This scale consists of eight pitches, with seven steps. **Half steps** (or **semitones**), the smallest interval commonly used in Western music, occur between the third and fourth pitches, and between the seventh and eighth. Slightly larger **whole steps** (or **whole tones**), which contain two half steps, occur elsewhere in the scale. Our version of "The Star-Spangled Banner" consists almost exclusively of pitches from this scale.

The minor scale based on C—that is, a C-minor scale—also consists of half steps and whole steps, but they occur in a different order, as Figure 1.10 shows.

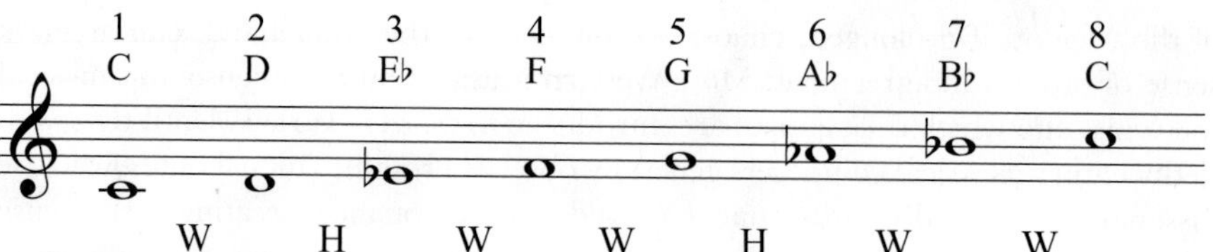

FIG. 1.10 C-minor scale.

The main distinguishing feature of the minor scale is its third pitch, which is always one half-step lower than the corresponding third pitch of the major scale. This change affects the basic character of the scale; for many, it sounds dark and somewhat melancholy in comparison to the major scale, which sounds bright and cheerful. We can hear this difference in many well-known melodies based on minor scales, such as "We Three Kings" and "When Johnny Comes Marching Home Again" ("The Ants Go Marching One by One"). In "We Three Kings," the lower third occurs on "kings"; in "When Johnny Comes Marching Home Again," the lower third occurs on "home":

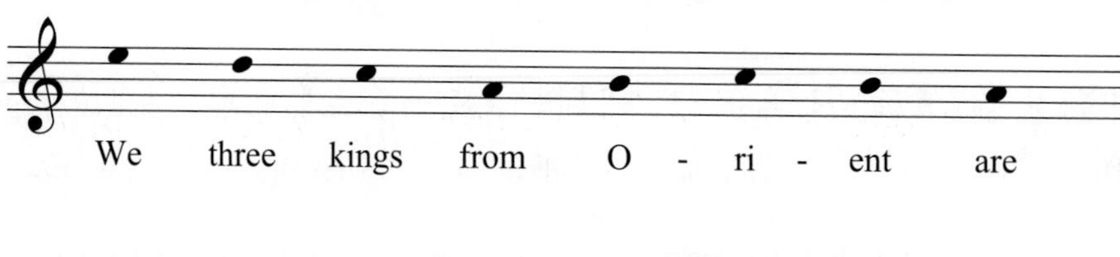

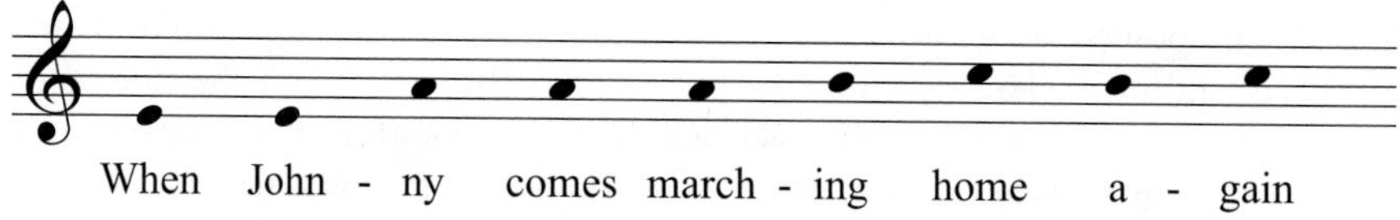

In contrast, the carol "Joy to the World" offers a good example of the raised major third. The melody begins with a descending major scale, in which the raised third appears on "Lord":

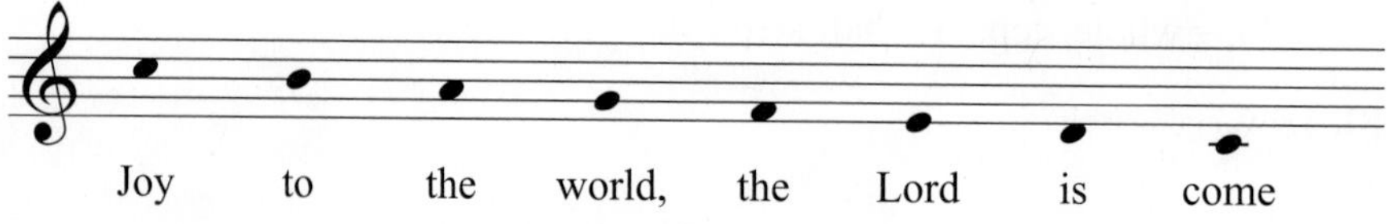

THE CHROMATIC SCALE

If we take the pitches represented by the seven letter names (A, B, C, D, E, F, and G; think, the seven white keys of the piano), and add five more pitches (think, the five black keys of the piano), we end up with twelve different pitches before we start duplicating the letter names one octave higher. Put another way, in Western music we divide the octave into twelve steps, each of which we define as a half-step (or semitone). Two half steps make up a whole step (or whole tone). Figure 1.11 shows the twelve steps, starting on "middle" C.

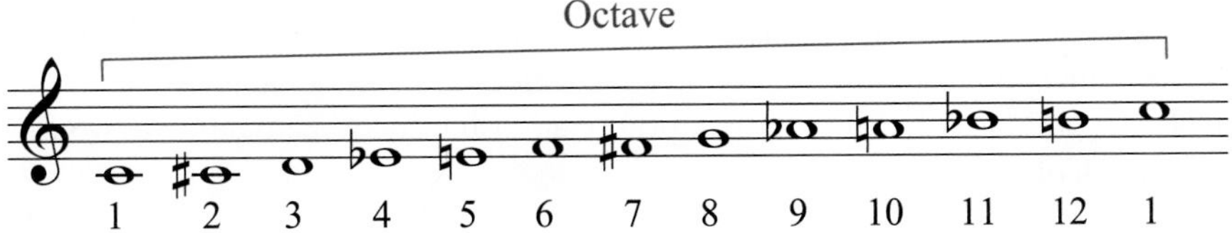

FIG. 1.11 The chromatic scale.

Larry Todd demonstrates the chromatic scale.

Taken together, these twelve steps constitute the **chromatic scale**. Music of some non-Western cultures might divide the octave differently, using, for example, intervals smaller than a half-step. And, we should add, some Western composers bent on experimenting have used divisions of the octave other than the chromatic scale. But the vast majority of the music you will hear, and almost all the music

MAKING CONNECTIONS *Alternative Scales*

Although we take the major and minor scales for granted—they are, in effect, default choices for most of the Western music we hear—there are other possible ways to devise scales. For example, folk music of various cultures often uses what are known as *gapped scales*, similar to a major scale. One of the most common is the *pentatonic scale*, which features only five different pitches per octave, instead of seven (Fig. MC 1.2).

FIG. MC 1.1 Pentatonic scale.

By the twentieth century, several composers were actively seeking other alternatives to the major and minor scales, then thought to be too traditional and outmoded for modernist tastes. One alternative was to divide the octave equally into six whole steps, in order to produce what came to be known as a *whole-tone scale* (Fig. MC 1.2).

FIG. MC 1.2 Whole-tone scale.

Still other twentieth-century composers went even further, and tried to "emancipate" all twelve pitches of the chromatic scale, so that they could be used in various configurations before any were repeated. This radically new type of music came to be known as *twelve-tone music* (see p. 432).

The need to experiment has led composers to explore many alternatives to the major and minor scales. Nevertheless, the major and minor scales have survived, more or less intact, and still form the basis of much of today's music.

described in this book, recognizes the division of the octave into twelve half-steps. This division is commonplace in the music we hear every day.

Whether simple or complex, melodies are an essential part of the Western musical experience. One might think that, given the limited number of pitches in the major and minor scales, eventually composers would exhaust all the great melodies. But it turns out that the possibilities for crafting a memorable tune are seemingly endless. Melodies involve not just selecting pitches but varying the types of intervals (conjunct and disjunct) and preparing a melodic climax or cadence. They also involve rhythm, which concerns temporal relationships between pitches, as we will discuss in Chapter 2.

check your **KNOWLEDGE**

1. What is a pitch? What is the difference between a fundamental pitch and a partial?
2. What is a melody? How many possible melodies could be written?
3. What is an interval? What is the difference between a half step and a whole step?
4. What is a scale? How many different types of scales are there?

CHAPTER

Rhythm, Meter, Texture, and Dynamics

Pitches, though essential, are just one dimension of music. A second dimension is **rhythm**, the succession of sound durations. In our daily lives, we experience countless examples of rhythm, from heartbeats to speech to ocean waves. In music, rhythm refers specifically to the durations of pitches and silences. In "The Star-Spangled

Banner," for example, the pitches for "say," "can," and "you" are shorter than the pitch for "see":

Oh, say, can you see

Rhythmic Values

Different types of notes indicate different relative pitch lengths, or rhythmic values, in Western music:

- The longest value normally used is the oval-shaped **whole note** (𝅝).
- A whole note equals two **half notes**, ovals with stems attached (𝅗𝅥𝅗𝅥).
- A half note equals two **quarter notes**, solid note heads with stems (♩♩).
- A quarter note equals two **eighth notes**, which have flags attached to the stems or are beamed together (♪♪ or ♫).
- By adding more flags or beams, we can represent shorter rhythmic values, such as sixteenth notes and thirty-second notes.

Figure 2.1 summarizes the most frequently encountered types of rhythmic values.

FIG. 2.1 Rhythmic values (binary division).

Notice that these rhythmic values divide into groups of two: that is, a whole note equals *two* half notes; a half note equals *two* quarter notes. However, by placing a **dot** directly after the note head, we can divide notes into groups of three. In a **dotted note**, the dot extends the note by adding half of its value. Thus, a dotted whole note (𝅝.) equals *three* half notes; a dotted half note (𝅗𝅥.) equals *three* quarter notes, and so on (see Fig. 2.2).

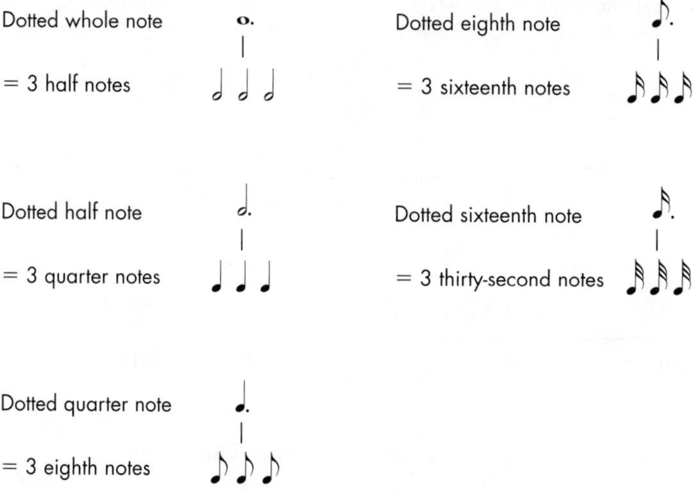

FIG. 2.2 Rhythmic values (ternary division).

We can alter rhythmic values in other ways as well. For example, a curved symbol known as a **tie** joins two notes to produce a rhythmic value equal to the sum of the individual values; a quarter note tied to an eighth note is equivalent to three held eighth notes.

Triplets are groups of three notes marked by the numeral 3, indicating that they have the same duration as two notes of the same value. Thus, a triplet of three eighth notes, , has the same value as two eighth notes, .

Finally, composers often use silence in measured quantities known as **rests**, which have their own set of symbols (see Fig. 2.3).

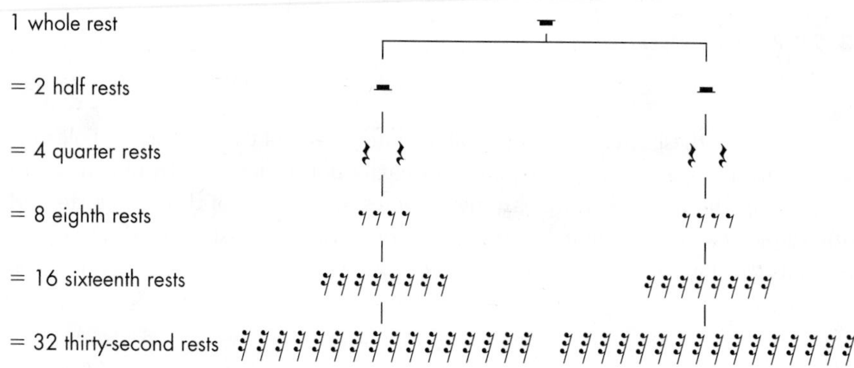

FIG. 2.3 Rests (binary division).

As with note values, rests normally divide in two. For example, a quarter rest, 𝄽, equals *two* eighth rests, 𝄾𝄾. As you might expect, adding a dot to a rest produces a division in three. Thus, a dotted eighth rest, 𝄾., equals *three* sixteenth rests (see Fig. 2.4).

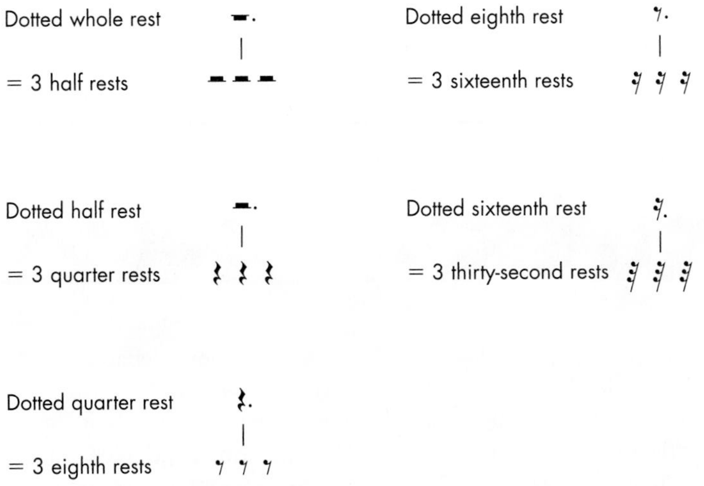

FIG. 2.4 Rests (ternary division).

Tempo Markings

These basic rhythmic values are the building blocks of Western rhythm, just as pitches drawn from scales are the building blocks of Western melodies. By themselves, however, rhythmic values do not tell performers all they need to know, as there is no absolute standard for measuring them. The durations of these values are relative, but performers still need to determine, for example, how long to hold a whole note. Consequently, composers often indicate the **tempo**—the basic pace of their music—by providing **tempo markings**. Once performers know the tempo, they can determine the actual duration of rhythmic values in a performance.

Finding the right tempo can be a challenging task. If the tempo is too fast, the music rushes by, blurring details into a jumble that the listener cannot understand. But if the tempo is too slow, the listener dwells too long on individual notes and loses the overall continuity of the music. Of course, setting the tempo is subject to the individual preferences of performers, whose interpretations of tempo markings can vary significantly.

Often, the tempo marking is just one word added above the beginning of the music: **allegro** (fast), or **adagio** (slow), for example. Table 2.1 lists some common tempo markings, all drawn from Italian, a convention dating back hundreds of years.

Composers can more precisely indicate tempo by using a **metronome**, a clocklike mechanism with a sliding scale. A metronome can produce ticking sounds at varying rates of speed, depending on the user who can adjust the rate either by moving a sliding weight (in a traditional, mechanical device) or by programming the desired speed (in a digital metronome). By following metronome markings, performers can accurately realize composers' intentions about tempo.

TABLE 2.1 Common Tempo Markings

Presto: Very fast	Andante: Moderately slow
Vivace: Lively	Largo: Slow
Allegro: Fast	Adagio: Slow
Allegretto: Moderately fast	Lento: Slow
Moderato: Moderately	Grave: Slow, gravely

MAKING CONNECTIONS *The Metronome*

Mechanical metronome.

How do musicians keep track of time? If you were Ludwig van Beethoven living in Vienna in 1816, you tried the metronome, a new device introduced by the German inventor/entrepreneur Johann Nepomuk Mälzel (1772–1838). Mälzel specialized in building musical machines, and he eventually constructed an entire mechanical orchestra that he called a Panharmonicon. He even talked Beethoven into writing a piece for it.

Mälzel wasn't the first to experiment with using a pendulum-powered device to measure musical time; that honor fell to German clockmaker Diedrich Nikolaus Winkel. But Mälzel improved on Winkel's device by adding the ability to set the pendulum's beat accurately, and in this modified form it was first manufactured in 1815. Mälzel's metronome had a pendulum with a movable weight that could decrease or increase the rate of ticking sounds, generated by a coiled spring. Beethoven was among the first composers to specify tempos by providing metronome markings.

Musicians have long debated the merits of the metronome. As an aid for mastering fast tempos, it is invaluable. But for many, the regular ticking interferes with the need for flexibility in performance. Still, Mälzel's metronome has enjoyed an afterlife the inventor could not have foreseen. Click tracks, which emit regular series of beats and are common in popular music, were developed in the 1930s for early sound movies as a way to synchronize music with film. In the same era, American composer Henry Cowell developed a complex metronome he called a Rhythmicon; it could play multiple rhythms simultaneously. And in 1962 the Romanian composer György Ligeti composed a "symphonic poem" for 100 metronomes. Once set in motion, they ticked continuously until their springs were exhausted, marking the end of the work.

Today, electronic metronomes have essentially rendered mechanical models obsolete. They have the advantage of producing extremely precise tempos.

Pulse or Beat

Whatever the tempo marking, performers must set the basic pulse, or **beat**, of the composition. When we listen to music, we usually sense an underlying series of beats. A common analogy compares beats to the footsteps of a marching band. Some types of music, such as marches, have beats in groups of two: One-two, One-two, and so on. Other types of music, for example waltzes, have beats in groups of three: One-two-three, One-two-three, and so on.

To return to "The Star-Spangled Banner," we can mark off its beats by placing them beneath the text, where they fall into groups of three. Our example shows how some words are held for exactly one beat, as in "say," "can," and "you." Other words, such as "see" and "light," are held for two beats each, while "by" and "the" are held for less than one beat each.

Oh, say, can you see by the dawn's ear - ly light What so
x | x x x | x x x | x x x | x x x |

proud - ly we hailed at the twi - light's last gleam - ing?
| x x x | x x x | x x x | x x

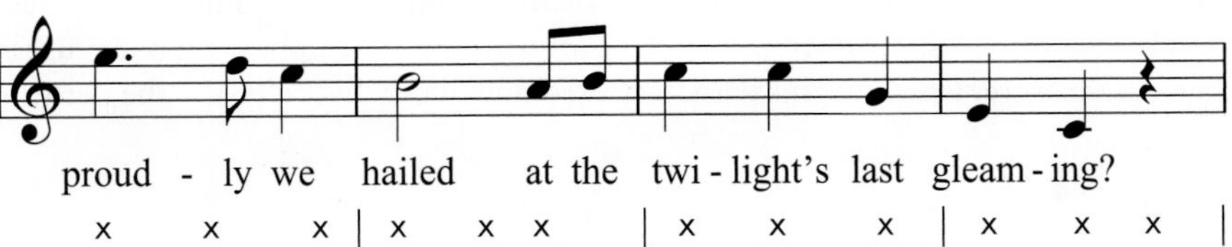

Try making a similar chart for a favorite song of your own. Is the underlying beat pattern in groups of two or three?

Measures

Most Western music is **metrical**: its rhythms are organized into equal segments of time, known as **measures** (or **bars**), which contain regular beat patterns known as **meters**. Naturally felt **accents** mark off the beginning of each pattern. Here is a succession of nine undifferentiated beats, with no indication of meter:

x x x x x x x x x

By stressing the first beat and then every third following beat, we create three groups of three beats each, and establish a sense of meter:

X x x **X** x x **X** x x

1 2 3 **1** 2 3 **1** 2 3

By convention, vertical lines known as **measure lines** (or **bar lines**) mark off these metrical divisions:

|x x x | x x x | x x x|

UPBEATS AND DOWNBEATS

The natural accent falls on the first beat, or **downbeat**, of each measure, while the other beats within each measure remain relatively unaccented. The last of these "weak" beats in each measure is known as an **upbeat**. The upbeat prepares us for the next measure, which begins with a stressed downbeat that refreshes the pattern:

|**x** x x | **x** x x |

Downbeat Upbeat Downbeat Upbeat

Stressed beats thus divide musical time into repeating patterns. Sometimes, though, a composer may disrupt the meter by placing stresses off the downbeat. In the next example, the stress falls on the second and fourth beat of each measure instead of on the first beat. This technique is known as **syncopation**, in which the accent appears at an unexpected place:

Syncopated pattern	1	**2**	3	**4**	1	**2**	3	**4**
Beats	x	**x**	x	**x**	x	**x**	x	**x**

This particular syncopated pattern is familiar in most rock music, in jazz, and in many other genres of popular music as well.

METER

Western music has three basic types of meter:

- **duple meter**, with two beats per measure;
- **triple meter**, with three beats per measure; and
- **compound meter**, which subdivide beats into smaller groupings of three.

Marches are an example of duple meter. A common variant of duple meter (sometimes known as **quadruple meter**) has four beats per measure. The third beat receives a slight stress, in addition to the stronger stress of the downbeat: **one**-two-*three*-four, **one**-two-*three*-four. Examples of this meter include "America the Beautiful" and "O Canada." Here is a line from "America the Beautiful" with its beats marked off. Notice how this melody begins with an unstressed upbeat:

A-|	mer-	i-ca!	A-|	mer-	i-ca!	God|	shed	his	grace	on|	Thee
four	**one** two	*three*	four	**one** two	*three*	four	**one**	two	*three*	four	**one**, and so on.

Examples of triple meter include waltzes and "The Star-Spangled Banner"; their beat pattern is: **one**–two–three, **one**–two–three.

Finally, in compound meter, the number of beats per measures (two, three, or four) subdivides into smaller groups of three, producing groupings of six, nine, and twelve divisions. Stephen Foster's song "Beautiful Dreamer," for example, has three beats per measure, which subdivide into groups of three each, for a total of nine divisions per measure: **one**–two-three–*four*–five-six–*seven*–eight–nine.

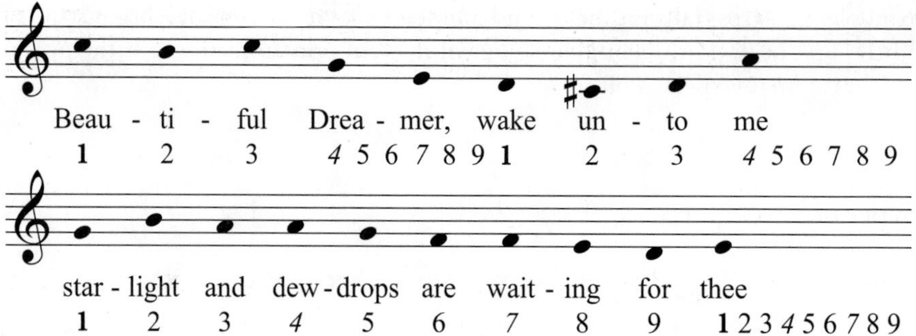
Beau - ti - ful Drea - mer, wake un - to me
1 2 3 4 5 6 7 8 9 1 2 3 4 5 6 7 8 9
star - light and dew - drops are wait - ing for thee
1 2 3 4 5 6 7 8 9 1 2 3 4 5 6 7 8 9

TIME SIGNATURES

In music notation, we specify the meter by a **time signature**, which appears as a fraction for two numbers: for example, $\frac{2}{4}$, $\frac{3}{4}$, and $\frac{6}{8}$. In duple and triple meters, the upper number indicates how many beats each measure has; the lower number indicates the rhythmic value assigned to each beat. Thus, in $\frac{2}{4}$ (duple meter), each measure has two beats, and each beat is equivalent to a quarter note.

In compound meters, the upper number indicates how many divisions each measure has. In $\frac{6}{8}$, each measure has six divisions, and each division is equivalent to an eighth note (there are two beats, each with three divisions—**1** 2 3 *4* 5 6). Other time signatures include $\frac{4}{4}$ (also indicated as **C**, for **common time**), $\frac{2}{2}$ (also indicated as ¢, for **cut time**), and compound meters such as $\frac{9}{8}$ and $\frac{12}{8}$.

All these meters—duple, triple, and compound—have regular beat patterns. From time to time, however, composers experiment with asymmetrical meters such as $\frac{5}{4}$ or $\frac{7}{8}$. In $\frac{5}{4}$, each measure has five beats (each equivalent to a quarter note), usually divided into groups of three and two, or two and three.

|**x** x x *x* x | **x** x x *x* x|

1 2 3 *4* 5 **1** 2 3 *4* 5

|**x** x *x* x x | **x** x *x* x x|

1 2 *3* 4 5 **1** 2 *3* 4 5

Why might composers choose asymmetrical meters? In large part, it is to escape the regularity of conventional meters, the "tyranny of the bar line" that dispenses music in evenly spaced blocks of sound. Still, most of the music we hear relies on a small number of duple, triple, and compound meters based on simple rhythmic relationships that are easy to follow.

MAKING CONNECTIONS *Many Meters: Igor, Nicolas, Serge, and* The Rite of Spring

In 1913, the ballet *The Rite of Spring* premiered in Paris. The challenging new ballet was accompanied by an equally radical piece of music, written by a young Russian composer named Igor Stravinsky. One of the hallmarks of this piece is its constantly changing meters, indicated by different sections being written in entirely different time signatures. The music was so jarring that riots were said to have broken out at the premiere, and Stravinsky himself had to be hustled out of the hall.

Several years later, in 1921, a young Russian musician named Nicolas Slonimsky was working in Paris as an assistant to the Russian conductor Serge Koussevitzky. In his autobiography *Perfect Pitch*, Slonimsky explains that Koussevitzky despaired of being able to conduct the work because of its many meter changes. Slonimsky came up with a unique solution to the problem. Just as in mathematics—where fractions of different values can be reconciled through finding a common denominator—Slonimsky worked out a way to rewrite sections of the score. He changed the bar lines and used a single time signature, making it easier to conduct.

When Koussevitzky saw the reworked score, he exclaimed to Nicolas, "You have a genius for mathematics!" Nicolas rather sheepishly admitted that this genius was "no more than the ability to add fractions." Koussevitzky used the reworked score for the rest of his career, passing it down to the American composer and conductor Leonard Bernstein. In 1984, Bernstein wrote to Nicolas that he "admired and revered and honored [him]" for facilitating his own efforts to conduct the work. (See Chapter 42 for a further discussion of *The Rite of Spring.*)

A contemporary ballet performance of *The Rite of Spring*.

Musical texture is like a fabric of sound.

If rhythm is the temporal glue that binds pitches together, meter channels the music into a measured temporal flow. Meter is how we make sense of musical time, by dividing it into easily perceived, regular beats.

Texture

How do composers decide how many notes to write, how many different rhythms to use? Often these decisions are affected by the **texture** of the music, that is, the type of fabric of sound that the composer chooses to use. Textures can be quite sparse or dense and complex. Put simply, a composer can write just a single line of music (imagine a single thread), or several lines of music that are sounding simultaneously (imagine a denser fabric of different threads). There are three basic musical textures: monophony, polyphony, and homophony. We introduce the first two briefly here; a discussion of homophony follows in the section on harmony.

MONOPHONIC TEXTURE

So far, we have been exploring single lines of music, a simple texture known as **monophony** (adjective *monophonic*, meaning "one voice"). In monophony, one musician performs a single line of music, or several musicians perform a single line of music in unison. For centuries, monophonic music was the prevalent type in the West.

POLYPHONIC TEXTURE AND COUNTERPOINT

Sometime around the tenth century, a new texture emerged that transformed Western music. This type of music, called **polyphony** (adjective *polyphonic*, meaning "several voices"), involves multiple sounding lines. The art of fitting one line of music against another, different line is called **counterpoint** (adjective *contrapuntal*, from a Latin phrase meaning "note against note"). Often, the terms *polyphony* and *counterpoint* are interchanged. (See Chapter 10, p. 74, for an extended discussion.)

In a polyphonic texture known as **imitative counterpoint**, after one line begins, it is "imitated" by other lines of music, typically one at a time. The texture gradually increases in complexity from one to two and then more parts. Sometimes, the **imitation** is literal, as in a type of music known as a **canon** (examples include "Row, Row, Row Your Boat" and "Three Blind Mice," also known as **rounds**). In Figure 2.5, the opening of "Row, Row, Row Your Boat," we can see the identical contours of the three parts as they enter, one at a time.

In **non-imitative counterpoint**, the different parts are relatively independent; the second part shares no material with the first. In the following, imaginary example, we hear the passage as one line of music set against another, different one. In other words, the second part does not imitate the first:

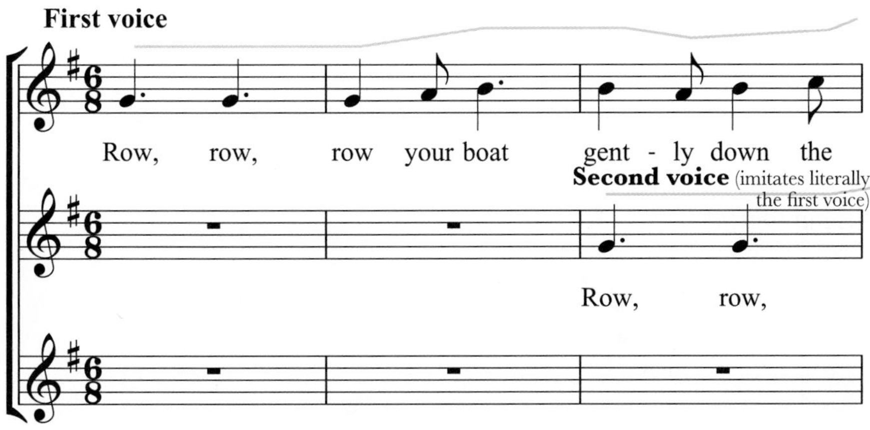

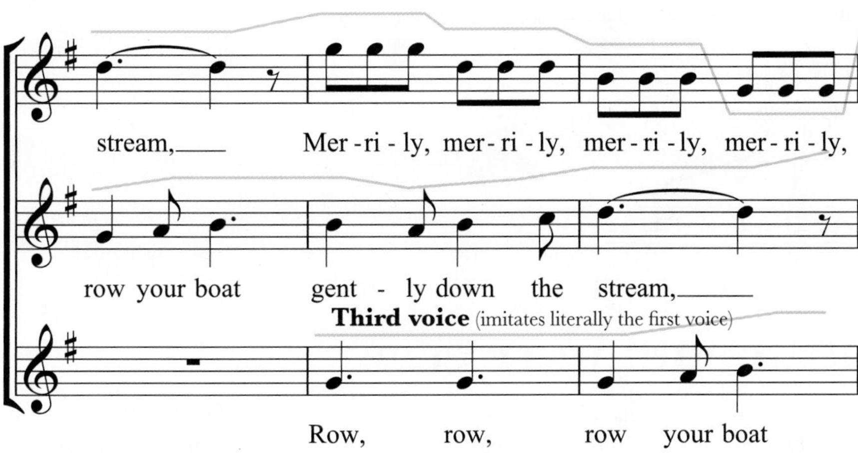

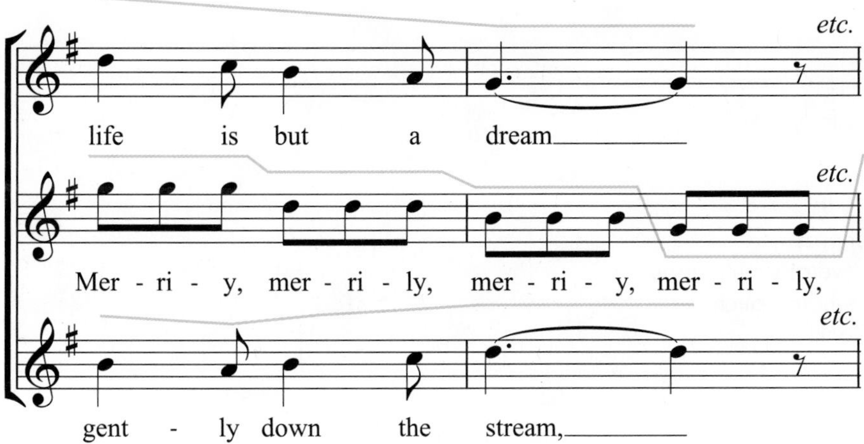

FIG. 2.5 Round, "Row, Row, Row Your Boat," an example of strict imitative polyphony.

Harmony

While counterpoint is the art of setting lines of music against each other, **harmony** is the art of using **chords**—combinations of two or more pitches that sound simultaneously, not one after the other.

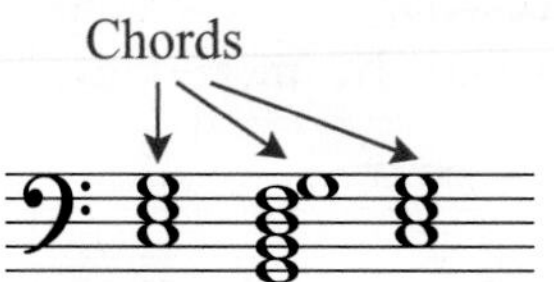

HOMOPHONIC TEXTURE

Chords often appear in a texture known as **homophony** (or "similar" voices). Homophony typically features a melody supported by chords, as when a guitarist playing chords accompanies a singer. Here is an abstract example:

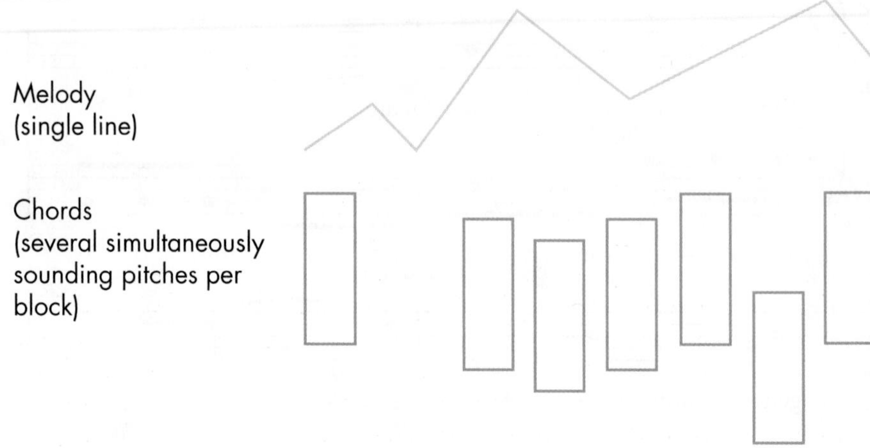

The singer's melody is "harmonized" by the chords of the lower parts. For example, we can harmonize the first two phrases of "The Star-Spangled Banner" by adding chords beneath the melody:

Like polyphony, homophony involves several parts moving against one another. There is a basic distinction, however. In polyphony, we hear the music as separate lines moving in time. In homophony, we hear the music as a succession of simultaneously sounding chords. Polyphony emphasizes the horizontal direction of musical lines, like separate threads running through a musical fabric. Homophony highlights chords, like blocks of color in fabric.

THE TRIAD

Since the mid-fifteenth century, the basic type of chord in Western harmony has been a three-note chord known as a **triad**, constructed by stacking two thirds together, for instance, C-E and E-G, to form the triad C-E-G:

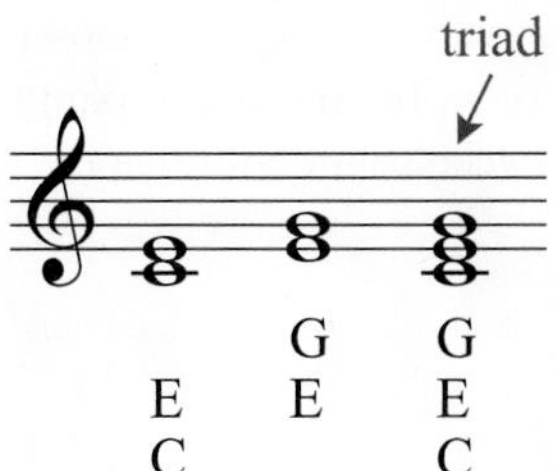

HARMONIC PROGRESSION

Over the years, rules have developed governing the progression from one chord to the next. Two concepts critical to harmonic progressions are consonance and dissonance. We have already distinguished between consonant and dissonant intervals (see Chapter 1, p. 11). In harmony, we extend the idea to consonant and dissonant chords. Some chords are consonant; to our ears, they sound stable and pleasant. Other harmonies are dissonant, and may sound unstable or harsh. As a general rule, a dissonant harmony progresses to a consonant harmony that "resolves" the tension of the dissonance.

Tonality

Tonality (adjective **tonal**) is a system of musical organization that depends on a network of harmonic relationships, all centered on consonant triads. These relationships revolve around a tonic triad that establishes the key (see p. 13). Most of the music we hear, whether popular or classical, uses tonality, which was developed in the seventeenth century. (For an in-depth discussion of tonality, see Chapter 19.)

Dynamics

When we describe a pitch, we can identify how high or low it is and how long it lasts, but we can describe other features as well. One is the relative loudness or softness of a pitch, or **dynamics**. By convention, we use Italian terms to designate dynamics levels (see Table 2.2).

Paul Klee's *Dynamic Gradation* (1923) uses colors of various intensities to suggest a range of dynamics.

Like tempo markings (see p. 19), dynamics levels are not absolute. What one musician might hear as ***forte*** (loud), another musician might hear as *mezzo* ***piano*** or ***forte*** (half loud). Sometimes changes in dynamics are abrupt—for instance, a sudden move from *fortissimo* (very loud) to ***piano*** (soft).

Composers also have another option: changing dynamics by *gradually* increasing the sound (**crescendo**) or *gradually* decreasing it (**decrescendo**, also **diminuendo**). And finally, some composers have pushed the outer limits of dynamics. For example, in the nineteenth century, Beethoven and Schubert occasionally called for triple forte (***fff***) to make a dramatic effect. By contrast, Russian composer Tchaikovsky notated a barely perceptible quintuple piano (***ppppp***), blurring the boundary between sound and silence.

TABLE 2.2 Dynamics Levels

pianissimo	***pp***	very soft
piano	***p***	soft
mezzo piano	***mp***	half soft
mezzo forte	***mf***	half loud
forte	***f***	loud
fortissimo	***ff***	very loud

MAKING CONNECTIONS *The Sound of Silence*

Modern American composer John Cage noted that music consists of two primary elements: sounds and silence. Although we might not think much about it, silence can play just as dynamic a role in a composition as does sound. Think back about the opening of Beethoven's Fifth Symphony. The famous four-note motive—Dah-Dah-Dah-DAH!— is followed by a brief silence before being dramatically repeated a step lower. The silence is just as important as is the sound to the impact of the opening of this piece. Cage used the idea of composing with silence in his famous 1952 piece 4′33″. In its three movements, a pianist sits largely in silence, without touching the keys. The performance opens with the lid closing over the keyboard. Toward the end of each movement, the lid is opened and then closed again to mark the start of the next movement. Cage hoped to get his audience to listen intently to the silence that made up the performance itself, as well as to sounds that are occurring all the time all around us. He made the point that there truly is no such thing as "absolute" silence.

The John Cage Trust has posted an iPhone app that enables anyone to create a version of 4′33″ by recording ambient sounds and then uploading the composition. There are various versions available for listening at the official John Cage website.

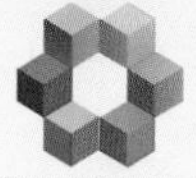

Follow the link to the John Cage website to experience the 4′33″ app.

check your **KNOWLEDGE**

1. What are the differences between rhythm, tempo, and meter?
2. What are the three primary types of musical textures, and what distinguishes them from one another?
3. What are the three types of meter, and what distinguishes them from one another?
4. What is a chord, and what role does it play in harmony?
5. What role do dynamics play in music?

CHAPTER

Timbre, Instruments, and Ensembles

Discussions of music often focus on pitch, rhythm, and dynamics. But how a sound is produced also plays a vital role in our musical experiences.

Timbre

Timbre (also known as *tone color*) is the quality of sound that differentiates one instrument from another. Several variables can affect it, such as the size and material of the instrument and how the instrument is played—how loudly or softly and whether in a high or low register. Timbre is what enables us to distinguish the sweet sound of a violin from the wooden sound of a xylophone or the thud of a bass drum. A composer's selection of a particular instrument can influence our perception of a piece in profound ways. In addition, blending different instruments together allows composers to explore a range of musical colors.

The Voice

The human voice is the most common musical instrument. Its individual qualities are determined by the vocal chords, a pair of mucous membranes folded within the throat. Every person's vocal chords are uniquely formed in terms of shape, thickness, and other features. When we sing, air from the lungs, acting as a bellows, flows through the vocal chords, causing them to vibrate. The resulting musical sound is then shaped by the throat, mouth, and nose. The range of pitches each voice can produce is determined by the tension of the vocal chords: the looser they are, the lower the pitch; the tauter they are, the higher.

We classify vocal ranges into the following categories, from highest to lowest:

Women: **soprano, contralto, alto**
Men: **tenor, baritone, bass**

The Family of Musical Instruments

Over the centuries, composers have written music for many different instruments, each with its own timbre. There are different systems for classifying Western instruments, though a common one organizes them into five groups:

1) **Idiophones** are made of solid materials that produce sounds when struck, rubbed, or shaken. Among them are the cymbal, gong, and xylophone.
2) **Membranophones** are instruments with tautly stretched membranes that vibrate to produce sounds. Examples include the timpani (kettledrums), bass drum, and snare drum.
3) **Aerophones** are instruments that use columns of air to produce sounds. This group includes wind and brass instruments (e.g. the flute, trumpet, and trombone) and the organ. Some aerophones have *reeds*, strips of pliable cane, set into the mouthpiece (e.g., saxophone, clarinet, oboe).
4) **Chordophones** are instruments with strings. Among them are the guitar, harp, violin, and piano.
5) **Electrophones** are instruments that generate sound electronically. Examples include the modern electronic organ, synthesizers, and computer programs.

Dashboard

Watch videos of musical instruments from each of these categories.

These five divisions are not perfect. A piano has strings that are struck by hammers, and so, technically, it combines aspects of idiophones and chordophones. An electric guitar uses electricity to amplify its sound but generally is considered a chordophone.

A second system for classifying common Western instruments divides them into four basic categories (Figure 3.1):

1) The **woodwinds** are aerophones, many but not all of which are constructed of wood. The most common include the flute and piccolo (which, before the twentieth century, were constructed of wood instead of metal), oboe and English horn, clarinet and bass clarinet, and bassoon and contrabassoon.
2) **Brass instruments** are aerophones made of metal. The most common include the trumpet, French horn, trombone, and tuba.
3) The **string instruments** are chordophones that include the violin, viola, cello, and double bass (also known as the string bass or contrabass).
4) The **percussion** group is made up of membranophones and idiophones, including instruments that produce distinct pitches—for example, timpani, xylophone, and tubular bells—and instruments that produce indefinite sounds—for example, cymbals, gongs, and triangle.

Note that a piano could be classified as either a string or a percussion instrument.

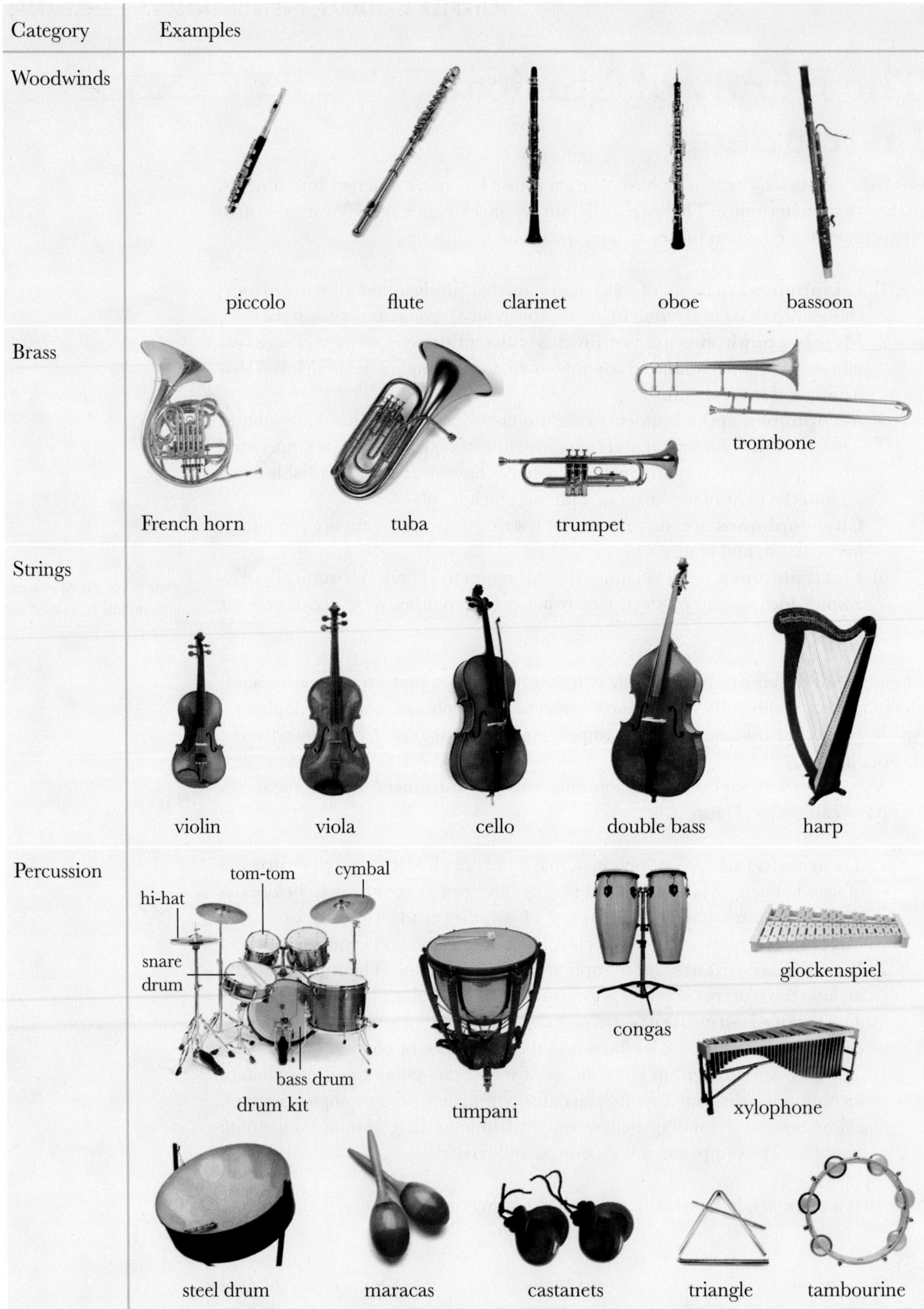

FIG. 3.1 Common Western instruments by group.

Finally, we may conveniently compare instruments according to their range—that is, how high or low they play. Figure 3.2 locates the approximate ranges of many common instruments in relation to the piano keyboard. The lowest sounding instruments include the contrabassoon, a woodwind instrument that can match the lowest pitches of the piano. At the other extreme is the piccolo, whose piercing high range matches the high pitches of the piano.

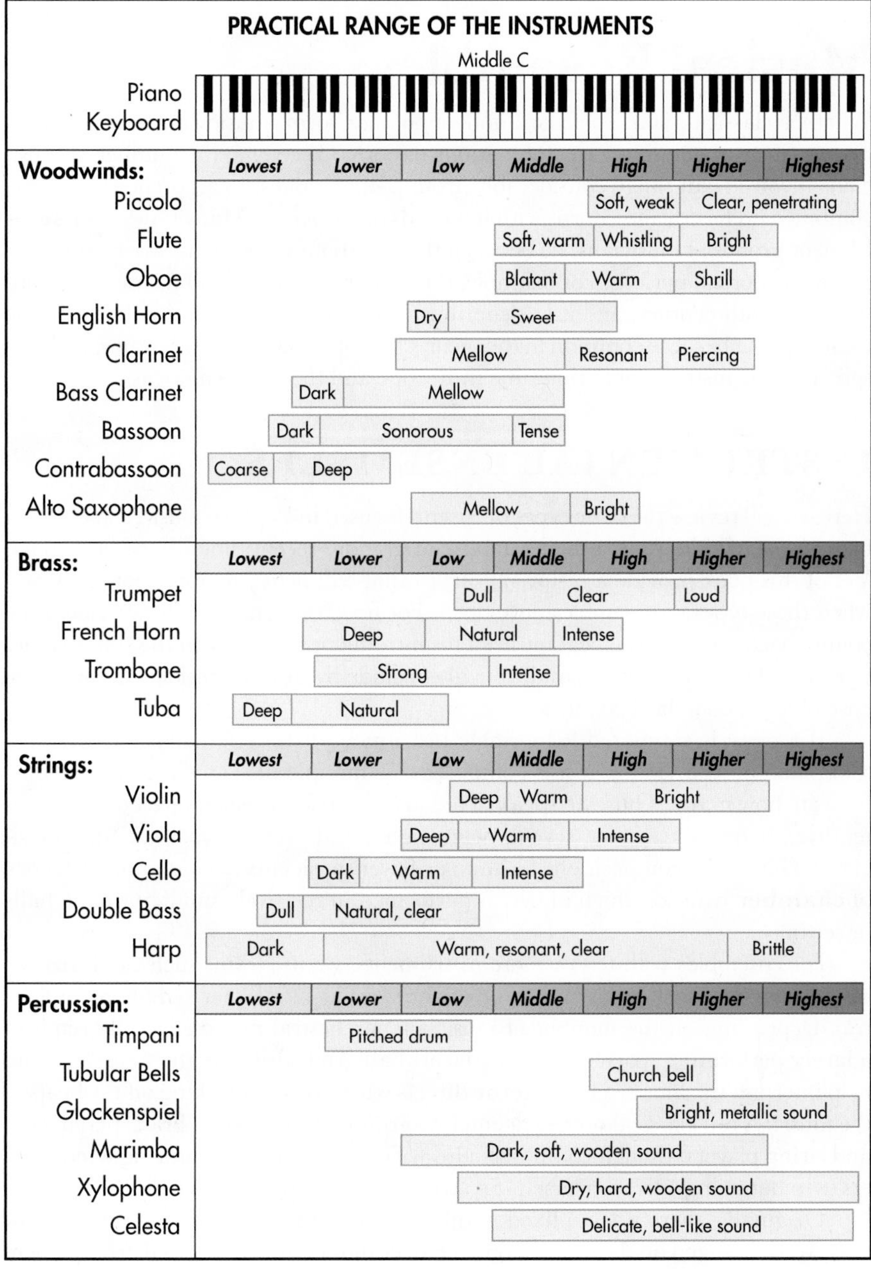

FIG. 3.2 Ranges of common instruments in relation to the keyboard.

In addition to range, each instrument has its own timbre. The plucked sound of a harp, for instance, is noticeably different from the nasal sound of an oboe. These differences in timbre have to do with how instruments produce their pitches. It is a complex topic that brings us back to pitch, where we began in Chapter 1. In brief, each instrument balances in different ways the fundamental of a pitch and its secondary partials. These different balances account for what makes a trumpet sound like a trumpet, or a violin like a violin.

Musical Ensembles

Whether classical, jazz, rock, or another popular form, music can be written for singers, instrumentalists, or combinations of both. Of course, the number of musicians involved can range considerably, from a single soloist to an orchestra, or to a combined orchestra and chorus with hundreds of musicians. Many types of **ensembles**, or groups of musicians, lie between these extremes, and many are common to specific historical periods. For example, the modern orchestra did not develop until the eighteenth century, and it has continued to evolve since then. Similarly, music for solo piano became common in the second half of the eighteenth century, with the spread of the instrument at that time in Europe and then the Americas.

INSTRUMENTAL ENSEMBLES

Here we will review the basic types of ensembles used in Western music, some dating back to the Middle Ages, others established in more recent times. Parts II through VII of this book provide a historical survey that will help you appreciate how and when these types of ensembles developed. For now, though, we will describe some common examples in classical music. This introduction starts with the simplest and moves to the more complex, and we will conclude by briefly considering the use of ensembles in non-classical music.

If a piece is composed for a single instrument, it is designated it as *solo* (e.g., solo piano or solo violin). If it is composed for multiple instruments, the title may indicate how many. Thus, we speak of a duo (two), trio (three), quartet (four), quintet (five), sextet (six), septet (seven), octet (eight), and even a nonet (for nine musicians). Generally, compositions for nine or fewer musicians belong to the category of **chamber music**, which ideally is performed in relatively small, intimate halls or settings.

Julliard String Quartet.

For ensembles with ten or more instruments, we use terms such as **chamber orchestra** (for smaller ensembles) or **orchestra** (as in a larger symphony orchestra). Depending on the number of musicians, orchestral music generally requires a larger performing space such as a concert hall. To coordinate the musicians and help interpret the music, a **conductor** directs with a baton, marking off the beats of the music. A full classical orchestra employs groups of woodwind, brass, percussion, and string players, though composers also write for orchestras featuring wind players (without strings), or, conversely, for string orchestra (without winds).

Originally, there was no fixed number of instruments in an orchestra or how they were arranged on the stage. However, over the centuries, a formal arrangement of the instruments has developed, as shown in Figure 3.3. The strings—as the lead instruments that often carry the melody—are most prominently featured.

Moscow Symphony Orchestra.

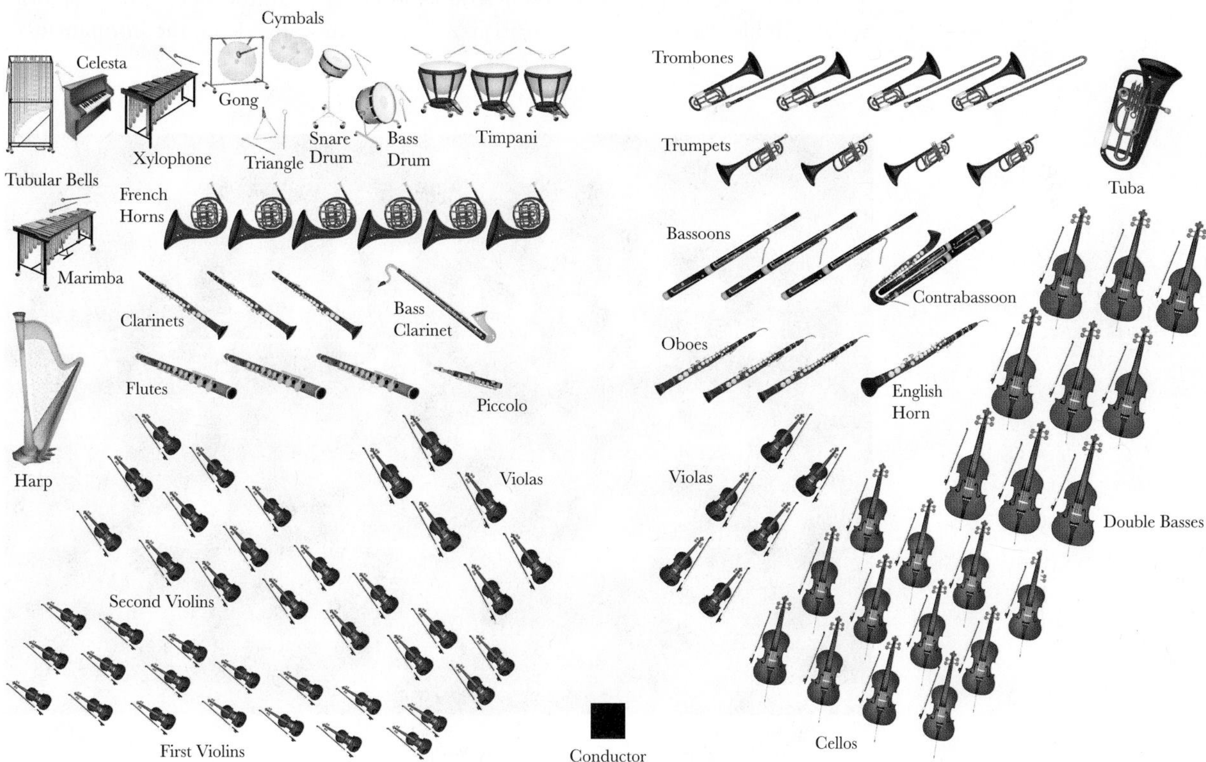

FIG. 3.3 Typical arrangement of orchestral instruments.

Finally, a familiar American institution is the marching band, typically consisting of wind and percussion players who march at athletic events and play in parades. They are a throwback to an earlier era in which bands had a military purpose, such as in the American Civil War. These bands represent the age-old idea that music could instill courage in soldiers entering combat.

VOCAL ENSEMBLES

In the case of vocal music, composers can write for solo voice (i.e., unaccompanied voice), or for a singer accompanied by an instrument or instrumental ensemble. The most common pairing is a singer accompanied by a piano in a performance of a song. Vocal ensembles can be identified as duos, trios, quartets, and so on, depending on the number of soloists involved.

If the composer requires a large group of singers, we refer to a **chorus**, typically consisting of female and male musicians divided according to their range into parts for soprano, alto, tenor, and bass (designated as S, A, T, and B). Choral music can also be written for a female chorus (S, A), or male chorus (T, B). If the chorus is relatively small, we may refer to it as a **choir**, often associated with sacred music for a church service.

MIXED ENSEMBLES

Some compositions join together vocal and instrumental musicians, such as a chorus performing together with an orchestra. Non-classical music often mixes soloists and ensembles as well. For instance, jazz settings can range from the intimate (e.g.,

A chorus performs at Lincoln Center in New York.

trio, quartet, quintet) to a larger group comprising a jazz band or orchestra. Jazz ensembles generally divide into a reed section (saxophones, clarinets), a brass section (trumpets, trombones), and a rhythm section (percussion, piano, string bass, guitar). In the age of the "big bands" of the 1930s and 1940s, these ensembles could reach twenty or so musicians. Rock music, on the other hand, tends to use smaller ensembles, with amplified guitars, percussion, and synthesized keyboard.

The size and composition of an ensemble have a powerful effect on our perception of the music. In general, if an orchestra or larger band of musicians is involved, we tend to view the music being performed as a shared social experience, and we relate to the musicians as a group. If, on the other hand, the ensemble is small, we tend to focus more on the individual musicians, and we may identify with the music in a more personal way.

(a) Large orchestra and chorus; (b) Count Basie and his big band; (c) the Beatles on *The Ed Sullivan Show.*

Benjamin Britten, *The Young Person's Guide to the Orchestra* (1946)

The English composer Benjamin Britten (1913–1976) wrote *The Young Person's Guide to the Orchestra* in 1946 to showcase the instruments of the modern orchestra. Suitable for music lovers of all ages, this impressive work offers an opportunity to compare the timbres of instruments. It is organized into the four main divisions of the orchestra: woodwinds, brass, strings, and percussion (**Listening Map 1**).

The work begins with a stately theme borrowed from a seventeenth-century English composer, Henry Purcell (ca. 1659–1695; see also p. 150). First the entire orchestra presents the theme, with the four groups blended together. Still, it is possible to pick out the colors and timbres of individual instruments: the tapping of the snare drum, the brittle strokes of the xylophone, the shrill tones of the piccolo, for instance.

Next, Britten separates the four groups, allowing Purcell's theme to emerge first in a woodwind choir, then in the brass, strings, and percussion. Rounding out this section of the *Guide* is another repetition of the theme for full orchestra.

Britten devotes the heart of the composition to a series of thirteen variations on the theme, each one tailor-made for a different instrument or instrumental group. The variations feature first the woodwinds, then strings, brass, and percussion. He uses different timbres to vary the melody. (Variations are a way of altering some aspect of the theme while retaining other features. Chapters 18, pp. 121–123 and 31, pp. 225–227, will discuss theme and variations as a form.)

After having disassembled the orchestra into its constituent parts, Britten reverses course for the conclusion of the piece. He chooses a Baroque form known as a *fugue* (see p. 169), in which the parts enter individually to build gradually layers of complexity. To help us find our way, Britten retraces the order of instruments that we have already heard in the thirteen variations: woodwinds, strings, brass, and percussion. Finally, he revives Purcell's original theme in the brass, bringing the composition to a triumphant conclusion.

check your KNOWLEDGE

1. What is timbre, and why is it important to our understanding of music?
2. What are two common ways of classifying musical instruments?
3. What is your favorite instrument, and why? How would you describe its range?
4. How do ensembles differ in classical music from jazz or rock? In what ways are they similar?

LISTENING MAP 1

BENJAMIN BRITTEN, *The Young Person's Guide to the Orchestra*

{1946}

FORM	Orchestral work
METER	Triple
TEMPO	Stately, dance like
SCORING	Full orchestra
OVERVIEW	*The Young Person's Guide to the Orchestra* showcases the basic timbres and ranges of the instruments, as well as the role each plays within the full orchestra. It was originally composed for use in an educational film but has since become a favorite in the concert hall. Written in three parts—an introduction, variations by instrumental group, and a concluding fugue—the work highlights the four major sections of the orchestra.

why to LISTEN

Besides its educational value, *The Young Person's Guide to the Orchestra* is a stirring composition. By borrowing his theme from the seventeenth-century British composer Henry Purcell, Britten was paying homage to an earlier period of British history. This piece was composed just as World War II was ending, when Britain was emerging from a long battle against the forces of Nazi Germany. *The Young Person's Guide* is thus both an instructive work and a tribute to the endurance of British culture.

first LISTEN

INTRODUCTION	VARIATIONS	FUGUE
0:00	**1:58**	**13:48**
Purcell's theme is stated by each part of the orchestra in succession.	Each section of the orchestra, broken down into 13 key instruments, plays a variation on the main theme.	Each of the 13 featured instruments plays the theme in counterpoint, capped by a final statement from the brass set against the fugue.

Continued

a deeper **LISTEN**

TIME	SECTION	LISTEN FOR THIS
0:00	**Part 1:** Theme (by Henry Purcell), stated by the full orchestra	Woodwinds Brass Strings Percussion Full orchestra **Allegro maestoso e largamente**
1:58	**Part 2:** Variations on Purcell's Theme	Woodwind variations 1. Flutes and piccolo 2. Oboes 3. Clarinets 4. Bassoons Brass variations 10. French horns 11. Trumpets 12. Trombones and tuba String variations 5. Violins 6. Violas 7. Cellos 8. Double bass 9. Harp Percussion, extended variation 13. Timpani, bass drum, cymbals, tambourine, triangle, snare drum, wood block, xylophone, castanets, gong, whip
13:48	**Part 3:** Fugue	Rapid entrances of Britten's fugal theme in the same order as variations 1–13 **Allegro maestoso e largamente** Reintroduction of Purcell's theme in the brass, set against the fugue

CHAPTER 4

Musical Form

In Chapters 1–3, we examined the basic concepts of pitch, rhythm, dynamics, and timbre, essential facets of music. Now we broaden our introduction to take up the question of **form**, the overarching plan that holds a piece together. Music flows over time, and when we look at a notated score, we can see the shape of what occurs during a performance.

To grasp the concept of form, it may help to think of its function in the visual arts. A painting, for example, may have compositional patterns that give it structure. A building may have a recognizable plan with repeating patterns, especially evident in blueprints. Musical form is similar. In fact, architects commonly use terms borrowed from music to describe the formal features of their buildings, such as rhythm, dynamics, or harmony. The German poet Goethe also made the connection by describing architecture as "frozen music."

There are many different forms used in music, and later in the book we will describe the most important ones in detail. Here, we will simply introduce some basic principles of how Western composers have used form to unify and shape their music.

Binary and Ternary Form

One way to think about musical form is as a compromise between the competing needs of *unity* and *variety*. Obviously, if a composition consisted of just one chord repeated endlessly, unity would be achieved, but we would find the music boring. On the other hand, if the composition consisted of different chords seemingly chosen at random, the need for variety would be met, but the music would be chaotic. Musical forms have thus developed largely to strike a balance between these two needs. So a composition using a particular musical form will typically have certain elements that return (e.g., a theme, a series of harmonies, a passage of several measures) according to some plan. Form gives the work a unified shape while offering sufficient variety to maintain our interest.

We can demonstrate the balancing of unity and variety with a few examples. In **binary form**, usually represented using capital letters in its simplest version as *AB*, we encounter two different sections of music (Fig. 4.1). There may be some similarities between the two, but essentially our brain processes the music as dividing into two portions, roughly of equal weight, *A* and *B*. To make the form especially clear, composers often repeat each section, resulting in *AA BB*, or, using what are called **repeat marks**, ‖: *A* :‖ *B* :‖.

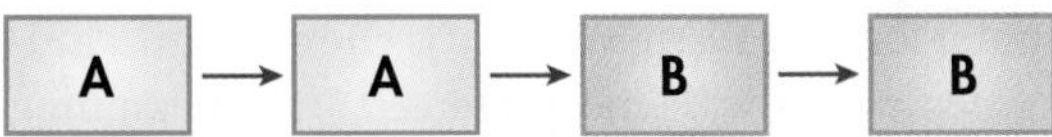

FIG. 4.1 Binary form.

MAKING CONNECTIONS *Musical Form in Architecture and Painting*

Two architects of the Italian Renaissance, Leon Battista Alberti (1404–1472) and Andrea Palladio (1508–1580), were famous for their use of musical proportions. In the fifteenth century, Alberti regarded musicians as "masters of numbers." He wrote a treatise on architecture in which he used the ratios of consonant musical intervals to establish proportions for physical spaces. In the sixteenth century, Andrea Palladio produced a treatise identifying seven of the "most harmonious" proportions to be used in constructing rooms. Several of these proportions aligned with Pythagorean ratios that the ancient Greeks had used to understand music (see Chapter 1).

We also see echoes of musical form in painting. For example, the twentieth-century French artist Georges Braque created a series of works attempting to distill the essence of musical structure in visual terms. To give texture to his vision, he added bits of paper, cardboard, and other objects to painted canvases.

One of Palladio's Italian villas. Note how the play of arches and classical columns creates a balanced, proportioned design.

Braque, *Musical Forms*, 1918.

In **ternary form**, there are three sections, of which the third is a repetition, either exact or modified, of the first. Ternary form is represented as *ABA*, or, if the second statement of *A* is modified somewhat, *ABA′*. This is a symmetrical, balanced form, but it has variety, owing to the placing of a new section, *B*, in its center.

FIG. 4.2 Ternary form.

Yet another example of a common form in Western music is **theme and variations** (Fig. 4.3). Here the unifying element is the theme, presented at the beginning of the composition, and sometimes repeated at the end, as if completing a musical circle. The variations (there can be as many as the composer decides) provide the variety by altering details or some aspect of the theme, such as its melodic shape, rhythm, meter, or harmonic accompaniment. Different composers will treat the art of variation differently. Some adhere rather closely to the theme, emphasizing its unifying aspect, while others may take us further and further away from it, satisfying our need for diversity.

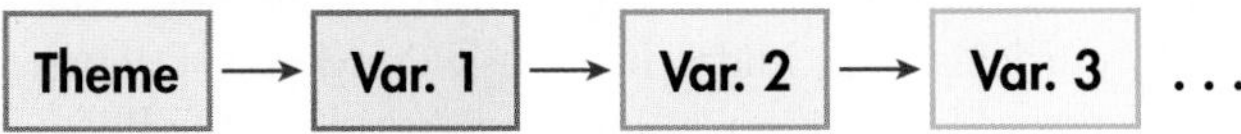

FIG. 4.3 Theme-and-variations form.

check your KNOWLEDGE

1. What is form, and how does it function in different arts?
2. What basic principle underlies musical form?
3. Compare and contrast binary form, ternary form, and theme and variations.

Classical Music and Historical Styles

Since the fall of Rome in 476 CE, Western music has inspired listeners. Along the way, a rich, complex tradition of art music developed in the soaring cathedrals of the Middle Ages, the festive Renaissance courts of emerging nation-states, and the sprawling urban centers of the Industrial Revolution. Binding all this music together has been the persistent idea that art music has value beyond its own time. A stirring performance of Beethoven's Fifth Symphony can surely produce as enthusiastic a response today as it did at its Viennese premiere some 200 years ago. Composers like Beethoven crafted compositions that enhanced listeners' enjoyment through repeated listening, deepening the music's significance.

What Is Classical Music?

Art music is sometimes described as "highbrow" and "serious," but the most common term for it is *classical*. This word derives from a Latin term that referred to the upper class in ancient Roman society. *Classical* was eventually co-opted to mean "excellent" and came to be applied to art music that composers, musicians, critics, and audiences deemed worthy of preservation.

At first glance, the idea of "classical" music seems flawed. Are there not "excellent" examples of jazz, rock, musicals, rap, and other musical styles? Of course. And what about non-Western music? Is the music of Japanese *Noh* plays, the Beijing opera, Balinese *gamelan* and *kora* of central Africa inferior to Western **classical music**? Of course not. Ultimately, judgments about music are subjective, changing as fashions come and go. Still, the idea of preferring this or that piece of music, film, or painting is embedded in our culture. To demonstrate, we need only consider another common term, derived from *classical*, and that is *classic*.

The idea of the classic has penetrated deep into our culture. Car buffs certainly have ideas about what qualifies as a classic automobile, and wine connoisseurs routinely make pronouncements about classic vintages. There are classic rock songs, classic films, and classic books. And there are certainly plenty of ways to mark something as exemplary. Society, it seems, has a vested interested in setting aside the very best in a given pursuit or product.

It might seem a stretch to compare works of classical music to mass-produced beverages, but the process of labeling them classics is not dissimilar. We might debate what qualifies a movie or Final Four basketball game as a classic, but we would probably concede the term's usefulness. In classical music, many concertgoers would grant that Handel's *Water Music*, Mozart's opera *The Marriage of Figaro*, and Musorgsky's *Pictures at an Exhibition*—all discussed in this book—are classics. This music has survived generations of shifting tastes and still resonates, not just

MAKING CONNECTIONS *The Classic in Popular Culture*

At the height of the "cola wars" in 1985, a well-known American corporation reformulated its product as "New Coke" in an attempt to reverse declining market share. Almost overnight, millions of consumers began protesting. Within months, the original formula returned as "Classic Coke," revalidating the old, familiar product. A hundred-year-old beverage thus became a "classic."

in concert halls, but also on the Internet, in ringtones, and as the soundtracks for video games.

The Classical-Popular Connection

We often regard classical and popular music as polar opposites. According to this view, classical music is for a highly educated audience; popular music is for the common person and mass consumption. But, as it turns out, classical and popular music *are* interrelated and occupy a connected musical continuum. Virtually all the major composers of Western classical music drew on the popular music of their own time. In the eighteenth century, Haydn incorporated folk tunes and popular dance styles into his symphonies, even though he usually wrote those symphonies for listeners at the European courts. And for one of the most celebrated operas of all time, *Carmen* (1875), the French composer Georges Bizet composed a *habanera*, a sensual dance first popularized in Havana, Cuba. These examples belong to classical music, yet they simultaneously embrace popular forms of music making.

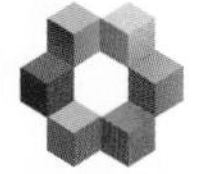

Dashboard

Watch a clip from *Psycho* to see how the score supports the mood of the film.

The twentieth century produced compelling examples of how popular music forged links to classical music. Jazz, which many regard as America's indigenous classical music, emerged as an authentic art form. Introduced in New Orleans as a fusion of different popular styles, jazz experienced within a few decades a remarkable transformation into an art form. "Classical" composers took note, and several incorporated jazz styles into their music. In the 1920s–1930s, composers like George Gershwin and Aaron Copland borrowed rhythms and harmonies from jazz in their compositions. During the 1950s, the "third stream" movement in jazz included many collaborations between classical and jazz musicians.

Film music is another form that has been influenced by classical styles. Several pioneering film composers of the Golden Age of Hollywood (ca. 1935–1955) were classically trained musicians who had emigrated from Europe. In their film scores, they borrowed techniques from nineteenth-century opera. For example, in films an invisible symphonic orchestra often plays the background music. In the opera house, the stage substituted for the screen, and the orchestra was semi-concealed in a pit.

Perhaps the most famous use of classical music in film is in Alfred Hitchcock's 1960 classic, *Psycho.* The entire score, by composer Bernard Herrmann, borrows heavily from the early twentieth-century composers Arnold Schoenberg and his followers (see Part VII). Its use of jarring harmonies and unusual combinations of instruments and timbres connects the techniques of twentieth-century classical music to the world of popular entertainment.

Popular music is thus not disconnected from classical music, and classical music is not necessarily elitist music. Rather, the two remain in dialogue with each other, as they have for centuries. Nevertheless, though most students are comfortable with current types of popular music, they encounter barriers to appreciating classical music. There are several reasons:

- First, the complexities of classical music notation can be off-putting.
- Second, classical compositions, especially those lasting several hours, place significant demands on our listening.
- Third, some classical music, especially of the twentieth century, explores radical alternatives to our common notions about pitch, rhythm, melody, and harmony.
- Fourth, most classical music is "old" music, from historical periods well removed from our own time.

So before we begin our account of Western classical music by time-traveling back to the Middle Ages, we'll give a short overview of the main historical periods, to help you better orient yourself as you begin this journey.

Classical Music Periods

Scholars continue to debate how to divide Western history into distinct periods, and that debate is particularly vigorous when it comes to the arts. Especially difficult to fathom is the present time, and how it fits into the grand historical sweep of the centuries. There is as yet no clear consensus about where twenty-first-century music is heading. Does it still maintain strong ties to the twentieth century, or is it on the threshold of a new historical period?

All that said, we will divide our discussion of the Western classical music tradition into seven sections (Figure 5.1):

1) *The Middle Ages (ca. 450–1450).* By far the longest period, the Middle Ages (also known as the medieval period) spanned roughly a thousand years. During much of this time, Western music was largely monophonic (using one line of music by itself). The birth of polyphony (different musical lines sounding simultaneously) somewhere around the ninth or tenth century marked a major milestone in Western music. Musicians now had to think harmonically *and* melodically. In addition, composers had to devise a system of musical notation to keep all the musical parts coordinated and synchronized. Medieval music uses scales called *modes*, and the system of musical organization based on these scales is called *modality*.
2) *The Renaissance (ca. 1450–1600).* Viewed as a cultural rebirth, the Renaissance returned to classical antiquity for inspiration. With the rise of humanism, the arts shifted toward humanity as a worthwhile object of study. In music, composers now began to develop individual styles of writing, and

composers—along with painters, sculptors, and architects—became celebrated for their accomplishments (facilitated by the invention of the printing press in the fifteenth century, and the beginnings of music publishing). During the Renaissance, composers began using what we recognize as our modern major and minor scales, as well as harmonies that we recognize as our modern major and minor triads.

3) *The Baroque period (ca. 1600–1750).* A reaction against the balance and proportion of Renaissance music, the Baroque unleashed the power of music to capture the emotions in direct and forceful ways. The Baroque saw the great rise of instrumental music, as well as music written for mixed vocal and instrumental ensembles. Other innovations included the widespread recognition of the bass line as a foundational element of music. Most critically, a new system of musical organization named *tonality* emerged. This system is based on the major and minor scales, the triads built upon them, and the keys they generate. Still in widespread use today, tonality replaced the modality of the Middle Ages and Renaissance.
4) *The Classical period (ca. 1750–1800).* A reaction against the exuberance and emotional drive of the Baroque, the Classical period returned to simpler, less emotionally charged music. It captured the spirit of the Enlightenment, a broad-based movement in the arts and letters that celebrated humanity's powers of reasoning. Classical composers projected in their music clear, tuneful themes supported by harmonies, balanced proportions, and symmetrical forms. Though by far the shortest of the main historical periods, the Classical period produced two of music's greatest composers, Haydn and Mozart.
5) *The Romantic period (1800s).* In reaction to the balance and design of the Classical period, nineteenth-century Romanticism explored the subjective nature of music. The Romantics tested the ability of music to express ideas and emotions as a separate form of language, a language of abstract sounds rather than one tied to written texts. Music was now elevated in the hierarchy of the arts. Romantic composers rejected set rules and procedures, and instead viewed their music ideally as a spontaneous art, powered and limited only by the imagination. Romanticism was challenged by other "isms" in the nineteenth century (for instance, nationalism, realism, and impressionism), but it held sway over many composers throughout the century.
6) *The modern era (ca. 1900–1970s).* Much of the twentieth century was, in turn, a reaction against the nineteenth century and the legacies of romanticism. The broad term to describe this reaction is "modernism." This music celebrated the modernity of twentieth-century life and its accelerating technological transformations (aviation, radio, television, computers, the Internet, etc.). However, it also articulated the period's harsh realities, including the horrors of two catastrophic world wars (1914–1918 and 1939–1945). In music, the break from the nineteenth century meant that composers explored new ways of organizing their work, including abandoning altogether the 300-year-old system of tonality. Especially after the Second World War, composers turned to new musical resources: generating and recording sounds in an electronic studio, for instance, or incorporating elements of chance into music. As music became increasingly avant-garde, new, and original, modernism reached a critical stage, probably somewhere around the 1970s. And that precipitated another reaction.

Middle Ages

ca. 450–1450

Monophony gives way to polyphony (ca. tenth century)

Renaissance

ca. 1450–1600

Composers recognized as individual creators; gradual introduction of tonal harmony

Baroque period

ca. 1600–1750

Complex melodies and forms; turbulent, emotional music; development of modern tonality

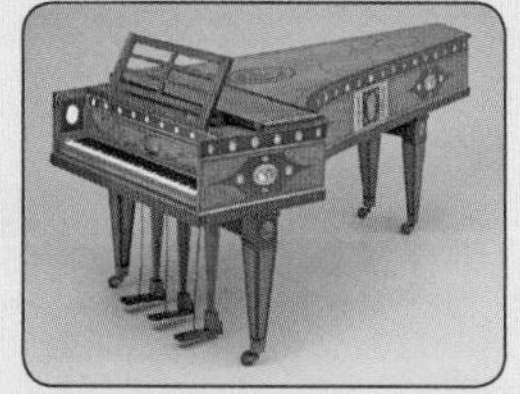

Classical period

ca. 1750–1800

Balanced forms; more graceful, simpler melodies

Romantic period

1800s

Self-expression valued more highly than following Classical rules

Modern era

1900–1970s

New scales and harmonies reflecting modern life, abandonment of tonality

Postmodernism

1970s–today

Revival of older styles combined with emphasis on exploration

FIG. 5.1 Overview of stylistic periods in Western music.

7) *Postmodernism (beginning somewhere around the 1970s or 1980s).* Postmodernism is a catch-all term to describe a break from the high-water mark of modernism in the twentieth century. In music it suggests a return to older styles while also emphasizing musical experimentation. As these words are being written, we are still experiencing postmodernism and discovering where it is leading us.

check your **KNOWLEDGE**

1. How do you understand the term "classic"? Can you think of three examples (e.g., products, books, films) that you regard as classics? Why?
2. How do classical music and popular music intersect? How are they different?
3. Write down a word or two that summarizes for you each of the seven Western musical periods. Repeat this exercise at the end of the semester.

CHAPTER

How to Listen

What do we listen for in music? Is the experience primarily emotional, intellectual, or spiritual? There is no correct answer, because music can operate on any or all of these levels, separately or together. But to perceive them, we need to develop strategies of listening, and we might begin by considering the listening experience itself.

The Listening Experience

Most of our listening is casual. We are all familiar with the constant presence of music as sonic background: the ringtones of cell phones; the background music in stores, elevators, and doctors' offices; the catchy jingles advertisers employ to promote their products. We hear these musical intrusions into our environment but generally pay them no heed and probably develop little emotional connection with them.

In contrast, how do we listen to music that we deliberately choose? Here, we are more attentive. There might be a phrase or harmony that piques our curiosity, a favorite line or two of text in a song that is meaningful. If the piece is among our favorites, we return to it repeatedly, so that we become emotionally attached to it.

Classical music rewards repeated listening. But because classical music can operate on different levels simultaneously, the experience can be challenging. One way to enhance our listening skills is to develop a basic vocabulary for understanding how the music is put together, how its various parts all come together to produce a coherent, satisfying work of art. Developing this vocabulary was our primary concern in Chapters 1 and 2, where we introduced elements common to Western classical music (and much popular music). But for classical music to survive—to become classic—it must also communicate to its listeners in a direct, meaningful way, even beyond the vocabulary that might define it. It should have qualities that relate to our varied human experiences and that encourage us to investigate it further. To illustrate, let's consider one brief example that is typical of such a classic.

Listening to John Philip Sousa's "The Stars and Stripes Forever"

Our choice is a celebrated American concert march for wind band, "The Stars and Stripes Forever" (**Listening Map 2**). The piece was composed in 1897 by John Philip Sousa, who led the Marine Corps Band and became America's venerated "March King."

His most popular composition immediately acquired patriotic overtones. Soon after the outbreak of the Spanish-American War in 1898, Sousa fitted a rousing text to be sung to the march. It reads in part: "Hurrah for the flag of the free, may it wave as our standard forever." The composition became so fixed in American culture that in 1987 Congress declared it the national march of the United States. It's hard to imagine a Fourth of July parade without "The Stars and Stripes Forever," and Sousa's march is now commonly played after a presidential address or speech. It has become part of popular music, yet it displays the craft of a composer trained in classical techniques. Sousa's work built bridges between popular and classical traditions.

Dashboard

Watch the U.S. Marine Band perform "The Stars and Stripes Forever."

To approach Sousa's "The Stars and Stripes Forever," first listen unassisted once or twice to gather some impressions. As you allow the music to wash over you, consider some basic questions. Is it fast or slow, loud or soft, or both? Does it use a high range or a low range? Do particular melodies, rhythms, or instruments stand out? The next step is to listen while following the Listening Map, where we offer a thumbnail sketch of the piece, with descriptions of its significant events. So that you can follow along more easily, the relevant timings for the recording appear on the left.

"The Stars and Stripes Forever" begins with a brief introduction for the full band. Like a military call to attention, this arresting opening prepares us for the first strain of the march, featuring a lively melody heard in the high register (①). Supporting it are lower instruments that fall into the two-beat patterns typical of marches. (As you listen to the music, try counting 1-2, 1-2, 1-2, and imagine the footsteps of a marching band.) This melody is repeated, until the second strain commences (②). Here Sousa offers a more emphatic melody, ratchets up the intensity, and repeats the second strain. We then proceed to a new section, known as the *trio*, where the music drops down to a softer level (③). In contrast to the first and second strains, the trio

brings a new theme that is at once more subdued. But at 1:43 it is interrupted by a "break," where the sound level suddenly increases as we hear dramatic exchanges between the low and high instruments (④). Now we return to the trio melody, played full bore as the climax of the piece, with new countermelodies in the shrill piccolo and booming trombones adding complexity to the music and intensifying its effect. Sousa then repeats the break and brings back the trio (⑤) before concluding the march with a triumphant, crashing chord.

Admittedly, our summary contains some details. There are several sections and repeats to track, and different levels of loudness and softness. Is there a simpler way to distill the main events of the composition? To do so, we can use *A*, *B*, and *C* for the first strain, second strain, and trio. Here we see that Sousa designed the composition to give extra weight to the trio. Unlike many marches, in which the opening material returns after a trio, Sousa's march is oriented *toward* the trio, the ultimate, boisterous goal of this patriotic march.

Is it necessary to grasp all these details in order to enjoy "The Stars and Stripes Forever"? Not at all. Different analyses could highlight other points: how Sousa assigns different starring roles to different instruments in the band at different points, for example. Still, our Listening Map reveals the basic plan of the piece. Try now, as you listen, to recognize the various sections, their melodies, and the supporting structure. Notice how individual instruments briefly emerge to shine separately before resuming their supporting roles. If you can sense how the music seems to embody the American motto *e pluribus unum* ("out of many, one"), you will have succeeded in enriching your listening experience.

LISTENING MAP 2

JOHN PHILIP SOUSA, "The Stars and Stripes Forever" {1897}

FORM	March (3 parts)
METER	Quadruple
TEMPO	March-like
SCORING	Brass band
OVERVIEW	Sousa's "Stars and Stripes Forever" is a classic example of an American march. Played by a brass band, it is broken into three parts: two contrasting themes (A and B), followed by a trio (C), the focal point of the composition. The trio itself is repeated three times, with a dramatic "break" occurring between each repetition. The simple four-beat rhythm ideally suits the rhythmic footsteps of soldiers.

why to LISTEN

Many patriotic songs celebrate America, including "The Star-Spangled Banner" and "My Country, 'Tis of Thee" ("America"). But "The Stars and Stripes Forever" is one of the few instrumental pieces—if not the only one—to capture the American spirit without using a single word. It embodies the swaggering pride and power of the nation at a time when the United States was entering the world stage. Like reading the Declaration of Independence or visiting Washington, D.C., hearing this piece gives great insights into the American character.

first LISTEN

INTRODUCTION	A	B	C (TRIO)	BREAK	C (TRIO)	BREAK	C (TRIO)
0:00	0:05	0:37	1:10	1:43	2:09	2:41	3:07
Full orchestra plays a brief "call to attention"	First theme	Second theme	Third theme (trio)	Interchange between high and low instruments	With piccolo countermelody		Final, triumphant return of third theme

a deeper LISTEN

TIME	SECTION	LISTEN FOR THIS
0:00	Introduction	Call to attention played by the entire orchestra, Full texture, ***ff***, tonic key  ***ff***
0:05	A	① First strain: Lively high theme supported by lower instruments in two-beat (1-2, 1-2) patterns, ***ff*** ***ff*** 
0:21		First strain repeats
0:37	B	② Second strain: More emphatic melody; emphasizes woodwinds and piccolos 
0:54		Second strain repeats: More emphatic with added brass
1:10	C	③ Trio: New lyrical melody, softer; ***p***, new key  ***p***
1:43	Break	④ Dramatic break: Dramatic exchanges between high and low instruments  ***ff***
2:09	C	Trio repeats with countermelody played by the piccolos above the main melody stated softly by the brass
2:41	Break	Dramatic break repeats
3:07	C	⑤ Final statement of trio, loudest sound level, with addition of countermelodies in piccolo and trombones

check your **KNOWLEDGE**

1. Describe the difference between listening to music casually and attentively.
2. Do you have a favorite piece of music that captures your attention?
3. How does Sousa use form in *The Stars and Stripes Forever* to build a sense of climax?

PART I SUMMARY: THE ELEMENTS OF MUSIC

- There are several different aspects of sound that composers manipulate in writing music, involving primarily pitch, rhythm, texture, dynamics, and timbre.
    - *Pitch* concerns the relative height of a musical sound, shown in Western music through a system of notation that uses notes to place pitches on a five-line staff.
    - *Rhythm* affects the duration of pitches.
    - *Texture* describes the relative thickness or complexity of the musical fabric.
    - *Dynamics* regulate the intensity of the sound (how loud, how soft).
    - *Timbre* refers to the quality of the sound (what makes a piano sound like a piano, a trumpet like a trumpet, etc.).

- In addition to these aspects, composers work with different musical forms, or blueprint-like plans, for unifying the music while providing variety.

- Since the seventeenth century, most Western music has used a system known as *tonality*, based on the major and minor scales. It has also used three-note chords, or *triads*, built on the pitches of those scales. The study of chords and how to progress from one to another is known as *harmony*, the vertical aspect of music. The study of setting one musical line against another line is known as *counterpoint*, which emphasizes the horizontal aspect of music.

- Music can be written for a soloist or a small group of soloists, or for larger ensembles such as an orchestra, band, or chorus.

- Classical music is the general term used to describe Western art music from the medieval period to the present.
    - The distinction between classical and popular/traditional music that has been made in the past is no longer as commonly held today. Scholars have shown that classical composers have always borrowed from popular melodies, rhythms, and harmonies. In turn, popular music has been influenced by classical styles.

- For convenience, the history of classical music has been divided into several major periods or eras.
    - The medieval and Renaissance periods traced the development from monophony (single melodies played or sung together) to polyphony (the addition of one or more additional melodic parts). Much of this music was based on modal scales and harmonies.
    - The Baroque period saw the introduction of modern tonality and harmony. Baroque music was characterized by ornate melodies and complex musical structures. This music often is interpreted to be highly emotional and turbulent.
    - The Classical era saw a return to more regular forms and simpler melodies. Its two greatest composers were Haydn and Mozart, imitated by the young Beethoven.
    - The Romantic period saw an increased emphasis on personal expression. Romantic composers rejected earlier rules to explore the range and depth of their own creativity.

- The modern era (twentieth century) introduced new ways of organizing pitch, scale, and harmony. This music was meant to reflect both the rapid technological changes occurring as well as the increasing horror at the cost of war, environmental change, and the threat of nuclear annihilation.
- Postmodernism (1970–today) represents both a return to more traditional forms as well as a continued interest in experimentation and self-expression.

- There is a difference between casually listening to music and listening attentively.
  - Attentive listening involves listening without any other distractions (such as searching the web or texting on your cell phone).
  - Attentive listening often requires that you listen to a piece more than once.
  - We can increase our pleasure from music by listening for the basic elements of melody, rhythm, and harmony, as well as by understanding a composition's form.

KEY TERMS

accent 22
accidental 9
adagio 19
aerophone 33
allegro 19
alto 32
baritone 32
bass 32
bass clef 7
beat 21
binary form 43
brass instruments 33
cadence 10
canon 26
chamber music 36
chamber orchestra 36
choir 38
chord 28
chordophone 33
chorus 38
chromatic scale 15
classical music 46
clef 7
common time 24
compound meter 23
conductor 36
conjunct motion 11
consonance 11
contralto 32
counterpoint (contrapuntal) 26
crescendo 30
cut time 24
decrescendo 30
diminuendo 30
disjunct motion 11
dissonance 11
dotted note 17
downbeat 22
duple meter 23
dynamics 30
eighth note 17
electrophone 33
ensemble 36
flat 8
form 43
forte 30
frequency 4
fundamental pitch 4
half note 17
half step (or semitone) 13
harmonic 4
harmony 28
homophony 28
idiophone 33
imitation 26
imitative counterpoint 26
interval 10
key 13
key signature 9
ledger lines 6
major scale 13
measure (or bar) 22
measure line (or bar line) 22
melody 9
membranophone 33
meter (metrical) 22
metronome 19
minor scale 13
monophony 26
natural sign 8
noise 45
non-imitative counterpoint 26
notation 6
note 6
octave 7
orchestra 36
overtone 4
partial 4
percussion 33
phrase 10
piano 30
pitch 4
polyphony 26
quadruple meter 23

PART

The Middle Ages

All of creation is a song of praise to God. —HILDEGARD OF BINGEN

Illuminated fourteenth-century chant manuscript.

The first flowering of Western music sprang from the expanse of time known as the Middle Ages (or medieval era), roughly the fifth to the mid-fifteenth century. Renaissance thinkers looking back on this era saw it as one of stagnation, a wasteland separating classical antiquity from their own golden age. They dismissed the early medieval centuries, which were wracked by political instability and dire poverty, as the "Dark Ages." Neither did they admire the later medieval centuries, termed "Gothic." (The name derives from the Goths, marauding Germanic tribes who had periodically ravaged the Roman Empire from the third century on.)

Aachen Cathedral in Germany, with Romanesque decoration.

Today historians view the Middle Ages more positively and recognize its contributions to Western culture. The first major event marking the era was the fall of the Roman Empire to a Germanic chieftain in 476 CE. While the next few centuries remained politically unstable and chaotic, by the seventh and eighth centuries a Germanic tribe known as the Franks was consolidating its power. By the eighth and ninth centuries, the arts began to enjoy a vigorous revival. The powerful emperor of the Franks, Charlemagne (r. 768–814), introduced measures to promote literacy, though he was himself unable to write. In the tenth and eleventh centuries, the art of manuscript illustration (called *illumination*) reached new heights. Monasteries and cathedrals rose in the Romanesque style, with massive walls and rounded arches. In the Gothic style (from the mid-twelfth to the early fifteenth century), the emphasis shifted to soaring arches, vaulted ceilings, and shimmering panels of stained glass.

The late Middle Ages saw the chartering of the first European universities. Meanwhile, the spreading Christian philosophy drew on the ancient Greeks as well as the church fathers. And over all those centuries of cultural awakening, Western art music grew steadily more versatile and complex.

Strasbourg Cathedral, France. Constructed of sandstone between 1176 and 1439, the cathedral remains the tallest extant structure from the Middle Ages.

WHY LISTEN TO *Medieval Music?*

To many modern ears, medieval music sounds utterly foreign. The melodies appear to be simple; there is limited, if any, harmony; and the music follows its own sense of time, as if not from this world. So why study it?

One reason is that, despite its remoteness from us, medieval music has retained a significant link to the present. Much of it was written for the Roman Catholic Church, to support early Christian worship. Working over centuries, anonymous musicians crafted thousands of sacred chants that have endured in an unbroken, rich tradition. The practice of chanting—of singing texts to repeated melodic patterns—is common to several faiths and cultures, Western and non-Western. Its mesmerizing force and allure are something that we understand today, whether celebrating a Mass, listening to Tibetan or Navajo chant, or participating in a crowd's athletic chant at a stadium. In medieval Christianity, chanting was a means of communicating sacred texts and transporting participants into a trance-like state. It could heighten spiritual awareness, including contemplation of the hereafter. And there was good enough reason for chant—life was difficult and woefully short, and prayer assisted by chanting was a source of comfort.

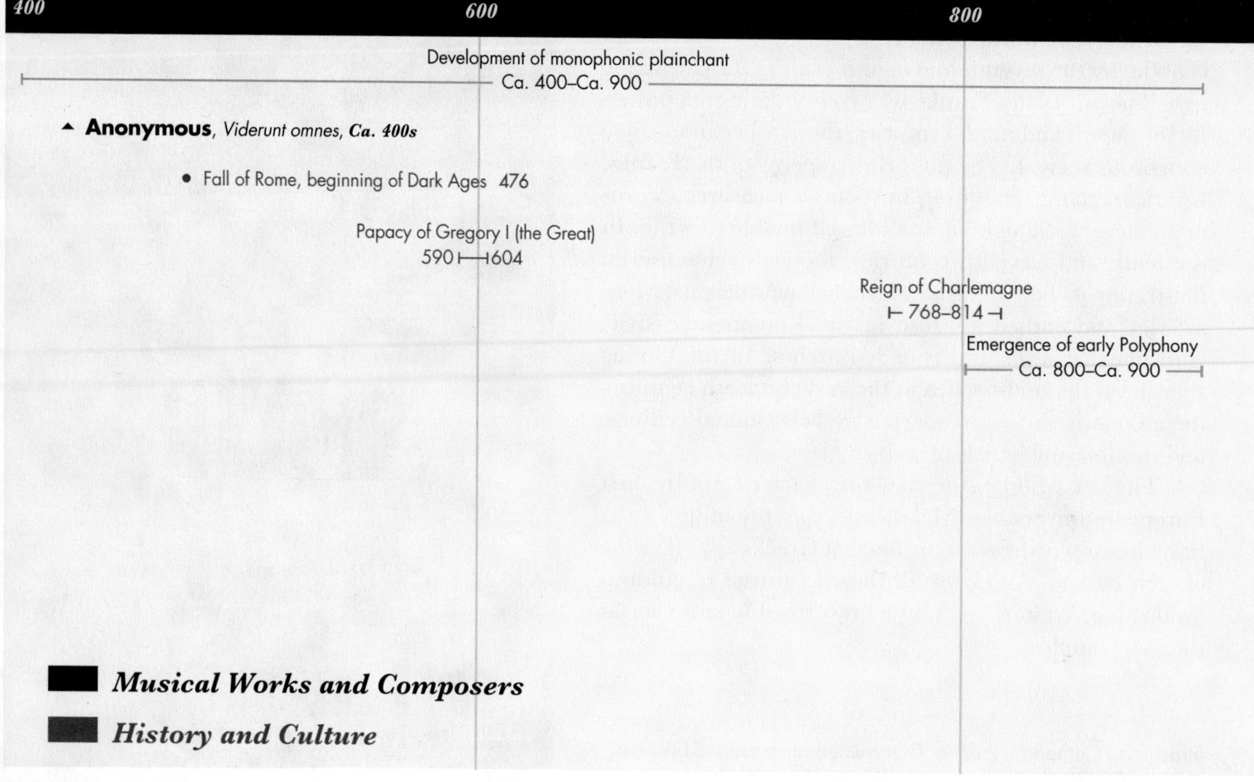

This music was designed to influence the participants' mindset, to direct their thoughts away from concerns of earthly life and toward heaven. Medieval music tends to move deliberately and at its own pace—not ours. Its melodies are compact, with limited range or movement.

Are there any similarities in today's music? Consider these parallels:

- The practice of chanting during meditation in Zen Buddhism
- Centuries-old prayers and chants in other faiths, including Judaism and Islam, still performed at different times each day as part of religious observances
- Any music used for personal meditation or to create a special atmosphere or personal space apart from the concerns of daily life

Another reason to study medieval music is that it represents the first major step in the development of Western classical music. Even within the confines of the Middle Ages, we can see developments in music—for example, from single-note melodies to basic harmonies—critical to the course of Western music over the next centuries. Our current system of musical notation originated with medieval scribes notating melodies on parchment manuscripts. The story of how this music developed is worth tracing, and in the West it began in earnest during the Middle Ages.

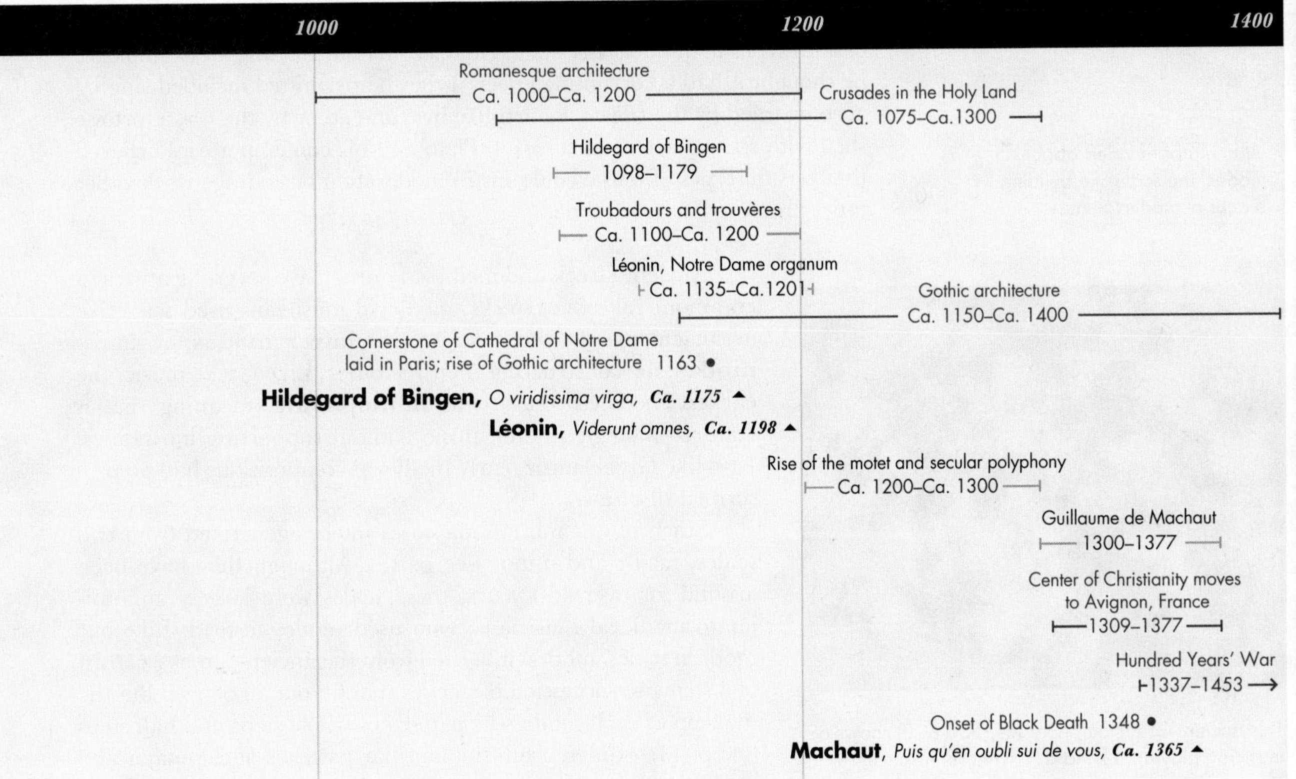

CHAPTER

7 Origins of Medieval Music

We know regrettably little about ancient Greek music and even less about ancient Roman music. We do know, however, that the music of the Middle Ages owed a considerable debt to the music of antiquity, especially Greek music. For that reason, our exploration of Western music begins here.

Early medieval musicians borrowed from the Greeks three key ideas:

1) *The distinction between consonance and dissonance*: This is the concept that certain musical intervals (see p. 11) are fundamentally pleasing and stable (**consonant**), while others are harsh and unstable (**dissonant**).
2) *The "music of the spheres"*: This is the idea that the stars and planets move in musical harmony, emitting inaudible humming that expresses simple mathematical ratios.
3) *The emotional and moral power of music*: The philosopher Plato (fourth century BCE) was so concerned about the power of music that he permitted only certain types in his ideal city-state. He rejected flute playing, for example, as he thought it had a corrupting effect. Types he permitted included singing accompanied by the *kithara*, a harp-like instrument, or by the *lyre*, a tortoise shell with strings stretched across it. Plato and his contemporaries believed that certain types of music could instill moderation or courage while other types promoted moral decline.

Dashboard

Watch a brief video about modes, the scale-like building blocks of medieval music.

This ancient Greek amphora (ca. 530 BCE) shows a musician playing a kithara, a lyre-like instrument with strings that were plucked.

Ancient Greek and medieval music have several features in common. Like the Greeks, medieval musicians used scale-like arrangements of pitches, known as **church modes**, or simply **modes**, for constructing their melodies. Like Greek music, the earliest medieval music was **monophonic**, meaning that it featured a single line of music without supporting harmonies. Also like Greek music, early medieval compositions had no prescribed rhythms.

Much of our music today uses pitches generated from two scales, major and minor (see p. 13). Although they have been around for over 450 years, these scales were largely unfamiliar to medieval musicians, who used modes instead. Like our modern scales, modes (inherited from the ancient Greeks) consist of a stepwise succession of pitches that fill out an octave. But the makeup of each mode—its pattern of whole steps and half steps (see p. 13)—differs from the familiar patterns of the major and minor scales.

check your KNOWLEDGE

1. Which concepts did medieval musicians adapt from Greek music theory?
2. Which three features did early medieval music share with Greek music?

CHAPTER 8 Music for the Christian Church

The bulk of medieval music has been lost. Illiteracy was then widespread, so most music was not preserved. But the Roman Catholic Church had a vested interest in spreading its sacred **liturgy**, or the texts and music used in worship. Much of the surviving music from the Middle Ages is notated music with church Latin texts. Our narrative of Western classical music begins here, with the music of the Roman Catholic Church.

For a few centuries, this church music—known collectively as **plainsong**, **plainchant**, or simply **chant**—was passed down orally, perhaps with hand signals used as teaching aids. Then, sometime in the first half of the ninth century, innovation came in the form of **neumes**—dashes, dots, and curved, hook-like figures that could be used to represent musical tones.

Scribes added these symbols above lines of text carefully copied onto manuscripts. We owe the origins of Western musical notation to the diligence of scribes working in monastic libraries. This striking innovation captured the ethereal pitches of plainchant and revolutionized the transmission of the music.

Neumes from an early Western manuscript, placed above the text *Jubilate Deo* ("Praise God").

Pope Gregory receiving divine inspiration in the form of a dove.

Gregorian Chant

Around 600, Pope Gregory I (r. 590–604) began setting standards for the liturgy and encouraging uniform practices in singing chant. According to legend, a divinely inspired Gregory notated the chant melodies himself. Medieval artists showed him copying this music while the dove of the Holy Spirit sang the sacred chants into his ear. In time, this authorized plainchant of the church became known as **Gregorian chant**.

To modern listeners, Gregorian chant requires a leap of faith:

- This music is not based on the major and minor scales familiar to us in classical and popular music, but on archaic-sounding church modes.
- In some chants, the musicians sing in **unison** (together), while in others they divide into two groups that alternate. In still others, known as **responsorial**, a soloist may alternate with the choir.
- There are no recurring rhythmic patterns in Gregorian chant to help orient us in time.
- There are no notated instruments blending with the human voice.
- Without harmony, the chant, isolated as a single melodic strand, seems to float in and out of our consciousness, as if not of this time or place.

Upon closer inspection, we can find in the sacred chants some basic principles of musical organization that remained relevant centuries later in Western classical music.

Slowly accumulating over several centuries, Gregorian chant originated in the rural monastic outposts that dotted Europe and the English Isles. This sacred music resounded too in the cathedrals that came to tower over new urban centers, including Paris, Milan, and Rome. Just as generations of anonymous artisans built the great medieval cathedrals, so generations of anonymous musicians created an enormous body of chants meant to endure. Like the Gothic cathedrals reaching toward the heavens, monophonic plainchants were intended as sonic sculptures that glorified God and transcended time.

The Divine Office and the Mass

In the Roman Catholic Church, the singing of plainchant supported two types of rituals:

1) The **Divine Office**, which was an extended series of services, beginning about 4:00 a.m. and continuing at regular intervals throughout the day and evening. These services were practiced chiefly in monasteries and featured readings of Scriptures and prayers, in addition to singing of psalms, other Scriptures, and hymns.
2) The **Mass**, which was celebrated in the morning, usually around 9:00 a.m. This complex ritual was, and is, the symbolic recreation of Christ's Last Supper with the twelve apostles. Just as a priest and congregation do today, in the Middle Ages they would share consecrated bread and wine, the body

and blood of Christ, in Holy Communion. Early on, this daily affirmation of faith became the most solemn, elaborate service of the church.

The Mass consisted of readings from Scripture, prayers, and sung chants, divided into two types:

1) The chants of the **Proper**, which changed from day to day and were sung to texts appropriate for the feast or saint being celebrated. (Thus, chants for the Blessed Virgin Mary or Advent differ from those for St. Paul or Easter.) Many Proper chants are ornate and include portions intended for trained musicians. The main Proper chants in a Mass are the *Introit* (for the entry of the clergy), *Gradual* (usually psalm verses chanted on the steps, or *gradus*, of the altar), celebratory *Alleluia* (or, during Lent, a penitential *Tract*), *Offertory* (for the offering), and *Communion.*
2) The chants of the **Ordinary**, which, by contrast, used the same texts from day to day. They include the *Kyrie eleison* ("Lord, have mercy"), *Gloria in excelsis Deo* ("Glory to God in the highest"), *Credo* ("I believe," the creed, or profession of faith), *Sanctus* ("Holy, holy, holy Lord"), and *Agnus Dei* ("Lamb of God"). Ordinary chants are generally simpler than Proper chants.

Table 8.1 summarizes the Proper and Ordinary chants and shows how they are arranged within the musical portions of the Mass.

Taken together, the Proper and Ordinary chants constituted the music for the Mass. In this complex ritual, chanted music was woven together with the spoken prayers, petitions, Gospel readings, and other texts of the service. The Proper and Ordinary chants, along with those for the Divine Office, were compiled by medieval scribes in lavish chant books, where thousands of melodies were frozen in notation for all time.

TABLE 8.1 Musical Portions of the Mass

PROPER (TEXTS CHANGE FROM DAY TO DAY, ACCORDING TO THE FEAST OR SAINT CELEBRATED)	**ORDINARY** (TEXTS REMAIN THE SAME FROM DAY TO DAY)
1. *Introit*	
	2. *Kyrie eleison* 3. *Gloria*
4. *Gradual* 5. *Alleluia* or *Tract*	
	6. *Credo*
7. *Offertory*	
	8. *Sanctus* 9. *Agnus Dei*
10. *Communion*	

Medieval Christmas Music: *Viderunt omnes*

Illuminated miniature showing a celebration of the Christmas Mass at the Sainte-Chapelle, Paris.

When we think of Christmas music today, we often think of Christmas carols as an all-too-familiar part of Western culture. We might hear them while attending a church service, while listening to a group of roving carolers, or while shopping at a mall. But while a few Christmas carols have old roots, the most popular ones originated much more recently. In the Middle Ages, the high point of celebrating Christmas would have been the Mass for Christmas Day, for which a substantial body of plainchant was gradually created. A good example of medieval Christmas music is the anonymous chant *Viderunt omnes*, which dates back to the fifth century (**Listening Map 3**).

Not until the fourth century CE was Christmas observed on December 25, a date chosen in part to incorporate ancient Roman rituals recognizing the winter solstice. (Our tradition of Christmas lights has a remote connection to these early efforts to turn back the darkness.) Medieval Christmas traditions that we still recognize today include the yule log and nativity scenes. Medieval carols were often accompanied by dancing and merrymaking, both of which, however, were initially banned within the church. An elaborate liturgy evolved for the Mass on Christmas (which literally means "the Mass of Christ")—so elaborate that three Masses were celebrated, at midnight, dawn, and during the day.

Viderunt omnes was one of many chants specified to be sung at Christmas. It is an ornate example of a **gradual**, a Proper chant sung or recited between the Epistle and Gospel readings in the Mass. In what are known as **melismas**, several notes are sung to one syllable, often to reflect the meaning of the text (①, ② in the Deeper Listen that follows). To us today, the chant sounds exotic but distantly familiar. In part, that is because it uses an ancient mode, or scale, similar but not quite identical to our modern major or minor scales.

check your **KNOWLEDGE**

1. How did Pope Gregory influence the development of Gregorian chant?
2. Which musical elements make Gregorian chant sound foreign to modern listeners?
3. Which Catholic rituals did plainchant support?
4. What is the difference between the Proper and Ordinary of the Mass?
5. How does *Viderunt omnes* celebrate the spirit of Christmas?

Listening Map 3

ANONYMOUS, *Viderunt omnes* ("All the Ends of the Earth")

{ **FIFTH CENTURY** }

FORM	ABA (Respond-Verse-Respond)
TEXTURE	Monophonic
GENRE	Plainchant (Gradual)
SCORING	Voices (sometimes a soloist, sometimes a choir)
OVERVIEW	The anonymous plainchant *Viderunt omnes* is a gradual designated for Mass on Christmas Day. It has three sections: 1. Respond (A) 2. Verse (B) 3. Repeat of the Respond (A) The Respond and the Verse each begin with music for a soloist, answered by the choir. The overall form takes the symmetrical shape of ABA.

why to LISTEN

Much of *Viderunt omnes* hovers around certain pitches. Still, the anonymous composer invested this text with a melodic subtlety that we can appreciate today. The chant focuses its hypnotic effect on a single melodic line: we hear pitches moving in succession, one after the other, with no competing harmonies or other lines of music. In this concentrated, rarified musical world, individual pitches assume considerable significance. Sometimes the chant appears almost static. But sometimes it moves nimbly through a greater range, creating captivating soaring and swooping effects.

first LISTEN

A RESPOND	B VERSE	A RESPOND
0:00	**1:07**	**(not included)**
Soloist followed by choir	Soloist followed by choir	Soloist followed by choir

Continued

a deeper LISTEN

TIME	SECTION	PERFORMER AND TEXT	TRANSLATION
0:00	A Respond	**Soloist:** *Viderunt omnes* ① Melisma on omnes Soloist Vi - de - runt o - - - - - mnes	All the ends of the earth have seen
0:10		**Choir:** *fines terrae salutare Dei nostri: jubilate Deo omnis terra*	the salvation of our Lord: Rejoice in the Lord, all the earth.
1:07	B Verse	**Soloist:** *Notum fecit Do-mi-nus* ② Melisma on *do* Soloist No tum fe - cit Do - - - - - - - - - mi nus	The Lord has made known
1:40		*Salutare suum: ante conspectum gentium revelavit* **[Choir:]** *justitiam suam.*	His salvation: before the sight of nations. He has revealed His justice.
2:07	A Respond	**Soloist:** *Viderunt omnes*	

CHAPTER

Hildegard of Bingen

We will never know who composed *Viderunt omnes*, nor, for that matter, the vast majority of Gregorian chant. Only a few names of musicians associated with Gregorian chant have come down to us. Since this music was dedicated to sacred worship, its purpose was to glorify God, not to celebrate human artistic creativity. Authorship, which we take for granted, was then a largely unfamiliar concept.

One extraordinary exception was Hildegard of Bingen (1098–1179), the founder of a convent on a gentle slope overlooking the Rhine River in what is now Germany. She was the tenth child of noble parents who offered their daughter to the church as a *tithe*, or "one tenth," of their worldly possessions. At age fourteen she took vows and entered a convent, where Benedictine nuns educated her.

Hildegard writes down her visions after being touched by a heavenly fire, watched by the monk Volmar.

Early in life Hildegard began experiencing ecstatic, riddle-like visions, later recorded in her writings and illustrations. One revealed God slaying the serpent Satan with a sword, another the abundant greenery of nature, and yet another choirs of angels praising the Lord. In one particularly startling vision, flames descended from heaven, touched her in her monastic cell, and revealed to her the meaning of the Scriptures. Following this epiphany, Hildegard devoted herself primarily to writing poetry and music, composing nearly eighty chants. She also produced commentaries on natural history and medicine, as well as a musical morality play with music, about the Devil's attempts to win a soul. Emperors and popes sought the advice of the versatile Hildegard, who became a celebrity in her own time. She preached sermons to large gatherings, one of the few women in the twelfth century to do so.

Hildegard's interests ranged widely, from theology to poetry and the natural sciences. She wrote about issues of social justice, helping the poor, and mankind's duty to preserve the natural world as part of God's creation. All of these subjects resonated in a remarkable revival of her work late in the twentieth century, on the 900th anniversary of her birth. Her writings were widely translated and her music released on best-selling CDs. In her afterlife Hildegard came to appeal to a wide diversity of followers: mystics, feminists, and members of the New Age movement among them.

Dashboard

Read an excerpt from Hildegard of Bingen's writings.

Hildegard created her own melodies and texts for use in the Divine Office and Mass. She described herself as a "feather floating on the breath of God" and offered her music as a medium for divine inspiration. An example of her art is *O viridissima virga* (**Listening Map 4**), a Proper chant for Masses in honor of the Virgin Mary. She describes Mary as a branch of the Tree of Jesse, which is a depiction of Christ's ancestors. The subject was readily familiar to Hildegard through its widespread use in medieval art, including illuminated manuscripts, embroidery, paintings, and magnificent stained glass panels.

LISTENING MAP 4

HILDEGARD OF BINGEN, *O viridissima virga* ("O Greenest Branch")

{ **TWELFTH CENTURY** }

GENRE	Plainchant
TEXTURE	Monophonic
OVERVIEW	Filling her text with images of spring, Hildegard likens Christ to a "beautiful flower" in parched lands. The poem has seven sections, ranging from two to six lines of free verse. No two sections of music are alike; instead, fresh portions of chant accompany the changing textual images. There is, however, one unifying musical device: each section of chant begins and ends on the same pitch (1), so that the music seems to sprout forth from a common source, like foliage from the Tree of Jesse. Her music matches the shifting images by employing a simple, devotional style, with one or two pitches per syllable. Still, she does not miss occasional opportunities for melismas, as on *ple-* of *plena* ("full"; (2)) and *al-* of *altissimo* ("in the highest"; (3)).

why to LISTEN

Unlike most of the composers discussed in this book, Hildegard was unusual in the breadth of her interests—she was a poet, musician, composer, abbess, and prolific writer and illustrator. Such versatility was rare, indeed, in the twelfth or, for that matter, any century. The gift to write poetry is special, as is the gift to write music. When they are shared in one person, the results can be extraordinary. As you read Hildegard's poem, and listen to her music, ask yourself whether her text may have inspired her music or vice versa.

first LISTEN

1	2	3	4	5	6	7
0:00	**0:39**	**1:32**	**2:11**	**2:36**	**3:46**	**4:38**
1st Verse	2nd Verse Begins on same note as 1st verse, but has a different length	3rd Verse Begins on same note as 2nd verse, but has a different length	4th Verse Begins on same note as 3rd verse, but has a different length	5th Verse Begins on same note as 4th verse, but has a different length	6th Verse Begins on same note as 5th verse, but has a different length	7th Verse Begins on same note as 6th verse, but has a different length

a deeper LISTEN

TIME	VERSE	LISTEN FOR THIS	LYRICS	TRANSLATION
0:00	1	(1) Sections begin and end on same pitch	*O viridissima virga, ave* *quae in ventoso flabro sciscitationis* *sanctorum prodisti.* O vi - ri - dis - si - ma vir - ga, a - ve quae in ven - to - so	*Hail, O greenest branch* *who sprang forth in the airy breezes* *of the saints' inquiries.*
0:39	2		*Cum venit tempus,* *quod tu floruisti* *in ramis tuis,* *ave, ave sit tibi,* *quia calor solis in te sudavit* *sicut odor balsami.*	*Since the time has come* *for you to flourish* *amidst your boughs,* *hail, hail to you,* *because the heat of the sun exuded* *from you like the aroma of balm.*
1:32	3		*Nam in te floruit pulcher flos* *qui odorem dedit omnibus aromatibus* *quae arida erant.*	*For a beautiful flower blossomed* *in you which gave a scent* *to all arid perfumes.*
2:11	4	(2) Melisma on *ple-* ("full")	*Et illa apparuerunt omnia* *in viriditate plena.*	*And all those have appeared* *in their full greenery*
2:36	5		*Unde celi dederunt rorem super gramen* *et omnis terra leta facta est,* *quoniam viscera ipsius frumentum protulerunt* *et quoniam volucres celi* *nidos in ipsa habuerunt,*	*Whence the skies gave dew on the pasture,* *and all the earth was made joyful,* *because her womb produced grain,* *and because the birds of the heaven* *have made their nests in her.*
3:46	6		*Deinde facta est esca hominibus* *et gaudium magnum epulantium,* *inde, o suavis virgo,* *in te non deficit ullum gaudium.*	*Then the harvest was prepared for Man,* *and a great rejoicing of banqueters,* *whence, O sweet Virgin,* *no joy is lacking in you.*
4:38	7	(3) Melisma on *al-*	*Hec omnia Eva contempsit.* *Nunc autem laus sit altissimo.*	*All these things Eve dismissed.* *Now let praise be to you in the highest.*

check your KNOWLEDGE

1. How are melismas effectively used in *Viderunt omnes?*
2. Why is Hildegard of Bingen so important in the history of medieval music?
3. What is the central metaphor in *O viridissima virga?* How does the musical setting reflect this theme?
4. Compare *Viderunt omnes* and *O viridissima virga.* What do they have in common musically? What are some differences, if any?

CHAPTER

10 Léonin and the Rise of Polyphony

For much of the Middle Ages, **monophony**—having only a single melodic line—was the defining feature of music. But by the ninth century, a few centuries before Hildegard composed her visionary chants, a radically different type of music was developing. In **polyphony** (literally, "many voices"), multiple musical lines are heard simultaneously, so that they compete for our attention. It emerged in a few experimental centers of Gregorian chant in England, France, and Spain. The development of polyphony was arguably *the* decisive event in Western music history.

The turn to polyphony during the Middle Ages opened up new terrains in Western music. By setting different musical lines against each other, composers began practicing the art of **counterpoint** ("note against note"; see p. 26). Over time, counterpoint evolved into a powerful musical discipline that enabled composers to achieve an extraordinary degree of inventiveness simply not supported by monophony.

The origins of Western polyphony are obscure, and its first composers anonymous. We do know, however, that these composers must have been educated church clerics, because the new music required notation. The first preserved examples consisted of a newly created musical line suspended above bits of Gregorian chant, suggesting that polyphony indeed originated in the church. By adding a second line to Gregorian chant, composers unlocked a pathway to a new musical dimension.

Instead of considering music just as a succession of single pitches in time, one after the other, they now had to place pitches also heard vertically, at the same time. This posed a new and exciting challenge: to create music that was pleasing in harmony as well as in melody.

As polyphony became more complex, there was a need to regulate the rhythms of the music, so that vertically sounding pitches could align in harmonies, or **chords**. No longer solely dependent on Gregorian chant, church musicians were now free to supplement chants with their own, decorative musical lines. In turn, the spread of polyphony throughout the West encouraged training composers who could produce it for sacred music.

In the late twelfth and early thirteenth centuries, church polyphony, known as **organum**, coalesced into a vibrant style of music making centered in Paris. The city was undergoing a cultural awakening: during this era, the Sorbonne University was chartered, and the great Cathedral of Notre Dame ("Our Lady") was being built. The cornerstone of Notre Dame was laid in 1163, and construction continued into the fourteenth century. The impressive finished cathedral, where polyphony was performed, features a radiant rose window, twin towers, and gravity-defying flying buttresses.

Early Notre Dame polyphony is attributed to the composer Léonin, described as the "best maker" of organum. Léonin lived from about 1135 to at least 1201 and was likely a priest and a poet as well as a composer. He gathered his compositions into a volume known as the *Magnus liber*, or *Great Book*. His successor, Perotin (active around 1200), also made significant contributions to polyphony.

Léonin created polyphony for Proper chants, such as the anonymous *Viderunt omnes*, which we examined earlier. His contribution was to add a new part above the solo sections of chant sung at the beginnings of the Respond and Verse (review **Listening Map 3**). The other sections of chant were assigned to the choir and were

Cathedral of Notre Dame, Paris (1163–ca. 1350). (a) Side view, showing the flying buttresses. (b) Façade.

MAKING CONNECTIONS *Gothic Cathedrals and Polyphonic Architecture*

The twelfth century brought the building of great Gothic cathedrals, which rose like medieval skyscrapers to dominate the urban areas of Europe. Though named after the Goths—a Germanic tribe who had sacked Rome centuries before—the new architectural style was first established in northern French realms. In Paris, Pope Alexander III attended the laying of the cornerstone for Notre Dame in 1163.

Gothic cathedrals were feats of engineering, advanced by three innovations:

1) the pointed arch, which redistributed weight so as seemingly to defy gravity;
2) the flying buttress, which offered external support that allowed for taller buildings; and
3) the ribbed vault, which required less structural support, allowing for more stained glass windows.

As the seat (*cathedra* in Latin) of bishops, cathedrals were meant to represent the house of God on earth. Their vast spaces, fantastic designs, and soaring towers and spires vaulting to the heavens transported worshipers from their daily cares to a purely spiritual world.

It is not surprising that early on, cathedrals became centers of the new polyphony in music. Just as Gothic designs created dramatic vertical spaces, polyphony liberated a vertical harmonic dimension for musicians to explore. The relatively modest two-voiced experiments of Léonin in organum were soon replaced by the more ambitious compositions of his successor Pérotin. By the early thirteenth century Pérotin was adding two or three newly composed parts above the sacred plainchant. As this swirling new music filled the cavernous interior of Notre Dame in Paris, listeners must have felt that the very architecture was coming alive.

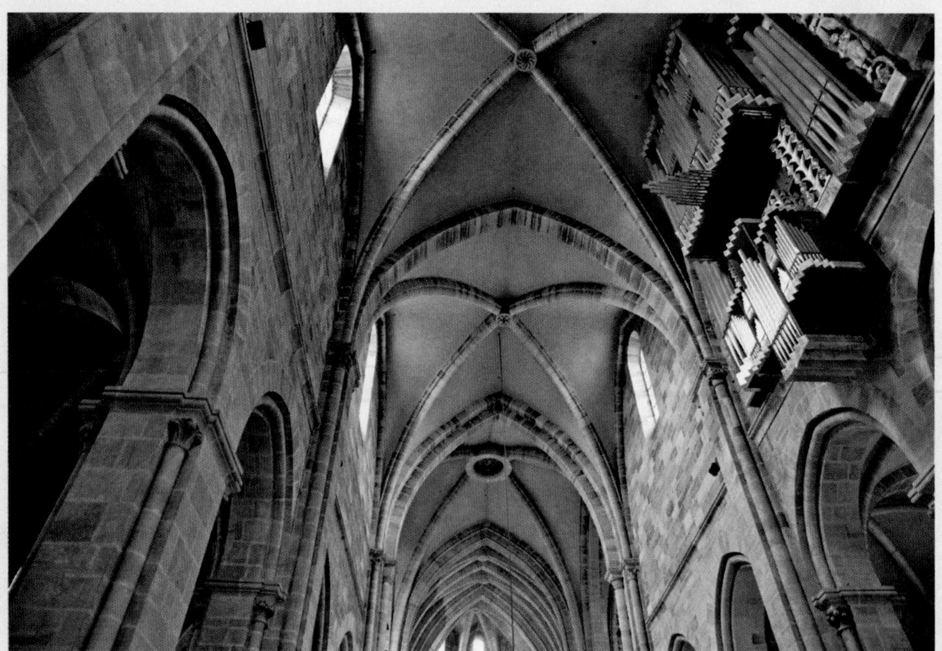

Interior of Bamberg Cathedral, Germany, showing vaulted arch ceilings and pointed archways.

sung as monophony, as they had been for centuries. The result thus combined the new with the old, alternating passages of ornate, two-part polyphony with bare, monophonic chant.

Though we know little about Léonin's life, the new type of Notre Dame polyphony he helped create changed Western music to its core. Now listeners received multiple channels of music at once, combining and separating in dynamic interplays of sounds. What had been relatively dull, gray tones were transformed into vibrant colors.

Musicians have always needed the freedom to experiment, to discover new creative solutions. In the Middle Ages, polyphony represented an entirely new world to explore. It took the musical art to previously unimagined levels of complexity.

Léonin's setting of the opening Respond of *Viderunt omnes* (**Listening Map 5**) adds a new voice above the chant and displays two types of polyphony:

- In the first type, the lower voice (a tenor, from the Latin for "hold") holds the note of chant while the upper voice executes melodic flourishes.
- In the second type (at the melisma on the *o-* of *omnes*), the tenor speeds up, approaching the pace of the upper voice.

At the conclusion of *omnes* the upper and lower voices form a **cadence**, or close, a restful and consonant coming together. With this pause we reach the end of the solo (and hence the polyphonic) portion of the Respond. Now the fifth-century monophonic chant holds sway until the beginning of the Verse (not in the recording or diagram). At that point, Léonin's animated polyphony again springs to life.

As Léonin and other early composers of polyphony realized, the new style required a new system of rhythms and a way of notating them to keep the voices in sync. As you listen to the opening of *Viderunt omnes*, you will soon distinguish two rhythmic layers. The first is the slower-moving lower voice (the chant), which often holds individual pitches for several seconds. The second layer is the more nimble upper voice, which generally moves in faster patterns of long and short pitches. Léonin's music thus has a rhythmic dimension that adds another layer of complexity and satisfies our need to organize musical time.

check your KNOWLEDGE

1. Why was the development of polyphony so important in the history of Western music?
2. What is counterpoint, and what did it offer composers?
3. How did Léonin transform the plainchant *Viderunt omnes?*
4. What are the two types of polyphony that Léonin used in *Viderunt omnes?*

LISTENING MAP 5

LÉONIN, First Respond from *Viderunt omnes* ("All the Ends of the Earth")

{TWELFTH CENTURY}

GENRE	Organum
TEXTURE	Polyphony alternating with monophony
FORM	ABA (Respond-Verse-Respond); shown here is the opening Respond
OVERVIEW	This brief excerpt from Léonin's *Viderunt omnes* (the Respond, or first section) lasts only two minutes or so, but it neatly encapsulates several key features of Western art music. This excerpt begins in polyphony, with Léonin's added voice above the chant (①), and a second type of polyphony, in which the chant (in the lower voice) speeds up (②). The music then returns to the first type of polyphony (③) before shifting to monophony as the chant continues by itself (④). Listening gives us the opportunity to compare the enriched sounds of polyphony (in two types) with the unadorned strand of monophony.

why to LISTEN

This excerpt addresses a central concern of Western music: harmony. In adding a second voice to the chant, Léonin had to decide which intervals would sound simultaneously, and when. Perhaps not surprisingly, his choices reflected the preferences of medieval musicians for consonant intervals such as the octave, fifth, and fourth.

But what makes this music special? Léonin carved out a new creative space. He did in the twelfth century what many Western composers and performers would later do across many centuries. He took some existing musical material—here a fifth-century chant, sanctioned by the Church—and added to it his own, new material, by placing over it an entirely new line of music. In a similar way, many classical composers and jazz musicians take a pre-existent theme and build their own compositions upon it. The paradoxical needs to compose freely, yet also to observe traditions and rules about how to compose, are a key element of Western music. In twelfth-century Notre Dame polyphony, we already have a glimpse of that process.

first LISTEN

POLYPHONY (FIRST TYPE)	POLYPHONY (SECOND TYPE)	POLYPHONY (FIRST TYPE)	MONOPHONY
0:00	**0:49**	**0:58**	**1:23**
First type of polyphony (lower voice holds the chant)	Second type of polyphony (lower voice speeds up)	First type of polyphony returns	Monophony; chant alone

a deeper LISTEN

TIME	TEXTURE	LISTEN FOR THIS	TEXT	TRANSLATION
0:00	Polyphony (first type)	① New upper part by Léonin, with melodic flourishes; slow chant in lower voice (tenor) Upper part: Vi - - - - - - - Tenor (chant): Vi - - - - - - - *(First pitch of chant)*	*Vi-* *-de-* *-runt*	*All the ends of the earth have seen*
0:49	Polyphony (second type)	② Melisma on *o-* of *omnes*; lower voice speeds up Upper part: O - - - - - - - Tenor (chant): O - - - - - - -	*o-*	
0:58	Polyphony (first type)	③ Tenor returns to slow chant; cadence at conclusion of *omnes*	*-mnes*	
1:23	Monophony	④ Choir sings rest of Respond in monophony	*fines terrae salutare Dei nostri* *jubilate Deo omnis terra*	the salvation of our Lord: Rejoice in the Lord, all the earth.

CHAPTER

Secular Medieval Music

So far, we have been describing sacred music for worship. But music also flourished outside the cathedrals and monasteries: in aristocratic courts, in slowly forming urban centers, and in thinly populated rural expanses where workers tilled the fields. This music took the form of music for court occasions, secular love songs, and

Medieval dance, as illustrated in an eleventh-century French manuscript.

dances and other types of popular entertainment. One dance form that has come down to us from the thirteenth and fourteenth centuries is the **estampie**, a stamping dance popular in France and Italy. All of this secular music was not as carefully preserved as sacred chant. Instead, it was largely transmitted by oral tradition or improvised as needed. Much of this music was sung, with or without instruments, but some—for example dance music—was intended for instruments alone.

Musical Instruments

View demonstration videos of medieval musical instruments.

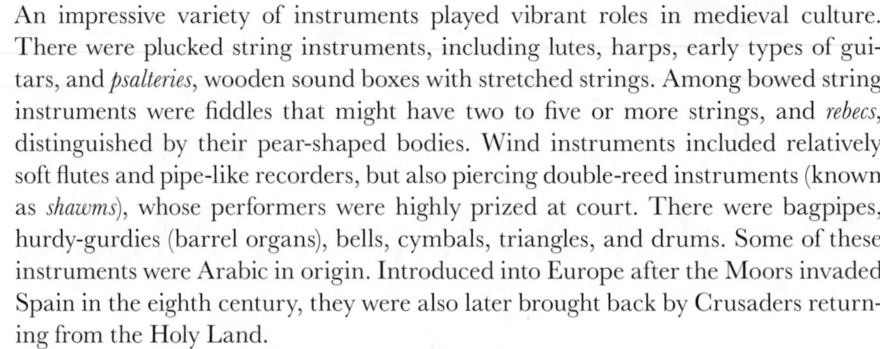

An impressive variety of instruments played vibrant roles in medieval culture. There were plucked string instruments, including lutes, harps, early types of guitars, and *psalteries*, wooden sound boxes with stretched strings. Among bowed string instruments were fiddles that might have two to five or more strings, and *rebecs*, distinguished by their pear-shaped bodies. Wind instruments included relatively soft flutes and pipe-like recorders, but also piercing double-reed instruments (known as *shawms*), whose performers were highly prized at court. There were bagpipes, hurdy-gurdies (barrel organs), bells, cymbals, triangles, and drums. Some of these instruments were Arabic in origin. Introduced into Europe after the Moors invaded Spain in the eighth century, they were also later brought back by Crusaders returning from the Holy Land.

By far the most complex medieval instrument was the organ. Indeed, for centuries the organ was the most imposing mechanical device of any kind. In some cases, hardy assistants operated the bellows, generating such wind pressure that the organist had to strike the keys forcibly. Musicians also played much smaller organs that could be transported or held in one's lap.

Today we can only guess how all these instruments were used. But already in the Middle Ages we see the division of Western music into vocal music, instrumental music, and music for voices and instruments together. These categories apply to most music discussed in this book.

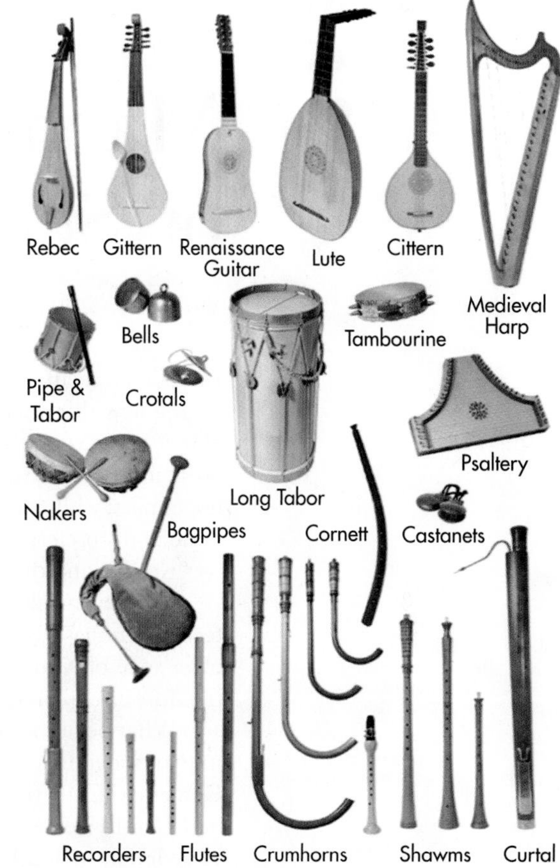

A variety of medieval musical instruments.

Secular Medieval Song

Much secular vocal music from the Middle Ages was performed in European courts. The nobility lived in fortress-like castles where they observed a strict social code of behavior known as **chivalry**. This word brings to mind knights in shining armor—and in fact it derives from the French *chevalier* (knight). The code of chivalry promoted the virtues of honor, valor, and fidelity. Women were idealized as "noble damsels" according to the rules of **courtly love**, a medieval tradition of love between a knight and a noblewoman.

Courtly love found creative outlets in two secular French repertories of the eleventh century:

1) In the southern region of what is now France, poet-musicians called **troubadours** wrote epic poems and composed songs about the Crusades (military campaigns in the Holy Land supported by the Catholic Church from 1095 until 1272) and courtly love. Some troubadours were noblemen, while others were commoners.
2) In the north, the troubadours' counterparts were known as the **trouvères**. Outside French realms, secular song took root in England, Italy, and Germany. The German **Minnesingers**, for example, sang of *Minne*, a spiritualized version of love.

Read an introduction to troubadours and their music, told from the perspective of one: Beatriz, Countess of Dia.

check your KNOWLEDGE

1. How was secular music different from music written for the church, and how did it develop?
2. Where did secular song first develop, and who performed it?

CHAPTER

Machaut and the Rise of Secular Polyphony

Polyphonic secular music was relatively late to emerge outside the church. It did so in a new thirteenth-century French genre known as the **motet**, a type of polyphonic vocal composition with some ties to the old Notre Dame organum. At first, poets simply took two-part sacred pieces and added new Latin or French texts to the upper part, while preserving the Latin chant in the tenor part. Increasingly, French became the preferred language in these compositions (*motet* derives from *mot*, French for "word"), and the texts became more and more secular in tone.

The new musical style, known as the ***Ars nova***, or new art, became in the fourteenth century rhythmically quite complex and sophisticated. In contrast to the older style of Notre Dame polyphony, with its fixed, repetitive rhythmic patterns, the *Ars nova* explored independent rhythms in different voices.

What began as an offshoot of the old Notre Dame polyphony now developed into an independent variety of secular polyphony performed outside the Church. Contributing to the new secular tone was the waning influence of the Catholic Church. Between 1309 and 1377, the papacy was centered not in Rome but in Avignon in southeastern France, where it fell under French influence. Then, between 1378 and 1417, a great schism (or break) followed as popes in Rome and "antipopes" in Avignon struggled for control.

Meanwhile, large-scale events shook Europe. At mid-century, the Black Death, a pandemic bubonic plague, killed a third of the population. And for much of the fourteenth century and beyond, France and England fought the devastating Hundred Years' War.

By the fourteenth century, secular polyphony had spread far, from Paris to England and Italy. Its principal representative was Guillaume de Machaut (ca. 1300–1377), a court diplomat who served French and Bohemian kings. For many years, he worked as a cleric at the cathedral of Rheims in the Champagne district, some 100 miles east of Paris.

Machaut produced a sizable quantity of music: all told, about 150 compositions. By far the most substantial is a polyphonic setting of the Ordinary of the Mass, which established a precedent for composers to follow for centuries. Most, though, are French secular works, including motets for three and four parts, and many love songs, known as **chansons**, in one, two, or three parts.

As we observed in the case of Hildegard of Bingen, it is rare in Western history when a major composer was also a major poet. Guillaume de Machaut probably leads this short list. Renowned as the premier French poet of his time, he was admired by no less a figure than Geoffrey Chaucer, author of the *Canterbury Tales*. Machaut's lyrics featured puns, references to contemporary events, and subtle, shifting metrical patterns. He wrote hundreds of poems, many of them in the *trouvère* tradition of courtly love, using the standard templates of medieval secular poetry. He also produced several long, narrative poems, some of which were interspersed with his love songs. All of his secular poetry was written in French, not Latin, which was reserved for the Church and for elevated literary styles. The turn to vernacular styles as legitimate outlets for literary works was a significant development in the later Middle Ages.

Guillaume de Machaut writing music.

Machaut set many of his poems to music, either as monophony, or as polyphony with two or three voices. His settings show an intimate relationship to his poems, so much that you might ask whether he was first a musician or a poet. However one decides this question, Machaut's two talents combined to produce some of the most creative and distinctive art of the fourteenth century.

Machaut's secular love songs, such as *Puis qu'en oubli sui de vous* (**Listening Map 6**), afford a distinctly intimate view of his art. This type of chanson is known as a **rondeau**, which features a recurring refrain heard in its entirety at the beginning and end of the composition. The rondeau is thus circular in structure, as suggested by its derivation from the French word *ronde*, or round.

Today, Machaut's music sounds unfamiliar. Its melodies are angular, its harmonies jarring, and its jostling rhythms unpredictable. We miss our usual chords, with their mellow, sweet-sounding thirds. But only decades after Machaut's death, English composers began introducing triads into their music. Exported to the Continent, this lush, new style revolutionized European music as the Middle Ages came to an end, and helped define the music of a new age: the Renaissance.

check your KNOWLEDGE

1. How did early secular polyphony develop?
2. What distinguished the songs written by Machaut, and why was he so important in the development of secular song?

LISTENING MAP 6

MACHAUT, *Puis qu'en oubli sui de vous* ("Since you have forgotten me")

{CA. 1365}

GENRE	Chanson
TEXTURE	Three-part polyphony
FORM	Rondeau: ABaAabAB
OVERVIEW	The form of this song is ABaAabAB, where AB represents the refrain, and the lowercase a and b the same music set to new, rhyming lines of texts. Notice the simple but elegant symmetry of the form. The composition begins and ends with the same music and text, which comes to a full cadence on a consonant chord (①) and (②), but for variety Machaut introduces new text for the third, fifth, and sixth lines.

why to LISTEN

Many of Machaut's poems and musical settings dwell on love and its unpredictable course. Usually he presents his songs from a male point of view that either praises the female beloved or chastises her for fickleness or infidelity. But in *Puis qu'en oubli sui de vous*, the perspective is turned, so that the poem and music support the perspective of a lady lamenting her lover's disloyalty.

This wistful chanson of a forgotten lover may be at some level autobiographical. Late in life Machaut fell in love with a young noblewoman named Péronne, but their relationship was unfulfilled, as he wrote in a narrative poem. Pitched in a low, dark register, Machaut's melody is supported by two lower parts. These mostly remain in the background but occasionally assert some independence by clashing harmonically or rhythmically with the melody. The means are simple, but the result is a poignant song that captures the human need to love, and to be loved.

first LISTEN

AB	a	A	ab	AB
0:00	**0:25**	**0:38**	**0:52**	**1:17**
Refrain	Same melody as A with new lyrics	Repeat of A	Same melodies as A and B with new lyrics	Refrain repeated

a deeper **LISTEN**

TIME	VERSE	LISTEN FOR THIS	LYRICS	TRANSLATION
0:00	**A**	(1) Vocal part accompanied by two lower-sounding instrumental parts Puis qu'en ou— bli sui de vous, dous a - mis	*Puis qu'en oubli sui de vous dous amis,*	Since you have forgotten me, sweet friend,
0:14	**B**		*Vie amoureuse et joie a dieu commant.*	I commend a life of love and joy to God.
0:25	**a**		*Mar vi le jour que m'amour en vous mis,*	I curse the day I placed my love with you,
0:38	**A**		*Puis qu'en oubli sui de vous dous amis,*	Since you have forgotten me, sweet friend,
0:52	**a**		*Mais ce tenray que je vous ay promis,*	But I will keep what I promised you,
1:06	**b**		*C'est que jamais n'aray nul autre amant,*	That I will never have another lover,
1:17	**A**		*Puis qu'en oubli sui de vous dous amis,*	Since you have forgotten me, sweet friend,
1:31	**B**	(2) All three parts come to a cadence on a consonant chord	*Vie amoureuse et joie a dieu commant.*	I commend a life of love and joy to God.

PART II SUMMARY: THE MIDDLE AGES

- Early Western music spans the Middle Ages, a long stretch of time from roughly the fifth to mid-fifteenth centuries.
- Most surviving medieval music was intended for services of the Catholic Church, including the Divine Office, typically performed in monasteries, and the Mass.
- The church developed Western musical notation to preserve thousands of sacred melodies sung to Latin texts, known as Gregorian chant, plainchant, or, simply, chant. These melodies were preserved in parchment manuscripts that were often lavishly illustrated, or illuminated.
- Chant is monophonic, meaning that it has a single melodic line.
- Some time around the ninth century, composers began adding extra lines of music to monophonic chant, producing early examples of polyphony. This development fundamentally changed the course of Western music. Composers of polyphony now had to conceive their music harmonically (vertically) as well as melodically (horizontally).
- The discovery of polyphony led to improvements in notation, so that musicians could coordinate simultaneously sounding musical parts.
- Outside the church, a tradition of monophonic and polyphonic music developed using secular instead of sacred texts.
- Most composers of medieval music were anonymous; among the leading named composers were Hildegard of Bingen, Léonin, and Guillaume de Machaut.

KEY TERMS

Ars nova 82
cadence 77
chanson 82
chant 65
chivalry 81
chord 75
church modes 64
consonant 64
counterpoint 74
courtly love 81
dissonant 64
Divine Office 66
estampie 80
gradual 68
Gregorian chant 66
liturgy 65
Mass 66
melisma 68
Minnesingers 81
mode 64
monophony 64, 74
motet 82
neume 65
Ordinary 67
organum 75
plainchant (plainsong) 65
polyphony 74
Proper 67
rondeau 83
troubadour, trouvère 81

KEY COMPOSERS

Hildegard of Bingen (1098–1179)
Léonin (ca. 1135–1201)
Guillaume de Machaut (ca. 1300–1377)

MUSICAL JOURNEYS
Kora Music of the Mandinka People of the Gambia

The Gambia is located in West Africa and is the smallest country on the continent. Various ethnic groups live in the country, with the Mandinka making up the largest population. The westernmost branch of the widespread Mande people, the Mandinka have a variety of music genres. Like most other Gambian ethnic groups, their society is organized into different classes of people. *Griots* are primarily hereditary professionals who specialize in playing music and performing works in praise of local leaders or relating history. Professional musicians are known as *jali* (pl. *jalolu*), and their music is referred to as *jaliyaa*.

In the past, jalolu served as court musicians, genealogists, oral historians, and even diplomats for leaders at all levels. They enjoyed permanent patronage; that is, individual leaders were obliged to support them. Jalolu would only marry other jalolus, ensuring that knowledge of the profession remained within the families. (Today marriages between jali and non-jali are far more common, and the music is taught in schools.) As the sole providers of their services, jalolu enjoyed a privileged position in Mandinka society, one that gave them power to criticize as well as to praise. Traditional jaliyaa is still performed at events such as child-namings, weddings, and religious celebrations. Although permanent patronage is now rare, today's politicians, businessmen, and religious leaders still regard jaliyaa as the music for their social class.

A male jali typically learns to sing and to play one of three melodic instruments, according to his particular family tradition. Although the jali women (*jali musolu*) do not play melodic instruments, they are highly trained and excellent singers. They play the *neo* or *karinya*, a tubular iron bell struck with an iron rod.

The most widespread instrument played by the male jali in the Gambia is the *kora*, a twenty-one-string bridge harp. Its body is made of a large half-calabash gourd, covered with cowhide to form the sound table. The body is pierced by a stout wooden pole, which forms both the neck and tailpiece. The player holds the instrument with the sound table facing him, the back of the calabash dome facing the listeners, and the neck towering above him. The cowhide forming the sound table also extends part way over the gourd, and is studded with decorative chrome tacks and cut with a sound hole. Extending downward from collars along the neck, the strings separate into two groups and pass over each side of a tall bridge mounted on the sound table. Below the bridge, the strings are knotted to anchor strings with a weaver's knot, and the anchors in turn are looped around an iron ring in the tailpiece. The collars (sing. *konso*) are raised or lowered to tune the strings. The strings (sing. *julo*) were once made of thin strips of antelope or cowhide twisted to form a round cross section, but since the introduction of nylon have been made of fishing line. The bright sound and durability of nylon have been factors in the kora's rise as a versatile and popular instrument.

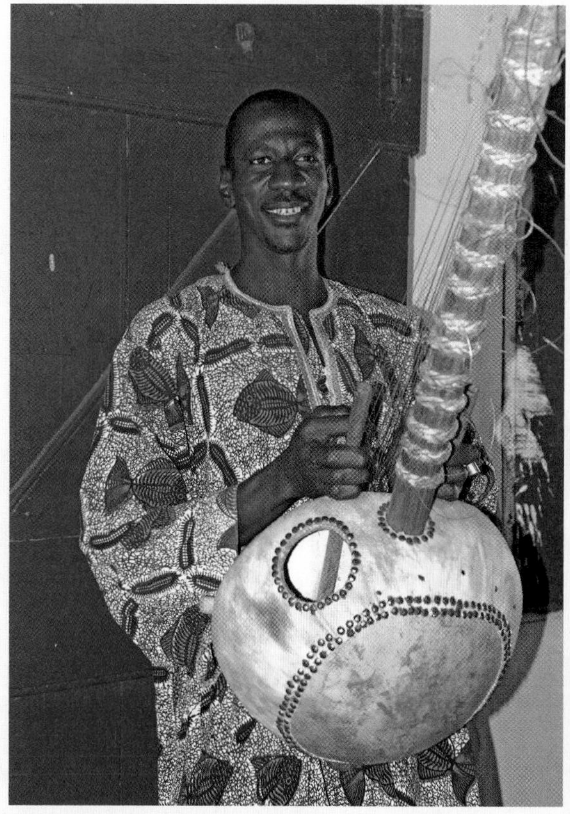

Gambian musician playing the kora.

According to legend, the kora was first played by Jali Madi Wuleng. One version of the story relates that while walking in the forest one day he heard beautiful music. Seeking its origin, he found a jinn (a genie or spirit) playing the kora. The jinn agreed to teach him to play if he would marry his daughter and remain in the spirit world forever. Wuleng agreed, but after some years escaped and brought the kora to the Mandinka.

Jaliyaa includes praise, historical narrative, and musical performance. The musical component of jaliyaa consists of a repertory of praise songs that celebrates the achievements of past heroes and contemporary figures. The basic vocal line (*donkilo*) is supported by a repeated musical figure (an **ostinato**) that kora players call the *kumbengo*. A typical kumbengo consists of a short melody in two contrasting parts. *Hemiolas*, interlocking rhythms and offset accents, create rhythmic interest. The basic *donkilo* line is used mainly as a choral refrain. The bulk of a song consists of long improvised recitations, called *sataro*, that incorporate proverbs, philosophical commentary, and formal and spontaneous praise for the individuals present at a performance.

In the 1990s Mandinka jaliyaa, especially kora jaliyaa, emerged as one of the most familiar West African sounds in the international world of Afro-pop music. Among the best-known musicians is Foday Musa Suso (b. 1953). A band leader, vocalist and kora player, Suso was born into a long-established and distinguished line of Mandinkan jalis. He moved first to Germany and then to Chicago, where he formed the Mandingo Griot Society, a loose aggregation of African, Caribbean, and American musicians playing a dance-based fusion of rock, funk, reggae, and traditional Gambian styles. Since the group disbanded, Suso has collaborated with a number of contemporary jazz/pop performers, including producer Bill Laswell and keyboard player/composer Herbie Hancock. He now divides his time between Chicago, New York, and the Gambia, combining the roles of traditional griot (see **Listening Map I.1**) and high-tech Western fusionist.

LISTENING MAP *I.1*

"Jula Jekere," performed by FODAY MUSA SUSO, recorded by VERNA GILLIS, 1978

FORM	Gambian praise song
METER	Free meter opening; regular meter during main song
TEMPO	Regular bass
SCORING	Kora (strung harp) and vocalist
OVERVIEW	"Jula Jekere" follows a basic song structure: it opens with an instrumental improvised introduction which is nonrhythmical; then the kora introduces the main melodic theme with a regular beat, which is the basis of the song performed by the vocalist; and finally there is a concluding improvisation. The singing is half chanted, half sung, as its purpose is to relate a key story in the life of the people, rather than to carry the melody.

why to **LISTEN**

Gambian kora players (or jalis) are celebrated storytellers. They help preserve the history of their local culture through their songs, and their work is highly prized. "Jula Jekere" tells the story of a nineteenth-century businessman/tradesman (*jula*) named Jekere Bayo. Through his dealings, he gained great status and wealth, and many myths arose around him. Jekere came to own many slaves and had many followers, and he used his jalis to spread the message about his power and wealth. Traditionally, prayer services were performed at the end of the Muslim month of fasting (or Ramadan). It was said that Jekere was so wealthy that he established separate services a week later, with hundreds of animals sacrificed. According to legend, only the singing by one of his jalis of this song stopped him from also sacrificing his hundred slaves.

first **LISTEN**

OPENING IMPROVISATION	MELODY/THEME	VOCAL/INSTRUMENTALS	INSTRUMENTAL
0:00	**1:08**	**1:58**	**5:30**
Kora explores melody playing without regular bass accompaniment.	Kora establishes the melody and begins to play with rhythmic bass accompaniment.	Vocalist sings with kora accompaniment; vocal phrases and brief instrumental responses occur in sequence. Extended improvised instrumentals break up the regular return of the main melody sung by the vocalist.	Kora performs final improvisation and then regular rhythm ends as it plays a series of brief melodic phrases to conclude the piece.

a deeper **LISTEN**

TIME	SECTION	LISTEN FOR THIS
0:00	Opening improvisation (kora)	Opening melodic improvisation on the kora in free rhythm. No lower-range melodic pattern. At 0:18, listen for the descending melodic contour of each phrase, which is typical of kora improvisation.
0:43		Regular lower-range melodic pattern (kumbengo) appears, coupled with the establishment of an upper-range melodic idea. Regular beat established.
1:08	Melody/ theme (kora)	First statement of main melodic theme. The lower-range pattern remains steady, as the upper-range part becomes simpler and more regular. The melodic phrases become less rhythmically dense, and lower to a "vocal" range. At 1:22, we first hear the vocalist, humming to mimic the instrument's melody. 
1:39		The upper-range part shifts to extended improvisation with some syncopation. Main melody briefly returns in the upper-range part (1:55–1:57).
1:58	Vocal and kora	The vocalist enters, followed by instrumental reiteration of the main melody. The vocalist has a declamatory style, as if he is telling a story as much as singing it. After the first declamation, the instrument responds before the vocalist returns, and they continue to trade parts.
3:07	Instrumental	Instrumental improvisation in the upper range. Lower-range pattern remains consistent.
3:23		Kora returns to main upper-range melodic pattern.
3:44	Vocal and kora	Voice returns. Variation of the earlier upper-range melodic pattern.
4:11	Instrumental	Upper-range melodic improvisations.
4:26		Ascending motive improvisation in contrast to the usual descending melodic contour. Vocalist mimics the melodic line.
4:39	Vocal and kora	Vocalist returns with kora accompaniment. At 5:02 the vocalist sings along using nonsense syllables with upper-range melody of the instrument. Note the return to humming around 5:16.
5:30	Kora	Note the ascending motive improvisation as before (4:26).
5:42	Instrumental conclusion	The lower-range part stops as the music shifts to free rhythm. The fundamental rhythm changes at about 5:50 as the track fades out.

PART

The Renaissance

Next to the word of God, music merits the highest praise. —MARTIN LUTHER

Renaissance musicians from the sixteenth century.

The Renaissance was an age of revival in arts and letters. It began in Italy around 1450 and, spreading throughout Western Europe, continued until around 1600. Writers, artists, and musicians of the Renaissance saw themselves as agents of a cultural rebirth inspired by their rediscovery of classical antiquity. We can trace many of our modern attitudes—our curiosity about the world, our interest in human affairs and the human spirit—to the Renaissance worldview.

Central to the Renaissance was the concept of **humanism**, which emphasized human achievements and values. This system of thought was inspired by ancient Greek and Roman works. In ancient Rome the orator Cicero had defined humanity (*humanitas*, from which we derive "humanities") as the proper pursuit of mankind.

Renaissance thinkers adopted this idea, which became one of the defining features of the Renaissance.

The idea of rebirth was also prominent, especially in the arts. Medieval music was dismissed as unworthy, and the state of the visual arts after the fall of Rome in 476 was compared to an aging body. The revival that began with a long line of Italian artists and architects—Leonardo da Vinci, Raphael, and Michelangelo among them—was likened to a miraculous rebirth. At the center of this artistic fever stood the "universal" or "Renaissance man," a well-rounded figure educated in the humanities, versed in classical literature, and skilled in arms and athletics. Leonardo da Vinci (1452–1519) was the ultimate example. His extraordinary achievements as a scientist, artist, inventor, and musician set him apart even among his many talented contemporaries.

Although the humanists embraced classical antiquity, they still glorified the creations of God. The humanists' new focus on Greek and Roman civilization came from their readings of the early church fathers, who in turn were influenced by the great classical thinkers. The humanists studied ancient ruins, statues, and coins. While not rejecting Christian beliefs, the humanists took a more flexible view of Christian teachings than medieval thinkers. For them mankind was no longer limited to contemplating the hereafter, but also a creative agent that could explore and marvel at the here and now.

Painters and sculptors depicted the human figure in realistic detail and developed individual styles. They humanized art by using **linear perspective**, which

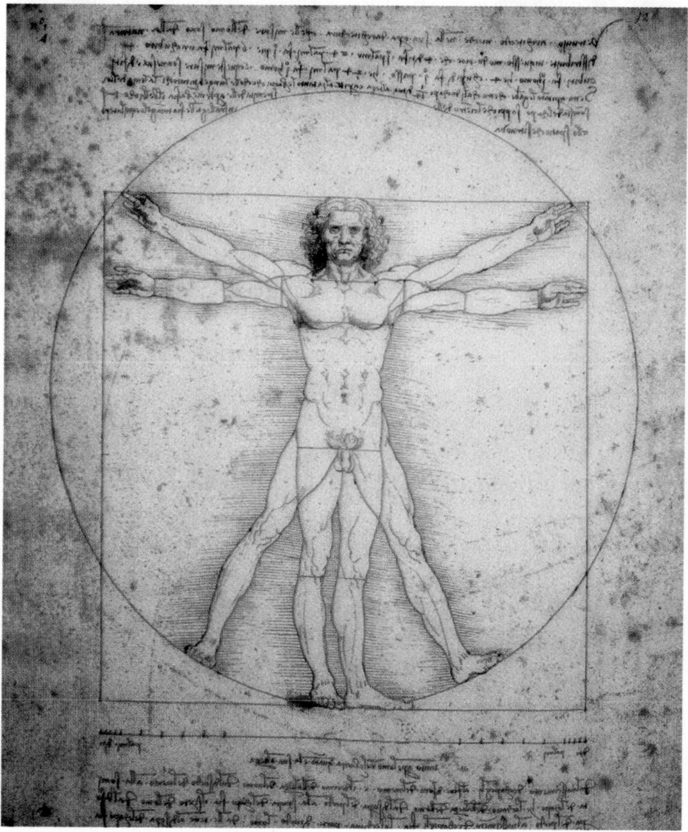

Vitruvian Man, a drawing by Leonardo da Vinci of an ideally proportioned human figure, named after the ancient Roman architect Vitruvius.

Masaccio, Madonna and Child with St. Anne, ca. 1424.

enabled them to render objects on their flat canvases to suggest real depth. This technique was probably introduced by the Florentine artist Masaccio in the 1420s and then developed by his contemporaries.

Composers, too, came to see themselves as individual creators rather than anonymous artisans. Josquin Desprez, perhaps the greatest musical genius of the period, wrote a motet that concealed his own name in an acrostic, spelled out by the first letter of each line of text. This musical signature reflected a new attitude about music, now emerging as an art practiced by composers with personal, engaging styles.

Today, we tend to view the Renaissance as a transition to modern times. Feudalism, supported by a land-based economy, was giving way to nation-states such as England, France, and Spain, ruled by monarchs. In Italy, the great city-states of Florence, Milan, and Venice were rising. The spread of international trade in turn promoted a new class of wealthy merchants and bankers, including the Medici family of Florence (see the Making Connections box on p. 105). Whereas previously church and state had been the primary supporters of the arts, the newly prosperous merchant class began to produce important patrons as well. Artists were now tasked with creating individual portraits, and musicians were commissioned to compose music for specific occasions. This new prominence given to the arts contrasted with medieval practices. Then, the church had required music to serve its needs. Individual creation was not celebrated. During the medieval era, much music outside the church was not preserved in notation and simply lost.

The growth of science and technology also had a significant impact on the Renaissance world. Columbus, Magellan, and other explorers ventured out onto the oceans, doubling the area of the world known to Europeans.

Copernicus revolutionized scientific thought by asserting that the earth revolved around the sun, not the sun around the earth. Galileo tinkered with designs for a helicopter-like flying machine and diving apparatus. The invention of printing provided the means to spread knowledge—and music—on an unprecedented scale. Earlier music had been written by hand and stored in monasteries, where few had access to it. The invention of movable type and the ability to print music opened up access for an ever-expanding public.

The Renaissance valued a new human curiosity about the world and humankind's place in it. The medieval worldview, in which the present was a time of self-denial and preparation for the hereafter, gave way to a burst of confidence in humanity's capabilities. With the dawning of the new age, composers rose to the new challenge. They still wrote music to praise God, but they also wrote music to celebrate human experience, both trivial and exalted.

A Note about Historical Periods

Columbus landing on Hispaniola in 1492.

We need to remember that the names and time spans of historical periods such as the Renaissance or Baroque were chosen only well after the periods themselves. To make sense of the sweep of history, historians have long sought to identify broad periods of time unified by developments in politics, science and technology, and the arts. But how we view these periods continuously shifts over time, so that their very names and chronology remain subject to debate and revision. Because history is a living process, we should not think of these periods as static and fixed.

Broad historical changes do not rigidly follow the steady march of a calendar, either. While we often say that the medieval period ended around 1450, there is nothing particularly special about that year. No sudden flash of light in 1450 heralded the start of the Renaissance. Change occurred gradually at different times in different places. The Renaissance that began in Italy around 1450 took a while to reach distant corners of Europe. And because Renaissance attitudes continued to change, Renaissance art and music could vary considerably in style and content from one region to another.

In short, rather than understand the Renaissance as a timeline with fixed endpoints, we might better think of it as a movement held together by certain ideas. It resembles a flowing stream shaped by several currents, each dynamically influencing the others, which created an ever-changing whole.

WHY LISTEN TO *Renaissance Music?*

If to our ears medieval music can sound remote, austere, and off-putting, Renaissance music is somehow more familiar and closer to music as we know it today. Briefly told, during the Renaissance four innovations occurred that decisively altered the character and sound of music, effectively modernizing it:

1) In addition to the older medieval church modes, composers began using two new modes, later recognized as our major and minor scales (see p. 13).
2) In choosing harmonies, composers began preferring **triads** (three-note chords; see p. 29), still the building blocks of most music we hear today.

3) The appearance of musical notation changed considerably. Standard modern features of writing music were widely adopted, including separate note heads, stems, and beams to connect notes.
4) In addition to fourths and fifths, thirds and sixths came to be considered consonant.

Much Renaissance music was vocal and tied to specific texts carrying specific meanings. The subjects of Renaissance songs—often courtship and love—are familiar to us today. In addition to vocal music, the fifteenth and sixteenth centuries witnessed the rise of Western music written for instruments alone. This division between vocal and instrumental categories continued on down through the centuries. (In the Baroque period, following the Renaissance, a third category arose that joined vocal and instrumental forces.)

Finally, during the Renaissance attitudes toward music fundamentally changed. More and more, composers and musicians practiced distinctive, individual styles of writing and performing. And as these new perspectives were taking root, the advent of printing altered how music was distributed. In short, music was now a valuable commodity that could be marketed and sold on a broad scale.

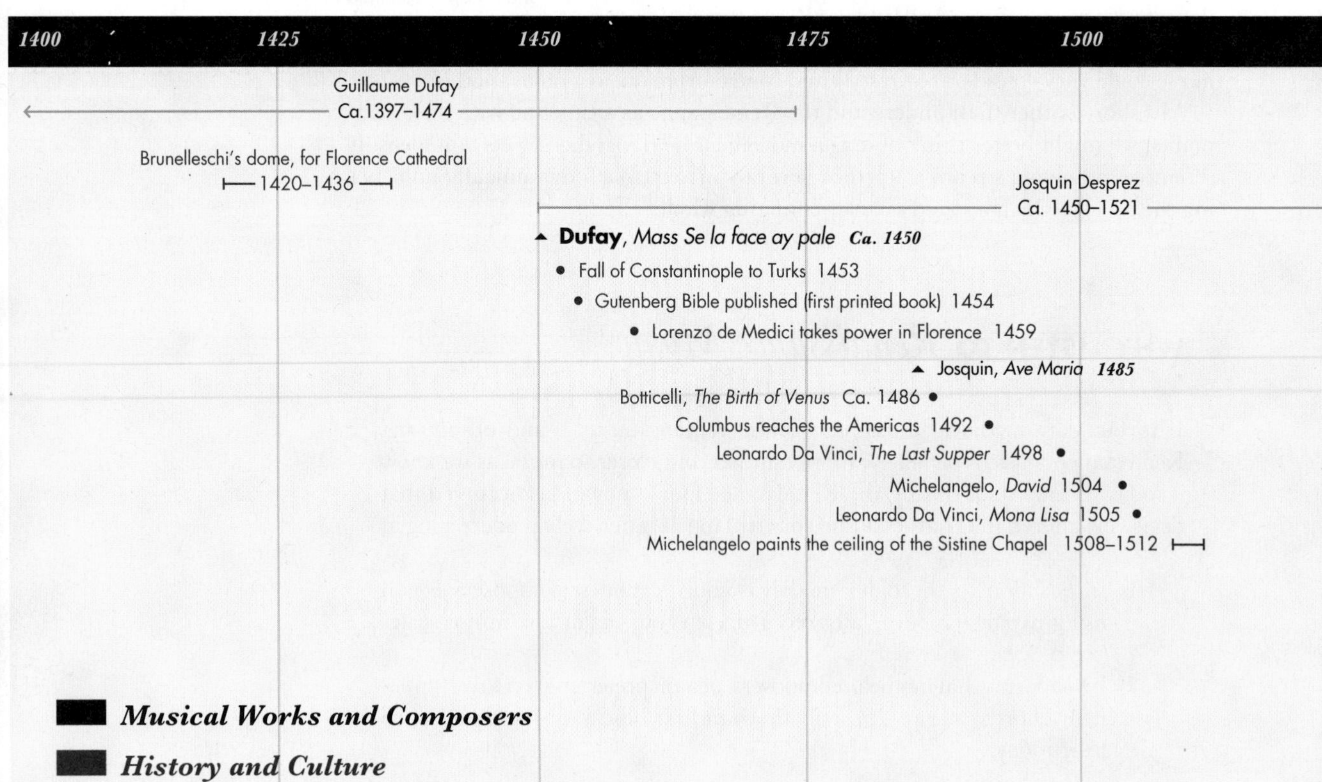

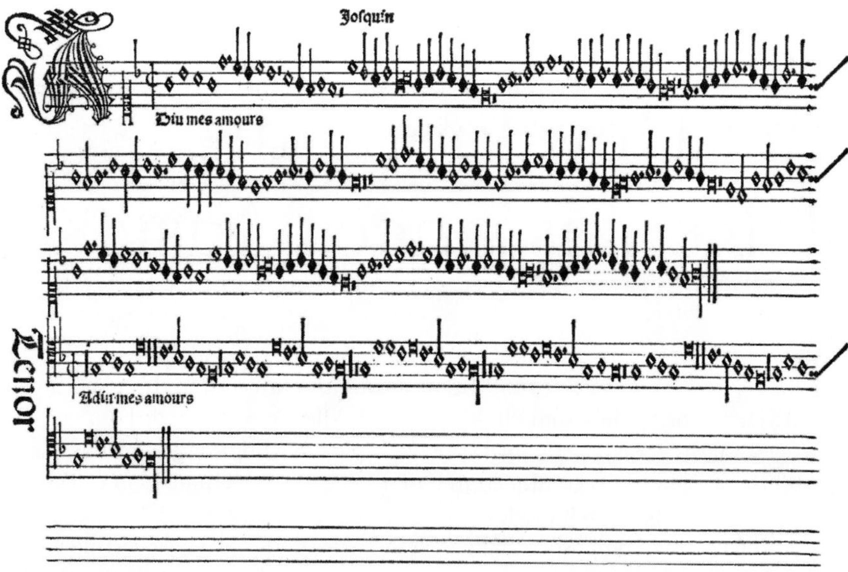

Page from an early music publication by Petrucci of Josquin's *Adieu, mes amours*. Although this notation may appear foreign to our eyes, it represents the addition of many modern features, including note heads and stems.

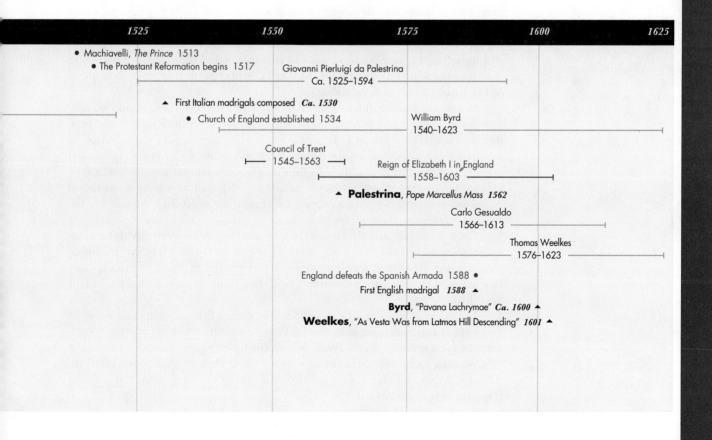

1525	1550	1575	1600	1625

- • Machiavelli, *The Prince* 1513
- • The Protestant Reformation begins 1517
- Giovanni Pierluigi da Palestrina Ca. 1525–1594
- ▲ First Italian madrigals composed ***Ca. 1530***
- • Church of England established 1534
- William Byrd 1540–1623
- Council of Trent 1545–1563
- Reign of Elizabeth I in England 1558–1603
- ▲ **Palestrina**, *Pope Marcellus Mass* ***1562***
- Carlo Gesualdo 1566–1613
- Thomas Weelkes 1576–1623
- England defeats the Spanish Armada 1588 •
- First English madrigal ***1588*** ▲
- **Byrd**, "Pavana Lachrymae" ***Ca. 1600*** ▲
- **Weelkes**, "As Vesta Was from Latmos Hill Descending" ***1601*** ▲

CHAPTER

13

The Development of Renaissance Music

Music underwent a genuine revitalization during the fifteenth and sixteenth centuries. Even so, for a while some links to the Middle Ages endured. For example, composers still drew on courtly love poetry of the late Middle Ages for their secular vocal music. They also continued to base their sacred polyphony on Gregorian plainchant and to use church modes.

But Renaissance composers challenged these ties to the past by asserting a newfound freedom and willingness to experiment. One result was that music steadily rose in stature among the fine arts. Composers now created large-scale works that demanded fresh approaches to musical structure. Eventually, the centuries-old authority of Gregorian plainchant eased its grip on sacred music. More and more, composers used their imagination rather than plainchant to set sacred texts.

Generally, medieval composers had started with one voice and then added parts to it in succession. Renaissance composers, in contrast, began thinking of all the parts of their music simultaneously as they created their works. Instead of focusing on each part separately, they conceived of a unified musical web of sound, in which the various strands supported and strengthened one another. Driving these changes were new ideas about **harmony** and **counterpoint** that made their music sound distinct from medieval music.

Among the most significant innovations of Renaissance music were two new modes that became our modern major and minor scales. It took quite some time for musicians to understand how revolutionary these new modes were. Indeed, it required about two centuries, during the Baroque era, for a new system of musical organization (tonality; see p. 30) to be fully developed based on the major and minor scales. (Tonality effectively replaced modality, which had held sway in medieval music for centuries.) Renaissance composers began the process by introducing the two new modes into their music.

These musicians also developed fresh approaches to harmony. By using *triads* (three notes stacked as thirds and played together; e.g., C-E-G), they created music that sounded richer than medieval music. Chords based on thirds are much more familiar to modern ears than medieval chords that featured intervals such as fourths and fifths.

The evidence suggests that early fifteenth-century English composers were the first to start experimenting with triads. They brought this new style to the Continent, where it quickly spread. Soon, Renaissance composers—unable to resist the new, pleasing sound of triad harmonies—were filling their compositions with them. This new approach to harmony would become the basis for most of the classical and popular music that followed.

MAKING CONNECTIONS *The Renaissance Rediscovers Classical Antiquity*

One powerful current that ran through the Renaissance was a renewed effort to celebrate Greek and Roman antiquity. Of all the arts, architecture and sculpture showed this connection most directly. Ruins of classical buildings and statues had survived through the centuries in Italy, reminders of the Roman Empire's past glory. Leading Italian architects and sculptors patiently studied the elements of symmetry and proportion in the ruins, seeking to apply them to their own art. A splendid example of Renaissance architecture is the Tempietto of Donato Bramante, probably begun in Rome around 1502. Commissioned by King Ferdinand and Queen Isabella of Spain to mark the presumed site of Saint Peter's crucifixion, this structure resembles a pagan temple from antiquity.

Renaissance painting and literature also found inspiration in classical themes. Artists took up portraiture as a new genre, typically showing their subjects in profile based on models from ancient coins. In literature, classical (as opposed to medieval) Latin became standard, as did the genres of classical poetry and drama: the epic poem, tragedy, and comedy, for example.

In Renaissance music, the classical connection was not as direct as in the other arts, owing to a lack of surviving examples. Yet some Renaissance musicians scoured ancient texts for evidence of how music had been created and performed centuries before. Others took the classical ideas of balance and order and applied them to musical composition. In addition, Renaissance humanists reaffirmed the ancient Greek idea that music could powerfully shape and influence human behavior. What this meant for composers was a new attention to how music could reflect the meaning of texts.

Bramante, Tempietto. Note the symmetrical design and use of a dome, influenced by Greek and Roman architecture.

check your **KNOWLEDGE**

1. Which features of medieval music continued to influence Renaissance composers?
2. Which musical innovations did Renaissance composers introduce?

CHAPTER

Guillaume Dufay and the Franco-Flemish Style

Guillaume Dufay (ca. 1397–1474).

Dashboard

Watch a video by Larry Todd about cantus firmus.

We usually think of Italy as the wellspring of the Renaissance. But in music it arose in Belgium, Holland, and particularly northeastern France. Composers left these homelands to work in Italy, where their transplanted art took root. They filled the ranks of musicians at the Papal Chapel in Rome and worked at Italian courts and chapels well into the sixteenth century. Only then did Italy produce native composers of the first rank.

Through much of the fifteenth century, what became known as the Franco-Flemish style centered on the powerful duchy of Burgundy. Many famous musicians of the day were associated with the Burgundian court, including one whose music bridged the end of the Middle Ages and the early Renaissance, Guillaume Dufay (ca. 1397–1474).

Born probably near Brussels, Dufay was a choirboy at the cathedral of Cambrai before he traveled south to Italy, where he served aristocratic patrons and sang in the papal choir. Periodically returning to Cambrai, he eventually settled there at the height of his fame, probably in the 1460s. Dufay belonged to a new generation of musicians in great demand, a sign of the enhanced status of music. He created music for high-profile events, including a motet for the 1436 consecration of Filippo Brunelleschi's stunning engineering feat, the dome of the Florence Cathedral.

Dufay composed secular chansons based on love poetry that had medieval origins. But their graceful melodic lines were uniquely his own. Much of his remaining music was devoted to the sacred genres of the motet and Mass. In several motets, Dufay followed the medieval technique of constructing the work around a slow-moving tenor part (the next-to-lowest-sounding part; see p. 77) that supported other, faster-moving parts. But he also employed forward-looking techniques: he varied his textures from carefully designed duets to denser thickets of four or five parts. In some cases, he had the individual parts imitate one another. And, in a bold departure from medieval practice, he occasionally used secular melodies, including his own, as foundations for his sacred Masses.

Dufay probably composed his *Mass Se la face ay pale* (**Listening Map 7**) around 1450, toward the middle of his career. By Dufay's time, the polyphonic Mass had developed into a multimovement cycle of the Ordinary (see p. 67) built around a recurring melodic line known as a **cantus firmus** ("fixed voice"). Typically a sacred plainchant, the cantus firmus appeared prominently in one voice in each movement, unifying the whole composition. For the cantus firmus of the *Mass Se la face ay pale*, Dufay strikingly chose a secular melody from a love song he composed

MAKING CONNECTIONS *Brunelleschi's Dome*

One of the great architectural icons of the early Renaissance, the dome of Florence Cathedral was constructed by Filippo Brunelleschi between 1420 and 1436. As it slowly rose to dominate the skyline, it came to represent the newfound prestige and wealth of the city-state. Its creator was a hot-tempered but secretive goldsmith untrained in the craft of architecture. He responded to an urgent call for a workable design to cover the open crossing of the two arms of the unfinished cathedral. Brunelleschi designed a free-standing, gravity-defying cupola, or dome, that could successfully enclose the vast space above the altar. It spanned 150 feet across and hovered 180 feet above the ground.

At the time, Brunelleschi's vision seemed utterly impossible to build. He proposed to raise the dome like an egg that could stand on its own, without using an interior scaffolding to support the work. Inspired in part by the circular designs of ancient Roman buildings, the cupola actually comprised two domes, one inside the other. These were shaped into an octagonal format by four enormous Gothic arches that met perfectly in the middle. Some four million bricks were required to complete the structure. To prevent them from developing fissures over time and collapsing, Brunelleschi instructed his masons to use an ingenious herringbone pattern.

When Pope Eugenius IV consecrated the cathedral in 1436, the Papal Choir performed a grand motet composed for the occasion by Guillaume Dufay. In four large sections plus a breathtaking conclusion on "Amen," Dufay's motet displays a grand musical architecture. It is well proportioned, in keeping with Brunelleschi's towering accomplishment.

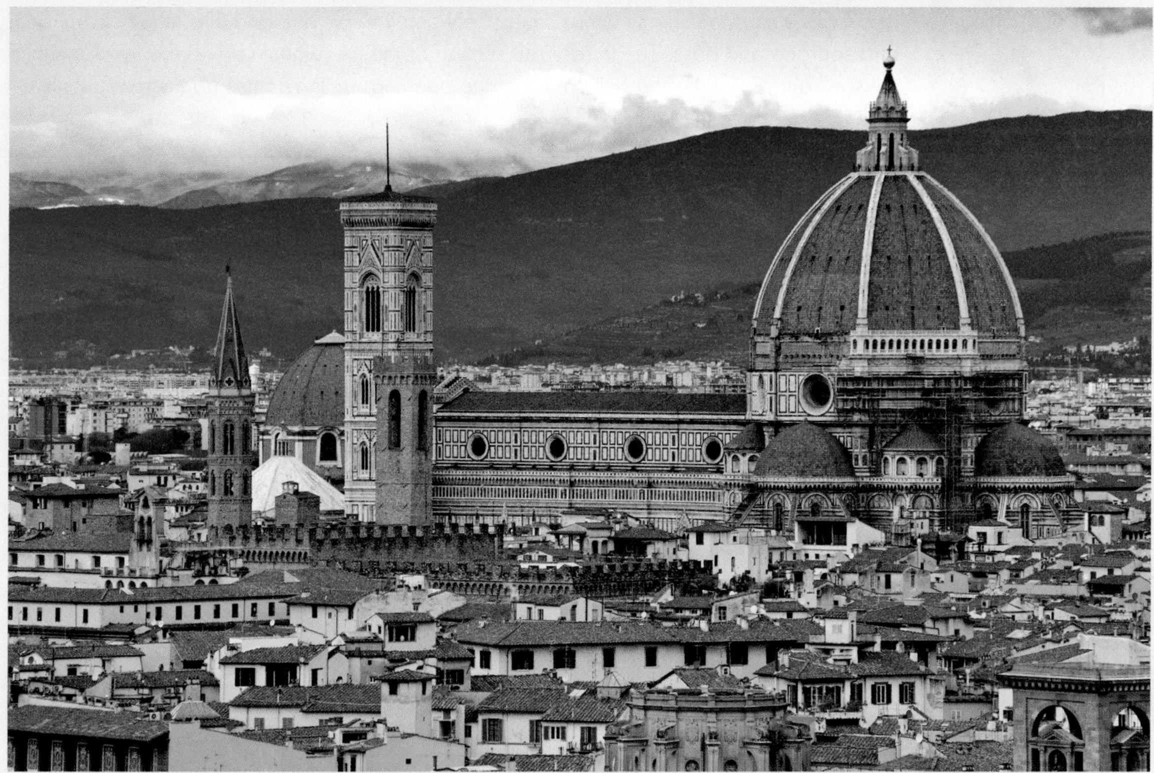

Florence Cathedral. Brunelleschi's dome is on the right end of the structure.

LISTENING MAP 7

GUILLAUME DUFAY, *Mass Se la face ay pale*, Kyrie {CA. 1450}

FORM	ABA
TEXTURE	Polyphony
GENRE	Mass
SCORING	Voices
OVERVIEW	The text of the Kyrie falls into three sections: "Kyrie eleison" ("Lord, have mercy"); "Christe eleison" ("Christ, have mercy"); and "Kyrie eleison" ("Lord, have mercy"). The overall plan is thus ABA, a symmetrical design that Dufay's music highlights. For the first and third sections, on "Kyrie eleison," he employs the full chorus, with the slowly moving cantus firmus—the melody of his love song—in the tenor voice (1 and 3). But for the second section, on "Christe eleison," Dufay aims for contrast: here the cantus firmus in the tenor voice drops out (2). In contrast to the full-bodied "Kyrie eleison," the "Christe eleison" offers intimate duets between the soprano and alto, alto and bass, and soprano and bass. The third, final section of the movement revives the text "Kyrie eleison" and reinstates the rich sound of the opening, as the cantus firmus reasserts its ceremonial role in the tenor.

why to LISTEN

Dufay's sacred Mass is notable for its use of a melody from one of his secular love songs. Some theories have been advanced to explain Dufay's unusual choice. One is that he may have composed the Mass for use in an aristocratic court wedding. Another is that he designed the composition as an offering to Mary, so that the love-song cantus firmus reflected her veneration. Either explanation could help account for the appearance of a popular song in a Mass, the musical highpoint of Catholic worship. No matter Dufay's motivation, the technique represented a new freedom. The idea of creating sacred music based on secular materials responded to the purely musical concerns of the composer.

first LISTEN

A	B	A
0:00	**2:12**	**3:23**
Full chorus; melody in tenor voice	Two-part polyphony; tenor voice drops out	Full chorus; melody in tenor voice

 *a deeper* **LISTEN**

TIME	SECTION	LISTEN FOR THIS	TEXT	TRANSLATION
0:00	**A**	Four-part polyphony (soprano, alto, tenor, bass); (1) cantus firmus (main melody) in tenor with slow note values Dufay - Missa Se la face ay pale, Kyrie Tenor Ky - ri - e	*Kyrie eleison*	Lord have mercy
2:12	**B**	Two-part polyphony with duets between soprano and alto, alto and bass, and soprano and bass; (2) cantus firmus in tenor drops out	*Christe eleison*	Christ have mercy
3:23	**A**	Four-part polyphony resumes; (3) cantus firmus reinstated in tenor in slow note values	*Kyrie eleison*	Lord have mercy

by the same name (Figure 14.1). This choice in a sacred Mass shows how humanistic values were becoming increasingly important in fifteenth-century music.

Se la face ay pa - le, La cause est a - mer

FIG. 14.1 The melody of Dufay's love song *Se la face ay pale,* the basis of his Mass.

Dashboard

Listen to the original song *Se la face ay pale* that inspired Dufay's Mass setting.

Dufay wrote his Mass for a small choral ensemble in four parts (soprano, alto, tenor, and bass). Generally, the tenor sang the cantus firmus in slow-moving pitches while the three other parts wove around it a tapestry of faster-moving, freely composed counterpoint. What Dufay originally conceived as a nimble love song now took on a solemn tone, to the repeating strains of "Kyrie eleison."

In earlier medieval music, the tenor had generally served as the lowest-sounding part of a composition. In Dufay's Mass, however, the tenor took its place above an even lower-sounding bass voice. Working independently of the tenor, the bass reinforced the pitches of the upper three voices.

check your **KNOWLEDGE**

1. Which region produced the first Renaissance composers? Where did they first find employment?
2. How did Dufay represent a new generation of musicians?
3. How did Dufay's music carry forward medieval traditions?
4. Which innovations did Dufay's music introduce?

CHAPTER 15 Josquin Desprez

Josquin Desprez (ca. 1450–1521).

After Dufay, several generations of Franco-Flemish composers excelled at writing sacred polyphony. Josquin Desprez (ca. 1450–1521) brought it to new heights in the sixteenth century, and his style became associated with the High Renaissance. Like Dufay, Josquin (known by his first name) was active in France and Italy. He perfected a new style of polyphony, with short musical themes, or **motives**, exchanged and imitated among the parts, which would influence the art of counterpoint for centuries to come.

We know little about Josquin's early years. Most likely he was born about 1450 near Picardy, in northern France. By the 1480s he was living in Italy, where he sang at the cathedral in Milan and enjoyed the patronage of the ruling ducal family. Later he joined the Papal Choir in Rome and briefly entered the service of the Duke of Ferrara. The duke was an important patron of the arts who, like Lorenzo the Magnificent in Florence, hired highly skilled Franco-Flemish composers to work at his court. When a plague broke out, Josquin left Ferrara to retire in his homeland, on what is now the border of France and Belgium.

A celebrity who was compared to Michelangelo, Josquin commanded a generous salary. He earned a reputation for composing according to his own schedule, rather than deferring to his patron's will. Years after his death, this reputation led the Protestant reformer Martin Luther to describe Josquin as the "master of the notes," bending them to his will.

Josquin's fame as a composer spread throughout Western Europe and survived long after his death. Owing to the development of the printing press by Johannes Gutenberg around 1440, music publishing began and quickly accelerated near the beginning of the sixteenth century. This major innovation contributed greatly to Josquin's reputation. Late in the fifteenth century, chant books—for centuries

MAKING CONNECTIONS *Lorenzo the Magnificent*

The Renaissance era was marked by a significant growth in trade among the Italian city-states and the new European nation states. For trade to be successful, there had to be a means of providing credit to those buying goods so that sellers could trust that they would eventually be paid for their wares. The Medici family of Florence was among the first to tackle this problem, by establishing one of the most successful banks of the Renaissance. Their considerable wealth led them to become the true rulers of Florence, which they controlled in some capacity for centuries, beginning in the 1400s. The Medici produced popes and queens and were dedicated humanists and patrons of the arts. The most famous of these arts patrons was Lorenzo the Magnificent (r. 1449–1492), an accomplished equestrian, celebrated poet, and skilled musician who attracted to the city several leading musicians. Lorenzo played instruments and composed, and he lavished his family's wealth on buildings, libraries, pageantry, and commissioning art.

Among the many works and artists that he sponsored, Lorenzo had an indirect hand in the creation of one of the iconic paintings of the Renaissance, Botticelli's *Birth of Venus* (ca. 1486). It shows the Roman goddess of love being transported on a seashell by Zephyr, the west wind, and arriving at the island of Cyprus. Botticelli modeled his version of the goddess on the *Venus de Medici*, a marble statue from the first century BCE owned by the Medici. Not only would Lorenzo have provided Botticelli access to this ancient sculpture, he undoubtedly encouraged him to base his new model of female beauty on this Roman work.

Botticelli's *Birth of Venus*, ca. 1486.

Venus de Medici, first century BCE.

copied laboriously by hand—were already being printed from woodblocks. Then, in 1501, the Venetian printer Ottaviano Petrucci, the first successful music publisher, began setting polyphonic music with movable type. Between 1502 and 1516 Petrucci released several volumes of Josquin's Masses and motets, a clear sign of the composer's reputation. Josquin was among the first composers to benefit from having his works commercially released and available for purchase.

In 1502, Petrucci brought out a volume opening with one of Josquin's most beloved works, the motet *Ave Maria*, composed probably around 1485 (**Listening Map 8**). The opening text of this motet is drawn from the New Testament, Luke 1:28, where the archangel Gabriel greets Mary and informs her that she will give birth to Christ. What follows is a series of five greetings, each commencing with *Ave* (Hail), which mark events in Mary's life as celebrated in Catholic doctrine. In the concluding measures, we hear a simple plea, "O Mother of God, remember me," a common prayer found on gravestones and prayer books of the period.

Josquin carefully crafted each section of his motet to capture the nuances of the text. The opening greeting offers a fine example of **point of imitation** with four parts, in which one voice introduces a short melody that the other voices imitate one by one in turn. This simple but exquisite music slowly accumulates from one to four parts and gently descends from high to low registers.

By Josquin's time, the tradition of imitative polyphony in sacred choral music was well established. But Josquin also understood that sometimes simpler musical means could be just as powerful as the most ornate. So we find in his motet *Ave Maria* three types of texture. From the most complex to the simplest, they are:

1) imitative counterpoint involving all four voices;
2) pairings of voices; and
3) **block chords**, where the four parts align vertically in **homophony**, distinct clusters of sound.

check your **KNOWLEDGE**

1. Which innovations did Josquin introduce to the motet?
2. What new technology helped spread Josquin's music throughout Europe?
3. In his *Ave Maria*, how did Josquin craft his composition to match the text of the prayer?

LISTENING MAP 8

JOSQUIN DESPREZ, *Ave Maria*

{CA. 1485}

FORM	Six salutations to Mary and concluding prayer
TEXTURE	Polyphony
GENRE	Motet
SCORING	Voices
OVERVIEW	Josquin uses the soprano part to open the composition, followed by imitation in the alto, tenor, and bass (①). In contrast to the four-part polyphony of the opening, other sections of the work feature duets of two parts, with the soprano and alto, and the tenor and bass paired together (②). In a third type of texture, Josquin aligns the four parts vertically to sing in block chords, or homophony (③, ④).

why to LISTEN

Josquin's skill ensured a well-balanced composition. The voices explored the two poles of the musical art in the fifteenth century: polyphony (counterpoint, or setting musical lines against one another) and homophony (harmony, aligning the parts to form distinct vertical clusters of sound we know as chords). In the space of just a few minutes Josquin's composition compellingly summarizes the craft of the Renaissance composer.

first LISTEN

FOUR-PART POLYPHONY	PAIRED VOICES	PAIRED VOICES	PAIRED VOICES	CHORDS; RHYTHM CHANGE	PAIRED VOICES	CHORDS
0:00	**1:04**	**1:52**	**2:40**	**3:14**	**3:44**	**4:53**
Gabriel appears to Mary	Reference to Mary's own Immaculate Conception	Nativity of Mary	Annunciation (Gabriel's announcement to Mary)	Mary's purification	Mary's Assumption into heaven	Final prayer

Continued

a deeper **LISTEN**

TIME	LISTEN FOR THIS	TEXT	TRANSLATION
0:00	**① Four-part polyphony; each entrance thickens the texture**	*Ave Maria, gratia plena* *Dominus tecum, virgo serena.* Soprano: A - ve Ma - ri - a, Gra - Alto: A - ve Ma - ri - a, Tenor: A - ve Ma - ri - a, Bass: A - ve Ma -	Hail, Mary, full of grace, the Lord be with you, serene virgin.
1:04	**② Voices in pairs; texture thins out (soprano [S] and alto [A], and tenor [T] and bass [B]), then all four voices**	*Ave cuius conceptio* *solemni plena gaudio* *coelestia, terrestria* *nova replet laetitia.*	Hail, you whose conception full of solemn joy fills the heavens and earth with new rejoicing.
1:52	**Voices in pairs (S and A, T and B)**	*Ave cuius nativitas* *nostra fuit solemnitas* *ut Lucifer lux oriens* *verum solem praeveniens.*	Hail, you whose nativity was our solemnity, as the star arising in the morning precedes the true sun.
2:40	**Voices in pairs (S and A, T and B)**	*Ave pia humilitas sine* *viro faecunditas* *cuius annuntiatio* *nostra fuit salvatio.*	Hail, pious humility, fertile without man, whose annunciation was our salvation.
3:14	**③ Chords, change from duple to triple meter; block chords suggest unity and perfection**	*Ave vera virginitas* *immaculata castitas* *cuius purificatio* *nostra fuit purgatio.*	Hail, true virginity, immaculate chastity, whose purification was our purgation.

3:44	**Voices in pairs (S and A, T and B), return to duple meter**	*Ave praeclara omnibus* *angelicis virtutibus* *cuius fuit assumptio* *nostra glorificatio.*	Hail, most bright in all angelic virtues, whose assumption was our glorification.
4:53	**④ Chords, final prayer; twelve simple chords personalize the text**	*O Mater Dei, memento* *mei. Amen.* O ma - ter de - i, Me - men - to me - i, A - men.	O Mother of God, remember me. Amen.

Palestrina and the Counter-Reformation

CHAPTER 16

By the second half of the sixteenth century, native Italian composers were beginning to rival the long line of distinguished Franco-Flemish musicians. The leading Italian musician was Giovanni Pierluigi da Palestrina (ca. 1525–1594), who refined further the Franco-Flemish style of imitative polyphony. Born near Rome in his namesake town, he spent most of his adult life in the city. Palestrina held several positions as a choirmaster, including at the Vatican, where he served nearly a dozen popes.

Giovanni Pierluigi da Palestrina (ca. 1525–1594).

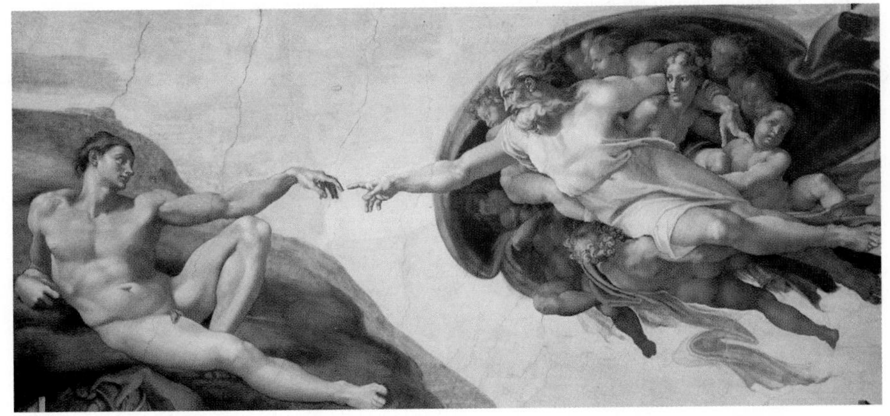

Palestrina composed works for the Sistine Chapel in the Vatican; shown here is Michelangelo's *The Creation of Adam* (ca. 1511–1512), a detail from the ceiling.

Palestrina's prolific output—among his works are 104 Masses and nearly 400 motets—reflects the spirit of the **Counter-Reformation**. This was the reaction of the Catholic Church to the **Protestant Reformation** which had been set in motion in 1517 by the German monk Martin Luther (see the Making Connections box on this page). The major event in the Counter-Reformation was the Council of Trent, convened by the pope in 1545 and in session off and on until 1563. The council's purpose was to reject certain beliefs of the new Protestant faith, reaffirm the sacraments of Catholicism, and correct the abuses of the church, some of which Luther had cited in his Ninety-Five Theses.

MAKING CONNECTIONS *Martin Luther and the Reformation*

Martin Luther, as painted by Lucas Cranach (1529).

In 1510 an Augustinian monk walked some 700 miles from the German town of Erfurt to Rome. Like so many faithful Catholics who had preceded him, he confessed his sins, did penance, and visited the holy sites of the Eternal City. His experience during his trip, however, would shake his faith to the core. While he said Mass, Italian priests chastised him to hurry. Luther then visited the "sacred steps" (*scala sancta*), on which Christ had reputedly walked. As Luther slowly climbed them on his knees, he recited an "Our Father" for each step. He believed that this act could help save a soul, perhaps a member of his own family, from purgatory. But when he reached the summit, he asked, "Who knows whether it is so?" Having arrived in Rome a priest, he departed a reformer.

On All Saints' Day in 1517, Luther nailed his Ninety-Five Theses to the door of the castle church in the German town of Wittenberg. This document outlined abuses in the Catholic Church, and it protested that by selling *indulgences* (papal grants of forgiveness), the Church was in effect selling salvation. Luther intended his action to prompt a debate among clerics, but what happened altered the course of history. Translated from Latin to German and other languages, the Theses were soon published. Copies spread like wildfire throughout Europe, a testament to the power of the recently invented printing press. Eventually Luther was declared an outlaw by the Holy Roman Emperor and excommunicated by the pope. The Protestant Reformation had begun.

These dramatic events altered the course of sacred music as well. Luther himself was a musician who played the lute and sang. Next to theology, he revered music as a gift from God that he believed drove away satanic forces. For the new Lutheran services, he wrote German texts for hymns. He probably composed several melodies as well, including the iconic expression of Protestantism, "A Mighty Fortress Is Our God." In the new Protestant faith, these hymns were sung not just by the clergy but by the congregation. Luther thus initiated the tradition of singing *chorales*, which have memorable melodies supported by block-like chords.

The bishops participating in the Council of Trent turned their attention to music as well. In 1555, Pope Marcellus II, who died after only a three-week reign, had directed the Papal Chapel singers to perform the sacred texts in a more dignified manner. By the 1560s, another pope was considering more severe measures, including a ban on polyphony and a return to singing unadorned plainchant. In response, Palestrina composed one of his greatest works, the *Pope Marcellus Mass* (**Listening Map 9**), published in 1562 and widely received as a defense of church polyphony.

In creating this work Palestrina chose not to use a cantus firmus. Instead, he freely composed the music, employing an expanded, six-part chorus requiring one soprano and one alto part, two tenor parts, and two bass parts. With this ensemble Palestrina explored imitative counterpoint and chordal homophony. He attained rich textures that surpassed the four-part polyphony of Josquin's *Ave Maria*. Nevertheless—and this was crucial to Palestrina's great accomplishment—the writing in the Mass remained clear, so that the music did not obscure the text.

The *Pope Marcellus Mass* became a standard to which other composers aspired. Although Palestrina's music is not as well known today, its influence extended historically well past the Renaissance, and geographically well beyond Italy. He may be the composer with the most enduring influence in the tradition of Western classical music.

The opening session of the Council of Trent in 1545.

check your **KNOWLEDGE**

1. What was the importance of the Counter-Reformation to Renaissance composers?
2. Why is Palestrina credited with perfecting imitative vocal polyphony in church music?
3. Which techniques did Palestrina use to emphasize the clear presentation of the text in his *Pope Marcellus Mass*?

LISTENING MAP 9

GIOVANNI PIERLUIGI DA PALESTRINA, *Pope Marcellus Mass*, Kyrie

{1562}

FORM	ABA
TEXTURE	6-part choir
GENRE	Mass
SCORING	Voices
OVERVIEW	The first movement of the *Pope Marcellus Mass*, the Kyrie, divides into the customary three sections ("Kyrie eleison," "Christe eleison," and "Kyrie eleison"). The Kyrie exhibits another distinctive feature of Palestrina's style. He prefers smooth, **stepwise motion** in his melodic lines—that is, motion in which a pitch moves to its neighboring pitch either above or below. Whenever he introduces a significant leap, he usually then fills in the space with stepwise motion in the opposite direction, as if to compensate. For all its complexity, Palestrina's music does not impede our ability to grasp the text. Instead, in accordance with the Council of Trent, the words "reach tranquilly into the ears and hearts of those who hear them."

why to LISTEN

The *Pope Marcellus Mass* weathered the test of time extremely well. To the generations of musicians who followed him, Palestrina was the upholder of *a cappella* music (vocal music *without* instruments) as the perfect art for communicating with God. He wrote church polyphony that did not obscure the delivery of sacred texts. The *Pope Marcellus Mass* thus continued the tradition of counterpoint that had effectively begun with Léonin in the twelfth century.

Later musicians admired Palestrina's Masses and motets as models. In 1725, the Austrian composer Joseph Fux wrote a counterpoint textbook based on Palestrina's music. Not only did Mozart and Beethoven study their counterpoint by using Fux's text, but so did countless later musicians, including this author.

first LISTEN

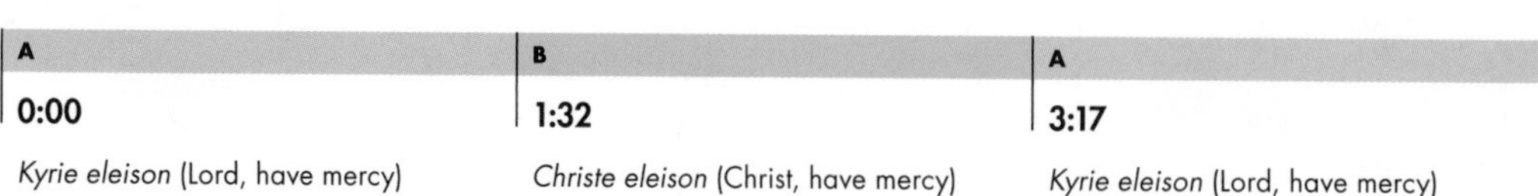

a deeper **LISTEN**

TIME	SECTION	TEXT	TRANSLATION
0:00	A	*Kyrie eleison* leap stepwise motion Ky - ri - e e - le - - - i - son Voices enter with ascending leaps followed by stepwise, descending motion	Lord, have mercy
1:32	B	*Christe eleison*	Christ, have mercy
3:17	A	*Kyrie eleison*	Lord, have mercy

New Currents: National Styles

Apart from sacred polyphony, lighter, secular music steadily gained currency during the sixteenth century. There were songs of all types—tuneful German *Lieder*; zesty Spanish *villancicos*; colorful French *chansons* filled with street and battle cries and birdsongs; English *consort songs*, in which a singer was accompanied by instruments; and Italian *frottolas* set to lighthearted, amorous poetry.

The Italian Madrigal

By far the most significant new secular genre was the Italian **madrigal**, typically composed for four or five parts, with one singer per part. What distinguished madrigals were their Italian (*not* Latin) texts of high literary quality, often drawn from poetry. To accompany these texts, composers used techniques drawn from sacred music. In particular, they applied imitative polyphony and chordal homophony to secular songs. Madrigalists were especially concerned with creating music that heightened the meaning of the texts, some of which could be quite serious.

The first wave of madrigals appeared during the 1530s from foreign and native composers working in Italy. As the century advanced, the genre evolved into a highly emotional form of musical expression. The most extreme composer of this music was Carlo Gesualdo, Prince of Venosa (1566–1613), nearly an exact contemporary of Shakespeare. Many of his madrigals still impress listeners as bizarre creations. Gesualdo confronts us with sharp melodic and rhythmic contrasts and jolting harmonic dissonances that tear apart the musical fabric. These works convey texts of unrelenting sorrow, and many were inspired by Gesualdo's own grief and depression. He is famous not only for his madrigals but for a vicious crime of passion: upon discovering his wife's infidelity, he gruesomely murdered her and her unfortunate lover.

Dashboard

Read about and listen to Gesualdo's most famous madrigal, *Moro, lasso, al mio duolo.*

MAKING CONNECTIONS

Art Imitates Life: The Shocking Music of Carlo Gesualdo, Prince of Venosa

Carlo Gesualdo (1566–1613).

Probably the most eccentric and original composer of the High Renaissance was the Italian Carlo Gesualdo, Prince of Venosa, also known as the Prince of Darkness. Gesualdo created madrigals in a style of arresting contrasts. He put triads together that bore little or no connection to one another, and he added pitches outside the traditional modes. He also used abrupt changes in rhythm and texture to create unpredictable music at once fragmented and spontaneous. His madrigals could be described as psychological music that explored in stark ways the dark underside of human emotions.

What drove Gesualdo's experiments was his obsession with strong texts of grief and pain, which may have reflected his sordid reality. He was presumed guilty of the gruesome murder of his first wife—who was also his cousin. She had taken a lover, keeping her affair secret from Gesualdo for two years. The story goes that when he discovered the pair, he killed them both and left their mutilated bodies on display before fleeing to his castle. As a nobleman, Gesualdo was immune to prosecution. Nevertheless, he feared retribution and had the land around his castle cleared of trees in order to afford a clear view of approaching danger.

Well after the Renaissance had expired, Gesualdo's shocking art attracted the attention of modernist composers in the twentieth century. They viewed him as an avant-garde musician centuries ahead of his time, who somehow anticipated their own "shocking" experiments. Shock effects in music became the order of the day for much experimental music of the twentieth century. They also were incorporated into jazz, rock, and many forms of popular music, not to mention "shock jock" radio broadcasting.

The English Madrigal

By Gesualdo's time, virtuoso singers were performing madrigals in courts and academies throughout Europe. The genre arrived in England in 1588, the year of the Spanish Armada's defeat. Italian madrigals were soon adapted into the distinct new genre of **English madrigals**, which had few literary pretensions and developed into a popular form of entertainment.

One of the most celebrated English madrigalists was Thomas Morley (ca. 1557–1602), an enterprising composer, organist, music publisher, and author. He wrote music for some of Shakespeare's plays, including "It was a lover and his lass" from *As You Like It*. In 1601 Morley collected two-dozen madrigals by English composers into a volume titled *The Triumphs of Oriana*. Its contents honor Elizabeth I, the Virgin Queen (r. 1558–1603), represented throughout by her nickname, Oriana. Those paying homage to the queen include Vesta (Roman goddess of the hearth), Diana (Roman goddess of the hunt), and satyrs, fauns, nymphs, and demigods.

Each madrigal in Morley's collection concludes with the lines "Then sang the shepherds and nymphs of Diana: Long live fair Oriana." Although the poetry is contrived, the composers enliven it with **madrigalisms**, or **word paintings**, musical turns of phrase that mirror the meanings of the text. For example, ascending and descending phrases suggest the ideas of rising and falling, fast and slow note values connote motion and rest, and harsh dissonances convey sadness and other strong emotions.

Among the madrigals chosen by Morley for *The Triumphs of Oriana* was "As Vesta Was from Latmos Hill Descending" (**Listening Map 10**) by Thomas Weelkes (1576–1623), who produced music filled with vibrant imagery. For several years Weelkes held a position as organist and choirmaster at Chichester Cathedral, although his chronic drunkenness eventually caused his dismissal. Weelkes also had a reputation for swearing, but he found quite another voice in his madrigals, often using his own texts.

Elizabeth I, ca. 1591.

Chichester Cathedral, where Thomas Weelkes worked.

THOMAS WEELKES, "As Vesta Was from Latmos Hill Descending"

{1601}

FORM	Sectional, according to the text
TEXTURE	Six-part choir: two sopranos, one alto, two tenors, and one bass
GENRE	English Madrigal
SCORING	Voices
OVERVIEW	"As Vesta Was from Latmos Hill Descending" is an entertaining madrigal typical of the English style. It requires a larger-than-normal ensemble, for which Weelkes wrote chordal passages in homophony and short sections of imitation. Weelkes uses word painting throughout this piece. For example, the words "descending" (1) and "running down amain" (3) inspired a plunging leap or falling, scale-like melody; "ascending" (2) is accompanied by a rising line. Sometimes the text literally prompts the musical response. When "Diana's darlings" abandon the goddess to greet Oriana, they depart "first two by two, then three by three together" (4)—that is, with two and then three vocal parts. The remaining solo voice suggests that the goddess is now "all alone" (5). The concluding line, "Long live fair Oriana," inspires a special treatment: an extended passage in imitative counterpoint (6). To emphasize the meaning—Elizabeth's long reign—Weelkes has the lowest voice, the bass, hold a pitch for several measures.

why to LISTEN

Weelkes's madrigal explores a fundamental question about the nature of music. To what degree can it convey specific meanings? That is, can a piece of music mean anything other than its succession of pitches, rhythms, and textures? The word paintings of High Renaissance madrigals suggest that it can, as the music mimics specific meanings of the text.

But later critics and thinkers drew a different conclusion: that music stands as an independent art *not* tied to meanings other than the sounds themselves. As you listen to Weelkes's madrigal, ask yourself whether you can fully enjoy the music just as music. Or do his word paintings enhance the experience by adding meaning?

first LISTEN

DESCENDING LEAP	ASCENDING LINE		IMITATION OF RUNNING	TWO PARTS, THEN THREE	SOLO VOICE, THEN MINGLED		COMPLEX INTERWOVEN LINES AND LONG HELD BASS NOTES
0:00	**0:26**	**0:42**	**1:04**	**1:25**	**1:42**	**2:13**	**2:31**
As Vesta . . .	She spied . . .	Attended on . . .	To whom . . .	First two . . .	Leaving their . . .	Then sang . . .	Long live . . .

a deeper **LISTEN**

TIME	LISTEN FOR THIS	TEXT
0:00	① Descending leap for "descending"	As Vesta was from Latmos hill descending, As Ves - ta was from Lat-mos hill descend - ing
0:26	② Ascending line for "ascending"	She spied a maiden Queen the same ascending she spied a maid - en Queen the same a-scend - - ing
0:42		Attended on by all the shepherds' swain,
1:04	③ Rapid descending lines, imitating running	To whom Diana's darlings came running down amain, Came run-ing down a-main, came run-ning down a-main
1:25	④ Two parts, then three	First two by two, then three by three together, First two by two, then
1:42	⑤ Solo part for "all alone"; voices mingle on "mingling"	Leaving their goddess all alone, hasted thither, And mingling with the shepherds of her train, With mirthful tunes her presence did entertain.
2:13		Then sang the shepherds and nymphs of Diana:
2:31	⑥ Extended passage in imitative counterpoint; long held notes in the bass	Long live fair Oriana. Long live fair O - ri - a - na,______

check your KNOWLEDGE

1. How and where did the madrigal first arise?
2. How did madrigal composers try to illustrate the texts that they set to music?
3. What distinguished the English madrigal from its Italian predecessors?
4. How did Thomas Weelkes use madrigal techniques in "As Vesta Was from Latmos Hill Descending" to depict the text?

CHAPTER 18 The Rise of Instrumental Music

One of the most important developments during the Renaissance was the rise of instrumental music. Not until the sixteenth century do we find substantial quantities of notated music intended solely for instruments. By the end of the century, composers were busily developing new, purely instrumental genres independent of vocal models.

At first, though, much of this new music involved adaptations of vocal compositions. Essentially, composers reworked motets, Mass settings, and secular genres such as the French chanson and Italian madrigal for performance by instruments alone. They created music for a variety of keyboard instruments, such as the organ and the **harpsichord** (see p. 155); several sizes of **lutes** (plucked string instruments with round bodies and long necks); and families of instruments such as **recorders** (woodwind instruments with whistle-type mouthpieces) and **viols** (bowed string instruments played upright).

Dashboard

Watch demonstration videos of Renaissance musical instruments.

In some instrumental music, composers used preexistent material as a cantus firmus, just as they had in their vocal music. Or, they invented a bass pattern, repeated several times throughout the composition to form a stable foundation. Above this bass line, they worked out ingenious melodic variations in the upper voices.

Another category of instrumental music, the dance movement, was especially popular during the sixteenth century. Often, slow and fast dances appeared in pairs. A common arrangement paired a **pavan**, a slow, ceremonial dance in **duple meter**, with a **galliard**, a sprightly, fast dance in **triple meter**.

Yet another instrumental genre was the **fantasia**, a polyphonic composition built around consecutive points of imitation. Still other instrumental pieces were improvisatory in character and likely served as short preludes to compositions in more serious styles.

A virginal (ca. 1600).

As the sixteenth century advanced, collections of lute, organ, and harpsichord music became common. In England, the works of Elizabethan keyboard composers were gathered into great anthologies such as the *Fitzwilliam Virginal Book*. This early seventeenth-century manuscript contains nearly 300 compositions suitable for the **virginal**, the English name for the harpsichord. The most famous Elizabethan composers are represented in the volume, but pride of place belongs to William Byrd (ca. 1540–1623), easily the most renowned and versatile English musician of the time.

As a young man Byrd was appointed organist to London's Chapel Royal, the royal family's place of worship. He loyally served the English court for more than fifty years. Byrd's career unfolded against the background of the English Reformation and establishment of the Anglican Church. The new church needed music for its services, and Byrd steadily produced motet-like anthems for them. However, his public career as an Anglican composer masked a secret: he belonged to the dissenting community of English Catholics who secretly practiced their faith. Byrd's private beliefs violated the law at the time, because England was officially a Protestant country. Nonetheless, Byrd composed about a hundred Latin motets for the principal feasts of the Catholic religion.

Among Byrd's instrumental music are about a hundred keyboard compositions, including many paired pavans and galliards, and variations on popular tunes. Byrd also produced a fine keyboard rendition of a popular song by John Dowland (1563–1626), "Flow My Tears," known as "Lachrymae" (Latin for "tears"; see **Listening Map 11**). It was widely transcribed by many composers in instrumental versions.

Byrd based this celebrated set of harpsichord variations on a composition by the Elizabethan lutenist John Dowland, who produced four volumes of popular lute songs and instrumental works. "Flow My Tears" originally appeared in 1596 as a piece for lute, and then as a song with text in 1600. The text was possibly by Dowland himself. Like Byrd, Dowland was a Catholic, though unlike Byrd, he did not enjoy the patronage of Queen Elizabeth. Instead, Dowland found favor at the Danish court and spent part of his career in France and Italy.

"Flow My Tears" is a sorrowful lament in five stanzas. Here is its first stanza:

Flow my tears, fall from your springs,
exilde for ever: Let me morne
where nights black bird hir sad infamy sings,
there let mee live forlorne.

Dowland captures the sadness of the text with expressive leaps and drooping, falling lines, and dissonant harmonies. The lute provides a discreet accompaniment of chords and occasionally ventures into delicate melodic detailing. The emphasis, however, is on the solo voice and its plaintive melody (see the first example in **Listening Map 11**).

MAKING CONNECTIONS *The English Reformation*

The Reformation powerfully altered the course of English history in unforeseen ways that merged politics and religion. When the Tudor monarch Henry VIII (r. 1509–1547) wanted to annul his marriage to Catherine of Aragon, the pope refused. In response, the king declared himself absolute monarch over "the realm of England." In 1533 the Archbishop of Canterbury annulled the marriage, and Henry VIII married Anne Boleyn (the second of his six wives). The next year the king became the head of the English, or Anglican, Church. The pope's excommunication of the king in 1538 finalized the split, and England was now officially a Protestant realm.

Money that formerly flowed from English monasteries to Rome was diverted to the crown. Catholics were persecuted, as a new liturgy for the Anglican Church slowly took shape. In 1549, during the reign of Edward VI (Henry's only son, who became king at age nine), the first Book of Common Prayer for the Anglican faith was published. But then, with the crowning of the Catholic Queen Mary (r. 1553–1558), history abruptly reversed itself. Now Protestants were burned at the stake as heretics, and the English crown briefly reverted to Catholicism until the death of "Bloody Mary," as the queen was dubbed. The pendulum swung once again when Elizabeth I, daughter of Henry VIII and Anne Boleyn, took the throne. Elizabeth reestablished the Anglican faith, only to be excommunicated by the pope in 1570.

The religious divide continued to play out in England well into the seventeenth century. During all these years of religious strife, English music was roiled by diverging attitudes toward the art. The more fervent wing of the English Reformation, Puritanism, tried diligently to separate English culture from anything papal. The great traditions of English cathedral choral music before the break with Rome were suppressed. The use of music in church services was severely limited. The remaining sacred music was stripped of anything resembling the polyphony that had been practiced in Europe for centuries.

Portrait of Henry VIII, by Hans Holbein the Younger (ca. 1538–1547).

For a composer such as William Byrd—a professed Catholic working in the Anglican Church—writing music to Latin sacred texts brought with it considerable risks. Fortunately for him, Queen Elizabeth was a moderate Protestant, and she used her authority to limit the influence of the most ardent supporters of the Reformation. Not only did she tolerate Catholic musicians such as Byrd, but at the Chapel Royal she cultivated a rich musical establishment. There, Byrd's art flourished. In 1575 the Queen even granted Byrd and another composer a patent that gave them the exclusive rights to print English music for twenty-one years.

LISTENING MAP 11

WILLIAM BYRD, "Pavana Lachrymae" for harpsichord solo (early seventeenth century), *based on John Dowland's* lute song "Flow My Tears"

{**1600**}

FORM	Theme and Variations
GENRE	Instrumental Solo based on a Pavan (slow dance)
SCORING	Harpsichord
OVERVIEW	Byrd reworked "Flow My Tears" for the harpsichord, probably sometime early in the seventeenth century. He used Dowland's memorable melody but also departed from it as his inspiration demanded. Because the original song resembles a pavan in its meter, mood, and structure, Byrd titled his rendition *Pavana Lachyrmae* and transformed the piece into a slow, dirge-like dance. It is divided into three main sections, which we'll label A, B, and C. In each section, Dowland's melody appears in the high register of the harpsichord, with embellishments and expressive details added by Byrd. Because the variations are based on the original, preceding melody, they are labeled A′, B′, and C′. The overall form thus is AA′BB′CC′.

why to LISTEN

In the musical form known as "Theme and Variation," a melody is introduced, and then increasingly elaborate variations follow. From the outset, Byrd embedded the idea of variation into "Flow My Tears." Each major section of Dowland's theme—A, B, and C—is followed by a variation, rather than simply repeated as in a traditional pavan.

The free variations move us further from the original theme, but not so far that we forget it. For instance, in A′, Byrd begins by extending the opening descent we have already heard in A, and by imitating it in the tenor register. The tenor part runs in counterpoint to the continuing statement of the melody by the upper voice.

Continued

first LISTEN

A/A′	B/B′	C/C′
0:00	1:35	2:50
First melody followed by variation	Second melody followed by variation	Third melody followed by variation

a deeper LISTEN

Byrd's composition is based on Dowland's lute song "Flow My Tears." Here is the opening of Dowland's composition:

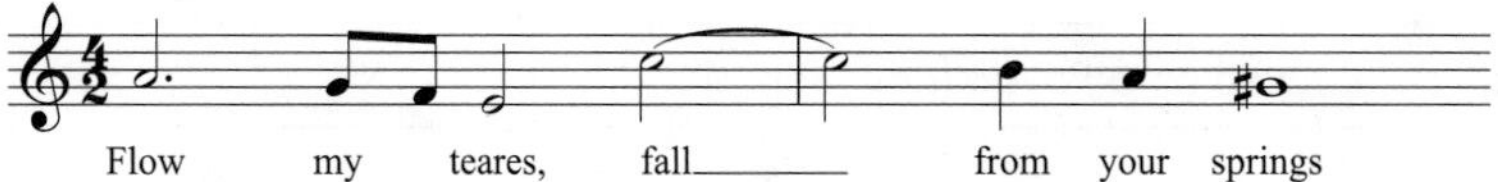

"Pavana Lachrymae," Byrd

TIME	SECTION	LISTEN FOR THIS
0:00	A	Theme in soprano part, imitated in tenor voice *(Melody)* Imitation in tenor
0:50	A′	Variation on A; series of faster falling pitches in the soprano, imitated by the tenor *(Variation)* Imitation in tenor
1:35	B	Second part of theme in soprano part
2:06	B′	Variation on B
2:50	C	Third part of theme in soprano part
3:33	C′	Variation on C

Remaining faithful to the theme but also subjecting it to variation is the hallmark of this composition by a master of the late Renaissance. And it is the hallmark of countless other variation sets practiced in the classical tradition by many composers we discuss in this book. But the technique of variation extends well beyond classical music to other art forms. The great jazz musicians, for example, find their inspiration by taking a preexistent theme and then varying it, sometimes to the point that the theme becomes more or less concealed. They set up a tension between the theme (the given) and the variations (in which they can express themselves more freely). What William Byrd practiced near the beginning of the seventeenth century was not utterly unrelated.

check your **KNOWLEDGE**

1. How did instrumental music develop during the Renaissance into a new genre?
2. Describe the new instrumental form of the fantasia? How did it differ from a dance movement?
3. What impact did the establishment of the Anglican Church have on the life and career of William Byrd?

PART III SUMMARY: THE RENAISSANCE

- The Renaissance was a cultural reawakening that arose in Italy around 1450 and continued for about 150 years.

- Renaissance art reflected a new interest in humanism, centered on the human mind and body. Composers used new modes, similar to our modern major and minor scales (p. 13), and triads (p. 13), so that their music sounds relatively modern to our ears.

- Franco-Flemish musicians, including Dufay and Josquin, flourished in parts of what are now France and Belgium. Many traveled to Italy, where they served in Italian courts and in the Papal Choir in Rome.

- The Italian composer Palestrina became identified with the music of the Counter-Reformation, the Catholic Church's response to the Protestant Reformation.

- The invention of printing facilitated the distribution of music and initiated the music trade.

- In sacred music, the principal genres were the mass and motet. In secular music, the madrigal became popular in Italy and was exported to England, where it was transformed into the English madrigal.

- Renaissance composers produced an increasing amount of music for instruments alone.

KEY TERMS

block chords 106
cantus firmus 100
counterpoint 98
Counter-Reformation 110
dissonance 115
duple meter 119
English madrigal 115
fantasia 119
galliard 119
harmony 98
harpsichord 118
homophony 106
humanism 92
linear perspective 93
lute 118
madrigal 115
motif (motives) 104
pavan 119
point of imitation 106
recorder 118
stepwise motion 112
triad 95
triple meter 119
viol 118
virginal 119
word painting 115

KEY COMPOSERS

Guillaume Dufay (1397–1474)
Josquin Desprez (ca. 1450–1521)
Giovanni Pierluigi da Palestrina (ca. 1525–1594)
William Byrd (ca. 1540–1623)
Carlo Gesualdo (1566–1613)
Thomas Weelkes (1576–1623)

MUSICAL JOURNEYS
The Sitār and Rāgas of India

Perhaps the best known world-music instrument is the sitār. Thanks to master performers like Ravi Shankar (1920–2012) and his daughter Anoushka (b. 1981), the sitār and its music has been heard in concert and on recordings since the 1950s. Shankar was one of the first Indian musicians to perform widely in the West, and besides performing traditional Indian music, he embraced Western musical styles, including jazz and rock. His famous student George Harrison (1943–2001) of the Beatles helped popularize the instrument among rock musicians through its use on recordings such as "Norwegian Wood." Harrison also produced

Ravi Shankar performs on the sitar in the 1970s.

a number of Shankar's recordings and featured him in his 1971 benefit Concert for Bangladesh. Shankar performed with two accompanying musicians. One played the Indian *sarod* (a stringed instrument that provides the underlying drone accompaniment to the sitār) and the other *tabla* (two small bowl-shaped drums).

The sitār is a large, fretted, long-necked lute. It is a prominent instrument of the classical music of the northern and central regions of South Asia. The name *sitār* is an Urdu transcription of *sihtār* ("three-stringed") from Persian, the court language of North India from the thirteenth century to the nineteenth.

Sitars are made of wood and a bulging gourd segment (though all-wood sitārs are sometimes found). The body has two main parts: the resonator or shell (*khol*); and the neck (*ḍā̃ḍ*, *daṇḍā*, *daṇḍī* "stick"). The shell is made of a dried gourd that provides a resonator; it is topped with a wooden soundboard. Many sitārs have a small second gourd resonator (S; *tumbā*) attached at the back of the neck below the nut. This is detachable, and adds little extra resonance to the instrument. The neck is a long, hollowed piece of wood, topped with a fingerboard. The frets are made of metal and arch over the fingerboard. The neck is topped with the peg head that holds the tuning pegs for the five principal strings. The strings are made of metal.

From the mid-nineteenth century, one or two thin strings began to be added, known today as *cikārī* (Hindi: "squeaking, gnat"). They are usually tuned to the first note of the scale. Another, later, nineteenth-century development is the addition of a dozen or so sympathetic strings (*taraf, tarab*: "side strings"). They pass underneath the movable frets. They are tuned to vibrate in sympathy with the plucked strings.

The player sits fully on the floor, left leg tucked flat beneath right, the shell supported in the hollow of his left foot. Some players sit cross-legged with the raised right thigh supporting the neck (requiring less pressure from the right arm); others keep it flat. The basic plucking style is a continuous through-movement of the right hand from the wrist, all four fingers held loosely together and supported by the thumb, mostly on the first string but often lightly brushing the second string simultaneously.

The primary repertory played by the sitār is known as the ***rāga*** (see **Listening Map I.2**). The term is derived from the Sanskrit word for the color "red," which symbolizes "passion" or "delight." Although in the West the term *rāga* is used to describe an individual piece, the rāga itself is simply a scale or mode on which the composition is based. Each rāga is characterized by a variety of melodic features. Besides the basic scale, the rāga includes rules governing the relative emphasis of the different scale notes and their sequence in ascending and descending orders. Distinctive ways of ornamenting or pitching particular notes and motifs or formulae from which complete melodies or improvisations can be constructed are also part of each rāga. Rāgas are normally attributed to divine rather than human origin. They are sometimes considered to exist in the form of deities or spirits, or to have magical or therapeutic properties. In North India each rāga is associated with a season or time of day at which it is normally performed.

The basic rāga form is in two parts: the *Ālāp*, an introductory section that opens in free rhythm; and the *Gat-toṛā*, which features the main tāl or rhythm of the piece. There are different subsections in each part; the opening Ālāp usually ends with a more rhythmic *joṙ* and *jhālā* sections. These sections further develop the rāga, and do add a basic rhythmic pulse, but they are not yet associated with the tala or rhythm of the main part of the rāga. It is only with the Gat-toṛā section that the rhythm pattern is introduced. This section gradually builds in speed from a slow introduction until finally reaching a virtuosic section of intense playing by the sitar and accompanying tabla, also called the jhālā.

LISTENING MAP *I.2*

Rag Nat Bhairav performed by SHAMIM AHMED KHAN, ZAKIR HUSSAIN, and AMANAT

FORM	Indian rāga
TEMPO	Opening free meter; main section: seven-beat tala divided 3/2/2
SCORING	Sitar (fretted plucked lute), tabla (pair of hand drums), tambura (fretless plucked lute)
OVERVIEW	A rāga is an instrumental piece that explores a specific scale and rhythm known as a rag. Each rag is associated with a specific emotion and is performed traditionally only at a specific time of day. The rāga is divided into two main sections: the Ālāp, which explores the basic scale and how each note is ornamented in a nonrhythmic setting; and the Gat-torā, which introduces the basic tala (or rhythm) and gradually increases in speed and intensity.

why to **LISTEN**

Rag Bhairav is one of the oldest of rāgas, and is one of the six main types of rāgas. *Rag Nat Bhairav*, heard here, is a variant of it, wedding its basic scale with one from the Rag Nat. Bhairav is associated with the god Siva, a powerful and somewhat terrifying figure in Hindu mythology. However, this rag is also associated with peaceful feelings fitting the early morning hours. (Traditionally, rāgas are intended for specific times of the day.)

Shamim Ahmed Khan (1938–2012) was a student of Ravi Shankar's. This performance mixes the traditional with more modern elements. Particularly unusual is the tabla solo toward the end of the piece. In a break with tradition, modern audiences have focused on the virtuosity of Indian musicians. Another nontraditional feature that one often hears today is the trading of rhythmic riffs between sitarist and tabla player, almost like jazz musicians.

first **LISTEN**

ĀLĀP	GAT-TORĀ	CONCLUSION
0:00	**1:39**	**8:57**
The sitarist explores the scale of the rāga, moving up in pitch, demonstrating how each note should be ornamented.	Sitar, tabla, and tambura. A series of passages rise and fall in intensity, exploring the main rhythm and melody. Climax in the energetic jhala section toward its end.	The intensity is broken, and the accompanists drop out as the sitarist plays a few notes.

a deeper LISTEN

TIME	SECTION	LISTEN FOR THIS
0:00	Ālāp	Tambura establishes the tonal center. "Sympathetic" string strum on the sitar highlights all of the pitches potentially used in the rāga performance.
0:04		Sitar enters with the melodic content. Free rhythm. Sa Re Ga - Ma - Pa Dha - Ni Ṡa
0:12		Repetitive strumming of the lower-pitched rhythm strings (commonly known as "jhala" strings) reinforces the tonal center. Background sounding of the tambura.
0:35		Characteristic bending of pitches to ornament the melody and move from one pitch to another.
0:56		**Jor:** Slight shift in rhythmic density and more regular pulsation of the melody and rhythm strings.
1:24		**Jhala:** Rhythmic density increases as the melodic range ascends, followed by a brief syncopated passage that signals the drummer of a shift to the next section.
1:39	Gat-torā	Slowing of melodic pulsation, thinner rhythmic density as the drum enters. At 1:45, pitch inflections of the drum, characteristic of tabla performance.
2:01		The musicians coordinate their musical accents.
2:12		The release of musical tension indicates the end of a melodic passage. At 2:40, quick strumming of sympathetic sitar strings. Drum pattern emphasizes underlying rhythmic cycle (i.e., tala), composed of seven beats divided 3/2/2 (*rupak tal*).
3:04		Brief shift in range and rhythmic density to build musical tension.
3:14		Musicians accend together to signal the close of the melodic passage.
4:19		Increase in rhythmic density and change in melodic content. Note how the melodic passages are of shorter duration.
5:33		Triple repetition of a melodic motive to signal the approach of the drum solo, as the sitar fades.
5:45		Tabla drum solo. Note the tambura continues to sound in the background.
6:28		**Jhala** begins: Tabla signals the sitar's return. The melodic content is more rhythmically dense than before the drum solo.
6:53		The duration of the closing melodic passage is shorter than its earlier version. Listen for the emphasis on single pitches, rather than melodic motives.
7:43		Use of triplets in the melody changes the rhythmic character of the performance and extends the closing phrase. At 8:41, dramatic increase in rhythmic density.
8:57	Conclusion	Series of repeated melodic motives signals the end of the performance.
9:05		Drummer is absent as the sitar musician plays a descending melodic line.

PART

The Baroque

Music wishes to be mistress of the air, not just of the water. —CLAUDIO MONTEVERDI

Painting by Giovanni Paolo Panini of a concert at Teatro Argentina in Rome (1747), celebrating the marriage of Louis the Dauphin of France to Marie-Josephe of Saxony.

Few terms for describing music and art are as fanciful as the **Baroque period**, from roughly 1600 to 1750. The name is likely to have derived from a Portuguese word for an irregularly shaped pearl. In music, this was a period of fundamental importance, spanning the rise of opera in the seventeenth century to the work of J. S. Bach and G. F. Handel in the eighteenth. Much of the period's art was characteristically grand, extravagant, and ornate.

The Baroque movement began in Italy. During the latter part of the sixteenth century, this emotional style began to challenge the serene balance of Renaissance art. Then, with the start of the seventeenth century, Baroque art emerged in all its grandeur. It was powerful and featured monumental, sometimes overwhelming effects. It was lavish, highly ornamented, and detailed. And it was an intensely charged art that captured the tortured passions of humankind.

First to popularize the Baroque style was a group of Italian artists. Among the innovators was Michelangelo Merisi (or Amerighi) da Caravaggio (1571–1610), whose life mirrored the high drama of Baroque art. He was often involved in street fights and occasionally jailed, and one bloody encounter in Rome led to his exile from the city. In his first celebrated painting, *The Calling of St. Matthew* (1599), Caravaggio depicts the moment when the tax collector Matthew is called upon by God. The painting is set in a darkened space, a tavern, where the only light originates from over the raised hand of Christ. Caravaggio captures the startled looks of Matthew and his companions as they turn to see the holy figure and experience his power.

Another key proponent of the Baroque style was artist and architect Gian Lorenzo Bernini (1598–1680). Working for several popes during the seventeenth century, Bernini made several improvements to St. Peter's Square and Basilica in the Vatican, the papal enclave within Rome. To surround the vast area before the basilica, he

The Calling of St Matthew, 1599, by Michelangelo Merisi da Caravaggio. Notice the dramatic use of light to convey the story.

Gian Lorenzo Bernini, *Throne of St. Peter*, the Vatican (1653), an ornate Baroque creation in marble, stucco, and bronze.

Diego Velázquez, *Las Meninas*, 1656. Velázquez was a key painter in the Spanish Baroque style.

created rows of gigantic columns supporting a long roof topped with monumental sculptures. Inside the cathedral, Bernini designed the Throne of St. Peter, a spectacular Baroque setting in marble, stucco, and bronze. Golden rays of light stream from its top, just above a highly ornate, three-dimensional relief depicting a mass of angels and seraphim.

From Italy, the Baroque spread throughout Western Europe. The Spanish Baroque found full expression in the brilliant portraits of Diego Velázquez, the official court painter of Philip IV. Meanwhile, the Netherlands, now emerging as a seafaring economic power, also enjoyed its golden century. Its southern regions were a center of the Counter-Reformation, the Catholic Church's response to the Protestant Reformation. There, the Flemish artist Peter Paul Rubens created heroic canvases on a grand scale, with glowing colors and a dynamic sense of movement and sweep. In the northern Netherlands (or Dutch Republic), a largely Protestant region, Baroque art culminated in the luminous paintings of Rembrandt, master of strong lighting effects and rich color. Rembrandt possessed an uncanny ability to capture not just the features but also the character of his subjects, including himself in dozens of revealing self-portraits.

In France, the seventeenth century was the "grand century" of Louis XIV, the Sun King, who ruled by divine right. The centerpiece of his power was Versailles, not far from Paris. Accommodating thousands, this colossal palace, with its glittering Hall of Mirrors, sweeping vistas, and elegant fountains and gardens, was the envy of European monarchs. The stately residence and seat of government impresses as a vast artwork in itself. Its exaggerated ornamentation and huge scale effectively projected the authority and enormous power of the French king.

The sciences made strong advances during the seventeenth century, which saw the invention of the telescope and microscope. Powerful minds were at work in all areas of scientific exploration, including Galileo Galilei (1564–1642) in astronomy and physics, René Descartes (1596–1650) in analytical geometry, William Harvey (1578–1657) in anatomy, and Isaac Newton (1642–1726) in calculus and physics. Their work dealt a death blow to the medieval worldview first challenged during the Renaissance. Descartes's pithy pronouncement "I think, therefore I am" opened the way to the eighteenth-century Age of Enlightenment.

Throughout the Baroque, composers created compelling music that reflected the emotionalism of the age. That music ranged from the dramatic operas of Monteverdi and Purcell to the polished chamber music of Corelli, the buoyant concertos of Vivaldi, the grand oratorios and operas of Handel, and the cerebral fugues of Bach.

Rembrandt van Rijn, *The Night Watch*, 1642. Rembrandt's ability to capture the character of his subjects is shown in the two brightly lit foreground figures.

The Palace of Versailles, a symbol of French king Louis XIV's power.

Watch a brief history of the building of Versailles.

WHY LISTEN TO *Baroque Music?*

Baroque music has several qualities to entice modern listeners. It projects a grandiosity and energy, and yet it plumbs the full range of intimate human emotions. Baroque music can be powerful, whimsical, and theatrical. Some have found parallels to its forward driving rhythms and strong bass lines in two twentieth-century art forms, jazz and rock. These modern forms can also explode with propulsive rhythms and yet remain anchored on foundational bass lines that help give the music its structure.

The characteristics of Baroque art and architecture—its ornate designs, complexity, and bizarre extremes—are echoed in Baroque music. In

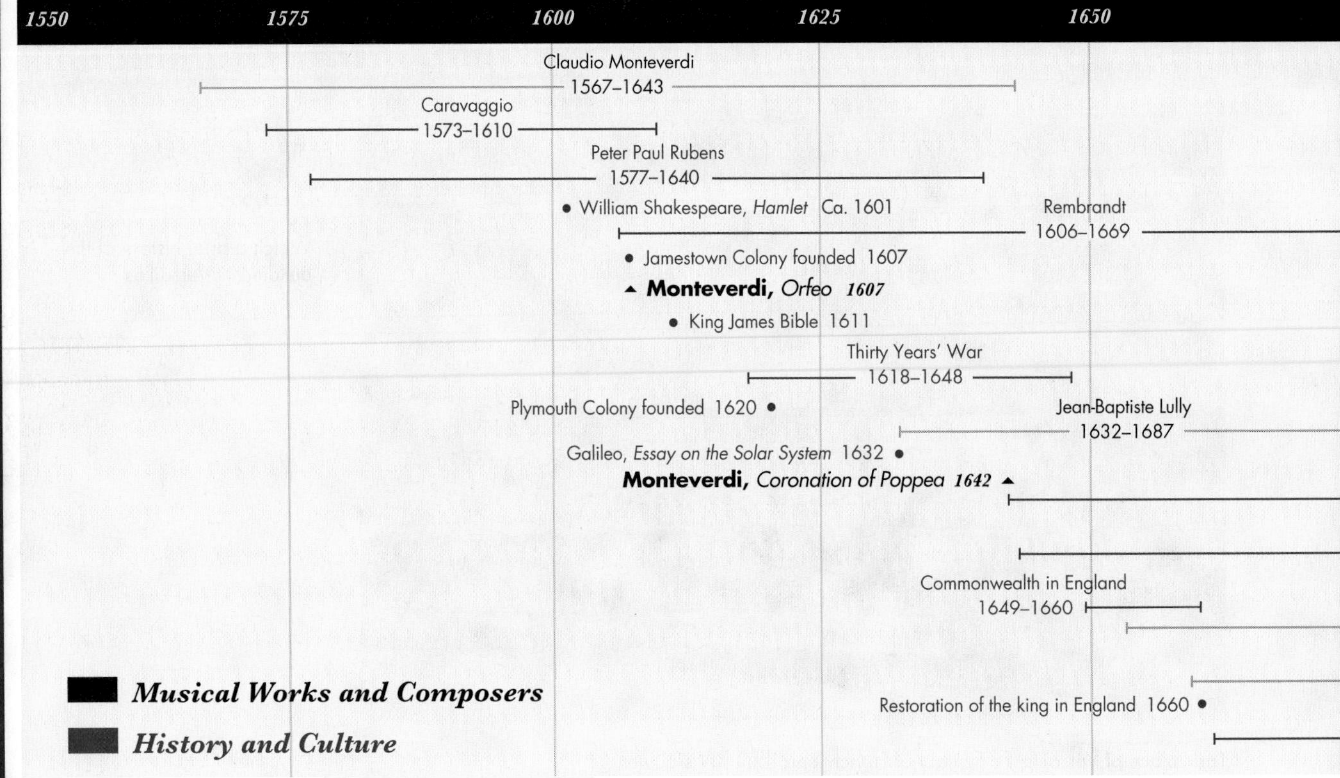

comparison, the Renaissance offered clean lines and measured proportions. There is an irrational edge to the Baroque, reminding us that not everything in human affairs is balanced, tidy, and perfect. Perhaps for that reason the Baroque has been revived from time to time down through history. Baroque-inspired architecture came into fashion in the later nineteenth century, for example, and Hollywood films in the twentieth sometimes offered spectacles reminiscent of the style. Early in the twentieth century, the remarkable musician Wanda Landowska made a highly successful career of reviving the harpsichord (a keyboard instrument that predates the piano). This Baroque instrument made another comeback during the 1960s, when bands such as the Beatles and the Rolling Stones featured it in their music.

Read about Landowska's twentieth-century revival of the harpsichord.

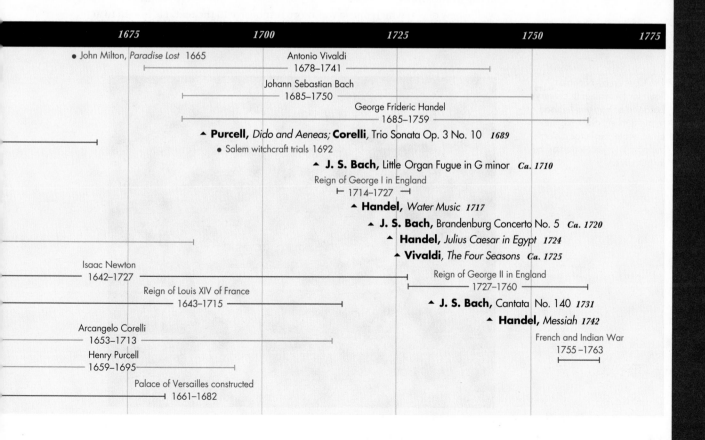

1675 *1700* *1725* *1750* *1775*

- John Milton, *Paradise Lost* 1665
- Antonio Vivaldi 1678–1741
- Johann Sebastian Bach 1685–1750
- George Frideric Handel 1685–1759
- ▲ **Purcell,** *Dido and Aeneas;* **Corelli,** Trio Sonata Op. 3 No. 10 *1689*
- Salem witchcraft trials 1692
- ▲ **J. S. Bach,** Little Organ Fugue in G minor *Ca. 1710*
- Reign of George I in England 1714–1727
- ▲ **Handel,** *Water Music* *1717*
- ▲ **J. S. Bach,** Brandenburg Concerto No. 5 *Ca. 1720*
- ▲ **Handel,** *Julius Caesar in Egypt* *1724*
- ▲ **Vivaldi**, *The Four Seasons* *Ca. 1725*
- Isaac Newton 1642–1727
- Reign of George II in England 1727–1760
- Reign of Louis XIV of France 1643–1715
- ▲ **J. S. Bach,** Cantata No. 140 *1731*
- ▲ **Handel,** *Messiah* *1742*
- Arcangelo Corelli 1653–1713
- French and Indian War 1755–1763
- Henry Purcell 1659–1695
- Palace of Versailles constructed 1661–1682

CHAPTER

19 Elements of Baroque Music

Running like a thread through the diverse styles of the Baroque is a compelling interest in human passions. Baroque painters exhibited this new emotionalism through their use of exaggerated shapes, dramatic lighting, and contorted human figures. Composers, in turn, used intense contrasts of loud and soft, complex melodic profiles with unanticipated twists and turns, and new rhythmic patterns. They set music to texts dealing with powerful emotional states such as love, rage, and sorrow.

Baroque composers were especially concerned with relating music and text. By the early decades of the seventeenth century, a basic change in musical style had taken place. As the Italian Baroque composer Claudio Monteverdi described it, the older style had favored multiple melodic lines that sometimes obscured the meaning of the text. This practice had reached its maturity in Renaissance polyphony, particularly in the works of Palestrina (see pp. 109–113). Monteverdi contrasted this style with a new one in which music was more responsive to the text. He aimed to achieve this goal in his music partly by focusing on a single melodic line accompanied by

The Concert by Nicholas Tournier (seventeenth century). Baroque composers focused on relating music and text; they often wrote music for a single melodic line accompanied by instruments.

instruments. Without the clutter of multiple melodic parts, he reasoned, the text could project clearly.

The techniques Baroque composers used contrasted strikingly with those of the Renaissance. In this chapter, we will discuss three elements of Baroque music:

1) Tonality (as opposed to modality, characteristic of medieval and Renaissance music)
2) A performance convention known as the *basso continuo*
3) New approaches to melody, rhythm, and dynamics

The Development of Tonality

For centuries, composers had respected the system of modality founded on the ancient church modes of the Middle Ages. Then, during the Renaissance, two new modes—our modern major and minor scales—gained favor. During the Baroque, these scales replaced the old church modes, and a new musical system of structuring melodies and harmonies—called **tonality** (see Chapter 2)—replaced modality. Once established, tonality reigned alone until the early twentieth century. And even though it was eventually challenged, tonality is still very much alive. In fact, most of the music we hear today, whether popular or classical music, is tonal.

Tonality is based on **triads**, the three-note chords separated by intervals of the third (for example, C-E-G, D-F-A, E-G-B, and so forth). In the Renaissance, composers had begun to explore triads, but not until the seventeenth century did this remarkably sophisticated new system emerge fully. Here we will briefly review the general principles of tonality, which is of paramount interest primarily because it has endured and is still in use. Thanks to musical developments from the Baroque era, triads are the building blocks of our contemporary musical experiences.

So just how does tonality work? We'll begin with a major scale, say C-major (see Chapter 1), shown in the following example. After writing out the C-major scale, we can build triads on each step:

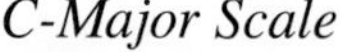

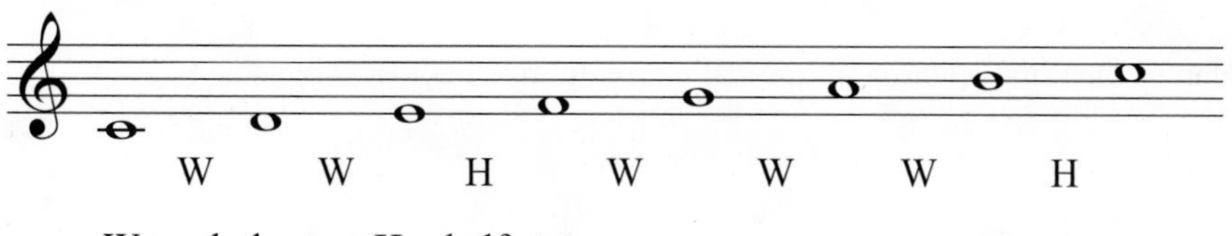

W = whole step; H = half step.

Triads on the C-Major Scale

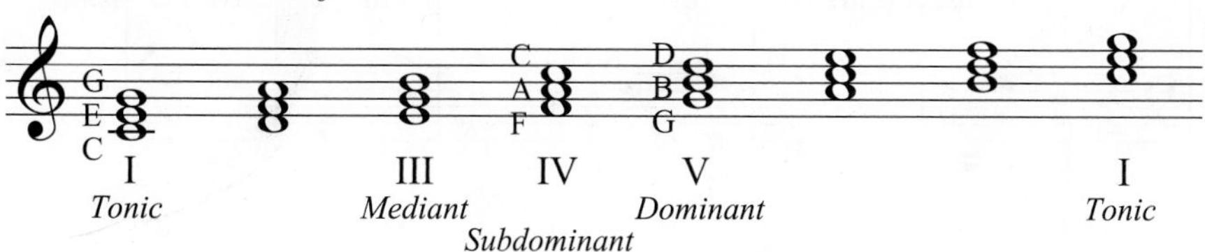

When we say a piece of music is in the **key** of C major, we mean that C, the lowest pitch of the C-major scale, serves as the center of the music. We call the triad built on C the **tonic** and use the Roman numeral I to identify it. In a piece of music in C major, then, we can expect to hear quite a few C-major triads. Usually, the piece will begin with I, and it will always end with I. What about the triads built on other steps of the C-major scale? Tonality sets up a hierarchy of these triads, so that not all have equal weight. After the tonic triad, the most important are those based on the fourth and fifth pitches of the scale, the **subdominant** (IV chord) and **dominant** (V chord), respectively. The tonic triad determines the key of a composition. Think of the tonic triad as the center of gravity, around which the subdominant and dominant triads revolve. The strongest association is between the tonic triad and the dominant triad. Next in importance is the subdominant triad, which works in conjunction with the tonic and dominant triads. Finally, all the triads derived from the scale may play roles in the **harmonic progressions**—the movement from one triad to another—throughout a tonal composition.

We can begin to see how triads function by considering part of a well-known melody, such as "Joy to the World." What concern us here are the triads that support the melody. We'll just focus on three—the tonic (I), subdominant (IV), and dominant (V):

Joy to the world

I IV I

The Lord is come,

IV I V I

Let earth receive her King

I IV IV V V I

Here is the same opening in musical notation, in the key of C major:

Baroque composers came to recognize the lowest-sounding line, or *bass line*, as the supporting line of harmonic progressions. In particular, they used certain bass-line patterns, or **cadences**, to announce an arrival in a particular key. The final progression of the preceding example, from dominant to tonic (V–I), represents a common cadence in the key of C major.

In the C-minor scale, the most important triads after the tonic are the dominant, **mediant** (on the third pitch), and subdominant triads:

C-minor Scale

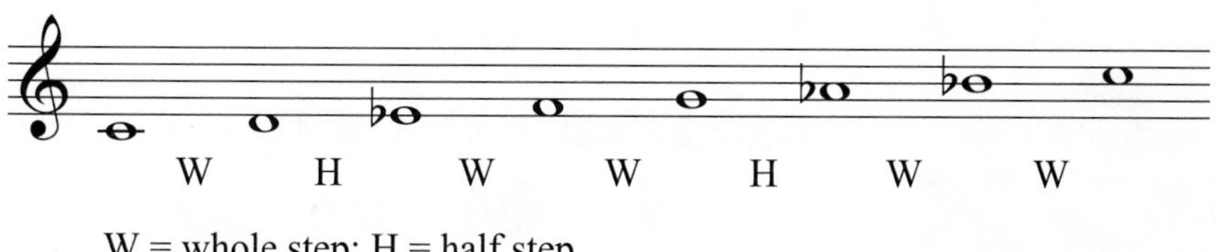

W = whole step; H = half step.

Triads on the C-minor Scale

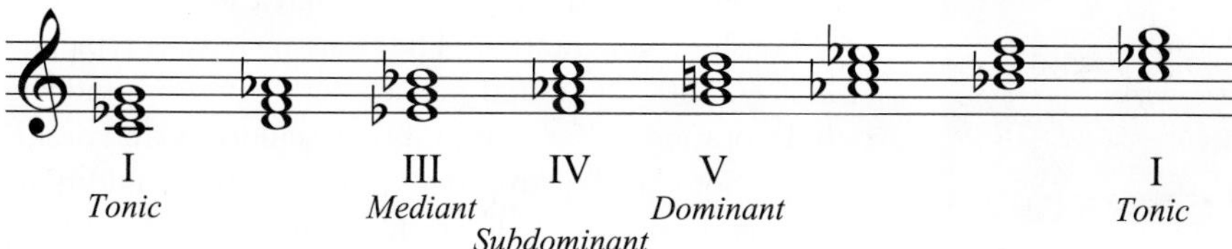

In the seventeenth century, tonality developed into a system of twenty-four keys: twelve major and twelve minor, each with its own series of triads. The major and minor keys were all **transpositions** of each other—that is, repetitions, starting on different pitches, of the same major or minor-scale pattern. During the Baroque, composers began to identify keys by **key signatures**, or listings of the sharps and flats needed for each key (see p. 9). We still follow that convention today.

Read more on the Baroque system of twenty-four keys, also known as the circle of fifths.

The Basso Continuo

A new performance technique called *basso continuo* (continuous bass), complemented the shift to tonality during the Baroque. The **basso continuo** (or simply, **continuo**) enabled composers to suggest harmonies above the bass part in a score. These shorthand notations, in the form of numbers, sharps, and flats, indicated which chords should be played, or realized, as the accompaniment. The practice, a defining feature of Baroque music, is similar to how jazz musicians today use charts to sketch the harmonic changes in a jazz composition.

In the Baroque period, performing the continuo required an instrument capable of playing chords (often a keyboard instrument such as a harpsichord or organ), and a bass instrument (for example, a cello or viol). The bass instrument played the bass

Princess Henriette of France (1727–1752), daughter of Louis XV, painted with bass viol by Jean-Marc Nattier; harpsichord in background. Performing the continuo required two such instruments: one to play the bass line alone, and one to add chords.

line, while the keyboard instrument played the bass line *and* the chords indicated by the numbers. The art of converting these numbers into sounding chords was known as **figured bass** or **thoroughbass**. Reading a figured bass, a trained musician could furnish a background of chords for the composition. Most Baroque compositions that we'll discuss include a figured bass performed by a supporting backdrop of continuo instruments.

Melody, Rhythm, and Dynamics in Baroque Music

Much of the appeal of Baroque music resides in the combined effect of its long, ornate melodies, driving rhythmic patterns, and forceful contrasts in dynamics.

Baroque melodies tend to be intricate and to display lavish ornamentation. The basic melody is typically enhanced with additional pitches that bring to mind the rich decoration of Baroque painting, sculpture, and architecture. Sometimes composers indicated these additions to the basic melody by liberally adding special signs, or **ornaments**, that alerted performers that they should add supplemental tones. One such ornament was the **trill**, indicated by the abbreviation **tr**, placed above a note. This sign directed musicians to alternate rapidly between the written note and the pitch immediately above, yielding a distinctive quivering effect.

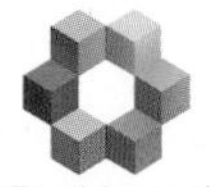

Dashboard

Watch a video on figured bass and how it developed.

By harnessing rhythm and meter, Baroque composers could achieve a driving energy in their music. Often they would begin by establishing a basic pulse through a repeated rhythmic pattern, which then prevailed throughout the piece. Furthermore, Baroque composers allied their rhythmic patterns with a strong sense of regularly recurring beats, or *meter*. Baroque music is distinguished by the historically first use of regular *bar lines*, which divide the music into recurring beat patterns.

Yet another innovative feature of Baroque music concerned the treatment of dynamics. For the first time composers specified contrasting levels of sound in their scores. The directions ***piano*** (***p***; soft) and ***forte*** (***f***; loud) became common. Usually, composers maintained one dynamic level for a long section of a piece, before making a shift. Each succeeding shift would mark a greater increase or decrease in volume, in a technique known as **terraced dynamics**—a step-like change from soft to loud, or loud to soft. These shifts could be quite striking, and helped composers regulate the dramatic pacing in their music.

Above all, treatments of melody, rhythm, and dynamics supported a primary goal of Baroque composers: to highlight unity of mood within a composition. In essence, each musical piece captured a particular emotion, such as rage, joy, sorrow, or grief. To that end, composers developed musical "figures of speech" to represent various moods. Sighing was expressed through drooping, two-note figures; rage through widely flung melodies filled with dramatic leaps. By using symbolic figures, composers sought to convey the human passions that figured so prominently in the arts and letters of the Baroque.

check your KNOWLEDGE

1. What are the major differences between medieval/Renaissance modality and Baroque tonality?
2. How are keys derived from the major or minor scales? What are the main triads for each type of scale?
3. What is the *basso continuo*? What role did it play in Baroque music?
4. How did composers' use of melody, rhythm, and dynamics reflect the new Baroque concerns with expressing human emotions?

CHAPTER

Claudio Monteverdi and the Rise of Italian Opera

The first great Baroque composer was the bold and innovative Italian Claudio Monteverdi (1567–1643), who began his career by absorbing the styles of late Renaissance music. A prodigy who published his first music at age fifteen, he worked for more than twenty years at the ducal court of Mantua. In 1613 he assumed a far more illustrious post as music director of the bejeweled cathedral of St. Mark's in Venice. Here he wrote sacred music and also served the Doge, or leader of the Venetian republic. For some thirty years Monteverdi remained in Venice, where he proved his versatility as a composer by producing madrigals

Claudio Monteverdi (1567–1643).

(for voices alone and for voices with instruments), organizing and writing music for sacred services, and establishing himself as the first master of an entirely new musical genre, opera. Monteverdi did not write much music for instruments alone, but his imaginative blending of instruments into vocal music was groundbreaking.

Monteverdi was heir to the style of late Renaissance polyphony. He collected his finely crafted works into four volumes of **a cappella** madrigals, for voices alone. But with the fifth volume, published in 1605, he began experimenting with a continuo section to accompany the vocal ensemble. In subsequent madrigals, Monteverdi enhanced the role of instruments so that they also played individual parts. His most successful experiments with mixed scorings were the "songs of war" and "songs of love," which appeared in his eighth volume of madrigals in 1638. The "songs of war" feature rapidly repeated instrumental figures in what Monteverdi termed the "agitated style," his musical representation of the passion of anger.

Monteverdi's sacred choral music exemplified another facet of his genius. His great collection of Vesper settings from 1610 showcases different styles and genres, including the older polyphonic Mass and **polychoral** choruses. Here, Monteverdi divided the vocal forces into two answering choruses, an arrangement that suited the echoing interior recesses of St. Mark's. Monteverdi's sacred music includes portions that blend voices and instruments, and intimate settings for solo voice and continuo. Such striking syntheses of old and new positioned him as the principal figure in the transition from the Renaissance to the Baroque. Still, his most influential achievements were in a strikingly new genre of music known as opera.

An **opera** is a dramatic work set to continuous music and acted out on a stage with singers, costumes, and scenery. Typically, an opera calls for solo singers and an orchestra, and may require a chorus as well. A librettist writes the text of the drama, known as the **libretto** (Italian for "little book"), which divides, like a play, into acts and scenes. A composer sets the libretto to music. The emergence of opera around the beginning of the seventeenth century marks a milestone in music history. Now music was directly allied with drama to produce a sophisticated combination. This new genre arose in Italy as a form of court entertainment and then began spreading outside the courts through Western Europe.

By the end of the sixteenth century, the stage had been set for opera through lavish theatrical court entertainments. A group of Florentine noblemen revived an ancient Greek dramatic practice known as **monody**, in which actors spoke their lines in a heightened style resembling singing. Composers began imitating this practice by setting texts to a single vocal line accompanied by a small continuo section of instruments. Monody allowed listeners to concentrate on a vocal line that brought the text into sharp relief.

Responding to these ideas, composers wrote music on pastoral subjects taken from Greek mythology, and opera was born. The first masterpiece in the new genre was Monteverdi's opera *Orfeo* (*Orpheus*), produced in 1607 for the duke of Mantua.

Dashboard

Watch a modern performance of "Possente Spirto" from *Orfeo*.

The Orpheus myth is an ideal subject for an opera. In classical mythology, Orpheus was the follower (or son) of the god Apollo. Poet *and* musician, Orpheus set his verses to music so moving that he could induce animals and inanimate objects to do his will. Like the new musical style of monody, he embodied the persuasive power of song.

MAKING CONNECTIONS *St. Mark's Basilica, Venice*

Among the centers of Christian worship with a storied musical tradition is the centuries-old Basilica of St. Mark's in Venice (it became a cathedral in the early nineteenth century). Its founding goes back to the ninth century, when Venetian merchantmen stole relics of St. Mark from Alexandria in Egypt and brought them to the budding city. Venice was then a province of the Eastern Orthodox Church in Byzantium, and its patron saint was the Greek saint Theodore. But because St. Mark had served as a missionary to the northern Adriatic region of Italy, he was venerated in Venice and became an ideal patron saint for the increasingly wealthy city-state.

St. Mark's was built in a Byzantine style that externally owed allegiance to the Eastern Orthodox Church. Over centuries the edifice became encrusted with precious stones—opal, mother of pearl, marbles, rubies, and gold—much of it brought back as plunder from the Crusades in the Middle Ages. At first sight, the structure makes an overwhelming impression, leaving many visitors speechless.

Inside the cathedral, visitors confront a wonderland of mosaics decorating five domed cupolas and raised galleries. To magnify the effects of light reaching the interior, each mosaic piece is set at a slight angle. And as musicians discovered, the recesses and separate galleries of the interior (laid out in the form of a Greek cross, with four sides of the same length) are ideal for capturing special musical echo effects. Even before Monteverdi arrived in 1613, composers had begun experimenting with *cori spezzati*, or "separated choirs," placed in the galleries. The architecture encouraged exploring musical dynamics through coordinated shifts between levels of sound, sometimes indicated in the music by the instruction "echo."

St. Mark's Basilica.

Orpheus in the underworld with Charon the ferryman, shown on a sixteenth-century Italian plate.

In Monteverdi's opera, Orfeo tries to win back his wife, Eurydice, who has died from a serpent's bite and is now in the underworld. Orfeo journeys there and gains her release. There is a condition, however: he must not look back at her while they return to the upper world. But he cannot resist, and when he does look back, he loses her again. Here the libretto departs from the myth: Apollo comforts Orfeo over his loss and transports him to the heavens, so that he can gaze forever upon his wife. (According to the myth, instead of this relatively happy ending, Orfeo meets a violent end.)

In much of this pioneering score, Monteverdi uses the monodic style of solo singing with continuo accompaniment. But he also includes lively choruses for the pastoral setting of Orfeo's homeland, subdued choruses for the shadowy underworld, and instrumental dances and movements as the scenes require. Monteverdi matches the diversity of the music with an elaborate ensemble of instruments, or **orchestra**.

As Act III opens, Orfeo has been accompanied by Speranza (Hope) to the entrance of the underworld, where he hopes to rescue his wife. But Speranza soon departs, and Orpheus is left alone. This passage unfolds in what is known as **recitative** (*recitativo* in Italian), the vocal style characteristic of the new monody. In recitative, the melodic line conforms to the inflections and accents of the text—its natural "ups" and "downs." Recitative was the essential dramatic ingredient of early opera. Because it imitated the spontaneity of speech, it was a highly flexible style. Moreover, recitative enabled the composer to convey a good deal of text rapidly and efficiently. Still, there were occasions that required more formal, structured, and melodic music.

One such occasion that demanded a more melodic treatment is Orfeo's following entreaty to Charon, the dramatic center of the opera. Charon, who ferries the souls of the dead across the river Styx into the underworld, has told Orfeo to abandon his journey. After a somber instrumental introduction, Orfeo begins his memorable monologue, "Possente spirto" ("O powerful spirit," **Listening Map 12**). Here Orfeo's appeal to Charon unfolds as a series of variations over a repeating bass line, with each variation sung to progressively more persuasive stanzas of poetry. Only with a last, desperate plea to the spirits of the underworld does Orfeo finally lull Charon to sleep. The fabled poet-musician then crosses the river, intent on reclaiming Eurydice with the sheer power of song.

After *Orfeo*, Monteverdi continued to write operas, some of which have been lost. The major surviving opera of his late period is *The Coronation of Poppea* (*L'incoronazione di Poppea*, 1642), which marks another milestone in music history. Unlike *Orfeo*, written for a court entertainment, *Poppea* had its premiere in a public Venetian opera house. This change in venue anticipated a gradual shift in music from royal diversions to operas

MAKING CONNECTIONS *Orfeo* and the Rise of the Orchestra

The word *orchestra* comes from the Greek for the area before a stage, where a large group of musicians can support the dramatic action. Today, we have a rather fixed image of what constitutes an orchestra. Generally speaking, we envision dozens and dozens of musicians, playing string, brass, wind, and percussion instruments while they follow the cues and gestures of a baton-wielding conductor. But what did composers do before there were standardized orchestras or conductors? In two words, they improvised.

Monteverdi realized that a careful selection and use of instruments in his operas could enhance the power of the music and delivery of the words. For *Orfeo*, the composer required nearly forty musicians, but the entire band did not play together. Some musicians likely played behind the scenes, and some had quite specific roles and played only during certain parts of the opera. Monteverdi seems to have organized the instruments into two basic categories: those for a *basso continuo* group, providing the bass line and harmonic foundation of the music; and those for melodic solos. *Orfeo*'s orchestra includes a string section of violins and viols, several trombones and trumpets, and other wind instruments, such as recorders and cornetts, wood instruments with cup-shaped mouthpieces that produced a piercing, nasal tone. For his continuo section, Monteverdi calls at different times for harpsichords, a double harp (a harp with two sets of strings), *chitarroni* (lute-like instruments with elongated necks), and small chamber organs (two with wooden pipes and one, known as a *regal*, with reeds).

Monteverdi was quite sensitive to the timbre, or quality of sound, of specific instruments. He viewed his orchestra as a rich palette of tone colors that he could exploit, depending on the dramatic situation on stage. In *Orfeo*, he draws selectively on its resources, associating instrumental colors with particular characters and settings. He uses the harsh reed organ to accompany Charon, ferryman for the dead. By contrast, Orfeo sings with a range of softer instrumental options, such as violins, cornetts, and a double harp. Here, in the subtle decisions of an early seventeenth-century Baroque composer, we can find many of the origins of the large ensemble we know today as the modern orchestra.

(a) Cornetts and (b) chittarone.

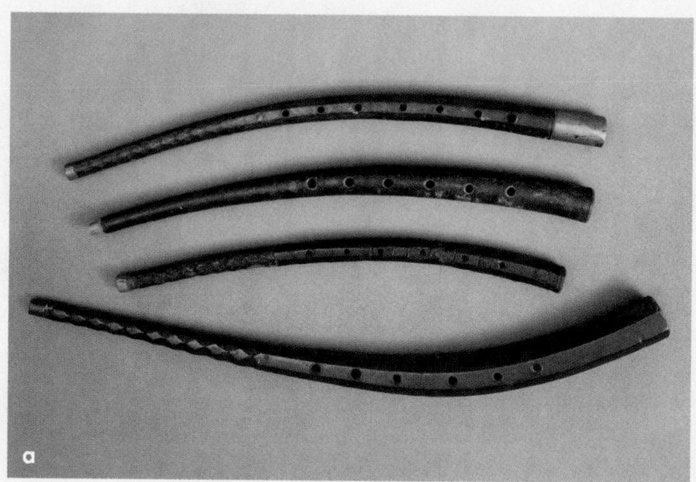
a

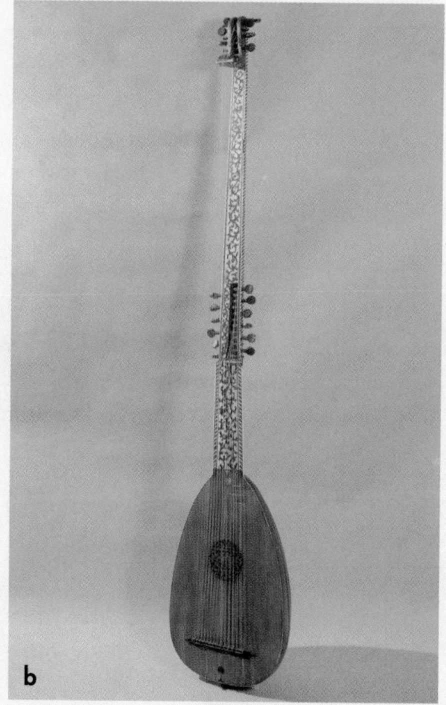
b

LISTENING MAP 12

MONTEVERDI, *Orfeo*, Act III, "Possente spirto" ("O Powerful Spirit"), excerpt

{1607}

FORM	Aria
GENRE	Baroque opera
SCORING	Voice accompanied by orchestra
OVERVIEW	Orfeo's plea to Charon, ferryman for the dead ("Possente spirto"), inspired the most sophisticated music of the entire opera. Here, Orfeo sings a series of increasingly ornamented variations as he seeks to enter the underworld. Its guardian remains unmoved, however, until Orfeo returns to a simpler yet more forceful style. Throughout, the musical instruments accompanying Orfeo mirror his passionate plea with their own variations performed between the verses. Excerpted here are the instrumental introduction and first three variations of the scene.

why to LISTEN

Still performed today, over 400 years after its premiere, Monteverdi's *Orfeo* can lay claim to being the longest-lived opera in classical music. Usually, operas come and go as fashions inevitably change, but *Orfeo* holds a special allure for listeners. Why is that? Setting aside its revered place in Baroque music, the opera has taken on a much broader significance because it is *about music itself*, about its universal power to move, agitate, and calm. In addition, we are still moved by the compelling story of Orfeo's attempts to vanquish death and reunite with his wife.

Monteverdi recognized that "Possente spirto," Orfeo's confrontation with Charon, was the crux of the opera. He called it a "righteous prayer" and poured his artistry into this little masterpiece. Monteverdi's emphasis on the voice, reinforced by the instruments to convey emotion, make this scene compelling, moving, and, above all, human.

first LISTEN

INTRODUCTION	VARIATION 1	INSTRUMENTAL INTERLUDE	VARIATION 2	INSTRUMENTAL INTERLUDE	VARIATION 3	INSTRUMENTAL INTERLUDE
0:00	0:32	2:05	2:34	3:46	4:02	5:42

a deeper **LISTEN**

TIME	SECTION	LISTEN FOR THIS	TEXT	TRANSLATION
0:00	**Instrumental introduction**	The music sets the somber mood of the underworld		
0:32	**Variation 1**	Orfeo accompanied by organ with wooden pipes and continuo, with two solo violins	*Possente spirto, e formidabil nume,* *Senza cui far passaggio a l'altra riva* *Alma da corpo sciolta invan presume.*	O powerful spirit, and formidable divinity, without whose aid passage to the other shore Is denied the soul severed from the body.
		Orfeo Pos - sen - te spir - - - to Continuo 3 e for-mi-da - solo violin solo violin		
2:05	**Interlude**	Two violins		
2:34	**Variation 2**	Orfeo accompanied by organ and continuo instrument, with two solo cornets	*Non viv'io, no, che poi di vita è priva.* *Mia cara sposa, il cor non è piu meco,* *E senza cor com'essor può ch'io viva?*	I live no more, since my dear spouse is taken from life, I have no heart, and without a heart how can I still live?
3:46	**Interlude**	Cornetts		
4:02	**Variation 3**	Orfeo accompanied by organ and continuo instrument, with solo double harp	*A lei volt' ho il cammin per l'aer cieco* *A l'Inferno non già, ch'ovunque stasis* *Tanta bellezza, il Paradiso ha seco.*	For her sake I have found my way through the blinding air, Not yet in Hades, for wherever is found such beauty, Paradise accompanies her.
5:42	**Interlude**	Double harp		

written for a public who purchased tickets. For his subject, Monteverdi turned to a scandalous chapter in Roman history: the reign of Emperor Nero (54–68 CE). According to legend, Nero "fiddled" while Rome burned, destroyed his real and imagined rivals on a whim, and possibly even murdered his mother. The alleged murder was to help clear the way for marrying his mistress, Poppea, after whom Monteverdi named his opera. For her part, Poppea intrigued against Nero's first wife, the empress Octavia, and ultimately succeeded in having her deposed. Monteverdi's ability to capture the emotions of a wealth of characters again provides considerable evidence of his musical and dramatic genius. The opera reflects as well the hypercharged emotionalism of Baroque music.

check your **KNOWLEDGE**

1. How do Monteverdi's madrigals reflect his debts to Renaissance music? How do they announce a new Baroque style?
2. What is an opera? How did the new genre develop?
3. Why is the Orpheus myth a particularly compelling choice for an opera?
4. What is a recitative? How does it differ from other types of melody?
5. How did Monteverdi use vocal and instrumental elements to display different emotions in Orpheus's solo "Possente spirto" ("O powerful spirit")?

CHAPTER

21 The Spread of Opera

By the middle of the seventeenth century, opera had spread throughout Italy and abroad. The opening of public opera houses made opera accessible to new, music-loving audiences. In addition, two types of solo vocal music now became standard. Recitative, the hallmark of early Italian opera, was reserved for texts that carried the dramatic action. A second, more melodic type of solo music, known as an **aria** (or air), was used for texts in which the characters paused to react to the unfolding drama. Often, a dry, rapid recitative introduced a lyrical, tuneful aria.

Opera in France

In France, opera arrived relatively late in the seventeenth century, for various reasons. **Ballet**—a dramatic form of dance that tells a story through the movements of dancers with musical accompaniment—was already a well-entrenched form of court entertainment. The composer responsible for establishing French opera was actually an Italian, G. B. Lulli, better known as Jean-Baptiste Lully (1632–1687). A royal patent granted by Louis XIV guaranteed Lully absolute control over French operas, of which he created more than a dozen. He typically began his operas with an orchestral **overture**, or introduction. It opened with stately rhythms to mark the entrance and presence of the king in the audience, and continued with a livelier section in imitative counterpoint. This coupling of the two sections (overture and imitative counterpoint), a style known as the **French overture**, found favor among later Baroque composers, French and foreign.

Jean-Baptiste Lully (1632–1687).

MAKING CONNECTIONS *Music as Royal Power: Lully at the Court of Louis XIV*

Among the European monarchs who ruled by "divine right," Louis XIV (self-styled as the "Sun King") enjoyed an especially long reign, from 1643 to 1715. It was Louis XIV who finished the massive palace of Versailles outside of Paris, with its glittering Hall of Mirrors and vast gardens. Versailles became the seat of the French court in 1682, and there an elaborate court etiquette developed and played out on a grand scale. Hundreds of officials attended to the king's every whim.

Louis XIV (r. 1643–1715) as Apollo, the Sun God.

Louis was heavily invested in the arts and surrounded himself with the most eminent French playwrights, poets, musicians, and dancers. In official portraits, he is often shown with a turned, exposed ankle, indicating his love of dance, particularly the minuet. While dancing in one of the spectacular court ballets, Louis met a young Italian dancer and composer named Giovanni Battista Lulli. Within a few years, Lulli (who later became a French citizen and changed his name to Lully) had decisively affected the course of French Baroque music, largely owing to the king's patronage.

Opera was slow to come to France. Many French musicians, including Lully, first thought that the French language was not as suitable for the new genre as Italian. But he altered his opinion when he heard an opera by one of his rivals. Soon Lully managed to secure a monopoly over French operas, and he used his newfound power to reign over the musical establishment, an absolute monarch in his own right. Between 1673 and 1687 Lully composed fourteen operas, about one a year. They were all tragedies on a grand scale that befit the Sun King. They were also carefully calculated to celebrate the monarch's absolute reign, and thus served as propaganda to glorify the French state. A severe taskmaster, Lully demanded the very best from his musicians. His own tragic exit came after he accidentally injured his foot while beating time with a pole in front of his orchestra. The wound became infected, and he died from gangrene.

Henry Purcell and English Opera

Henry Purcell (1659–1695).

In England, opera also arrived late in the seventeenth century. The English court had its own favorite form of entertainment, the **masque**, a spectacle featuring poetry, music, and elaborate sets and stage machinery. Masked players, sometimes members of the nobility, did not speak. (Shakespeare alluded to the masque tradition in a few of his plays.) These performances often centered on allegorical subjects such as peace or love, and they became popular in English theaters. However, in time opera began to establish a foothold in English musical culture. Henry Purcell (1659–1695), one of England's most distinguished composers, composed masques that increasingly took on the trappings of opera. These semi-operas, as they are described, involved dramatic plays interrupted by musical, masque-like episodes.

During his short career (he died at the age of thirty-six), Purcell was the organist of Westminster Abbey and of the Chapel Royal. He composed instrumental works, **anthems** (sacred compositions for the Anglican Church), ceremonial pieces for court, and dramatic operas. Purcell is remembered today mainly for *Dido and Aeneas* (1689), the first important English opera to use music throughout to unify a dramatic whole. Lasting under an hour, the opera contains a French-style overture, recitatives, airs, ensembles, choruses, dances, and instrumental interludes.

Purcell took for his subject the tragic love affair of Dido and Aeneas as related in Virgil's epic poem *The Aeneid*. Aeneas, forced to flee Troy while the Greeks sack the city, sets out to fulfill his destiny—to found Rome. Along the way, he lands at Carthage on the coast of North Africa, and falls in love with its queen, Dido. In Virgil's version, the messenger god Mercury appears and orders Aeneas to leave Carthage. In despair, Dido impales herself on his sword and then burns herself on a funeral pyre as Aeneas's fleet prepares to depart. The English version of Purcell's opera deviates somewhat from Virgil's account. Instead of Mercury intervening, a band of witches conspires to destroy Dido and Aeneas's love affair, and Dido dies of grief. (In Purcell's time, witchcraft had some contemporary relevance: the hysteria of the Salem witch trials would play out just a few years later.)

The most dramatic moment in Purcell's opera comes in its final scene, when Dido performs her lament "When I Am Laid in Earth." "To your promised empire fly, and let forsaken Dido die," she exclaims during her last meeting with Aeneas. Then, after she compels him to exit, a somber chorus prepares her solo by singing, "Great minds against themselves conspire. And shun the cure they most desire." Dido delivers a short recitative addressed to her sister, Belinda. The supple music mirrors the expressive nuances of the text as Dido, overcome by grief, welcomes death. Her steadily descending line is accompanied only by a figured-bass line, played, according to Baroque practice, by a continuo section of a bass instrument and harpsichord.

For the air that follows Dido's recitative (see **Listening Map 13**), Purcell employs a small chamber orchestra of strings. The strings accompany the vocal melody, while a descending bass pattern repeats several times underneath. This technique of grounding music over an unchanging bass pattern is known as a **ground bass** (or **basso ostinato**, literally "obstinate bass"). Monteverdi and other Italian opera composers had prized this technique, which then developed further in later Baroque instrumental music.

Rubens, *Death of Dido.*

check your **KNOWLEDGE**

1. How did opera spread from Italy to England and France?
2. What is a ground bass? How does Purcell use this technique to build tension in the accompaniment to Dido's "When I Am Laid in Earth"?
3. How does the shape of the melody reflect the subject matter of "When I Am Laid in Earth"?

LISTENING MAP 13

PURCELL, *Dido and Aeneas*, Act III, "When I Am Laid in Earth"

{1689}

FORM	Ground bass and ten variations, arranged in pairs
GENRE	English opera
SCORING	Voice accompanied by orchestra
OVERVIEW	Purcell's air begins as a descending chromatic line, often used in Baroque music to represent poignant grief. At first the pattern is alone in the bass (1); then, Dido sings her mournful text against relentless repetitions of the pattern (2). Her somber music falls into eight variations grouped into four pairs. The recurring statements of the ground bass build up a powerful tension released only by Dido's farewell, "Remember me!" After her final, eighth variation, the orchestra continues with two more drooping variations that suggest sighs (3). Pulled ever downward, the clashing string parts produce a highly dissonant, tense music. This lament conveys the nobility of the queen as it elegantly translates into music her tragic ending.

why to LISTEN

Dido's "When I Am Laid in Earth" shows several similarities to Monteverdi's "Possente spirto," examined in Chapter 20. Both use a basso ostinato and unfold as a series of variations over a fixed bass. Both use instruments: a string orchestra in Purcell, a *basso continuo* ensemble with shifting, echoing solo instruments in Monteverdi. And both represent the dramatic crux of the respective operas, but with this distinction: If Monteverdi's scene is about the power of music to move us, Purcell's is about capturing a particular emotion—grief.

first LISTEN

INTRODUCTION	VARIATIONS 1–8	VARIATIONS 9–10
0:00	0:14	3:00
	Dido and orchestra	Orchestra

a deeper **LISTEN**

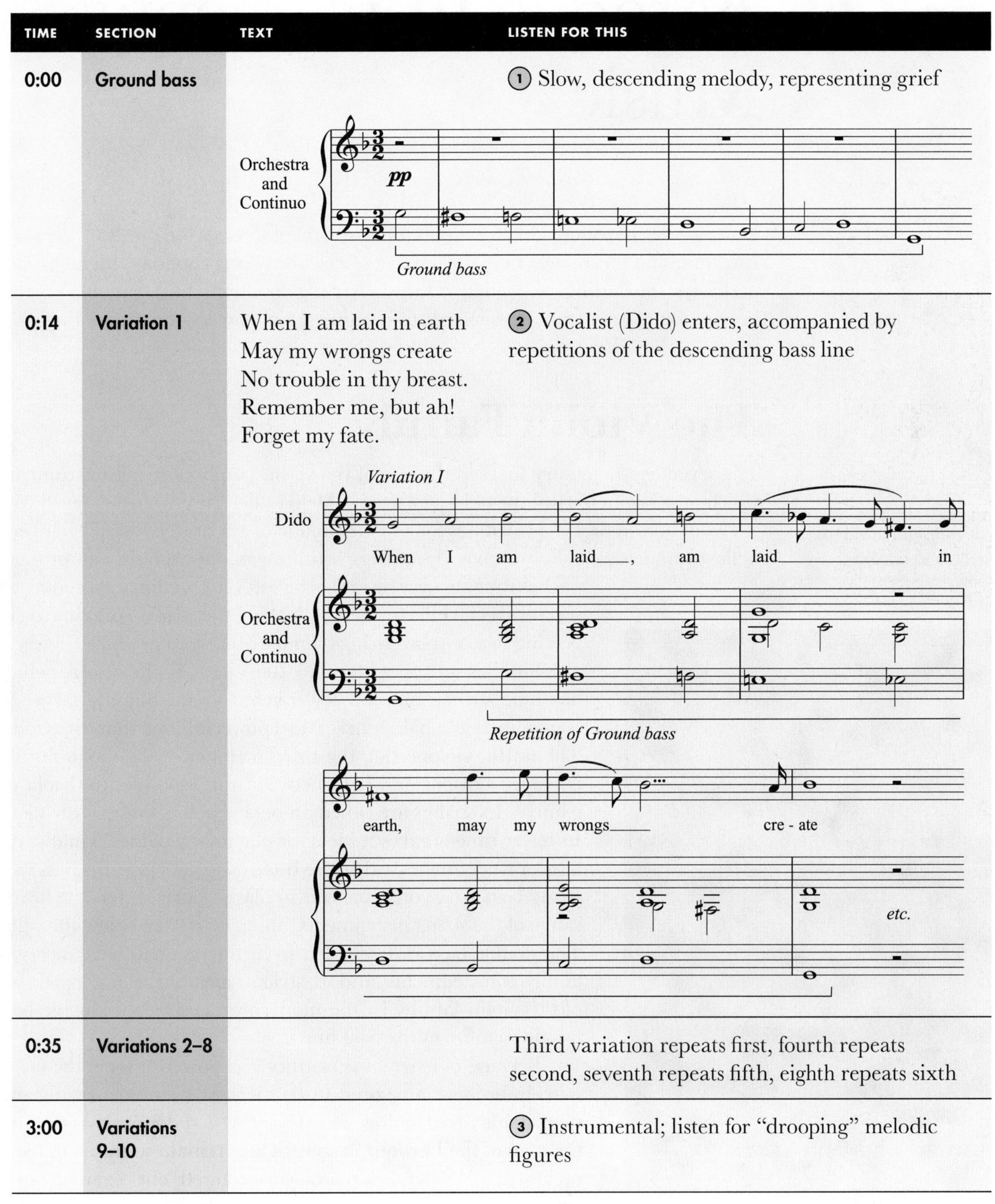

TIME	SECTION	TEXT	LISTEN FOR THIS
0:00	Ground bass		① Slow, descending melody, representing grief
0:14	Variation 1	When I am laid in earth May my wrongs create No trouble in thy breast. Remember me, but ah! Forget my fate.	② Vocalist (Dido) enters, accompanied by repetitions of the descending bass line
0:35	Variations 2–8		Third variation repeats first, fourth repeats second, seventh repeats fifth, eighth repeats sixth
3:00	Variations 9–10		③ Instrumental; listen for "drooping" melodic figures

CHAPTER 22 Baroque Instrumental Music

During the Baroque, great schools of instrumentalists arose in Italy, France, England, and Germany. This was an age of celebrated **virtuosos**—highly skilled performers including the Italian violinists Arcangelo Corelli and Antonio Vivaldi, in addition to lutenists, harpsichordists, organists, viol players, and opera singers.

Dashboard

Watch demonstration videos of the violin and related instruments.

The Violin Family

The seventeenth century marked the rise of the violin family of string instruments, which now began to rival the older viol family. Held under the chin, and played with a bow of horsehair, the **violin** has four strings (made of gut or steel) stretched over a hollow wooden case. By stopping the strings with fingers, the violinist can produce pitches ranging over several octaves. At the violinist's disposal are several special effects such as plucking the strings (**pizzicato**), or bowing two or more strings simultaneously to produce chords.

Counterclockwise from top: violin, viola, and cello.

Similar in appearance to the violin is the **viola**, which has four strings tuned a few pitches lower. Slightly larger in frame, the viola has a darker, less powerful tone than the violin. The **cello** (violoncello), the third member of the violin family, is played upright and held between the legs (like the viola da gamba). Its strings are tuned an octave below those of the viola. Its lower range makes it ideal for playing bass lines. Finally, the large, rather unwieldy **double bass** (also known as the bass viol, string bass, and contrabass), also played upright, has the lowest range of the string instruments, about an octave below the cello. The double bass is descended from the older Renaissance viol family of instruments, and so, strictly speaking, is not a member of the violin family. In the modern orchestra, the double bass usually reinforces the bass line.

Because of its great versatility and powerful tone, the violin quickly became a favored instrument of virtuosos. String sections made up of violins, violas, cellos, and double bass became the core of the Baroque orchestra and remain so in the modern orchestra. (We have already encountered one example of a string orchestra in the selection from Purcell's *Dido and Aeneas* in Chapter 21.)

The Harpsichord

Harpsichord (1634).

Two keyboard instruments, the harpsichord and organ, became prominent during the Baroque era. The **harpsichord** is an instrument in which keys activate a mechanism that plucks strings (unlike the modern piano, in which hammers strike the strings). The plucking agent was a small piece of stiff quill fixed to a strip of wood known as a jack. When the musician depressed a key, the jack was forced upward so that the quill plucked a string. When the musician released the key, the jack fell back to its original position and a small piece of cloth muted the string.

The origins of the harpsichord actually go back to the Middle Ages, and the earliest notated harpsichord music is from the sixteenth century, but the instrument's heyday was the Baroque. This era boasted a long line of harpsichord craftsmen along with celebrated virtuosos who composed for the instrument, including J. S. Bach and G. F. Handel. (For an example by Bach, see his Brandenburg Concerto No. 5, discussed in Chapter 25, in which the harpsichord figures prominently as a solo instrument.)

Because of their versatility, harpsichords were the workhorse of Baroque music. They could play a bass line and supply harmonies above it, according to the *basso continuo* practice, and thus provide a dependable support and backdrop to the music. They could not, however, offer extreme dynamic levels of soft and loud sounds. In the second half of the eighteenth century, harpsichords were displaced and then eclipsed by the new fortepiano (see p. 217), forerunner of our modern piano.

The Organ

Pipe organ (1738) in the Grote Kerk, Haarlem, Netherlands.

Known as the king of instruments, the **organ** makes an impressive range of sounds when air travels through tuned pipes. The air is generated by a bellows and controlled by one or more keyboards and usually a set of pedals. When it enters the pipes, it sets in motion vibrations that create sounds.

The ancient Greeks and Romans had hydraulic organs operated by a water-pumping mechanism. As early as the tenth century, an organ celebrated for its strong sound was in use in the monastery of Winchester in England. The most brilliant period of organ construction came during the Baroque. By the seventeenth century, great organs were filling European cathedrals and churches with rich blends of sound. Their ornate architectural designs provided visual counterparts to the music.

The most impressive Baroque organs had several keyboards, a pedal board, and ranks of pipes of different tone color

Dashboard

Watch a video about the organ, the most complex of Baroque instruments.

and pitch that could be engaged by knobs known as stops. At the time, these great machines were of unequaled complexity. Bach, the most celebrated organist of his time, was well versed in the technical design of organs.

New Musical Genres

New musical genres developed to accommodate the new virtuosity of instrumentalists. The term **sonata** (from Italian meaning "to sound," as opposed to "to sing") described a variety of pieces for one or a few instruments. Some Baroque instrumental music retained ties to older vocal music. In particular, the imitative polyphony of the Renaissance carried over to new genres well suited to keyboard instruments, on which performers could sustain several musical lines in complex textures.

Other instrumental types included virtuoso variations on ground-bass patterns, many of them drawn from dances of the period. Still other compositions, including the **prelude**, often introduced a more substantial instrumental work, and were more freely conceived in the style of improvisations.

Finally, many Baroque instrumental pieces were composed as dances and assembled into great collections. Eventually, a selection of several dances arranged in some order came to be known as a **suite** (from the French for "following").

By the middle of the seventeenth century, the older Renaissance coupling of slow and fast dances was giving way to suites of four dances of different characters. The preferred form for these dances was a two-part plan known as **binary form**. As the name implies, binary form consists of two sections, each of which is repeated. We may label the two sections *A* and *B*, and represent the overall form as *AABB*, or by using **repeat marks**, as ‖: *A* :‖‖: *B* :‖. In binary-form dances, the two sections are cut from the same musical cloth; in effect, the composer spins the whole dance from the same basic thread. The *A* and *B* sections differ, however, in their key plan. The *A* section begins in the tonic key, but as it approaches the end of the section, it **modulates**, or changes key, from the tonic to a second key (often the dominant). The *B* section reverses the process; here, we begin in the second key, and then, through another modulation, return to the tonic key.

Baroque suites offered a rich diversity of dances, some of which betrayed their colorful national origins. The **allemande** was a German dance in *duple meter*, while the **courante** was a fast French dance in *triple meter*. Other dances included the **sarabande**, a slow dance in triple meter that may have been brought to Spain and Europe from Latin America, and the **gigue**, a lively dance in *compound meter* related to the English jig.

Most Baroque suites were written for a solo instrument such as a harpsichord. But in the seventeenth century composers also began to produce suite-like series of dances for small groups of chamber ensembles. The most important was the **trio sonata**, introduced in Italy, which featured two solo treble instruments (often violins) and a bass instrument. In addition, a continuo instrument, usually a harpsichord or organ, played the bass line and filled in the harmonies. Thus, despite its name, the trio sonata usually required *four* musicians.

Arcangelo Corelli

Arcangelo Corelli (1653–1713).

The outstanding composer of trio sonatas was Arcangelo Corelli (1653–1713). After an apprenticeship in Bologna, Italy, Corelli spent most of his career in Rome, where he enjoyed the patronage of the Church and amassed a considerable fortune. The composer was celebrated for his serene, angelic demeanor. He rose to become the leading violinist of his time as well as a highly sought-out violin teacher. Corelli's reputation was secured through the wide distribution of his instrumental music, published in six collections between 1681 and 1714 as Opus 1 through Opus 6. (Corelli was among the first composers to use the word *opus*, from the Latin for "work.") Op. 1–4 contained trio sonatas, while Op. 5 offered sonatas for solo violin and continuo. Op. 6 was a collection of twelve concertos, a Baroque instrumental genre discussed below and on pp. 174–78.

By Corelli's time, a distinction had emerged between instrumental compositions for church services and those for chamber settings. Accordingly, half of Corelli's trio sonatas bear the title **sonata da chiesa** (church sonata), and the other half the title **sonata da camera** (chamber sonata). Church sonatas are generally in four movements. Although they may favor dance types common in the suite, church sonatas tend to use more complex musical textures that feature counterpoint. His chamber sonatas, on the other hand, are generally dance suites in three or four movements written in a lighter style.

Corelli's Trio Sonata, Op. 3 No. 10, is a church sonata, and each of its four movements presents its own thematic material and bass line. Like a dance suite, the movements are performed at different tempos, in this case fast-fast-slow-fast (see **Listening Map 14**). Two violins play the top two lines, while a bass instrument plays the third line. An organ also plays the bass line, while realizing chords from the figured bass, filling in the gap between the bass line and the violins.

The Baroque Concerto

Corelli was among the first Baroque composers to develop another new genre, the **concerto**, designed to showcase virtuosity in a more social context, *with* an orchestra. The main type of Baroque concerto was the **concerto grosso** (large concerto). It pitted a small group of soloists (a **concertino**) against a larger group of musicians (generally string players and a harpsichord) that made up the orchestra. The exchanges between these two groups gave the new instrumental genre dramatic pacing and musical vitality.

Usually Baroque concertos were written in three separate movements: fast, slow, and fast. The outer movements often employed **ritornello form**, in which an orchestral opening theme (a **ritornello**, plural *ritornelli*) returned throughout between soloist passages. If we label the ritornelli R, and the solo sections S, the resulting form looks like this:

R S R S R S R . . . (depending on how many ritornelli and solo sections the composer included)

LISTENING MAP 14

CORELLI, Trio Sonata in A minor, Op. 3 No. 10 {1689}

FORM	Church sonata in four movements
SCORING	Two violins, bass instrument, and organ
OVERVIEW	Written in four movements (fast-fast-slow-fast), Corelli's Trio Sonata in A minor features two violins accompanied by a bass and organ. The first movement, *Vivace*, introduces a stately theme in both violins. This leads to the lively second movement, with an interchange of themes between the two violins. The third movement, *Adagio*, is slower, with the two violins stating intertwining, ascending melodies. The sonata closes with a jig-like *Allegro*, which ends with a drop in dynamics as the piece concludes.

why to LISTEN

Instrumental music was around long before Corelli, but he is the first composer we have discussed who did *not* write vocal music. He preferred instead to focus on music featuring his favored instrument, the violin. Corelli was the first major composer internationally acclaimed for his instrumental compositions, which served as models for generations of musicians to come. So when we listen to his trio sonatas, we should ask ourselves what we expect not only from Corelli, but from instrumental music in general.

The violin can, in its own magical way, imitate the human voice and stir powerful human emotions. Baroque music was designed to do just that, with or without a text. So, in listening to Corelli's trio sonata, imagine the two solo violins engaging in a musical dialogue, with the first violin (Corelli's instrument) dominating, but the second violin occasionally having its say. And think of the four movements as projecting four contrasting moods, again not specified in words, but no less compelling. We might describe them as (1) stately and grand, (2) serious and involved, (3) introverted and pensive, and (4) animated and spirited.

first LISTEN

1: VIVACE	2: ALLEGRO	3: ADAGIO	4: ALLEGRO
0:00	**0:51**	**2:13**	**2:51**
Stately and lively introduction	Fast movement; imitation between two violins and bass	Slow, expressive melodic interchanges between two violins	Jig-like finale

a deeper **LISTEN**

TIME	SECTION	LISTEN FOR THIS
0:00	First Movement: Vivace	Brief introductory movement (repeated); chords and majestic rhythms, led by violin I
0:51	Second Movement: Allegro	Fast movement in imitative style, launched by entries of violin I, violin II, and the bass Violin I etc. Violin II etc. Bass
2:13	Third Movement: Adagio	Brief, slow movement with expressive exchanges between violins I and II, climbing higher in pitch
2:51	Fourth Movement: Allegro	Jig-like fast movement in binary form, with each section repeated and with imitation between violins I and II; closes with sudden drop from loud to soft dynamics Violin I etc. Violin II

What gives ritornello form its vitality is the contrast between the alternating sections. The fully orchestrated ritornelli are centered on particular keys and reuse thematic material announced in the first ritornello. The solo sections are much freer, and may include passages filled with virtuoso figurations. Typically, the solos are harmonically unstable, traversing a series of keys, and are thus not as anchored or predictable as the ritornelli.

check your KNOWLEDGE

1. Which new musical genres arose in Baroque instrumental music of the seventeenth century?
2. How did Arcangelo Corelli help popularize the violin as the new primary string instrument of the Baroque era?
3. What is the difference between a *sonata da chiesa* and a *sonata da camera*?
4. What provides the drama in the Baroque concerto grosso?

CHAPTER

23 Antonio Vivaldi

Antonio Vivaldi (1678–1741).

Watch a brief video on playing the violin.

The most productive and arguably most imaginative composer of Baroque concertos was Antonio Vivaldi (1678–1741). He produced nearly 500 of them, in addition to sacred music and some forty operas. Although he was an ordained priest (nicknamed the "Red Priest" because of his flowing red hair), Vivaldi served principally as music director of a Venetian orphanage/convent for girls. On Sundays and holidays, his highly trained, cloistered orchestra of pupils played his compositions. While performing, the forty or so young women were half concealed in a gallery behind latticework, as it was not considered proper for them to be seen in public performance. Vivaldi's orchestral concerts became quite renowned in Italy and abroad, attracting tourists to Venice. His scores were soon in such demand that he traveled extensively and won international fame.

Vivaldi once boasted that he could compose a concerto faster than a copyist could write out its parts (there is some evidence that he composed one of his operas in only five days). A distinguished violinist, he explored the technical resources of his instrument in hundreds of violin concertos. Many of these works featured rapidly played passages, covering the full range of the instrument and demanding a high level of skill from the performer. Vivaldi also wrote for less commonly used string and wind instruments such as the mandolin, the bassoon, and the piccolo. His output included not only concerti grossi but also solo concertos (those for one solo instrument and an orchestra), which eventually became the standard in the eighteenth century.

Vivaldi gave fanciful titles to several concertos. He was an important proponent of **program music**: instrumental music that was meant to tell a story or explore different nonmusical ideas, identified or hinted at by the title. He wrote concertos that evoked violent tempests, nocturnal settings, and dream states, and a series that imitated birds such as the goldfinch and cuckoo. There is even one concerto alluringly titled *Pleasure.*

Most famous of all are his *Four Seasons,* a cycle of four concertos for solo violin and orchestra that depict spring, summer, fall, and winter. The score was published around 1725 accompanied by four anonymous sonnets, possibly written by the composer himself, which yield valuable clues about the music's meaning. Vivaldi included lines from the sonnets within the appropriate part of the score, as if to encourage the soloist to contemplate the poetry while performing the music. The composer even wrote supplementary verbal cues into the score, including one tag for a persistent orchestral figure to suggest a barking dog in the slow movement of *Spring.*

Detail from the eighteenth-century painting *Spring* by Antonio Diziani.

The four sonnets celebrate a natural, rural world. In *Spring,* we experience birdcalls, murmuring brooks, a thunderstorm, and a peasants' dance. *Summer* depicts the stifling heat, languid breezes, and swarms of flies, while in *Fall* we encounter intoxicated peasants and a rousing hunt. Finally, *Winter* brings ice, bone-chilling cold, and chattering teeth.

Vivaldi intended to establish a series of one-to-one correspondences between his score and the poems. In our earlier discussion of the Renaissance madrigal (see p. 115), we encountered a similar technique, word painting. There, however, the technique was driven by a vocal text. In *The Four Seasons,* there is no sung text, just instruments. But there are also the four sonnets, presumably meant to be read before a performance, to enhance our understanding of the music.

Program music is most explicit when it imitates something that itself makes sounds. Here, we consider the first movement of *Spring* (**Listening Map 15**). When the solo violin trills on its high string a few measures into *Spring,* the sounds actually resemble birdcalls. These trills musically interpret the second line of the sonnet, "Greeted by birds with cheerful song." To represent the thunder of the sixth line, rapidly repeated pitches create the effect of an agitated rumbling. To convey the joyfulness of spring in the first line, there is no one-to-one equivalent, but the bright orchestral opening connotes a joyful mood.

Down through the centuries, musicians and scholars have debated the extent to which music can depict things, ideas, and subjects that lie beyond the notes. But many composers found inspiration in techniques similar to Vivaldi's. Less than seventy years after his death, another composer, Ludwig van Beethoven, included birdcalls and thunder in his "Pastoral" Symphony. Like *The Four Seasons,* it became one of the most celebrated pieces of classical music.

LISTENING MAP 15

VIVALDI, *Spring* from *The Four Seasons*, Op. 8 No. 1, First Movement

{CA. 1725}

FORM	Ritornello
GENRE	Concerto (first movement)
SCORING	Solo violin, string orchestra, and harpsichord (continuo)
OVERVIEW	The first movement of *Spring* mirrors the imagery of the included sonnet: Spring has joyfully come (1) Greeted by birds with cheerful song, (2) And springs, stirred by gentle breezes, Flow with sweet murmuring. (3) Covering the sky with a black cloak. Lightning and thunder announce the season. (4) When they have dispersed, the little birds Return to enchant with their singing. (5) In ritornello form, the movement alternates between five ritornelli for the entire ensemble and four passages that feature the solo violin.

why to LISTEN

As a celebrated example of Baroque program music, *The Four Seasons* raises again the questions of what we expect from music, and what music can or cannot provide. Strictly speaking, *The Four Seasons* is a collection of four concertos, just a miniscule fraction of Vivaldi's total output of more than 500. But the special title alerts us to the principal reason to listen: Vivaldi meant *The Four Seasons* to be about the seasons of the year, not just the notes on the page. Even going as far as marking particular passages with lines of poetry, he was musically celebrating the spring, summer, fall, and winter seasons.

first LISTEN

RITORNELLO 1	SOLO 1	RIT. 2	SOLO 2	RIT. 3	SOLO 3	RIT . 4	SOL. 4	RIT. 5
0:00	0:35	1:10	1:51	2:19	2:28	2:44	2:55	3:10
Advent of spring	Birdcalls	Murmuring streams	Lightning and thunder	Minor-key interlude	Birdcalls	Modified spring theme	Violin solo with continuo; ascending notes	Orchestral conclusion

a deeper **LISTEN**

TIME	SECTION	LISTEN FOR THIS
0:00	**Ritornello 1** (tonic key): The return of spring	① Sprightly opening featuring full orchestra; two ideas, (*a*) and (*b*), each performed ***f*** and then ***p*** *a* … ***f*** … etc. *b* … ***f*** … etc.
0:35	**Solo 1:** Birdcalls	② Trills and high notes in solo violin to simulate birdcalls
1:10	**Ritornello 2** (tonic key): Murmuring streams	③ Orchestra repeats (*b*) (***f***) from Ritornello 1, then introduces a flowing figure to suggest a stream (***p***), and concludes with (*b*) (***f***)
1:51	**Solo 2:** Lightning and thunder	④ Rapid pitches and sweeping scales in orchestra depict a thunderstorm; rapid passagework in the high register of the solo violin
2:19	**Ritornello 3** (minor key)	Orchestra repeats (*b*) (***f***), but in a minor key
2:28	**Solo 3:** Birdcalls	⑤ More birdcalls in the solo violin, answered by violins
2:44	**Ritornello 4** (tonic key)	Orchestra reuses a modified version of (*a*)
2:55	**Solo 4**	Final solo with ascending, running figure in the violin supported by the continuo
3:10	**Ritornello 5** (tonic key)	Final ritornello, based on (*a*), performed ***f*** and then ***p***

Vivaldi enjoyed great acclaim during his lifetime but died in poverty. His vast quantity of music was more or less forgotten until its rediscovery in the twentieth century. But what an extraordinary posthumous comeback. At last count, there are over 200 recordings of *The Four Seasons*, snippets of which have been appropriated for motion pictures, commercials, and ringtones. Vivaldi's enduring fame has proved a double-edged sword: critics complain that much of his music is repetitive, and filled with threadbare, theatrical effects. That may be, but in his day, reports of his great technique and imaginative concertos reached well beyond Italy. This news caught the attention of a German musician then studying the new Italian concertos. His name was Johann Sebastian Bach.

check your KNOWLEDGE

1. Why was Antonio Vivaldi so important in the history of the Baroque concerto?
2. What is program music?
3. How does Vivaldi relate the music of *The Four Seasons* to the sonnet that accompanies it? How successful is the composer?
4. Listen to a performance of one of the other concertos from *The Four Seasons* and compare it to *Spring*. Which musical techniques do the pieces share in common?
5. Imagine listening to Vivaldi's *Spring* without knowing anything about the title or the sonnet. Can you enjoy the music as music, or is the title indispensable to understanding it?

CHAPTER

24 Johann Sebastian Bach's Life and Career

Johann Sebastian Bach (1685–1750).

With Johann Sebastian Bach we reach a figure so dominant that he came to be viewed as embodying Baroque music. Further, some see his work as summing up developments in Western music extending back to the Renaissance. In German, *Bach* means "brook," but as Ludwig van Beethoven proclaimed, "His name should be ocean, not brook!" Beethoven was just one among many admirers who studied Bach's music deeply. Indeed, it is difficult to name a major composer from Mozart on who did not have ties to Bach's legacy. It is equally difficult to name a major earlier composer who cast such a long shadow on the course of European music.

Today, aspiring classical musicians test their skill on J. S. Bach's keyboard works, especially *The Well-Tempered Clavier.* These two encyclopedic cycles of pieces written in all twenty-four major and minor keys—forty-eight pieces in all—are among the most intellectually challenging keyboard pieces ever composed. Bach's church cantatas (in the hundreds), his St. Matthew and St. John Passions, and his Mass in B minor may well be the greatest achievements of Western sacred music. His concertos, suites, and organ compositions exemplify Baroque instrumental music in all its intensity and finery. And his late masterpieces, *The Musical Offering* and *The Art of Fugue*, are monuments to the art of counterpoint.

Acclaim did not always greet Bach during his lifetime or immediately afterward, however. In his day, he was known as a brilliant church organist, but he enjoyed little international standing as a composer. One reason is that, unlike his great contemporary Handel (see Chapter 27), Bach did not travel much, but lived and worked within a fairly small area of central Germany. Few composers matched his productivity, although, incredibly, little of his music was published at the time of his death. Full recognition of his achievement came later, in the nineteenth and twentieth centuries. When he died in 1750, he was quickly forgotten, and few had any sense of the full scope of his work.

Bach's Early Life and Career Beginnings

Johann Sebastian Bach (1685–1750) came from a long line of musicians reaching back into the sixteenth century. In turn, several of Bach's own children—he fathered twenty—carried on that tradition. He once boasted that he could assemble a worthy musical ensemble just by calling on members of his own family. In fact, two of his sons, Carl Philipp Emanuel and Johann Christian Bach, were better known during their lifetimes than their father.

J. S. Bach was born in Eisenach, a small town in central Germany. He probably received his first musical instruction from his father, who died when the boy was ten, leaving him to be raised by an elder brother. After assuming minor posts as an organist near Eisenach, in 1708 Bach became court organist in Weimar. There, he maintained and repaired organs while composing the majority of his organ works. One celebrated work he possibly composed in Weimar was the Toccata and Fugue in D minor. (A **toccata** was a baroque instrumental composition, typically for harpsichord or organ, in a virtuoso, free style). Today this music can be heard in films, rock music, and video games.

The Move to Cöthen

In 1717 Bach was offered a new position at the court of Cöthen, today about two hours' drive from Weimar. The Duke of Weimar did not immediately release him from service, however, and in fact had him imprisoned. Ultimately, he did grant the composer his freedom, and Bach and his family moved on to Cöthen.

As music director in Cöthen (1717–1723), Bach wrote instrumental works for the music-loving prince. The composer gathered many of them into collections, including six cello suites, the first volume of *The Well-Tempered Clavier*, and the six Brandenburg Concertos. He also produced keyboard pieces to help his second wife, Anna Magdalena, master the instrument. She was a professional singer who bore thirteen of Bach's children.

MAKING CONNECTIONS *The Afterlife of Bach's Toccata and Fugue in D Minor*

Scholars debate whether Bach truly wrote this famous example of Baroque organ music, or whether he only arranged it for the organ. Either way, the piece became indelibly associated with Bach, but only well after his death in 1750. Not until the 1830s was the piece even published. Later on, other musicians weighed in with their own versions. The American conductor Leopold Stokowski made one for full orchestra, used in the opening scene of Walt Disney's classic animated film *Fantasia* (1940).

Phantom of the Opera, poster for the 1962 film, which featured the Toccata in D minor.

The composition also took on an association with the supernatural and horror. It was featured in the 1932 film version of Robert Louis Stevenson's *Strange Case of Dr. Jekyll and Mr. Hyde* and in the 1934 horror film *The Black Cat* with Boris Karloff. In *20,000 Leagues under the Sea* (1954) and *The Mysterious Island* (1961), two popular films based on Jules Verne's science fiction, the mysterious Captain Nemo plays Bach on the organ. And finally, in the horror film version of *Phantom of the Opera* (1962), the loner phantom plays the Toccata in his lair beneath the opera house.

Whoever originally wrote the Toccata and Fugue probably had no intention of creating eerie music. But Hollywood saw to that, helping propel Bach to the top of the classical charts.

Final Years in Leipzig

In 1723 the family moved to Leipzig (pronounced "Lipe-tzig"), where he served as music director. He was responsible for composing music for the city's civic functions and principal churches, including St. Thomas, where his remains are now buried. He was also expected to instruct Latin at the Thomas School, an adjacent boarding school for boys. It was a task he particularly disliked.

Since the Reformation, Leipzig had enjoyed a rich musical tradition. Bach was determined not only to preserve but also improve the city's music life. The local authorities found his musical standards too high, however. Inevitably, tensions arose over his ambitious musical plans for the city. Still, he remained in Leipzig for nearly thirty years, where he coped with a demanding work schedule.

For the weekly church services, which often lasted nearly four hours, Bach produced organ preludes, motets, and chorale arrangements. His major contributions were cycles of **cantatas**, medium-length narrative works for chorus, soloists, and orchestra. These compositions served as the musical highpoint of the service and generally followed the reading of the Gospel text. In his first two years in Leipzig, Bach wrote a new cantata every week. In all, he composed nearly 300 cantatas, or five annual cycles, of which about 100 are lost. For several years, he also directed

MAKING CONNECTIONS *Bach's Children and Wives*

Between 1708 and 1742 Bach fathered twenty (yes, twenty) children, of whom only half survived to adulthood. Several became musicians who had important careers of their own, including Wilhelm Friedemann Bach, Carl Philipp Emanuel Bach, and Johann Christian Bach. (A five-year-old prodigy, Mozart, met J.C., known as the "London Bach," and played duets with him.)

Seven of Bach's children were from his first marriage, to Maria Barbara Bach, about whom little is known, other than that she came from a musical family. Her passing was a tragic shock. In 1720 the composer accompanied his employer, the Prince of Cöthen, to a holiday at a spa. Bach returned several weeks later only to learn that his previously healthy wife had died suddenly and was already buried. After the composer remarried, he had thirteen more children with Anna Magdalena Bach, a singer and skilled musician who produced copies of her husband's music.

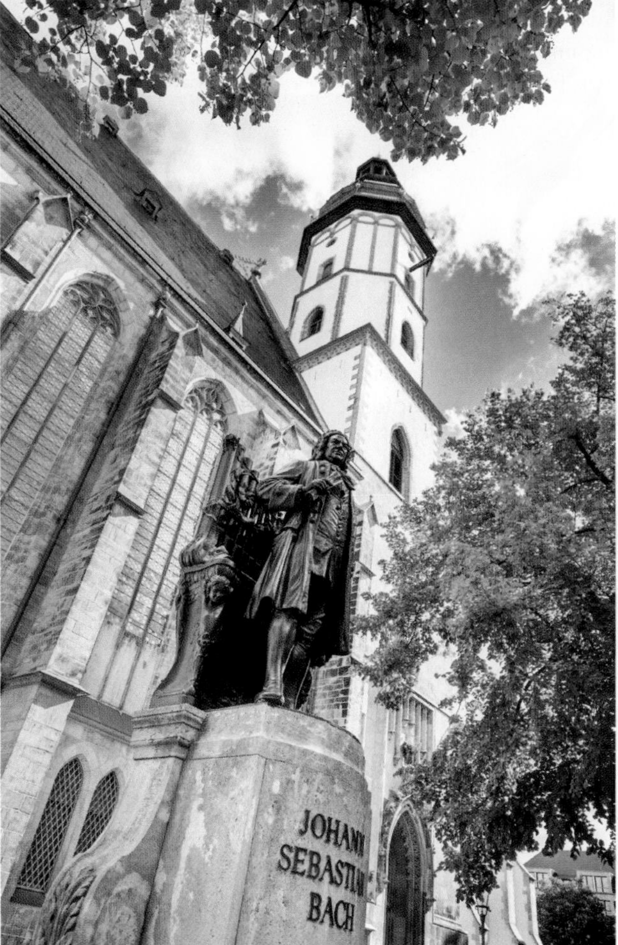

A statue of Bach by Carl Seffner stands outside the St. Thomas Church in Leipzig, Germany.

the *Collegium musicum*, an ensemble of professional musicians and university students who performed weekly public concerts.

Toward the end of his life, in 1747, Bach visited the Prussian court of Frederick the Great in Potsdam, near Berlin. There he improvised on a subject invented by Frederick, a "royal theme" that formed the basis of Bach's *Musical Offering.* During the 1740s, he was also at work on another monumental instrumental cycle, *The Art of Fugue.* He intended its closing theme to be a contrapuntal treatment of the letters of his own name. In German musical notation, B-A-C-H corresponds to these notes:

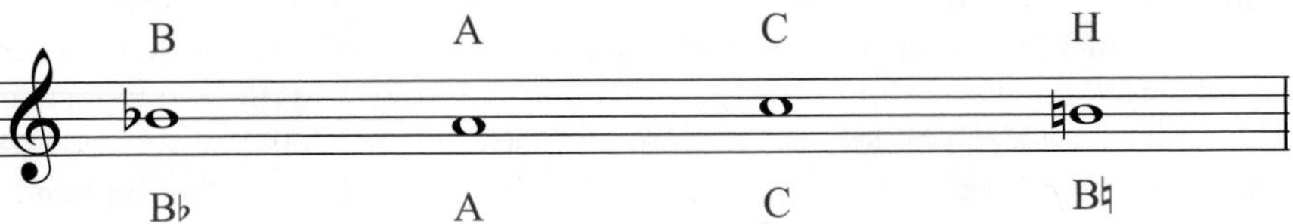

Ex. 24.1

During his last years Bach suffered from gradual vision loss. When he died in 1750, he left to posterity the unfinished *Art of Fugue.* Incredibly, the great bulk of his music—the official catalogue runs to over 1,100 compositions—existed only in manuscript and quickly fell into obscurity. It was almost a century before much of it was fully rediscovered.

check your KNOWLEDGE

1. Why is Bach considered to be one of the greatest composers of classical music?
2. Describe the three main periods of Bach's life, based on where he lived and worked.
3. How did Bach's compositions reflect his responsibilities as a working composer during each period of his life?

Bach's Instrumental Music

CHAPTER 25

Bach reigned supreme in the field of Baroque solo keyboard music and produced a vast quantity for the organ and for the harpsichord. He also wrote a considerable amount of chamber and orchestral music. He was equally versatile in all the principal instrumental genres of the day, whether writing short preludes, or longer sonatas, suites, trio sonatas, or concertos. And he could write for solo instruments, small chamber ensembles, or orchestras. Among his most impressive achievements were several compositions for solo violin and solo cello, that is, without any accompanying instruments. Bach seems to have set these works as a particular challenge, to test, for example, what a solo violin, unassisted by other instruments, could do.

Watch a performance of Bach's Violin Sonata No. 2 in A minor, BWV 1003, Andante, played by Katharina Uhde, violin.

As impressive as this output was, however, there was one Baroque genre in which he excelled above all others. **Fugues** are an intellectually demanding display of counterpoint, a complex musical puzzle to be solved, yet Bach could produce them almost on demand. Viewed as the summit of counterpoint, fugues appealed especially to connoisseurs trained to appreciate their intricacies. But by the time Bach died, fugues—at least the more formal, academic types—were falling out of fashion. This trend may be one reason why Bach's skillful examples faded for a while, only to be rediscovered when his music was eventually reclaimed from oblivion.

Page from the first edition of *The Art of Fugue* by J. S. Bach, published in 1752. The engraver added the floral decorations to fill out the page.

Bach and the Fugue

The fugue, which can be either an instrumental or vocal composition, is descended from the rich tradition of Renaissance imitative polyphony. The word itself comes from the Latin *fuga*, meaning "flight." (In the field of psychiatry, a "dissociative fugue" or "fugue state," is a disorder in which patients temporarily lose their sense of identity and often wander.) In a fugue, separate musical lines, or parts, successively state a theme known as the **subject**, the basis for the entire composition. The number of parts determines the complexity of the fugue. In a common arrangement, the fugue has four parts: soprano, alto, tenor, and bass. (These terms are used regardless of whether the fugue calls for vocal or instrumental performers.) Most fugues range from two to four or five parts, and more parts means greater complexity.

Bach's fugues begin with the **fugal exposition**: one part starts alone by announcing the subject in the tonic key. The second part then presents the subject in the dominant key, in a statement called the **answer**. Then, the remaining parts enter, alternating between the subject and the answer, until every part has appeared. Figure 25.1 shows a fugal exposition in four parts, with a subject in the soprano, an answer in the tenor, another statement of the subject in the alto, and another answer in the bass.

		(New or derived material)		
Soprano	Subject ________	~~~~~~~~~~~~~~~~		
Alto			Subject ________	~~~~~
Tenor		Answer ________	~~~~~~~~~~	
Bass				Answer ________

FIG. 25.1 Typical Exposition for Fugue in Four Parts. *Note that the parts may enter in other orders.*

With each new entrance, the listener has to begin following more and more parts, which can become a demanding proposition.

After the exposition, the rest of a fugue generally consists of passages known as **episodes**, which alternate with additional statements of the subject. The material of the episodes may be new or derived from the subject. While the subjects are centered on specific keys, the episodes tend to be harmonically flexible and unstable.

Controlling all the subjects and episodes is challenging enough, yet Bach sometimes added further layers of complexity. In **mirror inversion**, he reversed the melodic shape of the subject, so that it appeared upside down. In **augmentation**, he doubled the rhythmic values of the subject, slowing it down to a leisurely pace. In **diminution**, he cut the rhythmic values in half, so that it sped up. And in **stretto** (from the Italian for "narrow"), he collapsed the distance between entries of the subject so that they overlapped tightly. One technique Bach frequently used was the **pedal point**, in which one pitch is held for several measures while the other voices continue above or around it. All these special fugal techniques reinforce the idea that fugues are an intellectual pursuit: they appeal to the rational, problem-solving parts of our brains. In the hands of a great composer such as Bach, fugues can also evoke a powerful emotional response. Here we explore one of Bach's most celebrated organ works, known as the Little Fugue in G minor (**Listening Map 16**). Bach wrote it sometime during his Weimar period (1708–1717).

MAKING CONNECTIONS *Fugues beyond Music*

While fugues are strongly associated with the Baroque compositions of J. S. Bach, their complex patterns occasionally have inspired nonmusical examples. In the nineteenth century, the English essayist Thomas De Quincey, who experimented with opium, drew on similar forms to structure his writings. He even described one of his drug-induced hallucinations as a "dream fugue." In the twentieth century, James Joyce revealed that an episode in his epic, stream-of-consciousness novel *Ulysses* (1922) used a fugal structure. Then there was Aldous Huxley's complex novel *Point Counter Point* (1928), though it is unclear whether he intended his literary counterpoint as specifically fugal.

Modernist twentieth-century painters found connections between fugues and abstract colors and shapes. Shown here are two paintings titled *Fugue*: one by Russian artist Wassily Kandinsky (1914) and one by German artist Josef Albers (1925). What parallels do you see between Kandinsky's repeating curvilinear motifs and Bach's Fugue in G minor? How about between the fugue and Albers's geometric dash-like patterns?

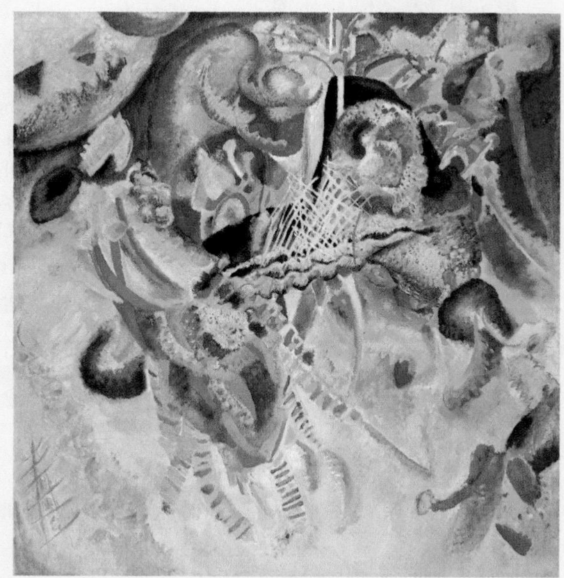

Wassily Kandinsky, *Fugue* (1914).

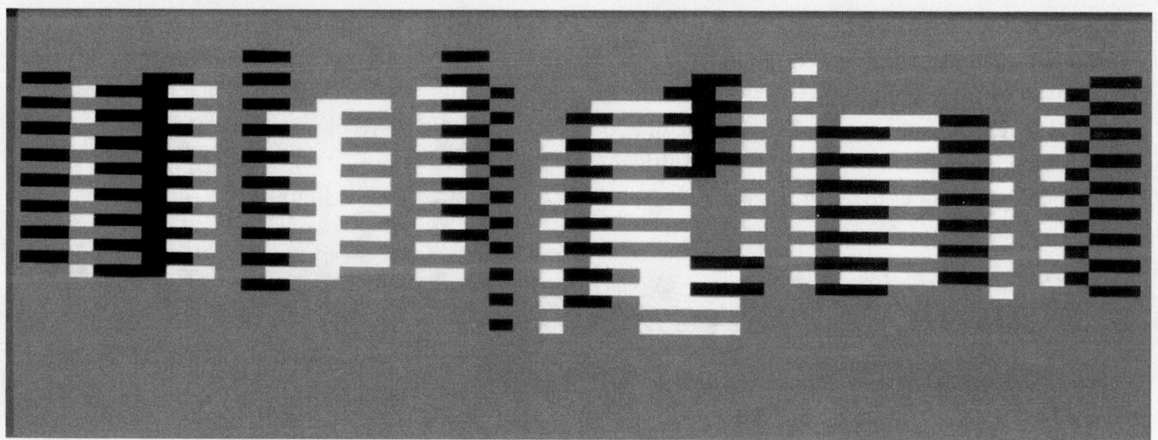

Josef Albers, *Fugue* (1925).

LISTENING MAP 16

J.S. BACH, *"Little" Fugue in G minor for Organ* {CA. 1708–1717}

FORM	Four-part fugue
SCORING	Organ
OVERVIEW	In the exposition (opening) of this fugue, the subject and answer alternate in parts of descending order: soprano, alto, tenor, and bass (1). Having established the conversation among the four parts, Bach alternates episodes with entries of the subject, sustaining an energetic, rhythmic flow. All told, the subject appears nine times: four in the exposition, then five more times scattered throughout the composition. The most unusual subject entry is the fifth, divided between the tenor and soprano parts, above a pedal point in the bass (2). After the last, sturdy entrance appears in the bass, Bach ends with a surprise: instead of a final minor chord, he substitutes a bright major chord (3). Baroque composers often used this device to give works in minor keys a strong sense of closure by unexpectedly using the major-key version of the tonic.

why to LISTEN

The abstract reasoning needed to solve math problems is not unlike that needed to compose or analyze fugues. Performing and listening to music such as a fugue, which especially emphasizes counterpoint, stimulates the mathematically inclined areas of our brains. No wonder, then, that Bach was compared to one of the most profound scientific geniuses of all time, Isaac Newton.

There is something inherently beautiful and satisfying about how the parts of Bach's Little Fugue in G minor fit together. Like the colors of a kaleidoscope, they reshape themselves in ever new combinations. The entire composition is unified around the fugal subject, which we hear nine times. That's the predictable, stable element of the music: we know that the subject will return. We do not know where it will appear, however. Bach's fugue thus offers both repetitions and variety, and also something more. As the Irish playwright and music critic G. B. Shaw observed, Bach's fugues can somehow "summon all the emotions that have been worthily expressed in music."

first LISTEN

EXPOSITION	ALTERNATING SUBJECTS AND EPISODES	FINAL CHORD
0:00	**1:20**	**4:10**
Statement of main theme in soprano, alto, tenor, and bass	Subject recurs in various voices that alternate with freer passages known as episodes.	Ends in surprise major chord

a deeper LISTEN

TIME	PART	LISTEN FOR THIS
0:00	Fugal exposition (subjects 1–4)	① Main theme stated in alternating subjects and answers in parts of descending order. The subject begins with a soprano part (S) outlining the tonic triad before shifting to faster pitches. The answer then enters in the alto (A) below, followed by the subject in the tenor (T), then an answer in the bass (B), which is played in the pedals of the organ. S (tonic) 4 A 2 (dominant) T 3 (tonic) B 4 (dominant)
1:20	Episode 1	Free section
1:32	Subject 5	② Subject stated in tenor, continuing in soprano, with pedal point in bass
1:51	Episode 2	
2:01	Subject 6	Alto
2:17	Episode 3	
2:29	Subject 7	Bass
2:45	Episode 4	
3:03	Subject 8	Soprano
3:20	Episode 5	
3:51	Subject 9	
4:10	Final chord	③ Surprise final major chord

Bach's Concertos

Though Bach was later prized by German nationalists, he was quite international in his approach to music. He did not travel beyond German realms, but he could imitate English or French tastes in his music, and he was a serious student of Italian Baroque music. When composing his concertos, Bach drew on Corelli and Vivaldi. He followed their use of contrasting orchestral and solo groups, and took over the *ritornello* principle of recurring, refrain-like sections (see pp. 157). Several of Bach's concertos are for one or more harpsichords and orchestra, or for one or more violins and orchestra.

His masterpieces in the genre are the six Brandenburg Concertos, dedicated to Christian Ludwig, the Margrave (hereditary noble title for certain German princes) of Brandenburg (a territory surrounding Berlin). During a visit to Berlin, Bach had played for the margrave, who requested some compositions. In response, Bach sent the Brandenburg Concertos in 1721, with a formal dedication written *not* in German but in French, the preferred language at court. Dating these concertos is difficult, but most likely they were composed before 1721 and then selected by the composer for the margrave.

The Brandenburg Concertos feature an assortment of solo instruments accompanied by a string orchestra and continuo. For instance, the brightly hued No. 2 groups a trumpet, a recorder, an oboe, and a violin, while No. 4 offers softer tints from its solo group of one violin and two recorders. In the case of the Fifth Brandenburg Concerto, the orchestra consists of strings in four parts (first and second violins, violas, and cellos and double bass), while the solo group consists of a flute, violin, and harpsichord. The harpsichord actually plays two roles: one as a continuo instrument, and one as a solo instrument (the first such use in a concerto).

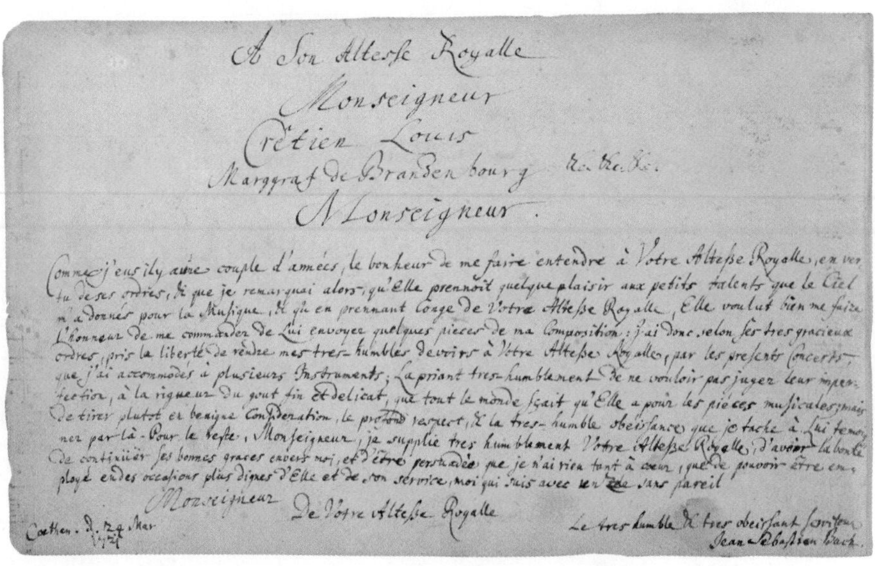

A Son Altesse Royalle
Monseigneur
Cretien Louis
Marggraf de Brandenbourg &c. &c. &c.
Monseigneur.

Comme j'eus il y a une couple d'années, le bonheur de me faire entendre à Votre Altesse Royalle, en vertu de ses ordres, & que je remarquai alors, qu'Elle prennoit quelque plaisir aux petits talents que le Ciel m'a donnés pour la Musique, & qu'en prennant Congé de Votre Altesse Royalle, Elle voulut bien me faire l'honneur de me commander de Lui envoyer quelques pieces de ma Composition: j'ai donc selon ses tres gracieux ordres, pris la liberté de rendre mes tres-humbles devoirs à Votre Altesse Royalle, par les presents Concerts, que j'ai accommodés à plusieurs Instruments; La priant tres-humblement de ne vouloir pas juger leur imperfection, à la rigueur du gout fin et delicat, que tout le monde sçait qu'Elle a pour les pieces musicales; mais de tirer plutot en benigne Consideration, le profond respect, & la tres-humble obeissance que je tache à Lui temoigner par là. Pour le reste, Monseigneur, je supplie tres humblement Votre Altesse Royalle, d'avoir la bonté de continuer ses bonnes graces envers moi, et d'être persuadée que je n'ai rien tant à cœur, que de pouvoir être employé en des occasions plus dignes d'Elle et de son service, moi qui suis avec un zele sans pareil

Monseigneur
De Votre Altesse Royalle
Le tres humble & tres obeissant serviteur
Jean Sebastien Bach.

Coethen. d. 24 Mar. 1721

Handwritten dedication of Bach's Brandenburg Concertos to Christian Ludwig, Margrave of Brandenburg, 1721.

This harpsichord was made by Jean-Paul Rouaud after the French maker Nicolas Dumont, 1707. A harpsichord part is prominently featured in Bach's Brandenburg Concerto No. 5 as a solo instrument.

Brandenburg Concerto No. 5 has three movements: fast, slow, and fast. The first movement (see **Listening Map 17**) follows the ritornello principle common in Italian Baroque concertos. It features breath-taking solos, particularly for the harpsichord.

Toward the end of the first movement, the harpsichordist performs a dramatic **cadenza** (an extended, virtuoso passage for a soloist alone).

check your **KNOWLEDGE**

1. What is a fugue? How is it structured?
2. What are some techniques that Bach employed in his fugues? How did these increase their complexity?
3. Which elements did Bach carry forward from the Italian concerto grosso in his Brandenburg Concertos?
4. What is unusual about the way Bach uses the harpsichord in the Fifth Brandenburg Concerto?

LISTENING MAP 17

J.S. BACH, Brandenburg Concerto No. 5 in D major, First Movement

{1721 OR EARLIER}

FORM	Ritornello form, alternating between orchestra and soloists
SCORING	Violin, flute, harpsichord, and orchestra
OVERVIEW	The main body of the movement alternates between solo sections and statements of the ritornello for the orchestra. In all, there are seventeen sections in this chain-like movement—nine ritornelli (R) for orchestra and eight solos (S). The first and last ritornelli, R1 and R9, present complete statements of the ritornello theme in the tonic key. Like tonal pillars, they support the endpoints of the structure. In contrast, R2–R8 offer abbreviated statements of the ritornello in different keys. As we proceed into the movement, the solos become more prominent. But these exchanges pale in comparison to the final solo, S8. The rapid harpsichord scales return as Bach thins out the texture to prepare for the cadenza. Much of this harpsichord cadenza unfolds above a pedal point in the bass register, building tension that resolves with the return of the orchestra in the tonic key (R9).

why to LISTEN

To describe Bach as a musical multitasker is no mere cliché. He approached composition as a musical challenge to be solved in multiple ways. So the six Brandenburg Concertos offer six different ways of writing concertos after the Italian concerto grosso model. Each had its own combination of instruments. The Fifth Brandenburg brilliantly shows how Bach's music could operate simultaneously on different levels. For example, in the first movement, the harpsichord, though just one instrument, plays two roles—it can blend into the orchestra, or it can emerge as a virtuoso soloist. In the second movement, there is no orchestra, just three soloists. Effectively, Bach changed genres from concerto to chamber music. And for the third movement, with the orchestra now restored, Bach wrote a gigue-like dance as if it were a fugue. Nothing is ever simple or straightforward in Bach, which is precisely why his music is so challenging. It pushes the human mind to new levels of envisioning and understanding music. And that is why his music can be so rewarding, and why we should listen.

first LISTEN

RITORNELLO/SOLO 1	RITORNELLOS/SOLOS 2–8	RITORNELLO 9
0:00	**0:49**	**8:44**
Statement of theme (ritornello) by orchestra, followed by solo section	Abbreviated ritornello theme alternating with solos, including harpsichord	Return of full theme by the orchestra

a deeper **LISTEN**

TIME	SECTION	LISTEN FOR THIS
0:00	R1	Complete statement of ritornello on the tonic, played by the full orchestra; pulsating rhythms; harpsichord serves as a continuo instrument Ascending skips then descending scale; music reaches two cresting pitches. **Allegro** *Skips* *Scale* crest
0:25	S1	Short motive exchanged between flute and violin; harpsichord emerges as a solo instrument, sustaining the rhythmic energy Flute Violin Harpsichord
0:49	R2	Abbreviated
0:54	S2	
1:13	R3	Abbreviated
1:19	S3	
1:37	R4	Abbreviated
1:42	S4	Harpsichord more prominent, breaks into rapid, sweeping runs
2:19	R5	Abbreviated
2:25	S5	Extended solo; new motive exchanged between the flute and violin
3:56	R6	Abbreviated
4:01	S6	

Continued

TIME	SECTION	LISTEN FOR THIS
4:42	R7	Abbreviated
4:52	S7	
5:17	R8	Abbreviated
5:23	S8	Rapid figurations in the harpsichord; orchestra and soloists drop out; harpsichord performs a long cadenza; pedal point in the bass
8:44	R9	Final, complete statement of ritornello on the tonic

R = Ritornello; S = Solo

CHAPTER 26 Bach's Sacred Music

Bach was a devout Lutheran composer, and as the Leipzig music director for nearly thirty years, he provided music for Sunday services. He is remembered especially for his post at the St. Thomas Church and its affiliated school. Founded in 1212, the school was the residence of a boys' choir, which stills performs Bach's music regularly in the church. But Bach was also active at other Leipzig churches, in particular St. Nicholas, dating back to the very beginnings of the city in 1165. To serve the musical needs of both parish churches, he designed a grueling schedule of performances that alternated between the two.

Almost weekly, Bach composed a new **cantata**, a large-scale composition for vocal soloists, chorus, and orchestra on texts related to the weekly sermons and Gospel readings. Each annual cycle required about sixty cantatas for the Sunday services and special feast days. All told, he probably composed five annual cycles of cantatas, although only three cycles, about 200 cantatas, survive more or less intact.

Bach was well versed in the theology of his time and took his faith quite seriously. Upon finishing a composition, he habitually inscribed at the end "Soli Deo gratia" ("Praise be to God alone"). Bach's monumental St. Matthew Passion, which premiered at St. Thomas in 1727, is a musical depiction and commentary on the Passion of Christ. In preparing the manuscript, he took special care, using red ink for the texts drawn from the Bible and black for nonbiblical texts.

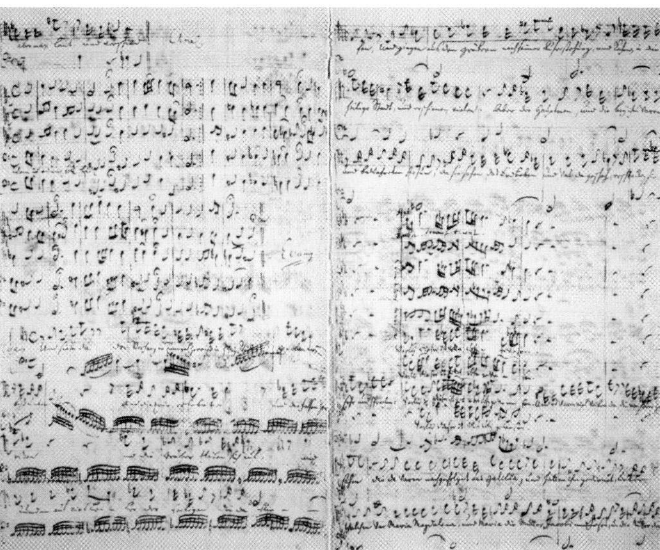

Handwritten score for Bach's St. Matthew Passion, with the biblical text in red.

Bach's Cantatas

Bach's cantatas (from *cantare*, "to sing") make up the largest part of his sacred music. The cantata arose in seventeenth-century Italy as a vocal composition in several movements, usually for solo voice and continuo accompaniment. Early Italian cantatas employed mostly secular texts. By the turn of the eighteenth century, however, German composers had begun writing cantatas with sacred texts and **chorales**, hymn tunes commonly used in Lutheran worship. German cantatas mixed choral movements with recitatives and arias for soloists. They were typically accompanied by a string orchestra that might be augmented by wind instruments and, on festive occasions, by brass and timpani.

Bach based many of his cantatas on Lutheran chorales, which formed a familiar part of the weekly worship. Throughout the seventeenth century, German composers had steadily continued writing chorales. Typically, Bach's **chorale cantatas** begin with a polyphonic choral movement built on a melody, and they conclude with a simple homophonic setting of the same melody. Between the endpoints, the individual movements often contain virtuoso music for solo singers and solo instruments. Usually, a recitative introduces a solo aria. The texts of these internal movements consist either of additional verses of the chorale or of devotional poetry.

Bach wrote his seven-movement Cantata No. 140 for performance in Leipzig several weeks before Christmas in 1731. The seven movements follow a carefully worked-out plan. The endpoints and center of the composition (movement nos. 1, 4, and 7) employ the chorale melody. The other movements (nos. 2–3, 5–6) form two pairs of recitatives and arias. The cantata is scored for solo singers, a chorus, and an orchestra that includes two oboes, an oboe da caccia (a lower-range oboe), a horn, a violino piccolo (a small violin), strings in four parts (first violins, second violins, violas, and bass instruments), and continuo.

The text of the chorale, written at the end of the sixteenth century, concerns Christ's parable of the ten wise and foolish virgins (Matthew 25). Five brought oil for their lamps; five did not. Only the wise (who had brought oil) were rewarded and could greet the bridegroom (the Savior), who arrived at midnight. The last line of the parable, "Keep awake then, for you never know the day or the hour," prompts the opening line of the chorale text, "Awaken, the voice summons us," a call for the faithful to be vigilant as they await Christ's Second Coming, the symbolic wedding. Figure 26.1 shows the famous chorale melody, still sung in Protestant churches, sometimes to the text "Sleepers, Wake." (See also **Listening Map 18**.)

This melody falls into several phrases, all coming to a pause or full ending. It fills out a three-part form, *AAB*. *A* presents the first three phrases, which are repeated. *B* continues with five more phrases, of which the last repeats the third phrase of *A*, giving the melody a rounded symmetry. This soaring melody reaches two high points that illustrate references in the text to the watchmen on high who await the Savior, and to the anticipated wedding of the Savior and the Soul.

MAKING CONNECTIONS *A Tale of Two Churches*

The St. Thomas and St. Nicholas Churches of Leipzig have long, storied histories, even beyond their association with Bach. In 1539 Martin Luther preached at St. Thomas, effectively bringing the Protestant Reformation to Leipzig. Several famous musicians who came after Bach either visited the church (Mozart, possibly Beethoven) or were connected with it through their employment (Mendelssohn). During the Napoleonic Wars in the early 1800s, the church served as an ammunition depot for Napoleon's armies and then a makeshift hospital for Germans. During the Second World War, it sustained damage when Allied bombs struck the bell tower. But it remains first and foremost a shrine for Bach lovers. The composer's remains were reinterred there in 1950, and outside stand two monuments to him.

The St. Nicholas Church played an unexpected role on the world stage in 1989, when it became the center of peaceful protests against the communist regime of East Germany. Even though the church was surrounded by the military and infiltrated by the Stasi (the secret police), the peaceful protests continued. The thousands of Leipzig citizens who held candles in the face of oppression are credited with helping topple the Berlin Wall, which had divided Germans for decades.

St. Thomas Church.

St. Nicholas Church.

FIG. 26.1 Chorale melody of Cantata No. 140.

LISTENING MAP 18

J. S. BACH, Cantata No. 140, *Wachet auf* (*Sleepers, Awake!*), First Movement

{1731}

FORM	Cantata
SCORING	A chorus and an orchestra, including two oboes, oboe da caccia, horn, violino piccolo, strings in four parts (first and second violins, violas, and bass instruments), and continuo
OVERVIEW	The cantata opens with the orchestra. Its driving energy comes from the steady tread of the bass line (known as a **walking bass**), which symbolically represents the approach of the Savior. In addition, Bach works with two thematic ideas: • (a), a rhythmic figure (long-short) associated with royalty • (b), a surging figure that eventually breaks into an extravagant flourish of ascending scales (1). Now the chorus enters. The sopranos sing the first phrase of the chorale in long notes, as the other choral voices embellish them by moving in more nimble rhythms (2). The mixture of these parts creates a rich polyphony. The orchestra sustains a backdrop of music drawn from the opening. Between the phrases of the chorale, the orchestra asserts its pulsing rhythms and soaring scales. And so the movement proceeds, with phrase after phrase of the chorale alternating with orchestral interludes. But one surprise awaits us. For the word "Alleluia," Bach introduces a fugal passage before the chorus turns to the ninth phrase of the chorale melody (3). By the end of this stately movement, the rich tapestry of polyphonic sound has prepared us for the arrival of Christ as Savior.

why to LISTEN

While the St. Matthew Passion was in many senses the epitome of Bach's career as a church musician, his hundreds of cantatas served a more practical function. They had to be composed rapidly, to meet the weekly demands of the Lutheran liturgical calendar. Nevertheless, Bach's devotion to his craft in these works is impressive, to say the least. A cantata such as No. 140 was designed as more than a musical interlude in the St. Thomas service for which it was written. What Bach accomplished here was a kind of musical sermon about the parable of the ten wise and foolish virgins. For the faithful, his music captures the essence of the parable. This music projects an avowedly Christian message, but it also represents Bach's attempt to capture the spiritual force of music.

first LISTEN

INTRODUCTION	1ST PHRASE/INTERLUDE	PHRASES 2–8/INTERLUDES	PHRASE 9/INTERLUDE	PHRASES 10–11/POSTLUDE
0:00	0:32	0:56	4:27	5:18
Orchestral introduction	Wachet auf . . .	Vocal phrases alternate with instrumental sections	Allelujah . . .	Final phrases/orchestral postlude

a deeper LISTEN

TIME	SECTION	TEXT	TRANSLATION	LISTEN FOR THIS
0:00	Orchestral Introduction			(1) Statement of two themes (a) and (b) with ground bass accompaniment a b
0:32	First chorale phrase	*Wachet auf, ruft uns die Stimme*	Awaken, the voice summons us	(2) Long notes in soprano, supported by chorus
0:49	Orchestral interlude			
0:56	Second chorale phrase	*Der Wächter sehr hoch auf der Zinne*	High atop the tower the watch-man calls,	
1:18	Orchestral interlude			
1:24	Third chorale phrase	*Wach auf, du Stadt Jerusalem!*	Awaken, O town of Jerusalem!	
1:44	Orchestral interlude			

Continued

TIME	SECTION	TEXT	TRANSLATION	LISTEN FOR THIS
2:14	Fourth chorale phrase	*Mitternacht heisst diese Stunde,*	This hour is midnight,	
2:33	Orchestral interlude			
2:39	Fifth chorale phrase	*Sie rufen uns mit hellem Munde:*	They summon us with cheer-ful voices:	
3:01	Orchestral interlude			
3:11	Sixth chorale phrase	*Wo seid ihr, klugen Jungfrauen?*	Where are you, wise virgins?	
3:29	Long orchestral interlude			
3:51	Seventh chorale phrase	*Wohl auf, der Bräutgam kommt,*	Arise, the bridegroom comes,	
4:06	Orchestral interlude			
4:11	Eighth chorale phrase	*Steht auf, die Lampen nehmt!*	Arise, and take your lamps!	
4:25	Orchestral interlude			
4:27	Ninth chorale phrase	*Alleluia*	Alleluia	(3) Choral fugal passage
5:11	Orchestral interlude			
5:18	Tenth chorale phrase	*Macht euch bereit zu der Hochzeit*	Prepare yourselves for the wedding,	Brief interlude at 5:30 and then repeats verse

TIME	SECTION	TEXT	TRANSLATION	LISTEN FOR THIS
5:51	Orchestral interlude			
5:54	Eleventh chorale phrase (same as third phrase)	*Ihr müsset ihm entgegengehn!*	You must go out to greet him!	
6:15	Orchestral postlude (repeat of introduction)			

Bach's Other Religious Music

By any measure, Bach's cantatas, to which he devoted the greater part of his career, are supreme creations in Western music. Still, he did write other sacred music that surpasses the cantatas in sheer scale. The imposing St. John Passion and St. Matthew Passion draw on scripture and devotional poetry to treat the Passion of Christ. These masterpieces match the scale of Handel's great oratorios (see Chapter 28). Unlike Handel's oratorios, however, Bach's Passions were written for church and use chorales, a feature that ties them to the chorale cantatas and to Lutheran worship.

More monumental is Bach's Mass in B minor, which cost him years of work. He began composing sections for the Latin Ordinary of the Mass (see p. 67) in the 1720s. Only toward the end of his life was he able to assemble the movements into this sprawling, complex work. The length of the Mass in B minor made it unsuitable for performance during a service. Bach seems to have intended it to demonstrate what a composer could do in setting the Mass, in an ideal vision of worship.

check your **KNOWLEDGE**

1. What is a cantata? How did it develop in Germany?
2. What is a chorale? How did it develop?
3. How did Bach incorporate a chorale melody into his Cantata No. 140?
4. What other types of religious works did Bach compose?
5. Why is Bach's Mass in B minor considered such a monumental and important work?

CHAPTER 27

George Frideric Handel

George Frideric Handel (1685–1759).

To close off our discussion of Baroque music, we turn to George Frideric Handel (1685–1759), Bach's great contemporary and the second master of the late Baroque. He was a man of the world who studied in Italy and worked in Germany before settling in England. Handel excelled in vividly rendering human dramas into music. He was known at first for his Italian operas. Later, he turned to oratorios (Chapter 28), which featured dramatic versions of biblical stories set to music. Handel's English oratorios became the basis of his continuing fame long after his death. Beginning in the nineteenth century, popular choral societies regularly performed oratorios such as *Israel in Egypt* and, most famous of all, *Messiah*.

A keyboard virtuoso, Handel astounded the English with his improvisations. In addition to keyboard suites, he wrote organ concertos for performance between the acts of his oratorios. Handel also created **occasional music**, or music for special occasions. His great instrumental work *Water Music* was performed during a royal outing on the Thames River. *The Music for the Royal Fireworks*, written for a large orchestra, celebrated a treaty ending one of the many wars that embroiled England and European monarchies.

MAKING CONNECTIONS *Handel versus Bach: Two Baroque Titans Compared*

Handel and Bach were both born into the Lutheran faith in central Germany; they were both distinguished virtuosos on the harpsichord and organ; and they became the leading representatives of the late Baroque in music. But their careers took decisively different turns. Well-traveled and cosmopolitan in outlook, Handel was an international celebrity, equally in his element composing Italian opera, English oratorios, Catholic and Anglican church music, and ceremonial anthems. Bach's sphere of activity remained centered in central Germany. He was a Lutheran church musician, and he devoted the greater part of his career to writing a staggering amount of music for the principal Leipzig parish churches.

Handel was a man of the theater, who understood how to use dramatic gestures in his music. Bach, on the other hand, though he showed power and drama in his music, took an introverted turn toward the learned forms of counterpoint. His many complex fugues challenged the intellectual abilities of most musicians. Handel was also a seasoned master of counterpoint, and he took the discipline quite seriously, but in comparison to Bach he was not showy about his learning.

Though Handel and Bach never met, both suffered a devastating condition in their last years—they went blind. By a twist of fate, they were patients of the same physician, a traveling, somewhat disreputable English surgeon named John Taylor. The surgeon operated on Bach in Leipzig and on Handel several years later in London but was unable to restore the sight of either.

Handel's Life and Career

King George I (r. 1714–1727).

Handel was born in Halle, a small Saxon town not far from Leipzig. His father, a barber-surgeon, sent him to the university to prepare for a law career. Not finding law to his liking, Handel moved to Hamburg, where he played violin in the municipal orchestra and began composing. In 1706 he traveled to Italy, chiefly to Florence and Rome, where he composed sacred music and well over 100 cantatas. Handel's supporters included Cardinal Ottoboni, a patron of Corelli who was taken by the unusual "fire and force" of the German's work. According to one observer, Handel even snatched Corelli's violin out of his hand to demonstrate how his music should be played.

In 1710 Handel became the music director to the court of Hanover. Its German ruler, Georg Ludwig, was later crowned King George I of England (r. 1714–1727). The terms of Handel's appointment allowed him to visit London, where he found favor at the court of Queen Anne. Handel took a position there, leaving Germany and his responsibilities in Hanover behind. In 1711 his opera *Rinaldo*, set during the eleventh-century First Crusade, premiered as the first Italian opera composed for England. The work was a great success though it also attracted its share of criticism. The critic Joseph Addison ridiculed the opera's special stage effects, including a release of sparrows: "There have been so many Flights of them let loose in this Opera, that it is feared the House will never get rid of them; . . . besides the Inconvenience which the Head of the Audience may sometimes suffer from them." (Apparently, the birds sometimes left their droppings on the unsuspecting audience.)

Handel remained in his adopted country for almost half a century, through the reigns of Queen Anne and King George I and II. In 1727 the composer became an English citizen. A portly man who wore a large, white wig, he cut an imposing figure. He guarded his privacy despite being an international celebrity, and lived quietly as a bachelor at his Georgian London residence. (Some 200 years later, the American rock guitarist Jimi Hendrix would live next door.)

For nearly three decades, Handel composed Italian operas, the preferred entertainment of English royalty and aristocracy. In 1720 he was named music director of the Royal Academy of Music, established as a profit-making enterprise to support the productions of Italian opera. Handel spent much of his time on administrative matters, attending to his Italian singers, and traveling to recruit the fashionable virtuosos demanded by the public.

Struggling with financial and artistic problems, Handel managed to keep his transplanted Italian opera alive well into the 1730s. By then, however, English audiences were beginning to tire of it, and in 1737 the academy closed its doors. The English had never been altogether comfortable listening to operas sung in a foreign language. In addition, they were uneasy with some Italian conventions, such as having sopranos or altos—among them

Handel's London residence at 25 Brook St., now a museum.

MAKING CONNECTIONS *Zadok the Priest and English Royalty*

Coronation of Queen Elizabeth II in 1953.

Handel served three English monarchs (Queen Anne, George I, and George II), and was often called upon to compose music for state functions. In 1727, he wrote four anthems for the coronation of George II. One of the last acts of George I had been to naturalize Handel, and so it was as an English citizen that Handel created these works, the most famous of which is *Zadok the Priest*. Based on the biblical account in 1 Kings, it explains how Zadok anointed Solomon the King of Israel. Though Handel's anthem lasts only five minutes or so, it is a dramatic, majestic work that has been performed during the anointing of every English monarch since George II.

castrati, castrated male singers—sing heroic male roles. The operas themselves had grown more and more stereotyped. English audiences disliked the typical "**exit aria**," in which a soloist would appeal to the audience for applause before abruptly exiting. Ultimately, London critics came to view Italian opera as a foreign threat to the established English theater.

Handel caricatured as an organ-playing pig in a 1754 engraving.

In 1732, Handel produced *Esther*, a first attempt at an English oratorio. *Esther* told the Old Testament story of the Jewish queen of Persia who saved her people from massacre. The Bishop of London ruled against producing *Esther* as an opera with full costumes, scenery, or staged action, which he felt would profane a sacred subject. Therefore, Handel had it performed "after the Manner of the coronation service," that is, sung by a large chorus in a concert setting. With its English text and uplifting biblical story, *Esther* scored a considerable success. Handel went on to compose nearly twenty oratorios, all presented in concert performance.

As a foreigner (a German in London), Handel was a frequent target of ridicule. His detractors caricatured his speech, his large size, and his voracious eating habits ("Nature," one observer noted, "required a great supply of sustenance to support so huge a mass"); in one illustration, he was shown as a "harmonious boar." Yet Handel prevailed against his critics. A man of firm will and shrewd business sense, he died in 1759 a wealthy man. He was buried in Westminster Abbey, the final resting place of England's most distinguished poets and musicians, and three thousand mourners attended his funeral. In the nineteenth century, Charles Dickens would be buried alongside him.

In 1717, the death of the Catholic Queen Anne led to a momentous change in the English monarchy. Queen Anne left no surviving heirs, so Parliament decreed that the throne would pass to a Protestant line. Her closest Protestant relative was the German prince-elector of the House of Hanover, Georg Ludwig, who became George I. Handel once again served his former employer.

According to an early Handel biographer, the composer created his *Water Music* in 1717 to gain the favor of the new king, who had been angered when the composer left his service in 1710. It is also possible that Handel wrote this orchestral music, now his most famous, for a public relations event promoting the king. George I planned a grand pageant to introduce himself to the British people, a party on the Thames River that would be easily visible and audible to Londoners within sight and earshot of the river.

As the royal party drifted upriver on a stately barge draped with banners, a group of smaller vessels followed. On one barge were Handel and fifty musicians merrily playing oboes, bassoons, trumpets, French horns, and strings. The sound of Handel's floating orchestra must have impressed the throngs of onlookers ashore. Entranced, the king called for the music to be encored twice.

Watch demonstration videos on the bassoon, trumpet, and French horn.

In its final version, *Water Music* comprises nearly two dozen pieces, most of which fall into common Baroque dance categories and are modest in length. There are also a few more extended pieces, including a festive two-part (slow-fast) overture based on the French style. Here we will explore two popular pieces from the collection (see **Listening Maps 19 and 20**).

Detail of an eighteenth-century painting by Canaletto showing a floating royal party on the Thames River in London. Handel composed the *Water Music* for a similar occasion.

LISTENING MAP 19

HANDEL, *Water Music: Air* in F major {1717}

FORM	Binary dance form (‖: :‖‖: :‖), with two sections, each repeated
SCORING	Orchestra with violin and oboe playing the melody
BASS	Baroque walking bass
OVERVIEW	The elegant Air in F major is a good example of the binary form (see p. 156) typically encountered in Baroque dances: ‖: tonic modulation second key :‖‖: return to tonic :‖ This miniature movement divides into two portions, each repeated and nearly equal in length. The melody, gently played by the violins and oboes, is accompanied by the other strings and supported by another example of a Baroque walking bass (①). Handel specified that the air be played three times, and for the middle statement added a few comments from the horns (②).

why to LISTEN

Handel's *Water Music* was written for a specific occasion, a leisurely royal outing in 1717 on the Thames River of King George I and his court. When we hear the *Water Music* today, in a recording or a concert hall, we are well removed from its original venue, not just in time but also acoustically. This was music designed for outdoor performance, so that its echoing sounds could freely resonate and mingle across the river. Meanwhile, the king slowly drifted upstream and surveyed his capital, and his subjects lined the shores to take in the pageantry.

Music outdoors works quite differently than indoors. Think of occasions when you have enjoyed hearing live music outdoors. How is the experience different from listening in a closed space, and how do your listening habits change as a result?

a deeper LISTEN

TIME	SECTION	LISTEN FOR THIS
0:00	Statement 1	① Melody in violins and oboes, supported by walking bass
1:11	Statement 2	② Melody in violins and oboes, added French horn parts
not included in recording	Statement 3	Return to original instrumentation: melody in violins and oboes

LISTENING MAP 20

HANDEL, *Water Music: Alla Hornpipe* {1717}

FORM	Three-part ABA
METER	Triple meter
SCORING	Orchestra divided into brass, woodwinds, and strings
OVERVIEW	*Alla Hornpipe* is a fast and colorful English dance in triple time. Here Handel assembled the full force of his orchestra, divided into three groups of brass (two trumpets, two French horns), woodwinds (two oboes, two bassoons), and strings. Initially, the oboes and violins seize the syncopated dance tune, which features vigorous accents against the beat (①). Then the orchestra drops out, and the trumpets and French horns playfully exchange the tune (②). The dance continues with orchestral sections and alternations between the trumpets and horns (③) before the full ensemble comes together to play a strong cadence in a major key (④). Next, a contrast: the brass fall silent, and our attention focuses on the woodwinds and strings. They introduce a fresh theme, in a minor key, but again marked by syncopations (⑤). Finally, the abbreviation *da capo* instructs the musicians to repeat the first section in the major key (⑥).

first LISTEN

A	B	A
0:00	0:58	1:54
Major key: first theme, full ensemble	Minor key: second theme, trumpets and horns drop out	Major key: first theme, full ensemble

a deeper LISTEN

TIME	SECTION	LISTEN FOR THIS
0:00	A (major key)	① Lively theme in triple time, woodwinds and strings 
0:15		② Theme exchanged between solo trumpets and French horns

Continued

TIME	SECTION	LISTEN FOR THIS
0:21		(3) Further orchestral interjections, solos for trumpets and French horns
0:56		(4) Cadence for full orchestra
0:58	B (minor key)	(5) New theme in minor key, trumpets and French horns drop out
1:54	A (da capo repeat, major key)	(6) Return to first theme, full ensemble

Handel and Italian Opera

By the time of the royal outing on the Thames, Handel was established in London as a composer of Italian opera. The main attractions of this genre were the ornate, stylized arias in which star singers reflected on the events of the unfolding drama. In *Giulio Cesare* (1724), Handel's most famous opera, the principal characters, Julius Caesar and Cleopatra, each sing eight arias, through which Handel fully developed their roles.

The preferred type of aria was the **da capo aria**, which consisted of two contrasting sections, *A* and *B*, followed by a repeat of the *A* section, resulting in the structure *ABA*. Though the **da capo** repetitions slowed the unfolding story, they allowed singers to showcase their voices through runs, trills, and other ornaments.

Stitched between the arias were recitatives—speech-like passages with simple continuo accompaniments—that laid out the dramatic action of the opera. To heighten the effect, Handel sometimes provided orchestral accompaniment for a recitative. Apart from arias and recitatives, Handel used ensembles, from duets to large-scale choruses; he was, in fact, one of the first to integrate choruses into Italian operas. To introduce his operas, he used orchestral overtures featuring majestic rhythms, thick chords, and animated fugal passages.

check your KNOWLEDGE

1. Compare and contrast the lives and careers of J. S. Bach and G. F. Handel.
2. What is binary form? How is it displayed in Handel's Air in F major?
3. How does Handel use different instruments in the *Alla Hornpipe* section of his *Water Music* to create dramatic contrasts in the piece?
4. Which innovations did Handel introduce to Italian opera?

CHAPTER

28

Handel and the English Oratorio

Handel's music solved one problem for London audiences, who had grown weary of performances in Italian. The English were naturally proud of their own culture and language, and Handel shrewdly sensed an opportunity when Italian opera began to fall out of favor there. His answer was to develop and embrace the English oratorio, which had English instead of Italian text.

Oratorios are large-scale, usually narrative musical works performed without costumes or scenery. Most of Handel's deal with biblical subjects, ranging from new treatments of Old Testament stories to the direct quotations of Scripture in *Messiah* and *Israel in Egypt*. Several of these works especially resonated among largely Protestant audiences. In one oratorio, *Judas Maccabaeus*, Handel found an Old Testament subject especially relevant to contemporary events. It concerned the warrior Judas Maccabaeus, who led a revolt against the Seleucid Empire and restored the Temple of Jerusalem in 164 BCE (commemorated in Judaism as Hanukah, the Festival of Lights). The oratorio's march-like chorus, "See the Conquering Hero Comes," was understood to celebrate the 1745 defeat of an uprising. In that episode, a grandson of James II, the last in the line of Stuart kings (see p. 194), unsuccessfully tried to restore the House of Stuart to the English throne.

In his oratorios, Handel abandoned the operatic conventions of theatrical staging, dramatic acting, and "exit arias." He greatly expanded the use of the chorus, however. The oratorios are filled with imposing choral movements, particularly in *Israel in Egypt* and *Messiah*. Sometimes, the chorus serves as a deliberative body that comments on the paused action, but it can also actively participate in the unfolding drama. Thus, in *Israel in Egypt*, grand choruses relate the tribulations of the Hebrew nation in exile. On other occasions, the chorus is directly engaged in the plot. In *Belshazzar*, based on the Book of Daniel, three distinctive types of choral music characterize the Babylonians, the Jews, and the Persians, the principal figures of that drama.

Far and away Handel's most popular oratorio is *Messiah*, composed in little more than three weeks in 1741. It was first performed in Dublin in 1742 as a benefit for Irish charities. To mount the performance, Handel had to overcome resistance from the author Jonathan Swift, who was dean of St. Patrick's Cathedral. Today, it is recognized as one of the great choral works of all time, and is performed annually at Christmas and Easter.

Dashboard

Listen to selected entries in the BBC's Hallelujah Chorus contest.

As an oratorio, Handel's *Messiah* introduces us to a different kind of listening experience. While oratorios can be quite dramatic and might seem to tell stories (like an opera but without scenery and costumes), they more closely resemble epic poems. Dating back to classical antiquity, epic poems, such as those of Homer and Virgil, presented larger-than-life events. They did so with a moralizing purpose, calculated more to uplift readers than merely to entertain them.

MAKING CONNECTIONS *Handel, the Duke of Cumberland, and Bonnie Prince Charlie*

Bonnie Prince Charlie.

Beginning with the Glorious Revolution of 1688, the English monarchy had faced the threat of uprisings from the Jacobites, supporters of James II, who sought to restore the Stuart line of monarchs. In 1745 that threat finally materialized when a grandson of James II, Charles Edward Stuart (a.k.a. "the Young Pretender" or "Bonnie Prince Charlie"), landed in Scotland with French support to organize a rebellion. After entering Edinburgh unopposed, the Prince marched south with an army of six thousand, including Scottish Highlanders and English loyal to the Stuarts, and began an ill-fated invasion of England. Though he intended to move on London, he advanced only as far as Derby in the East Midlands region of England before deciding to turn back to Scotland. Meanwhile, the English monarch, George II, sent his son, the Duke of Cumberland, to pursue the invaders. Cumberland decisively defeated them at the Battle of Culloden in Scotland in 1746. Bonnie Prince Charlie escaped, traveling disguised across the Scottish moors before taking a frigate back to France. The Duke of Cumberland showed no mercy to Jacobite sympathizers and became known as the Butcher of Cumberland. But in London he was regaled as a hero who had saved the country, and was honored in the chorus from Handel's oratorio *Judas Maccabaeus.*

Handel's tomb in Westminster Abbey, London.

Messiah consists of three parts, which comment on the incarnation (birth), passion (Crucifixion), resurrection of Christ, and the promise of redemption. The oratorio begins with a French overture. True to Handel's preference for choruses, nearly half of the fifty-three parts are sung by the full chorus, with the rest being solo arias. Among the best-known arias is "I Know That My Redeemer Liveth"; the notes of its opening measures were sculpted into Handel's monument in Westminster Abbey, for all visitors to see. Although soloists sing these arias, *Messiah* has no parts for individual characters and does not tell a story in a conventional sense. Rather, its overall theme remains the redemption of mankind through the life and work of Christ.

Here we look closely at two favorites from *Messiah*, the aria "Rejoice Greatly, O Daughter of Zion" and the Hallelujah Chorus (**Listening Maps 21 and 22**).

MAKING CONNECTIONS *Handel's* Messiah *and Jonathan Swift*

One of the most celebrated English writers and satirists of all time, Jonathan Swift wrote the novel *Gulliver's Travels* (1726) while he was the dean of St. Patrick's Cathedral in Dublin, center of the Anglican Church in Ireland. By the time Handel arrived in 1742 to supervise the premiere of *Messiah*, the aging writer was in failing health. Swift suffered from Ménière's syndrome, an inner-ear disorder that plagued him with episodes of vertigo. He clashed with the world-famous composer of English oratorios, and just months later, he was declared of unsound mind.

Swift was, musically speaking, tone-deaf; he once wrote that he "knew nothing of music," and "would not give a farthing for all the music in the universe." Nevertheless, as dean he tried to keep a tight control over his choristers. When Handel recruited St. Patrick's choir members to sing in *Messiah*, Swift reacted angrily and tried to have them punished for their "disobedience, rebellion, perfidy, and ingratitude." But the oratorio ultimately premiered at the New Music Hall on Fishamble Street and was an unqualified success. Several Dublin charities benefited from the proceeds, and the course of music history was changed.

St. Patrick's Cathedral, Dublin.

LISTENING MAP 21

HANDEL, *Messiah*, Aria, "Rejoice Greatly, O Daughter of Zion"

{1742}

FORM	Da capo aria (ABA′)
GENRE	English oratorio
SCORING	Soprano and orchestra
OVERVIEW	Placed toward the end of Part I, after the celebration of Christ's birth, this soprano aria displays Handel's Baroque craft at its most magnificent. Its text is drawn from the Old Testament Book of Zedekiah. It is a vivacious da capo aria with a twist: instead of simply repeating the opening portion, Handel rewrote it, so that he could modify some of its features. We thus encounter a varied repetition: ABA becomes ABA′.

why to LISTEN

Tracing a story in a linear fashion is not the primary goal of an oratorio. Oratorios concern great events in history, but they draw from them some universal message. In the case of *Messiah*, not intended to be performed in church, Handel did not have the option of setting the words of Christ. And so, while the first two parts of the oratorio generally concern Christ's birth, crucifixion, and resurrection, they do not tell the story as a narrative. Instead, they are a commentary on the Christian experience. This distinction is critical to understanding the oratorio and to adjusting our listening habits. As Handel himself is reported to have said, the purpose of his oratorio was not to entertain but to make his audience "better" in some way. The question to ask, as you listen, is how well Handel's music succeeds toward this end.

first LISTEN

A	B	A′
0:00	**1:32**	**2:41**
Orchestral introduction followed by soprano solo	Switch to minor key and more contemplative music	Return of the opening with slight variation

a deeper **LISTEN**

TIME	SECTION	LISTEN FOR THIS
0:00	A	**Orchestral introduction:** Energetic theme in major key with increasingly larger leaps expressing the joy of the coming of Christ Allegro; increasing leaps
0:18		**Soprano solo:** *Rejoice greatly, O daughter of Zion, shout O daughter of Jerusalem, Behold, thy king cometh unto thee.* Melisma on "Rejoice"; final repeat spreads the word over 49 notes extended melisma; re - joice
1:15		Cadence by the soprano leads to the orchestral postlude, a repeat of the joyous opening melody
1:32	B	Music shifts to minor key, *piano* dynamic level, slower rhythms and sustained tones He is the righ - - - teous Sa - viour **Soprano solo:** *He is the righteous Saviour, And he shall speak peace unto the heathen.*
2:41	A′	Abbreviated orchestral introduction, return of opening theme in major key
2:45		**Soprano solo:** (modified, more brilliant) *Rejoice greatly, O daughter of Zion, shout O daughter of Jerusalem, Behold, thy king cometh unto thee.*
3:55		Orchestral postlude

New minor melody

LISTENING MAP 22

HANDEL, *Messiah*, "Hallelujah Chorus"

{1742}

FORM	Chorus constructed on five musical ideas (*a*, *b*, *c*, *d*, and *e*)
GENRE	English oratorio
SCORING	Choir
OVERVIEW	The stirring Hallelujah chorus, which closes Part II, is easily the most celebrated movement of *Messiah*. Drawn from Revelation, the text announces the reign of the Lord and the resurrected Christ. It divides into five portions, each treated with a distinct musical motive.

first LISTEN

a	b	c	d	e	CONCLUSION
0:00	0:24	1:11	1:29	1:52	3:21
"Hallelujah . . ."	"For the Lord God . . ."	"The kingdom of . . ."	"And he shall reign . . ."	"King of kings . . ."	

a deeper LISTEN

TIME	SECTION	LISTEN FOR THIS
0:00	a	Brief orchestral introduction
0:06		Compact statements of "Hallelujah" sung by the chorus, immediately repeated, and compressed into statements on a single pitch

Allegro
a
Compression
Hal-le-lu-jah! Hal-le-lu-jah! Hal-le - lu-jah! Hal-le-lu-jah! Hal - le - lu-jah!

0:24	**b**	A stark figure sung in unison by the chorus; this new figure rises to the words "Lord God" before moving by wide leaps to suggest His great power *b* *leaps* For the Lord God Om-ni-po-tent reign-eth, Hal-le-lu-jah! Hal-le-lu-jah! *etc.*
0:47		Alternations between and combinations of *a* and *b*
1:11	**c**	Dramatic shifts in texture between low and high registers reflect the contrast between the "kingdom of the world" and the "Kingdom of our Lord and of His Christ" *c* The king - dom of this world
1:29	**d**	New subject in fugal style alternating between ascending and descending leaps *d* *tr* And He shall reign for ev - er and ev - er
1:52	**e**	Sopranos intone ascending pedal points: *(King of Kings, Lord of Lords)*, alternating with the choir singing "*Hallelujah*" . . .
2:31		Culminating combinations of (*a*), (*d*), and (*e*)
3:21	**Conclusion**	Dramatic pause
3:23		Final "Amen" cadence

MAKING CONNECTIONS *Standing Up for Handel*

According to tradition, when *Messiah* was premiered in England in 1743, King George II attended the event. At the text "For the Lord God" in the Hallelujah Chorus, the king rose to his feet. Monarchs did not stand while others sat, and so the audience naturally rose en masse and started a time-honored tradition. There is actually no hard evidence that the king attended the premiere, but audiences have been standing during this rousing chorus, with and without monarchs, for more than 250 years.

check your **KNOWLEDGE**

1. What is an oratorio? How does it differ from an opera?
2. Why did Handel stop writing operas and turn to English oratorios?
3. What is the subject of Handel's *Messiah* and how does the music convey it?
4. What is the structure of the Hallelujah Chorus? How does it express the joyful theme of the Resurrection of Christ and the triumph of the Lord?

CHAPTER

29 The End of the Baroque

By the time Handel composed *Messiah*, the Baroque was transitioning to a more relaxed style designed to please. Increasingly, a distinction was made between a strict "high" style and a lighter, "free" style. The strict style was most appropriate for church music; the free style, suitable for less serious music, allowed composers room to experiment. As the eighteenth century advanced, the free style became popular in opera and instrumental music, and finally influenced church music as well.

Two terms, *rococo* and *galant*, are often applied to this light, transitional style that arose toward the middle of the eighteenth century. ***Rococo*** (from *rocaille*, French for small stones or shells) is best applied to the arts in France. The term originally described a decorative style that emerged in French architecture as early as the seventeenth century before taking hold in the eighteenth century. It featured shell-like motifs as graceful ornaments, in contrast to the heavier style of the full-blown Baroque. In music, rococo appeared in light forms of opera that featured dances and scenes from everyday life.

Rococo-style oval room in Hôtel Soubisse, Paris (1739).

Galant is also used to describe the light style of the time, in France and elsewhere. Composers of galant music rejected the complexities of the Baroque in favor of a supple melodic style with a simple, supporting bass line. Their music emphasized memorable melodies, with short repeated phrases, and tended to have uncomplicated harmonies. Composers favored simple forms such as binary-form dance movements, with two sections, each repeated.

By the 1730s the galant style was making inroads into the late Baroque style. In Italy, a new type of comic opera, **opera buffa**, began to challenge the well-entrenched serious opera, **opera seria**. Typically, opera buffa featured just a few characters who sang tuneful arias and recitatives punctuated by short, crisp phrases.

Bach and Handel were aware of these changes. Bach parodied the new style of comic opera in some entertaining cantatas, including his *Coffee Cantata* (ca. 1735), probably intended to be performed in a Leipzig coffee house. In the cantata, a distraught father tries to forbid his daughter from drinking coffee, but he fails to break her from her addiction. In England, John Gay's *The Beggar's Opera* (1728), with music by J. C. Pepusch, satirized the social order. It included roles for pickpockets and harlots and spoofed the conventions of Italian opera, the basis of Handel's livelihood. The popularity of *The Beggar's Opera* contributed to Handel's decision to turn from Italian opera to English oratorio.

Read about *The Beggar's Opera.*

Throughout this period, composers aspired more and more to create music of simplicity, charm, and clarity. The magnificent splendor of the Baroque gradually came to be viewed as overly ornate and emotional. Along with the other arts, music began to resist the extravagance of the Baroque. Increasingly, it showed signs of a powerful new intellectual direction in Western thought that would become known as the Enlightenment.

check your KNOWLEDGE ?

1. Which styles began to challenge the high Baroque in the eighteenth century?
2. What is opera buffa?

PART IV SUMMARY: THE BAROQUE

- In music history, the Baroque was a period that began in Italy around 1600, spread throughout Europe, and continued until about 1750.
  - During this period tonality, based on our modern major and minor scales and system of triads, developed. It replaced modality, based on the old church modes, of the medieval age and Renaissance.
  - Baroque music typically uses regular meters and bar lines.
  - Baroque composers began specifying in their scores dynamics markings, such as *piano* and *forte* (soft and loud).

- The Baroque marked the rise of opera, a drama with continuous music performed on a stage with sets and costumes, and using solo singers, orchestra, and occasionally a chorus.
  - Opera began in Italy and then spread to other regions; seventeenth-century opera composers included the Italian Claudio Monteverdi and Englishman Henry Purcell.

- The Baroque witnessed the rise of highly skilled virtuoso musicians and introduced several new genres of instrumental music.
  - The sonata was for one solo instrument or for a small group of instruments.
  - The prelude was a relatively short piece, often of an improvisatory character.
  - The suite was a collection of dance movements of different characters.
  - The trio sonata was a chamber work in several movements that featured two treble instruments supported by a bass and a continuo instrument.
  - The concerto grosso was an instrumental work, typically in three movements, that featured a group of soloists supported by an orchestra.
  - Leading Baroque composers of instrumental music were the violinists Arcangelo Corelli and Antonio Vivaldi.

- The music of the Baroque reached its height in the prolific career of the German J. S. Bach, who produced roughly a thousand compositions.
  - One of the leading organ and harpsichord virtuosos of his time, Bach wrote hundreds of instrumental works, including suites, concertos, and *The Well-Tempered Clavier*, two collections of preludes and fugues in every key.
  - Bach is often recognized as the greatest practitioner of the fugue, a work in imitative polyphonic style in which several parts introduce and develop a fugal subject.
  - Bach composed a vast quantity of sacred music, including hundreds of cantatas, works for chorus, orchestra, and solo vocalists.
  - Bach designed his cantatas for use in weekly Leipzig church services, and typically built them around chorales, Lutheran hymn tunes then in common use.
  - After he died, Bach's music was largely forgotten. The full rediscovery of his genius did not occur until the nineteenth and twentieth centuries.

- The German composer G. F. Handel, a second master of the late Baroque, worked primarily in England.
  - Handel composed Italian operas, but eventually developed a new genre, the English oratorio, the mainstay of his fame.

- Based on biblical subjects, Handel's oratorios used an orchestra, chorus, and vocal soloists, but unlike opera, did not require sets, costumes, and stage scenery.
- Handel also composed ceremonial music for royal occasions, including the coronations of English monarchs, and the *Water Music*, for a royal outing up the Thames River.
- By the time Handel died, Baroque music had begun to be challenged by a lighter, more accessible style that in turn would give rise to the Classical period.

KEY TERMS

a cappella 142
allemande 156
answer 170
anthem 150
aria 148
augmentation 170
ballet 149
Baroque 130
basso continuo 139
binary form 156
cadence 139
cadenza 175
cantata 166, 178
cello 150
chorale 179
chorale cantata 179
concertino 157
concerto 157
concerto grosso 157
continuo 139
courante 156
da capo 192
da capo aria 192
diminution 170
dominant 138
episode 170
exit aria 188
figured bass (thoroughbass) 140
forte (*f*) 140
French overture 149
fugal exposition 170
fugue 169
galant 201
gigue 156
ground bass (ostinato) 150
harmonic progression 138
harpsichord 155
key (tonality) 138
key signature 139
libretto 142
masque 150
mediant 139
mirror inversion 170
modulation 156
monody 142
occasional music 186
opera 142
opera buffa 201
opera seria 201
oratorio 193
orchestra 144
organ 155
ornament 140
overture 149
pedal point 170
piano (*p*) 140
pizzicato 150
polychoral 142
prelude 156
program music 161
recitative 144
repeat marks 156
ritornello 157
ritornello form 157
rococo 200
sarabande 156
sonata 156
sonata da camera 157
sonata da chiesa 157
stretto 170
subdominant 138
subject 170
suite 156
terraced dynamics 140
toccata 165
tonality 137
tonic 138
transposition 139
triad 137
trill 140
trio sonata 156
violin 154
virtuoso 154
walking bass 182

KEY COMPOSERS

Claudio Monteverdi (1567–1643)
Jean-Baptiste Lully (1632–1687)
Arcangelo Corelli (1653–1713)
Henry Purcell (1659–1695)
Antonio Vivaldi (1678–1741)
Johann Sebastian Bach (1685–1750)
George Frideric Handel (1685–1759)

MUSICAL JOURNEYS
The Classical Music of Persia (Iran)

Very few countries have such a long history of national and political identity as Persia (now known as Iran). The great empire of Persia, famed for its creative genius, was a meeting place of diverse cultural elements, yet it maintained its individuality.

Persian classical music developed from the music of urban and courtly tradition. The first historical evidence of music comes from the Sassanian dynasty (224–651 CE). The Persians possessed a high musical culture in which musicians enjoyed an exalted position at the imperial court. The most illustrious, Bārbad, is known to have devised seven royal modes (*khosrovāni*), thirty derivative modes (*lahn*), and 360 melodies (*dastān*), corresponding to the number of days in the week, month, and year of the Zoroastrian calendar.

The Arab conquest of the Persian empire began in 642 and eventually resulted in its incorporation within the greater Islamic empire. The Arabs valued Persian culture highly, and soon Persian musicians and musical scholars were to be found throughout the Muslim world.

From the beginning of the sixteenth century, the country became unified under the highly nationalistic Safavid dynasty (1501–1722). Persia became increasingly isolated from the rest of the Middle East, where Ottoman rule was paramount. The Safavids established the Shiʿa faith as the state religion, creating an even greater separation from other Muslim states. The Shiʿa religious leaders viewed music with suspicion because its effect on listeners could not be reasoned or theologically explained. Furthermore, music was generally seen as an accompaniment to frivolity and merriment, which could lead to impiety. Consequently, there was a gradual decline of musical scholarship from the sixteenth century to the mid-nineteenth. Within urban settings, music was gradually reduced to a private, quasi-clandestine art where solo performance and improvisation became the dominant features.

The comparatively fallow period from the sixteenth century to the nineteenth gave rise to a system that linked modes into groups known as *dastgāh*. The system of twelve dastgāhs, which represents the classical tradition as known today, is largely a legacy of nineteenth-century practices. This system is attributed to Mirzā Abdollāh (1845–1918), an eminent player and teacher of the *setār* (long-necked lute). The second dastgāh can be heard as the basis of the piece in **Listening Map I.3**.

Until the early twentieth century, performance of Persian classical music was limited to special occasions in private gatherings, mostly in aristocratic homes or at court. Religious constraints tended to prohibit large public forums for musical presentation. Since then, Westernization and the advent of recording, film, radio, and television combined to give music a wider social application. Increasing Westernization was the dominant feature of Iran under Pahlavi rule (1925–1979), and significant strides were made in promoting music as a social force.

With the 1979 revolution and political takeover by the fundamentalist religious faction, all public music was initially brought to a halt. Within a few years, however, a considerable softening in policy occurred. The Tehran Symphony Orchestra was revived, music schools began functioning again, and music was once again heard on radio and television. Yet pop music of all kinds is still held in disfavor, and women are banned from singing in public. At the same time, large numbers of Iranian expatriate musicians (particularly in the United States) continue to produce and market a vast quantity of popular music.

A wide variety of instruments has been used in Persian music. Evidence suggests Persia as the source of several musical instruments found throughout the region. Currently the most widely used instruments of classical music are: *setār, tār, santur, kamāncheh, ney,* and *tombak.*

The setār is a long-necked lute with a small pear-shaped soundbox and four strings. Its name signifies "three strings"; a fourth drone string has been added in more recent times. It has a range of two octaves and a fifth, and it is strummed with the nail of the right index finger. The tār has a tonal range identical with the setār. It has three double courses of strings (six strings in all); the first two courses serve a melodic function, while the third course serves as a drone. The tār has a double interconnected body covered with parchment. The larger resonating chambers, doubled melody strings, and use of a metal pick (instead of the fingernail) result in greater volume of sound, which has made the tār much more popular than the *setār.*

The santur is a small dulcimer with two layers of quadruple strings tuned in unison resting on movable bridges. It has a range of over three octaves and is played with delicate hammers made of rosewood. In the piece featured in Listening Map I.3, the santur is played by Mohammad Heydari (b. 1939). Heydari was a prominent player and teacher of the instrument in his native Iran until he went into exile following the 1979 revolution; he currently lives and performs in Los Angeles. The kamāncheh is a spike fiddle with four strings and a range of about three octaves. Its body is round and deep, with a skin-covered surface over which the bridge rests. Ney is the generic name for many types of flute. A wooden rim-blown flute called *ney-e haftband* has found its way into the classical tradition. It is obliquely held, with six finger holes and one thumb hole. The *tombak,* also called *dombak,* is a vase-shaped wooden drum, held horizontally on the lap and played with the fingers of both hands. As it is used for establishing rhythm, the *tombak* is also popularly called the *zarb* ("beat").

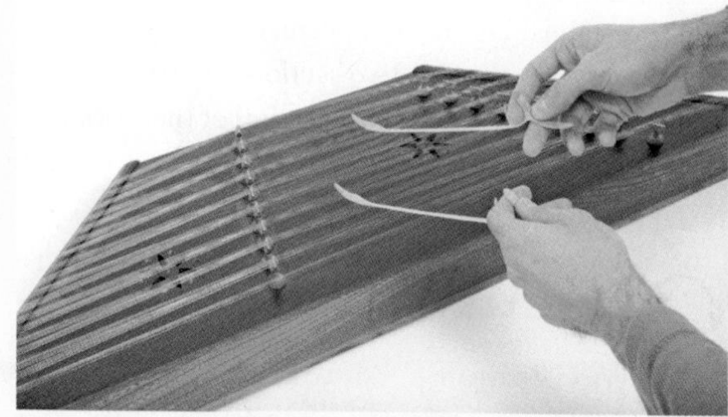

Persian santur.

Persian vocal music has a unique technique, which includes *tahrir,* a type of ornamentation with a quasi-yodeling effect and high falsetto notes. This difficult art has been declining since the beginning of the twentieth century, the era of notable singers Qamar and Tāherzāde.

LISTENING MAP *I.3*

"Avaz of Bayate Esfahan" (a secondary dastgāh of Homayoun), performed by MOHAMMAD HEYDARI, recorded by ELLA ZONIS, released in 1966

FORM	Persian dastgāh
METER	Improvisations are free (arhythmic); virtuoso sections have regular meter
TEMPO	Varies from very slow/contemplative to fast
DYNAMICS	Subdued but varying through the improvisations; louder in the virtuoso sections
SCORING	Santur (hammered dulcimer)
OVERVIEW	This composition is broadly broken into three main sections: an opening improvisation, which is rhythmically free; two brief virtuoso sections (separated by a short improvisation); and a concluding improvisation. The improvisations give the musician the opportunity to explore the nuances of the dastgāh (or scale). The middle virtuoso sections offer a strong contrast: they are in regular rhythm and are boldly played, with fast melodic runs replacing the briefer fragments of the improvisation sections.

why to LISTEN

This highly meditative introduction runs over four minutes before a regular rhythm and more dynamic "melody" emerge. The musician takes his time to work through a number of variations, establishing the tonal centers and range of the *dastgāh*, or scale. Two sections of virtuosic playing during the middle section of the work last only briefly before the player returns to a more contemplative improvisation. This structure seemingly turns the Western model upside down: the most exciting musical moments are brief, and they are bracketed by long sections of slow-moving improvisation. Try to put yourself into the contemplative mood of the music. Listen for the musician's many explorations in melody, rhythm, and timbre, and you may find yourself truly entranced.

first LISTEN

FREE IMPROVISATION	VIRTUOSO SECTION (*CHAHAR MEZRAB*)	FREE IMPROVISATION	VIRTUOSO SECTION	FREE IMPROVISATION	CONCLUSION
0:00	**4:27**	**5:10**	**5:38**	**6:16**	**7:20**
Establishment of the dastgāh's contours; variety in timbre; bursts of melody and implied rhythm	Metered section with rapid melodic passages and octave leaps; ends with brief silence	Return to melodic exploration; more contemplative mood	Regular rhythm returns in lower, contrasting range	Improvisation back to the original tonal center, gradually growing calmer	Ends ambiguously with no established tonal center

a deeper **LISTEN**

TIME	SECTION	LISTEN FOR THIS
0:00	Free improvisation	Monophonic explorations of the range and depth of the dastgāh (scale). Free rhythm as well as subtle variations of volume (dynamics) for musical expression. Use of ornaments and variety in texture (from sharp attack to more muted). Melodic motives in contrasting octaves (high, then low), such as the pairs at 0:16 and 0:21; 0:31 and 0:38; 1:41 and 1:45; and 1:55 and 2:04.
0:48		Emphasis on the tonal center (C). The performer improvises by connecting short melodic motives, rather than long passages emphasizing ascending or descending scales. Brief silences (as in 1:53–1:55).
2:11		Progression up the scale in bursts of ornamented melody. The dastgāh (scale) system is "neutral," utilizing "microtonal" pitches that do not suggest major or minor keys, as in Western tuning systems.
2:37		Brief ascending melodic contour as the tonal center shifts from (C) to (D).
3:07		"Call and answer" melodic motive exchange in octaves.
3:33		The tonal center has returned to (C) at 3:33, following a transitional sequence of melodic motives.
3:55		Emphasized lower octave, new tonal center (G). Rapid hammer work.
4:23		Brief return to (D) as the tonal emphasis, and then a brief silence.
4:27	"Virtuoso" section (chahar mezrab)	Begins with tonal center on (G). Busy passage with high rhythmic density and frequent jumps in octave. The virtuosic section concludes with the original tonal center (C). Ends with brief silence (5:05–5:09).
5:10	Free improvisation	Mood shifts again to more free improvisation, with tonal center back to (G).
5:38	Virtuoso section	Brief return of the "virtuosic" section in a lower octave, with (G) as the tonal center. Metered playing concludes with tonal center on (D).
6:16	Free improvisation	Back to free improvisation with an emphasis on the upper register to return to original tonal center (C). Improvisation continues emphasizing this concluding tonal center. Melodic explorations pick up speed and complexity (6:38–6:54; 6:57–7:09).
7:10		Slowing tempo.
7:20	Conclusion	The closing melodic motives emphasize the original tonal center (C), but the final phrases suggest a lack of resolution.

PART V

The Classical Period

Melody is the essence of music. —*ATTRIBUTED TO MOZART*

Portrait of young Wolfgang Amadeus Mozart performing with his father, Johann Georg Leopold, and his sister, Maria Anna (Nannerl), ca. 1763.

The Classical period extended roughly from 1750 through 1800. Its composers reacted against the intricate melodies and busy rhythms of the Baroque, instead favoring an accessible style marked by clear forms and balance. Centered on three major composers—Haydn, Mozart, and Beethoven—the Classical period eventually lent its name to the broader idea of art music. Thus, "classical" can refer to the music of Haydn, Mozart, Beethoven, and their contemporaries, but it can also refer to the entire tradition, from the medieval era to today. In contrast, the Classical period refers to a specific span of music history. Although the period lasted only about half a century, its influence on Western music endured well beyond.

The Classical period overlapped with a powerful philosophical and political movement known as the Enlightenment, which began with the scientific advances of Galileo, Newton, and others in the seventeenth century. During the eighteenth century, enlightened thinkers applied the same spirit of scientific inquiry to broader questions—how best to govern or lead a virtuous life, for example. They rejected what they saw as the superstitious beliefs of the past and instead valued reason, tolerance, and scientific inquiry. In *A Vindication of the Rights of Women* (1792), the English feminist Mary Wollstonecraft argued that women were equal to men and that reason was the only authority for the virtuous. For the German philosopher Immanuel Kant, whose motto was "dare to know," the enlightened person possessed an unquenched curiosity about the world.

Enlightenment thinkers such as Mary Wollstonecraft (shown here in a painting by Richard Rothwell) valued reason and explored questions of how to lead a virtuous life. Wollstonecraft asserted in *A Vindication of the Rights of Women* (1792) that women were equal to men.

That curiosity found outlets in new attempts to organize knowledge: the Swedish botanist Carl Linnaeus designed a system for classifying plants; the Englishman Samuel Johnson produced a two-thousand-page dictionary of the English language. Meanwhile, the Frenchman Denis Diderot labored for years over a massive encyclopedia (1751–1776). In response to Diderot's publication, a Scottish publisher brought out the *Encyclopaedia Britannica*, still available after many editions.

The new movement challenged absolute monarchs, who ruled by divine right and the authority of traditional institutions, including the Christian church. Could the Enlightenment's spirit of inquiry improve quality of life? Some rulers thought so, including Frederick the Great of Prussia (r. 1740–1786). His friendship with the French Enlightenment philosopher Voltaire (1694–1778) influenced the monarch's celebrated defense of civil liberties. On the other side of the Atlantic, Americans set down citizens' rights in the Declaration of Independence (1776). The American

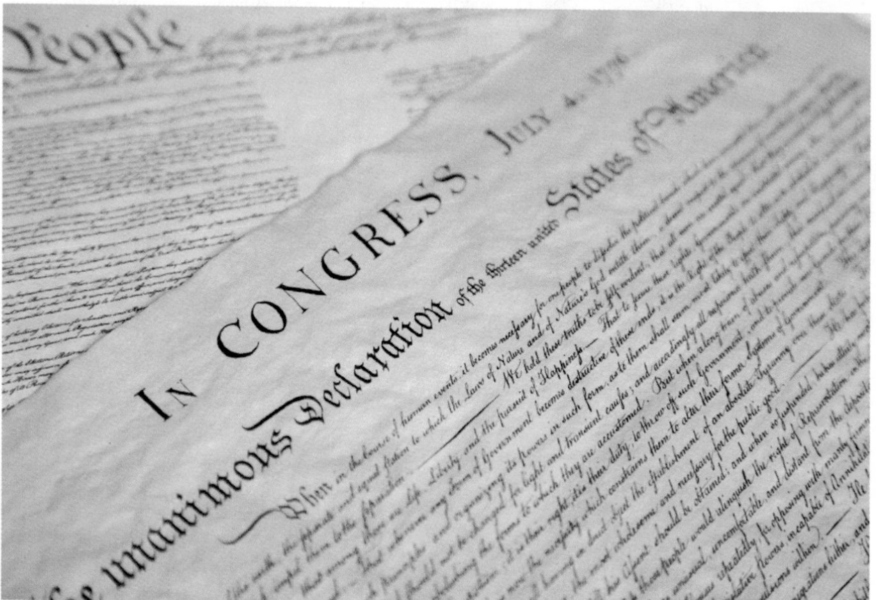

The 1776 Declaration of Independence proclaimed the United States an independent nation and set down the rights of American citizens.

Revolution and resulting founding of the United States not only demonstrated but tested the ideals of the Enlightenment, including its celebration of reason. Some optimistic observers suggested that by following this course, mankind would eventually achieve perfection.

In searching for that perfection, some artists turned to classical antiquity, which symbolized an earlier golden age. This trend is evident in works such as *The Death of Socrates* (1787) and *The Death of Marat* (1793) by the French painter Jacques-Louis David, which also reflected the political backdrop of revolution. The influential German art historian Johann Winckelmann wrote that contemporary artists should imitate the "noble simplicity and silent grandeur" found in Greek statues. In the 1730s and '40s, the rediscovery of the ancient cities of Herculaneum and Pompeii kindled new interest in Roman art. Architects eagerly took up Greek and Roman themes by modeling buildings on ancient temples, using balanced proportions, symmetrical columns, and clean lines. Classical revivals in architecture spread throughout Europe and then to America. The French architects of the Panthéon in Paris (completed in 1790) emulated the façade of the Roman Pantheon constructed in the second century CE. In turn, Thomas Jefferson captured some of its classical balance in several architectural designs, including one for his residence at Monticello.

The Death of Socrates by Jacques-Louis David (1787) represented a return to classical artistic styles while reflecting political themes.

Both (a) the Panthéon in Paris (1790) and (b) Thomas Jefferson's residence at Monticello (1772) echoed the classical balance of the Roman Pantheon (2 CE).

Music historians are divided on how they view the influence of this revival of classical antiquity on eighteenth-century music. Some argue that classicism had little effect on eighteenth-century music, given that composers of the time—unlike poets and architects—could not draw on ancient Greek and Roman models. Others, though, argue that the music of Haydn, Mozart, and the young Beethoven does show characteristics of classical art: poise, formal balance, and delight in beauty. This new emphasis was a reaction against the busy style of the Baroque and reflected the ideas of the Enlightenment.

There is another reason why the term "classical" appropriately describes the music of the latter eighteenth century. In the nineteenth century, composers began to view Haydn's and Mozart's music (and eventually Beethoven's) as timeless works of art that could serve as models, just as ancient artworks had for the eighteenth century. Eventually the new Classical music became the masterpieces that later composers used to measure their own progress and to define their search for independence.

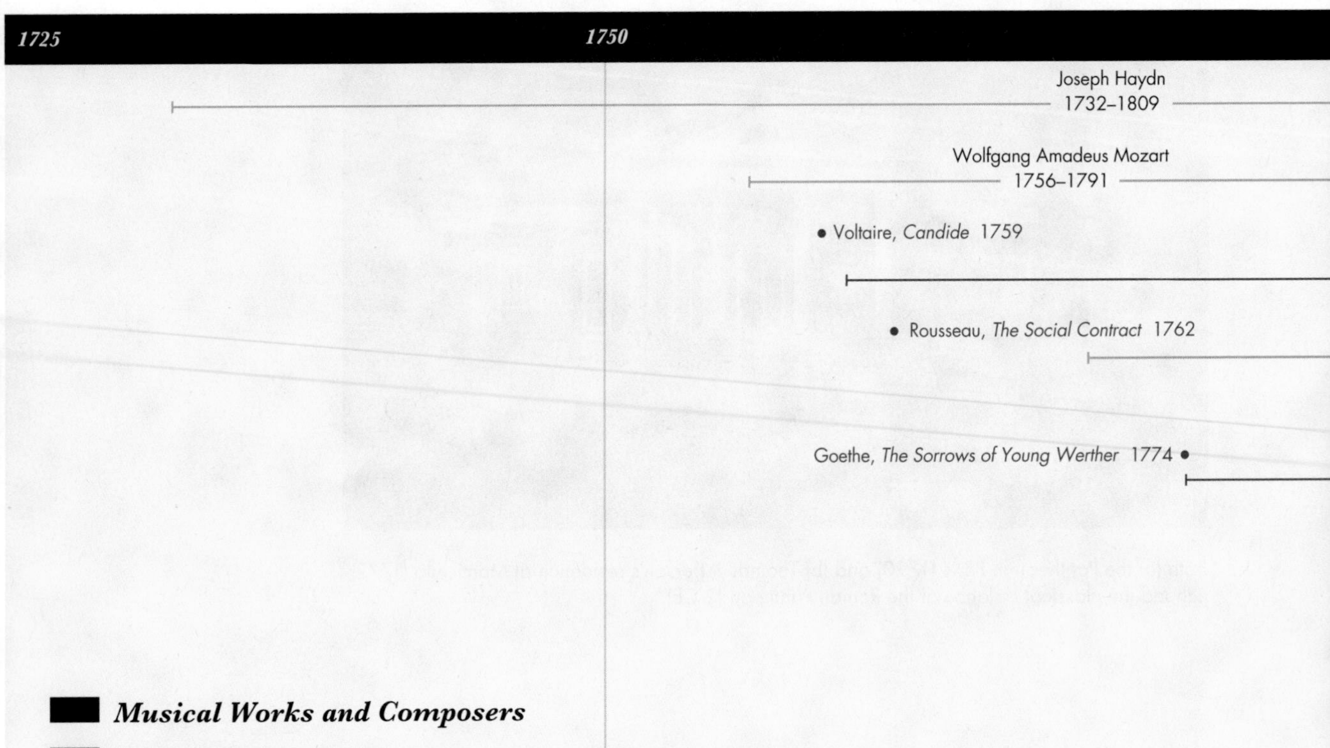

WHY LISTEN TO MUSIC FROM THE *Classical Period?*

Mozart was one of the most remarkable child prodigies of all time, and his music remains a popular symbol of the Classical period. His work is often depicted as nearly perfect, capable of overwhelming listeners with its sheer beauty. Along with his contemporary Haydn, Mozart valued classical features of balance, proportion, and symmetry. This music can offer a deeply moving experience, but it usually conveys emotions within an ordered structure. Although we are far removed from the eighteenth century, we can relate because we often crave order and balance. The compositions of Haydn and Mozart in particular bring us closer to that calming state. Classical music might not improve your IQ or spatial reasoning, despite some claims, but it clearly projects certain truths. It has the power to express emotions within a harmoniously proportioned and structured whole.

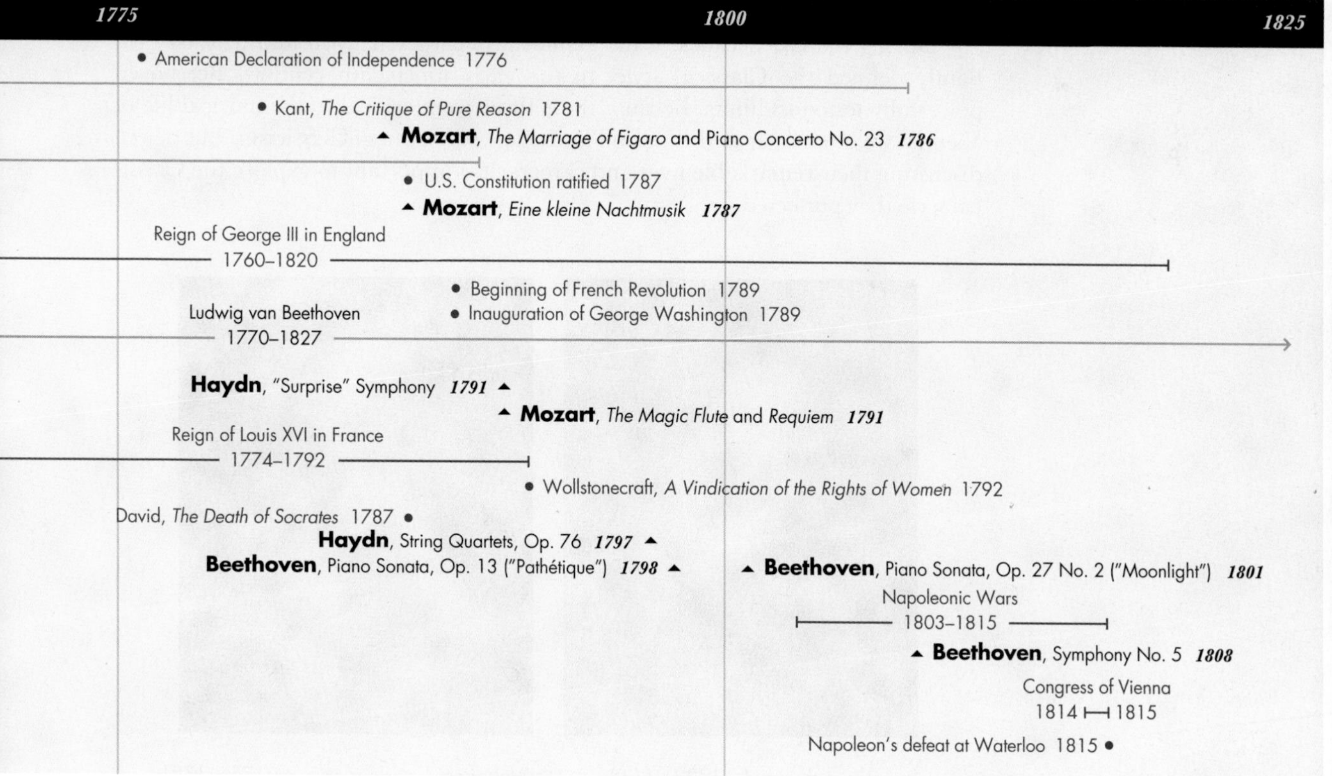

CHAPTER

Music in the Classical Period

The eighteenth-century Classical style was truly international and widely popular throughout Europe. Composers of this period approached melody, dynamics, rhythm, harmony, and texture in distinctive ways to separate their music from that of the Baroque period.

Franz Joseph Haydn (1732–1809) and Wolfgang Amadeus Mozart (1756–1791) were the most influential composers of the new classicism, but other eighteenth-century composers contributed to its style. Two sons of J. S. Bach—Carl Philip Emanuel (1714–1788) and Johann Christian (1735–1783)—were important forerunners of the new classicism, as was Christoph Willibald Gluck (1714–1787), who composed several successful Italian and French operas.

By mid-century, many composers were producing music for a new musical public. Though most composers still depended on royal patronage, public concerts were beginning to thrive in European cities. Music publishers were responding to the new market of musical amateurs within a rising middle class.

During the last decades of the eighteenth century, Haydn and Mozart brilliantly defined the Classical style; in the early nineteenth century, Beethoven powerfully tested its limits. Because these three were critical to the musical life of Vienna, we often refer to this period as the age of Viennese Classicism. But before discussing their remarkable lives and careers, it is important to explore the Classical style they perfected.

Franz Joseph Haydn (1732–1809).

Wolfgang Amadeus Mozart (1756–1791).

Melody in Classical Music

Baroque composers crafted elaborate melodies that ran on with little or no pause. In contrast, Classical composers favored melodies in short, balanced phrases. The opening of a celebrated theme from Haydn's "Surprise" Symphony illustrates this new approach.

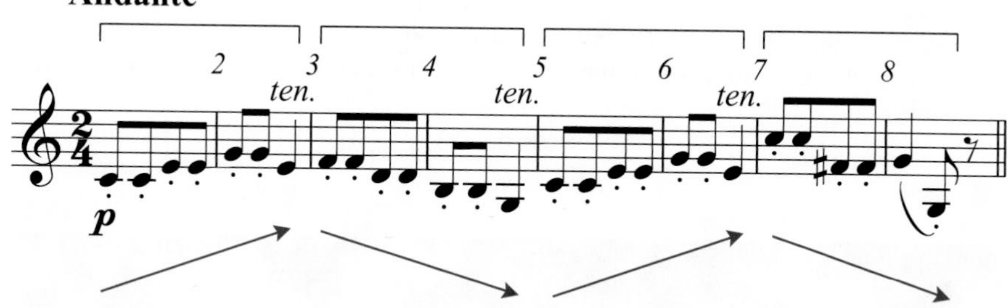

At first, Haydn's theme sounds straightforward. It falls into balanced pairs of measures. The melody ascends in the first two measures and descends in the next two. This pattern is repeated over the next four measures.

Another pattern can be seen in the way Haydn alternates the markings that tell the performers how to play the notes. He uses both **staccato** (detached) markings, shown by the dots below the notes, and **tenuto** (held) markings, shown by "*ten.*" above. The listener hears a series of clipped staccato notes interrupted every other bar by a longer, held note. This first part of the theme is performed at a soft (*piano*) level.

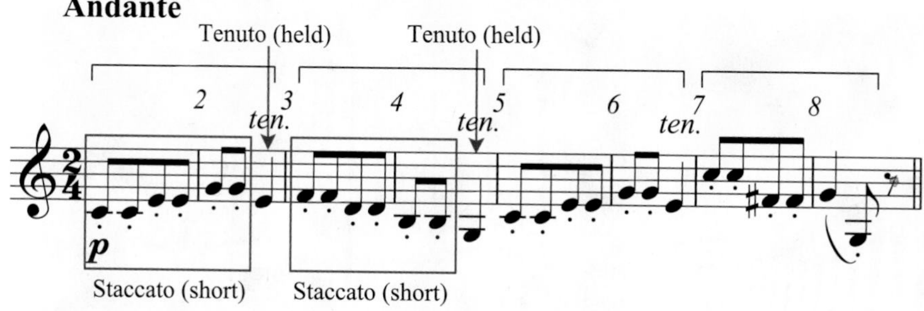

Next, Haydn begins repeating the melody with the dynamics dropped to a hushed *pianissimo*. Nothing disrupts the theme until an unexpected *fortissimo* chord at the end—Haydn's surprise, intended to rouse inattentive audiences.

Haydn's theme is an extreme example of the Classical style. It overstates the melodic symmetry in order to make a musical joke. The final orchestral crash jolts the balance of the theme, which has proceeded in regular, predictable units of two bars each.

MAKING CONNECTIONS *Balance in Neoclassical Art and Architecture*

The balance and symmetry of Classical music resonated with the ideals of the Enlightenment thinkers and their search for models of social and political harmony. That search led to another revival of classical antiquity, sometimes referred to as **neoclassicism**. If the Renaissance had marked the first return to ancient Rome and Greece in art and architecture, the Classical period marked the second. The harmonious geometry in the architecture of antiquity was now seen as reflecting Enlightenment ideals of civic virtue and new political orders. The democracy of ancient Athens and the Republic of ancient Rome were thought to offer alternatives to monarchy, and architecture responded in kind.

In Paris, Napoleon ordered the construction of La Madeleine, modeled on Roman temples, as a "temple of glory" for his victorious armies. In the United States, Thomas Jefferson used neoclassical architecture to celebrate American democracy. And in Berlin and Prague, music and architecture came together in two opera houses with neoclassical designs. At the Estates Theatre in Prague, Mozart premiered his opera *Don Giovanni* in 1787.

La Madeleine, Paris.

Estates Theater, Prague.

Many Classical themes consist of small parts that add up to larger symmetrical groupings. Composers seemed to be counting out the measures and distributing them into phrases that formed neatly balanced musical sentences. That is not exactly what they were doing, however. After all, Haydn inserted the explosive chord in his *Surprise* Symphony to *disrupt* the pattern. Still, many Classical themes do fall into regular, balanced portions, like a question and answer.

Dynamics in Classical Music

Classical composers changed dynamics more frequently than their Baroque predecessors, and they worked with a broader range of levels. About the middle of the eighteenth century, two new types of dynamics came into play: the **crescendo**, a gradual increase in dynamics, and the **decrescendo** (or **diminuendo**), a gradual decrease in dynamics. Classical composers often opened their orchestral music with attention-grabbing crescendos.

Also encouraging the use of gradually changing dynamics was the popularity of a new keyboard instrument, the **fortepiano** (literally, "loud-soft"). The forerunner of the modern piano, the fortepiano could produce fine shades of loud and soft. Firm pressure on the keys produced a loud sound; a more delicate touch, a soft sound. Musicians could easily create dramatic crescendos and diminuendos on the fortepiano. This option added a considerable variety to their music not possible with earlier keyboard instruments, such as the harpsichord.

THE FORTEPIANO

The forerunner of the modern piano was the fortepiano, invented by the Italian instrument maker Bartolomeo Cristofori around 1720. The breakthrough was a mechanism by which pressing the keys caused hammers to strike and rebound from the strings, allowing them to vibrate. Unlike harpsichords, which used a simpler mechanism that plucked the strings to generate an even level of sound, fortepianos had a range of dynamics. Cristofori's invention was slow to be embraced. J. S. Bach encountered some early fortepianos but did not write music specifically for the instrument. However, some of his children did. By the 1760s and 1770s, fortepianos were beginning to rival the older fixture of Baroque music, the harpsichord.

Cristofori fortepiano. This forerunner of the modern piano had a range of dynamics.

For all their novelty, fortepianos were quite different from modern pianos. Fortepianos had smaller ranges (generally about five octaves) and were smaller in size. They had less tension on their strings, which made them quieter than modern pianos. Today's concert grand piano has eighty-eight keys (more than seven octaves) and a reinforced interior iron frame, which accommodates more tension on the strings and allows for greater volume and a more penetrating sound.

Rhythm in Classical Music

Classical composers also separated their music from the Baroque through variety and contrast in their use of rhythm. For comparison, recall the opening of J. S. Bach's Fifth Brandenburg Concerto (see p. 177). The orchestra begins with a theme propelled by a stream of energetic sixteenth notes that is sustained through much of the movement. In contrast, Classical composers used greater rhythmic variety. They might begin a composition with one theme marked by its own rhythmic values, but later explore another theme with a very different rhythm pattern. This emphasis on rhythmic diversity keeps the music fresh and helps satisfy our need for variety in music.

Harmony and Texture in Classical Music

Haydn and Mozart often set their themes against simple chords, creating textures that were easier to follow than the involved designs of Baroque music. Classical composers might break up a chordal passage with some imitative counterpoint, for example. But they mostly reserved counterpoint, such as the fugue, for special purposes. Furthermore, Classical composers changed their harmonies less frequently than Baroque composers, often using just a few simple chords to reinforce the harmonic clarity of their music.

Classical composers also preferred major to minor keys. Haydn wrote over a hundred symphonies, yet only ten of them are in minor keys. Likewise, of Mozart's twenty-four piano concertos, only two are in minor keys. Baroque composers had associated minor keys with strong emotions. Classical composers favored the brighter major keys, perhaps with an ear to the popular demand for music pleasant to play and enjoyable to hear.

check your **KNOWLEDGE**

1. What are the main characteristics of Classical melodies? How are they different from melodies found in earlier styles?
2. What was new in the use of dynamics in the Classical period?
3. How did Classical composers develop the use of rhythm in new ways?
4. Which innovations did Classical composers make in their use of harmony and texture?
5. How did all of these changes reflect the overall approach of Classical composers? Compare this approach to those taken by composers in the Baroque period.

CHAPTER

31 Genres and Forms in Classical Music

Though Classical composers continued to explore musical genres inherited from the Baroque, such as the concerto and opera, they also developed new genres of their own. And they devised new musical forms to use in these new genres, forms that became associated with the Classical period but remained relevant for composers who followed.

New Instrumental Genres

The Classical period produced three new types of instrumental music:

1) the **symphony**, a large-scale work written for orchestra;
2) the **string quartet**, a composition for two violins, one viola, and one cello; and
3) the Classical **sonata**, a piece typically for one or two instruments, usually including a piano.

In the Classical period, symphonies were performed in relatively large venues, including aristocratic courts and concert halls. In contrast, the string quartet emerged in the Classical period as a favored type of chamber music, intended for intimate settings. Derived from Baroque models, Classical sonatas were another type of chamber music that gained popularity in the eighteenth century.

Symphonies, string quartets, and sonatas all feature several separate movements distinguished by their different tempos. A common arrangement is to have three movements in the order *fast–slow–very fast*. By adding a minuet, a stylized dance movement in a moderate tempo, composers extended the sequence to four movements, usually in the order of *fast–slow–minuet–very fast*. Each movement of these instrumental works features its own themes and a distinctive form.

The string quartet emerged as a favored type of chamber music. The artist has depicted Haydn in a light blue top coat, holding the first violin (fifth from the left).

Sonata Form

Sonata form was the most common instrumental form in the Classical period. Before continuing, it is important to distinguish between the terms *sonata* and *sonata form*:

- A *sonata* is an instrumental composition with several movements, for instance, Beethoven's "Moonlight" Sonata for piano in three movements.
- ***Sonata form*** is a specific form used in one or more movements of an instrumental composition, be it a sonata, string quartet, or symphony.

Most frequently, sonata form appears in the first or last movement of a work.

Other than the fugue, which rose to prominence during the Baroque period (see p. 169), sonata form is the most complex form we will encounter in our survey of Western music. But it is arguably the most important and common form used in classical music, at least from the eighteenth century on. What makes it so complex?

To appreciate sonata form, you have to pay attention to the overall structure of a composition (the "big picture") *and* the smaller details occurring within this picture. Part of the challenge lies in understanding these details, such as:

- keys and how they **modulate**, or change from the tonic to other keys;
- musical themes and how they can be similar or different; and
- how themes can be developed, altered, and restored.

Adding to the challenge, there is no such thing as a single "sonata form" just like there is no such thing as a perfect circle. Creative artists will not be bound by *any* set of rules, and composers are no exception. They can take the idea of the sonata form and use it as the basis for their own creative explorations.

In its simplest version, sonata form is broken down into three parts (Figure 31.1):

1) Exposition: the statement of the main themes
2) Development: the development of the main themes
3) Recapitulation: the final return to (or repetition of) the original themes

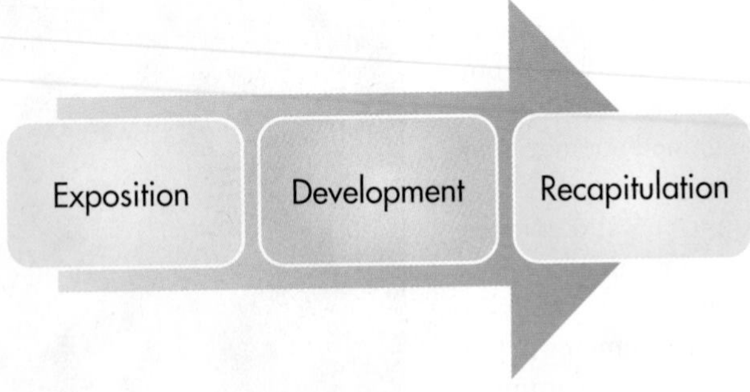

Figure 31.1 A simple representation of sonata form.

We can further break down this organization by examining what occurs in each of these parts. The first part of sonata form is called the **exposition** because it "exposes," or presents, the basic materials of the movement. Within the exposition, there are usually two major themes (or groups of themes). In the second part, the **development**, the composer develops one or more themes introduced in the exposition. Part of our enjoyment comes from marveling at how the composer cleverly reworks these themes in new and interesting ways, perhaps changing their rhythm and pitches, and placing them in a free range of keys. Finally, the third part, the **recapitulation** (or **reprise**), brings a fulfilling sense of closure. The relative freedom of the development gives way to restatements of the major themes and a return to a sense of order. The recapitulation helps close the entire section.

One way to understand sonata form is to compare it to another art form, such as a dramatic play or film. In the first few scenes, we typically meet the principal characters. In sonata form, these characters could correspond loosely to the principal themes of the composition, which are introduced in the exposition. Think of Romeo and Juliet, and imagine a composer representing them through different themes. Eventually some sort of dramatic conflict emerges: they love each other but cannot marry because of their feuding families. In sonata form, the idea of a dramatic conflict corresponds to the contrasting themes and keys presented in the exposition.

As the play continues, the conflict is developed and intensified, and it reaches a critical stage. Both Romeo and Juliet devise plans to overcome the obstacle that keeps them from being together. This process corresponds to the second main part of a sonata, the development, in which the composer develops the themes in various ways, and visits a succession of keys.

Eventually, in the closing scenes of the play, we reach some sense of resolution. This part corresponds to the recapitulation of the sonata, which restores the tonic key and corrects the imbalance of the development. In the tragedy of *Romeo and Juliet*, the resolution is not a happy one, yet it still provides a conclusion to the conflict. In a way, it reaffirms the play's opening message: the impossibility that these two "star-crossed lovers" will live a happy life together.

Juliet and Romeo in the 1968 film. In sonata form, these characters could correspond to the principal themes of the composition.

Keys and themes often seem to inhabit only the paper on which they are notated. But a piece of music can, in effect, "tell" a dramatic story, much like the story of our play. By comparing sonata form to the structure of a drama, we can begin to understand how it achieves its effects.

THE SONATA FORM IN ACTION

As composers worked with the sonata form, they continued to tinker with it to fit their own taste and personalities. One of the first things they did was to expand this three-part form by adding two optional sections: a stately **slow introduction,** which occurred before the exposition and prepared the listener for the rest of the movement, and a **coda** (from the Italian for "tail"), which occurred after the recapitulation and brought the movement to a conclusion (Figure 31.2).

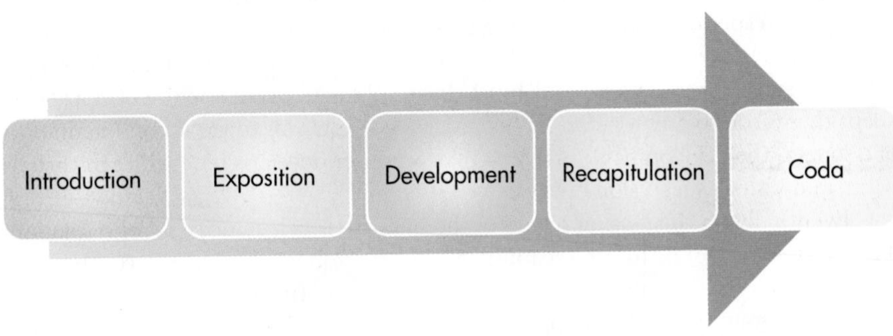

Figure 31.2 The expansion of sonata form to include an introduction and a coda.

At its simplest, the slow introduction consisted of just a few chords or brief portions of themes performed in a slow tempo followed by a pause. The shift to the fast tempo marked the beginning of the exposition. At the other end of the movement, the coda allowed the composer to provide a sense of closure to the music. At its simplest, the coda consisted of a few definitive chords. More elaborate codas could include dramatic excursions before reaching the final, unmistakable return to the tonic. The slow introduction and coda further reinforced the tonal tension and resolution as well as the formal symmetry that are hallmarks of Classical music.

Few composers in the Classical period matched Mozart's genius in applying sonata form. An especially clear example is the first movement of *Eine kleine Nachtmusik* (**Listening Map 23**), one of Mozart's most famous compositions, which has endured in popular culture through its use in films and commercials. Composed in 1787 for a small orchestra of strings, it is a **serenade**, music intended for an outdoor evening performance.

LISTENING MAP 23

MOZART, *Eine kleine Nachtmusik* (*A Little Night Music*), First Movement, Allegro

{1787}

FORM	Ternary sonata form
METER	Common time ($\frac{4}{4}$)
GENRE	Serenade
SCORING	String orchestra
OVERVIEW	The first movement of Mozart's *A Little Night Music* (*Eine kleine Nachtmusik*) perfectly models sonata form. It opens with an exposition consisting of a first, second and closing theme. The development section then elaborates on these themes. Finally, a recapitulation reinstates the original themes, and the piece closes with a brief coda.

why to LISTEN

We do not know why Mozart composed *Eine kleine Nachtmusik*. Presumably he intended the serenade as an evening entertainment for Austrian nobility. While it teaches us about sonata form, the charm of this music lies beyond merely this educational use. As one of Mozart's most popular works, it has found a wide variety of uses in commercials and soundtracks to twentieth-century films such as *Batman* (1989), *There's Something about Mary* (1998), and *Charlie's Angels: Full Throttle* (2003). Stephen Sondheim alluded to it in the title of his 1973 musical *A Little Night Music*, though this title was also inspired by an Ingmar Bergman film.

first LISTEN

EXPOSITION *REPEATED ONCE*	DEVELOPMENT	RECAPITULATION	CODA
0:00	**3:26**	**4:04**	**5:48**
First theme (tonic); bridge (changing keys); second theme (dominant); closing theme (dominant)	First theme (dominant) developed; modulations in key based on closing theme; brief turn to minor key before returning to tonic	Retraces 1-bridge-2-closing theme, now all in the tonic key	Short, ***f*** passage to conclude

Continued

a deeper LISTEN

TIME	SECTION	LISTEN FOR THIS
0:00	Exposition	**First Theme (tonic key)** Broken into three sections
		First Section ***f*** figure, entire orchestra 
0:10		**Second Section** Violins continue the melody 
0:21		**Third Section** Slower, ***p*** figure in the violins 
0:35		**Bridge (changing key)** Rising line in the violins, crescendo to *forte* leading to the second key; brief pause
0:53		**Second Theme (dominant key)** Graceful new theme in violins 
1:07		**Closing Theme (dominant key)** Texture thickens, dynamic level increases to *forte*, then drops to ***p*** New theme in violins 

TIME	SECTION	LISTEN FOR THIS
1:44	(Exposition repeated)	
3:26	Development	Opening measures of exposition restated in the dominant, then a series of modulations featuring the closing theme Brief turn to the minor, before the tonic key is announced
4:04	Recapitulation	Retraces the main events of the exposition while maintaining the tonic key
5:48	Coda	Short, *forte* passage with energetic figure in violins

Theme and Variations Form

Considerably easier to follow than sonata form is **theme and variations** form. It is often used in slow movements of Classical instrumental pieces. Unlike the first movement of *Eine kleine Nachtmusik*, which has several different themes, movements in theme and variations form generally focus on only one theme, the basis of the movement. It is heard at the beginning of the movement and then undergoes changes through a series of variations.

The slow movement of Haydn's "Surprise" Symphony provides an example of how a composer can vary his theme using this form (**Listening Map 24**). It begins with a theme in C major (①), followed by four variations and a coda.

Minuet and Trio

The **minuet and trio** was an aristocratic Baroque dance style made fashionable at the seventeenth-century French court of Louis XIV, where the so-called Sun King prided himself on his dancing abilities.

The word *minuet* may be derived from the French *menu*, meaning "small" or "slender," a reference to the small, graceful steps of the dance. Minuets were in a moderate tempo with triple ($\frac{3}{4}$) meter. During the eighteenth century, composers wrote minuets for dancing, but also used the form for their instrumental compositions, where they usually inserted it as the third of four movements. By mid-century, minuets were appearing in symphonies, string quartets, and sonatas—not for dancing, but for musical enjoyment.

There were two major sections in the Classical minuet: the minuet proper (*A*) and the trio (*B*) (Figure 31.3). The trio was nothing more than a second minuet. Its mood contrasted with that of the minuet proper, and often its key differed as well.

LISTENING MAP 24

HAYDN, Symphony No. 94 in G major ("Surprise"), Second Movement (Andante)

{1791}

FORM	Theme and variations
METER	Duple meter ($\frac{2}{4}$)
SCORING	Classical orchestra (winds, brass, timpani, and strings)
OVERVIEW	Haydn's celebrated movement contains a theme, four variations, and a coda. The theme, a deceptively simple melody, sets up an unexpected surprise midway. In the variations the composer alters different aspects of the theme—its melodic figurations, key, instruments that play the theme—to construct a movement that is at once dramatic, suspenseful, and mysterious.

first LISTEN

THEME	VARIATION 1	VARIATION 2	VARIATION 3	VARIATION 4	CODA
0:00	0:57	1:54	2:55	3:52	4:58
Tonic; two parts	Theme played by two violins	Theme in C minor	Returns to major; solos for oboe, then flute and oboe together	Full orchestra	Suspenseful chord announces the coda

a deeper LISTEN

TIME	SECTION	LISTEN FOR THIS
0:00	(1) **Theme (see p. 215):** (tonic major); two sections, each repeated	First section, C major: performed ***p***, then *repeated* ***pp*** with a *surprise* ***ff*** chord at the end Second section: performed ***p*** and repeated
0:57	**Variation 1**	The theme is clearly stated by the second violins. Haydn adds a faster moving part played by the first violins above it.
1:54	**Variation 2**	C minor, much of it played at a *forte* or *fortissimo* level. A moment of high drama with sweeping scales and stately rhythms, this variation transports us away from the simple theme that began the movement.

TIME	SECTION	LISTEN FOR THIS
2:55	Variation 3	Following a brief transition in the violins, the piece returns to C major. This variation features solos for the oboe and then flute and oboe together, as the violins play the theme below the soloists.
3:52	Variation 4	For the entire orchestra: The violins play running sets of notes while the winds and brass maintain the basic shape of the theme.
4:58	Coda	The orchestra pauses on a suspenseful chord, announcing the coda. The volume drops from ***ff*** to ***p*** and then to a hushed ***pp***. The opening bars of the theme are played quietly by the winds against subdued chords in the strings, like a fleeting memory of the melody.

After the trio, the original minuet was played again. The entire minuet thus assumed a three-part form: *minuet-trio-minuet* or *ABA*. Each section in turn was divided into three smaller sections, a-b-a′ for the minuet, and c-d-c′, with new music, for the trio. Finally, the smaller sections were fitted into a binary arrangement through the use of repeat signs: ‖: a :‖ ‖: b a′ :‖ and ‖: c :‖ ‖: d c′ :‖ (or, a a b a′ b a′, and c c d c′ d c′. Usually, the second performance of *A* occurred without the internal repeats.

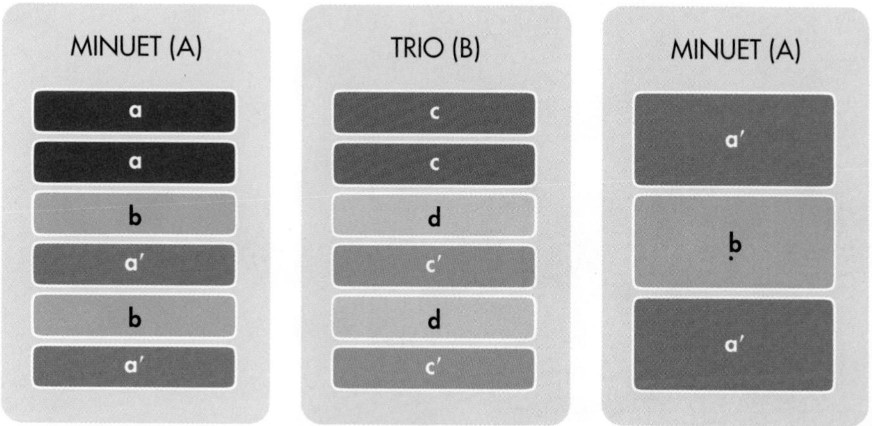

Figure 31.3 Form of the Classical minuet.

There is no better example of a concise minuet than the third movement of Mozart's *Eine kleine Nachtmusik*, which is a model of Classical symmetry (**Listening Map** 25).

MAKING CONNECTIONS *The Rise of the Minuet*

Louis XIV (see p. 149) was a monarch who took dancing rather seriously. He promoted ballets at his court of Versailles, surrounded himself with skilled dancers, and participated in dance spectacles. At one he appeared dressed as Apollo, the god of light, and afterward became known as the Sun King. Among Louis's favorite dances was the minuet, in which a couple performed small, elegant steps in an *S* or *Z* pattern.

Minuets became such a fixture of European court life that they started to be played as concert music. In the eighteenth century J. S. Bach included them in his dance suites, and they were heavily used by Classical composers. Haydn and Mozart wrote hundreds of minuets. Of Haydn's 104 symphonies, 96 have minuets, and Mozart even interrupted the finale of one of his piano concertos with an elegant minuet. But by the nineteenth century, the dance began falling out of fashion. As evidence of its decline in popularity, only two of Beethoven's nine symphonies have movements specified as minuets.

An eighteenth-century couple dancing a minuet depicted in a fresco by Giovanni Domenico Tiepolo, c. 1791.

LISTENING MAP 25

MOZART, *Eine kleine Nachtmusik*, K. 525, Third Movement (Allegretto)

{1787}

FORM	Minuet and trio
METER	Triple meter ($\frac{3}{4}$)
SCORING	String orchestra (first violins, second violins, violas, cellos, optional double basses)
OVERVIEW	Mozart's graceful minuet falls into clear phrases. The first part, A (①) is differentiated by dynamics (*forte*, *piano*, and *forte*) and performance styles (detached staccato and smooth legato). The contrasting trio, B, introduces a new key and theme (②), performed primarily legato, but also using contrasts in dynamics (now ***p***, ***f***, and ***p***). Finally, the piece concludes by returning to the original first part, A (③).

why to LISTEN

Minuets reached the height of their popularity as social dances during the eighteenth century. The courtly dances were performed at a moderate tempo and entertaining to watch. The music accompanying the dance typically offers hummable melodies and softly swaying rhythms.

Haydn and Mozart lavished great care upon their minuets. A fixture of aristocratic life, the minuet eventually came out of European courts into the broader musical culture. In particular Haydn might begin a minuet with elegant dance music, only to introduce in the trio a second dance that sounded like a folk song. His minuets wittily probed the lines separating Classical art music from the popular music of his day.

first LISTEN

MINUET (A)	TRIO (B)	MINUET (A)
0:00	**0:47**	**1:49**
(*a*): ***f***, staccato (*a*) repeated (*b*): ***p***, legato (*b*) and (*a*) repeated	(*c*): ***p***, legato (*c*) repeated (*d*): ***f*** (*c'*): ***p*** (*d*) and (*c'*) repeated	(*a*): ***f***, staccato (*a*) repeated (*b*): ***p***, legato (*b*) and (*a*) repeated

Continued

 *a deeper* **LISTEN**

TIME	SECTION	LISTEN FOR THIS
0:00	Minuet (A)	① The main (*a*) theme in violins, ***f***, with staccato pitches
0:12:		(*a*) repeated (*b*): ***p***, marked by smooth legato motion: modified return to (*a*), ***f*** (*b*) and (*a′*) repeated
0:47	Trio (B)	② The contrasting (*c*) melody: new theme in a new key, ***p***, legato
		(*c*) repeated (*d*): ***f*** (*c′*): ***p*** (*d*) and (*c′*) repeated
1:49	Minuet (A)	③ Return of the main (*a*) melody

Rondo Form

The **rondo** (literally "round") is a form based around a main theme that is periodically repeated throughout the movement. A rondo most frequently appears as the last movement of an instrumental work. This main theme is known as the **refrain** and is set in the tonic key. Other contrasting sections, known as **episodes**, introduce new keys and themes.

Composers devised different plans for their rondos. Sometimes they simply alternated the refrain (*A*) with a single episode (*B*) according to the plan *ABABA* (Figure 31.4).

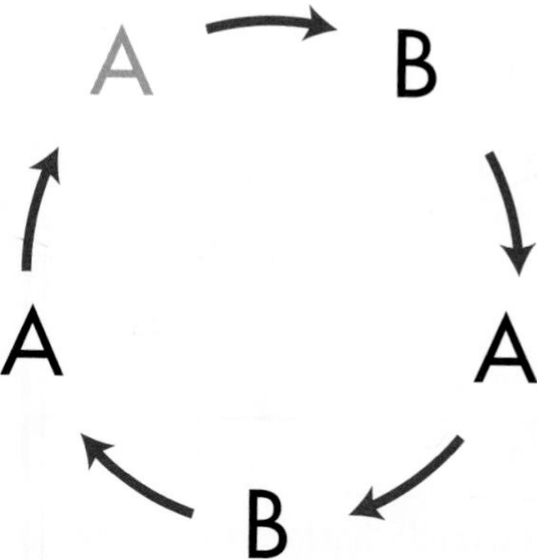

Figure 31.4 Simple rondo form.

Sometimes they devised more complex plans, such as this one, alternating between four refrains and three episodes (*B* and *C*) (Figure 31.5).

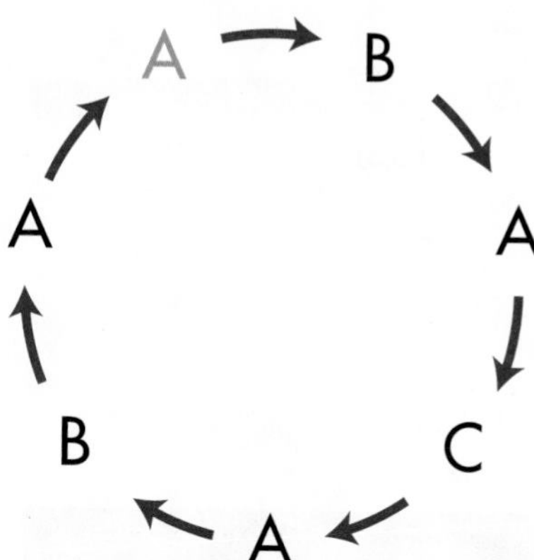

Figure 31.5 More complex rondo form.

This second plan offered Classical composers a symmetrical design—it traced the same sequence of events forward and backward—while also creating variety.

Haydn and Mozart generally composed their rondos in a lighter, more popular style than the "serious" movements in sonata form. But a rondo could offer high drama of its own, as in the last movement of Beethoven's "Pathétique" Sonata in C minor, Op. 13, composed in 1798 for piano (**Listening Map 26**).

LISTENING MAP 26

BEETHOVEN, Piano Sonata in C minor, Op. 13 ("Pathétique"), Third Movement (Allegro)

{1798}

FORM	Rondo
METER	$\frac{2}{2}$ or ¢
SCORING	Solo piano
OVERVIEW	The last movement of Beethoven's "Pathétique" Sonata is a rondo that falls into a symmetrical seven-part form: ABACABA. There are four statements of the opening refrain (A), an episode (B) that returns late in the movement, and another episode (C), that forms the midpoint of the movement. A, B, and C use differently profiled themes.

first LISTEN

A	B	A	C	A	B	A	CODA
0:00	0:29	1:14	1:35	2:29	2:46	3:31	4:11
Arched melody; tonic minor key	Lyrical theme; major key; lyrical theme		Slower, longer notes; major key				

a deeper LISTEN

TIME	SECTION	LISTEN FOR THIS
0:00	A Refrain (tonic minor)	First part of main theme pauses on a high note; second part pushes theme one pitch higher before gradually falling downward; modulates to new key

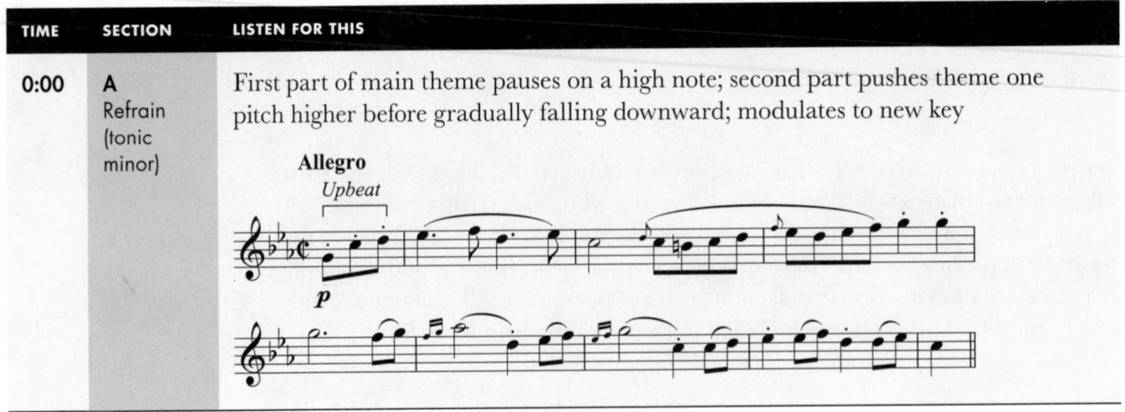

TIME	SECTION	LISTEN FOR THIS
0:29	**B** First episode (new major key)	Lyrical theme, dolce (sweetly); dramatic passages with cascading scale and pause  *dolce*
1:14	**A** Refrain (tonic minor)	Refrain theme  **Allegro** *Upbeat* ***p***
1:35	**C** Second episode (new major key)	Dramatic passages with cascading scale and pause; slower note values  ***p***
2:29	**A** Refrain (tonic minor)	
2:46	**B** First episode (tonic major)	
3:31	**A** Refrain (tonic minor)	
4:11	**Coda** (tonic minor)	

check your KNOWLEDGE

1. What are the three new instrumental forms that were introduced during the Classical period?
2. What is the difference between a sonata and sonata form?
3. What is the difference between the exposition, development, and recapitulation in ternary sonata form?
4. Define theme and variations. How is it different from sonata form?
5. How was minuet and trio form used by Classical composers?
6. How was rondo form used by Classical composers?

CHAPTER

32 Joseph Haydn

Understanding Haydn's music is essential to understanding the Classical style.

Of all the eighteenth-century Classical composers, the Austrian Joseph Haydn (1732–1809) enjoyed the widest international acclaim. His vast catalogue of music includes over 100 symphonies. There are nearly seventy string quartets, a genre he was the first to perfect. He also wrote hundreds of other chamber works, dozens of concertos, and sixty-odd keyboard sonatas, composed first for harpsichord and then for piano when it became fashionable. Haydn's vocal music includes operas, oratorios, and a large body of sacred music.

So celebrated was Haydn's music that dishonest publishers sold imitations of his work by lesser composers under his name. His music was widely performed in many countries, and his symphonies reached the American colonies. He received commissions from France, Spain, and Italy. All the while, his compositions were being regularly performed in Vienna, London, and Paris.

During his long life, Haydn witnessed significant changes in music. As a boy, he was familiar with Baroque music, which by the time he came of age had given way to a lighter style. During the 1770s, '80s, and '90s, he played a major role in shaping the Classical style. And by the time he died, much of Beethoven's revolutionary new music had been completed. Because Haydn's life and music sweeps across this spectrum of styles, understanding his music is essential to understanding the Classical style.

Haydn's Life and Music

Haydn was born in the southeastern part of Austria, near Hungary. As a child, he sang in the choir of St. Stephen's Cathedral in Vienna. In composition, he was largely self-taught. He pored over the latest keyboard music of Carl Philipp Emanuel Bach, but seems to have known none of the music of his father, Johann Sebastian Bach.

In 1761 Haydn gained a position at the court of Prince Paul Anton Esterházy, the head of an aristocratic Hungarian family. We learn much about Haydn's responsibilities—and those of court composers in general—from his contract with the prince. The prince expected Haydn to appear on command with his musicians, all wearing wigs, special uniforms, and white stockings. He composed music as the prince desired and for the prince's exclusive use. Haydn also served as librarian for the court orchestra and curator of the musical instruments, and he instructed the leisured ladies of the court in singing. In return, he received a salary and meals at the officers' table.

Prince Paul Anton was succeeded in 1762 by his brother, Nicholas "the Magnificent." In what is now Hungary, the new prince built a splendid palace called Esterháza. It boasted an ornate opera house, a marionette theater, a game preserve, and fountains. Designed to rival the magnificence of Versailles near Paris, the palace contained well over 100 rooms.

Haydn served Prince Nicholas for nearly thirty years. During that long employment, the composer worked steadily on symphonies, string quartets, and operas. Though slow at

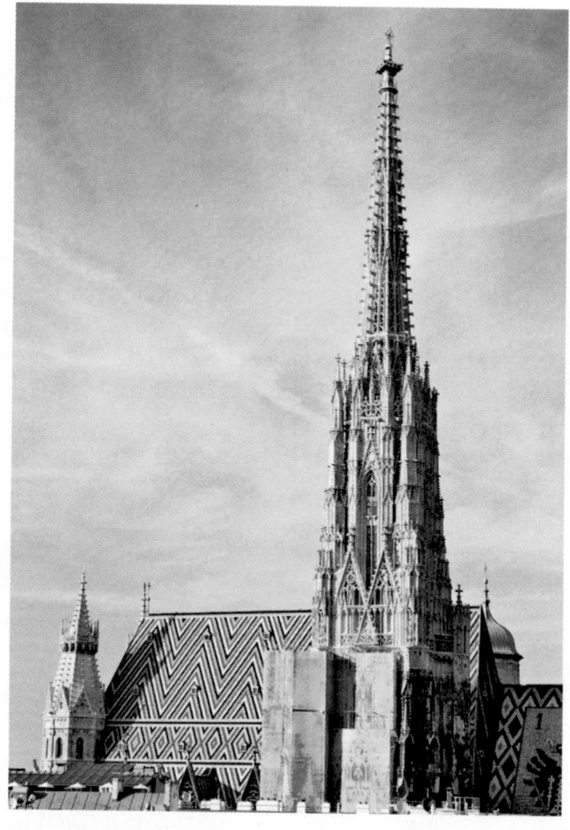

St. Stephen's Cathedral in Vienna, where the young Haydn sang in the choir.

Esterháza Palace, in what is now Hungary, where Haydn worked for nearly thirty years.

MAKING CONNECTIONS *The Esterházys and Haydn*

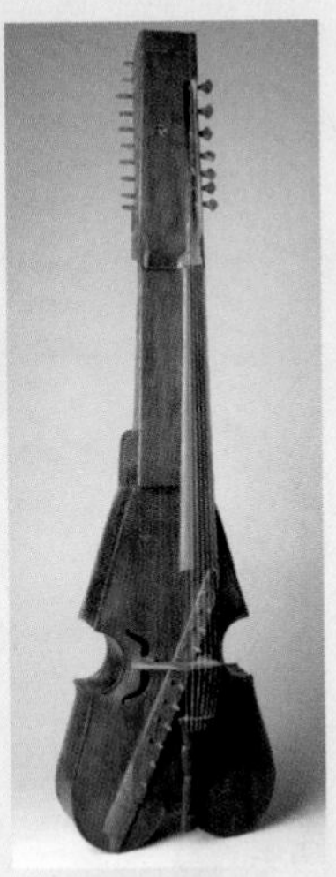

Baryton.

The Esterházys were a noble Hungarian family that had gained enormous wealth during the fifteenth century, eventually becoming the largest landowners in Hungary. Fiercely loyal to the Hapsburg emperors of Austria, they helped end the Turkish siege of Vienna in 1683. They were also dedicated patrons of the arts. Haydn served three Esterházy princes between 1761 and 1790. The second, Nicholas the Magnificent, was Haydn's principal patron and a serious musician as well. His preferred instrument was a little-known string instrument called the baryton. Played with a bow, it resembled a cello but had several more strings, including some that resonated freely from its back. Haydn wrote hundreds of chamber works on command that featured the baryton, all the property of, and in homage to, Nicholas.

first to develop his craft, within a few years of joining the Esterházy court Haydn was producing symphonies of remarkable variety and freshness. He wrote symphonies in three and four movements, symphonies that borrowed from Baroque genres, and symphonies that ended with fugues—in short, he tried one approach after another as he searched for his individual style.

In the late 1760s, Haydn began composing music in a heightened, serious style, marked by sudden dramatic changes in texture and dynamics, wide leaps in melodic lines, and abrupt pauses. Several works were in minor keys, which was unusual for the time. The most remarkable composition of this period is the "Farewell" Symphony (No. 45) of 1772, a unique work with a special purpose. Isolated at Esterháza, Haydn's musicians had been away from their families for a long time and were eager to obtain leave to return home. In response, Haydn used the symphony's last movement to petition the prince. What began as an energetic movement unexpectedly ground to a halt and gave way to an additional slow movement. Here, one by one, the instrumental parts began to drop out as the musicians symbolically bade farewell, leaving just two violins to complete the symphony with delicate, barely audible chords. The prince got the message and granted the musicians their leave the very next day.

Haydn once joked that the isolation of Esterháza forced him to become original. Still, his label as the father of the symphony is not accurate. By the time he began writing symphonies two basic types were already common:

- The Italian symphony was in three movements, in the sequence of *fast–slow–fast.*
- The Austrian/German symphony was in four movements, of which the second or third was typically a minuet and trio.

Haydn experimented with both types and eventually adopted the four-movement symphony as his favorite.

By the 1770s, Haydn's reputation was spreading through Europe. The Empress Maria Theresa remarked that in order to enjoy good opera she had to leave Vienna and journey to Esterháza. There she could also hear Haydn's latest symphonies, musical dramas that worked out their conflicts within the orchestra instead of on the stage.

Within a few years, Haydn began to reject the highly charged character of works such as the "Farewell" Symphony. Later in the decade, he began accepting commissions and releasing his music to publishers in Austria and abroad. In the mid-1780s Haydn was asked to write six symphonies for a concert series in Paris (the Paris symphonies, Nos. 82–87). Haydn was fully freed from his obligations to the Esterházy court when Prince Nicholas died in 1790. He now became a celebrity among composers, writing music for public consumption. Johann Peter Salomon, an enterprising violinist, visited Haydn in Vienna and persuaded him to compose music for public concerts in London. Haydn's freedom allowed him to make two trips to England, where he won acclaim in the press, received an honorary doctorate from Oxford University, and had audiences with King George III. The fruits of his visits to England were the twelve grand London symphonies (Nos. 93–104), the culmination of his symphonic style.

Haydn spent his last years in Vienna. Impressed by Handel's oratorios in England, Haydn composed two masterful works, *The Creation* and *The Seasons*. He premiered these in Vienna at the turn of the nineteenth century. He also finished a series of six Masses for soloists, chorus, and orchestra. These powerful compositions joined the rich traditions of sacred polyphony with the elaborate forms of the Classical symphony.

MAKING CONNECTIONS *Haydn in England*

By 1791, when Haydn arrived in England to premiere the first of his *London* Symphonies, he was an international celebrity whose music was being performed throughout Europe, as well as in Russia and the United States. Haydn's twelve *London* Symphonies were enthusiastically received by Londoners, and he was embraced as the "Shakespeare of music." Carefully playing upon his audience's expectations, Haydn offered symphonies filled with unexpected surprises, theatrical gestures, and quickly changing moods. Like Shakespeare, the composer combined moments of high tragedy with moments of comic relief. He also included full measures of irony, wit, and humor, all in a style that transcended national borders.

Hanover Square Rooms for concerts, London.

Although the Latin texts of these Masses were many centuries old, Haydn connected them to contemporary events. He used the titles *Mass in Time of War* and *Mass in Times of Great Need* because much of Europe was at war with Napoleon's advancing armies. Haydn's final days coincided with the occupation of Vienna by Napoleon's troops in 1809. In respect, a French honor guard was posted at his house. When Haydn died, the Requiem Mass composed by his great contemporary and friend, Mozart, was performed at the memorial service.

Haydn and the Classical Orchestra

Haydn's orchestras were much smaller than the orchestras we know today. The heart of the ensemble was the string section—first violins, second violins, violas, cellos, and double bass. Typically, the first violins carried the theme and the cellos and double bass played the bass line. The second violins and violas filled the gap between theme and bass line with chords or other material. To provide different instrumental colors, Haydn added a small number of woodwind and brass instruments, often just two oboes and two French horns. Oboes could carry melodic lines themselves or double the first violin part. Or the oboes could join the French horns to play harmonies to support the busy string section. For an especially festive symphony, Haydn would enlarge the orchestra by adding two trumpets and two timpani as well as more woodwinds, such as a flute or bassoon. At Esterháza, he directed an ensemble of about twenty to twenty-five musicians. An orchestra this size was much closer to the ensembles used by J. S. Bach than to a modern orchestra of about 100 musicians.

Eighteenth-century orchestras were not directed by a conductor standing on a podium with a baton. Usually, the leader of the first violin section gave the musicians their cues. Haydn himself participated from a harpsichord, playing the bass line with his left hand and improvising chords with his right (a throwback to Baroque continuo practice; see Chapter 19).

The large scale of Haydn's late symphonies led to the expansion of the Classical orchestra. In London, Haydn wrote for an orchestra of some forty musicians. Along with two oboes, the London symphonies require paired flutes and bassoons as standard members of the woodwind section. Some of these symphonies also require two clarinets. Haydn enlarged the brass section by regularly adding two trumpets to the two horns, and he routinely wrote parts for two timpani.

Haydn's late symphonies also reorganized the lower range of the string section by separating the cellos from the double basses. The double basses continued to play the bass line, but the cellos became increasingly independent. Haydn was now writing for a five-part string ensemble instead of for the four-part ensemble of his earlier symphonies. Table 32.1 summarizes the Classical orchestra used by Haydn, Mozart, Beethoven, and other early nineteenth-century composers.

Haydn's late symphonies were designed to respond to the tastes of his public audiences. He delighted the new concertgoers with seductive dance rhythms, charming tunes, and all sorts of special effects. The popular "Surprise" Symphony is titled after the celebrated *fortissimo* chord in the slow movement (see p. 216). But, like other late symphonies, the "Surprise" entertains the listener with many other unpredictable twists and turns—it is, in effect, a symphony of surprises. Its last

TABLE 32.1 The High Classical Orchestra (ca. 1790)

Woodwinds	Two flutes Two oboes Two clarinets Two bassoons
Brass	Two horns Two trumpets
Percussion	Two timpani
Strings (several per part)	Violin I Violin II Viola Cello Double bass
Harpsichord (used as continuo instrument)	

Dashboard

Watch demonstration videos of the instruments of the orchestra.

movement ingeniously solves a problem of form by combining elements of sonata form and rondo, yielding a highly entertaining hybrid of the two. In the process, he trips up the listener's musical expectations as well (**Listening Map 27**).

The movement begins with a catchy soft theme (*A*) in the violins in a major key (①). The theme divides into two portions. Haydn repeats the first portion, giving the overall theme a miniature binary structure, *a a b*. Marked by a distinctive opening two-note segment and always performed ***p***, this theme functions throughout the movement as a refrain. At the conclusion of this theme, Haydn launches into a vigorous *forte* passage. Rapid sweeping runs in the violins modulate from the tonic to a second key. After this passage ends with a bar of rest, he introduces a new compact theme in the second key. Performed ***p***, this new theme represents the *B* section, or first episode in a rondo form (②). Another busy passage for full orchestra ranging from *fortissimo* to *pianissimo* brings us back to the tonic key and the refrain (*A*).

So far, the movement proceeds like a rondo, with three clear sections in the order *A B A*. But now Haydn departs from the expected course. First, he shortens the second statement of *A*. Then, instead of treating the next section, *C*, as a second episode with its own theme, he writes an extended section based on the first theme. This extended section is performed *forte* and filled with animated passages for the strings. This "new" section modulates unpredictably like the development section of a sonata form, making it seem as if the rondo form has been left behind. *A* then returns in the tonic key, momentarily tipping the balance toward the rondo form, but the energetic modulations resume as Haydn develops his opening theme in the minor instead of major mode. After this dramatic center of the movement quiets down, Haydn brings back the refrain (*A*) and first episode (*B*) in the tonic, restoring the normal order of events in a rondo.

The last statement of *A* turns into a brief coda with surprises of its own, including a dramatic timpani roll. The final measures forcefully assert the tonic, but in one final surprise, Haydn writes two ***p*** chords in the winds before two decisive ***ff*** chords for the whole orchestra. These dynamic jolts trigger memories of the orchestral crash in the slow movement (see p. 216), further enhancing our delight at being surprised.

LISTENING MAP 27

HAYDN, Symphony No. 94 in G major ("Surprise"), Fourth Movement (Allegro Molto)

{1791}

FORM	Hybrid of rondo and sonata form
METER	$\frac{2}{4}$
SCORING	Classical orchestra (winds, brass, timpani, and strings)
OVERVIEW	The fourth movement of Haydn's "Surprise" Symphony begins as a rondo with a refrain (A), episode (B), and refrain (A). The music then departs in a section that sounds more like the development of a sonata form (C). When the refrain inevitably comes back, the movement once again resembles a rondo.

why to LISTEN

Haydn was a master of using surprise, wit, and humor in his music. The Classical style that he developed and perfected generally emphasized grace, symmetry, and orderly design, but the composer was also capable of disrupting his listeners' expectations in a way that added to their enjoyment. The finale of the *Surprise* Symphony is a case in point. Here Haydn deliberately blurs the formal outlines of the music. Is it a rondo? Is it in sonata form? The music fits now into one form, and now into the other, encouraging us to guess about how the movement will end. The symphony is designed to keep us on edge and to explore how music can surprise us with the unexpected.

first LISTEN

RONDO-LIKE FORM	SONATA-LIKE DEVELOPMENT	RONDO-LIKE FORM
0:00	**1:42**	**2:46**
A-B-A themes seem to follow a rondo-like form.	New development section introduced, breaking out of the rondo-like introduction (C-A-C)	Return to the original form (ABA coda).

a deeper LISTEN

TIME	FORM	SECTION	LISTEN FOR THIS
0:00	Rondo-like form	A	(1) Refrain in tonic in miniature binary form: 𝄆 𝄇 ‖ First portion in violins, ***p*** (repeated in violins with flute) Second portion **Allegro di molto**
0:35		Transition	Rapid ***f*** passages in violins, modulating; measure of rest
1:08		B	(2) Episode with new theme, ***p***, in second key
1:19		Transition	Rapid ***f*** passages in violins, then ***ff*** chords, dropping to ***p*** and ***pp***
1:35		A	Abridged statement of refrain in tonic, ***p***
1:42	Sonata-like development	C	Like a development section of sonata form, modulating with ***f*** passages
2:13		A	Abridged statement of refrain in tonic, ***p***
2:20		C	Resumption of development-like section with *A* treated in the minor mode ***f*** and ***ff***, then diminuendo
2:46	Rondo-like form	A	Refrain in the tonic major
3:03		Transition	Rapid ***f*** passages in violins; measure of rest
3:11		B	Episode with second theme, ***p***, in tonic key; brief ***f*** transition
3:27		A (Coda)	Refrain (modified) in the tonic key in the winds, ***p***, against a timpani roll and dramatic crescendo Feigned modulation, return to the tonic key; rapid passages, ***ff*** chords, then two ***p*** chords in the winds, and two ***ff*** chords for the entire orchestra

Haydn and the String Quartet

Along with his symphonies, Haydn is remembered for the string quartets that span his long career. He was the first master of this new genre, combining its instruments in a great variety of ways. In his quartets, the first violin might play the melody accompanied by the second violin, viola, and cello, or the ensemble might divide into two pairs of instruments. In yet another arrangement, the four instruments might engage as equal partners in imitative counterpoint. Haydn's mature quartets realized the full potential of the ensemble. The poet Goethe's comparison of a string quartet to a conversation among four equals is an apt description of Haydn's mature quartets, in which all four musicians often participate in a rich exchange of material.

During the 1780s, Haydn had the opportunity in Vienna to play through quartets with his considerably younger friend Mozart. Haydn would take the first violin part, and Mozart, the viola part. No doubt these casual performances prompted animated discussions about the music by these two equals.

The six quartets of Opus 76, composed in 1797, mark the summit of Haydn's achievement in this genre. The third quartet, known as the "Emperor," is in four movements, like most string quartets. The first and fourth movements are in sonata form, the second consists of a theme and four variations, and the third is a minuet and trio. The second movement is constructed upon one of Haydn's most celebrated themes (see **Listening Map 28**).

Haydn originally composed the theme of the second movement for a hymn marking the birthday of the Austrian emperor Francis II, in 1797. The composer then reused the theme without its text for the slow movement of his "Emperor" quartet. The theme consists of three phrases: *a*, *b*, and *c*. Phrases *a* and *c* are repeated so that the overall shape is *aabcc* (1).

In each of the four variations that follow, the entire theme appears in one instrument while other instruments accompany it. Haydn thus keeps the emperor's theme intact but surrounds it with varied textures, rhythms, registers, and accompaniments. Initially, the theme is entrusted to the first violin. In the variations, it moves to the second violin, cello, and viola, before returning to the first violin. The theme itself and the fourth variation are scored in a homophonic texture for the full ensemble. Variation 1 uses only two instruments, and variations 2 and 3 require, for the most part, three instruments.

Rhythmically, the first variation has an active part for the first violin; the second and third variations flow along in slower notes; and the fourth variation (like the theme itself) moves mostly in even notes. Toward the end, the fourth variation shifts to a high range, setting it off from the earlier variations. Haydn never departs from the tonic key, and he limits his dynamics to soft levels for the length of this exquisite movement.

Austrian emperor Francis II.

LISTENING MAP 28

HAYDN, String Quartet in G major, Op. 76 No. 3 ("Emperor"), Second Movement (Poco adagio, cantabile)

{1797}

FORM	Theme and four variations
METER	Duple ($\frac{2}{2}$)
SCORING	First violin, second violin, viola, cello
OVERVIEW	The second movement of Haydn's "Emperor" string quartet uses a theme that the composer originally wrote for the birthday of the Austrian emperor. The theme is initially presented by the first violin, the leader of the quartet. In the following four variations, the theme then moves through all four instruments, in the order of second violin, cello, viola, and (again) the first violin. The other instruments present varied material against the theme.

why to LISTEN

Great melodies are always memorable, and the theme of the slow movement to Haydn's "Emperor" string quartet is no exception. It is not difficult to imagine why this theme, which uses repetition but also contrast, later served as the national anthem for two countries. But there is a second reason why we should listen to this music. Haydn's use of the "Emperor's Hymn" as part of a string quartet provides an example of the best chamber music that the Classical period had to offer. In this intimate conversation between four string instruments, the first violin leads the way, as the emperor's voice. The other three musicians tend to play supporting roles, but all four instruments state and vary the theme. They are treated as equals, even if they ultimately yield to the first violin, who bows to the emperor. The theme remains constant, but the combinations of instruments change, providing variety.

first LISTEN

THEME	VARIATION 1	VARIATION 2	VARIATION 3	VARIATION 4
0:00	1:36	2:55	4:24	5:55
Stated by first violin	Second violin	Cello	Viola	First violin

Continued

a deeper LISTEN

TIME	SECTION	LISTEN FOR THIS
0:00	Theme	① **Theme:** In five phrases (stated by **violin 1**): *aabcc* **Poco adagio, cantabile** *a* — Pause on high pitch — *a* Same high pitch set off by fermata (pause) — *b* — Climax *c* — *c* — Smooth return to starting pitch (tonic) *p* *fz* *pp* * ∾, sign for an arnament known as a turn
1:36	Variation 1	Theme in **violin 2**, ***p***, accompanied by ornamental line in violin 1
2:55	Variation 2	Theme in **cello**, ***p***, accompanied by the other instruments
4:24	Variation 3	Theme in **viola**, ***p***, accompanied by the other instruments
5:55	Variation 4	Theme in **violin 1**, ***p*** but ending ***pp***, accompanied by the other instruments

Haydn's Influence

Haydn's influence was extraordinary, both during and after his lifetime. Building on the accomplishments of lesser figures, he established the symphony and the string quartet as the two most important genres of Classical instrumental music. Mozart and Beethoven drew freely on his contributions, as did countless other composers. International in appeal, his music communicated through its warmth, wit, and humanity. It reached new public audiences and represented the best the Classical period could offer.

MAKING CONNECTIONS *The Politics of Haydn's "Emperor's Hymn"*

When Haydn composed his "Emperor's Hymn" for the birthday of Francis II in 1797, he could scarcely have imagined how the melody would be revived in later times. In 1848, the German poet Hoffmann von Fallersleben wrote a poem to be sung to Haydn's melody with the text "Deutschland, Deutschland über alles" ("Germany, Germany above all else"). Like many liberal thinkers of the time, von Fallersleben advocated for the unification of Germany under a constitution that guaranteed basic civil rights for its citizens (unification did not happen until 1871). Then, in the twentieth century, Haydn's melody did double duty as the Austrian anthem (with a different text) and the German anthem. With the rise to power of the Nazis, the text "Deutschland, Deutschland über alles" took on a considerably more sinister meaning. After the Second World War, the anthem was banned until 1952. Today it is sung with only the third verse of von Fallersleben's poem, which speaks of unity, justice, and freedom.

check your **KNOWLEDGE**

1. Haydn's life stretched across three major musical styles. What were these styles, and how did Haydn's works change as each new style developed?
2. What role did patronage play in Haydn's life? What were the benefits and problems associated with being employed by his patron?
3. How did the makeup of the orchestra change during Haydn's lifetime? What influence did his works have on these changes?
4. How did Haydn's "Surprise" symphony reflect the height of the Classical symphony?
5. How did Haydn revolutionize the string quartet? How does his "Emperor" quartet reflect these changes?

CHAPTER

33 Wolfgang Amadeus Mozart

Wolfgang Amadeus Mozart as a child at the fortepiano.

The career of Wolfgang Amadeus Mozart (1756–1791) contrasted sharply with Haydn's. A child prodigy, Mozart began composing when he was only five years old; Haydn developed his craft later in life. Mozart was one of the leading keyboard virtuosos of his time; Haydn never won acclaim as a soloist. Finally, though Mozart earned a considerable income, he died in debt at age thirty-five; Haydn lived a long life and reaped the rewards of a successful international career.

Still, the two composers had much in common and greatly admired each other's music. Younger by twenty-four years, Mozart honored his friend by dedicating a series of string quartets to him. Haydn declared that Mozart was the greatest composer alive. Crushed by the news of Mozart's death, Haydn paid tribute by arranging for his music to be published.

Mozart's Life and Career

Mozart was born into a musical family in Salzburg, Austria. His father, Leopold, served as composer and violinist in the court of the city's ruling prince-archbishop. His older sister, Maria Anna (known as "Nannerl"), distinguished herself at the keyboard and composed, though regrettably none of her music has survived. As Nannerl was learning to play the harpsichord, three-year-old Wolfgang began picking out melodies and chords, relying on his uncanny musical ear to identify pitches. Proclaimed by his father to be the miracle that God allowed to be born in Salzburg, Wolfgang was soon improvising at the keyboard with astonishing facility. He could play blindfolded or with his hands covered and was equally adept at the violin.

Nannerl Mozart, Wolfgang's sister, age eleven.

Devoted to nurturing his children's talents, Leopold took his family on an international tour in 1763 that brought them as far as London. Along the way, they visited royal courts, where the children entertained the nobility. The seven-year-old Wolfgang performed at the Palace of Versailles before Louis XV and in London before George III. With his sister, he met Johann Christian Bach, youngest son of J. S. Bach, and sat on his lap while Bach improvised at the keyboard. After returning to Salzburg, the boy gave new evidence of his musical gifts. When the archbishop doubted the young child's abilities, Mozart was confined to a room to write a sacred work without assistance. He easily completed the task.

Wolfgang next went with his father to Italy. During Holy Week in 1770, he astonished observers at the Sistine Chapel in Rome by writing down from memory a choral work he had heard only once. More important for Leopold, Wolfgang began earning commissions to compose Italian operas, providing income to help the family's finances.

When the archbishop in Salzburg died, his successor, Hieronymus, reorganized his orchestra and engaged Mozart to join the court musicians in 1772. Like Haydn at Esterháza, Mozart composed music on command, including church music and serenades for visiting dignitaries, but he chafed at the archbishop's strictness. In search of a new post, he traveled with his mother to Germany and France but without success. Sadly, his mother died while they were in Paris, and Mozart had to break the news to his father.

In 1781, Mozart wrote an Italian opera to be presented in Munich. The premiere was a success, but the archbishop ordered Mozart back to his service, a demand Wolfgang resented. Matters went from bad to worse until the archbishop angrily dismissed the rebellious composer. Mozart decided to seek his fortune primarily as a freelance musician in Vienna, where he lived and worked for most of the last ten years of his life.

Mozart's move to Vienna marked a turning pointing in his career. He earned income from private lessons and commissions. He also gave concerts, selling tickets to the public from his own residence. During the Viennese years, he quickly turned out piano concertos for his own concerts. He created an extraordinary series of masterpieces, but Mozart's manuscripts reveal just how hectic his life was. Some piano parts for his concertos were left blank or thinly sketched, to be filled in when he performed them in concert. In Vienna, Mozart also joined a secret society known

Engraving of Vienna in the 1780s.

as the Freemasons, allowing him to make useful connections with members of the local nobility.

Despite his rapid output, in his last years Mozart lived beyond his means and had to borrow from friends, among them some fellow Freemasons. Even as he lay on his deathbed, Mozart was working feverishly on the Requiem Mass in D minor. An anonymous visitor commissioned the work, apparently on behalf of a count who intended to perform the work as his own. Mozart left this exquisite work unfinished. According to one account he was singing the timpani part when he died. Others tried to complete it, including his friend and pupil Franz Xavier Süssmayr, who provided the version that is most often performed today. The mystery surrounding the composition added to its allure, with many believing that Mozart conceived it as his own requiem.

Read parts of Mozart's letters.

When Mozart died, possibly from rheumatic fever, he was buried outside Vienna in an unmarked grave reserved for commoners. To this day, his remains have not been found, though controversy has swirled around a skull thought to have been Mozart's. DNA testing of the skull has so far proven inconclusive.

The range of Mozart's music is part of the staggering achievement compressed into his short life. He wrote over 600 compositions, which were catalogued in the nineteenth century by Ludwig von Köchel. (The *K* numbers used to identify Mozart's compositions are in honor of Köchel.)

MAKING CONNECTIONS *Mozart as Freemason*

Masonic banner.

How did Mozart spend his time apart from music? For entertainment, he often attended the theater or played cards, and he was especially fond of billiards. In order to mix into the higher levels of society, he dressed in fine attire. He also became a Freemason, joining a Viennese lodge in 1784 and remaining an active Mason until he died. Freemasonry was a secret male society dedicated to Enlightenment ideals of tolerance, freedom, and humanitarianism. It attracted members of the middle and leisured classes in Europe. Among its ranks were musicians and statesmen, including Haydn, and in the young American republic, George Washington and Benjamin Franklin. Freemasonry had not always been well received, but the Austrian emperor Joseph II tolerated the lodges. The movement was popular in Vienna, where it attracted not only commoners such as Mozart but nobility as well.

Members were initiated through a series of rites and moved through various ranks on their way to becoming master masons. For Mozart, Freemasonry offered a social outlet and an unrestricted space where he could exchange ideas freely. He also was intrigued with the rituals of the movement and composed several works specifically for use in lodges. His final opera, *The Magic Flute*, is viewed as especially rich in Masonic symbolism.

Several of Mozart's many operas—he wrote his first at age twelve—are performed often, including the Italian operas *The Marriage of Figaro* and *Don Giovanni*, and the German operas *The Abduction from the Seraglio* and *The Magic Flute*. There is also a wealth of sacred music, including the unfinished masterpiece, the Requiem in D minor. Among the many symphonies are the pensive No. 40 in G minor and the brilliant No. 41 in C major, known as the "Jupiter." Mozart wrote nearly forty

MAKING CONNECTIONS *Mozart and Posterity*

Soon after Mozart's death, legends began clustering around his memory. According to the most sensational, an envious court composer, Antonio Salieri (1750–1825), had poisoned Mozart. Salieri consistently denied the rumor, and there was no evidence to support it. Nevertheless, in the nineteenth century the Russian playwright Pushkin kept the legend alive in a short play about the two composers. Later, the Russian composer Rimsky-Korsakov composed a short opera perpetuating it. In the twentieth century Peter Shaffer wrote a play (*Amadeus*, 1979) based on the Pushkin and Rimsky-Korsakov works. Shaffer's depictions of Mozart and Salieri made for great drama. Mozart was portrayed as a divinely inspired genius at odds with his rude and immature behavior, while Salieri was a mediocre composer struggling to come to terms with Mozart's unique musical gifts. The play became a major film in 1984 that won eight Academy Awards.

Some critics argued that Shaffer's interpretation of Mozart was not supported by the historical record. Still, the theme of Mozart as an extraordinary prodigy stimulated no end of discussion and inspired countless writers, musicians, and artists. The mystery surrounding Mozart's death at age thirty-five only reinforced the idea that the prodigy was a child who had never grown up.

Mozart and Salieri as portrayed in the 1984 film *Amadeus*.

concertos, many of them for piano and orchestra. He crafted string quintets and quartets, piano trios, violin sonatas, music for wind ensembles, and, of course, music for solo piano. There is even music for mechanical clock and for glass harmonica, an odd instrument that required performers to rub glasses filled with water in order to produce eerily resonant pitches.

Mozart and the Classical Concerto

Mozart was *the* extraordinary pianist of his age, with few virtuosos approaching his command of the instrument. He produced a substantial amount of piano music, including a brilliant series of two dozen piano concertos that showcased the instrument. Mozart was not the first to write concertos for piano and orchestra, but he was the first to develop the piano concerto into a powerfully expressive and popular genre of the Classical style.

The Classical three-movement concerto that Mozart perfected was a combination of the older Baroque concerto and Classical sonata form. From the Baroque concerto, he retained the idea of a concerto being a contest between an orchestra and a soloist. From sonata form, Mozart took the three-part division of exposition, development, and recapitulation. This division is most clearly apparent in the first movements of his concertos.

Among Mozart's most popular concertos is Piano Concerto No. 23 in A major, K. 488. It was composed in 1786, possibly for Barbara Ployer, daughter of a wealthy Salzburg merchant and one of Mozart's students. The concerto's memorable themes range from the gentle lyricism of the first movement to the intense brooding melancholy of the slow movement and the lighthearted playfulness of the rondo finale. Mozart's restricts himself to five woodwinds in the orchestra (one flute, two clarinets, and two bassoons). He uses these instruments for soft, muted wind colors that enrich and play off against the strings.

The first movement illustrates the marriage of Baroque elements with sonata form (**Listening Map 29**). In it, Mozart works with four sections for the orchestra (called **tutti**, Italian for "all," here abbreviated T) and three main **solo** sections (S), which feature the soloist with light orchestral accompaniment:

This plan fits into a modified Classical sonata form:

Exposition 1	Exposition 2	Development	Recapitulation
T1	S1 T2	S2	T3 S3 T4

An autograph manuscript by Mozart includes a doodled sketch of his favorite student, Barbara Ployer.

One of the highlights of this movement is the piano **cadenza** that occurs toward the end. Stately orchestral chords and a solemn pause prepare us for the cadenza. It then erupts into rushing scales, sweeping sets of notes, and intense trills. Ordinarily, Mozart improvised his cadenzas during performances, without bothering to write them down. His cadenza for this movement has survived, however, giving us a good idea of his brilliant keyboard skills. When it is over, the orchestra brings the movement to a strong conclusion.

Mozart and Italian Opera

Italian opera continued to dominate the opera houses of Mozart's Vienna as it did elsewhere in Europe. One of the leading composers of Italian opera was the German C. W. Gluck (1714–1787), who worked in Vienna and Paris and also wrote French operas. In the 1760s and 1770s, Gluck pushed for major changes to serious opera. Gluck wanted the music to serve the drama. He believed that the overture should mirror the drama about to unfold on stage, and that arias should not interfere with the unfolding of the story. As a result, Gluck did not use da capo arias (see p. 192), which had allowed singers to stop the drama with cadenzas that showed off their voices. Above all, Gluck advocated for a "beautiful simplicity" in serious opera, in keeping with the neoclassicism of his time.

C. W. Gluck, whose reforms to the genre of serious opera inspired Mozart.

Gluck's reforms were not lost on Mozart, who met the elder composer. Mozart was inspired by some scenes from Gluck's operas and used elements from them in his own operas. Mozart composed both serious opera (**opera seria**) and comic

MOZART, Piano Concerto No. 23 in A major, K. 488, First Movement (Allegro)

{1786}

FORM	Synthesis of Classical sonata form and Baroque concerto form, alternating between sections for the orchestra (T) and piano (S)
METER	Common time ($\frac{4}{4}$)
SCORING	Woodwinds (one flute, two clarinets, two bassoons), brass (two French horns), strings
OVERVIEW	The first movement of Mozart's Piano Concerto No. 23 in A major alternates between sections that feature the orchestra (T) and piano (S). All told, there are seven main sections (T1 S1 T2 S2 T3 S3 T4), and they trace, in their presentations of themes and keys, the main events of a movement in Classical sonata form. One especially distinctive feature is the interruption of the last orchestral section (T4) to accommodate a virtuoso cadenza for the piano alone.

why to LISTEN

Traditionally, concertos are about virtuosity: a skilled soloist is set against an orchestra and assigned impressive and technically challenging displays of notes. And indeed some concertos pursue the idea of virtuosity to an extreme and leave us wondering, "How does the soloist do that?" As probably the greatest pianist of his age, Mozart was certainly capable of technically demanding passages. But there is another reason to admire and listen to his concertos. In a larger sense, they offer a study in group interactions. In the case of the Piano Concerto No. 23 in A major, the pianist is the individual and the orchestra is the group. As you listen to this exquisite music, try to follow the shifting relationships between the pianist and orchestra. Note how the piano often asserts its independence from the orchestra. Note too how the piano sometimes works harmoniously with the orchestra. There is much more going on in Mozart's music than just the notes on the page—the concerto can be heard almost as study of social relationships and the individual's role in a group.

first LISTEN

DOUBLE EXPOSITION			
ORCHESTRAL EXPOSITION	**SOLO EXPOSITION**	**DEVELOPMENT**	**RECAPITULATION**
0:00	**2:01**	**4:28**	**5:54**
T1	S1 T2	S2	T3 S3 T4-cadenza—T4

T = Tutti (Full orchestra); S = Piano Solo

a deeper LISTEN

TIME	PART	TUTTI (FULL ORCHESTRA)/ SOLOIST	LISTEN FOR THIS
0:00	Orchestral exposition	T1	First theme in tonic key (*a*), ***p***  Allegro
0:31			Transition, ***f***
0:53			Second theme in tonic key (*b*), ***p***  Closing passage, ***f***
2:01	Exposition featuring soloist	S1	First theme in tonic key (*a*), ornamented in piano, ***p*** Bridge, ***f***, modulating to second key Second theme in second key (*b*), ***p*** Closing passage, with trill in piano
4:06		T2	Brief orchestral passage; a new theme in second key (*c*) 
4:28	Development	S2	Ornamented version of *c* for the piano; exchanges between woodwinds and piano as the music modulates through several keys Ascending scale in the piano
5:54	Recapitulation: Short	T3	First theme in tonic key (*a*), ***p***

Continued

TIME	PART	TUTTI (FULL ORCHESTRA)/ SOLOIST	LISTEN FOR THIS
6:09	Recapitulation: Extended	S3	First theme in tonic key (*a*), ***p*** Transition, ***f*** Second theme in tonic key (*b*), ***p*** Closing passage in tonic, ***f***, with restatement of new theme (*c*) Trill in piano
8:26		T4	Based on closing passage, ***f***, and new theme (*c*), ***p***; then orchestral chords
8:53		Piano cadenza	Ending with a trill
9:57		T4	Closing measures in the tonic key for orchestra

opera (**opera buffa**). His best-known Italian operas, *The Marriage of Figaro* and *Don Giovanni*, are viewed as comic operas even though they mingle serious and comic characters. Mozart excelled in vividly portraying the nobility and members of the servant class. Far from being stock figures, the characters in his operas spring to life through his music and play out familiar human dramas.

The Marriage of Figaro is based on a French play by Pierre-Augustin Beaumarchais. Beaumarchais's play mocked the aristocracy, so the French monarch banned the play from Parisian stages. But it caught Mozart's attention in Vienna, and he decided to turn it into an opera. In just six weeks, he produced a score of over 400 pages of music without knowing whether the censors would ever allow it to be performed. Like the French monarch, the Austrian emperor banned public productions of Beaumarchais's play. However, the libretto prepared by Mozart's collaborator Lorenzo da Ponte (1749–1838) softened Beaumarchais's most controversial passages, and it reached the stage in Vienna in 1786. It is now regarded as one of the greatest operas of all time.

Mozart built much of *The Marriage of Figaro* on solo arias and recitatives—the common ingredients of Italian opera—but he also used duets, trios, and larger ensembles. He carefully selected these formats to present contrasting views of the characters with telling effect. Each of the four acts of the opera builds in tension to a finale, where Mozart masterfully constructs ensembles that bring main characters on stage until it seems to overflow with singers. A forceful quickening of the tempo speeds the finales to dramatic conclusions.

The opening scenes of the first act demonstrate how Mozart draws his characters. An energetic overture uses bustling string figures, animated wind interjections, and crescendo effects to create a sense of suspense and intrigue. In the first two scenes, we meet Figaro (bass) and Susanna (soprano), servants of the Count and Countess Almaviva, who hold court near Seville, Spain. Figaro and Susanna are to be married later that day, and the count has assigned them quarters next to his own rooms. Figaro is content with the arrangement, but Susanna fears that the count may be planning to seduce her while Figaro is away. When the countess summons Susanna with her bell, Figaro decides to outwit the count.

A contemporary production of Mozart's *The Marriage of Figaro* at the Metropolitan Opera in New York.

This action takes place in the first two scenes, which are split into two duets and recitatives for Susanna and Figaro (Scene 1), and a recitative and a solo for Figaro (Scene 2):

Scene 1 (Figaro and Susanna)	**Scene 2** (Figaro alone)
Duet	Recitative
Recitative	Cavatina
Duet	
Recitative	

Mozart cleverly ties the two scenes together by using the French horns of the orchestra in multiple musical metaphors. Horn fanfares that symbolize the power of the nobility appear in the first duet. When they reappear in the second duet, they suggest the count's bell that draws Figaro away from his wife, whom the count plans to seduce. And when they appear in Figaro's **cavatina** (a short setting for voice and orchestra typically less complex than an aria), they suggest the horns of Figaro as the would-be cuckolded husband.

The second duet between Figaro and Susanna (**Listening Map 30**) begins innocently enough with a cheerful melody in the bassoon picked up by Figaro, who describes the convenience of living near his master. If the countess summons Susanna with her hand bell (imitated by delicate tinkling in the flutes and oboes) (1), Susanna can quickly attend to her mistress. And if the count summons Figaro (imitated by the heavier horns and bassoons) (2), he too can quickly respond.

Dashboard

Watch a video of a modern performance of "Se a Casa Madama."

But now the music briefly takes on a more sinister tone as Susanna offers a contrasting point of view. What if the count should send Figaro away? Then the count could easily reach her quarters. Here Figaro interrupts Susanna, and the music comes to a halt. She resumes singing at a hushed level, becoming more earnest. If Figaro wishes to learn more, he must set aside any suspicion of her wrongdoing. Though doubtful, he agrees. The duet ends by dropping down to *pianissimo* as it gently refers to the music of the opening.

MOZART, *The Marriage of Figaro*, K. 492, Act I, Scene 1, Figaro and Susanna, "Se a casa madama" ("If my lady needs you")

{1786}

FORM	Duet
METER	$\frac{2}{4}$
SCORING	Figaro (bass), Susanna (soprano), and orchestra (two flutes, two oboes, two bassoons, two French horns, and strings)
OVERVIEW	Mozart's duet (more precisely, "little duet") begins with a brief orchestral passage before Figaro enters. The music takes on a more serious tone when Susanna responds. Eventually, the two sing together.

why to LISTEN

Mozart's opera *The Marriage of Figaro* has long been a staple of major opera houses due to the excellence of Mozart's music and Lorenzo da Ponte's libretto. But under slightly different circumstances, the opera might not have reached the stage during Mozart's lifetime. *The Marriage of Figaro* offers a social critique of class relations. The story of a servant outwitting his privileged master was not guaranteed to pass the censors in the years leading up to the French Revolution. The opera would almost certainly not have been performed in Paris, where the original French play had been banned. And even in Vienna, the enlightened monarch Joseph II banned the play, but allowed the opera to go forward. Mozart used music to push the boundaries of what was acceptable. He was able to explore ideas that would have been regarded as politically dangerous when presented without the music. The composer versus the censor: it is an age-old game that reminds us of the power of music.

first LISTEN

ORCHESTRAL INTRODUCTION	FIGARO	FIGARO	ORCHESTRA	ORCHESTRA	FIGARO	FIGARO	SUSANNA/ FIGARO/ BOTH	ORCHESTRAL CONCLUSION
0:00	0:04	0:23	0:31	0:38	0:42	1:07	1:23	2:27
	Se a caso madama . . .	*Vien . . .*	Horns and bassoon	Minor key	*Così se il mattino . . .*	*Susanna, pian, pian.*	*Ascolta . . .*	

a deeper **LISTEN**

TIME	SECTION/ SINGER	LISTEN FOR THIS	TEXT	TRANSLATION
0:00	**Orchestral introduction**	Melody in bassoon		
0:04	**Figaro**	Figaro's entrance, picks up bassoon melody; (1) countess's handbell	*Se a caso madama/ La notte ti chiama/ Din din: in due passi/ Da quella puoi gir.*	If my lady needs you at night, ding-ding! In two steps you're there.
0:23	**Figaro**	Flutes and oboes; (2) count's bell	*Vien poi l'occasione/ ce vuolmi il padrone/ Don don: in tre salti/ Lo vado a servir.*	Sometimes my lord needs me, dong-dong! In three leaps I'm there.
0:31	**Orchestra**	Horns and bassoons		
0:38	**Orchestra**	Music turns briefly toward minor key; additional references to the handbell and bell		
0:42	**Figaro**		*Così se il mattino/ Il caro Contino,/ Din din, e ti manda/ Tre miglia lontan/ Don don e a mia porta/ Il diavol lo porta./ Don don, ed ecco in tre salti . . .*	Suppose one morning, our dear little count, dong-dong, sends you three miles away. Dong-dong! And the devil might bring him to my door. Dong-dong! And in three leaps . . .
1:07	**Figaro**	Figaro interrupts Susanna	*Susanna, pian, pian.*	Susanna, softly, softly.
1:23	**Susanna/ Figaro/ both**	Susanna, then Figaro, then Susanna and Figaro together	Susanna: *Ascolta.* Figaro: *Fa presto.* Susanna: *Se udir brami il resto/ Discaccia I sospetti/ Che torto mi fan.* Figaro: *Udir bramo il resto:/ I dubbi, I sospetti/ Gelare mi fari.*	Susanna: Listen. Figaro: Be quick. Susanna: If you wish to hear the rest, put away doubts of my honor. Figaro: I wish to hear the rest, doubts and suspicions are chilling my heart.
2:27	**Orchestral conclusion**	Reference to music of the opening, with a diminuendo to ***pp***		

In the recitative that follows Figaro and Susanna's duet, the orchestra drops out, leaving the harpsichord to accompany the singers. Through animated exchanges with Figaro, Susanna now explains that the count intends to revive an ancient custom that allows him to visit her the night before her wedding. She leaves to attend the countess, while Figaro, in a short recitative opening the second scene, devises his strategy.

Dashboard

Watch a video of a modern performance of "Se vuol ballare"

He will pretend to play the dutiful servant, but will trick the count into dancing to the servant's tune. Considering how to do this, Figaro sings a cavatina, "Se vuol ballare." This cavatina is divided into three parts, in the order *ABA′* (**Listening Map 31**). In the *A* section, Figaro (alone on stage) imagines inviting the count to dance (①). The horns present the enticing melody accompanied by strings playing **pizzicato** (by plucking rather than by using the bow). Mozart uses the pizzicato effect to represent Figaro's onstage guitar. The *A* section has a moderately fast tempo, $\frac{3}{4}$ meter, and perfectly balanced phrases. All these features suggest that most aristocratic of dances—the minuet. But in the *B* section, where Figaro describes setting a trap for the count, the tempo shifts to a rapid *presto* and less-refined dance in $\frac{2}{4}$ meter (②). Here, Figaro sings in short, crisp phrases as he becomes angrier. Then, with the return of the *A* section, considerably shortened, we return to the world of the courtly minuet and of Figaro the servant. But a brisk coda in $\frac{2}{4}$ reminds us again of his intentions. "Se vuol ballare" is a masterpiece of characterization.

Mozart and German Opera

Dashboard

Watch a performance by Larry Todd of Mozart's Turkish Rondo.

In Germany, a native operatic tradition was relatively slow to develop. Italian opera and French drama ruled German stages during much of the eighteenth century. One type of German opera did take hold, however: the **singspiel**, a comic opera with tuneful solo numbers and spoken dialogue instead of recitative. In 1778 the Austrian emperor, Joseph II, established a national theater in Vienna to promote German opera. One of the emperor's first commissions went to Mozart for a singspiel titled *The Abduction from the Seraglio.* It premiered in 1782 and was based on a then-fashionable Turkish subject. Mozart's most famous singspiel, though, was *The Magic Flute*, which premiered in Vienna just months before his death.

The Magic Flute focuses on the moral education of Tamino, a young prince. In the first scene, three women dressed in black save him from a serpent and ask him to rescue Pamina, the daughter of the Queen of the Night. Accompanying Tamino on his mission is Papageno, a bird catcher, who gets a magic set of bells from the women in black. The women also offer Tamino a magic flute to protect him against dangers along the way.

Tamino and Papageno reach the court of Sarastro, who is holding Pamina, only to discover that he is an enlightened man. As the opera continues, Tamino and Pamina are eventually united, the plotting Queen of the Night is defeated, and Tamino and Pamina are welcomed into Sarastro's priestly temple.

The Magic Flute is a Masonic allegory about the triumph of reason over superstition. Both the score and the libretto have many references to Masonic beliefs. The overture begins with three chords, representing the applicant knocking on the door of the Masonic temple for admission. Several parts of the opera are in keys associated with Masonic numerology. Finally, there is music for winds in several passages that suggest the wind bands used in Masonic rituals. All of these features inspired

LISTENING MAP 31

MOZART, *The Marriage of Figaro*, K. 492, Act I, Scene 2, Figaro, "Se vuol ballare" ("If you want to dance") {1786}

FORM	Cavatina
METER	$\frac{3}{4}$
SCORING	Figaro and orchestra (two oboes, two bassoons, two French horns, and strings)
OVERVIEW	Figaro's charming cavatina alternates between two types of music that underscore class distinctions in the opera. At first, Figaro alludes to the courtly style of the minuet, associated with his rival, the count. Then, the music breaks into a popular dance, associated with the servant class, before resuming the leisured minuet.

first LISTEN

A (ALLEGRETTO $\frac{3}{4}$)	B (PRESTO $\frac{2}{4}$)	A′ (ALLEGRETTO $\frac{3}{4}$)	CODA
0:00	**1:34**	**2:03**	**2:32**
Minuet-like melody, played softly	Energetic popular dance, gradually increasing in volume	Return to opening theme, shortened and reworked	Brief melody based on B, played loudly, used to end the piece

a deeper LISTEN

TIME	SECTION	TEXT	TRANSLATION	LISTEN FOR THIS
0:00	**A** (Allegretto [moderately fast], $\frac{3}{4}$ meter)	*Se vuol ballare* *signor Contino,* *il chitarrino* *le suonerò.* *Se vuol venire,* *nella mia scuola,* *la capriola* *le insegnerò.* *Saprò, ma piano* *meglio ogni arcano,* *dissimulando* *scoprir potrò!*	If you want to dance, my little count, on my little guitar I'll accompany you. If you want to enroll in my school, capers I'll show you. Yes, I shall know, but carefully all these plots by stealth I'll unveil more successfully!	Minuet-like effect **Instruments:** Horns, pizzicato strings (representing Figaro's guitar) **Dynamics:** ***p***

Continued

TIME	SECTION	TEXT	TRANSLATION	LISTEN FOR THIS
		Allegretto ① Figaro invites the count to dance Se vuol bal - la - re, si-gnor Con - ti-no, se vuol bal - la - re, si-gnor Con - ti-no,		
1:34	**B** (Presto [very fast], 2/4 meter)	*L'arte schermendo,* *l'arte adoprando,* *di quà pungendo,* *di là scherzando,* *tutte le macchine* *rovescierò.* **Presto** ② Figaro sets a trap for the count L'ar -te scher-men do, l'ar-te a-do-pran-do, di quà pun-gen-do, di là scher-zan-do,	Disguising my craft, exploiting my craft, pinching here, jesting there, all his machinations I shall reverse.	Short, repeated phrases **Dynamics:** crescendo to *forte*
2:03	**A′** (Allegretto 3/4)	*Se vuol ballare*, for and so on	If you want to dance, for and so on	Shortened and reworked **Dynamics:** ***p***
2:32	**Coda** (Presto 2/4)			Based on *B* **Dynamics:** *forte*

the poet Goethe, himself a Mason, to comment that only Masons could fully grasp Mozart's opera.

Mozart matched a broad range of styles with his characters. Papageno sings irresistibly charming melodies that resemble folk tunes. Tamino and Pamina, on the other hand, sing elegant music in a heightened style. On the most serious level is Sarastro's music, which is noble and measured.

Quite apart from these characters is the Queen of the Night, whose role is drawn from serious opera. Her most dramatic entrance comes in the final act when she arrives at Sarastro's temple to foment a rebellion and incite Pamina to kill Sarastro (①). The Queen's rising hatred erupts in a "rage aria" (**Listening Map 32**), with melodic lines broken by wide leaps and energized by driving rhythms (②). The strings accompany her melody with bristling repeated notes, underscoring the aria's agitated style.

In the Queen of the Night's rage aria, Mozart makes extreme demands on the singer. In some passages, he pushes the soprano to the very limits of her high range. The form of the aria in three parts of unequal length is equally striking. The first section quickly modulates from the tonic to the second key. The second section acts as a transition to the return of the tonic. And the third, which re-establishes the tonic, is drastically restricted, as if to suggest the Queen being consumed by her own fury. This explosive music stands in striking contrast to the deliberate, reasoned tone of Sarastro's music, which ultimately prevails.

MOZART, *The Magic Flute*, K. 620, Act II, Scene 3, Queen of the Night, "Der Hölle Rache" ("Vengeance of Hell") {1791}

FORM	Aria
METER	$\frac{4}{4}$
SCORING	Queen of the Night (soprano) and orchestra (two flutes, two oboes, two bassoons, two French horns, two trumpets, two timpani, and strings)
OVERVIEW	This celebrated "rage aria" contains music that pushes the stylistic limits of Mozart's time. The virtuoso soprano part is extremely demanding and tests the extreme high range of the singer. And the accompanying orchestral music seethes with energy and drama.

why to LISTEN

If *The Marriage of Figaro* uses music to offer a critique of class society, *The Magic Flute* uses music in a different way, as allegory. This is a magical morality tale about good and evil. Here the force of good is symbolized by the enlightened Sarastro, who presides over a temple (a not-so-hidden reference to Freemasonry). In opposition, the force of evil is personified by the Queen of the Night. Between these extreme personifications of good and evil, the opera charts the moral progress of Prince Tamino and Pamina, who arrive at the temple and successfully find enlightenment. Throughout the opera, Mozart adapts his score to fit the needs of the allegory. Careful listeners can grasp a rich musical symbolism that supports this timeless tale of good and evil.

first LISTEN

BRIEF ORCHESTRAL INTRODUCTION	PART 1	BRIEF ORCHESTRAL INTERLUDE	PART 2	DRAMATIC PAUSE	PART 3
0:00	0:03	1:11	1:19	2:13	2:16
	Agitated melody with wide vocal leaps; modulates to second key		Rage continues; transition back to tonic key		Very short conclusion; final oath

Continued

a deeper LISTEN

TIME	SECTION	TEXT	TRANSLATION
		PART 1	
0:00	Brief orchestral introduction with agitated string chords		
0:03	Queen of the Night enters	*Der Hölle Rache kocht in meinem Herzen* *Tod und Verzweiflung flammet um mich her!* *Fühlt nicht durch dich Sarastro Todesschmerzen,* *so bist du meine Tochter nimmermehr* **Allegro assai** ① Wide leaps Der Höl - le Ra - che kocht in mei-nem Her - zen, ② Solo reaches into a very high register mehr	Vengeance of hell is roused in my heart, Death and despair burn all around me! If Sarastro does not feel the pains of death at your hand, Then you are no longer my daughter.
1:11	Brief orchestral interlude		
		PART 2	
1:19	Transition, modulating from second key back to the tonic	*Verstossen sei auf ewig, verlassen sei auf ewig,* *Zertrümmert sei'n auf ewig alle Bande der Natur,* *Wenn nicht durch dich Sarastro wird erblassen!*	Be outcast forever, be abandoned forever, All bonds of nature destroyed forever, If Sarastro is not destroyed by you!
2:13	Music comes to a dramatic pause		
		PART 3	
2:16	Very short concluding section in the tonic	*Hört! Rachegötter!* *Hört der Mutter Schwur!*	Hear me, gods of vengeance! Hear a mother's oath!

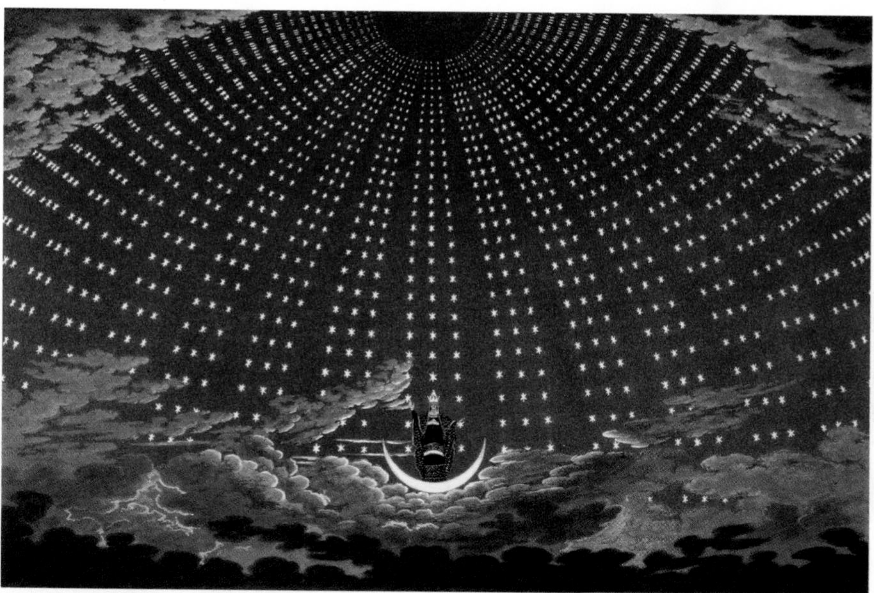

The starlit abode of the Queen of the Night. Stage design by Karl Schinkel for an 1815 production of *The Magic Flute* in Berlin.

Mozart's Legacy

Later generations continued to assess the magnitude of Mozart's genius. He is remembered as a great keyboard virtuoso and a prodigious composer of astonishing skill. His music is filled with melodies of unequaled beauty, and it is truly international in scope, bringing together a variety of styles and genres. With masterpieces in nearly every genre, his body of work assured the rise of German music into the nineteenth century. No one benefited more from Mozart's music than did Beethoven, the greatest piano virtuoso of his age.

check your **KNOWLEDGE**

1. Compare and contrast the life stories of Haydn and Mozart.
2. How did Mozart change the Classical concerto? Which elements of Baroque style and sonata form did he use?
3. How did Mozart adapt music in *The Marriage of Figaro* to depict individual characters?
4. How did *The Magic Flute* build on the German singspiel tradition?

CHAPTER

34 Ludwig van Beethoven

Ludwig van Beethoven (1770–1827).

Few composers changed music as decisively as Ludwig van Beethoven (1770–1827). His powerful scores, filled with strong dissonances but also heartfelt melodies, mapped the depths of human emotions and mirrored the fast-changing times in which he lived. Heir of Haydn's and Mozart's musical legacies, Beethoven exhausted and broke away from their high Classical style. He went on to define a new heroic style and influenced nearly every major composer who followed him.

Beethoven's music cast long shadows over the next several generations of composers. His symphonies set new models for the genre. Many composers, among them Franz Schubert, Felix Mendelssohn, Robert Schumann, and Johannes Brahms, were awed by his achievement and labored to create symphonies that might live up to his legacy. Even the number of symphonies he composed—nine—became a goal, with composers such as Schubert, Dvořák, Bruckner, and Mahler attempting to exceed the legendary number. Composers also took inspiration for their own chamber music from Beethoven's sixteen string quartets. Finally, generations of pianists matched their skill against Beethoven's challenging thirty-two piano sonatas.

Beethoven's career spans three stylistic periods:

1) his early period, which lasted up to 1802;
2) his middle period, between 1803 and 1814; and
3) his late period, between 1815 and 1827.

These periods roughly coincide with

1) Beethoven's youth in Bonn and early years in Vienna;
2) the continuing, devastating loss of his hearing; and
3) his last years, in which he composed from total deafness.

In terms of European history and culture, the three periods correspond roughly to:

1) the waning of the Enlightenment and outbreak of the French Revolution;
2) the rise of Napoleon after the French Revolution and his final defeat at the Battle of Waterloo in 1815; and
3) the Restoration after Napoleon, a conservative and reactionary period in Europe, ushered in by the Congress of Vienna in 1815.

Beethoven began his career by emulating the Classical style Mozart and Haydn had perfected during the 1780s and 1790s. But, by the time of his death, his music had moved beyond Classicism and was exploring Romantic ideals (see Part VI).

Beethoven's strong personality and eccentricities contributed greatly to his mystique as a suffering Romantic artist. He was a social recluse who was tormented by the great tragedy of his life, his deafness. Audiences still hear a forthright record of his life's struggles in his music. And his compositions can be understood as a compelling musical autobiography that won a new artistic independence for musicians who followed him.

Beethoven's Early Period

Beethoven was born in 1770 in Bonn, then part of a German territory loyal to the Austrian emperor. As a boy, he displayed uncommon musical gifts, leading some to compare him to Mozart. Still, Beethoven's childhood was miserable. His father, a pianist and singer, drank heavily and forced Beethoven to practice the piano for hours on end. Despite these rough beginnings, by 1784 Beethoven was serving at court as an organist; five years later, he joined the court orchestra as a violist.

Beethoven's early compositions were of uneven quality, although at age twenty he wrote an impressive funeral cantata in memory of Joseph II, the Austrian emperor (Holy Roman Emperor from 1765 to 1790). The cantata recounted Joseph's good works and faith in mankind's progress. Fifteen years later Beethoven reused part of the cantata in his opera *Fidelio* for the stirring dungeon scene, in which political prisoners yearn for freedom. Beethoven's reuse of the material was a powerful reminder of his support of the humanitarian ideals of the Enlightenment.

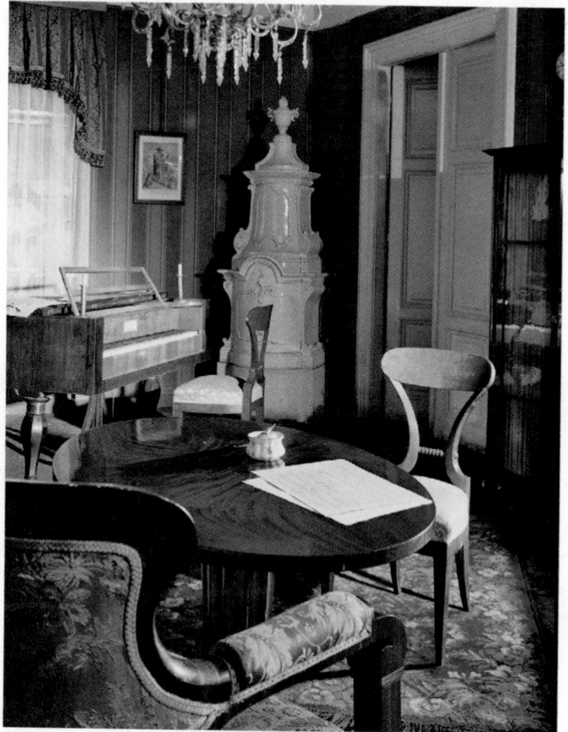

Beethoven would have had his lessons with Haydn in a room similar to this one from the same period (note the fortepiano).

In 1792 Beethoven moved to Vienna, the same city where he may have met Mozart during an earlier visit. Now, nearly a year after Mozart's death, Beethoven began studying composition with Haydn. The teacher-student relationship was problematic, lasting only about a year. During his time in Vienna, Beethoven appeared as a virtuoso pianist in aristocratic salons, where his performances inspired memories of Mozart. Beethoven also began to compose large works using the Classical genres, including several piano sonatas, two piano concertos, an ambitious set of string quartets, and his first symphony. These works owe much to Haydn and Mozart, but we hear unmistakable signs of Beethoven's emerging style within them: severe and frequent contrasts in dynamics; disruptive syncopated rhythms; and a relentless, driving energy.

One of Beethoven's best-known works from his early period, the "Moonlight" Sonata (1801), anticipated the music of his middle period. Beethoven once dismissed the work

MAKING CONNECTIONS *Beethoven and Haydn*

Most of Beethoven's personal relationships became strained at some point, and his relationship with Haydn was no exception. The two had very different temperaments. Haydn, who was used to dressing in formal eighteenth-century clothing, had excelled as a court musician. Beethoven, who dressed shabbily and had never taken an official court position, was strongly independent. Beethoven would go as far as to criticize the Viennese nobility, even though, ironically, he was dependent on their patronage.

Beethoven studied counterpoint with Haydn for about a year in Vienna, between Haydn's two journeys to London, but found his teaching old-fashioned and rejected some of the advice Haydn offered. Beethoven dedicated compositions to Haydn but refused to acknowledge him as a teacher. And, later in life, when Beethoven was asked who his favorite composer was, he passed over both Haydn and Mozart and chose the Baroque composer Handel.

Watch a video on improvisation in music, including Beethoven's "Moonlight" Sonata.

as unimportant. However, this sonata is remarkable because it breaks free from established models. In the work, Beethoven seemed to be deliberately reaching beyond the limits of the Classical sonata. In earlier sonatas, Beethoven had favored the typical Classical plans of three or four movements: *fast–slow–fast*, or *fast–slow–minuet–fast*. But after the turn to the nineteenth century, he grew more daring, treating each new sonata as an opportunity for experimentation.

The "Moonlight" Sonata has three movements, marked Very Slow and Sustained (*Adagio sostenuto*), Relatively Fast (*Allegretto*), and Very Fast and Agitated (*Presto agitato*).

Manuscript page from Beethoven's "Moonlight" Sonata.

Of the three, the first movement is the freest in form and played very softly throughout. The *Allegretto*, composed in a major key, functions as an interlude between the pensive *Adagio sostenuto* and explosive *Presto agitato*. The third movement, in the same minor key as the first, is composed in sonata form. Agitated in character, the third movement erupts with rapidly sweeping, ascending melodies. The movement features a much broader dynamic range than the first two: from a hushed *pianissimo* to an energetic *fortissimo*.

The first movement of the sonata (**Listening Map 33**) opens with brooding triplets played in the middle register of the piano, accompanied by a quietly descending bass line written in octaves (①). Above the triplets, Beethoven presents an unfinished-sounding melody that hovers around a single repeated pitch (②).

Falling into several phrases, the melody transports us away from the sonata's starting point in the tonic key. Then we hear the restless triplets of the accompaniment played over a pedal point in the bass. Beethoven is preparing us for the return of the tonic key and the reappearance of the melody's beginning. A coda rounds out the movement, with a hint of the melody now submerged in the low register of the piano. Overall, the form of the movement is *A*–Transition–*A′*. As the listening chart shows, these sections are framed by the introduction and coda.

Beethoven instructed that the movement be played delicately and *senza sordini* (without the piano's damper pedal). The dampers are strips of felt that rest on the strings. When a pianist depresses a key, a small hammer strikes the strings for that key. Once the key is lifted, the damper stops the strings from sounding. The damper pedal disables the dampers so that the strings continue to ring even after their keys are lifted. On the modern piano, depressing the pedal can create a muddy, blended sound as more notes are played. But when used on the more delicate fortepiano of Beethoven's time, the effect can be captivating.

Beethoven's Middle Period

Early in the nineteenth century Beethoven announced his intention to seek a "new manner" in his music. Despite the innovations of works such as the "Moonlight" Sonata, he may have felt he relied too much on the musical style of Haydn and Mozart in his early music. In his middle period, he began experimenting freely and in the process found his own voice.

Another issue influenced his new manner: during his late twenties Beethoven had begun losing his hearing. The deterioration was gradual, and as late as 1815, he was still attempting to perform in public. The psychological consequences of his hearing loss, however, were overwhelming. He despaired over the failure of the one sense in which, as he put it, he should have been whole. He contemplated suicide, but he ultimately decided to live for his art and entered his most productive period.

He quickly composed a bold new series of instrumental works with strikingly dramatic, heroic characters. Among these works are many of his most famous instrumental compositions, including the Cello Sonata in A major, Op. 69 (1808). Its four movements include (1) an opening with a cello solo before the piano enters; (2) a madcap scherzo with accents off the beat; (3) a short, lyrical slow movement; and (4) a climactic finale. Here Beethoven sets up a conflict between the singing qualities of the cello and piano and their ability to create percussive, persistent rhythmic effects by simply repeating single pitches.

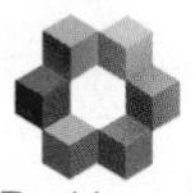
Dashboard

Watch a performance of Beethoven's Cello Sonata in A major, Op. 69.

LISTENING MAP 33

BEETHOVEN, Piano Sonata in C-sharp minor, Op. 27 No. 2 (“Moonlight”), First Movement (Adagio sostenuto)

{1801}

FORM	Free sonata form
METER	$\frac{2}{2}$
SCORING	Solo piano
OVERVIEW	The "Moonlight" Sonata is named after the subdued dynamic range and blurry sonorities of its first movement. The music suggests a free application of sonata form, which is why Beethoven likened it to a fantasy.

why to LISTEN

Why is the “Moonlight” Sonata one of Beethoven’s most famous compositions? Part of it has to do with the allure of the title, which describes the extraordinary first movement. This is, according to popular imagination, nocturnal music with a mysterious, dreamlike quality. The truth is, though, that Beethoven never used that title, instead providing the subtitle “like a fantasy.” Though not as picturesque as “Moonlight,” his description emphasizes that the piece enjoys a freedom of form even though it is part of a sonata. We can easily imagine Beethoven improvising the opening bars of the first movement and then letting the music wander, without concerning himself too much about formalistic restrictions. The “Moonlight” Sonata captures the shifting relationship between artistic freedom and structure in a compelling, meaningful way.

first LISTEN

INTRO	A	B (TRANSITION)	A′	CODA
0:00	**0:21**	**2:21**	**3:04**	**4:26**
Triplets in treble; descending bass line	Short melodic phrase centering on a few notes, followed by several more phrases, moving away from the tonic	Triplets in treble played against a bass pedal point	Return of main melody and tonic key, with triplet accompaniment	Triplets in treble, with hint of main melody in bass

 *a deeper* **LISTEN**

TIME	SECTION	LISTEN FOR THIS
0:00	Introduction	**Adagio sostenuto** Si deve suonare tutto questo pezzo delicatissimamente e senza sordini ① Triplets against octaves in the bass; tonic key *sempre* ***pp*** *e senza sordini*
0:21	A	Tonic, then touching on other keys ② Melodic phrases enter ***pp***
2:21	B (Transition)	Ascending, then descending triplets over a pedal point
3:04	A′	Return of melody and triplet accompaniment; return of tonic
4:26	Coda	Triplet accompaniment with vestiges of melody in the bass; tonic

Beethoven also explored his dynamic "new manner" on the broader canvas of the symphony. Between 1803 and 1808, he concentrated his symphonic innovations in three monumental compositions: the "Eroica" (Heroic) Symphony (No. 3), the Fifth Symphony, and the "Pastoral" Symphony (No. 6). In these works, Beethoven moved past the limits of the Classical symphony and produced music on an unprecedentedly grand scale. His four major innovations were:

1) expanding movements to a length well beyond those of Haydn and Mozart's symphonies,
2) building up the orchestra by adding woodwind and brass instruments,
3) designing symphonies to express a story or message beyond the music, and
4) linking certain movements so that they are performed without the traditional break between them.

Beethoven began experimenting with these innovations in the Third Symphony, which he dedicated at first to Napoleon Bonaparte. Beethoven saw Napoleon as a hero who had championed the common people and promoted the ideals of

MAKING CONNECTIONS *Napoleon as Romantic Figure*

The remarkable rise of Napoleon (1769–1821) from obscurity to major world leader as the self-proclaimed emperor of France is one of the incredible stories of the nineteenth century. He was born on the island of Corsica and rose through the ranks of the French military. When he first came to power after the French Revolution in the late 1790s, he supported the idea of a French Republic. However, by 1804 he had become an emperor just as despotic as the absolute monarchies he overthrew. So, why was Beethoven originally prepared to dedicate his Third Symphony to Napoleon?

Jacques-Louis David, *Napoleon Crossing the Alps* (1801).

While Beethoven was writing his Third Symphony in 1803, Austria was officially at peace with France, and he was thinking of moving to Paris to advance his career. He was also attracted to France because, like many liberal thinkers of the time, he was caught up by the romanticized image of Napoleon. Many saw Napoleon as a commoner who had risen from modest origins to greatness through self-reliance and individual achievement. The image of the French leader as a Romantic hero took many forms, from painting to literature and music. But after Napoleon was defeated at Waterloo in 1815, his fall was swift and definitive. The English poet Byron, who had identified with the idea of Napoleonic greatness, wrote these lines of jaded disappointment in his *Ode to Napoleon Bonaparte*:

> 'Tis done—but yesterday a King!
> And armed with Kings to strive—
> And now thou art a nameless thing:
> So abject—yet alive!

liberty and equality. But when Napoleon declared himself Emperor of France in 1804, Beethoven scratched out the dedication on his score and renamed the Third Symphony the "Eroica."

The "Eroica" Symphony is marked by nearly constant conflict and contrast, heightening its heroic character. The long and intense first movement features dissonant harmonies and clashing rhythms. The second movement is a solemn funeral march, while the third movement, in sharp contrast, is a joyful fast-paced scherzo. The complex fourth movement is the crowning conclusion to the symphony. Beethoven drew the theme of this movement from his ballet *The Creatures of Prometheus*, which celebrates the heroic deeds of the Greek mythological figure who brought fire and civilization to mankind. The symphony begins in a world of tragedy that culminates in the funeral march, a symbolic "death of a hero." It then moves on to the world of comedy in the scherzo and enlightenment in the triumphant finale.

Beethoven's Fifth Symphony in C minor

The mighty Fifth Symphony—perhaps Beethoven's best-known composition—is similar in mood to the "Eroica." It depicts a musical struggle that eventually resolves in a victorious finale. The symphony begins with a first theme constructed from a famous four-note **motive**, a burst of three short notes followed by a held note that brings the music to a halt:

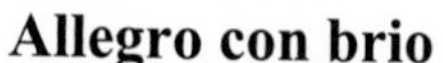

This basic short-short-short-long motive introduces a musical contradiction that is at work throughout the symphony. The three rapid notes propel the music forward, only to come to an abrupt halt on the fourth note. The dynamic forward energy is thus opposed by an unexpected pause, a pattern that plays out again and again in all four movements. Here are some examples:

- In the recapitulation of the first movement, the orchestra suddenly pauses for a brief oboe cadenza.
- In the second movement, a pause occurs near the exact midpoint.
- In the third movement, we hear only a few bars before the orchestra pauses.
- And in the finale, the use of a pause is even more dramatic. Beethoven suddenly interrupts the triumphant music by reviving material from the third movement.

We have little reliable evidence about Beethoven's intended meaning in the Fifth Symphony, but that has not stopped generations of critics and music lovers from seeing the work as a narrative of triumph over adversity. According to one interpretation, Beethoven meant the opening short-short-short-long motive to represent Fate knocking at the door, perhaps as a reference to his devastating hearing loss. A few years before composing the symphony Beethoven had written that he would "seize Fate by the throat; it shall not bend or crush me completely." Indeed, if anything, the first movement seems to depict a struggle with the famous motive. More generally, the writer and composer E. T. A. Hoffmann proclaimed the symphony as a powerful example of Romantic music. Hoffmann described the symphony as

MAKING CONNECTIONS *Finding Meaning in Beethoven's Fifth Symphony*

The idea of "Fate knocking at the door" at the beginning of the Fifth Symphony is one of the most enduring legends about Beethoven's music, but the question remains: did it originate from the composer himself? The only source we have indicating it was Beethoven's idea is the recollections of the composer's secretary and biographer, Anton Schindler. But Schindler is remembered as an unreliable witness, and his claim may not be true.

The truth has never really mattered to audiences. So compelling, forceful, and unprecedented was Beethoven's Fifth that people soon agreed: the symphony *had* to be about something more than just the notes on the page. The idea of a struggle resulting in a victorious celebration was evident in the music itself. Fate knocking at the door seemed a reasonable way to describe the opening. The story took hold and has remained a fixture in the popular reception of the composer.

But to complicate matters, we also have a different account from one of Beethoven's students, Carl Czerny. Czerny maintained that the famous opening of the symphony came from the birdsong of the yellowhammer, which the composer had heard during his walks in the countryside around Vienna. Sure enough, the yellowhammer call has several repeated pitches that occasionally drop down. But somehow the yellowhammer didn't quite measure up to the knocking of Fate in the popular imagination, and Czerny's story soon was forgotten.

Yet another way to find meaning in Beethoven's symphony emerged in 1941 in a context Beethoven would never have foreseen. During the Second World War, the Allies started using the letter *v* to stand for the ultimate victory over the Nazis. In Morse code, *v* is represented by dot-dot-dot-dash, which is identical to short-short-short-long rhythm of the symphony's four-note motive. Soon radio broadcasts were featuring the opening of the symphony as a coded way of strengthening the Allies' resolve to win. More than 100 years after it was written, Beethoven's music was enlisted in the Allied cause, showing the endurance of his music and the continuing need to find meaning within it.

Beethoven's student Carl Czerny maintained that the Fifth Symphony owed a debt to the song of the yellowhammer.

"frightening," "mysterious," and "sinister," adjectives that suggested just how far Beethoven had moved from the refined Classical style of Haydn and Mozart.

FIRST MOVEMENT (*ALLEGRO CON BRIO*)

The first movement of the Fifth Symphony (**Listening Map 34**) is written in sonata form. In it, Beethoven packs the celebrated short-short-short-long motive into nearly every bar to give the music an overriding sense of urgency and drama. We may wonder how a mere four notes command such power. The opening motive's powerful effect is accomplished in three ways:

1) The fermata (𝄐) on the fourth note interrupts the energetic attack of the first three notes. We cannot be certain about the direction the rhythm will take (①).
2) The fermata holds the fourth note for longer than its usual value, making it hard to sense the beat pattern.
3) The orchestra plays the motive in unison. Without any clue from the harmony, the tonic key is a mystery.

From this explosive beginning, and the four-note motive, Beethoven constructs his first theme, allowing the first movement to surge forward with the exposition, only to be interrupted periodically. The second theme is announced *fortissimo* in a contrasting key by the French horn (②). It expands the motive to a slightly longer, more insistent pattern—short-short-short-long-long-long—that momentarily breaks the flow of the rhythm. While the second theme continues in a gentle, lyrical vein, the original motive reappears in the bass line (③). Then, the motive unfolds in a forceful series of statements cascading downward from the high range of the winds, bringing the exposition to an exciting close. Another dramatic pause—two bars of silence—interrupts the music before the repeat of the exposition.

Beethoven begins the development section by reusing the four-note motive and its dramatic pause, this time with slight changes to the melody that prepare for a series of modulations. He guides the motive through numerous repetitions that gradually build in intensity and dissonance. When the repetitions reach their climax, the motive shrinks from four to two notes and finally to one note. This one note piece of the motive is exchanged in chords between the winds and strings (④) as the dynamics drop from *fortissimo* to *pianissimo.* This quiet section is the eerie calm before the storm. Suddenly, the four-note motive erupts *fortissimo*, and we reach the recapitulation, decisively marked by the now familiar fermata.

Beethoven has one more surprise in store for us. Just a few bars into the recapitulation, the orchestra halts, and the oboe offers a plaintive cadenza in an *Adagio*, not *Allegro* tempo (⑤). It is as if time stands still so that Beethoven can briefly explore the dimensions of the pause. Then the music resumes its wild course, retracing the events of the exposition, but with the second theme now stated in the tonic major, C major. However, instead of maintaining the major key, the music veers off into a coda that quickly reasserts the original tonic of C minor. Unlike the restrained codas of Haydn and Mozart, Beethoven's coda is quite long. In it, he presents many more statements of the four-note motive, including a new closing figure with exchanges between the wind and strings (⑥). Finally, we reach the insistent ending of the movement, which Beethoven emphasizes with eleven chords. This choice is another contrast with Mozart and Haydn, who might have found four or five chords sufficient. This type of emphatic ending is typical of Beethoven's middle period, and its emphatic, heroic style.

LISTENING MAP 34

BEETHOVEN, Symphony No. 5 in C minor, First Movement (Allegro con brio)

{1808}

FORM	Sonata form
METER	Duple
SCORING	Full orchestra (two flutes, two oboes, two clarinets, two bassoons, two French horns, two trumpets, two timpani, and strings; in the last movement Beethoven adds piccolo, contrabassoon, and three trombones)
OVERVIEW	Four notes (short-short-short-long, with a pause) are all that Beethoven needed to build an entire symphonic movement in sonata form. The two themes of the exposition use the telltale rhythm, and nearly every measure of the movement conveys its restless energy

why to LISTEN

It is nearly impossible *not* to listen to the Fifth Symphony because it so often appears in popular culture. Even if you have never heard all four movements of the Fifth, you have more than likely heard the famous first four notes that provide the basis for the entire composition. Soon after its first performance, the music took on an iconic significance that has lasted some two hundred years.

And there are no signs that the power of this music will fade any time soon. Whether you embrace the well-worn idea that the opening represents Fate knocking at the door, this masterpiece seems to communicate Beethoven's personal struggle to overcome adversity. That is a human narrative to which many can relate.

first LISTEN

EXPOSITION	DEVELOPMENT	RECAPITULATION	CODA
0:00	**2:40**	**4:00**	**5:46**
First four-note theme; modulates to second six-note theme (new key); Closing return to four-note theme	Exploration of four-note motive	First motif returns, followed by brief cadenza to second theme	Return to tonic leads to coda in tonic minor; four-note motive interrupted by new theme exchanged by winds and strings before emphatic ending

a deeper LISTEN

TIME	SECTION	LISTEN FOR THIS
0:00	Exposition	**First Theme** (Tonic minor key) ① Four-note motive (short-short-short-long) ending in a pause (𝄐) and immediately repeated one step lower with another pause Allegro con brio *ff*
0:06		Several more repetitions of motive, leading to more pauses and repetitions of motive Brief modulation
0:41		**Second Theme** (second key) ② Motive expanded to six notes (short-short-short-long-long-long) in the French horn *ff*
0:44		③ Lyrical extension of second theme, with four-note motive as accompaniment in the bass *p*
0:52		Music builds in intensity
1:11		**Closing** Cascading repetitions of four-note motive in winds; chords, rests
1:20		**(EXPOSITION REPEATED)**

Continued

TIME	SECTION	LISTEN FOR THIS
2:40	Development	Four-note motive (short-short-short-long) in horns and pause; several statements of motive, modulating, building in intensity
3:26		(4) Rupture of motive into paired chords, then individual chords exchanged between winds and strings with diminuendo from ***ff*** to ***pp*** 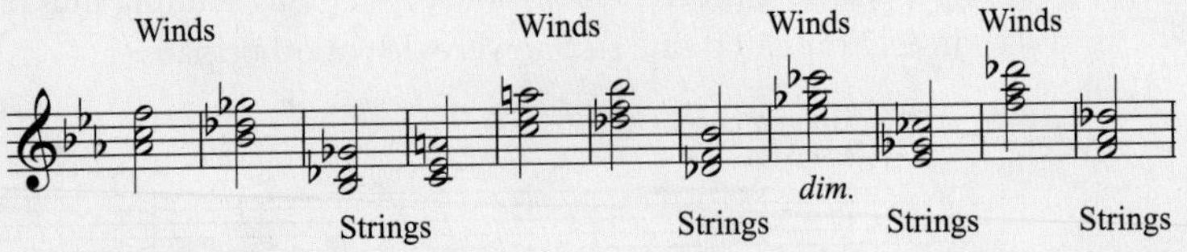 Winds Winds Winds Winds Strings Strings *dim.* Strings Strings
3:47		Four-note motive suddenly reemerges, ***ff***
4:00	Recapitulation	**First Theme (tonic minor)** Four-note motive and pause, repeated, with pause; music resumes then
4:16		(5) Brief oboe cadenza  ***f***
4:28		**Music resumes**
4:48		**Second Theme (tonic major)**
5:30		**Closing** Expected ending in tonic major is diverted
5:46	Coda	Return to tonic minor with frequent pounding repetitions of four-note motive
5:57		(6) New closing figure with exchanges between winds and strings  ***sf*** ***sf***
6:28		Two statements of opening motive with two pauses
6:36		Sudden drop from ***ff*** to ***pp***, interrupted by final bars, ending with eleven ***ff*** chords

SECOND MOVEMENT (*ANDANTE CON MOTO*)

After the dramatic first movement, the symphony continues with a slow variation movement based on a graceful theme in a major key (**Listening Map 35**). Heard first in the cellos and violas, this theme (*A*) continues in the winds and then the violins (1). In contrast to the brisk duple meter of the first movement, the *Andante* moves in a gentle triple meter. It proceeds with classical restraint until the music suddenly swerves from the A-flat major key of the opening to C major. Now the trumpets and horns blare out a *fortissimo* **fanfare** (*B*), a short, ceremonial flourish typically played by brass instruments. This particular fanfare displays a distinctive four-note motive (short-short-short-long) (2) that reworks the familiar four-note motive from the first movement so that it fits into triple meter:

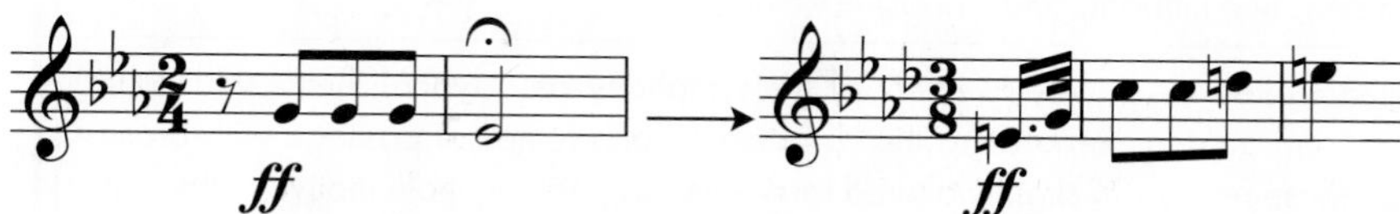

A soft, mysterious transition returns us to the original key of A-flat major as Beethoven launches a series of four variations. The first two variations add ornamental notes in progressively faster rhythms (3 and 4). The third variation turns the movement to a minor key. And the fourth variation carries the theme in the violins while the winds imitate it a measure later. A coda, initially pushing the tempo faster before settling back to the *Andante con moto*, rounds out the movement.

THIRD MOVEMENT (*ALLEGRO*)

Beethoven usually labeled the third movement of his symphonies a minuet or scherzo. But in the Fifth Symphony he provided just the tempo marking, *Allegro* (**Listening Map 36**). Nothing in this movement suggests the courtly world of the minuet. And if Beethoven conceived the movement as a scherzo, it begins in a most unusual way. First we hear a *pianissimo* figure in the low strings answered by the violins before a halt on yet another fermata (1). The starting and stopping of this *A* section is like a distorted memory of the first movement. The halting melody continues until the real theme emerges *fortissimo* in the horns (2). The real theme is yet another variant of the familiar short-short-short-long motive, again adapted so that it fits into the triple meter of the movement. The militant-sounding theme has a darker quality than the humorous themes of a typical scherzo.

LISTENING MAP 35

BEETHOVEN, Symphony No. 5 in C minor, Second Movement (Andante con moto)

{1808}

FORM	Theme and variations
METER	Triple
SCORING	Full orchestra (two flutes, two oboes, two clarinets, two bassoons, two French horns, two trumpets, two timpani, and strings)
OVERVIEW	Beethoven crafted the slow movement of his symphony as a lyrical theme with four variations and a coda. Separating the variations is a ceremonial passage with brass fanfares. These revive—in slightly altered form—the original four-note motive of the first movement.

first LISTEN

THEME	VAR. 1	VAR. 2	VAR. 3	VAR. 4	CODA
0:00	1:50	3:39	6:09	6:48	7:33
First statements of A–B	A: Faster, ornamental notes; B repeated	A: Even faster; B repeated	A: Minor key, in winds	A: Return to major, theme traded by violins and winds	Briefly faster then returns to original rhythm

a deeper LISTEN

TIME	SECTION	LISTEN FOR THIS
0:00	Theme (*Andante con moto*)	① **A:** Theme in violas and cellos, then flute, and finally violins; first key  *p*
1:10		② **B:** Short-short-short-long motive, swerves from first key to C major with fanfare-like statement in trumpets and horns  *ff* *sf*

TIME	SECTION	LISTEN FOR THIS
1:26		Transition with diminuendo leading back to first key
1:50	Variation 1	(3) **A:** Theme ornamented with slightly faster notes (first key) 
2:57		**B:** Fanfare-like motive in trumpets and horns (C major)
3:13		Transition leading back to first key
3:39	Variation 2	(4) **A:** Theme ornamented with even faster notes (first key) 
4:47		Pause; transition featuring woodwinds
5:27		**B:** Fanfare-like motive in trumpets and horns (C major)
6:09	Variation 3	**A:** Theme in woodwinds in minor key
6:48	Variation 4	**A:** Theme in violins imitated by woodwinds
7:33	Coda	Slightly faster tempo, then original *Andante con moto* tempo

In contrast, the trio (*B*), written in a bright C major, has a playful character in keeping with a scherzo. Here Beethoven writes a mock **fugato**, or small-scale fugue, with a bustling theme that rises from the lower strings to reach its height in the violins ((3)). The return of *A* revives the sinister tone of the opening of the movement. However, the music now seems disembodied because Beethoven brings the dynamics level in the strings down to *pianissimo* and instructs them to play the principal theme pizzicato (by plucking rather than by using the bow). This results in an uncanny echo of the formerly robust horn theme. When the orchestra seems to reach the movement's final cadence, the strings hold the tonic pitch at a barely audible triple *piano* (*ppp*) level. But this is not an ending, for the muffled timpani continue to tap out the four-note motive. Eventually the motive blends into constant timpani strokes as the violins hint at the mysterious opening motive of the movement, pushing it higher and higher. Finally, a dramatic crescendo spills over into the triumphant final movement, which begins with radiant C-major harmonies.

LISTENING MAP 36

BEETHOVEN, Symphony No. 5 in C minor, Third Movement (Allegro)

{1808}

FORM	Scherzo with trio
METER	Triple
SCORING	Full orchestra (two flutes, two oboes, two clarinets, two bassoons, two French horns, two trumpets, two timpani, and strings)
OVERVIEW	In the third movement, the four-note motive returns in yet another guise, to introduce a *fortissimo* theme in the French horns. Contrasting with its heavy-handedness is the comical nature of the middle section, the trio, which enters as a playful fugato (small-scale fugue).

first LISTEN

SCHERZO (A), C MINOR	TRIO (B), C MAJOR	SCHERZO (A′), C MINOR	TRANSITION TO FINALE	FINALE
0:00	**1:44**	**3:13**	**4:21**	**4:54**
Halting introductory theme (cellos and basses) alternates with second four-note theme (horns)	Binary form: ‖: :‖‖: :‖ Mock fugal section played by strings	Modified, A′ Intro theme (cellos and basses) and horn theme now played by pizzicato strings	Strings hold note as timpani taps out four-note rhythm	Triumphant beginning of finale

a deeper LISTEN

TIME	SECTION	LISTEN FOR THIS
0:00	Scherzo (A), C minor	① Introductory ***pp*** theme in cellos and basses, answered by violins, with two pauses

TIME	SECTION	LISTEN FOR THIS
0:18		② French horn theme (*ff*) based on four-note short-short-short-long motive 
0:36		Introductory *pp* theme with pauses and crescendo to
0:56		French horn theme (*f*)
1:13		Introductory *pp* theme extended, this time without pauses
1:38		Full orchestra ends with horn theme (*ff*)
1:44	**Trio (B), C major (binary form): ‖: :‖‖: :‖**	③ New theme in strings: mock fugato (*f*) with four entries in the cellos and basses, then violas, second violins, and first violins 
1:58		Repeat of first section
2:14		Fugato continues with second section (*f*)
2:42		Repeat of second section written out, beginning *f* but then moving to *p* and *pp*
3:13	**Scherzo (Modified, A′), C minor**	Return of introductory *pp* theme in cellos and basses with two pauses
3:30		Pizzicato (plucked) violins now take over the former French horn theme, *pp*
4:21	**Transition to Finale**	Strings hold the tonic pitch while the timpani play the four-note motive
4:41		Motive collapses into individual timpani strokes while the violins hint at the introductory *pp* theme
4:54	**Finale**	Rapid crescendo, leading to the finale

FOURTH MOVEMENT (*ALLEGRO*)

Beethoven's linking of the third and fourth movements is one of the most striking features of the Fifth Symphony. This simple but forceful device shatters the mold of the Classical symphony. The suspenseful transition from C minor to C major underscores how Beethoven viewed the movements of his symphony as interconnected parts of a whole. Beethoven prepares for the triumphant finale in C major by introducing passages in C major in the slow movement and in the trio of the third movement.

To give the finale extra weight, Beethoven reinforces the orchestra by adding three trombones, a piccolo (a small flute that plays in a very high range), and a contrabassoon (a bassoon that plays in an especially low range). While the trombones strengthen the brass section and add a solemn tone, the piccolo and contrabassoon extend the high and low ranges of the orchestra. The addition of these instruments to the orchestra as the symphony turns from C minor to C major gives the sound a pronounced muscular quality.

Cast in sonata form, the finale reflects Beethoven's heroic style at its most magnificent (**Listening Map 37**). The two main themes of the exposition are simple:

1) The march-like first theme presents the pitches of the C-major triad in ascending order (①).
2) The second theme, introduced by a crisp upbeat of three quick notes, offers yet another variant of the fundamental short-short-short-long motive (②).

Beethoven devotes much of the development section to exploring the second theme. He takes this theme through a series of modulations that build steadily in intensity, all pulling us toward the recapitulation. However, before the recapitulation can occur, the music comes to a grinding halt. Then, another complete surprise: instead of the recapitulation, we here the sinister C-minor music of the scherzo played *pianissimo*, a distant reminder of where we have been. A dramatic crescendo leads us to the real recapitulation and its bright, affirming C-major hues.

How to end this colossal movement was Beethoven's ultimate challenge. He overcame it by writing a stirring coda that concludes not just the movement but the entire symphony. This coda frustrates our search for closure several times. One after another, final-sounding C-major chords are played as if the piece were ending, only to delay the final notes. Finally, the ending comes after an unrelenting pounding away at the tonic harmony. The ending resolves all of the dissonance and tension of the entire symphony in one of the most thrilling moments in music.

Beethoven's Late Period

By 1814 Napoleon's France had fallen to a coalition of England, Prussia, Austria, and Russia. The victorious allies organized the Congress of Vienna to redraw the map of Europe in what was perhaps the first true international summit. During the Congress of Vienna, Beethoven composed patriotic pieces to celebrate the Allies' victories, but his music now seemed to lack the dramatic power of the middle-period

LISTENING MAP 37

BEETHOVEN, Symphony No. 5 in C minor, Fourth Movement (Allegro)

{1808}

FORM	Sonata form
METER	Common time, $\frac{4}{4}$
SCORING	Full orchestra (one piccolo, two flutes, two oboes, two clarinets, two bassoons, one contrabassoon, two French horns, two trumpets, three trombones, two timpani, and strings)
OVERVIEW	For the finale, Beethoven devised a dramatic sonata-form movement that concludes the entire work. The finale also revisits elements of the earlier movements in innovative ways.

first LISTEN

EXPOSITION	EXPOSITION REPEATED	DEVELOPMENT	RECAPITULATION	CODA
0:00	**2:03**	**4:14**	**6:15**	**8:02**
Introduction of first march-like theme (tonic) and second short-short-short-long theme (second key)		Development of second theme	Restatement of first and second themes (now both in the tonic key)	False endings leading to final triumphant and insistent statement of the major harmony

a deeper LISTEN

TIME	SECTION	LISTEN FOR THIS
0:00	**Exposition**	① First theme: march-like, ***ff***, C major **Allegro** ***ff***
0:36		Bridge, modulating to second key

Continued

TIME	SECTION	LISTEN FOR THIS
1:03		② Second theme, second key, short-short-short-long motive  Violins *ff* *p* *crescendo*
1:31		Closing passage, second key
2:03	(Repeat of Exposition)	
4:14	Development	Development of second theme, modulating through several keys
5:42		Grand pause as if preparing for recapitulation
5:53		Recall of music from scherzo, minor key, ***pp***
6:19		Dramatic crescendo
6:15	Recapitulation	First theme, tonic key
6:51		Bridge
7:22		Second theme, tonic key
7:51		Closing passage, tonic key
8:02	Coda	Several sections that fail to reach the final cadence
9:46		Tempo accelerates through a transition to *Presto*
10:10		Final statement of first theme
10:38		Final pounding away at the tonic harmony

music, and these pieces were promptly forgotten. Almost completely deaf, he withdrew more and more from public life. A contemporary publication called *The Harmonicon* described the sadness of Beethoven's situation: "His extreme reserve towards strangers, which is carried to such excess . . . prevents him from displaying those excellent qualities, which, under a forbidding exterior, he is known to possess." He communicated with visitors by receiving written notes and then answering them verbally. Increasingly, the music of this period grew abstract and difficult for Beethoven's contemporaries to understand.

The first few years of the late period were surprisingly unproductive. Then, during 1823 and 1824, Beethoven finished two major works that had occupied him for years. The first, the *Missa Solemnis* (1823), was a majestic setting of the Mass on a large scale. Beethoven intended the work for one of his royal patrons and students, the Archduke Rudolph, to honor the archduke's 1819 appointment as Archbishop of Olmütz. Beethoven was unable to finish the Mass in time for the ceremony, however, and its completion required several more years of work. The second major work completed during this time was his Ninth Symphony (1824).

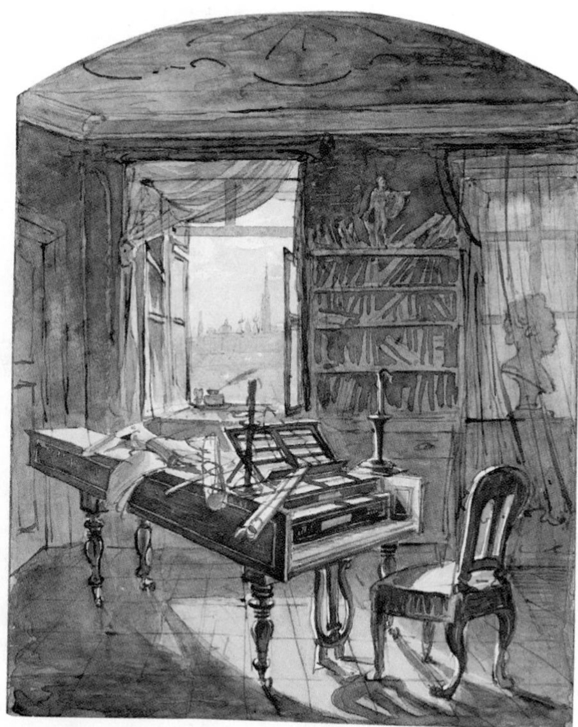

Sketch of Beethoven's study in Vienna.

The revolutionary Ninth Symphony presented a fundamentally new idea of the symphony and deeply influenced symphonic composition well into the twentieth century. Following the symphony's first three movements for orchestra was an enormous finale, inspired by Friedrich von Schiller's ode to universal brotherhood, the "Ode to Joy" (*An die Freude*). Beethoven's finale is nearly one thousand measures in length and takes more time to perform than some entire symphonies of Haydn or Mozart. The work also stands out because it was the first time vocal soloists and a chorus were used in a symphony. Despite its imposing complexity, the finale of the Ninth Symphony essentially unfolds as a series of variations on a simple melody: the "Ode to Joy." The melody transcended national barriers to become a melody known throughout the world. In 1989, the "Ode to Joy" gained additional meaning as an "Ode to Freedom" when Leonard Bernstein performed the symphony in Berlin after the Berlin Wall was opened and being torn down.

In his very last years, Beethoven wrote a series of six string quartets. By that time, he was fully dependent on his inner ear and memory of sound. In a sense, he was composing for himself rather than for others. The quartets reveal the primary qualities of Beethoven's late style: complex counterpoint, melodies of great lyrical beauty, and startling contrasts. Though these forward-looking works were misunderstood and initially rejected by many critics, they were warmly embraced by the generation of Romantic composers who followed him.

Beethoven's Death and Funeral

One might expect the composer of so much dramatic music to make a dramatic exit from this world. According to the accounts of his death, Beethoven did not disappoint. Shortly before he died on March 26, 1827, he was reported to have said in Latin, "Applaud, friends, the comedy is finished" before dying in the midst of a raging thunderstorm. An autopsy was performed, but the cause of death was not

Beethoven's funeral procession, as painted by Franz Stoeber (1827). Tens of thousands were in attendance.

clear. Several possibilities have been advanced, including lead poisoning, liver disease brought on by alcoholism, and kidney failure, to list just a few.

Although Beethoven lived a reclusive life in his last years, tens of thousands of Viennese turned out for his funeral, which was held on a scale usually reserved for the nobility. Among the pallbearers were several musicians, including the young composer Schubert, who would die within a year at the Mozartean age of thirty-one. The Austrian poet and playwright Franz Grillparzer delivered a eulogy not just for Beethoven but for the passing of an age as well.

Beethoven's Legacy

Beethoven was the crucial link between eighteenth-century Classicism and nineteenth-century Romanticism. He began by thoroughly understanding and mastering the Classical idioms of Haydn and Mozart, yet he soon transcended those idioms. For the composers who followed him, Beethoven's music took on a highly romanticized, mythical stature. He was viewed as a titan who created in solitude. In Beethoven's scores, the Romantics found a new expressive power and a statement of his unbending commitment to art. Understandably, they could not resist claiming Beethoven as one of their own.

MAKING CONNECTIONS *Eulogizing Beethoven*

The following is an excerpt from Franz Grillparzer's eulogy at Beethoven's funeral, March 29, 1827:

> As we stand here at the grave of this departed, we are, as it were, the representatives of a whole nation, of the entire German people, mourning the fall of the one highly celebrated half of what remained to us of the vanished splendor of native art, the flower of our country's spirit. True, the hero of poetry in the German language [Goethe] is with us still—and long may he remain with us! But the last Master of resounding song, the sweet lips that gave expression to the art of tones, the heir and successor of Handel's and Bach's, of Haydn's and Mozart's immortal fame, has ended his life, and we stand weeping beside the tattered strings of the silent instrument.

check your **KNOWLEDGE**

1. Compare the life stories of Beethoven, Haydn, and Mozart. How were they similar and different?
2. What were the three major periods of Beethoven's life as a composer? Describe how his music changed over time.
3. How does Beethoven's "Moonlight" Sonata break away from the Classical sonata?
4. Describe the innovations that Beethoven introduced in his Fifth Symphony. Why is it considered among his greatest works?
5. How did Beethoven's music change in the late period of his life? What new innovations did he introduce?

PART V SUMMARY: THE CLASSICAL PERIOD

- The Classical period witnessed a reaction against the complexities of Baroque music.
  - Broadly international in scope, Classical music culminated in the work of three composers active in Vienna: Joseph Haydn, Wolfgang Amadeus Mozart, and Ludwig van Beethoven.

- The Classical style favored melodies that divided into balanced phrases. It employed rhythmic variety and used new effects in dynamics, such as the crescendo and diminuendo.

- New genres included the symphony (for orchestra), string quartet (for two violins, one viola, and one cello), and Classical sonata (usually for one or two instruments, including a piano).
  - Each genre consisted of separate movements, usually in the sequence of *fast–slow–very fast* or *fast–slow-minuet and trio–very fast.*

- Classical composers used different forms within the movements of their instrumental works, including Classical sonata form, theme and variations, minuet and trio, and rondo.

- Joseph Haydn was the first great figure of Viennese Classicism.
  - A prolific composer who wrote in every genre of the time, Haydn produced over a thousand compositions.
  - Among his principal contributions is his long series of symphonies for orchestra and his string quartets for two violins, viola, and cello.

- Wolfgang Amadeus Mozart was the second great figure of Viennese Classicism.
  - A child prodigy and virtuoso pianist, Mozart composed in every genre of the time to produce over 600 compositions during his short career.
  - Among his contributions are symphonies, chamber music, piano concertos and piano music, Italian and German operas, and sacred music.

- The music of Ludwig van Beethoven linked the eighteenth-century classicism of Haydn and Mozart to nineteenth-century Romanticism.
  - Beethoven's career unfolded in Vienna, where he established himself as a piano virtuoso worthy of Mozart and as the dominant composer of the time.

- Beethoven's compositions are usually divided into three periods:
  - An early period, when he mastered the Classical style of Haydn and Mozart.
  - A middle period, when he wrote most of his revolutionary, heroic music.
  - A late period, when, imprisoned by total deafness, he created increasingly abstract, experimental music.

KEY TERMS

bridge 224
cadenza 251
cavatina 255
closing passage 224
coda 222
crescendo 217
decrescendo (diminuendo) 217
development 221
episode 230
exposition 220
fanfare 277
fortepiano 217
fugato 279
minuet and trio 225
modulate 220
motive 271
neoclassicism 216
opera buffa 254
opera seria 251
pizzicato 258
recapitulation (or reprise) 221
refrain 230
rondo 230
serenade 222
singspiel 258
slow introduction 222
solo 250
sonata 219
sonata form 220
staccato 215
string quartet 219
symphony 219
tenuto 215
theme and variations 225
tutti 250

KEY COMPOSERS

Joseph Haydn (1732–1809)
Wolfgang Amadeus Mozart (1756–1791)
Ludwig van Beethoven (1770–1827)

MUSICAL JOURNEYS
Beijing Opera

Beijing (Peking) opera is one of the most highly developed Chinese opera forms. Its popularity since the early twentieth century has given it the status of national opera of the People's Republic of China.

Although its roots go much deeper, the form underwent significant developments in the late nineteenth century as a result of imperial patronage. The early decades of the twentieth century are considered Beijing opera's golden age. Until the outbreak of war with Japan in 1937, the tradition remained extremely vital, with its practitioners actively involved in artistic experimentation. Many of the schools of performance that developed during this prewar period continue to dominate contemporary practice. In addition, works from this era comprise a large portion of today's standard repertory.

The composition of a single opera involved not only a librettist (who wrote the text) and musicians (who set the text) but actors. All of the major actors of the golden age were involved in the composition of new operas and the revision of old ones. They influenced textual and melodic construction in addition to designing their individual dances.

A Beijing opera performance.

Social activists viewed Beijing opera as a potentially powerful vehicle for social and political change. The Beijing opera reform movement—at its height from approximately 1908 to 1917—was one such campaign. Activists involved with it believed that the theater served as a classroom for the largely illiterate masses. Progressive performers staged new operas called *shizhuang jingju* (contemporary-costume Beijing opera), the texts of which often focused on contemporary social problems. The staging of these dramas employed realistic scenery, and actors wore costumes based on current clothing styles. Until this era of widespread social change, women had been virtually excluded from the theater, both as performers and as spectators. A number of all-female troupes were active in the early 1900s, but they performed mostly at private gatherings and not in public theaters.

Unrest in China from 1937 to 1949 significantly disrupted the performance and creation of Beijing opera. After the establishment of the communist People's Republic of China in 1949, the style was reformed according to the ideology of Mao Zedong. Mao demanded that Beijing opera should serve the "workers, peasants and soldiers," not the upper classes. It was his belief that art should help convert the masses to communism. The reformers made changes to the texts and performance conventions to emphasize patriotism, democracy, and equality between the sexes. They also created new operas on contemporary themes.

Until 1963 traditional opera flourished alongside the new communist-themed works. However, during the Cultural Revolution (1966–1976), when a political upheaval intended to emphasize Maoist beliefs, traditional works were strictly banned and were replaced by state-approved "model operas" (*yangbanxi*). After the Cultural Revolution came to a halt in 1976, the traditional repertory slowly reclaimed its place on the stage.

Tune Families and Instruments

Most traditional Beijing opera music belongs to either the *xipi* or *erhuang* tune families, groups of interrelated melodies. Xipi and erhuang may be thought of as counterparts of the Western modes (see Chapter 7). While they share the same basic scale, their cadential pitches are different, as are other crucial melodic and rhythmic features. Their dramatic associations are also distinct: erhuang is typically used in serious or melancholy situations, whereas xipi is heard in livelier, happier circumstances. Both xipi and erhuang have a number of different song types. Songs belonging to the same family share tonal, modal, and large structural features, but they vary in terms of metrical structure, tempo, melodic detail, and specific dramatic or emotional associations.

Purely percussive music constitutes another important kind of Beijing opera music. Percussion patterns punctuate the actors' speech and movement, provide sound effects, and mark the structural divisions of an opera, including its beginning, ending, and scene changes.

The traditional orchestra is made up of two main sections, the *wenchang* ("civil section"), which plays the melody; and the wuchang ("martial section"), which contains percussion instruments. The core *wenchang* instruments are *jinghu, jing erhu,* and *yueqin.* The jinghu and the jing erhu have two strings and are played with a bow. The timbre of the jinghu is sharp and piercing, in contrast to the more mellow and sonorous jing erhu, which is pitched an octave lower. The jing erhu is only used to accompany female and young male roles. The *yueqin* is a short-necked plucked lute with a large round body and two to four strings.

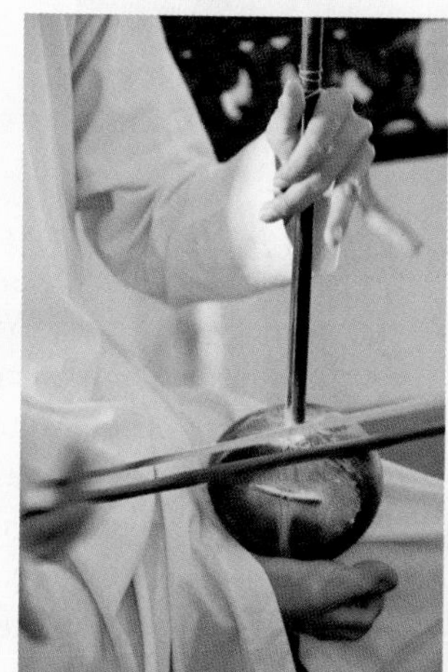

A musician playing an *erhu*.

Four players form the core of the wuchang. The leader plays both a drum called the *danpigu* and the clappers (an instrument that claps together two small boards) and is responsible for leading and signaling the entire ensemble. The danpigu is a small, single-headed drum that sits on a large three-legged stand and is played with bamboo sticks. A small gong, a large gong, and a pair of cymbals round out the rest of the wuchang, and other musical instruments may be added.

The Ruse of the Empty City

One classic Beijing opera is *The Ruse of the Empty City* (**Listening Map I.4**). Its plot is based on a story set in the period of the Three Kingdoms (220–265 CE) as related in a fourteenth-century Chinese historical novel. It is set in the Kingdom of Shu, which was ruled from Xicheng (the Western City) by its premier, Zhuge Liang. Sensing that the kingdom was growing weak, the general Sima Yi from the nearby Wei kingdom marched an army toward the city. To protect his people, Zhuge Liang opened the city gates and urged all of his citizens to hide. Zhuge Liang himself posed as a scholar and sat on the city's gate playing the *ch'in* (a stringed lute). At first, Sima Yi hesitated, knowing that Zhuge Liang was a powerful opponent and fearing that the "empty city" might be a trap. He retreated but was then convinced to return to lay siege to the city; meanwhile Zhuge Liang had time to call in reinforcements, and the siege was defeated.

LISTENING MAP *I.4*

Beijing Opera: Solo sung by GENERAL SIMA YI, from *The Ruse of the Empty City: A Traditional Peking Opera,* released in 1960

FORM	Beijing opera
SCORING	Male vocals; percussion instruments: "rising" high-pitch gong (*xiao luo*), "falling" low-pitch gong (*da luo*), cymbals, woodblock; and melodic instruments: jinghu (high-range fiddle, i.e., bowed lute), yueqin (plucked lute)
OVERVIEW	A vocal solo from a traditional Beijing opera, accompanied by both the melody and percussion instruments. This selection is sung by Sima Yi as he stands at the city gates. His soldiers urge him to attack, but Sima Yi is concerned by the seemingly empty city and hesitates. He vows to meet the forces of Zhuge Liang as an equal.

why to LISTEN

Beijing opera—like Western opera—is a highly stylized form of musical performance. On first listen, the instrument tonalities and clattering percussion may strike your ears as bizarre. The singing is stylized, as is the singing in Italian opera and other Western music. For example, a death-metal vocalist's style is just as calculated as that of a Beijing opera singer; they are both artistic artifices designed to express specific emotional or narrative states.

In Beijing opera, the ancient-sounding music and singing go hand in hand with the larger-than-life mythical stories that the operas tell. These are not everyday people engaged in normal activities; these are godlike men and women struggling with greater concerns, drawn from the rich history and mythology of China. The music of these godlike heroes is thus anything but ordinary.

first LISTEN

INSTRUMENTAL INTRODUCTION	SONG	CONCLUSION
0:00	**0:23**	**2:27**
Instruments set the scene for the action, playing without rhythm; melody and rhythm are then introduced.	Vocalist's verses alternate with instrumental interludes.	Instruments and the vocalist perform in free rhythm to signal end of section.

TIME	SECTION	LISTEN FOR THIS
0:00	Instrumental Introduction	Contrasting "rising" and "falling" pitched gongs, typically highlighting actors' movement. The woodblock sounds along with the upper-ranged gong, while the cymbals follow the lower-ranged gong.
0:12		Melodic ensemble (fiddle and plucked lute) enters.
0:23	Song	**Vocal: First verse** Vocalist portraying Sima Yi enters. The fiddle plays a matching melodic line with some variation.
0:36		**Instrumental** Interlude initiated by the percussion instruments.
0:45		**Vocal: Second verse** Vocalist returns with instrumental accompaniment.
0:57		**Instrumental** Interlude without gongs or cymbals.
1:05		**Vocal: Third verse** Vocalist returns with instrumental accompaniment.
1:15		**Instrumental** Interlude without gongs or cymbals.
1:24		**Vocal: Fourth verse** Vocalist with instrumental accompaniment.
1:35		**Instrumental**
1:42		**Vocal: Fifth verse** Vocalist with instrumental accompaniment; extends pitches in the closing phrase (1:51).
1:53		**Instruments and Vocalists** Falling gong followed by vocal shouts portraying Sima Yi's soldiers—"*Sa! Sa! Sa!*" ("Kill! Kill! Kill!")—urging him to invade the city.
2:00		**Instrumental** The full ensemble punctuates movement of the main actor as he moves across the stage for his final verse.
2:09		**Vocal: Sixth verse** The vocalist returns with the full ensemble. Increased rhythmic density of the vocal line, as well as melodic variations between vocalist and melodic instruments. Extended verse At 2:25, all performers briefly stop as the woodblock sounds two clicks to signal the closing phrase.
2:27	Conclusion	Shift to free rhythm as the vocalist and melodic instruments extend the duration of their melodic pitches. At 2:35, gongs and cymbals punctuate the end of the piece.

PART

The Romantic Period

All art constantly aspires towards the condition of music. —WALTER PATER

Caspar David Friedrich, *The Wanderer above a Sea of Fog* (1817).

When you think of the word *romantic*, what images come to mind? Today the term most often describes a certain expression of love, especially in the early stages of a relationship. But in the arts, *Romantic* has many other meanings. In music, the Romantic movement of the early nineteenth century erupted in reaction to the Classical era's emphasis on balance and symmetry. Romantic artists—particularly

Eugène Delacroix's painting *Liberty Leading the People* (1830), an idealized and symbolic representation of the July Revolution in France, captured the spirit of Romanticism.

writers and painters—were drawn to nature, finding in it the same awe-inspiring grandeur and beauty that previous generations had found in religion. Rather than emphasizing form and balance, the Romantic artists found new inspiration in the freedom of nature. Classical constraint gave way to unbounded feeling; rational thought, to the free play of emotions.

The term *Romantic* comes from *roman*, a type of medieval poem written in one of the Romance languages. Around 1800, German critics detected features of the *roman*—its emphasis on romance, the fantastic, and the supernatural—in the literature of their own time. They called this literature "Romantic" because they thought it was influenced by medieval models rather the models from classical antiquity that influenced eighteenth-century literature. Critics began to sharpen the distinction between Classical and Romantic art. Classical art tended toward objective beauty and formal purity. Romantic art tended toward subjective content and the mixing of different forms and genres. Classical art suggested the mechanical and finite; Romantic art, the natural and the infinite.

As the nineteenth century progressed, *Romantic* gained additional meanings, until at last it described a great variety of new art and literature. Romantic art and literature displayed the following hallmarks:

- Fascination with the gothic
- Freeing of the imagination and its irrational forces
- Emphasis on emotions

- Celebration of originality
- Yearning for the infinite

Romantic acquired so many meanings that it eventually lost much of its usefulness for describing the arts of this period. But it has endured as a label for the nineteenth-century reaction against Classicism.

Romanticism was not a unified movement. It pursued different paths in different parts of Europe, primarily in Germany, France, and England. One German forerunner was the *Sturm und Drang* (*Storm and Stress*) movement of the 1770s. The *Sturm and Drang* produced plays and novels with highly emotional characters, who often met tragic ends. One writer touched by the *Sturm und Drang* was Johann Wolfgang von Goethe (1749–1832). His sensational novel *The Sorrows of Young Werther* (1774) concerns a young man who kills himself in a fit of lovesick despair. A free spirit, Werther prefers art that expresses genius and is not bound by rules. His behavior and outlook clash with the enlightened, rationalist thought of the Classical period, and anticipate the attitudes of Romantic writers and artists who followed in the nineteenth century. Goethe's novel was an immediate bestseller, and its influence spread throughout Europe. Young men began dressing like Werther, wearing a blue jacket and yellow pants, and some of the most disillusioned even took their own lives, as life imitated art.

In France, an important influence on the Romantic movement was the philosopher Jean-Jacques Rousseau (1712–1778), who exposed his candid feelings in his *Confessions* (1782). Rousseau viewed his work as a kind of diary-like autobiography that recorded his personal feelings with a frankness freed from the conventions of literary style. In his philosophical writings, Rousseau viewed modern mankind as corrupted by civilization, and our distant ancestors as "noble savages" who had lived in an innocent state of nature. Rousseau's ideas about civilization forecast the French Revolution, which unleashed its full fury in 1789. The revolution not only tore the fabric of French society but also advanced new views about the role of the modern artist.

The Dream of Ossian (1813) by Jean-Auguste-Dominique Ingres. Ossian—supposedly a hero from Celtic mythology—became a powerful Romantic symbol in the hands of Romantic artists.

In England, too, the arts underwent profound change. Artists moved toward new models that focused on local sources and personal expression. An unusual influence was one of the great literary forgeries of all time. In the 1760s, readers were introduced to Ossian, a mythic Celtic poet from the third century BCE. Ossian was actually the invention of the enterprising Scotsman James Macpherson (1736–1796). Macpherson pieced together bits of epic poetry from the Greeks and Romans and set them in Ireland and Scotland to create the so-called Ossianic poems. He then passed them off as parts of an original Celtic epic poem, crediting himself only as its "translator." The work described the pre-civilized world of the Celts, as well as their wars and interactions with supernatural figures. An Ossianic craze followed the release of Macpherson's work and quickly spread beyond England. Goethe's Werther declared that Ossian had replaced Homer in his heart, and Napoleon carried a copy of Ossian with him during his campaigns.

What all these authors shared was a reaction against eighteenth-century Enlightened thought. The Romantics overturned the Classical notion that art imitated external objects or ideas and that artists should follow time-honored models. Newly empowered, the Romantics countered thought that a work of art generated its own creative energy. Instead of imitating the world, art expressed the artist's highly original experiences of it. The Romantics relied on their own feelings and genius. And for them what counted was not the objective form of art but its subjective content.

Responses to these revolutionary ideas were wide ranging. In England, William Wordsworth (1770–1850) declared that poetry expressed the spontaneous outpouring of feelings. He and fellow Romantic Samuel Taylor Coleridge (1772–1834) published *The Lyrical Ballads* (1798), which embodied the Romantic spirit. Wordsworth's "Tintern Abbey," the final poem in the collection, combined the gothic setting of a ruined, twelfth-century abbey and a fascination with the natural world. Also

Tintern Abbey, the Transept (ca. 1795) by J. M. W. Turner. Its haunted location was the subject of a famous poem by Wordsworth.

appearing in the collection, Coleridge's "Rime of the Ancient Mariner" is a perfect example of the Romantics' focus on the individual. Its story of a mariner haunted by his act of shooting an albatross combines the Romantic views of the supernatural and an individual struggling with deep feelings of guilt.

In France, the writer Victor Hugo (1802–1885) defined Romanticism as "liberalism in nature." Hugo's most famous novel, *Les Misérables*, celebrates a representative man, Jean Valjean, who clashes with the rules and conventions of society. In America, Nathaniel Hawthorne (1804–1864) and Edgar Allan Poe (1809–1849) found inspiration in the occult and grotesque, and in individuals depicted as "outsiders." Hawthorne's main character in his novel *The Scarlet Letter*, Hester Prynne, refuses to name the father of her child, the product of an adulterous relationship. Her challenge to social norms creates turmoil in the Puritanical society of Boston where she lives. Hawthorne's contemporary Poe is famous for numerous stories that focused on the macabre, but again also featured outlawed heroes who defied societal constraints. All these examples show the Romantics' determination to explore new ways of expressing their diverse subjective experiences. Romantic composers explored these experiences as well, and attempted to release the full range of their emotional world in a colorful language of tones.

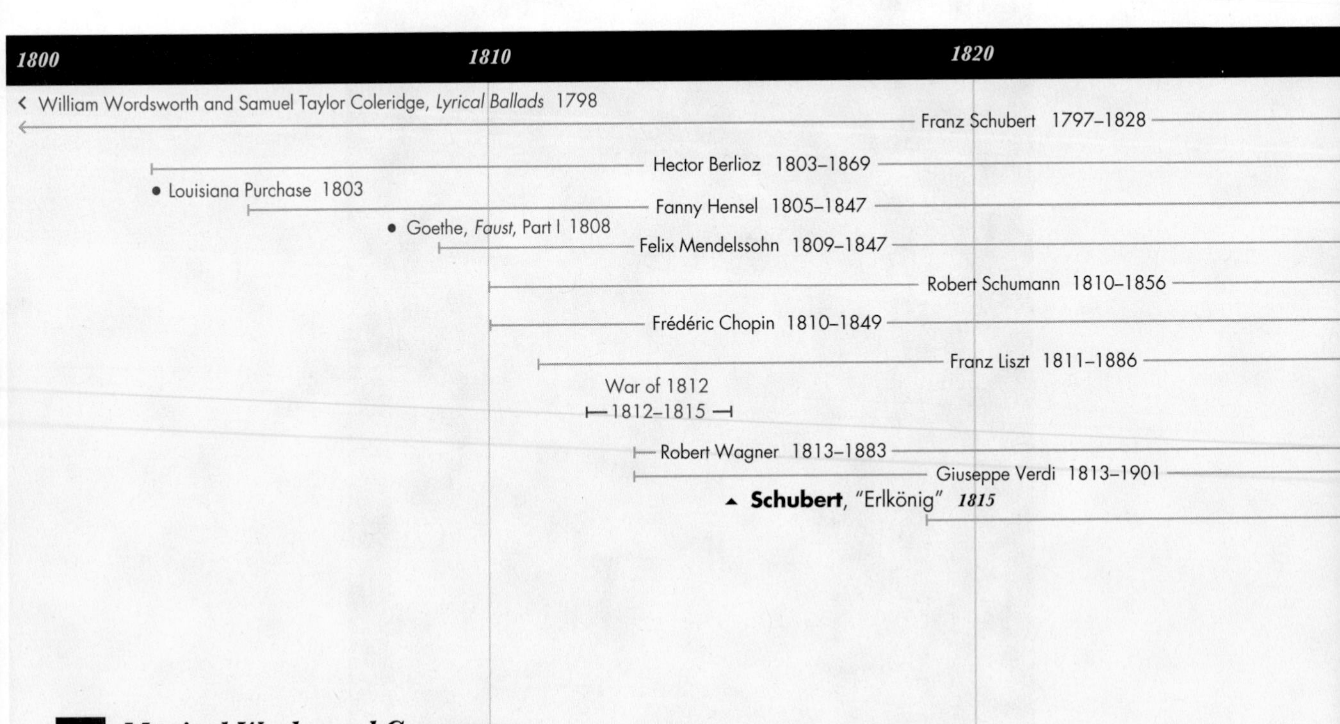

WHY LISTEN TO *Romantic Music?*

Somewhere in the second half of the eighteenth century, the status of music began to rise among the arts. Until then, music had often been regarded as a diversion because of its association with subjective emotional experiences. But with the transformation brought on by the Romantic movement—including its new interest in subjectivity—music acquired new allure and prestige. By the late nineteenth century, music's position among the arts had changed considerably. The influential English critic Walter Payter captured music's new importance when he wrote that "all art constantly aspires towards the condition of music."

Today we have lost much of the Romantics' enthusiasm for seeing the world primarily through our subjective feelings. But we are still very much aware of music's power to express and appeal to our emotions directly and meaningfully. This sense that music can communicate in a way that words cannot is a nod to nineteenth-century Romanticism, and a compelling reason why we should listen.

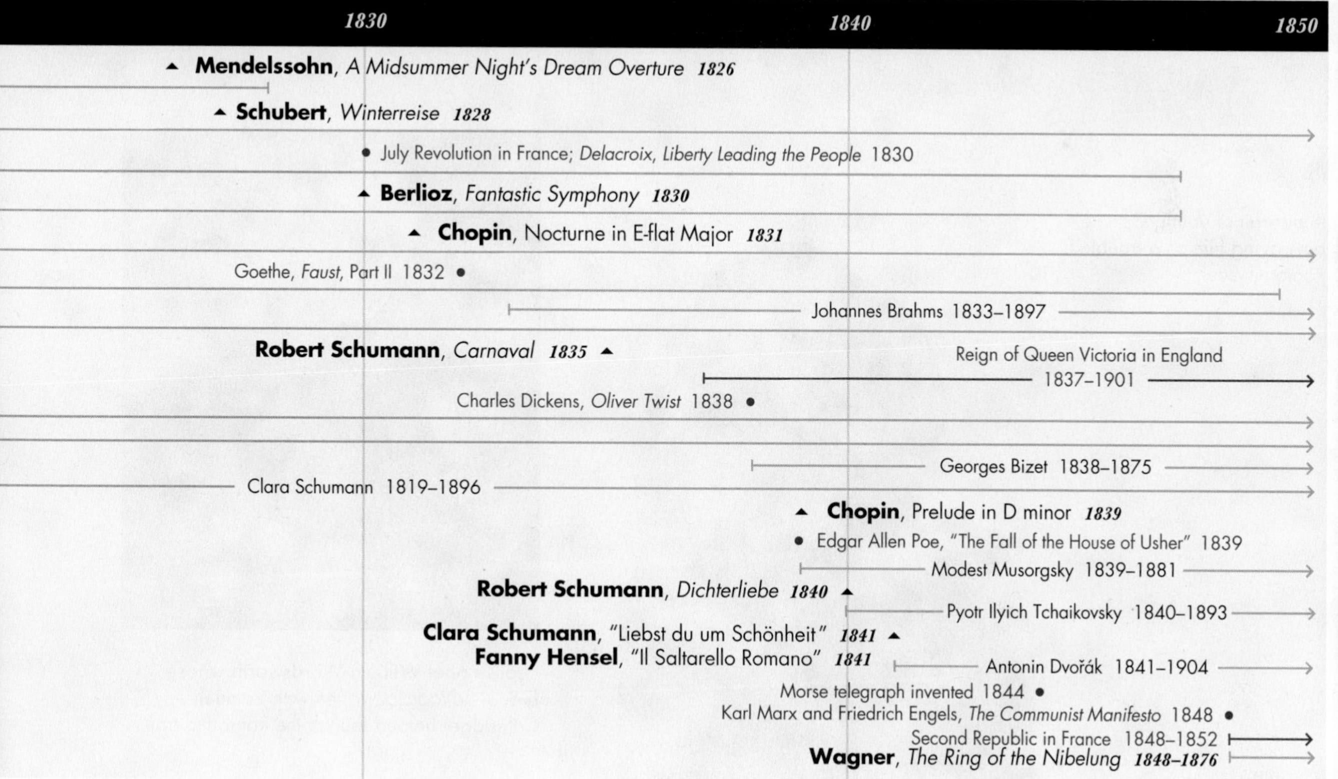

Continued

1850	1860	1870
• Nathaniel Hawthorne, *The Scarlet Letter* 1850		
▲ **Verdi**, *Rigoletto* *1851*		
	▲ **Liszt**, *Petrarch Sonnet No. 104* *1858*	
← Hector Berlioz 1803–1869		
	American Civil War 1861–1865	
	▲ **Wagner**, *Tristan and Isolde* *1865*	
← Robert Schumann 1810–1856		
		Mussorgsky, *Pictures at an Exhibition* *1874* ▲
		Bizet, *Carmen* *1875* ▲
← Johannes Brahms 1833–1897		
← Franz Liszt 1811–1886		
← Reign of Queen Victoria in England 1837–1901		
	Gustav Mahler 1860–1911	
← Richard Wagner 1813–1883		
← Giuseppe Verdi 1813–1901		
← Georges Bizet 1838–1875		
← Clara Schumann 1819–1896		
← Modest Mussorgsky 1839–1881		
← Pyotr Ilyich Tchaikovsky 1840–1893		
← Antonin Dvořák 1841–1904		
← Second Republic in France 1848–1852		
← **Wagner**, *The Ring of the Nibelung* *1848–1876*		

A portrait of young Goethe, portraying him as a troubled, Romantic soul.

English poet William Wordsworth whose *Lyrical Ballads* (cowritten with Samuel Coleridge) helped launch the Romantic age.

1880 1890 1900

Richard Strauss 1864–1949

▲ **Brahms**, Violin Concerto in D major *1879*

▲ **Tchaikovsky**, *Romeo and Juliet* *1880*

▲ **Strauss**, *Death and Transfiguration* *1890*

▲ **Dvořák**, Symphony No. 9 *1893*

Musical Works and Composers

History and Culture

Karl Marx, whose revolutionary ideas about government helped spawn twentieth-century communism.

Edgar Allen Poe, American poet and essayist, whose image as a tortured writer fit well into the Romantic movement.

CHAPTER 35 Music in the Romantic Period

Franz Liszt conducts at a concert in Budapest, 1865.

In the same way the term "romantic" acquired many different meanings, Romantic music included a diverse group of composers with individual styles of expression. Still, several telltale signs distinguish Romantic music from eighteenth-century Classical music. Composers of the Romantic period had distinctive approaches to melody, dynamics, rhythm, harmony, form, and timbre.

During the nineteenth century, the social status of composers changed. Now less dependent for their livelihoods on European courts, composers found support in a growing middle class that attended public concerts. Many cities established their own civic orchestras to satisfy this growing consumer base. Of course, the same economic forces that created the new artistic freedom posed challenges. Few composers could survive by selling their music, and many had to find other ways to support themselves. Some gave lessons, others went on concert tours, and still others turned to music journalism. In the concert halls and opera houses, they struggled to find new audiences to support their art. But however they pursued their careers, Romantic composers exploited their new freedom with energy and daring.

The nineteenth century is sometimes described as the century of Romantic music, but this is an oversimplification. Signs of musical Romanticism emerged in the late eighteenth century, and the movement was more or less over by the mid-1800s. Increasingly after 1850, new directions in the arts, including realism, naturalism, symbolism, and impressionism, challenged Romanticism. By the end of the century, composers were creating music fundamentally different from the Romantic music of the first half of the century.

Even at the height of Romanticism, music had lingering ties to Classicism. Nearly every Romantic composer was indebted in some way to the music of the great Viennese Classicists. The Romantics' relationship to this music was different for each composer. Some relied heavily on classical forms while others strove to break cleanly from the past. The most accurate way of understanding nineteenth-century music is to acknowledge the presence of both movements. Classicism and Romanticism were like two intertwining strands, with Romanticism increasingly more prominent, and Classicism less so. Nineteenth-century composers transformed the Classical style and romanticized the legacies of Haydn, Mozart, and Beethoven to create a new kind of music.

Melody in Romantic Music

Romantic composers valued music that was spontaneous. Generally avoiding the tidy, balanced phrases of Classical melodies, they created freer melodies that suggested imbalance and unpredictability.

A vivid example is the opening melody of Frédéric Chopin's Prelude in D minor for piano (see also p. 333). It begins simply enough with a three-note descending figure. From this opening, Chopin spins out an agitated melody, intense and passionate, that unfolds in two parts:

Chopin: Prélude in D minor, Op. 28 No. 24

The first part consists of a phrase that crests on the downbeat of bar 3. The second phrase (beginning in bar 5) retraces the three-note descent from the beginning, but now stretches to a higher range, peaking on the downbeat of bar 7. Chopin then extends and intensifies this second phrase. To finish off the second phrase, he adds a totally unanticipated gesture in the twelfth measure: a rushing scale that climbs three octaves before breaking off abruptly in the highest reach of the piano. What begins as a singable melody quickly turns into a fantasy playable only on the piano.

Dynamics and Expression Marks in Romantic Music

Romantic composers also set off their music from the Classical period by exploring a wide range of dynamics. Instead of just using the traditional range of dynamics from, say, *pianissimo* (***pp***, for very soft) to *fortissimo* (***ff***, for very loud), they now added more extreme markings—***fff***, for example, or even ***ppppp***, to suggest nothing more than a hint of a whisper of a sound. They used dynamics to help reinforce an impression of spontaneity. The opening of Chopin's prelude again serves as a good example. Chopin begins *forte* only to subside immediately through a *diminuendo.* Then, the second and third bars swell and ebb in volume. Finally, Chopin gradually increases the intensity, adding three more crescendos, the last accompanying the surging ascending scale.

In addition to bold, flexible treatments of dynamics, Romantic composers stamped their individuality onto their scores by adding expression markings to describe a mood. In an exquisite piano composition titled *By Lake Wallenstadt,* Franz Liszt designated the tempo as *Andante placido* (moderately, placidly). He went even further by adding these lines from the Romantic poet Lord Byron's *Childe Harold's Pilgrimage* (1818), a long narrative poem:

> Thy contrasted lake
> With the wild world I dwell in, is a thing,
> Which warns me, with its stillness, to forsake
> Earth's troubled waters for a purer spring.

These four lines invited performers and audiences to imagine themselves as tourists visiting the Swiss mountain lake, reading Byron's poetry, and listening to Liszt's music—a perfect example of Romantic escapism.

Not to be outdone, Liszt's contemporary Robert Schumann composed a Fantasy for piano that begins with the instruction, "to be performed throughout in a fantastic and passionate manner." Behind all these expression marks was a desire to allow music to probe what ultimately defied precise definition: the subjective world of the emotions.

J. M. W. Turner's painting of a scene from Lord Byron's narrative poem *Childe Harold's Pilgrimage.* Franz Liszt included lines from the poem in his piano composition titled *By Lake Wallenstadt.*

Tempo and Rhythm in Romantic Music

Romantic composers also took new liberties in their use of rhythm. They freely specified gradual changes in tempo, including the **ritard**, a reduction in speed, and **accelerando**, an increase in speed. This stretching and contracting of the basic pulse created a natural, variable rhythmic flow. Another technique that became common in the nineteenth century was **rubato**, a flexible approach to rhythm in which performers stretched or contracted the rhythmic values of a melody but without altering the overall pace. Rubato reflected the Romantics' preference for rhythmic spontaneity and gave the performer license to make rhythmic changes in a passage to add to its expressiveness.

Harmony and Tonality in Romantic Music

During the nineteenth century, the familiar tonal system of the Classical period was transformed. Classical tonality depended on a tonic triad supported by a group of related triads (see pp. 137–139). The most important of these was the dominant triad, which was built on the fifth pitch of the scale. Classical composers viewed tonality primarily as an orderly, rational system of musical planning. Romantic composers, on the other hand, used tonality as yet another agent of expression. Their compositions frequently visited a broad range of keys and introduced daring harmonic progressions well removed from the tonic. Romantic composers began moving away from the standard dominant-to-tonic progression of the Classical period in favor of other possibilities, such as key changes to a third above or below the tonic. In addition, they blurred the distinction between the major and minor modes by frequently mixing major and minor keys. Thus, a composition in C major might contain harmonies freely drawn from the key of C minor. Composers also intensified the use of dissonances, weakening the power of the tonic.

Tristan and Isolde, in an 1883 painting at Neuschwanstein Castle, Bavaria. Richard Wagner's 1865 music drama version is often seen as the culmination of German musical Romanticism.

Romantic composers extended the tonal system further by experimenting with new, colorful harmonies, especially with pitches drawn from the chromatic scale (see p. 15). Unfamiliar and novel, these chromatically tinged harmonies gave the music a raised sense of yearning and anticipation. And the more these harmonies were used in a composition, the more they challenged the idea of a secure tonic key.

As the nineteenth century progressed, all these innovations reached a critical stage of development in the work of Richard Wagner. His great music drama *Tristan and Isolde* (1865), often seen as the culmination of German musical Romanticism, introduced a new musical language. It features long stretches of chromatically charged music that masked the sense of key centers.

Wagner's innovative approach to harmonic and tonal planning fundamentally affected the course of nineteenth-century music. The next generation of composers adopted and extended his revolutionary approach. Indeed, by the end of the century, some composers were writing music that came close to abandoning stable tonal centers. Their work paved the way for the more radical experiments of twentieth-century modernism (see Part VII).

Forms and Genres in Romantic Music

Just as you might expect, the Romantic composers developed flexible approaches to musical form, again to make their music more spontaneous and expressive. Their compositions ranged from works of enormous size, many times the length of their Classical counterparts, to short pieces that lasted barely a minute or two. Some of Wagner's operas last upward of five hours, while one of Chopin's piano preludes, less than a minute. Wagner's gigantic operas pursued the Romantic ideal of the infinite by stretching their lengths to epic proportions. Miniature pieces impressed listeners as being created on the spur of the moment.

Throughout the nineteenth century, Classical musical genres still held sway. Composers continued to write sonatas, string quartets, concertos, symphonies, and operas, and they continued to use Classical forms, including sonata form, theme and variations, and rondo. But they filled the old Classical blueprints with highly original, subjective contents. Romanticism was, after all, a celebration of content over form. Composers now expressed their creative subjectivity by wholeheartedly exploring **program music** (see p. 161), instrumental music intended to evoke images or convey the impression of events that included descriptive titles and sometimes even detailed explanations to help guide listeners.

The range of these composers' imaginations was astonishing. Franz Liszt wrote a collection of piano pieces titled *Years of Pilgrimage*, inspired in part by his experiences in Switzerland and Italy. Mendelssohn produced dozens of *Songs without Words*, refined and expressive piano miniatures that resembled songs but lacked texts and vocal parts. Robert Schumann composed collections with titles such as *Fantasy Pieces*, *Night Pieces*, and *Scenes of Childhood*. On occasion, he titled his pieces only *after* he had composed them, letting the music suggest the meaning. Schumann's short piano pieces include "Soaring," "Whims," "The Prophetic Bird," and—most Romantic of all—the open-ended "Why?" Other nineteenth-century composers wrote orchestral music inspired by novels, poems, plays, historical subjects, paintings, myths, and exotic locales.

For the Romantics, program music was compatible with the traditional genres of instrumental music. Liszt wrote a piano concerto with the title *Dance of Death*, and Mendelssohn composed a Scotch Symphony, with allusions to Scottish history and folksong. Romantic composers did not always rely on traditional genres for their program music, however. On occasion, their inspiration produced new genres, most notably the **character piece**, short piano compositions with programmatic references, and the **concert overture**, a free-standing movement for orchestra that was often inspired by non-musical subjects (see Chapter 38).

MAKING CONNECTIONS *Romantic Content in Program Music*

In celebrating content over form in their music, Romantic composers considerably stretched expectations of what music could accomplish. When Franz Liszt finished his first symphony in 1854, instead of releasing it as his Symphony No. 1, he titled it "Faust" Symphony. Why? Because he designed the symphony to be about Goethe's great dramatic poem. Liszt conceived the three movements of the work as musical sketches of the principal characters: Faust, a restless scholar who signs a pact with the devil; Gretchen, an innocent woman whom he seduces; and Mephistopheles, the satanic character who agrees to grant Faust's desires in exchange for Faust's soul. Granted, the three movements of the symphony—fast, slow, and very fast—followed an old pattern familiar to Haydn and Mozart in the eighteenth century. However, instead of carefully focusing on using Classical forms such as sonata form, Liszt was more interested in tying his symphony to one of the great literary masterpieces of the nineteenth century. He was, in short, a confirmed composer of program music.

So were many of his contemporaries. Mendelssohn and Berlioz wrote music about their impressions of Italy, and Robert Schumann wrote colorful piano pieces with titles more literary than musical—*Papillons* (*Butterflies*), *Carnaval*, and *Dances of the League of David*. The Romantics were not at all modest in expanding the power of their music to treat non-musical subjects, including plays (Mendelssohn's Overture to *A Midsummer Night's Dream* about Shakespeare's play), paintings (Liszt's piano piece *Sposalizio* about Raphael's painting of the wedding of Mary and Joseph), and ancient Greek art (Liszt's *Orfeo*, an orchestral work inspired by a Greek vase depicting Orpheus). Program music allowed the Romantics to celebrate subjective content over objective form in a way that was limited only by their imaginations.

Faust and Mephistopheles. The tragic tale of how Faust sold his soul to the devil was a popular one among Romantic writers, artists, and composers.

Timbre and Tone Color in Romantic Music

Tone color—the timbre or quality of sound—fascinated the Romantics. They brought a new emphasis to the sensual aspects of sound in their music. Nowhere was their interest in tone color more evident than in orchestral music. Throughout the century, the size of orchestras continued to expand. New instruments were employed for special effects, and the brass section was strengthened considerably.

Orchestration—the art of organizing an ensemble's instrumental sections into shifting patterns of sounds—took its rightful place next to harmony and counterpoint as a musical discipline.

Encouraging the new interest in orchestration were technological advances of the Industrial Revolution, which led to modifications of instruments. In particular, valves were added to brass instruments. In the past, brass instruments had been limited in the variety of notes they could play. To play all the notes of the scale, brass players had to carry several different fittings to be inserted into their instruments. Adding valves enabled musicians to play the full chromatic scale on a single instrument so that they could play complex melodies. The increased melodic role of brass instruments in turn expanded the palette of instrumental colors available to composers.

This new appreciation of tone color fused sound and image and stimulated the Romantic imagination. Several nineteenth-century composers experienced this synthesis in an especially vivid way through a phenomenon known as **synesthesia**. This is where one sense—such as hearing sounds produced by instruments—stimulates a second sense, particularly vision. For example, Mendelssohn likened the timbres of trumpets and French horns to contrasting shades of blues and purples. Franz Liszt led the musicians of his orchestra in Weimar by cueing particular passages with specific colors, as if he actually saw colors while he conducted. This cross-sensory stimulation supported the Romantics' primary goal: to take flight in a world of sensuous music limited only by the imagination.

check your **KNOWLEDGE**

1. Describe Romanticism. What were the hallmarks of the movement?
2. How were Romantic composers influenced by the Viennese Classical composers? How did they assert their independence from Classical composers?
3. Give the key characteristics of Romantic music for each of these basic musical elements. Compare the similarities and differences for each element in the Classical and Romantic approaches.
   - **a.** melody
   - **b.** dynamics
   - **c.** rhythm
   - **d.** harmony and texture
   - **e.** form and genre
   - **f.** timbre

CHAPTER

Art Song 36

"Every composer is a poet, only of a higher stature." With these words, Robert Schumann elevated composers to the status of "tone-poets." For the Romantics, music was a language far richer and more suggestive than words. Felix Mendelssohn, when asked to explain the meaning of some of his piano pieces, replied that words alone were too vague and imprecise. The nineteenth-century philosopher Arthur Schopenhauer argued that texts served to unleash—not control—the imagination of composers. Their music, in short, was a powerful, independent language of emotions.

Romantic composers set many texts to music, and their century saw a great flowering of the art song. Art songs were especially popular in German-speaking areas, where they were known as **lieder** (pronounced *leeter*; singular, **lied**, pronounced *leet*). Lieder were vocal songs with German texts typically composed for a solo singer and piano. Sometimes several lieder were composed as part of a **song cycle,** an artistically unified set of songs grouped in a particular order to explore a particular theme or tell a story, or both.

Encouraging the remarkable burst of nineteenth-century song writing was the rise of German lyric poetry. It achieved extraordinary subtlety in the hands of Goethe, the preeminent figure in German arts and letters. His short, sensitively nuanced poems were ideally suited to the needs of Romantic composers, who valued above all else subjective, personal experiences in their music. In their lieder, Romantic composers wedded music and poetry. The music reflected the shifting nuances of the poetry while the poetry inspired a variety of melodic and harmonic ideas. Music and poetry were fused into a new genre, the Romantic art song.

Songwriters found their texts in many sources. Among the German poets, they turned to Goethe and Schiller, and also to younger German poets, especially Heinrich Heine, Joseph Eichendorff, and Wilhelm Müller. Folk poetry, with its timeless and universal themes, also provided a rich source of texts. Finally, some composers turned to British poetry. They drew on the celebrated Ossianic poems, the long narrative poems of Sir Walter Scott, the lyric poetry of Lord Byron, and the poems of Robert Burns, cast in common dialects evocative of Scottish folksong. Composers also used texts from the plays of Shakespeare, highly regarded in German areas since the eighteenth century.

Among the most prolific composers of art songs were Franz Peter Schubert, Robert Schumann, Johannes Brahms, and Hugo Wolf. The century also produced a number of distinguished women songwriters, among them Clara Schumann (wife of Robert Schumann), Fanny Hensel (sister of Felix Mendelssohn), and Josephine Lang.

MAKING CONNECTIONS *Lyric Poetry and Us*

The nineteenth century saw a great resurgence of lyric poetry. This art form traced its origins to the ancient Greeks, who wrote poems sung to the accompaniment of a lyre. In the nineteenth century, lyric poems were relatively short, consisting of a few stanzas in recurring poetic meters. Often set in the first person, they were designed to capture and express a personal feeling or emotional response. Not surprisingly, lyric poetry became a favorite medium for Romantic poets and composers alike. Here is one famous example of a lyric poem by Robert Burns:

Scottish poet Robert Burns (1759–1796).

O my Luve is like a red, red rose
That's newly sprung in June;
O my Luve is like the melody
That's sweetly played in tune.

So fair art thou, my bonnie lass,
So deep in luve am I;
And I will luve thee still, my dear,
Till a' the seas gang dry.

Till a' the seas gang dry, my dear,
And the rocks melt wi' the sun;
I will love thee still, my dear,
While the sands o' life shall run.

And fare thee weel, my only luve!
And fare thee weel awhile!
And I will come again, my luve,
Though it were ten thousand mile.

Today, lyric poetry is alive and well in popular culture. We need look no further than the top popular songs. They tend to be short and use texts (known, not accidentally, as *lyrics*) that fall into several stanzas, and they tend to focus on a particular feeling or emotional state.

Schubert's Life

Born in Vienna in 1797, Franz Schubert led a modest life for almost all his thirty-one years. By the time he died in 1828, his Lieder and piano pieces were popular in Austria, although full recognition of his genius and enormous catalogue of music came only later in the century.

Schubert received his first musical instruction from his father, a schoolmaster of modest means, who taught him to play the violin. When he was eleven years old, the boy was sent to an imperial monastery school for commoners. There he rapidly developed his musical abilities and came to the attention of Antonio Salieri, the aging court composer of Italian opera and Mozart's former rival (see Chapter 33). Young Schubert served as a choirboy in the imperial court chapel and played in the student orchestra. He pored over the scores of Mozart, Haydn, and, later on, Beethoven. Throughout his student years he composed fluently, relying on the generosity of an older student who gave him music paper, which Schubert was too poor to buy.

Franz Schubert (1797–1828).

When his voice broke, Schubert left the boarding school. His father had intended him to become a schoolteacher, and Schubert dutifully prepared for that career. For a few years, he taught in his father's school and sometimes gave music lessons to help support himself. Though teaching became increasingly time-consuming, Schubert produced an extraordinary amount of music. In 1814, at age seventeen, he wrote his first masterpiece, the song *Gretchen at the Spinning Wheel*, based on a famous poem from Goethe's *Faust.* Then, in 1815, Schubert set to music Goethe's popular **ballad** "Erlkönig" ("The Erlking"), a composition that would become one of his most famous. That same year, he produced over 140 other songs, 30 of them inspired by Goethe's poetry. The next year he wrote another 100 songs.

Eventually, Schubert resigned from teaching to devote himself to composition. However, in his last ten years, he suffered from syphilis, and his health steadily declined. Unlike Beethoven, Schubert had few patrons, and he failed to win a steady position in Vienna. Known to his friends as "little mushroom" (Schubert was not quite five feet tall), he did have the support and encouragement of a small group of young middle-class artists, musicians, and poets. These supporters gathered in the evenings to hear his latest work. But in the reactionary political environment of Vienna after the fall of Napoleon, such gatherings were suspect. For a time, Schubert and his friends were under surveillance by the secret police, and at one point he and five others were questioned and detained.

Schubert revered the music of Beethoven, although, incredibly, the paths of the two musicians rarely crossed in Vienna. At Beethoven's funeral, Schubert was among the torchbearers, but he survived the great musician by only a year or so. According to his wish, he was buried near Beethoven's grave.

Although Schubert is most often associated with the German art song—he crafted over 600—he was a remarkably versatile and prolific composer who completed nearly 400 other works. He tried his hand at opera, although he failed to mount a successful production. He also wrote sacred music and choral works. Besides vocal music, Schubert composed a large quantity of instrumental music, including numerous dance pieces and miniatures for piano. Many of these piano pieces were written for the so-called *Schubertiades*, the evening gatherings of his friends. Some of Schubert's best work is found in his piano sonatas, string quartets, and other chamber music, all worthy successors to Beethoven's masterpieces.

Schubert also wrote an impressive series of symphonies. The first few owe a great deal to the symphonies of Mozart and Haydn. The most famous, the *Unfinished* (No. 8), is actually one of several symphonic fragments Schubert left behind, and it did not appear in print until 1867. The Ninth Symphony, the *Great,* is a formidable large-scale work that shows clearly the influence of Beethoven. Its premiere, which took place more than ten years after Schubert's death, required the joint efforts of Robert Schumann, who found the manuscript in Vienna, and Mendelssohn, who conducted the work in Leipzig. Only about 100 of Schubert's compositions appeared in print during his lifetime. It remained for musicians of following generations—Robert Schumann, Mendelssohn, Liszt, and Brahms—to help establish Schubert's fame and his rightful place in music history.

A Schubertiade (gathering of Schubert's friends for an evening of music), as depicted by Moritz von Schwind. Schubert is shown playing the piano (center).

Schubert's Lieder

Dashboard

Read more about Schubert's song cycles.

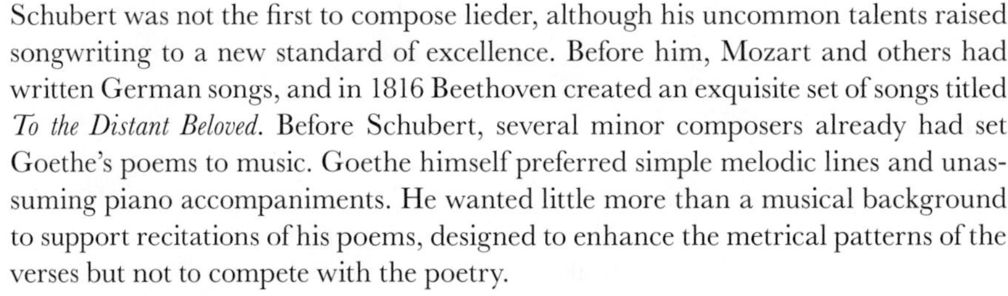

Schubert was not the first to compose lieder, although his uncommon talents raised songwriting to a new standard of excellence. Before him, Mozart and others had written German songs, and in 1816 Beethoven created an exquisite set of songs titled *To the Distant Beloved.* Before Schubert, several minor composers already had set Goethe's poems to music. Goethe himself preferred simple melodic lines and unassuming piano accompaniments. He wanted little more than a musical background to support recitations of his poems, designed to enhance the metrical patterns of the verses but not to compete with the poetry.

However, in Schubert's mature lieder, the music is far more than a simple accompaniment. Schubert's melodies are ideally suited to the singing voice and give a spontaneous musical expression to the poetry. The piano accompaniments, anything but unassuming, are often very complex. Schubert typically begins with a few introductory measures for just the piano. These measures introduce a short theme or a colorful harmonic progression to set the mood and prepare the listener for the poem. After the singer begins, Schubert typically employs a wealth of figurations in the piano to mirror and interpret the text.

Schubert produced songs at a staggering rate. On one day in October 1815, for example, he composed nine songs. Sometimes, he would write several using texts from one poet. For other stretches of his song writing, he turned quickly from one poet to another.

Many of Schubert's individual songs have long been popular favorites, such as "The Erlking," *The Trout, Ave Maria, Death and the Maiden,* and *To Music.* Schubert is especially remembered for his two great song cycles, *Die schöne Müllerin* (*The Lovely*

MAKING CONNECTIONS *Goethe and Music*

There is a certain irony that Goethe, whose poetry inspired countless settings from Romantic composers, once compared Romanticism to a disease. He had strong views about music and how his own poetry should be set in song. He preferred simple songs with modest musical accompaniment so that the poetry, not the music, remained the most important element. Romantic composers, however, had a different idea. Goethe was born early enough to witness Mozart in action as a child prodigy, and in the poet's declining years he welcomed another prodigy, Felix Mendelssohn-Bartholdy, into his circle in Weimar. Like Beethoven, whose music he admired, Goethe had one foot in the eighteenth century and the other in the nineteenth; in literature, he was a key transitional figure who connected two different ages.

Miller's Daughter), which contains twenty songs, and *Winterreise* (*Winter's Journey*), which contains twenty-four songs. Both cycles are based on the poetry of Wilhelm Müller and are unified by their narrative design and overall moods of rejected love and alienation.

Most of Schubert's lieder—and art songs in general—fall into three types. The **through-composed song** is an art song that uses new music for each stanza of the poem. Schubert generally employs this form for narrative poems or for poems with shifting moods that naturally require fresh music. The **strophic song** is an art song that reuses the same music from one stanza to the next. Schubert often chooses this form for non-narrative poems or poems displaying a unity of mood. The **modified strophic song** falls between the through-composed and strophic song. Its music for the first stanza repeats in subsequent stanzas but undergoes some variations, such as a change in key, a change in the accompaniment, or a slight revision of the vocal line.

Schubert's *Erlking*

Goethe's celebrated poem "Erlkönig" (German for "Elder King," a name given to the king of the elves, and usually written in English as "Erlking") is based on a Danish folk legend. It relates the story of a father's terrifying ride on horseback. His son is feverishly ill, and the father is racing to get him to home and safety. Clutching his son in his arm, the father reassures him that all will soon be well. Nonetheless, his son fears that the sinister Erlking is tormenting him and causing his pain. By the time the father reaches his destination and prepares to dismount, his son is dead.

Goethe's poem begins with verses for a narrator to set the scene and, at the end, to relate the horrifying outcome. The dialogue, though, is mostly between the father and son, with occasional interjections from the king of the elves. In adapting the poem into song (see **Listening Map 38**), Schubert's challenge was to compose

The Erlking, portrayed by Moritz von Schwind (ca. 1860).

dynamic music to capture the rhythm of the galloping horse. At the same time, he needed to distinguish the characters' different roles, which he did using subtle changes in range, key, and accompaniment. According to one of Schubert's friends, the composer was suddenly seized with inspiration after reading Goethe's poem, and quickly created the music in one sitting.

Schubert establishes the mood with a piano introduction that presents an unrelenting series of rapidly repeated triplets in the middle register—the galloping horse—and in the bass below a driving, rising motive (1). The music begins *pianissimo*, suggesting the sound of hoof beats approaching from the distance. Against these increasingly insistent rhythms, which continue until the very last measures of music, Schubert places the vocal part. Each character is given his own vocal range and character:

- The narrator sings in a medium range and minor mode.
- The father sings in a lower range, also in the minor mode;
- The son sings in a progressively higher range in a minor mode.
- The Erlking sings in a variable range, generally in a major key.

Schubert further distinguishes the Erlking by giving him a more melodious, seductive style. He also creates a slight shift in the accompaniment when the Erlking is singing (2).

LISTENING MAP 38

SCHUBERT, "Erlkönig" ("The Erlking")

{1815}

FORM	Ballad (through-composed)
METER	Quadruple
TEMPO	*Schnell* (fast)
SCORING	Voice and piano
OVERVIEW	Schubert's ballad, written when he was eighteen, captures in a single vocal line the four characters of Goethe's poem. They are the narrator, who introduces the story; the father, who rides a horse while clutching his feverish son; the son; and the imagined (or real?) Erlking, who torments the son. The piano, animated by a constant flow of restless triplets, conveys the galloping of the horse and suspenseful mood of the poem. Musical details shift in response to the drama played out in the poem.

why to LISTEN

Schubert uses these dramatic ingredients to create one of the great song settings of the Romantic age. It is as compelling in performance today as it was in Schubert's time. Using simple means, Schubert creates a dramatic crescendo effect. His music captures in turns the frenzied ride through the exhausting piano part, the mounting concern of the father and delusions of the son, and the entrancing music of the Erlking.

first LISTEN

PIANO INTRODUCTION	MAIN COMPOSITION	CONCLUSION
0:00	**0:22**	**3:56**
Driving triplets in the piano	Narrator's voice introduces the drama that involves the father, his son, and the imagined Erlking	Sudden, dramatic ending

Continued

a deeper LISTEN

TIME	SECTION	LISTEN FOR THIS	TEXT	TRANSLATION
0:00	Piano Intro	(1) **Rhythm:** Rapid repeated triplets against a rising figure in the bass **Key:** minor **Dynamics:** *pp* 		
0:22	Narrator		*Wer reitet so spät durch Nacht und Wind?* *Es ist der Vater mit seinem Kind;* *Er hat den Knaben wohl in dem Arm,* *Er fasst ihn sicher, er hält ihn warm.*	Who rides so late through night and wind? It is the father with his child. He grasps the boy in his arm, He holds him fast, he keeps him warm.
0:55	Father		*"Mein Sohn, was birgst du so bang dein Gesicht?"*	"My son, why is your face so troubled?"
1:03	Son		*"Siehst, Vater, du den Erlkönig nicht,* *den Erlkönig mit Kron' und Schweif?"*	"Father, do you not see the Erlking, The Erlking, with crown and train?"
1:19	Father		*"Mein Sohn, es ist ein Nebelreif."*	"My son, it is only a wisp of fog."
1:28	Erlking	(2) Shift to major key, slight shift in the accompaniment (repeated pitches in the bass against chords)	*"Du liebes Kind, komm, geh mit mir!* *Gar schöne Spiele spiel' ich mit dir,* *Manch bunte Blumen sind an dem Strand,* *Meine Mutter hat manch gülden Gewand."*	"You lovely child, come, go with me! I'll play lovely games with you, There are many bright flowers on the shore. My mother has many golden garments."

TIME	SECTION	LISTEN FOR THIS	TEXT	TRANSLATION
		"Du lie - - bes Kind, komm, geh mit mir!		
1:51	Son	Higher pitch level	*"Mein Vater, mein Vater, und hörest du nicht, Was Erlenkönig mir leise verspricht?"*	"My father, my father, and do you not hear what the Erlking promises me?"
2:04	Father		*"Sei ruhig, bleibe ruhig, mein Kind In dürren Blättern säuselt der Wind."*	"Be calm, stay calm, my child, The wind rustles the withered leaves."
2:13	Erlking	Major key, very soft, slight shift in accompaniment	*"Willst, feiner Knabe, du mit mir gehn? Meine Töchter sollen dich warten schön, Meine Töchter führen den nächtlichen Reihn, Und wiegen und tanzen und singen dich ein."*	"Fine boy, will you go with me? My lovely daughters wait for you, My daughters lead the nightly dance, and they will cradle and dance and sing you to sleep."
2:30	Son	Still higher pitch level	*"Mein Vater, mein Vater, und siehst du nicht dort Erlkönigs Töchter am düstern Ort?"*	"My father, my father, do you not see there the Erlking's daughters in the dark?"

Continued

TIME	SECTION	LISTEN FOR THIS	TEXT	TRANSLATION
2:43	Father		*"Mein Sohn, mein Sohn, ich seh' es genau, Es scheinen die alten Weiden so grau."*	"My son, my son, I see it all too well, The old willows appear so gray."
2:59	Erlking	*f*	*"Ich liebe dich, mich reizt deine schöne Gestalt, und bist du nicht willig, so brauch ich Gewalt."*	"I love you, your pretty face charms me, and if you are not willing, I will use force."
3:11	Son	Highest pitch level	*"Mein Vater, mein Vater, jetzt fasst er mich auf! Erlkönig hat mir ein Leids getan!"*	"My father, my father, now he grasps me! The Erlking has harmed me!"
3:25	Narrator		*Dem Vater grauset's, er reitet geschwind, Er hält in Armen das achzende Kind. Erreicht den Hof mit Muhe und Not, In seinen Armen das Kind war tot.*	The father shudders, he rides quickly, he holds in his arms the groaning child, he reaches the court, in his arms the child was dead.
3:56	Conclusion	Rapid triplets stop		

Robert Schumann

Robert Schumann (1810–1856).

The second great song composer of the nineteenth century, Robert Schumann, spent most of his career in the German cities of Leipzig, Dresden, and Düsseldorf. An impressionable youth devoted to music, Schumann had a particular fondness for Schubert's music and wept when he learned of the composer's death in 1828. Ten years later, Schumann visited Vienna and met Schubert's brother, who gave him access to Schubert's unpublished manuscripts. Schumann arranged for several to be performed and published. And, like Schubert, Schumann became a prolific composer of songs and song cycles, many of which are the equal of Schubert's.

Schumann was born in 1810 in Zwickau, Germany. Encouraged to read German literature by his father, a publisher and bookseller, Schumann experimented with writing on his own. He tried his hand at poetry and short stories, finding inspiration in the Romantic tales of E. T. A. Hoffmann and Jean Paul Richter. After his father's death, Schumann was sent to Leipzig to study law at the university but chose instead to study piano with Friedrich Wieck, a noted teacher and concert pianist. Planning to become a concert pianist, Schumann put in long hours of practice and composed difficult piano music for his performances. However, a hand injury ended his plans.

Wieck's best student was his own daughter, Clara, a child prodigy who soon emerged as a composer (see p. 320) and distinguished concert pianist. Nine years older than Clara, Schumann fell in love with her and asked Wieck for permission to marry her. For reasons that are still not clear, Wieck opposed the marriage and tried to discredit Schumann. Eventually, the matter was settled in court, which ruled in the couple's favor. Robert and Clara were married in 1840.

The year 1840 also marked a turning point in Schumann's career: he redirected his creative energies from piano music to songs and composed well over 100 lieder, many of them settings of Romantic love poetry. In the years that followed, he composed chamber and orchestral music, including four symphonies, and eventually took up choral music. He even tried opera, though, like Schubert, he failed to mount a successful production. For much of his early career, Schumann worked in Leipzig, where his circle included Mendelssohn, then the civic music director.

Dashboard

Read about and listen to Robert Schumann's *Carnaval*, Op. 9 ("Florestan").

After the Schumanns moved to Dresden for health reasons, a revolution broke out in 1849, and the couple fled the city with their children. By then, Schumann was suffering seriously from nervous breakdowns and mental depression. Attempting to improve his career, he accepted a post as the municipal music director of Düsseldorf but was not well suited to the job. Schumann was so nervous in front of crowds that he would tie the baton to his hand to avoid dropping it when conducting rehearsals or concerts. A bright moment in his life came in 1853, when the young composer Johannes Brahms knocked on his door with a letter of introduction. Schumann was among the first to recognize Brahms's genius, but by then Schumann's health had deteriorated significantly. Suffering from hallucinations, he tried to drown himself in the Rhine River. Fishermen rescued him, and he was committed to an asylum near Bonn. Forbidden to see Clara until just before his death, he was occasionally visited by Brahms. After Schumann's death in 1856 at the age of forty-six, Brahms remained Clara Schumann's devoted friend for over forty years.

Photograph of Clara and Robert Schumann, 1850.

Schumann's legacy includes not only his compositions but his work in music journalism. He was instrumental in founding the *New Journal for Music* in 1834 and worked for several years in Leipzig as its editor. Schumann became a champion of new music and young composers. As he wrote about musical life in Germany, he voiced his fear that music was being overly commercialized by performers focused on showmanship over musical quality. Schumann's ambitious literary efforts were matched by the Romantic spontaneity and color of his music, which marked the high point of German Romanticism in the first half of the nineteenth century.

Schumann's *Dichterliebe*, Op. 48

Dichterliebe (*Poet's Love*) is Schumann's most famous song cycle. It was inspired by Heinrich Heine's highly successful volume of poems titled *Book of Songs* (1827), which established the poet's career. His early Romantic poems inspired thousands of nineteenth-century songs. The *Book of Songs* brought together hundreds of his early poems, many of them dealing with unrequited love. Most of the poems were only two, three, or four stanzas long. Heine's poems were famous for their cutting irony and forceful imagery. None of that was lost on Schumann, who devised many imaginative ways to set the poems to music.

Schumann selected the texts for *Dichterliebe* from a section of *The Book of Songs* titled "Lyrical Intermezzo." In a prologue to this section (not set by Schumann), Heine introduces the poet, an old knight who is pining for his lost love. The set of poems begins with the awakening of the poet's love in springtime and then traces his eventual rejection and disillusionment. In the last poem—and the last song of *Dichterliebe*—the poet buries his grief and pain in an enormous coffin.

The opening song from *Dichterliebe* is the strophic setting "Im wunderschönen Monat Mai" ("In the Lovely Month of May," **Listening Map 39**). Heine's short poem tells of the awakening of love and unfulfilled desire. The poet uses two images, budding flowers and singing birds, to suggest the awakening of love. The only hint he gives that something may be amiss comes in the last two lines, where the poet speaks of his longing.

Clara Schumann

Clara Schumann (1819–1896).

Schumann's wife, Clara (1819–1896), was one of the most celebrated piano virtuosos of the nineteenth century, and her playing won acclaim throughout Europe, including in Paris and Vienna, and in Moscow. A child prodigy, Clara Wieck began to study piano at age five with her father. At age nine, she made her debut in Leipzig and a few years later premiered her piano concerto there with Mendelssohn conducting. Her compositions include stylish solo piano pieces designed for her own concerts, an impressive set of variations on a theme by Robert, several songs (some published under Robert's name), and a piano trio written for Mendelssohn's sister, Fanny Hensel, who died before she could accept the dedication.

After marrying Robert in 1840, Clara played fewer concerts and found less time to compose—hardly surprising, for between 1841 and 1854, she gave birth to eight children. Still, Clara occasionally went on concert tours, and she taught with her husband at the newly founded Leipzig Conservatory. After Robert's mental collapse, Clara raised their family herself. She returned to the concert stage and became a noted interpreter and editor of her husband's music, although she composed little after his death.

LISTENING MAP 39

ROBERT SCHUMANN, "Im wunderschönen Monat Mai" ("In the Lovely Month of May"), from *Dichterliebe (Poet's Love)*

{**1840**}

FORM	Strophic
METER	$\frac{2}{4}$
TEMPO	*Langsam, Zart* (slowly, tender)
SCORING	Voice and piano
OVERVIEW	Robert Schumann's song is strophic, meaning that it uses the same music for each stanza of the poem. It begins and ends with the piano, which introduces dissonant harmonies that never resolve to a consonant triad. This lack of resolution is Schumann's way of translating into music the "yearning and desire" of the poem.

why to LISTEN

Schumann stressed the intimate relationship between text and music and made his piano accompaniments indispensable to the songs. For example, sometimes he left the vocal part "unfinished" and concluded the song with the piano. He also unified his song cycles by artfully linking many of the songs, reusing motives or bits of thematic material from one song to the next. Like Schubert, Schumann constructed strophic, modified strophic, and through-composed lieder.

In this short song, Schumann frames the two stanzas with a piano introduction and postlude and separates them with an interlude for piano. In the interlude and the postlude, Schumann brings back the yearning music of the introduction. The song ends with a symbol of the poet's longing—a held, dissonant chord, which brings no closure but gives the piece an open-ended, Romantic quality.

Continued

first LISTEN

PIANO INTRODUCTION	STROPHE 1	PIANO INTERLUDE	STROPHE 2	PIANO POSTLUDE
0:00	0:12	0:35	0:45	1:08
Tends toward a minor key	Vocal line tends toward a major key			Conclusion without resolution of dissonance

a deeper LISTEN

TIME	SECTION	LISTEN FOR THIS	TEXT	TRANSLATION
0:00	Piano Intro	Harmonically vague and dissonant, tending toward a minor key; conveys sense of longing		
0:12	Strophe 1	Tending toward a major key; consonant harmony on "Mai"	*Im wunderschönen Monat Mai* *Als alle Knospen sprangen,* *Da ist in meinem Herzen* *Die Liebe aufgegangen.*	In the lovely month of May, while all the buds were bursting, then did love arise in my heart.
		p Im wun - der schö-nen Mo-nat Mai,		
0:35	Piano Interlude			
0:45	Strophe 2		*Im wunderschönen Monat Mai* *Als alle Vögel sangen,* *Da hab ich ihr gestanden* *Mein Sehnen und Verlangen.*	In the lovely month of May, while all the birds were singing, then did I confess to her my yearning and desire.

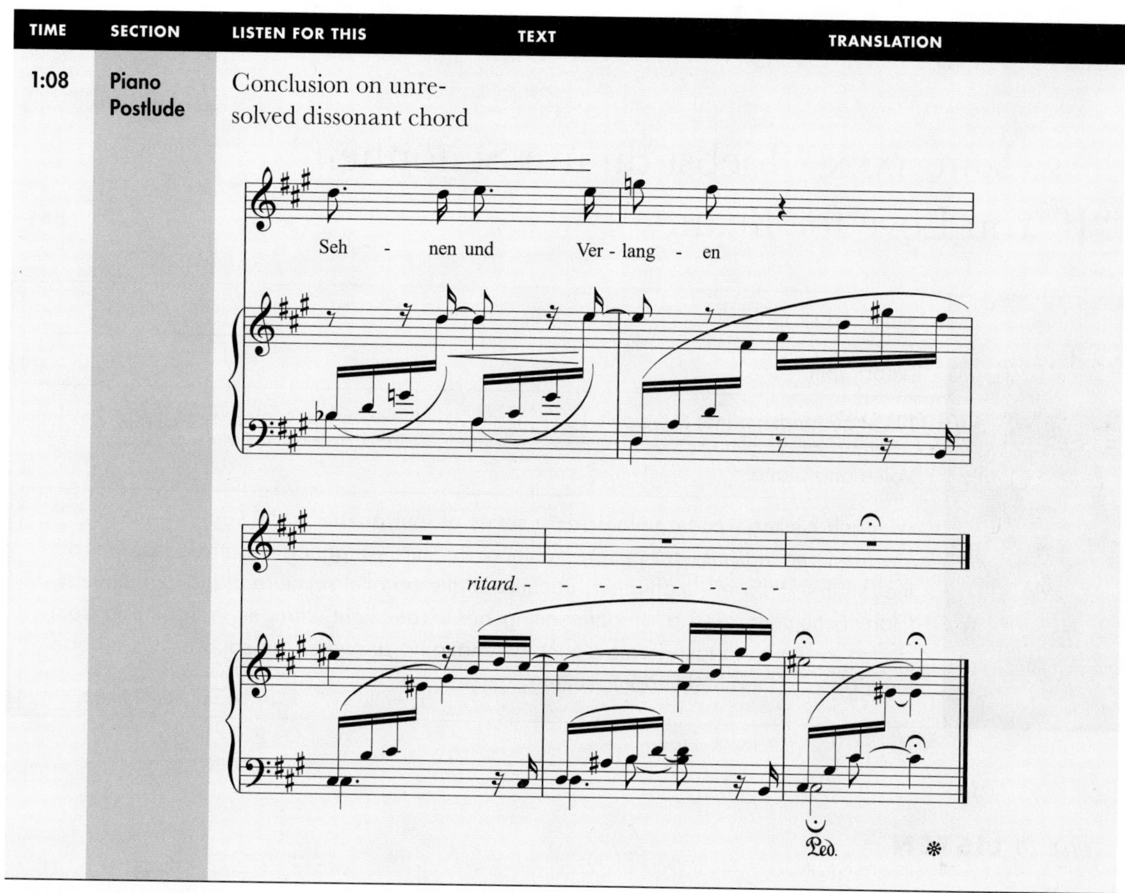
Seh - nen und Ver - lang - en
ritard.
Ped.

TIME	SECTION	LISTEN FOR THIS	TEXT	TRANSLATION
1:08	Piano Postlude	Conclusion on unresolved dissonant chord		

Clara Schumann, "Liebst du um Schönheit" ("If You Love for Beauty")

Among the gems of Clara Schumann's music is "If You Love for Beauty," one of three songs that she composed in 1841 for Robert while she was expecting their first child (**Listening Map 40**). Robert added nine more songs to the collection, all drawn from the poetic volume *Love's Springtime* by Friedrich Rückert. Eventually the twelve lieder appeared in print under Robert's name.

LISTENING MAP 40

CLARA SCHUMANN, "Liebst du um Schönheit" ("If You Love for Beauty")

{1841}

FORM	Modified strophic
METER	Quadruple
TEMPO	*Nicht zu langsam* (not too slowly)
SCORING	Voice and piano
OVERVIEW	Friedrich Rückert's poem unfolds as a series of four questions ("If you love for . . ."). The first three reasons—for beauty, youth, or treasure—trigger a negative response, but the fourth—for love—is affirmed. Because of the parallel structure of the four stanzas, Clara Schumann used a strophic setting but made slight changes in the music from stanza to stanza to take into account the changing answers. The song is thus a good example of a modified strophic setting.

why to LISTEN

In four similar stanzas, the poet lists three reasons not to love—for beauty, youth, and wealth—and one reason to love—for love itself. The parallel structure of the verses supports a strophic setting, with recurring music from stanza to stanza. However, the progression from beauty to youth, wealth, and love described in the text argues for slight changes to the underlying strophic design. For instance, the opening melody in the first strophe is slightly modified in the second. Clara made most of her adjustments in the second and fourth stanzas, so that the form can be represented as *AA′AA″*, with *A″* further set off by a shift to a slightly faster tempo. Framing the song are a brief piano introduction and slightly extended postlude. The piano has the final comment and suggests the eternity of love.

first LISTEN

SHORT PIANO INTRODUCTION	STROPHE 1	STROPHE 2	STROPHE 3	STROPHE 4	PIANO POSTLUDE
0:00	0:06	0:28	0:50	1:13	1:44
	A	A′	A	A″	

a deeper **LISTEN**

TIME	SECTION	LISTEN FOR THIS	TEXT	TRANSLATION
0:00	**Short, calm piano intro**			
0:06	**Strophe 1** **A**	Opening melody  *p* Liebst du um Schön- heit, o nicht mich lie - be!	*Liebst du um Schönheit,* *O nicht mich liebe!* *Liebe die Sonne,* *Sie trägt ein gold'nes Haar.*	If you love for beauty, Oh, do not love me! Love the sun that wears golden hair.
0:28	**Strophe 2** **A′**	Slight changes in vocal line  *mf* Liebst du um Schät- ze, o nicht— mich lie - be!	*Liebst du um Jugend,* *O nicht mich liebe!* *Liebe den Frühling,* *Der jung ist jedes Jahr!*	If you love for youth, Oh, do not love me! Love the spring that remains young each year!
0:50	**Strophe 3** **A**		*Liebst du um Schätze,* *O nicht mich liebe!* *Liebe die Meerfrau,* *Sie hat vielen Perlen klar!*	If you love for treasure, Oh, do not love me! Love the mermaid, she has many bright pearls!
1:13	**Strophe 4** **A″**	Slightly faster tempo	*Liebst du um Liebe,* *O ja mich liebe!* *Liebe mich immer,* *Dich, lieb' ich immerdar.*	If you love for love, Oh, do love me! Love me forever, you, I will love always.
1:44	**Piano Postlude**			

MAKING CONNECTIONS *Clara Schumann as Composer*

Few women musicians composed large-scale works in the nineteenth century. One was Emilie Mayer (1812–1883), who wrote eight symphonies, and another was Fanny Hensel (see Chapter 37). Before marrying Robert Schumann, Clara Wieck composed a virtuoso piano concerto, and she later produced an impressive piano trio. But after marrying Robert, Clara put her composing aside to support Robert's work and raise their large family. When she did find time to compose, Clara concentrated on solo piano pieces and songs, genres associated with music for the home.

Sadly, Clara dismissed her own efforts to write music. In her opinion, no woman had ever been able to compose successfully. In a similar way, the great English novelist George Eliot (Mary Anne Evans) observed that men could probably have improved most of the books written by women. These belittling comments mirrored the attitudes of the time, which minimized the creativity of women artists and relegated them to supporting, domestic roles. Many women musicians were effectively written out of history. Because of her fame as a pianist, Clara Schumann was never forgotten, but serious consideration of her own music was delayed until well into the twentieth century.

check your **KNOWLEDGE**

1. Why were Romantic composers attracted to the art song?
2. What are the three basic types of lieder? How are they distinguished? Why might a composer choose one type over another?
3. Compare the lives of Franz Schubert and Robert Schumann. How did each experience personal difficulties? Did these difficulties affect their musical output?
4. Why do you think Clara Schumann allowed her husband to put his name on some of the songs that she composed? What does this tell you about the role of women in nineteenth-century society?

CHAPTER

Piano Music 37

During the nineteenth century, the piano as we know it emerged as a powerfully expressive musical instrument. This was the great age of piano music. Most of the leading composers and performers were pianists, including the Schumanns, Frédéric Chopin, Franz Liszt, Felix Mendelssohn, Fanny Mendelssohn Hensel, and Johannes Brahms. Beethoven had launched his career in Vienna as a pianist and performed in public until deafness overtook him.

The modern piano was a product of the Industrial Revolution and the new technologies it brought. Reinforced with iron plates and rails, pianos could be built with greater tension on their strings than the eighteenth-century fortepianos known to Haydn and Mozart. These reinforcements increased the range of both pitches (how high and low) and volume (how soft and loud) a piano could play. A new type of key mechanism made it possible to repeat quickly an individual note by reducing the distance traveled by the hammer when it struck the string again.

Another innovation was the standardization of three foot pedals for the instrument. The damper, or sustaining pedal—which raised the dampers so that strings could resonate freely—permitted pianists to introduce fresh material with both hands while prolonging blurred layers of sound. The *una corda*, or soft pedal, enabled pianists to create fine shades of sound that contrasted with the louder dynamics now possible on the instrument. A third pedal, known as the *sostenuto* but not found on all pianos, was used to sustain individual notes.

A modern grand piano.

The modern piano was—and remains—an especially versatile instrument. Pianists could manage melodic material with one hand while weaving complex accompaniments with the other. Thanks to this capability, complex orchestral works could be arranged for the piano. Many composers created their orchestral music while working at the keyboard, where they could create a rough version of the music before finalizing the details of the full orchestral score.

In an age before sound recordings, the piano became an important means of spreading new music. Increasing numbers of middle-class European and American households had pianos. Not just sturdy pieces of furniture, they

MAKING CONNECTIONS *The Age of the Virtuoso*

Niccolò Paganini (1782–1840).

The nineteenth century was indeed an age of virtuosity. With its emphasis on individual expression, the idea of the virtuoso fit in well with the spirit of the Romantic period. Traveling throughout Europe and eventually the United States, these highly skilled musicians captivated audiences with their amazing performances. Many Romantic composers were themselves virtuosos who wrote spectacular compositions for their own performances. There were virtuosos for just about every instrument, although the majority were pianists. Some used their instruments in spectacular ways, like the violinist Italian Niccolò Paganini, who could play the violin held upside-down or with only one string. Others drew dazzling sounds and created passages so intricate that their audiences could only marvel at how they executed them. Grand soirées became fashionable in upper-class society, with several virtuosos competing against one another or joining together in a glittery gala finale.

The dominant piano virtuoso of the century was Franz Liszt (see p. 335), whose playing was so sensational that a special word, *Lisztomania*, was coined to describe it. But there were other virtuoso musicians who developed distinctive ways of performing and became celebrities in their day. One of Liszt's rivals, Sigismond Thalberg, was known as "Old Arpeggio." He had a particular way of playing a melody in the middle of the piano and surrounding it with dazzling arpeggiations above and below it. Audiences imagined that he must have had three or more hands to pull off this feat. Another pianist, Alexander Dreyschock, specialized in doubling the bass line in thunderous octaves. He developed this technique so that he could make an already difficult bass part from a Chopin étude still more difficult by playing it with rapid-fire, left-hand octaves. Like all virtuosos, these pianists shared a common drive to expand playing technique and test the limits of their instrument in new and daring ways.

became visible reminders of the enhanced cultural role that music enjoyed. To satisfy the growing demand for music making in the home, publishers offered music for pianists of all levels. And hosts of traveling concert pianists became well-known celebrities in their own right.

Frédéric Chopin

The Polish composer Frédéric Chopin (1810–1849) wrote piano music of exquisite refinement and brilliance. He was born to a French father and a Polish mother outside Warsaw, then part of Napoleon's French empire. He studied in Warsaw and played concerts in Austria and Germany before settling in Paris in 1831. Not long before his arrival, Romanticism had begun making a strong impact on the arts in France. Chopin spent most of his career in Paris. In 1848, to escape the upheaval of the political revolution there, he left France to tour briefly in England and Scotland. By that time, he was suffering from tuberculosis. Less than a year after returning to Paris, he died at age thirty-nine.

Daguerreotype of Frédéric Chopin from 1849, the year of his death.

During his eighteen years in Paris, Chopin withdrew from the demanding career of a public concert pianist. Frail in health, he preferred to compose and teach piano to French aristocrats, and he was a favorite at salons held in their lavish residences. During these evening salons, spontaneous music making took its place along with poetry readings and cultured conversation. Chopin's circle boasted an impressive group of musicians, artists, and writers. Among Chopin's friends were fellow virtuoso Franz Liszt (see pp. 335–339) and the unconventional composer Hector Berlioz (see pp. 352–360). Chopin also befriended Romantics in other artistic fields, such as the painter Eugène Delacroix and the writers Alfred de Musset, Honoré de Balzac, and Gustave Flaubert.

Chopin's circle also included the baroness Aurore Dudevant, who wrote a stream of novels under the pen name of George Sand. Chopin met her in 1836, and for eleven years she was his lover, counselor, and artistic companion. An early feminist, Sand surrounded herself with artists, had affairs with men and women, occasionally wore male attire, and took up cigar smoking. Chopin and Sand divided their time between Paris and Sand's summer estate 150 miles south of Paris, where Chopin composed much of his piano music.

Chopin focused almost exclusively on music for solo piano. His short, intimate piano pieces make up much of his finest work. They include stylized renditions of the **waltz** (in French, **valse**), a ballroom dance in triple meter, and two dances of Polish origin: the **polonaise**, an aristocratic dance in triple meter; and **mazurka**, a peasant dance also in triple meter. Chopin's nostalgia for his homeland, especially after the Russians crushed a Polish revolt in 1831, gives many of these works a feeling of melancholy. Chopin also composed nearly thirty **études**, short, highly polished exercises designed to explore the technical resources of the modern piano.

CHOPIN'S NOCTURNES AND PRELUDES

Among Chopin's most Romantic creations are his **nocturnes**, character pieces with singing melodic lines and gentle accompaniments that evoke night settings and dreams. One of Chopin's most famous is the Nocturne in E-flat major, Op. 9 No. 2 (**Listening Map 41**), written in 1831 for a Belgian pianist, Marie Pleyel.

In contrast to the dream-like Nocturne in E-flat major is Chopin's impetuous Prelude in D minor (**Listening Map 42**). It is the last of twenty-four preludes he released in 1839 as Op. 28, with one prelude for each of the twelve major and twelve minor keys. Chopin was not the first to compose keyboard **preludes**, which musicians typically used to warm up their fingers. Chopin's preludes followed the example of J. S. Bach's monumental *Well-Tempered Clavier*, two elaborate cycles of preludes and fugues in all the keys for a total of forty-eight pieces. However, Chopin's preludes are truly Romantic creations. They are preludes to

MAKING CONNECTIONS *A Double Portrait by Delacroix*

Within Chopin's circle was the French Romantic painter Eugène Delacroix (1798–1863), whose paintings featured bold uses of color (see *Liberty Leading the People* on p. 295). In 1838 Delacroix began work on a double portrait of Chopin and his lover, the baroness Aurore Dudevant, best known by her pseudonymn, George Sand. In the original design, the painting was to show Chopin playing a piano while she sat nearby, knitting and reacting to his music. But Delacroix never finished the painting. After his death the canvas was cut into two portions, doubtless to raise its value. The Chopin portrait ended up in the Louvre in Paris, while the Sand portrait found its home in a museum in Copenhagen.

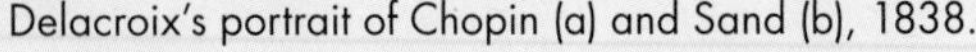

Delacroix's portrait of Chopin (a) and Sand (b), 1838.

nothing at all, except to whatever the listener's imagination provides. Taken individually, the preludes impress as short musical sketches or even unfinished fragments. Taken together, they form an enriching collection of nineteenth-century piano music. They are full of ever-changing styles, ranging from the simple and elemental to the complex and grand. One of the most dramatic, Chopin's Prelude in D minor, reveals the uninhibited, passionate side of his musical personality (**Listening Map 42**).

CHOPIN, Nocturne in E-flat major for Piano, Op. 9 No. 2

{1831}

FORM	AA'BA"BA"' Coda
METER	$^{12}_{8}$ compound meter
TEMPO	*Andante* (moderately slow)
SCORING	Piano solo
OVERVIEW	Chopin projects a singing melody in the right hand of the pianist with supporting chords from the left hand. The use of the damper pedal creates soft blurs of harmonies that add to the effect of a nocturnal setting.

why to LISTEN

Chopin's entrancing Nocturne in E-flat major illustrates the most imaginative aspects of his art. Against a gently rocking bass accompaniment, he places an expressive, singing melody in the soprano (*A*; ①). Noteworthy are the progressively wider leaps that push the melody higher and higher until it crests and gently descends. The meter Chopin chooses for his composition is $^{12}_{8}$, an example of compound meter (see p. 23), with twelve beats per measure, subdivided into four groups of three beats. The result is a soft, murmuring accompaniment that creates a gently flowing, liquid effect.

Repeating the opening melody, Chopin adds variety by embellishing it (②). A second theme in a new key (*B*; ③) serves only as a brief diversion from the original melody, which soon reappears with a fresh layer of ornamentation. The two themes continue to alternate before we reach the final section, an extended coda that climbs to the highest register of the piano in a dramatic, *fortissimo* climax. Now, for the first and only time, the steady, rocking accompaniment falls silent. Chopin indulges in a brief, brilliant cadenza before concluding with some soft chords.

first LISTEN

A	A'	B	A"	B	A"'	CODA
0:00	0:26	0:55	1:27	1:57	2:27	3:01
Singing theme	Theme with embellishment	New theme	Theme varied with new embellishments		Final varied statement of theme	Cadenza

Continued

a deeper LISTEN

TIME	SECTION	LISTEN FOR THIS
0:00	A	① Singing theme in tonic key with expressive leaps, against a rocking accompaniment in the bass  Andante espress. dolce
0:26	A′	② Return of opening theme in tonic key with added ornamentation 
0:55	B	③ Second theme in the soprano in a new key 
1:27	A″	Return of opening theme in tonic key with added ornamentation
1:57	B	Return of second theme
2:27	A‴	Return of opening theme in tonic key with new ornamentation
3:01	Coda	Melody moves to higher register, crescendo to ***ff***, with the melody appearing in octaves Music pauses; brilliant cadenza in the highest register of the piano, with diminuendo *to* ***pp*** and a few concluding chords

LISTENING MAP 42

CHOPIN, Prelude in D minor for Piano, Op. 28 No. 24

{1839}

FORM	Free, based on a melody and accompaniment developed through a variety of keys
METER	6/8
TEMPO	*Allegro appassionata* (Fast, passionately)
SCORING	Solo piano
OVERVIEW	Chopin begins with an agitated, widely spaced bass accompaniment that spins off a melody in the upper range of the piano. The melody is led through a succession of different keys, before culminating in a series of rapid descents to the low bass register.

why to LISTEN

The Prelude in D minor seems to teeter on the edge of a precipice. Several times rushing ascending scales and tumbling descents sweep across the keyboard. Driving the restless energy of the theme is a jagged five-note pattern in the accompaniment, which gives the music an unrelenting, frenzied quality (1). Chopin begins the prelude boldly in the tonic D minor (2). He next leads the theme through a wandering series of keys, each more searching than the last. The tonic returns a little more than midway through the piece, with the melody now projected in stark octaves against the swirling accompaniment. The climax comes with a tumultuous, rapid-fire descent in doubled thirds and a triple *forte* **stretto**, or increase in tempo, spilling over into the coda. Three more cascading descents plummet to the bass; then, the piece ends decisively with three booming pitches in the deep bass. Like the Nocturne in E-flat major, the Prelude in D minor lasts but a few moments. Chopin excelled at channeling his inspiration within relatively small musical spaces.

first LISTEN

TONIC KEY	NEW KEYS	TONIC KEY
0:00	0:40	1:45
Dramatic theme in treble set against rocking, passionate accompaniment	Theme led through different keys	Return of opening theme, climax, and dramatic close

Continued

a deeper LISTEN

TIME	SECTION	LISTEN FOR THIS
0:00	Tonic key	① Two measures of accompaniment in bass, *forte*, wide leaps 
0:03		② Irregular, climbing melody in soprano  **Allegro appassionato**
0:25		Ascending and descending runs, modulating
0:37	New key	Two measures of accompaniment in bass
0:40		Melody enters in new key, modulating
1:18	New key	Melody in new key, now rapidly modulating, leading to
1:45	Tonic key	Return of opening melody, now in octaves
1:52		Rapid, tumbling descent in thirds
2:17		Stretto (increase in tempo), triple forte, leading to
		Coda
2:19		Three sweeping, descending runs
2:37		Three accented, low bass notes

Franz Liszt

Franz Liszt (1811–1886).

Born in Hungary, the pianist Franz Liszt (1811–1886) came from a musical family. His father played a number of instruments, was employed by Prince Nicholas II of the Esterházys, and knew Haydn and Beethoven. Like many other composers, Liszt showed skill on the piano at an early age and was performing and composing before his teen years. In 1822, he moved to Vienna, where, according to legend, Beethoven embraced him. Settling in Paris in 1827, Liszt experienced the upheaval of the July Revolution in 1830. Seeking spiritual growth in this time of political instability, he turned to Catholicism and for a while attended meetings of a Utopian socialist sect. He also figured prominently in the artistic circle around George Sand, where he frequently encountered Chopin.

The most decisive event for Liszt during this period was a concert given in 1831 by Paganini, whose virtuosity on the violin took Paris by storm. Paganini had pushed violin technique to new, unimaginable limits. Indeed, some wondered if he had been taught by the devil, a notion encouraged by the violinist's gaunt, macabre appearance. Overwhelmed by Paganini's playing, Liszt set out to accomplish on the piano what Paganini had on the violin. One result was a set of piano études so difficult that Liszt later revised them to make them more playable. He gave several of these pieces vivid titles, including "Eroica" ("Heroic"), "Evening Harmonies," "Wild Hunt," and "Mazeppa," a keyboard rendition of the legend about a Cossack leader strapped by his enemies to a wild horse.

Between 1838 and 1848, Liszt played many concerts, journeying from Spain to Russia, from Ireland to Turkey. Everywhere, he impressed audiences with his extraordinary skill and showmanship. Liszt was the rock star of his time, and he gained a cult-like following. His ardent fans fought over relics such as his discarded handkerchiefs and cigar butts, and the poet Heinrich Heine coined the term "Lisztomania" to describe the electrifying effect he had on audiences. Liszt's repertoire included hundreds of fantasias and transcriptions for piano solo based on other composers' works, especially famous arias and scenes from operas. He also composed original music, including pieces inspired by his travels in Switzerland and Italy (*Années de Pèlerinage*, or *Years of Pilgrimage*) and a set of Hungarian rhapsodies filled with infectious melodies and rhythms drawn from gypsy music.

Countess Marie d'Agoult (pen name Daniel Stern; 1805–1876), who had three children with Liszt.

In 1848 Liszt settled in Weimar as the court conductor. For the next several years, he wrote serious, experimental music. During this period he finished his magnificent Piano Sonata, a reply to Beethoven's weighty sonatas, and began composing orchestral music (see p. 398). While in Weimar, Liszt promoted the music of Berlioz, Wagner (who married Liszt's daughter Cosima in 1870), and other progressive composers. During his later years, Liszt divided his time between Weimar, Rome (where he took the minor orders of the priesthood), and Budapest, where he was hailed as a Hungarian hero. Aspiring young pianists came from afar to study with Liszt, including American pupils who helped preserve his fiery performance style.

Liszt's personal life was as sensational as his music. During the 1830s he lived with the Countess Marie d'Agoult, a writer who used the pen name Daniel Stern and published a novel about their affair. For a few years, they lived together in Italy and Switzerland, occasionally returning to Paris. They had three children, but by the mid-1840s, the two had separated. Then, in 1847, Liszt met Carolyn Sayn-Wittgenstein, a Russian princess and prolific author. The two lived together in

MAKING CONNECTIONS *Lisztomania*

Liszt has sometimes been described as the first rock star in music history. Ken Russell's 1975 film *Lisztomania* drives this point home by casting Roger Daltrey, the flamboyant lead singer of The Who, as Liszt. Certainly, Liszt's charisma as a pianist and forceful stage personality were unlike anything the musical world had experienced. But just how did he transform himself into a major performing star that had such a sensational effect on his audiences?

- Liszt was a pianist of unprecedented skill, able to sight read music that was too difficult for most musicians to play with practice. Audiences stood on their chairs to get a glimpse of Liszt's acrobatic feats at the keyboard.
- Instead of sharing the stage with other musicians, as was the custom, Liszt turned the spotlight on himself. He was the first to play solo recitals, concerts in which he appeared alone.
- Liszt further heightened the focus on himself by reconfiguring the stage. Traditionally, pianists played with their backs to the audience, but he turned the instrument sideways so audiences viewed him from the side, in profile.
- He played mostly by memory, adding to his allure as a Romantic musician.
- Liszt always made a grand stage entrance. He typically arrived at concerts in impressive carriages and sometimes appeared in the dress uniform of a Hungarian military officer, with epaulets, sword, and scabbard.

Liszt understood, as did few of his rivals, how to create a buzz around his celebrity as the virtuoso of the century.

Audiences were driven to near-hysteria when Liszt performed, as shown in this contemporary print.

Dashboard

Watch Larry Todd discuss how composers use musical ciphers or codes.

Weimar, although the princess was still married. For several years, she attempted to secure a divorce and in 1861 appealed directly to the pope. Her request was denied, however, and she was never able to marry Liszt.

LISZT, PETRARCH SONNET NO. 104

Liszt once observed that music should spring from poetic ideas. His music indeed probes the mysterious relationship between music and non-musical subjects. A particularly compelling example is his exquisite Petrarch Sonnet No. 104 (**Listening Map 43**), a piano composition with a very unusual history. Attracted in the 1840s to the love sonnets of the medieval Italian poet Petrarch, Liszt selected several to set as songs with piano accompaniment. Liszt returned to the songs in the 1850s and converted them into pure piano compositions. Instead of having a vocalist sing Petrarch's text with piano accompaniment, Liszt now relied on the piano to express the rhythms, contours, and meanings of the poetry. What began as a song with text became a song without text—or, rather, a song with its "text" projected by the piano.

Fanny Hensel

Another virtuoso pianist-composer, Fanny Hensel (1805–1847), worked well apart from the public glare of Liszt's international career. Granddaughter of the eighteenth-century Jewish philosopher Moses Mendelssohn, she was the elder sister of Felix Mendelssohn-Bartholdy (see p. 343). Like her brother, Hensel was a child prodigy. She excelled in composing gem-like songs and short character pieces for piano, although she also produced substantial piano sonatas, chamber music, cantatas for chorus and orchestra, and an overture for orchestra. Her catalogue of music, mostly unknown until recently, runs to well over 400 compositions.

Fanny Hensel (1805–1847).

Unlike Clara Schumann, who hailed from a middle-class family and pursued a public career, Fanny Hensel was a member of the leisured upper class. She expected that music would be only a small part of her private domestic life. For many years she composed for her immediate circle, without plans to publish her music. (A few of her songs were silently incorporated into her brother's song collections, while a few others appeared anonymously.) But she did find an outlet for her creative energies in the music room of the family's Berlin residence, where 200 guests might gather to hear her concerts. Contemporary accounts describe Hensel's brilliance as a pianist, and her concerts were attended by celebrities such as Franz Liszt, the Danish author Hans Christian Andersen, and, of course, her brother. In 1846, Hensel began publishing selected works, only to die tragically of a stroke in 1847. The bulk of her music then disappeared from public view until late in the twentieth century.

Read an excerpt from Fanny Hensel's letters.

Although she did not appear on the concert stages of Europe, Hensel cultivated a refined musical taste. Her three favorite composers were J. S. Bach, Beethoven, and her brother, so she named her son Sebastian Ludwig Felix Hensel. She enjoyed debating with her brother the finer points of his scores, and her letters are filled with insightful critiques of the European concert scene. Her comments could be pithy yet also telling. She admired Chopin's music but wished that the frail musician could "bite back," perhaps expressing a desire for him to go beyond the pretty Romanticism of his work. She compared Paganini to a wild genius with the "appearance of a crazed murderer, and the movement of a monkey." An English friend of Hensel maintained that she felt far more than she said. Indeed, Hensel's music provided the release for a musical genius whose creativity was suppressed by the society of her time.

Hear Larry Todd discuss Hensel's life and work and perform her Allegretto Grazioso in E Major.

HENSEL, "IL SALTARELLO ROMANO" ("THE ROMAN SALTARELLO") IN A MINOR, OP. 6 NO. 4

A vivid example of Hensel's virtuoso style is "The Roman Saltarello," inspired by her visit to Italy in 1841 (**Listening Map 44**). The **saltarello** is a lively Italian folk dance in a fast triple meter, native to Naples. The dance spread to other regions of Italy, including Rome, where Hensel encountered it. A few years before Hensel wrote her piece, her brother incorporated a noisy saltarello into the finale of his "Italian" Symphony. He used the same key that his sister chose—A minor.

LISTENING MAP 43

LISZT, Petrarch Sonnet No. 104

{1858}

FORM	Modified strophic setting, with introduction, three strophes, and coda
METER	Quadruple (C)
TEMPO	*Agitato assai* (very agitated) in the introduction, *Adagio* in the three strophes and coda
SCORING	Solo piano
OVERVIEW	Liszt's composition is a piano arrangement of a song composed earlier for voice and piano on the text of Petrarch's Sonnet No. 104. The core of the piano version has three statements of a lyrical theme, modified with changes in accompaniment and the addition of virtuoso cadenzas. Petrarch's text appears separately, printed *before* the music.

why to LISTEN

Petrarch's poem concerns his unfulfilled, platonic love for a married noble woman named Laura. Like Petrarch, Liszt struggled with earthly and spiritual desires. To interpret the poem at the piano, the composer opted for a modified strophic arrangement. The dramatic introduction abruptly throws us into the composer's emotional world. It presents two contrasting types of music, Liszt's means of illustrating Petrarch's paradoxes. Initially marked Very Agitated (*Agitato assai*), the introduction begins with a highly dissonant rising passage (1). It then crescendos to the exact opposite: a dreamy *Adagio* that slowly descends through a ritard (2) to prepare us for the main theme (*A*, 3). Stated simply, with discrete rolled chords as the accompaniment, the lyrical theme divides into two parts, heard in the tenor and soprano registers (4). Two brilliant extended repetitions of the theme follow (*A′* and *A″*), each allowing Liszt to take greater advantage of the piano's resources. The theme then appears in the high register, accompanied by lush, echoing arpeggiations in the bass. Several times Liszt interrupts the theme to display his virtuosity in cadenzas bursting with rapid passagework and sparkling trills (5). The stately coda concludes the work in a more subdued style, with harmonies alternating ambiguously between consonant and dissonant chords (6), a final allusion to Petrarch's paradoxes.

first LISTEN

INTRODUCTION	STROPHE 1	STROPHE 2	STROPHE 3	CODA
0:00	0:29	1:34	2:31	4:26
Agitato assai section; Adagio section	A	A′	A″	

a deeper LISTEN

TIME	SECTION	LISTEN FOR THIS
0:00	Introduction	① *Agitato assai* (Very agitated)—rising, dissonant, accented passage
0:08		② *Adagio*—dreamy passage, ritard
0:29	Strophe 1 A	③ First statement of theme
1:10		④ Theme continues in tenor register
1:34	Strophe 2 A′	Theme repeated in soprano, against arpeggiations in bass
2:19		Cadenza
2:31	Strophe 3 A″	⑤ Another statement of the theme, ***ff***, marked "very passionately," with cadenza-like interruptions
3:34		Theme extended, cadenza and pause
4:26	Coda	⑥ In a stately style, alternating consonant and dissonant harmonies

LISTENING MAP 44

HENSEL, "Il Saltarello Romano" ("The Roman Saltarello") in A minor, Op. 6 No. 4

{1841}

FORM	Free, based on three statements of a dance melody
METER	$\frac{2}{4}$
TEMPO	*Allegro molto* (very fast)
SCORING	Solo piano
OVERVIEW	After a brief introduction, the dance gets under way with small leaps in the dance tune supported by crisp chords in the bass. There are three statements of the tune. The second is extended by excursions to different keys, while the third increases the tempo, propelling the music to a spirited ending.

why to LISTEN

The whirling contours of a single theme form the basis for the entire composition. Beginning in the tonic, Hensel leads the dizzying dance through various keys before returning to the tonic key and the theme, now marked at a faster tempo. The accelerating coda, filled with zesty dissonances, brings this delectable imitation of folk music to a rousing conclusion.

first LISTEN

INTRODUCTION	MAIN COMPOSITION	CODA
0:00	0:05	2:23
Main motive of the theme, with characteristic small leaps	Three statements of the dance melody	Acceleration

a deeper LISTEN

TIME	SECTION	LISTEN FOR THIS
0:00	Introduction	
0:05	Main composition	First statement of theme **A** in tonic
0:30		Second statement of **A** in tonic
0:44		**A** led through a succession of different keys
0:59		Theme **A** in the dominant
2:01		*Più presto*, third statement of **A** in tonic
2:23	Coda	Continuing to accelerate

check your KNOWLEDGE

1. What changes in the design of pianos inspired nineteenth-century composers?
2. Who were the virtuosos, and how did they help popularize the music of their era?
3. Compare Chopin's Nocturne in E-flat major and Prelude in D minor. How do they represent different aspects of the composer's style?
4. Compare the performing careers of Chopin, Liszt, and Fanny Hensel. How do you think these differences were reflected in their musical style and output?
5. While Chopin and Liszt were both celebrated in their day, Hensel's work went largely unknown for over 100 years. Why do you think this was so?

CHAPTER 38 Orchestral Music

Virtuosos such as Liszt showed that the piano could simulate the sounds and gestures of an entire orchestra. However, Romantic composers also searched for new ways to compose for real orchestras. The modern orchestra as we know it came of age in the nineteenth century. The works of two of the major orchestral composers show the progression of Romantic orchestral music. The German Felix Mendelssohn-Bartholdy developed a refined brand of Romanticism that retained ties to the Classical style, while the Frenchman Hector Berlioz took musical Romanticism to a new extreme level of expression.

The nineteenth century saw the transformation of the orchestra. The Classical orchestra was relatively small, with a modest number of woodwinds, brass, and strings organized into distinct groups. During the nineteenth century, the orchestra grew into a much larger, more versatile ensemble, with the size and makeup we know today. This expanded orchestra offered Romantic composers a much wider spectrum of instrumental colors.

Orchestral concert at Covent Garden Theatre, London, 1846. The nineteenth century saw the transformation of the orchestra into a large and versatile ensemble.

Orchestration—the art of scoring music for an orchestra—achieved new recognition. In 1843 Berlioz wrote a treatise on the topic. Among its more fanciful passages, the French composer imagined creating an orchestra with 467 instrumentalists and a 360-member chorus, for a total of 827 musicians. It might have 120 violins, many times the number available to Haydn. And it might exploit new instruments and new combinations of familiar instruments, such as 30 pianos accompanied by bells and other percussion. Never realized by the composer, Berlioz's vision reflected a bold view of the orchestra as its own instrument capable of a range of new effects inconceivable to earlier composers.

The growth of the orchestra created the need for someone to direct the musicians to achieve a coherent sound. This new figure was the orchestral conductor, who would gain importance and in many cases fame. Formerly, the concertmaster (typically a violinist) led the orchestra, or a musician would offer occasional cues from a keyboard instrument, as Haydn had in his time. But the increasing length and complexity of nineteenth-century orchestral scores demanded someone to focus on directing the music. The conductor now ruled over their musicians with a **baton**, a thin rod used to cue musicians, indicate changes in tempo and dynamics, and add dramatic flourishes to capture the audience's attention. Conductors rehearsed the orchestra, interpreted the works to be performed, and in the process injected their own personalities into the orchestra and its music. Individual conductors became famous and were associated with specific orchestras, leading to a new class of prized musicians.

Many leading composers of the nineteenth century were noted conductors as well. One of the first conductors to use a baton was Mendelssohn, who led a superb orchestra in Leipzig. Berlioz conducted in Paris and elsewhere, Robert Schumann in Düsseldorf, Brahms in Vienna, and Liszt in Weimar. Both Berlioz and Wagner wrote eloquently on the art of conducting and frequently directed their own music to ensure it was properly performed.

The genre of the symphony—brought to new heights by Haydn and Mozart and then transformed and enlarged by Beethoven—continued to attract nineteenth-century composers. Schubert, Mendelssohn, Robert Schumann, Berlioz, Liszt, and Brahms all struggled to create works that measured up to Beethoven's extraordinary symphonies. Many of these composers also favored the concert overture, a shorter, one-movement work inspired by a literary, dramatic, or other programmatic idea. Finally, many wrote concertos for solo instruments and orchestra, coupling the cult of the Romantic virtuoso soloist to the new orchestral virtuosity.

Felix Mendelssohn-Bartholdy

Felix Mendelssohn (1809–1847) came from a distinguished family. His grandfather, Moses Mendelssohn, was a well-known Jewish philosopher who had championed religious tolerance. The composer's father was a successful banker in Berlin. In 1816, the Mendelssohn children were baptized in the Protestant faith, and the family added a new surname, Bartholdy, to help assimilate them into Berlin society. Like his elder sister Fanny, Felix was a child prodigy with an acute musical ear and extraordinary ability. Likened to a second Mozart, he composed, played the piano, organ, violin, and viola, and conducted.

Felix Mendelssohn-Bartholdy (1809–1847).

The young composer received an excellent education. He studied with private tutors, mingled with celebrity musicians and literary figures, and attended the University of Berlin. Mendelssohn was especially devoted to the music of J. S. Bach, who was not well known or celebrated at the time. While still a young man, in 1829, Felix conducted a performance of Bach's St. Matthew Passion that helped inspire a revival of interest in Bach's works that continues today.

In 1825 and 1826, Mendelssohn produced his first two masterpieces, the Octet for string instruments and the Overture to *A Midsummer Night's Dream* for orchestra. In 1829, he made his debut performance in England. After the fashionable London concert season had ended, he spent the summer on a walking tour of Scotland. He visited Edinburgh and the Highlands before reaching Fingal's Cave in the Hebrides Islands off the Western coast of Scotland. The wild Scottish terrain inspired one of Mendelssohn's most Romantic works, the "Hebrides" Overture (also known as "Fingal's Cave" Overture).

Following his return to Berlin, Mendelssohn made a European tour, which took him to Austria, Italy, Switzerland, and France. In 1835, at age twenty-six, he moved to Leipzig to conduct the Gewandhaus Orchestra. Here, in the city of J. S. Bach, Mendelssohn oversaw public concerts performed by leading musicians of the time. He programmed contemporary music but also a healthy share of German music of the past—especially Bach, Handel, Mozart, and Beethoven. And he continued to compose critically acclaimed compositions, including the oratorio *St. Paul* (1836) and the Piano Trio in D minor, Op. 49 (1840).

MAKING CONNECTIONS *Mendelssohn as Conductor*

Besides making his mark as a composer, Mendelssohn helped popularize the modern orchestra by serving as a well-regarded conductor. Between 1829 and 1847, he frequently conducted the Philharmonic Society of London as well as large-scale music festivals in Germany and England. Near the end of his short life, he was even invited to New York, but was unable to make the long trip. The main post that he held from 1835 on was music director at Leipzig, which included leading an annual series of subscription concerts performed by the Gewandhaus Orchestra, still one of the premiere orchestras in the world. Founded in the eighteenth century, the orchestra originally performed in a hall used by clothing merchants (*Gewandhaus*). Under Mendelssohn's leadership, the orchestra became one of the best ensembles of the time and welcomed many leading nineteenth-century musicians to its concerts.

The original Leipzig Gewandhaus, where Mendelssohn performed, as painted by the composer.

Lake Thun, Switzerland, as painted in watercolor by Mendelssohn (1847).

A cultured man, Mendelssohn wrote poetry, mastered many languages, and was an accomplished painter. He was also a music educator and instrumental in founding the Leipzig Conservatory of Music, which attracted students from Europe and abroad. Among Mendelssohn's wide circle were Queen Victoria, the poet Goethe, the fairy-tale writer Hans Christian Andersen, and the composers Berlioz, Chopin, Robert and Clara Schumann, Liszt, Rossini, and Wagner.

Mendelssohn's interest in earlier music led him to study the works of Bach and Handel. From Bach's music, Mendelssohn learned the strict forms of counterpoint. From Handel's music, Mendelssohn learned how to write for choral ensembles. His enthusiasm for Handel's oratorios prompted Mendelssohn to create the oratorio *Elijah* (1846). He based the work largely on the Old Testament account in 1 Kings, and it was first performed at a music festival in Birmingham, England. After Handel's *Messiah*, Mendelssohn's *Elijah* ranks among the most successful oratorios of all time.

Because of his reliance on earlier music, Mendelssohn is generally viewed as a Classical-Romantic composer who combined the best qualities of these different musical periods. Yet much of his music is highly original and fully embodies the Romantic spirit. His *Lieder ohne Worte* (*Songs without Words*) are inspired Romantic miniatures for piano. Two of his symphonies, the "Scotch" (No. 3) and "Italian" (No. 4), allude to folk music and treat the orchestra to create a painting by subtly blending different instrumental timbres to suggest different tints of colors. The Violin Concerto in E minor, Op. 64 (1845), filled with passionate, soulful melodies and delicate gestures for the violin, is one of the great concertos for the instrument. Mendelssohn is at his most Romantic in his one-movement orchestral concert overtures, the most famous of which is the Overture to *A Midsummer Night's Dream*.

MENDELSSOHN, OVERTURE TO *A MIDSUMMER NIGHT'S DREAM*, OP. 21

Many Romantic composers found inspiration in Shakespeare's tragic and comic characters and supernatural worlds of ghosts, elves, and magic. In 1826, when Mendelssohn was only seventeen years old, he composed what he called a "brazen boldness": his Overture to *A Midsummer Night's Dream* (**Listening Map 45**). Despite its title—the music can be imagined as an overture to an unwritten opera based on Shakespeare's comedy by the same name—Mendelssohn declined to reveal a program for it. Instead, he left it to his listeners to imagine how his music related to the play.

Shakespeare's comedy unfolds around the wedding festivities of Theseus, Duke of Athens, and Hippolyta, Queen of the Amazons. Among their subjects are two pairs of lovers who have fled Athens for a nearby forest. The forest is also being visited by tradesmen who are secretly rehearsing a play for the wedding celebration, and by a hunting party of the Athenian royalty.

The forest is the enchanted realm of Oberon and Titania, the estranged king and queen of the elves. Oberon has sent his attendant Puck to subdue Titania with a magic love potion. The potion will make her fall in love with the next being she encounters. Puck gives the potion to Titania and causes her to fall in love with Bottom the Weaver, one of the tradesmen secretly rehearsing the play. As an added twist, Puck transforms Bottom's head into that of a donkey's. At the same time, the lovers are dosed with the potion in such a way that they switch partners.

J. N. Paton, *The Reconciliation of Oberon and Titania* (1847). Shakespeare's play inspired many Romantic painters as well as composers.

Eventually, the dramatic knot is untied, affairs are righted, and the mortals return to Athens to join in the wedding celebrations. In the epilogue, Puck, commenting on the magical nature of the story, notes that the play has been "no more yielding than a dream."

Mendelssohn wrote his overture in a modified sonata form. Into this form he wove several musical ideas, including motives, themes, and other materials linked to the play. We can identify six ideas:

1. Four mysterious, sustained chords, delicately scored for winds (*a*). Serving as a motto, these chords open the exposition and recapitulation, and they reappear at the conclusion. For Franz Liszt, they represented the audience entering a dream state and their awakening at the end of the work. In musical terms, the four chords prompt the remarkable motivic and thematic transformations that occur throughout the work and play on the comedy's central idea of mistaken identity and metamorphosis.
2. Scurrying music for the elves (staccato, *pianissimo* material for the strings, in a minor key; *b*).
3. Regal music for Theseus's court (*fortissimo*, for full orchestra, in a major key; *c*).
4. Smooth, lyrical music for the mortal lovers (*piano*, in a major key; *d*).
5. Music for the boorish tradesmen (complete with an imitation of Bottom's braying like a donkey; *e*).
6. Hunting calls for Theseus's party in the forest (*f*).

Listening Map 45 traces the progress of these motives through the composition.

The development, largely based on the elves' music (*b*), uses wide-ranging changes of keys to suggest the wanderings of the mortals in the forest. A ritard at the end of the development corresponds to a passage in the play where the exhausted lovers fall asleep. Then the magical four chords from the beginning (*a*) enter to signal the recapitulation. Its order of events essentially retraces the exposition, except that now Mendelssohn reserves the return of *c*, the music associated with the court of Athens, for the coda. When *c* appears, its former, bright regal sound is transformed into a softly scored, glowing melody. In the last scene of the play, the elves sneak into Theseus's court and have the final say. Similarly, Mendelssohn's overture ends with the four evocative chords of *a*, a last reference to the elves' supernatural spell.

Several years after Mendelssohn wrote his overture, the king of Prussia commissioned the composer to create additional music for the full play. For that occasion in 1843, he composed several new pieces, including a delicate scherzo to capture Titania's fairy, "swifter than the moon's sphere," and a softly lit nocturne for the lovers in the forest.

One piece from the incidental music deserves a special mention: the popular Wedding March that Mendelssohn composed for Theseus and Hippolyta. This festive composition began an unanticipated afterlife in 1858, when the English Princess Royal married the Crown Prince of Prussia to the strains of Mendelssohn's Wedding March. This event established a custom, and the piece has been played at millions of weddings ever since.

LISTENING MAP 45

MENDELSSOHN, Overture to *A Midsummer Night's Dream* Op. 21

{1826}

FORM	Modified sonata form
METER	$\frac{2}{2}$ duple meter (¢)
TEMPO	*Allegro di molto* (very fast)
SCORING	Orchestra (two flutes, two oboes, two clarinets, two bassoons, two French horns, two trumpets, ophicleide [obsolete brass instrument usually replaced by a tuba], two timpani, and strings)
OVERVIEW	Just as Shakespeare's comedy is about transformation and metamorphosis, on many levels Mendelssohn's overture plays on the idea of musical changes. Motives and themes appear in the overture and are constantly adapted and transformed. Mendelssohn wrote the composition in sonata form, but he made some adjustments to avoid conventional expectations. Chief among these adjustments are the four mysterious chords heard at the very beginning, at the beginning of the recapitulation, and finally at the very end. These chords represent the blurring of reality and illusion, and remind us, as does Puck in Shakespeare's closing lines, that the play is "no more yielding but a dream."

why to LISTEN

Mendelssohn's Overture to *A Midsummer Night's Dream* is one of the most remarkable achievements of any musical prodigy. He was only seventeen when he composed what was quickly seen as a masterpiece and remains among his most popular works. Not even Mozart had written anything of comparable significance by that age that has stood the test of time. The young Mendelssohn set himself a most difficult challenge: capturing Shakespeare's comedy in purely musical terms. He accomplished this task by creating distinctive types of music for the different characters: for example, for the elves, scurrying music; and for the lovers, a lyrical melody. And Mendelssohn prefaced and concluded his score with four soft, drawn-out chords, through which the audience enters and exits Shakespeare's transformed, dream-like state. The result is musical magic.

first LISTEN

MOTTO	EXPOSITION	DEVELOPMENT	MOTTO	RECAPITULATION	CODA	MOTTO
0:00	0:20	4:03	6:26	6:50	10:09	11:55
Four chords played softly (*a*)	Elves' music (*b*) Regal music (*c*) Lovers' music (*d*) Tradesmen's music (*e*) Hunting calls (*f*)	Loosely based on elves' music (*b*)	(*a*)	Elves' music (*b*) Lovers' music (*d*) Tradesmen's music (*e*)	Elves' Music (*b*) Regal Music transformed (c)	(*a*)

a deeper LISTEN

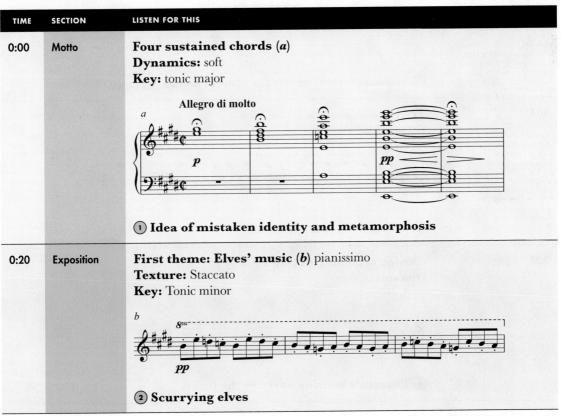

TIME	SECTION	LISTEN FOR THIS
0:00	Motto	**Four sustained chords (*a*)** **Dynamics:** soft **Key:** tonic major Allegro di molto *a* *p* *pp* ① **Idea of mistaken identity and metamorphosis**
0:20	Exposition	**First theme: Elves' music (*b*)** pianissimo **Texture:** Staccato **Key:** Tonic minor *b* 8va *pp* ② **Scurrying elves**

Continued

TIME	SECTION	LISTEN FOR THIS
1:09		**Bridge: Regal Athenian music (*c*)** **Key:** modulating (changing to a new key) *c*  *ff* ③ **Theseus's court**
2:18		**Second theme: Lovers' music (*d*)** **Dynamics:** soft **Key:** new major key *d*  ***p*** ④ **Smooth, lyrical music for mortal lovers**
3:14		**Tradesmen's music (*e*)** **Dynamics:** *fortissimo* *e*  *ff* ⑤ **Braying effect for Bottom**
3:38		**Closing section: Hunting calls (*f*)** **Dynamics:** forte *f* 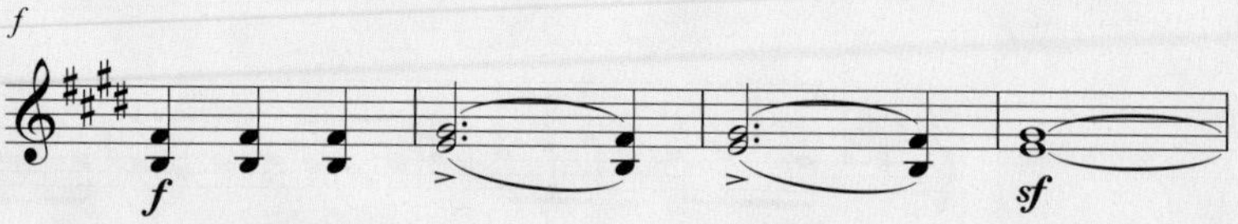 ***f*** *sf* ⑥ **Theseus's hunting party in the forest**
4:03	Development	**Largely based on elves' music (*b*)** **Dynamics:** mainly pianissimo **Key:** modulating through several keys Ritard and pause

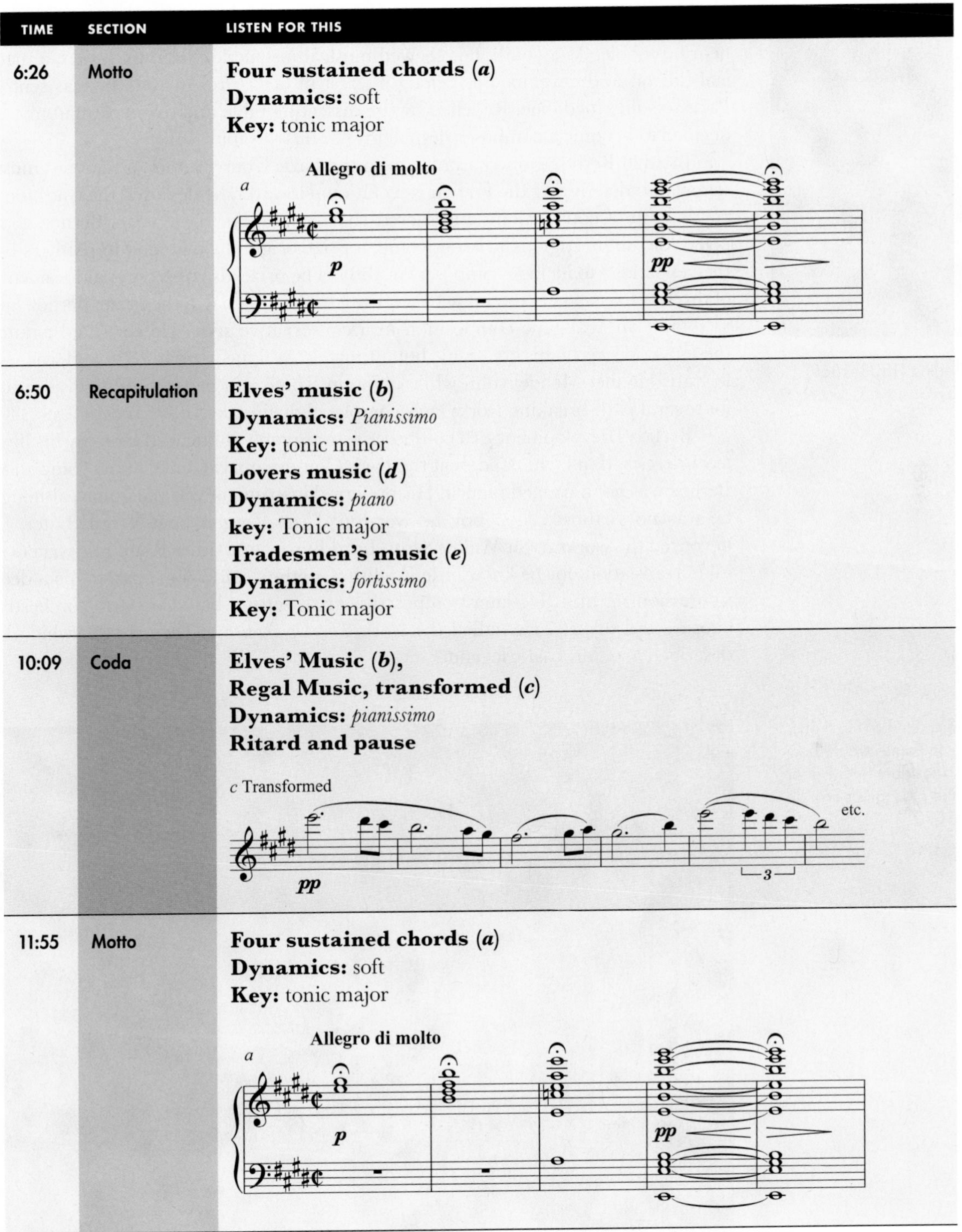

TIME	SECTION	LISTEN FOR THIS
6:26	Motto	**Four sustained chords (*a*)** **Dynamics:** soft **Key:** tonic major Allegro di molto *a* *p* *pp*
6:50	Recapitulation	**Elves' music (*b*)** **Dynamics:** *Pianissimo* **Key:** tonic minor **Lovers music (*d*)** **Dynamics:** *piano* **key:** Tonic major **Tradesmen's music (*e*)** **Dynamics:** *fortissimo* **Key:** Tonic major
10:09	Coda	**Elves' Music (*b*),** **Regal Music, transformed (*c*)** **Dynamics:** *pianissimo* **Ritard and pause** *c* Transformed *pp* 3 etc.
11:55	Motto	**Four sustained chords (*a*)** **Dynamics:** soft **Key:** tonic major Allegro di molto *a* *p* *pp*

Hector Berlioz

Hector Berlioz (1803–1869), painted by Gustave Courbet, 1850.

The French composer Hector Berlioz (1803–1869) was born in southeastern France, near Grenoble. As a youth, he received musical instruction from his father, a medical doctor, and developed a lifelong interest in literature. In 1821 he was sent to Paris to study medicine. Repelled by the dissecting table and tiring of anatomy, he decided to become a composer despite his parents' disapproval.

In 1826 Berlioz gained admission to the Paris Conservatory, a national music school founded during the French Revolution. However, he deplored the traditional curriculum of counterpoint and sacred vocal music. For three years Berlioz competed for the prestigious Prix de Rome, a prize originally awarded to painters but then expanded to include composers in 1803. The prize also offered a paid residency of three to five years at the French Academy in Rome. To win the prize, Berlioz had to submit an academic composition in a conservative style. He struggled against these restrictions on his creativity, but ultimately won the prize in 1830 and was sent to Italy. He met Mendelssohn while living in Rome and began finding inspiration for several path-breaking works later completed during the 1830s and 1840s.

Berlioz's development as a composer was arguably influenced more by his literary interests than by his studies at the Paris Conservatory. Unlike many composers, Berlioz was not a trained pianist. His preferred instrument was the guitar, although he was no virtuoso. As a boy he worshiped the Roman poet Virgil. Later, he devoured the works of Sir Walter Scott, Lord Byron, and other Romantic writers—all in translation, for he knew little English. Goethe's epic poem *Faust* made a deep impression on him. He later composed a great setting based on it for orchestra, chorus, and soloists. He called the work *The Damnation of Faust* (1846), which he described as a "dramatic legend."

Villa Medici, seat of the French Academy in Rome, where Berlioz was a resident fellow after winning the prestigious Prix de Rome in 1830.

All of Berlioz's important works have either a text or a musical program of some kind. Among his symphonies, *Harold in Italy* is based on Byron's *Childe Harold's Pilgrimage* and on Berlioz's own experiences in Italy. *Roméo et Juliette* is a large-scale "dramatic symphony" with vocal soloists and choral forces, based on Shakespeare's tragedy. Several orchestral overtures draw on Scott, Shakespeare, and Byron. Finally, Berlioz created librettos for his operas *The Trojans* and *Béatrice et Bénédict* based on Virgil's *The Aeneid* and Shakespeare's *Much Ado About Nothing*.

Harriet Smithson, Irish actress and wife of Berlioz.

In 1827 a troupe of English actors arrived in Paris to perform Shakespeare's plays. At the time, a literary debate was raging between the Romantic writers, led by Victor Hugo, and the academic defenders of traditional French drama. As Berlioz watched the performances, he sided with Romantic writers, who viewed Shakespeare's plays as a liberating alternative to French Classical drama. But there was another attraction for Berlioz: the Irish actress Harriet Smithson, who played Ophelia in *Hamlet* and Juliet in *Romeo and Juliet*. Berlioz resolved to marry her, although first he immortalized her in his revolutionary *Fantastic Symphony* (see Listening Map 46). After a stormy courtship, the two were married, though within a few years they divorced.

Read an excerpt from Berlioz's *Memoirs*.

To support himself, Berlioz became a journalist and published forceful, witty pieces of music criticism that satirized the shallowness of French culture and politics. In his *Memoirs*, an endearing account of his life, he did not hesitate to direct his critical gaze toward himself.

As orchestrator and conductor, Berlioz understood the potential of the modern orchestra as did only a few of his contemporaries. Berlioz's orchestra was much larger than those of the Classical period. Table 38.1, for example, summarizes the orchestra required by the *Fantastic Symphony*.

Reinforcing the paired woodwinds of the Classical orchestra are two more bassoons (for a total of four). Also, Berlioz occasionally calls for a piccolo and English horn, a double-reed instrument that resembles the oboe but plays in a lower range. He expands considerably the brass section. Four rather than two horns are required, and Berlioz calls for two cornets (an instrument similar to the trumpet but with a

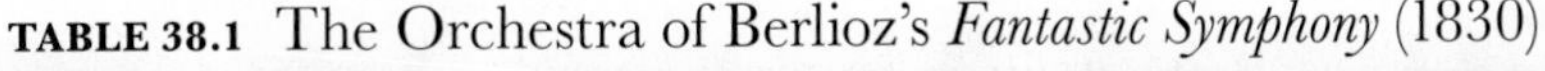

TABLE 38.1 The Orchestra of Berlioz's *Fantastic Symphony* (1830)

WOODWINDS	BRASS	PERCUSSION	STRINGS*
Two flutes (second doubles on piccolo)	Four horns	Timpani	First violins
Two oboes (second doubles on English horn)	Two cornets	Bass drum	Second violins
Two clarinets	Two trumpets	Snare drum	Violas
Four bassoons	Three trombones	Cymbals	Cellos
	Two ophicleides	Bells	Double bass
		Two harps	

* Strings are in five parts (further subdivisions employed).

less brilliant tone), two trumpets, three trombones, and two ophicleides (a bass brass instrument eventually replaced by the tuba). Berlioz's string section has five basic parts, as in Beethoven's symphonies, but he frequently explores further subdivisions of the strings into many additional parts. Finally, the percussion emerges as a section in its own right—along with the timpani, we find a bass drum, snare drum (a small, two-sided drum with wire strings stretched across the lower side), cymbals, bells, and two harps.

Berlioz's orchestral scores teem with new instrumental colors and special effects. He was especially adept at exploring the timbres of new or little-used woodwind, brass, and percussion instruments. He also coaxed new sounds from familiar instruments: for example, by having woodwind instruments play a **glissando**, or slide between pitches; by having an oboe play with its bell in a leather sack to produce a dull, muffled sound; or by having several timpani, tuned to different pitches, play dull, rumbling chords. He was constantly experimenting with subtle effects, such as writing especially sparse orchestral textures or requiring the violins to tap their strings with the wood of their bows to create a hollow, eerie effect.

FANTASTIC SYMPHONY

The sensational work that launched Berlioz's career was the *Fantastic Symphony* (*Symphonie fantastique*, 1830). Few critics praised the piece, and its radical nature inspired forceful attacks from conservative listeners. The young composer declared that the inspiration behind this symphony, or "musical drama" as he called it, was his tormented infatuation with Harriet Smithson. To explain the unusual course of his symphony, he drafted a detailed movement-by-movement program, distributed at the premiere to the audience. From this program we learn that after an attack of lovesick despair, an artist takes an overdose of opium. The music represents the drug's effects, portraying the artist's fantasies, hallucinations, and nightmares. In one bold stroke, Berlioz extended instrumental music to express the most intense personal feelings and the subconscious depths of the mind.

The primary musical influence on Berlioz's symphony was Beethoven's *Pastoral* Symphony. Both works are autobiographical, and both are in five movements, instead of the customary four. Berlioz's third movement, a slow movement, depicts a pastoral scene and even includes an allusion to Beethoven's symphony by simulating the sound of distant thunder. Berlioz, however, stretched the limitations of the program symphony by giving his imagination free reign.

First Movement: Reveries, Passions

The first movement expresses the artist's malaise before meeting his beloved and his experience of love at first sight. The long, slow, mournful introduction gives way to a passionate Allegro movement that announces her arrival, his "volcanic" love for her, his fits of jealousy, and his suffering. The Allegro is loosely based on sonata form. The notable first theme plays a special role as the ***idée fixe***, or "fixed idea," a melody that recurs in every movement of the symphony to represent the artist's beloved. Here is the melody in full:

Allegro agitato e appassionato assai

This arching melody breaks into three extended phrases. The first reaches two crests; the second takes a step figure (bracketed in the example) and pushes it to a climax; and the third descends from the highest pitch to bring the melody to a cadence.

In his notation of the idée fixe, Berlioz took pains to achieve the precise effect he had in mind. His numerous tempo markings include *animez* ("excited"), *retenu* ("held back"), and *a tempo con fuoco* ("in tempo with energy"). There are numerous expression markings as well: in the first four bars alone, three crescendos, a *poco sf* (an accent not quite as heavy as a normal *sforzando*), and a diminuendo. All of Berlioz's notation in the symphony was highly detailed, emphasizing the strong connection between the music and the ideas in the program.

MAKING CONNECTIONS *The Romantics and Opium*

One inspiration for *Fantastic Symphony* may have been Thomas De Quincey's *Confessions of an English Opium-Eater*, published in 1822. In that essay, De Quincey gave a frank examination of the "pleasures" and "pains" of opium, and specifically mentioned the role of music in his hallucinations:

> The dream commenced with a music which now I often heard in dreams—music of preparation and of awakening suspense . . . [then] a battle, a strife, an agony, was conducting—was evolving like a great drama, or piece of music; with which my sympathy was the more insupportable from my confusion as to its place, its cause, its nature, and its possible issue . . .

Many Romantic writers experimented with opium, which was used to relieve a variety of medical conditions, including anxiety, dental pain, neuralgia, dysentery, and hysteria. Some writers, like Samuel Taylor Coleridge, became addicted to the drug. He described his famous unfinished poem, *Kubla Khan*, as being "composed in a sort of reverie brought on by two grains of opium." Others, including John Keats, Edgar Allan Poe, and Charles Dickens, tried the "aspirin of the nineteenth century" from time to time. There seems little doubt that Hector Berlioz used it as well, although whether his *Fantastic Symphony* was made even more *fantastic* by the drug is unclear. After all, dream states, whether induced by opium or not, were familiar terrain of the Romantics.

Engraving for Samuel Taylor Coleridge's poem *Kubla Khan*, which may have been inspired by an opium dream.

Second Movement: A Ball

In the second movement the artist encounters his beloved at a ball. Berlioz writes, accordingly, an increasingly lively waltz in triple meter. Toward the middle of the movement, the *idée fixe* momentarily interrupts the graceful course of the waltz. The dance then resumes and breaks into an animated coda for the conclusion. The orchestra includes parts for at least four harps, and a lovely solo for the cornet. The orchestration is rich and varied, and at times creates a magical, shimmering effect.

Third Movement: Pastoral Scene

The artist now moves to the countryside, where on a lazy summer evening he listens to two shepherds piping a slow tune. Performing the duet are an oboe and English horn, with the oboe placed offstage to create a sense of distance. The music calms the artist and leads him to consider how he will woo his beloved. Birdcalls reminiscent of the slow movement of Beethoven's "Pastoral" Symphony reinforce the mood. Then the idée fixe reappears in yet another transformation, and the artist wonders whether he has been deceived. The melody ceases and quiet returns. After threatening rolls on timpani suggest distant thunder, the shepherds' tune is heard again, and the pastoral scene ends peacefully.

Fourth Movement: March to the Scaffold

The last two movements depict the nightmares of the artist's opium dream. In the fourth movement, he dreams that he has murdered his beloved and awaits execution for his crime. The music suggests the grim procession to the scaffold, with muffled brass, dull chords for the contrabass, and an insistent march-like rhythm in the timpani. A contrasting section features the bright, metallic sound of the full woodwind and brass, again accompanied by the thump of percussion. Near the end of the movement, a clarinet sounds the opening phrase of the idée fixe. However, it is rudely interrupted by a *fortissimo* chord as the guillotine falls, a grisly musical representation of decapitation. This horrifying scene concludes with pizzicato notes in the strings to suggest the drop of the severed head, followed by several bars of triumphant chords.

Fifth Movement: Dream of a Witches' Sabbath

The symphony culminates with a massive finale. In a ghoulish hallucination, the artist imagines himself at his own funeral, escorted by gruesome monsters and sorcerers. The beloved appears, transformed into a witchlike harlot. Solemn bells give way to a medieval plainchant, the sequence *Dies irae* from the Requiem Mass. Then, the witches join in a round dance. For the final section of the movement, Berlioz combines the *Dies irae* and the round dance, as shown in **Listening Map 46**.

The finale offers the most fantastic and wild music of the symphony. Dictating its loose, at times "chaotic" structure is the unusual narrative of the program. An eerie slow introduction sets the mood, with the strings divided into nine parts. Melodic fragments and dissonant harmonic textures appear and disappear, without stating a clear theme. These are the "strange noises" described in Berlioz's program, answered by other sinister utterances. As the introduction slowly dissolves, we hear the idée fixe from afar. In a macabre parody of the original melody, Berlioz employs a shrill clarinet to distort it. Now the noble melody turns into a lively dance tune, with snap-like embellishments and added trills (①). Turned into a sorceress, the beloved is wildly greeted by her companions as she takes her place at the artist's funeral.

In the second section of the finale, Berlioz managed to offend many French Catholics by introducing the sacred *Dies irae* into an undignified opium dream. Accompanying the chant are solemn bells, symbolizing the Church and its rituals. Berlioz divides the chant into three large portions: each is stated three times in successively faster notes and higher registers that turn the sacred chant into a caricature (②).

For the third section, the round dance of the witches, Berlioz mocks academic counterpoint by writing a boisterous fugue. It ignores many of the rules he had been instructed to follow at the Paris Conservatory. Each entrance of the fugal subject

HECTOR BERLIOZ, *Fantastic Symphony*, Finale, "Dream of a Witches' Sabbath"

{1830}

FORM	Free form, as suggested by the program
METER	C, later $\frac{6}{8}$
TEMPO	*Larghetto* (fairly slow), *Allegro* (brisk)
SCORING	Orchestra (one flute, one piccolo, two oboes, two clarinets, 4 bassoons, 4 French horns, two trumpets, two cornets, three trombones, two ophicleides, 4 timpani, one bass drum, snare drum, cymbals, two bells, two harps, and strings)
OVERVIEW	Like Mendelssohn and other Romantic composers, Berlioz was fascinated with dreams, and he designed the culminating finale of his *Fantastic Symphony* as an especially memorable one. Its disjointed nature—bits of themes appear, are blurred, distorted, or caricatured in some way—suggested the wayward course of a dream. And the sudden intrusion of the *Dies irae*, a sacred chant from the Requiem Mass certainly familiar to French Catholics, was bound to cause confusion and, for many, outrage. The music is filled with special effects—double basses made to sound like rumbling drums, violins that tap with the wood of their bows, timpani that play chords—all calculated to suggest the incoherent parts of a dream, and to test and explode the boundaries of good taste.

why to **LISTEN**

While Mendelssohn was reluctant to provide the program of his Overture to *A Midsummer Night's Dream*, Berlioz gave audiences one for his *Fantastic Symphony*. It was one thing to be able to detect elves in Mendelssohn's music without a written explanation. But for a symphony about a sensitive artist who takes an overdose of opium, the composer needed to explain the unusual course of the music. The symphony met a stormy reception at its premiere at the Paris Conservatory. Most critics attacked the score for its unusual effects, considered exaggerated and beyond the limits of what music could and should be about.

Regardless of how you react to Berlioz's score, there are at least two compelling reasons to listen. First, the composer's printed program set a new standard for what Romantic music could attempt to express. Second, it was a composition ahead of its time. Despite the initial rejection of the premiere in 1830, it was eventually accepted and welcomed into the canon of classical music. Today the symphony remains a standard of the concert hall.

first LISTEN

INTRODUCTION	ALLEGRO	CODA
0:00	1:19	9:45
Indistinct, dream-like orchestral textures	*Idée fixe* melody *Dies irae* chant Witches' Round Dance *Dies irae* and Round Dance combined	Animated tempo

a deeper LISTEN

TIME	SECTION	LISTEN FOR THIS
0:00	Slow Introduction	Texture: Muted strings, vague thematic fragments in winds and brass
1:19	Allegro	① *Idée fixe* melody, played and distorted twice by the clarinet Allegro *ppp*
2:50		Bells (and hint of theme of the Round Dance)
3:19	*Dies irae* chant	② Each phrase stated three times by low winds, then speeded up in the brass and woodwinds in higher registers DIES IRAE *f* Repeated in a higher register and sped up 8va *f* Repeated in a higher register and sped up *f*

Continued

TIME	SECTION	LISTEN FOR THIS
4:58	(hint of Round Dance)	
5:17	Witches' Round Dance	③ Free fugue-like passage that breaks down FUGAL SUBJECT
7:09	(hint of *Dies irae*)	
8:21	*Dies irae* and Round Dance combined	
9:45	Coda	Animated tempo

appears against grating, syncopated chords (③). The wild course of the fugue suggests the witches scurrying around the body of the artist.

Berlioz concludes his symphonic nightmare by combining the dance and the *Dies irae* in two different keys, adding to the musical chaos. At one point, the violins and the violas tap their strings with the wood of the bows for a special, unsettling effect (*col legno*). The striking juxtaposition of the dance and the *Dies irae* is another example of Berlioz's extraordinary experimentation that many of his contemporaries found very difficult to understand.

The first performance of the *Fantastic Symphony* brought swift critical responses. Robert Schumann hailed Berlioz as a master of the modern orchestra, although he admitted that at first glance the symphony looked like music turned upside down! At the other extreme, one reactionary Belgian critic labeled the symphony a "saturnalia of noise," devoid of art. From the start, the *Fantastic Symphony* drew Berlioz into the age-old controversy of innovation versus tradition. Despite the critics, Berlioz's innovations had lasting impact on symphonic music. The *Fantastic Symphony*'s detailed program, its free approach to musical form and thematic transformation, and its bold use of the modern orchestra all heavily influenced musical experimenters who followed.

check your **KNOWLEDGE**

1. How did the classical orchestra change during the nineteenth century? Why were Romantic composers interested in making these changes?
2. Describe how Mendelssohn's Overture to *A Midsummer's Night's Dream* was influenced by Shakespeare's play. Give specific references in the work and the additional incidental music that Mendelssohn composed later.
3. Why was Berlioz's *Fantastic Symphony* considered so radical when it premiered? Give specific examples of Berlioz's innovations found in the symphony's five movements.
4. Compare the life and music of Mendelssohn and Berlioz. What are the major similarities and differences in their biographies and music?

CHAPTER 39

Romantic Opera

Romantic opera was a showcase of fantastic plots, spectacular stage effects, huge orchestras, and singing that stretched the limits of the human voice. Part of its appeal was its wide range of subjects. Craving the unusual and fantastic, composers chose settings ranging from Roman Gaul to Aztec Mexico, to Scotland, India, and Egypt. They used librettos based on ancient legends or even created their own. They searched Romantic novels, plays, and poetry for their inspiration. In their operas, Romantic composers emphasized the same influences found in other Romantic music, including the supernatural and the freedom of nature.

One of the most popular Romantic operas was *Der Freischütz* (*The Freeshooter*, 1821) by the German composer Carl Maria von Weber. The subject is the age-old tale in which a mortal makes a compact with the devil. Weber's protagonist is a young hunter who accepts seven magic bullets from the devil so that he can win a marksmanship contest and the hand of Agathe, the daughter of the head forester. In the climactic scene, the devil misdirects Max's final shot toward Agathe, who miraculously survives. The intervention of a hermit-like holy man leads to a happy outcome. Weber's score teems with lyrical Romantic melodies, sinister dissonant chords for the devil, a chorus of unseen spirits, and radiant music for the hermit.

Scene from the opera *Der Freischütz* (*The Freeshooter,* 1821) by Carl Maria von Weber.

The original production included special stage effects such as flaming wheels that rolled across the stage and a mechanical owl that flapped its wings.

Another remarkable production was *La Muette de Portici* (*The Deaf Woman of Portici*), which premiered in Brussels in 1832. Set in seventeenth-century Italy, it told the story of an uprising against Spanish rule. Its climax depicted nothing less than the eruption of Mt. Vesuvius. Swept up with patriotic fervor, the Belgian audience poured out into the streets and began a revolution that led to the independence of Belgium from Dutch rule.

All these effects and plot twists required unusual and colorful music. Romantic composers rose to the occasion to create memorable music that equaled the excitement on the stage. Opera flourished throughout Europe during the nineteenth century, particularly in Italy, France, and Germany. It also succeeded in other regions, where distinctive national schools emerged. In each country, opera responded to Romanticism in different ways.

Italian Romantic Opera

The center of opera—Italy—had a distinguished tradition of over two centuries, and opera remained the most popular style of music in the nineteenth century. Most Italian composers devoted themselves to opera, writing for star singers, whose sensational careers dominated Italian stages. Composers shaped their operas around tuneful solo arias for these virtuosos to perform. They introduced these arias with recitatives and included the occasional ensemble or chorus for variety, but the focus remained on the star performers. Composers had little control over their operas once they reached the stage, and they were often cut or drastically changed, even to the point of substituting popular music from other operas to please a famous performer.

At the heart of Italian opera was *bel canto,* a style of singing that emphasized beautiful melodic lines against unobtrusive orchestral accompaniments. The showcase of *bel canto* was the aria. In the nineteenth century, the simple aria was supplanted by the **double aria**, which featured two parts: a slow lyrical section followed by a fast, brilliant section. Often a transition linked the two portions, and the entire work was labeled a **cavatina**. Frequently, the slow-fast cavatina was introduced by a recitative, yielding the common *Scena e cavatina*, or "scene and cavatina":

Recitative	Cavatina
	Slow, lyrical—transition—fast, brilliant

Typically, each principal character in an Italian opera sang at least one cavatina, which often marked the character's first entrance on stage.

The composer who established the conventions of Italian Romantic opera was Gioachino Rossini (1792–1868), creator of nearly forty serious and comic operas that premiered in the leading opera houses of Venice, Naples, Rome, and Milan. Rossini enjoyed a phenomenal popularity in Europe from about 1816 to 1830. A likeable man and a great lover of food, he even had culinary dishes named in his honor, such as *Tournedos Rossini*. His comic masterpiece, *Il barbiere di Siviglia* (*The Barber of Seville*, 1816) is filled with tuneful arias and crisp recitatives. Its rousing overture is especially celebrated.

In 1824, Rossini settled in Paris, where he wrote the French opera *Guillaume Tell* (*William Tell*, 1829), with its ever popular, dramatic overture. Then he abruptly left the stage and took up residence in Italy before returning to Paris in 1855. He spent his retirement composing sacred music and lighthearted piano pieces, but produced no new operas.

Gioachino Rossini (1792–1868).

Another successful Italian opera composer was Gaetano Donizetti (1797–1848). Remarkably prolific, Donizetti completed over seventy operas. It was said that he could turn out a new opera in a week or two, and cartoons of the time often showed him writing music on two sheets of paper, working with both hands. Among his most successful operas is *Lucia di Lammermoor* (1835), drawn from a novel by Sir Walter Scott.

Read about and listen to Bellini's Cavatina, "Casta Diva" from his opera *Norma*.

The third leading Italian composer was Vincenzo Bellini (1801–1835), who finished only ten serious operas during his tragically short career. His fame reached beyond Italy to France, England, and Germany. Bellini was known for expressively lyrical melodies that suggest the soulful elegance of Chopin. His masterpiece is *Norma*, which premiered in 1831 in Milan.

GIUSEPPE VERDI

The dominant composer of nineteenth-century Italian opera was Giuseppe Verdi (1813–1901). He was born near Busseto, an area of northern Italy then under French control. By age eight, Verdi was serving as an organist at two local churches, but in composition, he was slow to develop. When he applied at age nineteen to study at the music conservatory in Milan, he was rejected for, among other reasons, being too old and not advanced enough as a pianist.

Verdi had modest success with one of his early operas in Milan, although his early attempts gave little hint of what was to come. Indeed, one of his early operas was a total flop. His personal life was full of tragedies. Shortly after his young daughter and son died, his first wife died of encephalitis, inflammation of the brain. A turning point came in 1842, when he scored a major triumph with the opera *Nabucco*, based on the biblical account of Nebuchadnezzar and the Babylonian captivity. A stream of operas followed over the next ten years as Verdi turned to Schiller, Hugo, Byron, Shakespeare, and others for subjects. He later described this period as his time "in the galley" dedicated to developing and honing his craft. Reaching artistic maturity, he then produced a cluster of operas during the 1850s. Three of them remain among the most often performed operas today: *Rigoletto* (1851), *Il trovatore* (*The Troubadour*, 1853), and *La traviata* (*The Misguided Woman*, 1853).

Giuseppe Verdi (1813–1901).

Much of Verdi's long career—there is more than half a century between his first and last operas (1839–1893)—coincided with the *Risorgimento* (*Resurgence*), the great movement for the unification of Italy. After a series of small tremors, revolution erupted in 1848. Gradually, a unified country emerged from what had been a confusing mixture of separate city-states and territories, many under foreign control.

Victor Emmanuel II, king of Italy (r. 1861–1878). Verdi was an important figure in Italian nationalist politics leading up to the monarch's rule.

Verdi was an important figure in the revolution. Several of his operas deal with political oppression and inspired his countrymen. In *Nabucco*, for instance, the captive Hebrews sing a chorus that many heard as a rallying cry for Italian nationalism. In fact, patriots used Verdi's name in one of the slogans of the revolution, "*V*ittorio *E*mmanuel, *Rè D'I*talia" (Victor Emmanuel, King of Italy). Verdi rejoiced when the Austrians were driven out of Italy and replaced by a monarchy under Victor Emmanuel II in 1861; Verdi was named an honorary deputy in the new Italian parliament.

A tireless advocate for the rights of composers, Verdi insisted that his operas be published in authorized versions to combat musical piracy. With his publisher, Ricordi, Verdi became rich by taking full advantage of new copyright laws that protected the interests of composers. He was a composer of international standing whose operas were performed in London, Paris, and, of course, throughout Italy. Notably, his opera *Aida* premiered in 1871 in Cairo following the opening of the Suez Canal. The subject, a war between ancient Egypt and Ethiopia, inspired Verdi to create a lush musical score filled with pageantry and, when an opera house could afford it, even live elephants.

For several years after *Aida*, Verdi withdrew from public life. He led a leisured existence on an estate in northern Italy, where he quietly raised livestock. But he was not yet ready to retire. Moved by the death of the patriotic Italian novelist Alessandro Manzoni in 1874, Verdi composed a compelling, dramatic Requiem Mass. Then, at age seventy-four in 1887, he unexpectedly returned to the stage in triumph with the tragedy *Otello*, based on Shakespeare's play. He finished his final opera, *Falstaff*, in 1893 at age eighty. This last masterpiece was a comedy based on Shakespeare's *The Merry Wives of Windsor* and *Henry IV*. In each composition, Verdi continued to experiment in ways that challenged the conventions of Italian opera. Instead of dividing the music into distinct arias, recitatives, and ensembles, he produced long stretches of continuous music. The supple vocal lines of these scores often combine aria and recitative styles. Instead of the orchestra serving as background accompaniment to the singer, Verdi also increasingly used it as a powerful, expressive agent.

Rigoletto

One of his most successful operas is *Rigoletto*, finished in 1851, with an Italian libretto adapted from a play by Victor Hugo. Hugo's play concerns the sixteenth-century French monarch Francis I, who seduces the daughter of his court jester. That subject was risqué enough for officials to shut the play down after its Parisian premiere in 1832. But not quite twenty years later Verdi returned to the banned play for the subject for one of his operas of the 1850s. In Austrian-occupied Italy, he had to appease the censors by moving the setting of the opera to the Renaissance Italian court of the Duke of Mantua.

As the curtain rises on *Rigoletto*, we meet the duke, sung by a tenor, who woos the wives of his noblemen. When another nobleman accuses the duke of seducing the nobleman's daughter, the hunchbacked court jester Rigoletto, a baritone, mocks the nobleman and in turn is cursed by him.

A different side of Rigoletto emerges in a subsequent scene, when we meet his daughter Gilda, a soprano. She lives in seclusion, sheltered from the evils of the world by the protective jester. Eventually, Gilda is taken from Rigoletto's home and deceived into falling in love with the duke. In revenge, Rigoletto hires an assassin to kill the duke and deliver the body in a sack. But in the end, Gilda sacrifices herself to save the duke and is murdered instead. When Rigoletto, about to throw the body

Costume for Rigoletto, the hunchbacked court jester, in Verdi's 1851 opera.

into a river, hears the duke singing in the distance, he opens the sack to find his dying daughter. His revenge has failed tragically, and the curse is fulfilled.

"La donna è mobile," **Rigoletto,** *Act III*

What Rigoletto hears the duke singing is a reprise of "La donna è mobile" ("Woman is fickle"), which is first heard in the opening scene of Act III (**Listening Map 47**). "La donna è mobile" is a **canzone**, a song in strophic form. When the song is first heard, the duke has arrived at an inn to meet the seductive sister of the assassin Rigoletto has hired to kill the duke. Outside the inn, Gilda and Rigoletto watch through a window, in shock and mounting rage. The orchestra begins by briefly previewing the duke's memorable tune. When the duke begins singing, the full melody unfolds in short, catchy phrases in an irresistible, swaying triple meter. Near the melody's end, it reaches a climactic high note. Then, refrain-like, the orchestra repeats the opening bars, before receding into the background for the duke's second verse. At the song's conclusion, the orchestra states the tune once again, but now in a diminuendo, as the assassin appears to ask Rigoletto whether the duke should live or die. The song is straightforward and simple, but calculated with unerring accuracy to promote the drama.

Watch a concert production of this aria from *Rigoletto*.

LISTENING MAP 47

VERDI, *Rigoletto*, Act III, Canzone "La donna è mobile" ("Woman Is Fickle") {1851}

FORM	Strophic song
METER	$\frac{3}{8}$
TEMPO	*Allegretto* (fairly brisk)
SCORING	Tenor solo and orchestra (one piccolo, two flutes, two oboes, two clarinets, two bassoons, four French horns, two trumpets, three trombones, tuba, and strings)
OVERVIEW	Verdi uses the simplest means to maximum effect in this beloved number from *Rigoletto*. First, the orchestra introduces the tune, but only part of it, before pausing. Then the duke makes his entrance, and sings the tune twice, with a brief orchestral interlude.

why to LISTEN

At the core of every Verdi opera is human conflict acted out between passionate characters. Verdi's genius was to translate their dramatic collisions into engaging music, and to use vivid musical means to draw characters into sharp focus. The results were compelling dramas. Additionally, in keeping with the time-honored traditions of Italian opera, Verdi always emphasized the sheer beauty of the human voice and its expressive melodic capabilities. "La donna è mobile" is probably the most famous melody that he ever wrote. To prevent the premature release of what he sensed would be an instant hit, he did not rehearse it until the last possible moment.

first LISTEN

INTRODUCTION	STROPHE 1	ORCHESTRAL INTERLUDE	STROPHE 2
0:00	**0:14**	**1:04**	**1:16**
Preview of melody by orchestra Brief pause	Duke sings the melody; orchestra softly repeats and briefly pauses		Duke sings the melody; orchestra repeats opening of the melody, ***f***, then ***p*** and triple ***p***

 *a deeper* **LISTEN**

TIME	SECTION	LISTEN FOR THIS	TEXT	TRANSLATION
0:00	**Introduction**	Orchestral introduction softly previews opening of melody, and briefly pauses		
0:14	**Strophe 1 (duke's entrance)**	First statement of the melody	*La donna è mobile* *qual piuma al vento* *muta d'accento* *e di pensiero.* *Sempre un amabile* *leggiadro viso,* *in pianto, in riso,* *è menzognero.* *La donna è mobile,* etc.	Woman is fickle, like a wind-blown feather, she changes her accent and her thoughts. Always lovable and a pretty face, weeping or laughing, she lies. Woman is fickle, etc.
		con brio *legato* La donna è mo-bi-le qual piuma al ven - to, mut-a d'ac - cen - to e di pen		
1:04	**Orchestral interlude**	Orchestra softly repeats opening of melody, and briefly pauses		
1:16	**Strophe 2**		*È sempre misero* *chi a lei s'affida,* *chi le confida* *mal cauto il core!* *Pur mai non sentesi* *felice appieno* *chi su quell seno* *non liba amore!* *La donna è mobile,* [etc.]	Wretched always, he who believes in her, who recklessly confides his heart to her! And yet one does not feel entirely happy who does not imbibe of love at that breast! Woman is fickle, [etc.]

French Romantic Opera

In early nineteenth-century France, operas about political prisoners struck a chord with survivors of the horrific upheaval of the French Revolution. Luigi Cherubini (1760–1842)—an Italian composer who produced successful operas in Paris before 1800—wrote several examples known as "rescue operas." They derived from eighteenth-century French opera that had spoken dialogue in place of recitative, but still featured sung arias and choruses. Politics continued to mix with opera during the reign of Napoleon, when composers glorified the emperor by writing lavishly ceremonial operas.

After Napoleon, French opera changed course. More and more, composers catered to the newly prosperous middle-class. This trend was especially evident during the reign of the "Citizen King," Louis Philippe (r. 1830–1848), when French opera culminated in **grand opera**. This was opera mounted on a large scale, with grand historical themes, massive choruses, spectacular ballets, and impressive stage effects, such as depicting a shipwreck in a storm.

Several foreign composers produced grand operas in French or were influenced by the style (Rossini's *Guillaume Tell* of 1829 is one famous example). The leading practitioner of grand opera was the German Giacomo Meyerbeer (1791–1864), who settled in Paris. Meyerbeer had a good sense of what would impress French audiences. Typically in five long acts, his grand operas incorporate entertaining ballets—one even featured roller skaters to represent an ice-skating party. Most of his operas treat historical subjects drawn from European history. *Les Huguenots* (1836), for example, concerns the persecution of French Protestants in the sixteenth century.

Rossini's *Guillaume Tell* (*William Tell*, 1829) is a famous example of French grand opera.

The Parisian bourgeoisie loved grand opera, but the art form did not endure. In fact, nineteenth-century France did not produce any major opera composers who could rival the stature of Verdi or Wagner. Nevertheless, grand opera did yield innovations in stagecraft and orchestral effects that influenced major composers such as Verdi in Italy and Wagner in Germany.

German Romantic Opera

Before the Romantic era, Germany had no well-established operatic traditions, unlike Italy and France. Mozart had created a German masterpiece in his *Magic Flute* (1791, see p. 258), but he favored Italian opera. Beethoven managed to complete only one opera, *Fidelio* (1805), which cost him enormous effort. Although written in German, *Fidelio* is influenced by the French rescue opera, and its libretto is a translation of a French source.

German Romantic opera emerged during the opening decades of the nineteenth century. It was a further development of the singspiel, a type of German opera with spoken dialogue that Mozart had perfected in *The Magic Flute*. After

Mozart, Carl Maria von Weber (1786–1826) had great success with the 1821 premiere of his Romantic opera *Der Freischütz* (see p. 361). Performed throughout Europe, *Der Freischütz* was one of the most important early German Romantic operas. It influenced many composers, including Wagner.

RICHARD WAGNER

Richard Wagner (1813–1883).

No composer of the nineteenth century commanded at once greater fame and notoriety than Richard Wagner (1813–1883). He created revolutionary new operas that ran to several hours and employed enormous orchestral and theatrical resources. Wagner usually created his own librettos. He wrote pointed essays to promote his new ideas about music and art, which his admirers and detractors alike labeled the "Music of the Future." A great innovator in his bold use of chromatic harmony (see p. 305), Wagner pushed the traditional tonal system closer to its breaking point than ever before.

Wagner's life was as controversial as his music. Hounded by creditors, he accepted money from friends even though he could not repay them. He had affairs with his supporters' wives. German authorities regarded him as a subversive who associated with anarchists.

Born in Leipzig, Wagner displayed early on interests in music and the theater, and tried his hand at writing a play which he considered setting to music. Heavily influenced by Beethoven, he also composed an early symphony, which was largely forgotten after a handful of public performances. Wagner's career began modestly enough, with several minor posts directing opera in Germany and in what is now Latvia, but to evade his creditors, he moved to Paris in 1839. Seeking to capitalize on the popularity of grand opera, he wrote *Rienzi, or the Last Consul of Rome* (1842), a sprawling five-act opera no one in Paris was willing to produce. Instead, Wagner returned to Germany to oversee the opera's premiere. *Rienzi* was a tremendous success, and Wagner followed it with a series of operas that shared themes such as redemption and drew their plots from mythology. These operas included several frequently performed today, such as *Der fliegende Holländer* (*The Flying Dutchman*, 1843), *Tannhäuser* (1845), and *Lohengrin* (1850).

Lohengrin was premiered in Weimar with Liszt as conductor. Wagner was not present, however, having fled Germany on account of his role in the Dresden revolution of 1849. He spent the next several years exiled in Switzerland, writing essays about music, drama, and politics, including an anti-Semitic attack on Mendelssohn and Meyerbeer. During this time he also planned his gargantuan cycle of four operas, *Der Ring des Nibelungen* (*The Ring of the Nibelung*), which required more than a quarter of a century to bring to completion (1848–1876).

In his essays, Wagner examined the historical development of opera and set down his vision for the music of the future. For Wagner, opera was a serious art form originally conceived as drama set to music, with deep roots stretching back to the tragedies of Greek antiquity. But Wagner believed that opera had deviated from its role as high art, that it had been corrupted by the vanity of virtuoso singers and empty stage spectacles. In his new operas, Wagner wanted to reverse those developments in order to restore the dramatic integrity of opera. He would create works—**music dramas**, as he called them—unified in every respect toward a dramatic end. The music, libretto, stage design, and other ingredients would all contribute to

Set design for Wagner's sole comic opera, *Die Meistersinger von Nürnberg* (*The Mastersingers of Nuremberg*, 1865).

what Wagner's circle labeled the **Gesamtkunstwerk**, or "total art work." Wagner would realize this vision in the dramas of *The Ring*.

While shaping these theories, Wagner interrupted work on *The Ring* to compose two other major works. The first, *Tristan und Isolde* (1865), is based on a medieval romance from Arthurian legends and was heavily influenced by Wagner's reading of German philosophy. *Tristan and Isolde* contains some of Wagner's most experimental music and challenged the conventions of opera with its free-ranging chromatic lines, thick orchestral textures, complex networks of motives, and long stretches of continuous music. The second major work was his sole comic opera, *Die Meistersinger von Nürnberg* (*The Mastersingers of Nuremberg*, 1865), which portrays a sixteenth-century singers' guild. The plot sets a young knight's musical genius against critics who disapprove of his innovative art—and, by extension, of Wagner's reform of opera.

In Wagner's dramas, libretto and music combine in a continuous melodic flow, with none of the traditional breaks then common in Italian and French operas. Instead of dividing the drama between independent numbers, Wagner employed free "poetic-musical periods" of various lengths, each with its own complex character. The orchestra does not just accompany the singers but achieves its own dramatic power reminiscent of Beethoven's symphonies. Wagner's vocal lines are fully woven into the orchestral sound, and all musical elements act together to fulfill the overriding demands of the drama.

One of Wagner's major contributions was to enlarge the orchestra. He increased considerably the number of strings, and actually specified the number of violins, violas, and so on that he required. Instead of pairs of woodwinds, he wrote for triple and even quadruple woodwinds. He enlarged the brass section even more dramatically, calling for as many as eight horns in *The Ring*, four of which were specially designed and known as "Wagner tubas." Wagner was one of the first orchestral composers to exploit the tuba, a bass instrument that strengthened the lower range of the brass ensemble. Finally, he introduced elaborate parts for harps (the *Ring* cycle generally calls for six) and experimented with different percussion instruments. Table 39.1 gives the instrumentation of *Das Rheingold*, the first drama of *The Ring*; a comparison with the charts on pp. 239 and 353 sets Wagner's expansion of the orchestra in perspective.

Another major contribution of Wagner was his new approach to text setting. By writing his own librettos, Wagner did away with the traditional division of labor between librettist and composer, and retained complete control over the finished work. He preferred a flexible, free type of verse, with varying stresses per line. He also preferred repetitions of similar syllables or vowels rather than rhymes at the end of the lines.

To help unify his colossal scores, Wagner used an elaborate system of short musical motives, each of which was connected to some character or element in the drama. The term **leitmotif** ("leading motive") is generally applied for Wagner's motives, although the composer did not invent the term. Other composers had employed similar techniques before Wagner. For example, Mendelssohn used

TABLE 39.1 The Orchestra of Wagner's *Das Rheingold* (1854)

WOODWINDS	BRASS	PERCUSSION	STRINGS
Three flutes (third flute doubles as second piccolo)	Eight French horns	Four timpani	Sixteen first violins
One piccolo	Four "Wagner" tubas (tenor and bass, alternating with four of the horns)	Triangle	Sixteen second violins
Three oboes	One contrabass tuba	Cymbals	Twelve violas
One English horn (doubles as fourth oboe)	Three trumpets	Bass drum	Twelve cellos
Three clarinets	One bass trumpet	Gong	Eight double basses
One bass clarinet	Three trombones	Sixteen anvils of various sizes on stage	
Three bassoons	One contrabass trombone	Six harps (seventh on stage)	

specific motives in his Overture to *A Midsummer Night's Dream* (**Listening Map 45**), and Berlioz wove a recurring melody into all five movements of his *Fantastic Symphony* (**Listening Map 46**). However, Wagner magnified the idea, applying dozens of leitmotifs in his dramas. Wagner's disciples pored over his scores to identify prominent motives, which they gave names: for example, the "Nature," "Curse," and "Sword" motives. These motives filled the music of Wagner's *Ring*. Sometimes, two or three were heard together in a way that enriched the flow of the music. Wagner also used his motives as a powerful psychological tool that could condition audiences to anticipate a particular dramatic situation or entrance of a character. Above all, Wagner's motives gave unity to his scores, enabling him to tie together their musical and dramatic threads.

Wagner's Der Ring des Nibelungen (The Ring of the Nibelung)

Wagner remained in exile from Germany for more than ten years until 1860, when he received a partial amnesty. Then, in 1864, came a dramatic reversal of fortune when he met a devoted follower, Ludwig II (r. 1864–1886), the young king of Bavaria. Known as "Mad King Ludwig," this reclusive monarch lived in a fantasy world limited only by his imagination. He exhausted the Bavarian state treasury building Romantic medieval castles. The most famous of these is Neuschwanstein, which later served as the model for the castle at Disneyland. Ludwig paid Wagner's debts and funded the construction of the Bayreuth (pronounced *BY-roit*) Festival Theater, which was specifically designed for *The Ring*. About 140 miles from Munich, it became a Wagnerian shrine in which *The Ring* was annually staged.

Dashboard

Read about how Wagner's Ring was influenced by and has influenced other works of art.

MAKING CONNECTIONS *Musical Cues in Wagner and Beyond*

Wagner was not the first opera composer to create musical motives that could be associated with specific characters or dramatic ideas—we can find them in Mozart's *Don Giovanni*, for instance—but he was the first to develop them into a complex, sophisticated network, and to maximize their use. With his operas running up to five hours long, Wagner needed a way to give them shape and structure. What better way to do this than work into the music distinctive motives that could return periodically? These motives could either summarize for the audience dramatic action that had already taken place, or anticipate an event or character about to happen or appear on stage.

This simple but powerful musical technique later became a mainstay of the Hollywood film industry, and is still in use today. In the epic classic *Gone with the Wind* (1939), Tara's theme is indelibly associated with the Georgian plantation depicted in the film. Similarly, it is impossible to watch the space-fantasy classic *Star Wars* (1977) without being aware of the fanfare-like theme associated with Luke Skywalker.

Demand for tickets soon outstripped the supply; even today, concertgoers wait for five to ten years for tickets.

Performed over four evenings (nearly twenty hours of music in all), *The Ring* comprises a prologue, *Das Rheingold* (*The Rhinegold*), and three weighty dramas, *Die Walküre* (*The Valkyrie*), *Siegfried*, and *Götterdämmerung* (*The Twilight of the Gods*). After laboring for years over the libretto, drawn from Nordic mythology, Wagner spent twenty more years composing the scores, writing well over two thousand pages of music.

Ever since its first performance in 1876, this great cycle has attracted its champions and critics. While the American Mark Twain joked that Wagner's music was not as bad as it sounded, the English playwright George Bernard Shaw interpreted *The Ring* as an allegory that predicted the downfall of modern capitalism. The German philosopher Friedrich Nietzsche—a close friend of Wagner until the premiere of *The Ring*—may have formulated his concept of the superman from the work. In the twentieth century, Adolf Hitler found symbolic qualities for his Aryan race in Wagner's superhuman heroes. In literature, *The Ring* may have influenced the fantasy novels of the Englishman J. R. R. Tolkien, including *The Lord of the Rings*. The scope and size of Wagner's *Ring* were never equaled, and its musical style set a new standard that generations of young composers used to measure their own progress.

Bayreuth Festival Theater, which was specifically designed for Wagner's *Ring*.

For his four dramas, Wagner used mythology instead of history because he wanted his epic cycle to have timeless relevance. *The Ring* is a universe of many levels. First, there is the uncorrupted world of nature represented by the Rhine River. Above, there are the gods, who inhabit a fortress called Valhalla. Deep in the earth live the Nibelungs, a dwarfish race ruthlessly exploited by their master, Alberich. Finally, there is the world of mortals, through whom the drama is acted out.

The prologue, *Das Rheingold*, is in four continuous scenes. Containing about three hours of music, this is the shortest of the four works in the cycle. In the first scene, we encounter the Rhinemaidens, keepers of the gold, at the bottom of the river. By renouncing love, the dwarf Alberich manages to steal their treasure. The second scene transfers us to the craggy peaks overlooking the Rhine, where the gods have gathered. Two giants have finished building their fortress, Valhalla, and arrive to demand one of the goddesses as payment. But after learning that whoever possesses Rhinemaidens' gold controls the universe—they settle instead for the precious metal. In the third scene, the ruler of the gods, Wotan, and the demigod of fire, Loge, descend to the realm of the Nibelungs, and by trickery capture Alberich, who has already used the gold to make a magical ring and helmet. In the concluding, fourth scene, we return to Valhalla, where the giants claim the recovered hoard of gold. But Alberich has cursed it, and when the giants fight over the treasure, one is slain. Ignoring this omen, the gods enter Valhalla over a rainbow. *Das Rheingold* comes to a radiant conclusion with Wagner's music for "The Gods' Entrance into Valhalla" (**Listening Map 48**).

Wagner, Das Rheingold*, "The Gods' Entrance into Valhalla"*

Das Rheingold employs an elaborate network of some thirty motives. Each is associated with an idea, character, or object and undergoes musical changes that mirror the drama. One of the most important is the Nature motive. It is associated with the Rhine River and wells up from the depths of the orchestra. The motive is based on the most fundamental consonant harmony, the major triad.

The giants, Nibelungs, and various gods are also caught in Wagner's web of motives. Thus, in the final scene, when Donner, god of thunder, summons a storm to clear the turbulent heavens, he does so with a compact motive associated with his character. As the skies brighten, a rainbow appears, forming a bridge to Valhalla. Six harps now sustain a shimmering harmony as the Rainbow motive rises in the low strings (①). It, too, is based on a major triad, and appropriately resembles the Nature motive with which the work began. Appropriately, too, the Rainbow motive slowly rises and falls, forming an arch that paints in musical terms the rainbow that appears on stage.

Next, Valhalla is given its own motive, which, solemn and measured, is heard in brass chords (②). Somewhat reassured, the gods begin their procession into the fortress. At this point, Wagner introduces the Sword motive, which figures prominently in the next dramas of the cycle (③). In the radiant music that concludes *Das Rheingold*, a trumpet sounds the Sword motive with penetrating brilliance. The Sword motive is also based on a major triad, making it the final motive in a series that includes the Rainbow and all-encompassing Nature motives.

As the gods prepare to enter Valhalla, Loge, demigod of fire, has misgivings about their fate, and fears that they are rushing to their destruction. (Of course, it is his element, fire, that eventually consumes all at the end of *The Twilight of the Gods*.) Loge's motive is accompanied by chromatic slides up the scale, suggesting licking flames (④). Most unsettling of all, drifting up to the gods from the river below is the chorus of Rhinemaidens, who lament their lost treasure (⑤). Ignoring their plea, the gods cross the rainbow to take up residence in their magnificent new home.

Das Rheingold ends with the orchestra restating the Valhalla, Sword, and Rainbow motives simultaneously. For the moment, the gods are secure.

As the epic continues, Wotan, the king of the gods, as well as Alberich and others compete for control of the ring. Bound by contracts and treaties, Wotan must act through intermediaries. First, in *The Valkyrie*, Brünnhilde—one of Wotan's warrior daughters—tries to save the mortal Siegmund so that he might reclaim the gold. But Siegmund has unknowingly committed incest with his long-separated sister Sieglinde, and so must forfeit his life. By disobeying Wotan's command not to intervene to save Siegmund, Brünnhilde must give up her divinity and is put to sleep on top of a mountain, where Wotan encircles her with a ring of fire. In the next drama, Siegfried, son of Siegmund and Sieglinde, fashions a sword, recovers Alberich's golden ring, enters the ring of fire, and awakens Brünnhilde. But in the final drama, Siegfried is slain. Reclaiming the ring, Brünnhilde builds his funeral pyre and kills herself by riding her horse into the flames. The banks of the Rhine overflow, and the ring finally returns to the Rhinemaidens, completing Wagner's epic circle. But in the distance, Valhalla is consumed in an all-encompassing fire.

Arthur Rackham, illustration of the Rhinemaidens for Wagner's *Das Rheingold* (*The Rhinegold*), the first of four music dramas that constitute Wagner's *Ring*.

LISTENING MAP 48

WAGNER, *Das Rheingold*, concluding scene, "The Gods' Entrance into Valhalla"

{1854}

FORM	Free, determined by divisions in the text, and organized musically around recurring leitmotifs.
METER	Various meters
TEMPO	Various tempos
SCORING	Orchestra (one piccolo, three flutes, three oboes, one English horn, three clarinets, one bass clarinet, three bassoons, eight French horns, four tubas, one contrabass tuba, three trumpets, one bass trumpet, three trombones, one contrabass trombone, percussion, six harps, and strings).
OVERVIEW	The final scene of *Das Rheingold* shows Wagner's art at its most elaborate. As the gods prepare to enter their fortress Valhalla, we hear first the arching Rainbow motive, then the stately Valhalla motive, and, cutting through the lush textures, the Sword motive (anticipating dramatic action to come in the later music dramas of the *Ring*). Interrupting these three motives are Loge's chromatic slides, alluding to the fire that will eventually destroy the gods, and the Rhinemaidens' lament, with the observation that the gods above celebrate what is "false and rotten." Be that as it may, the gods cross the rainbow to a climax of the combined Rainbow, Valhalla, and Sword motives, as the curtain falls.

why to LISTEN

Probably more has been written about Wagner than any other nineteenth-century celebrity, whether a musician or not. The scope of his achievement, culminating in the four epic music dramas of *The Ring of the Nibelung*, is measureless. The controversies surrounding his career and music seem endless as well. However one assesses him, he was a musical genius who redefined and stretched Western tonality to its limits, preparing the experimental music of the twentieth century. He was also a composer who redefined our sense of musical time. Wagner wrote epic works—both the words *and* the music—that challenged the endurance of musicians and audiences alike. He needed this expansive platform to create his mythical worlds and present universal themes of timeless relevance. Attending a complete performance of the *Ring* cycle over a number of days is a truly special event.

Continued

 *first* **LISTEN**

RAINBOW MOTIVE	VALHALLA MOTIVE	SWORD MOTIVE	VALHALLA MOTIVE	LOGE'S MOTIVE	RHINEMAIDENS' SONG	RAINBOW, VALHALLA, AND SWORD MOTIVES
0:00	0:58	3:03	3:56	4:30	5:16	7:23

a deeper **LISTEN**

TIME	SECTION	LISTEN FOR THIS	TEXT	TRANSLATION
0:00	Rainbow Motive	① Arching melody rising and falling in the bass, accompanied by six harps, strings, and high woodwinds	**Froh** *Zur Burg führt die Brücke,* *leicht, doch fest eurem Fuss* *beschreitet kühn* *ihren schrecklosen Pfad!*	 To the castle leads the bridge, light, though firm to your feet; boldly cross your fearless path!
0:58	Valhalla Motive	② Chordal style in the brass	**Wotan** *Abendlich strahlt* *der Sonne Auge;* *in prächtiger Glut* *prangt glänzend die Burg.* *In des Morgens Scheine* *muthig erschimmernd* *lag sie herrenlos,* *hehr verlockend vor mir.* *Von Morgen bis Abend,* *in Müh' und Angst* *nicht wonnig ward sie gewonnen!* *Es naht die Nacht* *vor ihrem Neid* *biete sie Bergung nun.*	 In the evening shines the eye of the sun; in a magnificent glow the fortress shines bright. In the morning light glittering bravely it lay uninhabited, nobly enticing before me. From morning 'til evening in toil and anguish it was not happily won! Night approaches before its envy, may it now offer shelter.

TIME	SECTION	LISTEN FOR THIS	TEXT	TRANSLATION
3:03	Sword Motive	③ Rising triadic figure in the trumpet	**Wotan (cont'd)** *So grüss' ich die Burg,* *sicher vor Bang' und Grau'n!* *Folge mir, Frau;* *in Walhall wohne mit mir!*	So I greet the castle, safe from fear and trembling. Follow me, wife; Live with me in Valhalla!
3:56	Valhalla Motive		**Fricka** *Was deutet der Name?* *Nie, dünkt mich, hört ich ihn nennen.*	What means the name? Never, it seems, did I hear it named.
4:06		(The Gods begin to cross the rainbow.)	**Wotan** *Was mächtig der Furcht* *mein Muth mir erfand,* *wenn siegend es lebt,* *leg' es den Sinn dir dar.*	What, through the power of fear my courage conceived, if it lives in triumph its purpose will be revealed to you.
4:30	Loge's Motive	④ Chromatic sliding figures in the strings	**Loge** *Ihrem Ende eilen sie zu,* *die so stark im Bestehen sich wähnen.* *Fast schäm' ich mich* *mit ihnen zu schaffen;* *zur leckenden Lohe* *mich wieder zu wandeln,* *spür' ich lockende Lust;* *sie aufzuzehren* *die einst mich gezähmt,* *statt mit den Blinden* *blöd zu vergeh'n,* *und waren es göttlichste Götter!*	They hasten to their end, deluding themselves to be enduring, I am nearly ashamed to be involved with them, I have a strong urge to change myself again into licking flames and consume them all, who once controlled me instead of weakly perishing with the blind, even if they were the most divine gods!

Continued

TIME	SECTION	LISTEN FOR THIS	TEXT	TRANSLATION
			Nicht dumm dünkte mich das! *Bedenken will ich's:* *wer weiss, was ich thu'!*	That doesn't seem dumb to me! I'll ponder it. Who knows, what I will do?
		(As he prepares to follow the Gods, the song of the Rhinemaidens rises up from the depths of the valley below.)		
5:16	Rhinemaidens' Song	⑤ Choral lament	**Rhinemaidens** *Rheingold! Rheingold!* *Reines Gold!* *Wie lauter und hell* *leuchtetest hold du uns!*	Rhinegold! Rhinegold! Pure gold! How true and bright You did graciously shine upon us!
		Rhein - gold, Rhein - gold, rei - nes Gold!__		
5:34			**Wotan** *Welch' Klagen dringt zu mir her?*	What lamenting do I hear?
5:39			**Rhinemaidens** *Um dich, du klares,* *wir nun klagen,* *gebt uns das Gold.*	For you, bright one, we now mourn, give us the gold.
5:45			**Loge** *Des Rheines Kinder* *beklagen des Goldes Raub.*	The children of the Rhine lament the theft of the gold.
5:51			**Wotan** *Verwünschte Nicker!* *wehre ihrem Geneck!*	Cursed water-sprites! Stop their teasing!

TIME	SECTION	LISTEN FOR THIS	TEXT	TRANSLATION
6:03			**Loge** *Ihr da im Wasser!* *Was weint ihr herauf?* *Hört, was Wotan euch wünscht!* *Glänzt nicht mehr* *euch Mädchen das Gold,* *in der Götter neuem Glanze* *Sonn't euch selig fort an!*	 You there in the water! Why do you cry up to us? Hear what Wotan wants from you! Though the gold no longer shines on you maidens, in the new radiance of the gods you will bask comfortably henceforth!
6:34			**Rhinemaidens** *Rheingold! Rheingold!* *Reines Gold!* *O leuchtete noch* *in der Tiefe dein laut'rer Tand!* *Traulich und treu* *ist's nur in der Tiefe:* *falsch und feig* *ist was dort oben sich freut!*	 Rhinegold! Rhinegold! Pure Gold! Oh if only your pure finery Still sparkled in the deep! Familiar and true is the gold only in the deep; false and rotten is what rejoices above!
7:23	Rainbow, Valhalla, and Sword Motives	(As the Gods cross the rainbow to the fortress, the curtain falls.)		

Wagner's influence on music, drama, and European culture was incalculable. Wagnerian societies sprang up in Germany, France, and England. His music galvanized thinking about music, drama, and the arts. A large number of admirers—royalty, musicians, and writers among them—made pilgrimages to Bayreuth to hear his dramas.

Many composers imitated Wagner's lush style and use of motives. Others struggled to break free from his influence, such as the young French composer Debussy, intent upon exploring a radically new style of composing music. Regardless of the reaction to Wagner, his work was hugely significant to the course of music. His synthesis of the arts, his seamless musical forms, and his use of a boldly expanded orchestra all brought German musical Romanticism to its extraordinary culmination. And his influence deeply shaped twentieth-century popular culture. Hollywood employed film composers who were thoroughly trained in Wagner's music. Finally, we may trace the idea of film prequels and sequels, of epic science fiction and fantasy series based on mythological characters and races (for instance, *Star Wars*, *Star Trek*, *The Lord of the Rings*) to Wagner's monumental works.

check your **KNOWLEDGE**

1. Who were the four major composers of Italian opera? Which innovations did they introduce? Why is Verdi considered to be the most important of these composers?
2. Which new form of the aria did Italian opera composers develop? Describe its structure.
3. What distinguished French "grand opera" from other nineteenth-century types?
4. Wagner described his operas as "music dramas," while some critics used the term *Gesamtkunstwerk*. Define these terms and explain why they were appropriate to describe Wagner's works.
5. How did Wagner use myth to shape his works, particularly in the epic *Ring* cycle? How did his use of myth reflect and develop typical Romantic themes?

CHAPTER

Late Nineteenth-Century Music

Romanticism dominated much of the nineteenth century. However, increasingly during the second half of the century, two powerful forces reshaped European music and culture:

1) **Nationalism**, the conscious use of elements associated with a particular nation to create patriotic feelings, promoted new, distinctive styles in the arts. For example, Wagner was motivated to compose large-scale music dramas in part because of his political views, which supported a unified

Germany. Outside France, Italy, and Germany, where operas often reflected political agenda, nationalism also affected the course of music. Czechs, Slavs, Russians, Norwegians, and many others wrote music that defined emerging national identities.

2) **Realism** threatened to overwhelm the Romantics' faith in subjectivity with scientific, observable truth. Charles Dickens captured the new attitude in his character Thomas Gradgrind, a hardened schoolmaster who dryly says in the novel *Hard Times*, "Facts alone are wanted in life." Realist movements in literature and painting provided alternatives to Romanticism, which was becoming less relevant in a modernizing, mechanizing world.

Thomas Gradgrind and his two children, Louisa and Tom, from the novel *Hard Times* by Charles Dickens (1854).

Nationalism and realism challenged Romanticism in the later nineteenth century. Composers such as the Bohemian Antonín Dvořák and Russian Modest Mussorgsky used nationalism to separate their music from the mainline European Romantic tradition. At the same time, some composers, such as Johannes Brahms and Gustav Mahler, were nostalgic for the Romantic past, even as Romanticism was on the wane. While Mahler lived through the first decade of the twentieth century, long enough to engage with modernism (see Part VII), Brahms died just three years before the end of the nineteenth. Unrestrained yet poignant, Brahms's music captured the moods of a Romantic composer living in an increasingly un-Romantic age.

Johannes Brahms

Born in Hamburg, Johannes Brahms (1833–1897) was introduced to music at an early age by his father, a musician of modest means. We know little about Brahms's very early compositions, because he destroyed them as unworthy. A turning point for the young composer came in 1853, when Robert Schumann befriended him. In his critical writings, Schumann described Brahms as a "young eagle" about to soar with Haydn, Mozart, and Beethoven. Sadly, Schumann's death in 1856 cut short their friendship.

Johannes Brahms (1833–1897).

Brahms was an avid student of music history, who imitated Classical forms and diligently studied counterpoint. Though Wagner declared the symphony obsolete as a genre, Brahms put enormous effort into writing symphonies of great power and freshness. It wasn't until he was in his forties that he was able to complete his first symphony. Again, honoring tradition, he composed chamber music throughout his life, and, as one of the great pianists of the century, produced many impeccable works for the instrument.

Some viewed Brahms's music as a counterbalance to Wagner's "music of the future" and Liszt's commitment to program music. For those clinging to older values, he stood as a champion of musical conservatism, and as a composer who wrote what came to be known as **absolute music**. In Brahms's case, this meant writing sonatas, string quartets, and symphonies that could be appreciated in purely musical terms, without needing programs or literary titles. However, for those seeking "progress" in music, Brahms became an easy target for criticism. Another, more accurate view described Brahms's position in music history as two-sided. On the one hand, he continued to compose in the style of German musical Romanticism, as had

Vienna in the 1870s.

been practiced by Robert Schumann. On the other, he explored new approaches to thematic development with lasting influence. The twentieth-century modernist composer Arnold Schoenberg (see Chapters 41 and 42) later labeled Brahms a "progressive."

Appropriately, Brahms pursued most of his career in Vienna—the city of Haydn, Mozart, Beethoven, and Schubert. There, during the 1860s, he won fame as a pianist and conductor. In his later years, he also premiered his major compositions in the city. Among them were several orchestral works, including four symphonies and four concertos. His most ambitious composition, written after the death of his mother, was the *German Requiem* (1868). It was an imposing work for solo singers, chorus, and orchestra, with texts drawn from the Lutheran Bible.

Brahms freely acknowledged his debts to Beethoven. The First Symphony (1876) contains a theme that sounds much like Beethoven's famous "Ode to Joy" melody from the Ninth Symphony. When confronted with this similarity, Brahms replied, "Any jackass can see that." He also found inspiration in baroque and Classical music. In some orchestral works, he used fixed, repeating bass patterns, as if imitating a compositional technique from the Baroque. Brahms's works contain as well allusions to Handel and Haydn.

BRAHMS, VIOLIN CONCERTO IN D MAJOR, OP. 77, THIRD MOVEMENT

Brahms's Violin Concerto (1879) was written for his close friend, the Austro-Hungarian violinist Joseph Joachim (1831–1907), one of the great virtuosos of the nineteenth century. Its three movements (fast, slow, and fast) proudly show its connection to Classical traditions. Brahms set his concerto in D major, the key of Beethoven's Violin Concerto (1806), a work that Joachim had performed as a boy with Mendelssohn conducting. Following the Classical tradition, Brahms's concerto begins with a full exposition of the thematic material for orchestra alone before the soloist dramatically enters with a second exposition. Similarly, in the third movement (see **Listening Map 49**), Brahms employed a rondo form after the Classical templates Mozart and Beethoven followed in their concertos. But, in a nod to Brahms's own time, and in tribute to Joachim, the composer opened the finale with a theme reminiscent of Hungarian gypsy music.

Joseph Joachim (1831–1907).

This jovial refrain theme (*A*; ①) enters straightaway in the violin playing in **double stops**—bowing two strings simultaneously to produce two-note chords. The string section of the orchestra accompanies the theme with strumming, broken chords. Brahms splits the theme between the solo violin and orchestra, with the solo taking the lead and the orchestra answering. But the orchestra provides one unexpected twist by injecting accents that momentarily throw off the meter of the music.

The energetic second theme (*B*; ②) pits a forceful, rising line in the solo part against a descending line in the bass instruments (later reversed when the orchestra takes up the theme). When *A* returns, Brahms again inserts cross rhythms that disrupt the meter.

The gentle third theme (*C*; ③) appears first in the solo violin before being played by various instruments in the orchestra. Then Brahms returns to *B* and an exuberant statement of *A*, yielding the overall formal scheme *ABACBA*.

At this point, we expect to hear a solo cadenza. And, indeed, the composer includes one: the violinist begins to play triple and quadruple stops in a solo passage. But soon the orchestra reenters in a hushed backdrop to the soloist. The "cadenza" gradually builds in momentum, finishing in a cascading series of arpeggiations in the violin that prepare us for the coda.

Shifting to a brisk tempo, this stirring, march-like conclusion offers an accelerated summary of the movement by revisiting *A* and *B*. Near the end, the music briefly dies down before three definitive chords mark the rousing conclusion.

Nationalism in Music

For the diverse populations of Europe, nationalism was a declaration of their unique political, social, and cultural identities. During the nineteenth century, a series of unification and liberation movements swept across the Continent and beyond, and promoted new national styles. By the 1870s, Germany and Italy were finally unified as countries. Earlier in the century, Spanish rule was overthrown in South America, while Russian rule was resisted in Poland. In the Austrian Empire, Czech, Hungarian, Serb, and Croat nationalists challenged the dominant Austrian government. In the United States, the doctrine of Manifest Destiny promoted the nation's westward expansion to the Pacific Ocean.

Nationalism created the idea that literature, painting, and music should reflect special national and regional characters. Nationalism thus spurred new interest in native folklore, dance, and poetry. Composers drew on popular folk songs and rhythms of national dances, and they enriched Western tonality by exploring the

LISTENING MAP 49

BRAHMS, Violin Concerto in D major, Op. 77, Third Movement

{1879}

FORM	Rondo (ABACBA + Coda)
METER	$\frac{2}{4}$
TEMPO	*Allegro giocoso, ma non troppo vivace* (fast, jocose, but not too fast)
SCORING	Solo violin and orchestra (two flutes, two oboes, two clarinets, two bassoons, four French horns, two trumpets, two timpani, and strings)
OVERVIEW	Brahms constructed the finale of his violin concerto as a rondo, with the solo violin introducing the refrain at the outset, accompanied by the orchestra. The music is intended to suggest a Hungarian style of writing and performing, in homage to the Hungarian/Austrian violinist Joseph Joachim, for whom Brahms wrote the work.

why to LISTEN

Brahms's Violin Concerto neatly summarizes several important musical ideas from the late nineteenth century:

1) By writing his concerto in the same key as Beethoven's Violin Concerto (1806), and by choosing a rondo form for its finale, Brahms was placing his music in the Austro-German line of Classical music.
2) By writing a concerto, Brahms reexamined the role of virtuosity in the musical culture of his time.
3) By writing a finale that alluded to Hungarian gypsy music, Brahms was paying homage to Joseph Joachim's ethnic identity but also acknowledging the forceful role of nationalism.

first LISTEN

A	B	A	C	B	A	CADENZA	CODA
0:00	1:19	2:09	2:48	3:49	5:03	5:29	6:48
Main theme presented by solo violin	Ascending, scale-like theme		Third theme			Virtuosic violin part leading to . . .	march-like coda

a deeper LISTEN

TIME	SECTION	LISTEN FOR THIS
0:00	A	**Refrain (tonic key)** ① Theme in duple meter in solo violin in double stops (***f***), answered by orchestra, which injects cross accents to simulate triple meter **Allegro giocoso, ma non troppo** ***f***
1:19	B	**Second theme (dominant key)** ② Vigorous ascending line in solo violin (***ff***), answered by descending line in orchestra ***ff*** *energicamente*
2:09	A	**Refrain (tonic key)** Cross rhythms introduced so that the music temporarily shifts into triple meter
2:48	C	**Third theme (several keys)** ③ Gentle theme in triple meter introduced in violin (***p***), then in orchestra ***p*** *dolce*
3:49	B	**Second Theme (tonic key)**
5:03	A	**Refrain (tonic key)**
5:29	Cadenza	Violin begins with triple and quadruple stops, then orchestra offers a light accompaniment that gradually builds; cascading arpeggiations in solo violin lead to . . .
6:48	Coda	*Poco più presto* (a little faster) ***p*** March-like restatement of A and B rising in intensity from ***p*** to ***ff***; near the end the music dies down; three decisive ***f*** chords

MAKING CONNECTIONS *Nationalism in Art*

Just as nineteenth-century music responded to nationalism, so did nineteenth-century art. John Gast's *American Progress* (1872) depicts the toga-clad Columbia—a popular symbol of the United States—bringing light from the east as settlers push doggedly westward, fulfilling the idea of Manifest Destiny. The signs of "progress" include steamships, Conestoga wagons, the railroad, and the telegraph wire grasped by Columbia herself. Another female iconic image, this one promoting the ideals of French nationalism, appears in Eugène Delacroix's *Liberty Leading the People*, completed after the Revolution of 1830 that overthrew the monarchy of Charles X (see p. 295). According to reports, the artist said that although he had not fought for his country, he would paint for it.

John Gast's *American Progress* (1872).

colorful harmonies and nonconventional scales of folk music. Musical nationalism arguably made its strongest impact in regions trying to break free from the dominant European musical centers of Germany, Austria, France, and Italy. By 1900 several new national musical styles were established or beginning to emerge. Two of the most striking examples were Bohemia (now the Czech Republic) and Russia.

Antonín Dvořák

Antonín Dvořák (1841–1904).

Antonín Dvořák (pronounced *d-VOR-shock,* 1841–1904) was born in Bohemia, the Western portion of what is now the Czech Republic. Although then part of the Austrian Empire, Bohemia was powerfully affected by nationalism. During Dvořák's youth, the leading Czech composer was Bedřich Smetana (1824–1884), whose orchestral works and operas based on subjects from Czech history and folklore were especially popular.

In 1874 the Austrian government gave Dvořák a scholarship for music composition. Brahms served on the panel of judges and became Dvořák's friend and later arranged for the publication of Dvořák's compositions. Dvořák often used popular Slavic dances as the basis of his compositions. Some examples were the *dumka,* a slow, melancholic dance; the *furiant*, a fast dance marked by strong changes between duple and triple meters; and the *polka*, a lively dance in duple meter. Despite these strong nationalist influences, Dvořák was equally capable of writing music in traditional Germanic forms, as his nine symphonies show.

As Dvořák achieved international fame, he was invited to conduct his symphonies in England, and in 1892 he arrived in New York. There he served as director of New York's National Conservatory of Music, established in 1885 by the socialite Jeanette Thurber. During Dvořák's "American" period (1892–1895), he explored indigenous American music. He examined African-American spirituals and the music of American Indians, and incorporated his research into several compositions. Among them were chamber works, a patriotic cantata, and the composer's ninth and final symphony, subtitled "From the New World," and premiered in New York in 1893 at the recently opened Carnegie Hall.

DVOŘÁK, SYMPHONY NO. 9 ("FROM THE NEW WORLD"), SECOND MOVEMENT

In four sizable movements, this work follows the general sequence of many nineteenth-century symphonies. Dvořák gives his symphony a special American character, however, by writing melodies based on folk music scales. He also used lively rhythms, unusual harmonies, and colorful orchestrations drawn from the music he heard while living in the United States. For its second and third movements, Dvořák found inspiration in *The Song of Hiawatha* (1855), a poem by Henry Wadsworth Longfellow based on North American Indian legends.

MAKING CONNECTIONS *Jeanette Thurber and Music Patronage, Americanized*

Jeanette Meyers Thurber (1850–1946) was a wealthy American art patron who had studied music at the Paris Conservatory. Her principal ambition was to found an American music conservatory that could be expanded by opening additional branches across the country. She began by establishing the National Conservatory in New York in 1885 and hired Dvořák to direct it. He was offered the staggering salary of $15,000 (probably 200 times his annual income in Bohemia) and a first-class ticket to the United States, and he was promised summers off to compose. In exchange, the composer agreed to direct the school, teach pupils, and give six concerts a year. Although Thurber was not able to expand the conservatory to other cities, her vision and generosity did enable women and African-American students to study at the conservatory. One of them, the baritone Harry Burleigh, introduced Dvořák to African-American spirituals. For his part, Dvořák composed some of his greatest music in the United States, including the "New World" Symphony and Cello Concerto. And he did enjoy his summers off, spending time in 1893 in a Czech immigrant community in Spillville, Iowa. He led the conservatory for three years, before returning to Bohemia in 1895.

Jeannette Meyers Thurber, who founded the National Conservatory of Music in New York in 1885 and hired Dvořák to direct it.

Dvořák's subtle second movement (*Largo*) contains some of his loveliest music (**Listening Map 50**). It begins with seven solemn brass chords (*a*), pitched in a low register and played quite softly (*ppp*; ①). These chords slowly evolve before reaching the home key. They give way to the first theme, a haunting melody heard in the dark registers of an English horn (*b*; ②) accompanied by muted strings. Its soothing contours derive from the **pentatonic scale**, which is often associated with folk music. Somewhat like a major scale, a pentatonic scale has two gaps, shown in the example below:

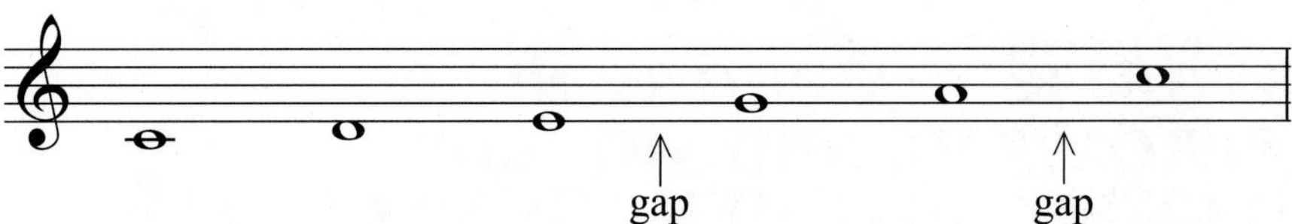

Ex. 40.1

The melody Dvořák created from this scale later became popular as the spiritual "Goin' Home," when one of his students fitted this text to the music:

Goin' home, goin' home, I'm a goin' home,
Quiet-like, some still day, I'm jes' goin' home.
It's not far, jes' close by,
Through an open door,
Work all done, care laid by,
Goin' to fear no more.

Dvořák's melody quickly spread outside concert halls, and was widely heard by non-musicians, so much so that it in effect acquired the status of folk music.

When the melody concludes, the opening chords return, this time in the woodwinds. Then the strings take up the melody, with muted horns playing its final notes. Turning to a slightly faster tempo, Dvořák introduces the central *B* section with a new melody in a minor key (*c*; ③). It begins with a descending figure. Next, the clarinets present a second idea that gently ascends and descends (*d*; ④). Toward the end of this section, Dvořák uses imitations of birdcalls and static drone effects to paint a pastoral scene. Beginning simply, this passage broadens through a crescendo to a *fortissimo* climax.

Now Dvořák recalls two themes from the first movement of his symphony (*e*; ⑤ and *f*; ⑥). Late nineteenth-century composers often reused the opening themes later in a work to help unify their multi-movement compositions. Finally, the familiar English-horn melody of *A* returns, and near the end of the movement, the majestic brass chords sound again.

Russian Music

For centuries, Russia had remained largely isolated from Europe. The first tsar to embrace Western culture was Peter the Great (r. 1689–1725), who as a young ruler visited Europe. He invited foreign musicians to work in his magnificent capital,

DVOŘÁK, Symphony No. 9 (“From the New World”), Second Movement, Largo {1893}

FORM	ABA form, bracketed by brass chords
METER	Quadruple (C)
TEMPO	*Largo* (slowly)
SCORING	Orchestra (two flutes, two oboes, two clarinets, two bassoons, four French horns, two trumpets, three trombones, one tuba, timpani, and strings)
OVERVIEW	The basic form of the movement is a ternary ABA, prefaced and followed by solemn brass chords. Before the return of A Dvořák writes a transitional section that brings back themes from the first movement of the symphony.

why to LISTEN

After coming to the United States, Dvořák used his art to explore the potential for a national American musical style. The America of 1893 was a land of immigrants, a melting pot of various nationalities. Truly “American” music would not emerge until the work of native composers in the twentieth century. Dvořák was the first major composer to ask: “Every nation has its music—there is Italian, German, French, Bohemian, Russian—why not American music?” When we listen to Dvořák’s *New World* Symphony, we hear a symphony of four movements that follows the outlines of many Classical symphonies. But prominent parts of the composition have more to do with folk music and American musical materials than with Classical tradition. It was Dvořák’s genius to be able to do both.

first LISTEN

BRASS CHORDS	A	B	TRANSITION	A	BRASS CHORDS
0:00	**0:41**	**4:33**	**7:58**	**9:00**	**11:01**
(*a*)	(*b*) English horn solo; (*a*) in woodwinds; (*b*) in strings, horns	(*c*) in flute and oboe; (*d*) in clarinet; (*c*), (*d*) in strings	recall of themes (*e*) and (*f*) from first movement	(*b*) in English horn; (*b*) in strings	(*a*)

Continued

a deeper **LISTEN**

TIME	SECTION	LISTEN FOR THIS
0:00	**Brass Chords (a)**	① Sequence of seven long chords played by the brass section; ***p*** *a* **Largo** ***ppp*** ***f*** *dim.*
0:41	**A**	② English horn solo (*b*), ***p***, major key *b* ***p***
2:22		Chords (*a*), now in woodwinds
2:48		Strings, horns (*b*), ***ppp***
4:33	**B**	③ Flute, oboe (*c*), minor key, ***pp*** *c* **Un poco più mosso (A bit faster)** ***pp*** ***f***
5:07		④ Clarinet (*d*), minor key, ***p*** *d* ***pp***
5:58		Strings, (*c*), (*d*)
7:58	**Transition**	Birdcalls, Crescendo to ***ff***

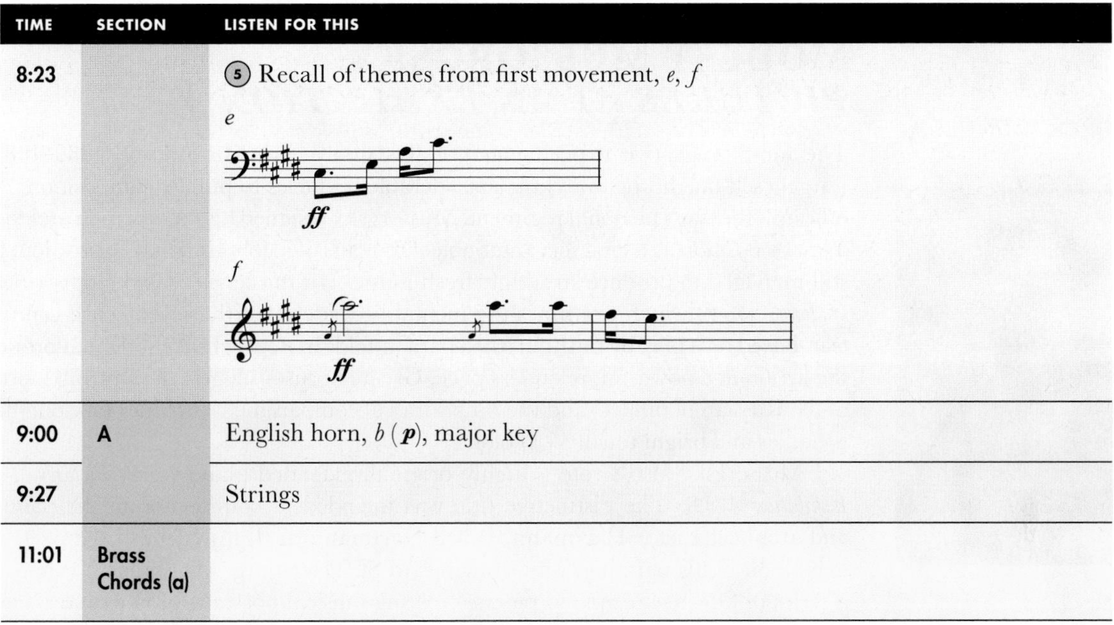

TIME	SECTION	LISTEN FOR THIS
8:23		(5) Recall of themes from first movement, *e*, *f* *e* ***ff*** *f* ***ff***
9:00	A	English horn, *b* (***p***), major key
9:27		Strings
11:01	Brass Chords (a)	

St. Petersburg, a practice continued by Catherine the Great (r. 1762–1796). During her reign, Italian opera was in demand, and French was the preferred language at court.

Some aspects of Russian life were slow to change. For centuries, the lower class of peasants, known as serfs, had been tied to a feudal system that required them to work the land of the elite property owners in exchange for a modest subsistence. Change finally came in 1861, when the Russian tsar emancipated the serfs. By this time, Russian was emerging as a literary language. Alexander Pushkin (1799–1837), often credited as the founder of modern Russian literature, wrote several influential works. His poems and plays served as the basis for several Russian operas. In later years, Pushkin concentrated on prose, as did a series of Russian novelists including Fyodor Dostoevsky (1821–1881) and Alexander Tolstoy (1828–1910), who produced monumental, realistic novels about the Russian homeland.

The Emancipation of the Russian Serfs by Alfons Marie Mucha.

By the second half of the century, many Russian composers were turning to native musical sources instead of Western models. In particular, a group of five composers, the "Mighty Handful" (*kuchka*), set out to create a national Russian style. Four of them were musical amateurs: César Cui, a military engineer; Alexander Borodin, a chemist; Modest Mussorgsky, an army cadet; and Nikolai Rimsky-Korsakov, a naval officer. Only one, Mily Alexeyevich Balakirev, was a professional musician. Partly because they lacked formal European training, they cultivated new, distinctively Russian manners in their compositions.

MODEST MUSSORGSKY: *PICTURES AT AN EXHIBITION*

Modest Mussorgsky (1839–1881).

The most innovative experimenter of this group was Mussorgsky (1839–1881). Largely self-taught, he overcame considerable obstacles to pursue composition. An officer in the tsar's personal regiment, Mussorgsky resigned his commission and took a minor position as a civil servant. Subject to bouts of alcoholism and depression, he still managed to produce strikingly fresh music. His masterpiece is the opera *Boris Godunov* (1874), which examines the mental breakdown of the seventeenth-century tsar. Based on a play by Pushkin, the opera unfolds in a speech-like style that propels the action at a powerful, relentless pace. Great choruses suggest the shifting moods of the Russian populace, and the orchestra's accompaniment provides folksong-like melodies and bright touches of color.

Mussorgsky also wrote a highly original, extended piano work, *Pictures at an Exhibition* (1874). The distinctive title was intended to commemorate the painter and architect Victor Hartmann. When Hartmann died, his friends organized an exhibition of his paintings and drawings in St. Petersburg. Mussorgsky composed a series of fifteen short piano pieces, creating musical portraits of Hartmann's art. Nearly fifty years later, in 1922, the French composer Maurice Ravel orchestrated Mussorgsky's score. Ravel's brilliant and colorful orchestral arrangement is now the most frequently performed version of *Pictures at an Exhibition.*

The composition begins with a leisurely "Promenade," meant to depict a spectator who strolls through the exhibition of Hartmann's art. Then each movement represents an individual artwork that the spectator pauses to admire. Mussorgsky conjures up vivid music that brings the static artwork to life and tells musical stories. Many of these movements depict everyday objects or scenes Hartmann had encountered during his own travels: a Russian toy nutcracker; a rich and a poor Russian Jew; a clock shaped like the hut of Baba-Yaga, a witch in Russian folk tales. In Mussorgsky's score, the promenade theme returns intermittently, transposed to different keys and reworked in some way, forming a series of interludes that help unify the composition. The opening "Promenade" and final movement (see **Listening Maps 51–52**) are both stamped with a Russian style distinct from European influences.

Stage design for Mussorgsky's opera *Boris Godunov* (1874).

Promenade

The first notable feature of Mussorgsky's promenade theme is its flexible meter. The composer alternates measures in $\frac{5}{4}$ and $\frac{6}{4}$. This mixture of meters goes against the Western preference for regular beat patterns. Coupled with the unusual beat patterns is Mussorgsky's use of a pentatonic scale, illustrated by the distinctive gaps in the melody. A third feature is the call-and-response pattern of the opening. This pattern is reinforced in Ravel's arrangement, in which a piercing solo trumpet prompts an answer from a brass choir. All these features are typical of Russian folk music.

LISTENING MAP 51

MUSSORGSKY, *Pictures at an Exhibition,* "Promenade" (1874) Orchestrated by MAURICE RAVEL {1922}

FORM	Free
METER	Chiefly $\frac{5}{4}$ and $\frac{6}{4}$
TEMPO	*Allegro giusto, nel modo russo; senza allegrezza, ma poco sostenuto*
SCORING	Orchestra (one piccolo, two flutes, three oboes, two clarinets, one bass clarinet, two bassoons, one contrabassoon, four French horns, two trumpets, three trombones, tuba, and strings)
OVERVIEW	Mussorgsky's "Promenade" is meant to accompany a visitor strolling in an art gallery and viewing the artworks of Victor Hartmann. The form is free but is organized around a melody that is introduced by a solo trumpet and then answered by other instruments.

a deeper LISTEN

TIME	LISTEN FOR THIS
0:00	Solo trumpet states "Promenade" theme, answered by brass chords 
0:17	Trumpet and brass continue to exchange the melody
0:35	String section enters, followed by the woodwind and brass
1:33	Brass repeat the promenade theme

The Great Gate of Kiev

Mussorgsky based his climactic finale on a sketch Hartmann had drawn for a monumental gate to the city of Kiev. Now the capital of the Ukraine, Kiev traces its roots back to the fifth century and was part of the Russian Empire when Mussorgsky was alive. Never realized, Hartmann's gate was meant to commemorate an assassination attempt in 1866 in St. Petersburg on the tsar Alexander II.

Mussorgsky's ceremonial music is structured as *ABABCA*. The first part, *A* (①), features brightly hued music based on a pentatonic melody. The melody of the next part, *B* (②), is based on a Russian Orthodox hymn. This is a fitting choice because Kiev is considered the birthplace of Christianity in Russia. Together, the two themes suggest a procession of pilgrims approaching and passing under the gate's grand arches. These two sections alternate. Then, we hear the ringing of the bells shown in Hartmann's sketch, with reverberating, clashing harmonies. Now, in a surprise move, Mussorgsky recalls the promenade theme. A spectator no more, he ultimately identifies with Hartmann's artwork and joins its procession. The movement ends with a triumphant restatement of *A*, realizing Hartmann's grandiose vision of the gate.

Mussorgsky based the finale of the piano suite *Pictures at an Exhibition* (1874) on a sketch by Victor Hartmann for a monumental gate to the city of Kiev.

LISTENING MAP 52

MUSSORGSKY, *Pictures at an Exhibition*, "The Great Gate of Kiev" (1874), orchestrated by MAURICE RAVEL {1922}

FORM	ABABCA
METER	Quadruple (C)
TEMPO	Allegro
SCORING	Orchestra (one piccolo, two flutes, three oboes, two clarinets, one bass clarinet, two bassoons, one contrabassoon, four French horns, three trumpets, three trombones, timpani, triangle, bass drum, tam-tam, cymbals, glockenspiel, bells, two harps, and strings)
OVERVIEW	For "The Great Gate of Kiev" Mussorgsky designed a rondo form. The ceremonial refrain (A) is heard three times. In B the composer cites a Russian Orthodox chant, and in C he brings back the promenade theme from the first movement.

why to LISTEN

Mussorgsky is a composer well removed from European musical Romanticism. In pursuing a new kind of Russian music, he was responding to some of the new literary movements of his time, including realism. His *Pictures at an Exhibition* are written to be objective musical photographs of Victor Hartmann's art works, not subjective, Romantic responses to them. The compositional techniques that Mussorgsky uses—pentatonic scales, unusual meters, freely applied dissonances—further distance his music from the mainstream European tradition. His music offered a viable alternative to Romanticism. And it inspired some of the early twentieth-century modernists attempting to separate themselves from the nineteenth century.

first LISTEN

A	B	A	B	C	A
0:00	**1:02**	**1:37**	**2:10**	**3:15**	**3:49**
Chordal theme	Russian Orthodox chant	Chordal theme	Russian Orthodox chant	Promenade theme from first movement	Chordal theme

Continued

 *a deeper* **LISTEN**

TIME	SECTION	LISTEN FOR THIS
0:00	A	① Ceremonial chordal theme with melody in top voice; brass
1:02	B	② Russian Orthodox chant, "As you are baptized in Christ," woodwinds
1:37	A	Repetition of chordal theme in brass, with faster accompanying figure in the strings
2:10	B	Repetition of chant in woodwinds
2:45	B	Simulation of the bells
3:15	C	Promenade theme from the first movement added in trumpet
3:49	A	Final, majestic statement of opening theme

PYOTR IL'YICH TCHAIKOVSKY

Pyotr Il'yich Tchaikovsky (1840–1893).

If Mussorgsky's music celebrated Russian nationalism and realism, the music of his great contemporary Pyotr Il'yich Tchaikovsky (1840–1893) presented strong ties to nineteenth-century European Romanticism. Tchaikovsky was certainly aware of the nationalist experiments of the "Mighty Handful." In fact, he wrote several distinctly Russian operas himself. Like his Russian contemporaries, Tchaikovsky used Russian folk songs and non-Western scales and harmonies. Still, Tchaikovsky remained outside the circle of the "Mighty Handful," creating music much closer to Brahms than to Mussorgsky.

Tchaikovsky showed an early aptitude for music, yet he attended the School of Jurisprudence in St. Petersburg in preparation for becoming a civil servant. For a while he worked as a clerk in the Ministry of Justice until 1863, when he resigned his post and enrolled in the newly founded St. Petersburg Conservatory. There, he received a thorough grounding in Western music. Later, he taught at the Moscow Conservatory.

Tchaikovsky's life was not a happy one. His mother's death when he was fourteen was a severe emotional blow, and he struggled throughout his life to come to terms with his homosexuality. He married one of his admirers, but the marriage failed. For many years, he carried on a platonic relationship with Madame

Nadezhda von Meck, a wealthy businesswoman who had inherited a railroad fortune. Devoted to the arts, she was Tchaikovsky's patron for thirteen years, enabling him to resign his conservatory post and to devote himself to composition. Although they corresponded regularly, they agreed not to meet. Then, in 1890, without explanation, Madame von Meck withdrew her support and broke off the correspondence.

In the last few years of the composer's life, Cambridge University honored him with a doctorate, and his music was performed in Europe, where it won Brahms's admiration. In 1891, during a tour in the United States, Tchaikovsky fell into a deep depression and longed to return to his homeland. The melancholy of his last years is especially evident in the powerful slow movement of his sixth and last symphony, the "Pathétique." He died at age fifty-three, under mysterious circumstances. According to one report, Tchaikovsky fell victim to cholera in St. Petersburg. According to another account, he committed suicide after a homosexual relationship had been exposed.

Madame Nadezhda von Meck, Tchaikovsky's patron for thirteen years.

Tchaikovsky composed six symphonies, some of which contain programmatic elements. For example, the Fourth concerns fate, and the Sixth ("Pathétique") is an intensely personal statement about life and death. Among his other works are a violin concerto and the First Piano Concerto, which quickly won favor after its premiere in Boston in 1875. Tchaikovsky also wrote music for three ballets, *Swan Lake* (1876), *The Sleeping Beauty* (1889), and the well-known *Nutcracker* (1892).

Among Tchaikovsky's most experimental and Romantic orchestral music are works based on Shakespeare's *Romeo and Juliet*, *The Tempest*, and *Hamlet*, which he described as orchestral fantasies.

Tchaikovsky, Romeo and Juliet *Fantasy-Overture*

In creating an orchestral overture about *Romeo and Juliet* (**Listening Map 53**), Tchaikovsky confronted the problem of relating a sonata-form movement to a Shakespeare tragedy. Rather than follow the play directly, he based his score on three essential elements: the "ancient grudge" of the warring Capulets and Montagues; the "star-crossed lovers," Romeo and Juliet; and Friar Lawrence, who mediates between the warring families and grants the lovers a brief time together before their tragic end.

Curiously, Tchaikovsky chose to begin with Friar Lawrence, although in Shakespeare's play this character appears mainly in the last act. In a slow introduction, dark woodwinds play the Friar's hymn-like melody (*a*; ①) in stately even notes. This solemn beginning yields to a dissonant passage for strings and horns, the first suggestion of conflict. Next, Tchaikovsky adds woodwinds and strings, and arpeggiations in the harp. Then he repeats this opening of the composition one pitch lower. The music gradually intensifies until it erupts in the passionate Allegro, which is the beginning of the exposition.

Depicting the feud, the first passage of the exposition (*b*; ②) is full of conflict. The music features strong dissonances, clashing rhythmic figures, contrasting orchestral groups (especially winds versus strings), and cymbal crashes. With the high woodwinds pitted against the low strings, theme *b* traces the bitter course of the feud.

The struggle breaks off, and Tchaikovsky introduces in the English horn and violas the celebrated lovers' theme (*c*; ③). This peaceful music is in a major key far removed from the minor key of the feud. A subdued lyrical passage for muted strings (*d*; ④) sustains the mood of tranquility. After restating *c* with more instruments, Tchaikovsky quietly concludes the exposition with a series of gently descending chords for the harp and light orchestral accompaniment.

The development section resumes the feud. Here Friar Lawrence's theme confronts the feud music through a variety of keys. The conflict grows in intensity, and at its climax a *fortissimo* statement of the Friar's theme in the trumpets prepares us for the recapitulation. We hear a shortened version of the feud theme (*b*) followed by the lovers' theme (*c*). The deep emotions of their love are expressed through the many changes in key in this section. But the resumption of the feud shatters the lovers' music, despite appearances of the Friar's motive in the brass. A timpani roll announces their deaths, and a somber coda depicts their funeral procession. Here, Tchaikovsky transforms the lovers' theme. First, it changes to become dirge-like before memories of the lyrical theme reappear in the high strings with soothing harp chords. Four *fortissimo* measures of chords conclude the work with a final allusion to the "ancient grudge."

Program Music of the Later Nineteenth Century

Much of Tchaikovsky's orchestral music was programmatic, that is, inspired by ideas outside music, such as a legend, a play, or poem. This feature tied these works to the earlier experiments of European Romantics. After Berlioz's *Fantastic Symphony* and Mendelssohn's concert overtures (see pp. 343–360), important contributions to orchestral program music came from Franz Liszt, who in 1848 settled in Weimar. There, he gave up his illustrious career as a piano virtuoso and turned wholeheartedly to composition. He wrote a bold series of orchestral works, usually in one continuous movement, that he termed "symphonic poems." Liszt drew on a wide variety of subjects, including Shakespeare's *Hamlet*, poems by Byron, Schiller, and Hugo, and the Orpheus legend. In each work a "poetic idea" determined the form and style of the music.

Liszt's forward-looking experiments opened up new possibilities for others to explore. One of these explorers was Richard Strauss (1864–1949), who worked in Germany and Austria, and lived long enough to experience the two cataclysmic world wars of the twentieth century. In the 1880s Strauss fell under Liszt's influence and began to write a series of what he labeled **tone poems**, extended, one-movement orchestral works with programmatic elements. Among them were *Don Juan*, a retelling of the Don Giovanni legend, and *Death and Transfiguration*. Strauss's other tone poems included *Till Eulenspiegel's Merry Pranks*, based on German folklore; *Don Quixote*, based on the novel by Cervantes; and the grandiose *Thus Spake Zarathustra*, inspired by Nietzsche's powerful philosophical work about the modern superman. (Its memorable opening crescendo achieved worldwide popularity when it was used in the 1968 science fiction film *2001: A Space Odyssey*.) Strauss wed Liszt's "poetic idea" with Classical music forms such as the sonata, rondo, and variations. Then, as the century came to its close, he changed course and turned his attention to writing operas in the lush chromatic language of Wagner. As we shall discover, his long career would take further unexpected turns in the twentieth century (see p. 452).

Richard Strauss (1864–1949).

LISTENING MAP 53

TCHAIKOVSKY, *Romeo and Juliet* {1880}

FORM	Sonata form with slow introduction and coda
METER	C
TEMPO	Various tempos
SCORING	Orchestra (one piccolo, two flutes, two oboes, one English horn, two clarinets, two bassoons, four French horns, two trumpets, three trombones, one tuba, timpani, cymbals, bass drum, harp, and strings)
OVERVIEW	Tchaikovsky's symphonic fantasy uses a modified sonata form with a slow introduction and extended coda serving as bookends. The three main thematic ideas represent Friar Lawrence (*a*), the feuding clans of the Montagues and Capulets (*b*), and the lovers, Romeo and Juliet (*c*).

why to LISTEN

Romeo and Juliet, the tragic tale of "star-crossed lovers" from rival families, is not only one of Shakespeare's most celebrated plays, but also one of the most famous love stories of all time. Little wonder that it has inspired numerous adaptations on stage and screen.

For the concert hall, Hector Berlioz composed his *Roméo et Juliette* in 1839 as a "dramatic symphony," with orchestra, vocal soloists, and choruses. In the twentieth century the Russian composer Sergei Prokofiev set the story as a ballet. What distinguishes Tchaikovsky's orchestral fantasy is that it uses only an orchestra—no words, no stage sets—to tell the story of Shakespeare's tragedy. In this way, his composition follows another purely orchestral rendering of a Shakespeare play, Mendelssohn's *Midsummer Night's Dream* Overture (see p. 346). But while Mendelssohn constructed a range of themes for the various characters of that play, Tchaikovsky concentrated his unforgettable music on three ideas: the feud between the families, the doomed love of Romeo and Juliet, and peacemaking of Friar Lawrence. Tchaikovsky's work makes us experience Shakespeare's tragedy as abstract ideas and emotions, but the result is just as powerful as any rendition of the play.

Continued

first LISTEN

INTRODUCTION	EXPOSITION	DEVELOPMENT	RECAPITULATION	CODA
0:00	5:06	10:28	12:43	16:56
Friar Lawrence theme (*a*)	feud theme (*b*) lovers' theme (*c*) lyrical passage (*d*) lovers' theme repeated (*c*)	feud (*b*) returns (*a*) reintroduced	(*b*) shortened (*c*) in full scoring resumption of feud (*b*)	fragments of (*c*), (*d*)

a deeper LISTEN

TIME	SECTION	LISTEN FOR THIS
0:00	Introduction	(*a*) (Friar Lawrence), ① chorale-like melody in winds *a* **Andante** *p* poco più *f*
4:00		Dissonant passage for strings and horn, then woodwinds and harp; crescendo to . . .
5:06	Exposition	②, (*b*) first theme in the tonic, depicting the feud, *f* *b* **Allegro** *f*
6:33		Transition
7:14		③, (*c*) second theme in a new key, lovers' music *c* *mf espr.*
7:33		④, (*d*) lyrical passage for muted strings *d* *Muted strings* *pp*

TIME	SECTION	LISTEN FOR THIS
8:19		(*c*) repeated with full scoring
9:25		Closing passage
10:28	**Development**	Resumption of the feud, with (*b*) in imitation between the treble and bass
10:40		Reintroduction of (*a*), ***ff***
12:43	**Recapitulation**	(*b*), shortened
13:49		(*c*), full scoring
15:43		(*b*), resumption of feud
16:47		Timpani roll announces the lovers' deaths
16:56	**Coda**	Funeral march, fragments of (*c*) against timpani stroke
18:47		(*c*) in the high strings
19:22		Timpani roll and conclusion in tonic major

RICHARD STRAUSS, *DEATH AND TRANSFIGURATION*

Strauss was only twenty-five when he composed *Death and Transfiguration*, an orchestral tone poem that offers a vision of the afterlife (**Listening Map 54**). The music describes a dying artist who, in his final hours, reviews his life. The artist is obsessed by his vision of an artistic Ideal, which he finally attains when his soul is transfigured at his death.

Strauss adapted sonata form to match his ambitious program. The work begins with an extended slow introduction in a minor key. A quietly pulsating figure in the strings and irregular timpani strokes suggest the artist's weak heartbeat as he lies on his deathbed. Gradually two motives emerge. The first (*a*; ①) descends from the high woodwinds. The second (*b*; ②), tenderly descends still further in the oboe and then solo violin.

The uneasy calm gives way to an agitated Allegro, the exposition of the sonata form. In this section, the artist awakens to agonizing pain. To illustrate the artist's suffering, Strauss couples an unsettling, syncopated motive in the low strings (*c*; ③) with dissonant harmonies. Instead of stating a predominant theme in the exposition, Strauss propels the music forward through a complicated network of clashing motives.

Cutting short this section, Strauss moves into the development, depicting a review of the artist's life. Motive *b* suggests infancy and childhood, followed by an energetic version of *a* in the brass to depict youth and manhood. Now the music becomes more intense, illustrating the artist's passionate striving toward the Ideal. Toward the end of the development, the rising theme associated with the Ideal (*d*; ④) finally emerges. We hear three statements of *d*, each in a higher key. Then, the slow introduction reappears, followed by an abbreviated recapitulation, returning to the artist on his deathbed. Forceful accents in the brass punctuate his final agony.

The broadly conceived final section—the transfiguration—is a large-scale coda dedicated to the theme of the Ideal. The conclusion begins softly, with stately suggestions of *d* in the brass accompanied by strokes of the tam-tam, a large gong suspended in a frame. Gradually, Strauss adds woodwinds and strings and introduces faster rhythmic values. The theme of the Ideal appears several times and stretches into the upper register of the violins. In the closing bars, we hear a breathtaking diminuendo as this exquisite Romantic vision of the transfigured artist recedes and fades.

At the end of his life, Strauss was haunted by his youthful tone poem. As he lay on his deathbed in 1949, he remarked that dying was just as he had composed it in *Death and Transfiguration.*

GUSTAV MAHLER

Other composers, including three active in Vienna, found individual ways to absorb the immense influence of Wagner's music:

- Hugo Wolf (1860–1903) devoted himself to writing intensely chromatic songs that explored the new boundaries of tonality established by Wagner.
- Anton Bruckner (1824–1896) completed an imposing series of nine symphonies written in a densely chromatic language that showed Wagner's influence. These symphonies follow the trend in late nineteenth-century music toward ever expanding scope and length.
- Gustav Mahler (1860–1911) pursued a similar direction by conceiving large-scale symphonies that arguably brought the German symphonic tradition to its culmination.

Gustav Mahler (1860–1911).

While a student in Vienna, Mahler absorbed fully the music of Wagner and philosophy of Schopenhauer and Nietzsche. Known first as a conductor, Mahler held several posts before settling down to direct the Vienna Opera from 1897 to 1907. He conducted during the winter seasons and then composed during his summer holidays.

Mahler's music reflects in detail the challenges of his tormented life. In 1897, partly to avoid discrimination against him because he was a Jew, he converted to Catholicism. In 1907 his elder daughter died, and a doctor diagnosed him with a heart condition. The victim of anti-Semitism, Mahler left Vienna to join the Metropolitan Opera in New York in 1908 and the New York Philharmonic in 1909. He returned to Vienna, where he died in 1911.

Mahler wrote orchestral song cycles as well as symphonies, and much of his music is best understood as a joining of the two genres. His symphonies are filled with warmly lyrical passages that seem to demand texts, and his song cycles feature

LISTENING MAP 54

RICHARD STRAUSS, Death and Transfiguration {1889}

FORM	Modified sonata form
METER	C
TEMPO	Various tempos
SCORING	Orchestra (three flutes, two oboes, one English horn, two clarinets, one bass clarinet, two bassoons, one contrabassoon, four French horns, three trumpets, three trombones, one tuba, timpani, tam-tam, two harps, and strings)
OVERVIEW	Like Tchaikovsky's *Romeo and Juliet*, Strauss's tone poem also uses a modified sonata form, expanded by a slow introduction and extended coda. In addition, the slow introduction returns before the recapitulation, so that there are six sections: slow introduction, exposition, development, return of slow introduction (abridged), recapitulation, and coda. They correspond to Strauss's program about an artist on his deathbed who reviews his life before dying and being transformed by a vision of the Ideal.

why to LISTEN

Strauss was in his twenties when he began composing orchestral tone poems. Extending Liszt's earlier experiments in his symphonic poems, Strauss took the concept of program music to a new level, broadening the scope of what the orchestra could attempt to describe. And so, Strauss's monumental *Thus Spake Zarathustra* was not only about Nietzsche's book of the same title, but also about German nineteenth-century philosophy in general. In the case of *Death and Transfiguration*, Strauss created the story line about a dying artist who reviews his life before meeting death and finally attaining the artistic Ideal that had evaded him in life. (Realizing that this topic would be difficult to understand, Strauss asked a friend to write a poem that would help audiences better interpret the music's meaning.) In the 1880s Strauss's experiments in program music were considered quite daring and, for the time, modern. As you listen to the music, consider how successfully the score communicates the subject, and whether Strauss himself was pursuing an unattainable Ideal in his score. Music that tests the boundaries of what music can do almost always offers a compelling reason to listen.

Continued

first LISTEN

SLOW INTRODUCTION	EXPOSITION	DEVELOPMENT	SLOW INTRODUCTION (SHORTENED)	RECAPITULATION (SHORTENED)	CODA
0:00	**4:49**	**8:34**	**14:56**	**15:45**	**16:31**
Motives (*a*), (*b*)	Motive (*c*)	Material based on motives (*b*), (*a*) Three statements of motive (*d*)			Transfiguration of the artist, based on (*d*)

a deeper LISTEN

TIME	SECTION	LISTEN FOR THIS
0:00	**Slow introduction**	① The dying artist, based on two motives, (*a*) . . . *a* **Largo** 8va **pp** *dolce (sweetly)* 3
2:18		. . . and (*b*) ② *b* **pp** *Sehr zart (very tenderly)*
4:49	**Exposition**	③ The artist awakens (agitated), motive (*c*); Tempo: allegro *c* **Allegro molto agitato (Fast, greatly agitated)** **ff**
8:34	**Development**	The artist reviews his life, based on (*b*) and (*a*)
12:47		④ Appearance of the Ideal, three statements of (*d*) *d* **Sehr breit (Very broadly)** **ff**

TIME	SECTION	LISTEN FOR THIS
14:56	Slow introduction (shortened)	The dying artist
15:45	Recapitulation (allegro, shortened)	Last agony and death of the artist
16:31	Coda (moderato)	Transfiguration of the artist, based on (*d*) (expansive, tam-tam)

a symphonic treatment of themes. Several of Mahler's symphonies combine orchestral and vocal forces, a feature that traces back to Beethoven's Ninth Symphony. Another influence on Mahler's compositions is the program music of Liszt and Strauss. Although Mahler did not compose tone poems, he based his symphonies on broadly philosophical programmatic concepts. The Second Symphony, in five lengthy movements, ends with a "Resurrection." The Fourth Symphony suggests the progression from earth to heaven and concludes with a strophic song that details the "virtues of heavenly life." In the finale of the Sixth, sometimes called the "Tragic," three "hammer blows of fate" correspond to tragedies in the composer's own life.

In addition to nine completed symphonies, Mahler left an unfinished tenth symphony written in a provocative, forward-looking musical language. He also composed three major song cycles: *Songs of a Wayfarer* (1896), *Songs on the Death of Children* (1904), and *The Song of the Earth* (1909). *The Song of the Earth* was based on Chinese poetry of the third century BCE, and explored non-Western scales and harmonies.

Songs of a Wayfarer (*Lieder eines fahrenden Gesellen,* 1896)

Mahler wrote the texts for this song cycle himself. He drew heavily on German folk poetry and earlier song cycles for inspiration—in particular, on Schubert's *Winterreise*, which also concerns a wanderer (see p. 313). But Mahler's approach was new and fresh. He fully exploited a wide range of orchestral colors and instrumental combinations. Moreover, each song of the cycle began in one key and ended in another, suggesting the wayfarer's restlessness and the composer's flexible approach to tonal organization.

Mahler's first song reveals reason for the wayfarer's wandering. He has been rejected by his lover, and he thinks of her on her wedding day and muses about his sorrow and the passing of spring. In the second song, the wayfarer wanders through dewy fields of flowers on a bright spring morning. The sun fills the world with light, contrasting with the wayfarer's sadness as he struggles to regain his lost happiness. The third song is violent in mood. The wayfarer compares his grief to a dagger stabbing his breast. He longs to be laid upon his funeral bier, freed from agony. The fourth song represents the wanderer's leave-taking from his beloved.

Solemn, dirge-like music suggests a funeral procession. Then, in an exquisite conclusion, Mahler invokes the image of a linden tree in whose shade the wanderer finally finds solace.

Perhaps the most celebrated of the four songs is the second (**Listening Map 55**). It is based on a gentle melody (*a*) that, after two initial leaps, rises up the scale. Mahler set the poem as a strophic song with four strophes but modified the music of the second, third, and fourth in various ways. The second strophe, for example, presents the theme in canon, with the vocal part leading and the cellos imitating the theme. There follows a lush orchestral interlude that departs from the tonic key of the opening. Strophes 3 (extended) and 4 (shortened) are each cast in a new key as the wayfarer continues on his journey. The final strophe, set in a slow tempo, remains incomplete, suggesting the wanderer's uncertainty. "Will my happiness now return?" he asks, only to answer, "No." The song ends with the brief emergence of a solo horn and solo violin and then a triple *piano* chord and arpeggio for the harp.

Mahler reused some of the material from this song in his First Symphony. Indeed, many of his symphonies either quote his songs or allude to literary ideas. A tone-poet, Mahler achieved in works of great depth and beauty the perfect union of language and music.

Europe at the Close of the Century

Throughout Europe, the last decades of the nineteenth century signaled the final stage in Romantic music, if not its eclipse. As early as mid-century, some French composers had begun turning away from operas on Romantic subjects to a lighter form of entertainment, the operetta. With their popular melodies and satirical tone, operettas were written more to entertain than to explore serious subjects. Later in the century, Georges Bizet's *Carmen* (1875), an opera in four acts with spoken dialogue, offered a more sobering alternative to Romanticism: a realistic treatment of Spanish gypsy life. Bizet filled his sensational score with catchy, sensual melodies, including a popular dance form, the **habanera**. After hearing *Carmen*, the philosopher Nietzsche, who was tiring of Wagner's heavy scores, remarked approvingly: "It is necessary to Mediterraneanize music." Nietzsche, like many others, was starting to reject the heavy German style of Wagner in favor of something more accessible.

Costume sketch for the title role in Bizet's opera *Carmen* (1875).

BIZET, *CARMEN*, HABANERA FROM ACT 1

Fame was initially not kind to Georges Bizet (1838–1875). A talented musician who studied at the Paris Conservatory, he was seventeen when he wrote an impressive symphony and won the Prix de Rome, which sent him to Italy for a few years. But after his return, he failed to achieve a lasting success in the opera house. His masterpiece, *Carmen*, initially earned only a lukewarm reception in Paris. Just months after the premiere, Bizet died of a heart attack at thirty-seven, unaware that his opera

MAHLER, *Songs of a Wayfarer*, No. 2 {1896}

FORM	Modified strophic song
METER	$\frac{2}{2}$ duple meter (¢)
TEMPO	In a leisurely tempo
SCORING	Voice and orchestra (one piccolo, two flutes, two oboes, one bass clarinet, two bassoons, four French horns, one trumpet, timpani, triangle, bells, harp, and strings)
OVERVIEW	The second of Mahler's *Songs of a Wayfarer* uses a poem that he probably wrote himself. He crafted a modified strophic setting, in which the main tune reappears from strophe to strophe, with changes in orchestration and texture, then in keys, before being shortened in the fourth strophe, and left as a fragment in the fifth. The orchestra offers comments between the first and second, second and third, and third and fourth strophes.

why to LISTEN

Mahler is one of the many composers who fell under Wagner's influence. Although Mahler did not write music dramas, he did write symphonies that required huge orchestras, and he composed chromatic music that would have been unthinkable without the model of Wagner's works. However, Mahler was not just a composer who brought Wagner's ideas to the genre of the symphony. He was also a master of nuance and delicate instrumental timbres. The *Songs of a Wayfarer* are a case in point. In the second song, the full orchestra is rarely used. Instead, Mahler extracts various instrumental colors: solos for the flute or violin, for example, or the soft shimmering sound of a triangle. These are bits of musical imagery that reflect the images of nature in the poem. In this way, Mahler showed how the smallest orchestral gestures could also be the most telling and greatly add to our appreciation of the music.

first LISTEN

STROPHE 1	ORCHESTRAL INTERLUDE	STROPHE 2	ORCHESTRAL INTERLUDE	STROPHE 3	ORCHESTRAL INTERLUDE	STROPHE 4	STROPHE 5
0:00	**0:38**	**0:45**	**1:19**	**1:36**	**2:26**	**2:37**	**3:10**
(*a*) (flute, voice)		(*a*) in voice and flute, imitated by cello		(*a*) in voice and violins		based on opening of (*a*)	shortened and incomplete

Continued

a deeper **LISTEN**

TIME	SECTION	LISTEN FOR THIS	TEXT	TRANSLATION
0:00	**Strophe 1**	(*a*) (flute, voice, ***p***), tonic major key	*Ging heut' Morgen über's Feld* *Tau noch auf den Gräsern hing* *Sprach zu mir der lust'ge Fink:* *Ei, du! Gelt?* *Guten Morgen!* *Ei, Gelt? Du!* *Wird's nicht eine schöne Welt?* *Schöne Welt? Zink! Zink!* *Schön und flink* *Wie mir doch die Welt gefällt!*	Went this morning through the fields, Dew still clinging to the grass, There spoke to me the merry finch: Hey, fine day, you? Good morning, then! Hey, fine day, you! Hasn't it turned into a lovely world? Lovely world? Chirp! Chirp! Lovely, sing! But how the world pleases me!
		a **In gemächlicher Bewegung (At a comfortable pace)** Ging heut' Mor-gen ü-ber's Feld, Tau noch auf den Grä-sern hing		
0:38	**Orchestral interlude**	crescendo to ***f***, diminuendo		
0:45	**Strophe 2**	(*a*) in voice and flute, imitated by cello, tonic major key	*Auch die Glockenblum' am Feld* *hat mir lustig, guter Ding',* *mit den Glöckchen, klinge, kling,* *ihren Morgengruß geschellt:* *"Wird's nicht eine schöne Welt?* *Kling, kling! Schönes Ding!* *Wie mir doch die Welt gefällt!* *Heia!"*	And the bluebells in the field merrily in good spirits with their little bells (ding, ding) pealed their morning greeting to me: "Isn't the world becoming beautiful? Ding, ding! Beautiful thing! But how the world pleases me! He Ho!"
1:19	**Orchestral interlude**	***f***, then diminuendo, departure from tonic key		

TIME	SECTION	LISTEN FOR THIS	TEXT	TRANSLATION
1:36	**Strophe 3 (extended)**	(*a*) in voice and violins (***pp***), new major key	*Und da fing im Sonnenschein* *gleich die Welt zu funkeln an;* *Alles Ton und Farbe gewann* *Im Sonnenschein!* *Blum' und Vogel, groß und klein!* *"Guten Tag,* *ist's nicht eine schöne Welt?* *Ei, du, gelt? Schöne Welt!"*	And then in the sunshine the world suddenly began to sparkle; all gained sound and color In the sunshine! Flowers and birds, large and small! "Good day, Isn't it a beautiful world? Hey, you, fine day? Lovely world!"
2:26	**Orchestral interlude**	ritard		
2:37	**Strophe 4 (shortened)**	based on opening of a (***p***), modulating	*Nun fängt auch mein Glück* *wohl an?*	Will my happiness now return?
3:10	**Strophe 5 (incomplete)**	Solo violin, horn, harp (***ppp***), new major key	*Nein, nein, das ich mein',* *Mir nimmer blühen kann!*	No, no, that I think can never bloom for me!

would become perhaps the most popular of all time, inspiring many films, musicals, and ballets.

Carmen is set in early nineteenth-century Spain. The title role is a young gypsy woman who possesses a raw sensuality. She seduces an army corporal, Don José, who deserts his post to marry her and join her circle of social outcasts and bandits. Soon enough Carmen leaves Don José for a bullfighter. Distraught, Don José stabs her to death.

The premiere of *Carmen* shocked and scandalized many Parisian opera patrons, who were accustomed instead to operas with sentimental plots and graceful ballets. But opinions on the opera changed as Romanticism ebbed and realism took hold in the arts. Further adding to the opera's appeal was Bizet's generous use of exotic melodies, including several that drew on Spanish popular music. There is no better example than the Habanera, sung by Carmen when she makes her first entrance in Act 1 (**Listening Map 56**). Emerging from a factory with a chorus of workers, she sings of love as an elusive bird that cannot be caught or tamed.

Dashboard

Watch a performance of this scene from *Carmen*.

Her music is based on the habanera, a type of Cuban dance first popularized in Spanish-occupied Havana during the early nineteenth century. Bizet begins by establishing a simple minor-keyed bass pattern of four notes (①), used throughout the entire number. Above this swaying accompaniment, Carmen sings a coyly descending chromatic line. (②). The chorus repeats her music, but now shifts from the minor to the parallel major key, while Carmen muses on the word *l'amour* ("love"). The next section, still in the major, is the refrain, sung first by Carmen and then by the chorus. Drawing herself into the song, she now compares love to a young, uninhibited gypsy. After the chorus warns, "Take guard," Carmen sings another strophe, answered again by the chorus and refrain, and driven by the alluring, hypnotic beat of the bass.

Poster for Puccini's opera *Madama Butterfly* (1904).

INSTRUMENTAL GENRES AND VERISMO OPERA

After France's humiliating defeat in the Franco-Prussian War of 1870–1871, a young generation of composers sought to raise the stature of French music by turning to instrumental genres such as the symphony. Among others, César Franck (a Belgian active in France, 1822–1890) and Camille Saint-Saëns (1836–1921) wrote important symphonies and other instrumental works. In Italy, opera remained the predominant genre, but now composers began to abandon the older conventions, such as the predictable set numbers and the subordination of the orchestra to the soloists. They instead began to favor continuous stretches of music and a more ambitious use of the orchestra. In the closing decades of the century, **verismo**, a strikingly realistic style of opera, came into style. *Cavalleria rusticana* by Pietro Mascagni and *Pagliacci* by Ruggiero Leoncavallo, still popular today, are outstanding examples of the new style. Giacomo Puccini (1858–1924) moved even more boldly toward realistic settings and stark, dramatic situations in his operas *La Bohème* (1896), *Tosca* (1900), and *Madama Butterfly* (1904). Their characters feature, respectively, a poor seamstress who dies of tuberculosis; a singer pursued by a Roman police chief; and a Japanese geisha who marries an American naval officer only to commit suicide after he abandons her.

Read about and listen to "Che gelida manina" from Puccini's *La Bohème*.

Finally, the expansion of tonality in the works of Wagner and other Romantic composers pushed the boundaries of musical harmony. The new century would bring an even bigger disruption when younger composers broke from using traditional harmonies entirely. Composers sensed that the aesthetic of expression—the lifeblood of Romanticism—had been exhausted. Eager to break the grip of Romanticism, they turned away from the legacy of the nineteenth century to seek new approaches to music in a new, modern age.

MAKING CONNECTIONS *The Afterlife of* La Bohème

Few operas have enjoyed as varied an afterlife as Puccini's *La Bohème*. Premiered in 1896 in Milan with the young Arturo Toscanini (1867–1957) conducting, its success promoted his career. Toscanini later became a household name in the United States thanks to his radio broadcasts and recordings. The opera was also associated with the great Italian tenor Enrico Caruso (1873–1921), who made many recordings of excerpts. Then in 1959, "Musetta's Waltz," one of the most popular numbers in the opera, crossed over into popular music as the basis of Della Reese's hit song "Don't You Know." And in 1996, the musical *Rent* opened on Broadway in New York, with a story line adapted from Puccini's opera. In the musical, the impoverished lovers Roger and Mimi live a bohemian existence in Greenwich Village in New York, where, instead of tuberculosis, they contend with AIDS.

LISTENING MAP 56

BIZET, *Carmen*, Act 1, Habanera

{1875}

FORM	Habanera (slow dance in duple meter, set as strophic song with refrain-like chorus)
METER	$\frac{2}{4}$
TEMPO	Allegretto, almost Andantino
SCORING	Soprano solo, chorus and orchestra
OVERVIEW	Bizet establishes the rocking pattern of the habanera with a four-note bass pattern that is repeated over and over. Above this pattern Carmen sings her descending chromatic melody, with occasional refrain-like replies from the chorus.

why to LISTEN

Bizet's *Carmen* received a lukewarm reception at its Paris premiere in 1875 but later became one of the most popular operas of all time. What accounted for this change? Bizet's masterpiece broke decisively with conventions, and in doing so initially encountered resistance, which was overcome as tastes changed. *Carmen* was one of the first operas to respond to the new movement of realism in the arts. Its subject, a sordid love affair between a gypsy seductress and a common soldier, was not what Parisian audiences expected. Bizet did little to soften the hard realities of his story. Some who heard the opera early on were entranced by its blend of exotic musical themes and sensuality, including Tchaikovsky and especially Johannes Brahms. In one year alone, Brahms saw the opera more than twenty times. You might suppose that Brahms, the leading representative of the Austro-Germanic tradition, would be the upholder of everything "serious" about classical music, but he, too, felt compelled to listen.

first LISTEN

INTRODUCTION	STROPHE 1	STROPHE 2
0:00	0:06	2:26
Four-note rocking pattern in bass	Carmen's descending chromatic melody, answered by chorus	

Continued

a deeper **LISTEN**

TIME	SECTION	LISTEN FOR THIS	TEXT	TRANSLATION
0:00	**Introduction**	① Fixed beat pattern established in bass Cellos *pp*		
0:06	**Strophe 1**	② Descending chromatic melody sung by Carmen, minor key L'amour est un oi-seau re-bel-le Que nul ne peut— ap-pri-voi-ser,	*L'amour est un oiseau rebelle* *que nul ne peut apprivoiser,* *et c'est bien en vain qu'on l'appelle,* *s'il lui convient de refuser.* *Rien n'y fait, menace ou prière,* *l'un parle bien, l'autre se tait,* *et c'est l'autre que je préfère.* *Il n'a rien dit, mais il me plait.*	Love is a rebellious bird that no one can tame, and one calls it in vain, if it conveniently refuses. Nothing works, neither threat nor prayer, one speaks well, another is silent. I prefer the latter. He says nothing, but pleases me.
0:39		Chorus repeats Carmen's music in major key, with comments by Carmen		
0:57		Refrain, sung by Carmen, major key	*L'amour est enfant de Bohème,* *il n'a jamais connu de loi.* *Si tu ne m'aimes pas, je t'aime.* *Si je t'aime, prends garde à toi!*	Love is a Bohemian child that has never known restraint. If you do not love me, I love you. If I love you, take guard!
1:39		Refrain repeated by chorus		

TIME	SECTION	LISTEN FOR THIS	TEXT	TRANSLATION
2:29	Strophe 2		*L'oiseau que tu croyais surprendre* *battit de l'aile et s'envola.*	The bird you thought you surprised beat its wings and flew away.
			L'amour est loin, tu peux l'attendre. *Tu ne l'attends plus, il est là!*	Love is distant, you can wait for it. When you don't wait for it, it is there!
			Tout autour de toi, vite, *Il vient, s'en va, puis il revient.* *Tu crois le tenir, il t'évite;* *tu crois l'éviter, il te tient!*	Quick, all around you, it comes, goes, then returns. You think you can grasp it, it escapes; you think it has escaped, it grasps you!

check your KNOWLEDGE

1. How did nationalism and realism make an impact on nineteenth-century music?
2. To what extent was Brahms indebted to eighteenth-century music? To what extent was he a Romantic composer?
3. Why was American music difficult to define in the later nineteenth century?
4. Compare some examples of later nineteenth-century program music and the sources of their inspiration.
5. Which innovations did composers test in later nineteenth-century orchestral music?
6. How would you describe music at the end of the nineteenth century?
7. What were the dominant musical genres in nineteenth-century France and Italy?

PART VI SUMMARY: THE ROMANTIC PERIOD

- Nineteenth-century Romanticism was a reaction in the arts against the eighteenth-century Enlightenment, and, in music, against the Classical style of Haydn and Mozart.

- Romantic composers celebrated subjective experiences and developed highly individual modes of expression.
  - They treated rhythm and meter flexibly.
  - Their melodies tended to be more freely formed than Classical melodies.
  - They extended the traditional range of dynamics to elevate the subjective content of their art.
  - They were attracted to program music, relating many of their works to non-musical subjects such as poems, plays, or paintings. Two new musical genres were the short character piece for piano and the orchestral concert overture.
  - They explored an enlarged range of keys and harmonies that gradually weakened the central authority of the tonic.

- A new musical genre, the art song, became popular, particularly in German-speaking areas. German lyric poetry inspired songs known as lieder. Notable composers in this genre included Franz Schubert, Robert Schumann, and Clara Wieck Schumann.

- New technological developments in the construction of pianos inspired a rich repertoire of music for the instrument.
  - Many virtuoso performers—including Frédéric Chopin, Franz Liszt, and Johannes Brahms—toured Europe, helping to popularize the piano.
  - Fanny Hensel, Felix Mendelssohn's sister, was another accomplished pianist and composer, though, unlike Clara Schumann, she did not have a public career.

- The Romantic era saw many innovations in orchestral music.
  - The orchestra expanded to include new instruments, allowing for greater variety in tone color.
  - Orchestration (the art of combining different instrumental sounds) gained in stature as composers explored novel instrumental effects in orchestras.
  - Felix Mendelssohn and Hector Berlioz were two key composers who helped transform nineteenth-century orchestral music.

- Romantic opera was a showcase of escapist plots, spectacular stage effects, huge orchestras, and singing that stretched the limits of the human voice.
  - In Italy opera remained the dominant nineteenth-century musical genre. The principal composers were Gioachino Rossini, Gaetano Donizetti, Vincenzo Bellini, and Giuseppe Verdi.
  - French nineteenth-century opera included "rescue" operas about the liberation of political prisoners. It also included "grand" operas, which were lavish productions in five acts and generally based on historical subjects.
  - The dominant nineteenth-century German composer of opera was Richard Wagner. His large-scale music dramas offered a new synthesis of the arts and powerfully transformed the course of classical music.

- Romanticism influenced much nineteenth-century music, but in the second half of the period, nationalism and realism increasingly affected music's evolution.
  - Several prominent composers were centered in Vienna, including Johannes Brahms, Richard Strauss, and Gustav Mahler.
  - Among the composers identified with nationalist movements was Antonín Dvořák in Bohemia.
  - In Russia, a group of five composers known as the "Mighty Handful," including Modest Mussorgsky, developed distinctive Russian musical styles largely independent of European models.
  - Another leading Russian composer, Peter Il'yich Tchaikovsky, wrote music stylistically closer to European traditions.
  - Composers who were influenced by realism included Musorgsky in Russia, Georges Bizet in France, and Giacomo Puccini in Italy.

KEY TERMS

absolute music 381
accelerando 305
ballad 311
baton 343
canzone 365
cavatina 362
character piece 306
concert overture 306
double aria 362
double stop 383
etude 329
Gesamtkunstwerk 370
glissando 354
grand opera 368
habanera 406
idée fixe 354
leitmotif 370
lieder 309
mazurka 329
modified strophic song 313
music drama 369
nationalism 380
nocturne 329
orchestration 308
pentatonic scale 388
polonaise 329
prelude 329
program music 306
realism 381
ritard 305
rubato 305
saltarello 337
song cycle 309
stretto 333
strophic song 313
synaesthesia 308
through-composed song 313
tone poem 398
verismo 410
waltz (valse) 329

KEY COMPOSERS

Gioachino Rossini (1792–1868)
Gaetano Donizetti (1797–1848)
Franz Schubert (1797–1828)
Vincenzo Bellini (1801–1835)
Hector Berlioz (1803–1869)
Fanny Hensel (1805–1847)
Felix Mendelssohn (1809–1847)
Frédéric Chopin (1810–1849)
Robert Schumann (1810–1856)
Franz Liszt (1811–1886)
Giuseppe Verdi (1813–1901)
Richard Wagner (1813–1883)
Clara Schumann (1819–1896)
Johannes Brahms (1833–1897)
Georges Bizet (1838–1875)
Modest Mussorgsky (1839–1881)
Pyotr Il'yich Tchaikovsky (1840–1893)
Antonín Dvořák (1841–1904)
Gustav Mahler (1860–1911)
Richard Strauss (1864–1949)

MUSICAL JOURNEYS
Balinese Gamelan

The term *gamelan* is used to describe various types of Indonesian orchestras. These vary in size, function, musical style, and instrumentation, but generally include tuned single bronze gongs, gong chimes, single- and multi-octave **metallophones** (metal-keyed xylophones), drums, flutes, bowed and plucked stringed instruments, a xylophone, small cymbals, and singers. Gamelan and similar ensembles can be found throughout the region, including in West Java, Central Java, East Java, and Bali.

Bronze kettledrums from the third and second centuries BCE found in Sumatra, Java, Bali and other parts of Southeast Asia suggest that a high level of workmanship in metal had been reached by that period. However, there is no evidence of a direct line of development between these drums and the bronze instruments of gamelan and related orchestras. Perishable instruments made of wood, leather, and bamboo probably have also existed in Southeast Asia since ancient times. The first evidence of the existence of gamelan ensembles comes around 800 CE. Xylophones, bamboo flutes, and double-headed drums are depicted in reliefs on the ninth-century Borobudur temple in central Java.

A gamelan orchestra in Bali, Indonesia, with metallophones.

Two primary tuning systems are used that distinguish different types of gamelan: a five-note system commonly called *sléndro* and a seven-note one called *pélog*. During the second half of the nineteenth century, both types of orchestra often performed together, particularly to accompany popular theatrical performances, like shadow-puppet plays. Known as *wayang kulit*, shadow puppets are two-dimensional flat figures that are made out of tooled leather that are manipulated using long rods. Held behind a screen and lit from behind, the shadows of the cutout figures are viewed by the audience.

Gamelan music often accompanies theatrical performances featuring shadow puppets.

Gamelan and related ensembles have traditionally been used to accompany religious rites and dances that have survived from pre-Muslim times (before about the fifteenth century CE). The instruments are shown respect; no one may walk over them, and special offerings of incense are made before an ensemble is played. In Java a gamelan is often given a revered name of its own. The gamelan's main function is to accompany ceremonial or religious rituals, held chiefly in the temples in Bali and in village or court environments in Java. Gamelan are played in rainmaking ceremonies in Central Javanese rice fields; in processional dance genres such as *réyog* in East Java; and for erotic dances such as that of the singer-dancer in *tayuban* in Java. They are also played to welcome guests at weddings and other ceremonies.

Gamelan Comes to the West

Ensemble performance on sets of gamelan instruments outside Southeast Asia began to occur only in the latter half of the nineteenth century, by visiting troupes that were predominantly from Java. The most famous is perhaps the group that performed at the "Java Village" at the 1889 Exposition Universelle in Paris, where Claude Debussy first encountered gamelan performance (see Chapter 42). Occasionally these groups left behind the instruments they brought with them. For example, the gamelan featured in the 1893 Chicago-based World's Columbian Exposition is currently housed at the Field Museum in Chicago.

The repertory performed by these groups was not limited to "traditional" regional gamelan material. The ensembles were part of larger commercial promotions of the region, and repertory often included material familiar to the audience at these expositions, in addition to traditional pieces. For example, the 1893 Chicago gamelan performed not only Javanese and Sudanese repertory, but also Western music including tunes such as "America" and "Yankee Doodle."

Balinese Gamelan

Gamelan in Bali are used primarily to accompany dance and dance-drama on religious and (in recent times) secular occasions. There are various large ensembles more commonly referred to as *gong.* The stately *gamelan gong* (or *gamelan gong gede*) may consist of metallophones (known as *gender* and *saron*), kettle gongs, gong chimes, double-headed "female" and "male" drums, suspended gongs of different sizes, and cymbals. Once a court ensemble of about forty instruments, it is now a village ensemble of some twenty-five instruments. The metallophones are paired and play the main "melody" in unison or octaves. They are tuned slightly out of phase with each other, giving the music a "shimmering" sound that is quite distinctive. The virtuoso *gamelan gong kebyar* has developed from the earlier *gamelan gong.* The term *kebyar* literally means "lightning" and refers to the dramatic quick tempos used in performance. This ensemble has expanded instrumentation and also has inspired the creation of new repertory for the orchestra.

The gamelan heard on the recording for **Listening Map I.5** was based in the court of the Puri of Peliatan, Prince Anak Agung Gdé Mandera. It consists of twenty-five musicians, drawn both from palace staff and the villagers, and professional dancers. This gamelan's instruments are made from a secret mixture of metals to form an alloy with a distinctive sound. The piece that they perform, "Pendet," is a ritual dance during which the female dancers toss flower petals. These petals symbolize the gods' oversight and protection of the people. It was developed over the last century or so, so is not as old as some other dance forms.

LISTENING MAP *1.5*

"Pendet," performed by GONG KEBYAR of PELIATAN, recorded by JACQUES BRUNET, released in 1971

FORM	Cyclical
METER	Duple
TEMPO	Alternating intense, quick passages with slower, contemplative ones
TIMBRE	"Shimmering"
PERFORMED BY	*Gamelan gong kebyar* composed of various bossed gongs, metallophones (i.e., xylophones with metal keys), cymbals, and a pair of hand barrel drums, as well as flutes
OVERVIEW	A modern ritual dance, "Pendet" is a typical contemporary gamelan performance. It features alternating sections of slow, contemplative music followed by rapidly performed, intensely emotional passages. Each melodic phrase is repeated, as are entire series of phrases, in recurring cycles, giving the piece its unique, nonlinear structure. The main gong player serves as a conductor, signaling the changes in rhythm and instrumental density.

why to LISTEN

Unlike Western music, which is linear (i.e., we can track a beginning, middle, and end), Balinese gamelan music is cyclical. The gamelan orchestra "cycles" through a series of units, varying moments of greater melodic intensity and instrumental texture with quieter, more contemplative moments. Just as individual melodic/rhythmic fragments are repeated, so are series of these phrases, so that there are cycles within cycles. Also, unlike the Western seven-note major/minor scales, this piece is based on a five-note, or "gapped," scale. Such scales are more typical of folk and traditional music than Western classical music and create a distinctive sound. Listen particularly to the main gong (or *ketuk*); this instrument serves as a kind of conductor, signaling changes in sections through either specific rhythmic cues or by dropping out entirely. Each player is in charge of a single instrument, often playing just one note in each passage, so that melodies are formed by players performing in sequence. This type of performance is called "interlocking," because each individual part is joined with all others to form the melody line.

first LISTEN

INTRODUCTION	FIRST THEME	TRANSITION/SECOND SECTION	THIRD SECTION	CONCLUSION
0:00	**0:03**	**0:35**	**2:02**	**4:24**
Very brief introduction on the saron (metal-keyed xylophone) alone	Entire ensemble plays together; first melodic theme and basic rhythmic pattern introduced	Short break signals a different theme played more slowly; flute joins the melody instruments	Alternating themes: first a repeated pattern that slowly grows in intensity, then a rapid series of notes	A return to relative calm, ending with a final shimmering note

 *a deeper* **LISTEN**

TIME	SECTION	LISTEN FOR THIS
0:00	Introduction	Introductory phrase played on a metallophone (*saron*).
0:02	First Theme	The majority of instruments enter. Main melodic phrase (1–2-flatted 4–2) established by midrange metallophones, steady beat established by a single bossed gong (*ketuk*). Punctuating gongs (*kempul*) sound every other beat in the background.
0:07		Crescendo (increasing volume) of the most rhythmically dense xylophones, then burst in volume as the full ensemble enters. At 0:18, note the musical "stutter" to anticipate the closing of a melodic passage.
0:21		Listen for the change in instrumentation as several instruments briefly stop playing to highlight the main melody again before the full ensemble returns.
0:35	Transition/ Second Section	Change of mood and melody as the instrumentation and rhythmic density change again. Missing "timekeeper" (*ketuk*) gong. At 0:46, flutes (*suling*) join in the main melody.
1:07		Brief increase in tempo indicates the closing of a melodic phrase.
1:36		Note how the timekeeper gong (along with ensemble) reduces its rhythmic density before dropping out entirely (1:44).
1:45		Transition; listen for the metallophones and flutes playing the same melodic line.
2:02	Third Section	Two main subsections alternate. The first begins slowly, consisting of a repeating pattern that grows in intensity (2:02–2:22). Then, there is a dramatic increase in rhythmic density, particularly of the higher-pitched metallophones from 2:23 to 2:32. At 2:23, sudden burst of melodic activity.
2:33		First theme with repeated patterns growing in intensity
3:17		Dramatic second theme
3:27		First theme
4:00		Second theme
4:24	Conclusion	Shift in mood through a change in instrumentation, slower tempo, and reduced rhythmic density.
4:31		"Shimmering" quality of the metallophones is heard on the sustained final pitch.

PART

The Modern Era

One must be absolutely modern. —ARTHUR RIMBAUD

Contrary to general belief, an artist is never ahead of his time, but most people are far behind theirs. —EDGARD VARÈSE

Pablo Picasso, *Les Demoiselles d'Avignon*, 1907.

Beginning in the late nineteenth and early twentieth centuries, a new movement in the arts took hold and profoundly altered the course of music. **Modernism** was a sharp break from the nineteenth century that promoted the new realities of the modern world, rather than a Romanticized notion of it. The resulting art seemed shockingly strange and different from what had come before.

Claude Monet, *Impression: Sunrise*, 1872.

Certainly there was nothing new about the idea of "modern" as opposed to "old" music. Western history had witnessed compositions that broke decisively from the past to offer innovations perceived as modern. When twelfth-century musicians set new parts against the traditional Gregorian chant, the resulting medieval organum must have seemed utterly strange and new (see Chapter 10). And when Berlioz premiered his *Fantastic Symphony* in 1830, its noisy passages and colorful combinations of instruments must have seemed radically modern as well (see Chapter 38). Both examples challenged previous assumptions about the limits of music.

Part of what propelled modernism forward was a dizzying succession of technological and scientific innovations that drastically changed people's day-to-day lives. New technologies—from telephones and phonographs in the early decades through the Internet and Wi-Fi in the later ones—opened new avenues of communication. New machines—from power tools and steam shovels to typewriters and eventually PCs—increased productivity and created more leisure time. Breakthroughs in medicine extended life expectancies.

Meanwhile, political movements challenged and changed the relationship between people and their governments. Citizens who felt increasingly unsettled in the changing modern world supported the rise of totalitarian regimes, such as Nazism in Germany and fascism in Italy. At first, these movements offered a sense of order and national pride, yet the price was brutal authoritarianism and war. Communism in the newly established Soviet Union promoted an idealized "workers' paradise" that emphasized group "well-being" over individual experience. All these trends influenced the arts in meaningful ways.

Three profoundly new scientific theories developed in the late nineteenth and early twentieth centuries: (1) evolution, (2) psychoanalysis, and (3) relativity. All

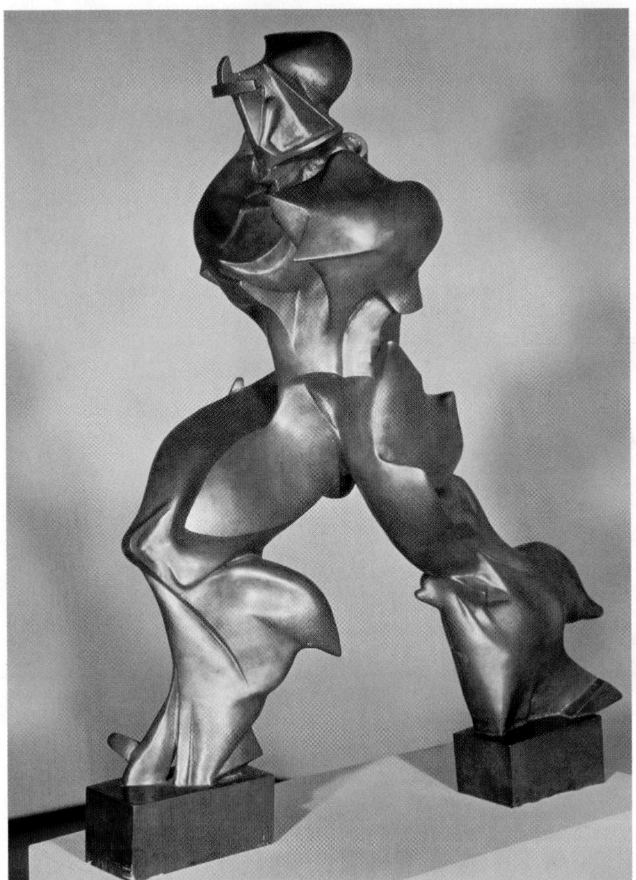

Umberto Boccioni, *Unique Forms of Continuity in Space*, 1913.

three theories undermined the idea that there was one overarching truth that did not change over time. The effects of these theories on society and the arts were enormous.

1) *Evolution*: In *On the Origin of Species* (1859), Charles Darwin (1809–1882) explained his theory that plant and animal life had evolved over time, with only the strongest surviving. As the nineteenth century closed, this basic idea became a social justification for racism and imperialism. Various nations engaged in empire-building around the globe, with profound consequences for the new century. The implications of Darwin's theory also removed a spiritual dimension and mystery from the general view of the world, one of the hallmarks of Romantic thought. For many, evolution was a direct assault on religious belief.
2) *Psychoanalysis*: Sigmund Freud (1856–1939) also had a significant impact on modernism. He proposed that humans were subject to irrational, subconscious forces, an idea which in turn suggested that society was less orderly than once thought. Freud's ideas about the role of sexuality in human behavior confronted head on the reserved social values of the nineteenth century.
3) *Relativity*: The physicist Albert Einstein (1879–1955) revolutionized our views about time and space with his theories of relativity (1905 and 1915). Einstein proposed that our perception of the world was based on our individual point

of view. To us, the world appears to be fixed and unchanging, but in fact it is constantly in motion. Einstein's ideas would influence several artistic movements, including **cubism** and Futurism.

Marcel Duchamp, *L.H.O.O.Q.*, 1919.

A range of artistic movements contributed to twentieth-century modernism in different ways, but they all emphasized a break from the past. Several movements were primarily associated with the visual arts, especially painting. Table VII.1 provides a brief overview of the major art movements and their impact.

All this agitation sent the arts onto strange new paths that led the modern world to unpredictable destinations. Within only a few decades, painters had abandoned the traditional use of perspective, poets and writers had begun to explore the unconscious in new ways, and many composers had abandoned the time-honored system of tonality. The catastrophic First World War, followed swiftly by another, had forever altered the old order. In the following decades, new waves of the avant-garde arose, made up of shifting alliances of writers, artists, composers, and philosophers. After the Second World War, the number of artistic movements continued to grow, from abstract expressionism, existentialism, op art, pop art, "happenings," and "performance art" to computer art and postmodernism. Succeeding generations explored new paths of artistic experimentation that stretched their audiences' comprehension to the limits.

And yet the arts survived as a necessary gauge of the human condition. As the arts grew bolder in their demands, more abstract in their nature, and more elusive in their meaning, a chasm widened between artists and the public. That alienation became especially meaningful for music and for the revolutions in sound it caused.

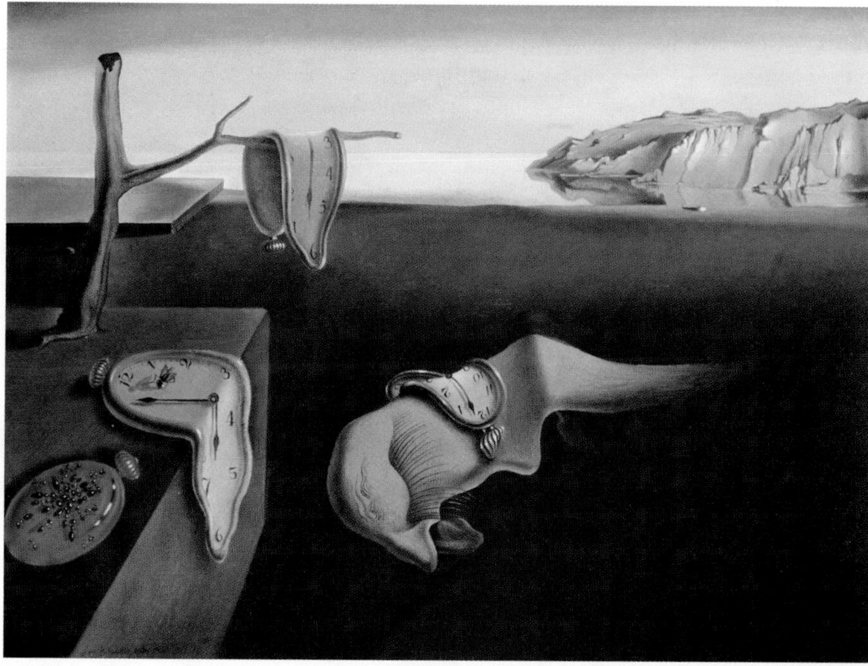
Salvador Dali, *The Persistence of Memory*, 1931.

TABLE VII.1 Major Art Movements of the Modern Era

YEARS	MOVEMENT	CENTER OF ACTIVITY	DESCRIPTION	SAMPLE WORK
1870s–1880s	**Impressionism**	France	Preferring to paint outdoors, impressionists studied the effects of light in an attempt to capture shifting appearances. They focused on both scenes of modern urban life and natural settings, featuring lily ponds, haystacks, or sunsets.	Monet, *Impression: Sunrise*, 1872 (p. 421)
1905–1920s	**Cubism**	France	Jointly developed by the painters Pablo Picasso and Georges Braque, cubism depicted real objects but rejected the centuries-old illusion of perspective. Instead of using flat canvases to simulate three-dimensional space, cubists broke up objects into cube-like, multidimensional facets, carefully arranged on the canvas.	Picasso, *Les Demoiselles d'Avignon*, 1907 (p. 420)
Ca. 1915–1930	**Futurism**	Italy	The Futurists' work highlighted the violent energy of modern life. They were impressed with the increased speed of communication, transportation, and scientific discovery that was a hallmark of the age. Luigi Russolo's *The Art of Noise* tied Futurism to experiments with expanding instrumentation and timbres available to modern composers.	Boccioni, *Unique Forms of Continuity in Space*, 1913 (p. 422)

YEARS	MOVEMENT	CENTER OF ACTIVITY	DESCRIPTION	SAMPLE WORK
1920s–1940	**Expressionism**	Germany	The expressionists attempted to portray how the artist's inner feelings colored the external world. Along with other artists of the period, they saw a relationship between musical sound and the perception of abstract colors and forms.	Kandinsky, *Improvisation No. 30* (Canons), 1913 (p. 447)
1916–1930s	**Dadaism** (from "dada," coined in 1916 as a nonsense word for "hobbyhorse")	France	Dadaism arose from a disillusioned generation of artists and writers after the First World War, who sought refuge in a paradoxically new art of anti-art—an absolute break from the failed past. Its aim was to free art from the constraints of nineteenth-century values, the same values that presumably had led the world to destruction. A leading practitioner was Marcel Duchamp, who challenged the division between art and non-art.	Duchamp, *L.H.O.O.Q.*, 1919 (p. 423)
1925–1940s	**Surrealism**	France	The surrealists sought to unleash the free play of the mind, its dreams and fleeting thoughts, and to reveal the truths of the unconscious through free association. They were strongly influenced by Freud's explorations.	Dali, *The Persistence of Memory*, 1931 (p. 423)

WHY LISTEN TO *Twentieth-Century Music?*

Sometimes taking risks wins universal admiration. But the modernists' explorations of new musical frontiers encountered substantial resistance at first. Indeed, twentieth-century avant-garde movements in music did more than strain the understanding of audiences; they increasingly alienated those audiences. The avant-garde became so innovative that, some critics argued, it eventually became irrelevant to modern and (now) postmodern life. In approaching modernism, we can focus on two basic questions: (1) why did so many listeners dislike modernist music; and (2) in view of this dislike, why should we listen to it?

In response to the first question, consider how musical traditions existing since the Renaissance have conditioned us to expect certain features in music. The idea of "consonant" and "dissonant" harmonies has been accepted for so long that it seems an eternal truth, rather than an arbitrary and now familiar categorization. When avant-garde music pushes the dissonance level too high,

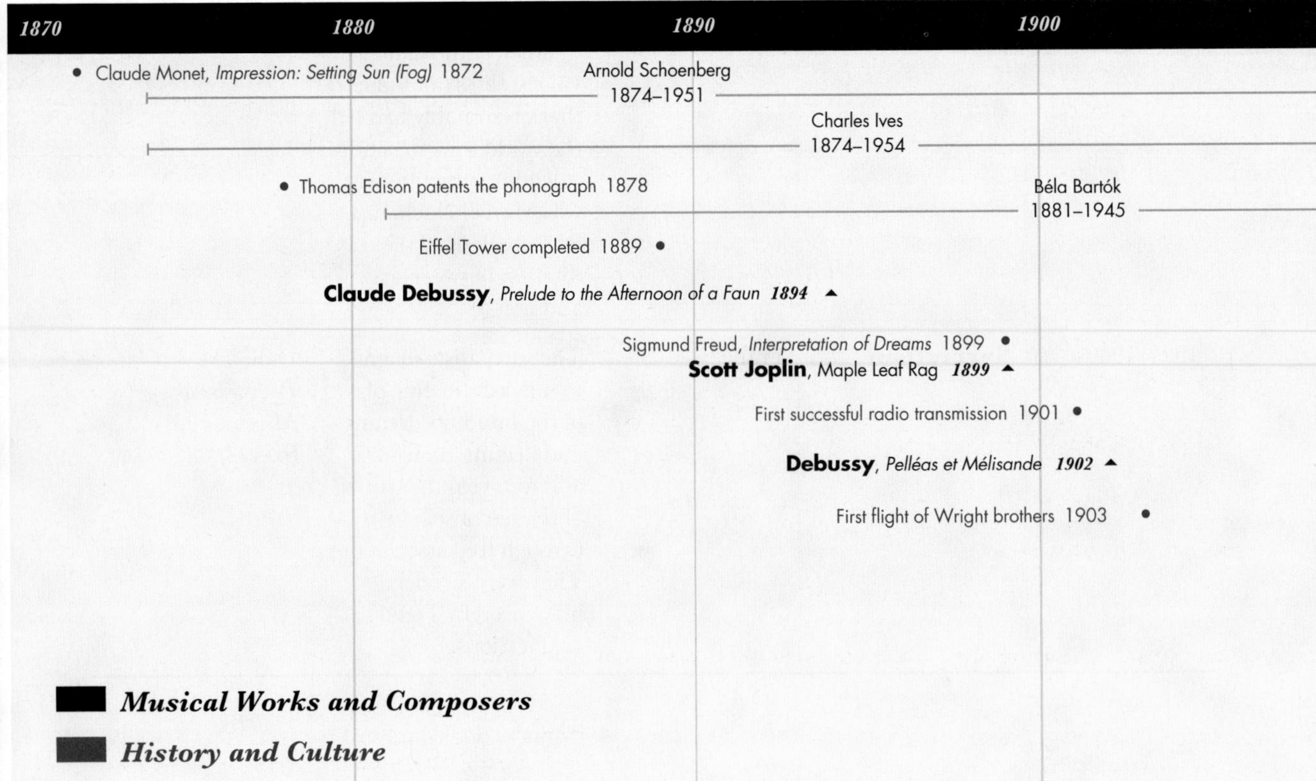

we cannot (or choose not to) cross the gap between our expectations and the reality of what we are hearing.

Modernism provided an escape from the troubles of the past, whether political, social, or cultural, and found value in the radically new. It led composers to take significant risks, as they explored an unfamiliar world of new sounds that collided with conventional ideas of beauty in art. Modernist music confronted audiences with a bold challenge: cling to the familiar, or explore uncertain new terrains of sound. It was a stark choice. Admittedly, not many were prepared to follow the experiments of composers who viewed themselves as musical pioneers. But just as Sir Edmund Hillary and Tenzing Norgay ascended Mt. Everest in 1953, or as American astronauts landed on the moon in 1969, the modernists also challenged our ideas about what was possible. They opened up new vistas of sound unthinkable to previous generations of musicians. Along the way they discovered new insights into the mystery of artistic creativity. Our natural curiosity about the unknown is reason enough to listen: sometimes in the most unfamiliar and least explored, we can find new perspectives on our own lives.

1910 | 1920 | 1930 | 1940

- Pablo Picasso, *Les Demoiselles d'Avignon* 1907
- Cubism 1908–1912
- First Futurist manifesto 1909
- **Ralph Vaughan Williams**, *Fantasia on a Theme by Thomas Tallis* ***1910***
- Marcel Duchamp, *Nude Descending a Staircase* 1912
- **Schoenberg**, *Pierrot lunaire* ***1913*** - **Stravinsky**, *The Rite of Spring* ***1913***
- First World War 1914–1918
- **Charles Ives**, *General William Booth Enters into Heaven* ***1914*** - **W. C. Handy**, *St. Louis Blues* ***1914***
- **Charles Ives**, *Concord Sonata* ***1915***
- Albert Einstein's general theory of relativity 1916
- Bolshevik Revolution in Russia 1917
- **Sergei Prokofiev**, "Classical" Symphony ***1917***
- James Joyce, *Ulysses* 1922
- Soviet Union established 1923
- **Alban Berg**, *Wozzeck* ***1923*** - **Varèse**, *Hyperprism* ***1923***
- Stalin rules Russia 1926–1953
- **George Gershwin**, *Rhapsody in Blue* ***1924***
- *The Jazz Singer*, first "talking" picture 1927
- **Louis Armstrong**, *"Struttin' with Some Barbecue"* ***1927***
- Discovery of penicillin 1928
- Stock market crash 1929 - Great Depression 1929
- **Stravinsky**, *Symphony of Psalms* ***1930*** - **Duke Ellington**, *Mood Indigo* ***1930***
- Presidency of Franklin Delano Roosevelt 1933–1945
- **Gershwin**, *Porgy and Bess* ***1935***
- **Bartók**, *Music for Strings, Percussion and Celesta* ***1936***
- **Dimitri Shostakovich**, Fifth Symphony ***1937***

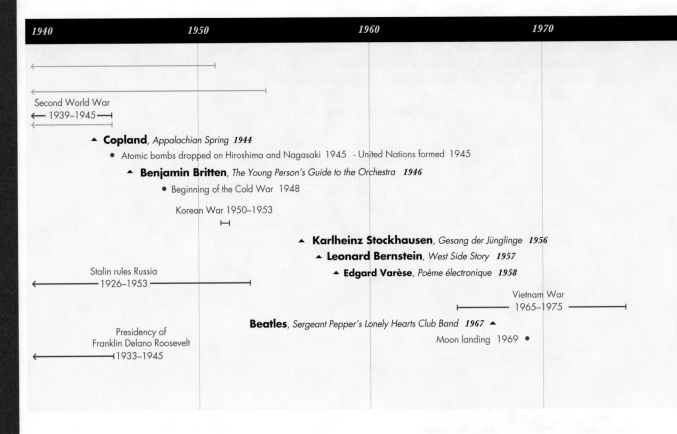

1940	1950	1960	1970

Second World War 1939–1945

▲ **Copland**, *Appalachian Spring* ***1944***

• Atomic bombs dropped on Hiroshima and Nagasaki 1945 - United Nations formed 1945

▲ **Benjamin Britten**, *The Young Person's Guide to the Orchestra* ***1946***

• Beginning of the Cold War 1948

Korean War 1950–1953

▲ **Karlheinz Stockhausen**, *Gesang der Jünglinge* ***1956***

▲ **Leonard Bernstein**, *West Side Story* ***1957***

▲ **Edgard Varèse**, *Poème électronique* ***1958***

Stalin rules Russia 1926–1953

Vietnam War 1965–1975

Beatles, *Sergeant Pepper's Lonely Hearts Club Band* ***1967*** ▲

Moon landing 1969 •

Presidency of Franklin Delano Roosevelt 1933–1945

Thomas Edison shown ca.1870 with an early dictating machine that was the first step in the development of the phonograph. The phonograph would revolutionize the way music was heard and performed in the twentieth century.

Vladimir Lenin was one of the leaders of the Bolshevik revolution that saw the overthrow of the Czar and the establishment of communism in Russia.

1980	1990	2000	2010

▲ **Ellen Zwilich**, *Concerto grosso* ***1985***

▲ **John Adams**, *Short Ride in a Fast Machine* ***1986***

• Fall of the Berlin Wall 1989

• Dissolution of the Soviet Union 1991

9/11 terrorist attacks in United States 2001 •

Wars in Afghanistan 2001–2014

Wars in Iraq 2003–2011

Sofia Gubaidulina, *Violin Concerto No. 2* ***2007*** ▲

Barrack Obama elected, first African-American president of the U.S 2008 •

Franklin D. Roosevelt led the country out of the Great Depression and through World War II.

Barack Obama was the first African-American elected to serve as president of the United States.

CHAPTER

Music in the Twentieth Century

After centuries of convention in Western music, twentieth-century composers abandoned tonality and explored new ways of approaching and organizing pitches and harmony. These innovations are modernism's most distinct feature. They are also what caused most of the difficulty for audiences. In addition, modernist composers experimented with new approaches to rhythm and timbre that drastically changed the way music was composed.

For centuries, composers had based their music on triads and the familiar major and minor scales, the building blocks of Western tonality. But by 1900, it had become clear to some composers that the old tonal system could not fully accommodate their musical ideas. In particular, Wagner and Liszt had devised new, flexible approaches to tonality that better suited their musical ideas. Significant parts of Wagner's works imply rather than clearly define key centers. And Liszt's late works often seem to abandon key signatures and drift into an ambiguous harmonic world. His experiments with testing the limits of tonality were ahead of their time. Only a few years after Wagner's and Liszt's deaths, tonality was on the verge of collapse.

Alternatives to Tonality

Late nineteenth-century composers such as Dvořák and Musorgsky experimented with scales outside the major and minor scales of the tonal system, including the five-tone pentatonic scale (see pp. 388, 392). Another special scale, the **whole-tone scale**, came into vogue toward the end of the century. The whole-tone scale divides the octave evenly into whole tones (or whole steps), instead of the mixture of whole and half steps found in the major and minor scales.

Whole-tone scale

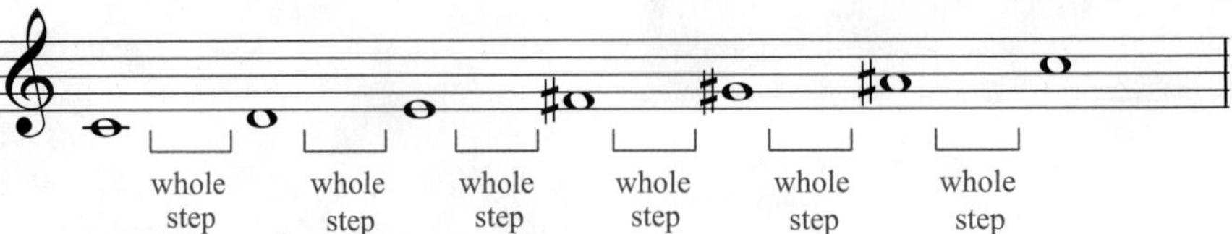

Composers such as Claude Debussy (see Chapter 42) based a number of works on whole-tone scales. Debussy used the scales to generate not just melodies, but also, by combining individual pitches of the scale, novel harmonies. The result was shimmering, impressionistic sounds that suggested for some listeners the light-filled works of Impressionist paintings.

Besides new scales, composers experimented with many new approaches to harmony that went well beyond the traditional use of major and minor triads. One new idea was **polytonality**, performing simultaneously unrelated harmonies from different keys. A celebrated polytonal passage occurs in the ballet *Petrushka* (1911) by the Russian composer Igor Stravinsky.

Russian dancer Vaslav Nijinsky in the title role of Stravinsky's ballet *Petrushka* (1911). The ballet features a celebrated polytonal passage, mimicking the grotesque, mechanical movements of the title character.

Stravinsky creates a swirling mass of dissonant sounds through this use of polytonality. When separated, the competing harmonies sound ordinary enough; but when combined, they create a distinctly unsettling, modern effect. The jarring harmonies are a perfect accompaniment for the character Petrushka, a wooden puppet that comes to life. His grotesque features and mechanical movements are reflected in the music itself.

Arguably the most provocative type of modern harmony was the **tone cluster**, a chord made up of several closely adjacent notes. This technique was developed by the ruggedly individualistic American composer Henry Cowell (1897–1965). Cowell used his forearms to strike adjacent keys at the piano, spanning an octave and more. In *Tides of Manaunaun* (1917), Cowell directed the pianist to execute a rolling series of tone clusters in the bass, intended to conjure up the Irish god of motion and waves. Initially regarded as the forefront of the avant-garde, tone clusters soon became common in twentieth-century classical and jazz compositions.

Dashboard

Watch Larry Todd demonstrate how modern composers use dissonance in music.

Arnold Schoenberg and the Rejection of Tonality

The growing freedom in harmonic organization reached a new extreme in the music of the Austro-Hungarian Arnold Schoenberg (1874–1951). Around 1908, Schoenberg began composing without key signatures and stopped using tonal triads. Schoenberg labeled his music "pantonal," meaning that it relied on all pitches of the chromatic scale, to signify its emancipation from tonality. He proclaimed tonality, the bedrock of Western music for centuries, to be obsolete, and dismissed conventional notions of consonance and dissonance as irrelevant in the new century.

Arnold Schoenberg in 1924.

Watch a video on tone rows.

Schoenberg's rejection of conventional tonality took place over a period of about twenty years, from roughly 1890 to 1910. In the first stage, his early, tonal music became increasingly chromatic and dissonant. However, Schoenberg kept this music just barely within the bounds of tonality by occasionally using triads. The decisive move to **pantonality** came when he abandoned the remaining triads altogether, creating music no longer grounded in tonality. Most listeners reacted to Schoenberg's pantonal compositions with bewilderment and shock. Music without tonal references was like a gravity-free field, in which listeners struggled to grasp floating strands of disordered pitches. In place of Schoenberg's term "pantonal," critics seized on the pejorative term *atonal* (**atonality**: "without tonality") to describe this music.

Through the First World War and beyond, Schoenberg continued to work in the atonal idiom, creating compositions that challenged both musicians and audiences. Then, in the 1920s, he devised a new approach that allowed him to impose order on his atonal music. Known as the **twelve-tone system**, it was Schoenberg's second great contribution to twentieth-century music.

To achieve an equal use of all twelve pitches, Schoenberg organized them into a *tone row*, or **series**. The **tone row** was a fixed sequence of the twelve chromatic pitches that allowed them to be used methodically in a composition before any one was repeated. Schoenberg's tone rows displayed a free mixture of intervals, while avoiding concentrations of pitches that outlined triads.

Schoenberg was able to create additional tone rows based on the original:

- By playing the basic row backward, he derived a second tone row known as the **retrograde**.
- By rewriting the original tone row upside-down, he produced a third tone row known as **inversion**, a mirror-like reflection of the original.
- Finally, by playing this third tone row backwards, he generated a fourth row known as **retrograde inversion**.

Of the new alternatives to tonality that emerged in the twentieth century, the twelve-tone system proved to be the most significant. Schoenberg introduced the

MAKING CONNECTIONS *Atonality and Soundtracks*

Schoenberg's atonal music often emphasizes the intervals of the second and seventh, which may sound dissonant, upsetting, or harsh. If you watch a horror, thriller, or science fiction film, there is a good chance that some of the music you hear is atonal. One particularly famous example is the screeching music for the shower scene in Hitchcock's *Psycho* (1960; see p. 47). In these films we understand and accept that the music is meant to reinforce our sense of heightened suspense, fear, dread, or anxiety. Music filled with pleasing consonances would simply not do the trick.

system to his students Alban Berg (1885–1935; see p. 451) and Anton von Webern (1883–1945; see p. 451), who explored its potential further during the 1930s and 1940s. In Europe and the United States, many composers developed the technique in new directions after the Second World War. Once considered revolutionary and at the vanguard of the radical extreme, the twelve-tone system was increasingly embraced by the musical establishment.

New Experiments with Rhythm and Timbre

Complementing Schoenberg's revolutionary treatments of pitch were modernists' efforts to change age-old ideas about rhythm and timbre. Twentieth-century composers rejected regular, recurring beat patterns in favor of asymmetrical divisions. Many of them embraced a technique known as **polyrhythm**, the layering of competing rhythms and meters. Some composers, such as Igor Stravinsky and the Hungarian Béla Bartók, gave their music a dynamic rhythmic energy by frequently changing meters within a composition.

Some composers turned their attention to the quality of sound itself—its timbre, or color. In 1911 Schoenberg coined the term ***Klangfarbenmelodie***—a composite German word meaning "sound-color-melody"—to emphasize the significance of timbre. In a bold exploration of this concept, Schoenberg altered instrumental scorings of slowly shifting atonal chords to suggest an ever rotating kaleidoscope of sound. The shifting colors of the music replaced the traditional role of pitch.

The pioneers of modern music avoided whatever they deemed to be too familiar in music. The eccentric French composer Eric Satie (1866–1925), protesting the tedium of academic musical forms, composed pieces with tongue-in-cheek titles such as "Three Pieces in the Form of a Pear." Stravinsky opened his ballet *The Rite of Spring* with a coarse, high note on a bassoon, an effect previously not heard in classical works. Schoenberg chose for his extraordinary atonal music lurid, expressionist subjects that were as shocking to his audiences as the new sounds themselves (see Chapter 42).

The decisive break from nineteenth-century music took place in the early years of the twentieth century. After the First World War, as if reacting against their own prewar radicalism, the leading composers redefined their relation to earlier traditions. Some embraced a direction known as **neoclassicism**, which refocused composers' interests on eighteenth-century musical elements (see Chapter 43). Others continued to cultivate national styles and were influenced by developments in popular music and jazz. Then, the end of the Second World War, followed by accelerating gains in technology, triggered a new round of experimentation and renewal that proved more radical than ever before.

check your KNOWLEDGE

1. How did twentieth-century music differ from earlier musical styles in its approach to melody, rhythm, and timbre?
2. Which alternatives to classical tonality developed in the early years of the twentieth century?
3. How did twentieth-century composers approach harmony differently from their predecessors?
4. How did Arnold Schoenberg revolutionize music through his championing of atonal and twelve-tone music?
5. Which new developments in rhythm and timbre accompanied the revolution in tonality?

CHAPTER

42 The Modernist Revolution

Several composers pioneered musical modernism. Born in the second half of the nineteenth century, they lived long enough in the twentieth to leave strong footprints on modern music. Three composers during this time were particularly innovative and influential:

1) Claude Debussy turned his subtly refined scores away from the dominant Austro-Germanic influences in European music.
2) Igor Stravinsky, a cosmopolitan figure who worked in Europe and the United States, revolutionized approaches to rhythmic structure and formal design.
3) Arnold Schoenberg created a radical innovation in sound through his determined exploration of atonality.

Paris (where Debussy and Stravinsky worked) and Vienna (where Schoenberg worked) were the hubs for these developments. The composers' experiments varied strikingly in scope, yet they expressed a common desire to discard the familiar. Not just in music but in other arts as well, Paris and Vienna teemed with revolutionary ideas as the seeds of modernism were sown.

Claude Debussy

Claude Debussy (1862–1918), painted by Marcel André Baschet, 1884.

Little in the background of Debussy (1862–1918) predicted his musical modernism. He trained at the Paris Conservatory, a revered and traditional institution, and won the Prix de Rome after impressing the judges with a standard cantata. His three years in Italy did not particularly inspire him. Like Berlioz half a century before, Debussy chafed at the conservative routine that he found there. And like many other musicians, Debussy made the pilgrimage to Bayreuth, Germany, to hear Wagner's music dramas. He did not find a meaningful path for himself through Wagner's music, however; instead, he saw it as a glorious sunset marking the end of a previous age. In his own music, Debussy rejected the dense textures, thick orchestration, and seriousness of Wagner's art.

As a young man, Debussy had visited Russia, where Tchaikovsky's eccentric patroness, Madame von Meck, employed him as a pianist. While there, Debussy studied Russian music, especially the works of Modest Musorgsky, whose style deeply influenced him. Another key inspiration occurred in 1889 when Debussy heard Indonesian musicians perform at the International Exposition in Paris. Playing a group of gongs and drums, known as a **gamelan**, the Indonesians' music was unlike anything that he had heard. These performers employed non-Western scales, including pentatonic scales (see p. 388). The fresh sounds of this exotic music and its idiosyncratic rhythmic patterns revealed further possibilities for him to explore. (See p. 416 for a discussion of gamelan music.) Yet another influence was Liszt's later, experimental music, in which Debussy found imaginative applications of whole-tone scales and harmonies. Intrigued by all these models, he strove to create a new kind of music. Declaring his artistic liberation, Debussy told a colleague that he was renouncing his faith in the C-major scale and in the tonal system that it symbolized.

Along with Maurice Ravel (1875–1937), Debussy is one of the composers most often labeled as an impressionist. However, Debussy did not associate directly with the impressionist painters. Although he often used imaginative titles for his compositions—for example, *Reflets dans l'eau* (*Reflections in the Water*)—his inspiration seems to have been more poetic than pictorial. Still, the shimmering harmonies of his compositions suggest the play of light and color in impressionist paintings.

Debussy once said that the ideal music drama should consist of a loose series of dreamlike scenes. This belief reveals his affinity to **symbolism**, a French movement of poets who aimed to create in their art impressions through suggestion rather than literal descriptions. The poem *L'après-midi d'un faune* (*The Afternoon of a Faun*) by Stéphane Mallarmé inspired Debussy to compose an orchestral work envisioned as a musical prelude to it. Though Debussy finished his score in 1894, it is generally accepted as a seminal work of twentieth-century modernism.

MAKING CONNECTIONS *The Eiffel Tower as Modernist Icon*

The Eiffel Tower.

Some 250 million tourists have visited the iconic Eiffel Tower since it opened in 1889. During its construction, the wrought iron tower became the center of a Parisian culture war that pitted tradition against innovation, the familiar against the unknown, and art against science and technology. A petition signed by 300 French painters, poets, musicians, and intellectuals demanded that the project be canceled. Its shadows, they feared, would obscure the great buildings of the city, such as Notre Dame and the Louvre.

Of course, the tower was built. Initially the plan was to dismantle it after twenty years, but it remains one of the most recognizable architectural structures of all time. Its original purpose was to stand as a gateway to the *Exposition universelle*, a world's fair held during the 100th anniversary of the French Revolution. Among the visitors was the twenty-seven-year-old composer Debussy, who was inspired by the Javanese gamelan ensemble he heard there.

PRELUDE TO THE AFTERNOON OF A FAUN (1894)

Debussy's Prelude may at first strike the listener as rather unassuming. It lasts only about ten minutes, rarely attains a *fortissimo* dynamic level, and uses a much smaller orchestra than the Wagnerian standard of the day. There are prominent parts for woodwinds and strings, but the brass section is reduced to just four horns. Debussy adds two harps and, near the end, introduces small finger cymbals that produce a delicate tinkling. He blends all these instrumental colors to evoke the pastoral, blissful world of Mallarmé's faun.

In the poem, the faun (a half-man, half-goat deity from Roman mythology) dreamily recalls his sexual adventures with woodland nymphs. But Mallarmé never makes clear whether those adventures have actually happened or whether the faun merely imagines them. The poem, which is suggestive rather than literal, moves back and forth between the present and the faun's recollection of the past. Debussy translates that suggestiveness into gentle distortions of melodies and harmonies, transporting us to the faun's mythological world.

The music begins with a gesture of understated but striking originality: a solo for flute, the modern symbol of the Greek panpipes (see **Listening Map 57**). Like a free improvisation, this dreamy solo (*a*; ①) seems tonally shapeless: it begins with nothing more than a slippery, descending chromatic fragment that retraces its steps.

MAKING CONNECTIONS *Symbolism*

Debussy associated with several French poets and writers who were part of the symbolist literary movement. One was Paul Verlaine (1844–1896), whose poem *Clair de lune* (*Moonlight*) inspired one of Debussy's most popular piano pieces. Another was Stéphane Mallarmé (1842–1898), who exercised tremendous influence in his attempt to liberate poetry from its traditional rhythms and rhyme schemes. In 1894 Mallarmé attended the premiere of Debussy's *Prelude to the Afternoon of a Faun* and was quite taken with the work. For Mallarmé, poetry and music were closely related. In his poetry, Mallarmé attempted to go beyond the literal meanings of the words, seeking to unleash sounds and rhythms that could form patterns and structures not unlike what music offered.

Answering the flute are a woodwind chord, a harp glissando like a cool summer breeze, and a melodic fragment played on the horn. From those materials, Debussy builds up the first section of the Prelude (*A*), which suggests a series of freely conceived variations on *a*. He avoids any direct repetition of thematic or harmonic material that might negate the poem's play between the imagined and the real. Instead, the music conjures up the faun's idyllic existence in a timeless, mythic-poetic world. With each variation, Debussy changes the faun's theme in some way, either by subtly altering its shape or by revising the harmonies or orchestration.

The *A* section contains four variations on the opening flute solo, like four shifting perspectives on the faun's memory of the past. The harmonies are vividly chromatic, effectively blurring our sense of a key center, although individual triads occasionally emerge. In addition, the composer incorporates whole-tone scales, which reinforce the sense of suspended tonality. A gentle swell and shift to a faster tempo prepare us for the central part (*B*), based on a haunting tonal melody (*b*; ②). First played by the woodwinds and then extended by the strings, this melody describes two descending phrases separated by an especially wide, expressive leap.

Costume sketch by Leon Bakst for the faun in Claude Debussy's ballet version of *The Afternoon of a Faun*, 1912.

Could this contrasting section, much of which uses tonal triads, represent the faun's recall of his experience? Perhaps, although Debussy then revives the opening flute melody (*A′*), and again leads it through four varied statements. The first two are in lengthened note values, accompanied by harp arpeggiations and gentle chords in the strings. The third and fourth are played in a slower tempo, accompanied by the antique cymbals and two solo violins. Finally, in the closing bars, muted horns sound a distant echo of the faun's melody, in a last, fleeting view of his world.

LISTENING MAP 57

DEBUSSY, *Prelude to the Afternoon of a Faun* {1894}

FORM	ABA′
METER	Chiefly $\frac{9}{8}$ and $\frac{3}{4}$, *très modéré* (very moderately)
SCORING	Orchestra (three flutes, two oboes, one English horn, two clarinets, two bassoons, four French horns, two harps, two antique cymbals, and strings
OVERVIEW	Debussy uses a three-part ABA′ form, but he overlays onto the A sections a series of free variations of the faun's melody, heard at the beginning in the flute. The music shifts between passages that use triads and keys, others that use whole-tone scales and harmonies, and still others that lie between these two types.

why to LISTEN

Much of the music we have studied in this book uses a basic dramatic model. A sense of musical conflict is established, allowed to run its course, and then resolved at the end. Recall Mozart's *Marriage of Figaro* (the Cavatina), Beethoven's Fifth Symphony, or Tchaikovsky's *Romeo and Juliet* as examples of dramatic approaches. But what if a composer chooses *not* to follow this model? Debussy was such a composer, and his music often circles around itself, even seeming to go nowhere. The *Prelude to the Afternoon of a Faun* begins lazily with a flute solo, then continues with variations on the theme, some so subtle that the music becomes almost static. In this kind of music, bold, dramatic gestures are replaced by suggestive allure. What is important, Debussy seems to be saying, is not always what you literally hear, but what is left unheard. This suggestiveness mirrors Mallarmé's poem, which does not trace a clear narrative, but depends on suggestion and nuance to achieve its dreamy effect. The symbolist model keeps us guessing, in the poem and in Debussy's music, and invites us to unlock our imaginations.

first LISTEN

A	B	A′	CLOSING
0:00	4:55	6:37	9:32
Chromatic melody played first on flute, then put through four variations	New theme in woodwinds, with stronger tonal feeling	Return to A, transposed to new key; slower rhythms	Distant echo of theme is heard in horns

a deeper **LISTEN**

TIME	SECTION	LISTEN FOR THIS
0:00	**A Moderate**	(1) Chromatic flute melody (*a*) *a* **Very moderate** *flute* ***p*** *sweetly and expressively*
0:25		Harp glissando, horn
1:00		Four free variations on (*a*)
3:18		More animated, swell to ***f*** and decrescendo, whole-tone harmonies
4:30		Ritard, *pianissimo*
4:55	**B Return to opening tempo**	(2) New theme (*b*) in woodwinds, with stronger tonal associations *b* ***p*** *espressive and very sustained* ***mf***
5:27		Animated, (*b*) in strings, swell to ***ff*** *B* in violin solo, decrescendo to ***p***
6:30		Ritard
6:37	**A′ Return to opening tempo**	(*a*) in flute (transposed, rhythmically altered)
6:55		(*a*) in oboe (transposed, rhythmically altered)
7:10		Languorous: (*a*) in flute (two statements), antique cymbals, two solo violins
9:32	**Closing**	Muted horns, ***ppp***

Most of Debussy's career unfolded in Paris. There he wrote several major orchestral works with evocative titles. Among them are the three orchestral Nocturnes (1899), *Nuages* (*Clouds*), *Fêtes* (*Festivals*), and *Sirènes* (*Sirens*); the "symphonic sketch" *La Mer* (*The Sea*, 1905); and the ballet *Jeux* (*Games*, 1913). Debussy also composed a substantial amount of piano music. The modernist chords, whole-tone passages, and delicate layers of sound Debussy demanded from the piano required a different kind of keyboard technique than that needed for tonal nineteenth-century piano music, centered on triads. As if realizing this need, Debussy composed a set of twelve distinctive etudes for the instrument, with each devoted to a particular technique required to play his music.

Despite Debussy's negative reaction to Wagner, the Frenchman's one complete opera, *Pelléas et Mélisande* (1902), has some curious ties to Wagner's *Tristan und Isolde*. Like Wagner's celebrated music drama, *Pelléas* uses continuous music and an intricate network of motives. But there the resemblance ends. Debussy envelops his understated score with delicate orchestral sounds. The stage action takes place behind a gauze screen that filters our perceptions of the drama. Finally, there are hardly any *forte* passages in the entire opera, in contrast to Wagner's full-blown scores.

Debussy led the French revolt against German music. Not all his countrymen supported his efforts, however. The composer Camille Saint-Saëns, for example, found Debussy's music pretty but unrefined, and the *Prelude to the Afternoon of a Faun* no more a piece of music than a painter's palette was a finished painting. Indeed, there is an unfinished, spontaneous quality about Debussy's scores. However, in rejecting time-honored notions about what unified a work of music, Debussy emerged as a composer of the modern age. And the unassuming melodic nuances of his faun prepared the way for even more far-reaching and revolutionary experiments in sound.

Igor Stravinsky

Igor Stravinsky (1882–1971).

Russian by birth, Igor Stravinsky (1882–1971) enjoyed a long career extending across much of the twentieth century. After attending law school, he took composition lessons from the celebrated composer Nikolai Rimsky-Korsakov. In 1910 Stravinsky arrived in Paris, where he developed his own revolutionary approach to composition. His first major efforts were the orchestral scores for two ballets, *The Firebird* (1910) and *Petrushka* (1911). These works were commissioned by Sergei Diaghilev, the founder of the famous *Ballets Russes*, a Russian dance company based in Paris. Stravinsky would continue to compose scores for the *Ballets Russes*, including *The Rite of Spring* (1913), *Pulcinella* (1920), *The Wedding* (1923), and *Oedipus Rex* (1927).

Stravinsky's *Firebird* is based on a Russian fairy tale. It tells of the adventures of Tsarevich Ivan, who encounters a benevolent fairy endowed with magical powers (the Firebird) and the evil magician Kastchei. The lush orchestration of the score and its opulent tonal language suggest the music of Rimsky-Korsakov.

Stravinsky turned to other Russian folk tales as his source for *Petrushka*, a ballet about a hapless puppet who comes to life and mingles with a group of colorful characters at a Russian fair. *Petrushka* is more adventuresome than *The Firebird*. Stravinsky uses snatches of Russian folk tunes and short motives that are repeated in different settings to produce a hypnotic effect. He is bold, too, in his treatment of harmony, experimenting with polytonality. In long passages, he freely mixes notes

MAKING CONNECTIONS *The* Ballets Russes

The *Ballets Russes* was the brainchild of Sergei Diaghilev (1872–1929), a cultured Russian impresario who managed his ballet company in Paris for twenty years, between 1909 and 1929. Diaghilev was a conservatory-trained musician who aspired to be a composer, but was advised against a career in music because he lacked sufficient talent. Instead, he found his creative space in the world of ballet. He revolutionized the art form by bringing together talented Russian dancers such as Anna Pavlova (1882–1931) and Vaslav Nijinsky (1889–1950); artists including Picasso and Matisse to design modern sets and costumes; and composers such as Stravinsky, Debussy, Ravel, and Prokofiev to produce daringly modern scores.

Diaghilev experimented with replacing the set dance numbers of traditional ballet with extended passages of pantomime, thereby allowing composers considerable latitude. Instead of the graceful movements of traditional ballet, Diaghilev's company offered unusual gestures and jumps that bordered on the sensational and sometimes provoked scandals. Diaghilev's troupe ushered in the age of modern dance, and most modern choreographers still trace their roots to the *Ballets Russes.*

Anna Pavlova (1882–1931), one of the most celebrated dancers of her time, member of the original company of the Ballets Russes.

of the C-major scale with unrelated harmonies without regard for their consonant or dissonant values.

Stravinsky's major early masterpiece, and the work that galvanized public opinion, was his third score for Diaghilev, *Le Sacre du printemps* (*The Rite of Spring*, 1913). Its creation, which the composer described as an "act of faith," required about two years of difficult work. The ballet's premiere threw the audience into an uproar and provoked a brawl between supporters and detractors. Many audience members found the main action of the ballet, in which a sacrificial virgin dances herself to death, utterly scandalous. Few critics spared their contempt for Stravinsky's modernist score. Driven by unrelenting rhythms, it called for an enormous orchestra (with quintuple woodwinds, augmented brass, and boisterous percussion sections) and teemed with primitive-sounding melodic fragments and clamorous harmonies. *The Rite of Spring* defiantly rejected traditional tonality and the Romantic aesthetic of expression that had defined the music of the nineteenth century.

Dashboard

Read some early reviews and reactions to *The Rite of Spring.*

STRAVINSKY, *THE RITE OF SPRING* (1913)

To have appreciated *The Rite of Spring,* Stravinsky's audience in 1913 would have had to abandon almost all their preconceptions about melody, harmony, form, and rhythm. Unlike Debussy, who coolly explored new musical resources through

Dance II, by Henri Matisse (1910), evokes a wild style similar to the "Dance of the Adolescents" in Stravinsky's *Rite of Spring*.

understated nuance, Stravinsky assaulted his listeners head-on, violating their expectations and subjecting them to sounds then deemed beyond the bounds of musical propriety. Like Debussy's *Prelude to the Afternoon of a Faun*, Stravinsky's score reflects a mythical, timeless world. We are introduced to that world not by innuendo, however, but by a forceful musical confrontation. Instead of the smooth sensuality of Debussy's faun, we experience the raw energy of a pagan Russian tribe.

The first part of the ballet, titled "The Adoration of the Earth," consists of an orchestral introduction and seven scenes connected without pause. Two of its most celebrated passages are the "Introduction" and the "Augurs of Spring: Dance of the Adolescents" (see **Listening Map 58**).

Stravinsky opens the "Introduction" with a solo for bassoon. However, the tune strains into the instrument's uppermost register, which composers generally avoid because of its piercing quality. This solo sounds more like a wild croaking than a refined theme. It is, in fact, built on a short motive of eight notes, which are immediately repeated with different rhythms (*a*; ①). Notice how the two pauses in the first measure disrupt the sense of a regular meter, and how the altered rhythms of the motive violate the sense of a regular beat. This free treatment of meter and rhythm is one of the distinctive traits of Stravinsky's style.

The bassoon is joined by a horn and then by clarinets, with each instrument asserting its own independent line in a kind of rough counterpoint. Stravinsky juxtaposes the bassoon motive with swelling and diminishing masses of woodwinds—suggesting the awakening of spring, or, as he described it, the "sublime uprising of Nature renewing herself." Eventually, he amasses a dense woodwind choir, with irregular orders of lines, meter, and rhythm. Suddenly, the music halts and the opening bassoon solo returns. Now a short motive plucked by the strings (*b*; ②) brings a transition to the first scene, the "Augurs of Spring: Dance of the Adolescents."

While the "Introduction" offers contrasting lines of woodwind colors, the "Augurs of Spring" focuses on rhythm. A single dissonant chord (*c*; ③) is repeated with numerous, varying rhythmic accents, which drives the dance forward with the pulsing lifeblood of spring. Stravinsky forces us to concentrate on pure rhythm as the essential principle of musical organization.

After two regular measures of vigorous chords in the strings, bold exclamations from the horns (shown by accents in the Listening Map) mark off the pulses into asymmetrical rhythmic groupings. The chord itself is made up of two traditional, although unrelated, triadic harmonies; heard together, they form unrelenting dissonant sonorities. The chords show no recurring rhythmic pattern; animating the music is the energy of the basic pulse—the chord—and not the predictable pattern of a traditional meter.

Occasionally, Stravinsky redistributes part of the chord in a broken arrangement (*b*; ②), previously heard in the strings in the transition to the scene, but now projected in the throaty register of an English horn. In addition, against the dissonant chords Stravinsky begins setting short, crisp fragments of melodies. We may pick out three (*d*, *e*, and *f*; ④–⑥), presented in turn by the bassoons, horns, and trumpet.

Against the throbbing backdrop of the chords, these fragments stand out as tonal reference points. They sound like folk songs that are just starting to take shape in a world of primitive harmonies. Additional instruments join in as the dance gains momentum. There is no definite break to mark the conclusion of the dance. Instead, the music eventually spills over into the next dance, the "Game of Abduction," which surges forward in an animated Presto tempo, also driven by a relentless rhythmic power.

Stravinsky playing *The Rite of Spring*, as depicted in a sketch by Jean Cocteau. Cocteau was a French poet and critic who attended the famous opening night performance of this work.

STRAVINSKY, *The Rite of Spring*, "Introduction" and "Augurs of Spring: Dance of the Adolescents" {1913}

FORM	Free
METER	Various, frequently shifting
SCORING	Orchestra (two piccolos, two flutes, one alto flute, three oboes, one English horn, four clarinets, one bass clarinet, three bassoons, two contrabassoons, eight French horns, one piccolo trumpet, four trumpets, three trombones, two tubas, timpani, cymbals, and strings)
OVERVIEW	The "Introduction" depicts the germinating of spring that spills over into the energetic "Augurs of Spring: Dance of the Adolescents." Both sections are freely formed and yet clearly structured. In the "Introduction" the opening high bassoon solo recurs periodically as a type of refrain. In the "Augurs of Spring: Dance of the Adolescents," Stravinsky derives his material from a pulsating chord, simply repeated for extended stretches in ever changing patterns of accents. Against these chords Stravinsky introduces various motives that sound like the beginnings of folk songs.

why to LISTEN

Music that provokes a scandal usually arouses our curiosity to listen, even if the scandal occurred more than a hundred years ago. There were many aspects of the premiere of *The Rite of Spring* in 1913 that shocked Parisians, but among the most conspicuous was Stravinsky's bold, new, and for many, violent approach to rhythm and meter. By changing the meter so frequently, Stravinsky essentially demolished a long-standing convention of Western music. In the noisy stretch of the score known as the "Augurs of Spring: Dance of the Adolescents" Stravinsky began with a crunching, dissonant chord. Then, by simply repeating it in unpredictable groups of beats, he filled out the pages of the section. Instead of giving us a theme, and then developing it, Stravinsky began by giving us only rhythm. In doing so he seemed to suggest that in the beginning was rhythm, the beating of life. His music forced listeners to concentrate on this facet of the musical experience, and to rethink how we perceive rhythm. The means were simple, but the result profound.

first LISTEN

INTRODUCTION	AUGURS OF SPRING: DANCE OF THE ADOLESCENTS
0:00	**3:35**
Main melody *(a)* played on bassoon	Fragments of folk-like melodies played against dissonant, regular chords

a deeper **LISTEN**

TIME	SECTION	LISTEN FOR THIS
0:00	Introduction	Based on *a*, bassoon solo ① *(a)* theme  *Bassoon* **Lento**
1:00		Free counterpoint in woodwinds, increasing in complexity
1:59		Pause
3:00		Return of *a* in bassoon
3:14		Transition figure in strings (*b*) ② *(b)* theme 
3:37	Augurs of Spring: Dance of the Adolescents	Irregular, dissonant chords (*c*) ③ *(c)* theme  *Horns* *Horns* *1 2 3 4 1 2 3 4 5 1 2 1 2 3 4 5*
4:24		*d* in bassoons against *c d* in bassoons against *c* ④ *(d)* theme  *Bassoon* ***f***
4:58		Pause
5:19		*e* in French horn against *b* ⑤ *(e)* theme  *Horn* ***mp***
5:56		*f* in trumpets against *b* ⑥ *(f)* theme  *Trumpet* ***mp***
6:21		*(e)* in flute against (*b*), several repetitions, with buildup of full orchestra; spills over into "Game of Abduction" at 6:57

Arnold Schoenberg

Arnold Schoenberg (1874–1951). This portrait was painted by Richard Gerstl, a Viennese artist who helped Schoenberg with his own paintings.

Of all the modernist composers, Arnold Schoenberg (1874–1951) posed the greatest challenges to critics and audiences alike. Still, his influence was deep. Schoenberg lived and worked primarily in Vienna and Berlin until 1933, when he emigrated to the United States to escape persecution by the Nazis. His early tonal compositions were in the late Romantic style that drew on Wagner's musical language. They culminated in *Gurrelieder* (*Songs of Gurre*, composed in 1903 but not premiered until 1913), a large-scale cantata for orchestra, soloists, several choruses, and narrator—hundreds of musicians in total. The score for *Gurrelieder* had so many parts that special music paper was printed just to fit them on the page. The cantata's text was based on a Danish legend about the medieval King Waldemar, his mistress Tove, and his jealous queen Helvig.

Early in his modernist phase Schoenberg was pushing beyond Wagner's style to explore new possibilities. In increasingly adventurous compositions such as the Chamber Symphony Op. 9 (1906), Schoenberg experimented with whole-tone scales and novel harmonies built upon the interval of the fourth.

In 1908, the composer broke decisively with tonality. The work that took this fateful step was the Second String Quartet, Op. 10. It began with key signatures and recognizable, if weakened, tonal features. But in the finale, Schoenberg added a soprano solo that prophetically begins, "I feel the air of another planet." Here, Schoenberg finally freed himself totally from the use of triads.

In his revolutionary new music, which he described as pantonality, Schoenberg generally avoided repeating adjacent pitches, preferring instead to choose freely from the twelve pitches of the chromatic scale (see Chapter 41). Schoenberg was convinced that pantonality—or atonality, as it became known—was the logical successor to the outworn system of tonality. He regarded his music as an inevitable historical development, and he took great pains to relate it to the work of earlier composers such as Wagner and Brahms. Although on first hearing Schoenberg's music seems worlds removed from the late nineteenth century, the links are there, even if obscured in the thick textures of atonal melodies and harmonies. For example, Schoenberg developed his themes in much the same way as Wagner or Brahms had. The difference was that Schoenberg's themes now lacked their harmonic reference points. Moreover, Schoenberg continued to cultivate the traditional forms favored by Brahms: sonata form, the rondo, and theme and variations, for example. Despite his radical new treatment of pitch, Schoenberg was unwilling to break completely from the traditions of German music.

Schoenberg's embrace of atonality corresponded roughly to the expressionist movement in German art, which used exaggeration to depict extreme, subjective emotions. An associate and friend of the Russian expressionist painter Wassily Kandinsky, Schoenberg himself painted brightly colored expressionist canvases, including some telling self-portraits. Like Kandinsky, he was fascinated with interplays between sound and color. Just as the expressionist painters distorted and ultimately abandoned realistic images, so Schoenberg distorted and ultimately rejected tonality.

Expressionism's emphasis on expression connects it with German Romanticism. Similarly, Schoenberg's provocative and highly emotional atonal works could also be traced to the Romantics. But the subjects of Schoenberg's expressive urges were uncompromisingly new: the psychological world of hidden, tormented feelings and the dark underside of the artist's subconscious. *Erwartung* (*Expectation*, 1909), a monodrama for soloist and orchestra, is about the hallucinations of a betrayed lover. The expressionist song cycle *Das Buch der hängenden Gärten* (*The Book of the Hanging Gardens*, 1909) is rich in sexual imagery and Freudian associations.

MAKING CONNECTIONS *Wassily Kandinsky and German Expressionism*

A pioneer of modern art who was influenced by Schoenberg's atonal music was the Russian painter Wassily Kandinsky (1866–1944). Evidence suggests that Kandinsky experienced synesthesia, a rare condition in which one sense triggers a reaction in another sense (colors can stimulate sounds, or sounds can stimulate tastes, for instance). In Kandinsky's case, color and sound were inseparable. While listening to one of Wagner's music dramas, and later to Schoenberg's atonal music, he reported seeing an entire range of colors.

Kandinsky, *Improvisation No. 30* (Canons), 1913.

Kandinsky worked principally in Germany, then moved to France, where he died during the Second World War. While in Germany in 1910, he began painting abstract watercolors, replacing realistic images with dabs of color and shapes, a watershed moment in the history of art. Like Schoenberg, Kandinsky was drawn to expressionism: the painter believed that colors could evoke deep psychological responses from the viewer, capturing a powerful and complex interior world. Painting, according to Kandinsky, should be abstract, like music. Not surprisingly, he titled his canvases using musical terms, such as Composition, Improvisation, or Fugue (see p. 171).

SCHOENBERG, *PIERROT LUNAIRE*, "VALSE DE CHOPIN" (1912)

One of the most impressive—and difficult—works from Schoenberg's atonal period is the song cycle *Pierrot lunaire* (*The Moonstruck Pierrot*). It uses for its text symbolist poetry by the Belgian Albert Giraud. Composed and performed in 1912 (after some forty rehearsals), the work is scored for a soprano and a small chamber ensemble of five musicians who play eight instruments: piano, flute/piccolo, clarinet/bass clarinet, violin/viola, and cello.

Schoenberg scored each song for soprano and a different ensemble of instruments. The soprano does not sing in the conventional sense but, rather, uses a technique known as ***Sprechstimme*** ("speaking voice"), located somewhere between speaking and singing. Sprechstimme became a powerful technique in Schoenberg's battery of expressionist devices. It embraces musical distortion: it has accurately notated rhythms, but is performed with uneven inflections in pitch.

Little Pierrot, by French expressionist Georges Rouault, ca. 1937. The tragic figure of the "sad clown" was a favorite among the expressionist painters and writers.

The subject of Schoenberg's song cycle is Pierrot, the stock "sad clown" character of pantomime. A moonstruck Pierrot is unmasked as a rejected, terror-stricken creature. The chamber ensemble weaves an intricate web of atonal sound around the poetry, which contains a series of shocking images. The twenty-one poems are loosely arranged in three groups of seven each. Schoenberg set them to miniature movements that generally last only a few minutes. Each poem consists of thirteen lines divided into four, four, and five lines, with refrain-like repetitions of lines from the first four.

The poem set in the fifth song, "Valse de Chopin," compares a melancholy waltz of the Polish composer to the bloodstained lips of an invalid. Chopin's waltz is not identified, and there is no waltz melody clearly recognizable in Schoenberg's music. Rather, the song is a freely composed atonal setting that suggests a grossly distorted version of a waltz. For the text and translation, see **Listening Map 59**.

This macabre movement is scored for flute, clarinet, and piano. For the third stanza, Schoenberg replaces the clarinet with the bass clarinet, whose lower range effectively distorts the original timbre of the ensemble, and turns Chopin's waltz into a "melancholy, dark waltz." The music, in the triple time of a waltz, begins with what sounds like a piano accompaniment to a clarinet line, in effect, an atonal waltz melody. In the poem, "chords of wild lust" interrupt the waltz; in the music, the melody and accompaniment give way to irregular piano chords. The stanzas are separated by instrumental interludes, and framed by a prelude and a postlude in which the piano accompaniment fades as the somber waltz dies away.

LISTENING MAP 59

SCHOENBERG, *Pierrot lunaire*, No. 5, "Valse de Chopin" {1912}

FORM	Free
METER	$\frac{3}{4}$ (slow waltz)
SCORING	Chamber ensemble (flute, clarinet/bass clarinet, soprano, and piano)
OVERVIEW	Schoenberg divides the text of thirteen lines into three parts of four, four, and five lines. These parts are framed by an instrumental introduction and postlude, and separated by brief instrumental interludes. Throughout the use of *Sprechstimme* in the vocal part plays off against shifting colors of the instruments in the chamber ensemble.

why to LISTEN

One hundred years and counting after the premiere, *Pierrot lunaire* continues to perplex listeners, if not with its atonal layers of sound, certainly with its use of *Sprechstimme* and kaleidoscopic juxtapositions of different instrumental timbres. Stravinsky—who admired Schoenberg's composition—focused in the *Rite of Spring* on rhythm; on the other hand, Schoenberg focused in *Pierrot lunaire* on the very quality of sound, by exchanging bits of material between the soprano and changing combinations of instruments. In Schoenberg's hands, these instruments could project different mixtures of colors. The soprano went even further, distorting her musical lines so that they became lodged somewhere between traditional singing and everyday speech. Perhaps, then, Schoenberg's score, certainly avant-garde for 1912, is not as unfamiliar as it might at first seem. It repays listening, as speech-like words become music, and music approaches speech.

first LISTEN

INTRODUCTION	LINES 1–4	INTERLUDE	LINES 5–8	INTERLUDE	LINES 9–13	POSTLUDE
0:00	**0:06**	**0:19**	**0:22**	**0:34**	**0:40**	**1:00**
Piano, clarinet, flute	Opening verse	Piano chords	2nd verse	Instrumental	Final, elongated verse; bass clarinet replaces clarinet	Orchestra plays the piano accompaniment fades to ending

Continued

 *a deeper* **LISTEN**

TIME	SECTION	TEXT/INSTRUMENTATION	TRANSLATION
0:00	Introduction	(piano, clarinet, and flute)	
0:06	Lines 1–4	***Wie ein blasser Tropfen Bluts*** ***färbt die Lippen einer Kranken,*** *also ruht auf diesen Tönen* *ein vernichtungssücht'ger Reiz.*	**Like a faint drop of blood** **coloring the lips of an invalid,** there rests in these tones A charm in search of negation.
0:19	Interlude	(chords in piano)	
0:22	Lines 5–8	*Wilder Lust Akkorde stören* *der Verzweiflung eisgen Traum.* ***Wie ein blasser Tropfen Bluts*** ***färbt die Lippen einer Kranken***	Chords of wild lust disturb the icy dreams of despair. **Like a faint drop of blood** **coloring the lips of an invalid.**
0:34	Interlude		
0:40	Lines 9–13	(clarinet changes to bass clarinet) *Heiss und jauchzend, süss und schmachtend* *melancholisch düstrer Walzer,* *kommst mir nimmer aus den Sinnen!* *Haftest mir an den Gedanken,* ***wie ein blasser Tropfen Bluts!***	 Hot and rejoicing, sweet and pining, melancholy, dark waltz. You never leave my senses! You seize my thoughts **like a faint drop of blood.**
1:00	Postlude	(piano)	

Alban Berg and Anton von Webern

Among Schoenberg's disciples were two students who followed his lead in exploring the new terrain of free atonality and twelve-tone music (see p. 432). Considerably less prolific than Schoenberg, Alban Berg (1885–1935) composed slowly and carefully. His principal works include two expressionist masterpieces, the operas *Wozzeck* (1923) and *Lulu* (left unfinished, its third act was not premiered until 1979). Berg also produced chamber works, a violin concerto, orchestral pieces, and songs. Although most of his music is atonal, it does not exhibit Schoenberg's uncompromisingly dissonant style. Rather, it features flowing melodies and lush harmonies, and even carries some fleeting touches of tonality.

Anton von Webern (1883–1945), Schoenberg's other celebrated disciple, was a serious student of the history of music. Many find his music overly intellectual and difficult to listen to and understand. Nonetheless, Webern took great pains, like his teacher, to justify the revolutionary character of his music by linking it to previous historical periods.

Webern crafted miniature instrumental and vocal compositions out of a minimum of notes, a few fragile moments of sound that seem imposed on silence. Schoenberg and Berg rarely worked within these severe limitations, preferring instead to work on larger scales. Webern labored intensively over individual pitches, carefully coordinating their individual rhythms, dynamics, articulations, and contours. On first hearing, his scores may sound like isolated points of sound in no particular order. Only after repeated hearings do patterns begin to emerge. Without question, Webern's music is intricate, but perhaps no more so than the music of J. S. Bach. And, despite its rigor, Webern's music is filled with feeling. He gave detailed performance instructions in his scores, all directed to expressive ends. Not one note is wasted.

In his later years, Webern developed an increasingly abstract style. His life ended tragically in 1945, when shortly after the Second World War officially ended, he was shot outside his home by a soldier occupying his Austrian town. Only in the 1950s was Webern's significance fully realized, as a generation of younger composers began emulating his discipline and exquisite control. They were joined by the aging Stravinsky, who diligently studied Webern's twelve-tone works and compared them to elegantly cut diamonds.

Alban Berg (1885–1935) and Anton von Webern (1883–1945).

check your KNOWLEDGE

1. What were the primary centers of revolutions in the arts at the dawn of the twentieth century? Why were these centers so important?
2. What were the musical influences on Claude Debussy, and how did they affect his music?
3. Compare Debussy's *Prelude to the Afternoon of a Faun* with Stravinsky's *The Rite of Spring.* What do these works have in common? What are some differences between them?
4. Which musical elements from the nineteenth century did Schoenberg carry forward in his own work? Which elements did he reject, and how did he replace them?
5. How did Schoenberg's students Berg and Webern advance Schoenberg's work? Which new elements did each introduce to the style?

CHAPTER

43 Neoclassicism

Costume for a character in Richard Strauss's neoclassical opera *Der Rosenkavalier* (1911).

In their zeal to break with the nineteenth century, Debussy, Stravinsky, and Schoenberg composed music that seemed brazenly new and modern, with no connection to the past. But there was a second option that some composers began to explore: neoclassicism. It involved revisiting the music of earlier periods *before* the nineteenth century, especially the Classical and Baroque periods, and reusing elements of their styles in modernist contexts.

To audiences of 1913, Stravinsky's *The Rite of Spring*, with its brutish rhythms and overwhelming power, must have seemed like an assault on the foundations of the music itself. Schoenberg's atonal scores, too, must have seemed like a wild foray into the uncharted realm of modernism. The early modernists were at first determined to break with the musical language of the late Romantic style. Increasingly after the First World War, however, their work became less focused on experimentation and more on reconsidering the musical past. They were especially attracted to the music of the eighteenth century and before. They found in this music a purity and rigor of approach that they felt had been overwhelmed by the excesses of the nineteenth-century composers.

These composers drew on the music of the pre-Romantic past to reinvigorate twentieth-century music. In 1909 Maurice Ravel wrote a minuet to suggest the style of Haydn, 100 years after his death. Richard Strauss, abandoning the dissonant tone of his operas *Salome* and *Elektra*, invoked Mozart's *Marriage of Figaro* in the delightfully elegant opera *Der Rosenkavalier* (1911). Brazilian composer Heitor Villa-Lobos explored similarities between the music of J. S. Bach and Brazilian **folk music** in a series of pieces titled *Bachianas brasileiras* (1930–1945).

The scope of neoclassicism was broad. Composers revived forms of counterpoint such as fugue and canon. They rediscovered baroque genres such as the suite, concerto, and oratorio, and redeployed standard classical forms such as the sonata form, minuet, and rondo (see Chapter 31). They wrote for intimate chamber ensembles, shunning the sprawling orchestral scores of the late nineteenth century. Stravinsky suggested that nineteenth-century composers had "overfed" their audiences with orchestral music that was too rich. The neoclassicists did not return wholeheartedly to using traditional tonality, however; their harmonies remained modern.

Sergei Prokofiev

After Stravinsky, the most significant new Russian composer was Sergei Prokofiev (1891–1953). He attended the St. Petersburg Conservatory before establishing himself as a concert pianist and writing several ballet scores for Diaghilev's company. When he was not touring as a pianist or composing, Prokofiev pursued his favorite hobby, chess, and became so skilled that he won a game from a chess master who had held the world title for several years during the 1920s. For many years, Prokofiev worked in the West, but unlike Stravinsky, who eventually settled in the United States, Prokofiev returned to Russia in 1936. There, during the Stalinist era, the composer was criticized for what the state authorities viewed as unacceptable "modernisms" in his music.

Sergei Prokofiev (1891–1953).

Prokofiev's style offers a mixture of percussive rhythmic effects and lyrical melodies with wide leaps. A versatile composer, he wrote operas, ballets, symphonies, concertos, chamber works, piano music, film scores, and a charming children's tale for narrator and orchestra, *Peter and the Wolf* (1936). Because Prokofiev worked in "old-school" Western genres, Stalinist critics warned that he should produce more patriotic music promoting the Russian motherland and its socialist revolution. **Socialist realism**, the dominant doctrine of the arts in the Soviet Union, required that music be accessible to the common worker and serve the state. Among Prokofiev's works that did win official approval was the Fifth Symphony, premiered by the composer early in 1945, in the closing months of the Second World War, as the Soviet Army was advancing through Poland during its final push to Berlin. The warm lyricism and singable melodic lines of the symphony were embraced, and Prokofiev's statement that the work was a "hymn to free and happy Man" was taken as an endorsement of socialist realism. But the authorities refused to mount his opera *War and Peace* (1943), based on Tolstoy's epic novel. Its premiere had to wait until after the composer's death, which, ironically, occurred on March 5, 1953, the same day the Russian dictator Stalin died.

Although Prokofiev never allied himself with any particular style of composition, strong neoclassical tendencies can be heard in his music. In fact, he called his First Symphony the "Classical." This exuberant early work of 1917, the year of the Russian Revolution, suggests how Haydn might have composed in the twentieth century. The result is a delightful translation of the eighteenth-century classical style into a modern musical language.

MAKING CONNECTIONS *Music in the Soviet Union*

In 1917 Nicholas II, last of the Romanov tsars who had ruled Russia for centuries, abdicated after the outbreak of the Russian Revolution. Vladimir Lenin, leader of the Russian Marxist Party known as the Bolsheviks (Russian for "the majority"), then seized power. In 1922 he announced the formation of the Soviet Union, dedicated to removing traces of capitalism in Russia and advancing a workers' state. After Lenin's death in 1924, a member of his circle, Joseph Stalin, consolidated power, took control of the party, now renamed the Communist Party, and ruled the Soviet Union until his death in 1953. Stalin conducted ruthless purges of his enemies, real and perceived, instituted ambitious plans to transform the Soviet Union from an agrarian to industrial economy, and led the country through the Second World War.

Russian dictator Joseph Stalin (1878–1953) ca. 1935.

These decades were an equally turbulent time for the arts. Although there was an initial flourishing of several avant-garde movements, the state began to restrict artistic expression. In music, the young Prokofiev composed several steely, modernist scores, including a ballet for Diaghilev's *Ballets Russes* intended to depict the modern industrialization of the Soviet Union. But when Prokofiev returned for good to his homeland in 1936, he found that the climate in the arts had changed. Two years before, Stalin had decreed that Soviet art must adhere to the ideals of *socialist realism*, meaning that it had to depict and glorify everyday scenes of the people, and promote the aims of the state. A composers' union was established to set further policies for Soviet music. Any composition deemed too complex, modernist, or abstract was denounced as bourgeois, decadent, and Western. Tuneful melodies, clear harmonies, and subjects that were little more than propaganda for the Soviet state were now required. More than once Prokofiev's music was rejected or censored as too Western and anti-Soviet, and in 1948 he had to write a public letter disavowing his earlier works.

PROKOFIEV, SYMPHONY NO. 1 IN D MAJOR ("CLASSICAL") (1917)

Prokofiev scored his Symphony No. 1 for a classical orchestra, with double woodwinds, two horns, two trumpets, timpani, and strings. The symphony is in four movements and has key signatures. The first movement (see **Listening Map 60**) is in sonata form as is the fourth. The second, slow movement is in *ABA* form; and the third, curiously, offers a Baroque dance known as a gavotte instead of a minuet.

Prokofiev begins with a rousing triadic ascent in D major, a stock figure used by Haydn and other Classical symphonists (*a*; ①). The scurrying first theme that follows is played by the strings. A flute then introduces the bridge subject (*b*; ②), which begins to modulate from the tonic to the dominant key. Following the Classical tradition, the contrasting second theme (*c*; ③) enters in the dominant key.

Prokofiev places the second theme in the high register of the violins, with a simple staccato accompaniment in the bassoon. Distinctly modern departures from Haydn's style are the gaping leaps in the melody and the "incorrect" harmonies of the accompaniment, a humorous parody of the Classical style. Prokofiev sustains this infectious melody and its jolting leaps through three statements. For the closing section of the exposition, he takes up the opening material and ends with sweeping descending scales and a strong cadence on the dominant. Again departing from Haydn's practice, he does not repeat the exposition.

A bar of rest allows us to catch our breath before the development begins. First, we hear *a* in the minor tonic and then *b* in a range of different keys. Next, the composer energetically exchanges *c* between the violins and the bass. Finally, the music approaches what promises to be the recapitulation. Prokofiev does indeed bring back the opening material, but in the wrong key. This deliberate "error" is a device known as a **false recapitulation**. As Prokofiev knew, Haydn himself had sometimes used it in his symphonies to confuse his unsuspecting listeners. After returning the music to the real tonic, Prokofiev continues the recapitulation according to the traditional plan. The result is a witty rediscovery of classical sonata form, filtered through a twentieth-century Russian's sensibility.

Stravinsky and Neoclassicism

From the end of the First World War to about 1950, Igor Stravinsky explored neoclassicism in a brilliant series of compositions that substituted intimate chamber ensembles for the enormous orchestra of his *Rite of Spring.* This economy of resources is particularly evident in *The Soldier's Tale* (*L'histoire du soldat*, 1918), a "dramatic spectacle" that is performed by a narrator, small group of instruments, and actors and a dancer.

Stravinsky's other neoclassical works borrowed largely from eighteenth-century models. The Dumbarton Oaks Concerto for chamber orchestra (1938) was inspired by Bach's Brandenburg Concertos, and thus is neo-Baroque in spirit. The Symphony in C (1940) was indebted to the symphonies of Haydn, whom Stravinsky revered as a "celestial power." Still other neoclassical works turned to classical mythology and antiquity. Among them were the ballet *Orpheus* (1948) and the opera-oratorio *Oedipus Rex* (1927), for which Stravinsky directed that the soloists appear on pedestals, to suggest the timelessness of Greek statues.

STRAVINSKY, *SYMPHONY OF PSALMS* (1930)

After the First World War, Stravinsky worked primarily in France and in 1934 became a French citizen. But new commissions led to American engagements. One was an invitation to write a work for the fiftieth anniversary of the Boston Symphony

LISTENING MAP 60

PROKOFIEV, "Classical" Symphony, First Movement {1917}

FORM	Sonata form
METER	$\frac{2}{2}$, Allegro
SCORING	Orchestra (two flutes, two oboes, two clarinets, two bassoons, two trumpets, two horns, timpani, and strings)
OVERVIEW	Prokofiev produced an entertaining movement that adheres fairly closely to Classical sonata form, with an exposition based on two contrasting themes in the tonic and dominant, a development, and a recapitulation. Nevertheless, occasional licenses in the harmonies and wide leaps in the melodic lines betray the twentieth-century features of the music, resulting in an engaging example of neoclassicism.

why to LISTEN

There are two principal reasons to listen to Prokofiev's "Classical" Symphony. One is its playful sense of time travel, as a twentieth-century composer tries to revive elements of the eighteenth-century Classical style. A second reason is the cross-cultural perspective of a Russian composer imitating and wittily parodying an Austro-Germanic style of writing. (Recall that Haydn's music was also filled with wit and humor.) As you listen to the symphony, can you identify which features sound like Haydn and which sound like Prokofiev? Does the viewpoint of a twentieth-century modernist Russian composer add to our enjoyment of Haydn's music? And, in turn, does Haydn's style put in bolder relief modernisms in Prokofiev's score? As a neoclassical work, Prokofiev's symphony is intended to square tradition with innovation—to remind listeners of the grand history of the genre as well as to suggest, perhaps, where the genre might still lead.

first LISTEN

EXPOSITION	DEVELOPMENT	RECAPITULATION
0:00	**1:46**	**2:53**
Statement of first theme (*a*), bridge (*b*), and second theme (*c*)	(*a*), (*b*), and (*c*) developed	Opens with "false" recapitulation of (*a*) (in the "wrong" key), but then returns to the tonic to complete the piece

a deeper LISTEN

TIME	SECTION	LISTEN FOR THIS
0:00	Exposition	① Rousing, ***ff*** ascent leading to **first theme** in the tonic (*a*) in the strings Allegro *rising triadic figure*
0:23		② **Bridge subject** in the flute (*b*)
0:57		③ Quiet **second theme** in the dominant (*c*) with gaping leaps in the violins, supported by bassoon *pp elegantly*
1:31		Rousing **closing section** in the dominant
1:44		One bar of rest
1:46	Development	(*a*) in the minor
1:57		(*b*) led through a variety of keys
2:15		(*c*) exchanged between the violins and bass
2:53	Recapitulation	First theme (*a*) appears in the "wrong key" (false recapitulation)
3:03		Bridge (*b*)
3:27		Second theme (*c*) in correct, tonic key
3:54		Rousing closing section in the tonic

in 1930. The result was Stravinsky's *Symphony of Psalms* in three movements, settings of verses from three psalms for chorus and orchestra. The orchestra consists of woodwind and brass sections, percussion (including harp and two pianos), and a reduced string section of cellos and double basses. Absent are the lush, Romantic sounds of violins and violas and the mellow colors of clarinets; instead, Stravinsky features the clear sonorities of the woodwind and brass. The psalm texts are stated in a way that recalls medieval chant (see Chapter 8). They are accompanied by compact, repeated orchestral figures. The work as a whole is intended as an impersonal, collective offering to God.

For the three movements (performed without a break) Stravinsky selected verses from Psalms 39, 40, and 150. The second movement ("I waited patiently for the Lord"), is a testament of faith based upon the opening three verses of Psalm 40 (see **Listening Map 61**). It is the most complex of the three parts.

The movement is designed as a fugue, more precisely a special kind of fugue known as a **double fugue**, because it has two fugal subjects instead of one. Stravinsky begins with the oboes and flutes, which introduce the first fugal subject (*a*; ①) in four alternating entries. Based on a compact motive of four notes, the subject is reinvented rhythmically through various repetitions. It then continues to sketch a descending angular line.

Next, the chorus enters performing the second fugal subject (*b*; ②), while portions of the first subject appear in the orchestra. The new subject begins with a descending skip followed by stepwise motion, but then leaps up on the word "Dominum" ("Lord"), written in the score in capital letters. Eventually, Stravinsky presents the second subject in tightly overlapping entries (stretto); then, he has the orchestra revive the first fugal subject. In the closing measures, he combines the two subjects, but brings the chorus to a soft, unison cadence on the same pitch. The symbolism is clear: the music charts a course from the depths of the "horrible pit" to the "new song" of praise, and of absolute trust in the Lord.

In 1939, not long after the outbreak of the Second World War, Stravinsky left France for the United States and would become an American citizen in 1945. As an international musical celebrity, he was well received, and eventually settled in Hollywood. He was invited to Harvard, where he delivered a series of lectures (in French) on music. They were published in English as his *Poetics of Music* (for an excerpt, see Making Connections on p. 461). But when he made an arrangement of "The Star Spangled Banner," the authorities found that his retouching of the standard harmonies violated a statute prohibiting changes to the anthem, and the composer was let go with a warning.

More troublesome was his relationship with Walt Disney, who paid him $5,000 for the rights to use *The Rite of Spring* in the animated film *Fantasia* (1940). Stravinsky had little say about the payment. Russia had not signed an international copyright convention, so Disney could use the music whether compensating the composer or not. But what made the relationship more strained was Disney's particular treatment of Stravinsky's score. Music meant for a ballet about spring rituals of pagan Russian tribes was now used in animated scenes showing the evolution of the earth and the appearance of dinosaurs, a linkage that Stravinsky found utterly "imbecilic."

STRAVINSKY, *Symphony of Psalms*, Second Movement (Psalm 40: 1–3)

{1930}

FORM	Fugue, using two subjects
METER	$\frac{4}{8}$
SCORING	Orchestra (one piccolo, four flutes, four oboes, one English horn, three bassoons, one contrabassoon, four French horns, one soprano trumpet, four trumpets, three trombones, one tuba, and strings) and chorus (sopranos, altos, tenors and basses)
OVERVIEW	Stravinsky designed the movement as a double fugue, with the first fugal subject being introduced by the orchestra, before the chorus takes up the second subject. Then in the closing section, the two subjects are juxtaposed and combined.

why to LISTEN

Symphony of Psalms is a masterpiece that explores the spiritual dimensions of music. Stravinsky himself was baptized in the Russian Orthodox faith, and he seems to have taken his faith quite seriously. He commented that in the *Symphony of Psalms* he intended not to write a symphony about the singing of psalms, but rather to bring the singing of psalms into the symphonic concert hall. That meant reducing references to late nineteenth-century music—the time period that gave rise to the Boston Symphony Orchestra in 1880—and finding inspiration instead in other historical periods. In the case of the second movement, Stravinsky turned to the austere world of fugal counterpoint. This was perhaps a nod to the Baroque complexities of J. S. Bach, but also an acknowledgment of the centuries-old tradition of imitative polyphony stretching back to the Renaissance. Elsewhere in the work the choral writing is often chant-like, focusing on simple pitch repetitions or formulaic patterns that invoke a medieval sound world. There is, too, a ritualistic quality to this music, which invites us to participate anonymously in a communal statement of faith in God.

first LISTEN

SUBJECT 1	SUBJECT 2	SUBJECT 2	SUBJECT 1	BAR OF REST	SUBJECTS 1 AND 2	END
0:00	1:58	3:41	4:26	5:04	5:06	6:25
In orchestra	Chorus; subject 1 referenced by orchestra	Chorus; subject 2 in S, A, T, B, then in stretto (overlapping parts)	Briefly returns in orchestra; pause		Subject 1 in orchestra; subject 2 in chorus	Unison cadence in chorus

Continued

a deeper **LISTEN**

TIME	PART/ DESCRIPTION	LISTEN FOR THIS	TEXT	TRANSLATION
0:00	Subject 1	(1) Orchestra, beginning with four entries in oboe, flute, flute, and oboe (*mf*) Oboe *mf* C E♭ B♮ D C E♭ B♮ D C E♭ B♮ D C E♭ B♮ D		
1:58	Subject 2	(2) Chorus, beginning with four entries in soprano, alto, tenor, and bass; references to subject 1 in orchestra (*mf*) Soprano *mf tranquil* Ex - pec - tans ex - pec - ta - vi DO - MI - NUM,—	1. *Expectans expectavi Dominum;* *et intendit mihi,* *et exaudivit preces meas.*	1. I waited patiently for the Lord; and he inclined unto me, and heard my cry.
			2. *Et eduxit me de lacu miseriae,* *et de luto faecis,*	2. He brought me up also out of a horrible pit, out of the miry clay,
3:41	Subject 2	Chorus in stretto (tight, overlapping entries in soprano, alto, tenor, and bass) (*p*)	*et statuit super petram pedes meos: et* *direxit gressus meos.*	and set my feet upon a rock, and established my goings.
4:26	Subject 1	Orchestra in stretto (*p*)		
5:04	Bar of rest			
5:06	Subjects 1 and 2	Subject 1 in orchestra, subject 2 in chorus (*ff*)	3. *Et immist in os meum canticum novum,* *carmen Deo nostro:* *Videbunt multi, videbunt et timebunt: et* *sperabunt in Domino.*	3. And he hath put a new song in my mouth, even praise unto our God: many shall see it, and fear: and shall trust in the Lord.
6:25	End	Unison cadence in chorus (*p*)		

MAKING CONNECTIONS *Stravinsky as Lecturer*

In 1940 Stravinsky gave a series of lectures at Harvard University, later published as *The Poetics of Music*, on various musical topics, including the phenomenon of music, the acts of composition and performance, and the status of music in the Soviet Union. Reading between the lines of these lectures, Stravinsky's core beliefs about music come through: music is a self-sufficient art that stands on its own. It didn't need to imitate the external world or express ideas, let alone be confined to political propaganda, as it was in his homeland, Russia.

The closing lines of Stravinsky's last lecture offers a grand vision of what music could be:

"Music," says the Chinese sage Seu-ma-tsen in his memoirs, "is what unifies." This bond of unity is never achieved without searching and hardship. But the need to create music must clear away all obstacles. . . . For the unity of the work has a resonance all its own. Its echo, caught by our soul, sounds nearer and nearer. Thus the consummated work spreads abroad to be communicated and finally flows back toward its source. The cycle, then, is closed. And that is how music comes to reveal itself as a form of communion with our fellow man—and with the Supreme Being.

Béla Bartók

Dashboard

Read about and listen to Bartók's Bagatelle Op. 6.

The Hungarian composer Béla Bartók (1881–1945) combined a neoclassical approach with a long-running interest in the folk music of his country. Trained as a concert pianist, he was deeply influenced by the music of Liszt. Still, realizing that Liszt's virtuoso style had little to do with authentic Hungarian folk music, Bartók set out to research that music for himself. He traveled extensively through rural Hungary recording folk melodies on an Edison phonograph, and transcribing them into musical notation. Nor did he stop there; he also gathered Slovakian, Rumanian, and Turkish folk melodies, some six thousand in all, before visiting Algeria in Northern Africa and adding another 200 more pieces to his collection. The use of modes, **microtones** (intervals smaller than a half-step), and asymmetrical rhythms in this folk music provided inspiration for many of Bartók's own compositions.

For many years, Bartók taught piano at the Budapest Royal Academy of Music, where he continued to compose and to research folk music. During the 1930s, alarmed by the rise of fascism in Germany and Italy, he sent his music to England to be published, and in 1940 he emigrated to the United States, becoming, like Stravinsky, an American citizen in 1945. In poor health, Bartók struggled to earn his livelihood through giving concerts. He was awarded a research appointment at Columbia University, and began work on a collection of Yugoslav folk music. When he died in 1945, he left several planned compositions unrealized.

Bartók's principal contribution was in instrumental music. He wrote three concertos for piano and one each for violin and viola. Of the piano concertos, the first (1926) features dissonant clusters of chromatic pitches in irregular rhythmic groupings. The second (1931) contains an elaborate display of contrapuntal techniques. The third (1945), sketched in Asheville, North Carolina, is a contemplative work written in the last year of Bartók's life. One other concerto deserves special mention: the Concerto for Orchestra (1943) extends the idea of virtuoso display to the entire orchestra and has become a classic of the modern orchestral repertoire.

Bartók's instrumental music includes many compositions for piano solo, among them the *Allegro barbaro* (1911), filled with percussive rhythms that look ahead to the *Rite of Spring*; a Sonata for piano (1926); and *Mikrokosmos*, a six-volume collection of short pieces of increasing difficulty. His six string quartets (1908–1939) are among the finest quartets written in the twentieth century; no less successful are the Sonata for Two Pianos and Two Percussionists (1937) and the *Music for String Instruments, Percussion and Celesta* (1936; see Listening Map 62).

Bartók neither fully accepted Schoenberg's atonality nor fully rejected traditional tonality. Rather, his music celebrated the inflections of folk music and incorporated distinctly new approaches to the problem of tonal organization. In works still using triadic harmonies, Bartók typically supplemented the tonics and dominants of nineteenth-century music with his own harmonies. In works not based on triadic harmonies, he suggested tonal centers by repeating individual pitches or clusters of pitches. Despite his innovative approaches to harmony, however, the composer often relied on traditional forms for his compositions, as did other neoclassic composers.

BARTÓK, *MUSIC FOR STRING INSTRUMENTS, PERCUSSION AND CELESTA* (1936)

Bartók conceived this four-movement neoclassic work for a small-sized chamber orchestra. It consists of two five-part string groups complemented by drums, cymbals, timpani, harp, piano, celesta (a small keyboard instrument in which hammers strike metal plates to produce tinkling sounds), and xylophone (a percussion instrument with a series of wooden bars struck by wooden mallets). In his own seating arrangement for this ensemble, Bartók suggests positioning the strings on the two sides of the stage, with the double basses at the back and percussion between the two string groups.

Despite the unusual scoring—there are no woodwinds or brass—Bartók extracts a wealth of special effects. For example, the string players perform with and without mutes, produce high-pitched harmonics (see p. 4) by lightly touching and bowing the strings, and in one passage strike the strings with the wood of their bows (*col legno*). Finally, they occasionally use pizzicato, including a special type in which the strings are snapped sharply against the fingerboard to create striking percussive effects.

Bartók uses the percussion instruments sparingly in the first movement, introducing a few one at a time. Only in later movements do they appear in various combinations. One special effect is the glissando, or slide, heard at various times in the piano, harp, and timpani (where it yields a kind of hollow, thudding sound). From time to time, the delicate colors of the celesta provide a soft metallic backdrop to the orchestra.

Béla Bartók (1881–1945) recording folk songs during his travels in Romania.

Of the four movements, the first is a fugue, the second is in sonata form, and the third and fourth are rondos. **Listening Map 62** lays out the plan of the third movement, a symmetrical five-part rondo in the form *ABCBA*. Separating its parts are four repetitions of the fugal subject from the first movement. Further reinforcing the symmetry of the movement is an eerie xylophone solo that frames the movement. It plays the same rhythms forward and backward, so that, like the rondo form, it describes a **palindrome** (a sequence that occurs in the same order forward and backward).

Of the five main sections of the movement, section *A* is based on a mournful figure in the strings (*a*; ①). Probably inspired by Hungarian folk music, it features a snap-like rhythmic pattern. In section *B* (②), the celesta and two solo violins take up a new theme to the accompaniment of crisp piano chords, and string glissandos and clusters of trills. Section *C* features fragments of the fugal subject in the strings, performed *pianissimo* and with each pitch repeated rapidly. They are accompanied by rapid glissandos in the piano, harp, and celesta. The section works up to a climax for the full ensemble. Then, as the movement reverses itself, Bartók brings back the *B* and *A* sections, with the material restated and compressed. The movement ends as it began, with the solitary xylophone solo.

It would be difficult to mistake the innovative qualities of Bartók's score, or to ignore the provocative edges of his music. And yet, Bartók allied his highly individual, modernist bent with a concern for formal balance and proportion, and a fascination with musical symmetry, qualities that reveal his embrace of neoclassicism.

MAKING CONNECTIONS *Palindromes and Musical Symmetries*

We do not know the original purpose of *palindromes* (from the Greek for "running back again"), a sequences of things that occur in the same order forward and backward—for example, the letters in "Madam, I'm Adam." Are they entertaining curiosities or something more serious?

Many composers have been drawn to palindromes. The twelve-tone composer Anton von Webern (see p. 450) was so taken by a set of Latin palindromes called the "magic square" that he tried to set it to music. Webern was celebrated for being obsessed with musical symmetries and unity, but he was not alone. In the fourteenth century Guillaume de Machaut (see p. 82) composed a piece with a text that gave away its structure: "Ma fin est mon commencement" ("My end is my beginning"), in which the music literally reverses course midway. J. S. Bach indulged in similar musical palindromes. Mozart was credited with writing a piece that could be played by two violinists, with one musician reading the score upside-down and backward. Twentieth-century musicologist and composer Nicolas Slonimsky even wrote a piece called the "Mobius Striptease." The score itself was written on a mobius strip—a piece of paper twisted and attached to itself—representing an unending surface and thus a melody that repeats itself forever.

Another composer who was entranced with musical symmetries was the Hungarian Béla Bartók. His music gives the sense that the notes are carefully positioned in some overarching symmetry that governs the music. Bartók often favored the interval of the **tritone**, that is, the distance that divides the octave exactly in half, with six half steps on either side.

He also favored forms that were symmetrical, for example an *ABCBA* rondo form. And he occasionally used strict palindromes, as in the opening of the third movement of the *Music for Strings, Percussion and Celesta*, where the xylophone solo is a literal rhythmic palindrome, collapsing in a few seconds the large-scale plan of the entire movement.

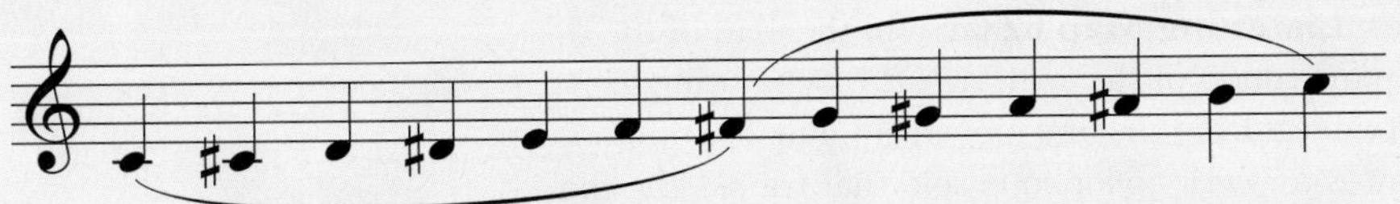

Division of the octave into two tritones.

check your KNOWLEDGE

1. Define neoclassicism. When and why did it develop? What was its relation to twentieth-century modernism?
2. How was Prokofiev's "Classical" Symphony representative of the neoclassicism movement? How did his approach differ from Stravinsky's?
3. Describe Stravinsky's *Symphony of Psalms*. Discuss its relation to the neoclassicism movement. Which unique features did Stravinsky incorporate in this work?
4. What was the influence of folk music on the music of Béla Bartók? How did this shape his approach to neoclassicism?

BARTÓK, *Music for String Instruments, Percussion and Celesta*, Third Movement

{1936}

FORM	Symmetrical five-part form, ABCBA
METER	$\frac{4}{4}$ (adagio)
SCORING	Chamber orchestra (timpani, xylophone, celesta, piano, harp, bass drum, tam-tam, and strings)
OVERVIEW	Bartók combines his preference for symmetrical forms and unity of purpose with music that simulates Hungarian folk music. In addition, the movement connects to the entire composition through its systematic recall of materials from the first movement.

why to LISTEN

Form and content in music are two ideas that we have encountered frequently. You might think that content usually wins out in the contest between the two. When you imagine a favorite piece of music, what are the impressions that first spring to mind? Probably not its form, but its content: a catchy melody or turn of phrase, for example, or some memorable harmonies. Bartók's *Music for Strings, Percussion and Celesta* certainly offers memorable content; attractive themes and rhythms abound that bring us close to the world of Hungarian folk music. But ordering the whole are symmetries of form that keep everything unified and in proportion. Form and content remain in a satisfying balance in this music, and remind us why we need both.

first LISTEN

Note xylophone solos open and close the work, at 0:00 and 7:08.

A	INTERLUDE	B	INTERLUDE	C	INTERLUDE	B	INTERLUDE	A
0:00	**2:04**	**2:13**	**3:28**	**3:36**	**5:19**	**5:31**	**6:22**	**6:41**
Xylophone solo followed by (*a*) theme	First phrase of fugal subject from first movement	(*b*) theme	Second phrase of fugal subject from first movement	(*c*) theme, dramatic crescendo and then diminuendo	Third phrase of fugal subject from first movement	(*b*) theme, slowing tempo	Fourth phrase of fugal subject from first movement	(*a*) theme

Continued

 *a deeper* **LISTEN**

TIME	SECTION	LISTEN FOR THIS
0:00	Xylophone solo (rhythmic palindrome)	Glissandos in timpani
0:28	A	① (*a*) in violas; strings, timpani *a* **Adagio** 3 ***p***
2:04	Interlude	Recall of fugue subject, first phrase, from first movement
2:13	B (gradually faster)	② (*b*) in celesta, two solo violins *b* ***mf*** *espr. (with expression)*
3:28	Interlude	Recall of fugue subject, second phrase, from first movement
3:36	C	Fragments of fugue subject, glissandos in celesta, harp, piano, powerful crescendo from ***pp*** to ***ff*** and diminuendo to ***pp***
5:19	Interlude	Recall of fugue subject, third phrase, from first movement
5:31	B (slower, resuming Adagio tempo)	(*b*) in strings, celesta
6:22	Interlude	Recall of fugue subject, fourth phrase, from first movement
6:41	A	(*a*) in strings, timpani
7:08	Xylophone solo (palindrome)	

National Styles

The eruption of nationalism in the nineteenth century led to the development of several new national musical styles, a process that continued into the twentieth century. You might think that national styles—based on the traditional folk music and folklore of particular ethnic regions—would be incompatible with the aims of modernism. But that was not necessarily the case. Several composers wrote music in national styles that impressed listeners as fresh and modern. The twentieth century also included a new flowering of English music and the striking case of Shostakovich in the Soviet Union.

During the twentieth century a cross section of composers working outside major European countries such as Germany, France, and Italy continued to explore and promote national styles. In Finland the music of Jean Sibelius (1865–1957) reflected the tide of nationalism that opposed Russian rule and secured his homeland's independence in 1917. So overtly patriotic was Sibelius's *Finlandia* for orchestra (1899) that initially it was banned by the Russian authorities. Sibelius also wrote programmatic tone poems based on the *Kalevala* saga, the Finnish national epic poem. His seven symphonies were generally dark and brooding in tone—again reflecting the national character—but firmly anchored in tonality. Following this

The Sibelius monument in Helsinki, Finland, aims to capture the essence of the composer's work.

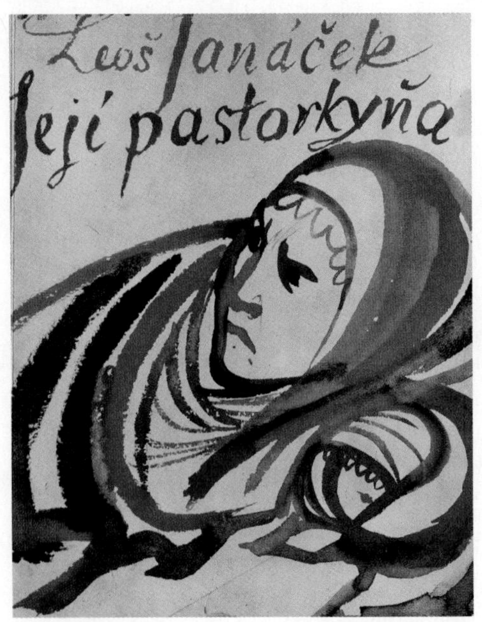

Cover of *Jenůfa*, 1904 opera by Leoš Janáček (1854–1928).

intense period of activity, around 1925 he withdrew from public life as Finland's most distinguished composer and entered a retirement of some thirty years.

In Czechoslovakia, newly formed as an independent country after the First World War, Dvořák was followed by Leoš Janáček (1854–1928), who was born in Moravia, the eastern district of the present Czech Republic. Janáček incorporated elements of Moravian folk music into a colorful style faithful to the accents of the Slavic dialect. His masterpiece was the Czech opera *Jenůfa* (1904), written in a realistic style, with melodies that approximated the irregular patterns of everyday speech.

The music of the Hungarian Béla Bartók, which exuded an uncompromising modernist spirit, also was deeply indebted to the folk music of his homeland. So important was traditional folk music to the composer that he formulated a three-point plan of how to use it in his own music:

1) By quoting melodies he had collected.
2) By composing new melodies that imitated folk music.
3) By writing in a freely modernist style that absorbed the flavor and idioms of folk music without citing or closely imitating them.

Dashboard

For one example of how Bartók reused a Slovakian melody, see the discussion of Bartók's Bagatelle.

Often joining Bartók in his research travels was his compatriot, Zoltán Kodály (1882–1967), whose opera, *Háry János* (1926) was inspired by Hungarian folk music. Kodály's art, Bartók declared, expressed the very spirit of their country.

Several composers in Latin countries also responded to nationalist sentiments. Manuel de Falla (1876–1946) wrote a number of popular works on Spanish subjects before the horrors of the Spanish Civil War (1936–1939) and victory of the dictator Francisco Franco led him to move to Argentina. The prolific Brazilian composer Heitor Villa-Lobos (1887–1959) employed popular Brazilian melodies and dances in extended series of works. And the Mexican Carlos Chávez (1899–1978) emerged in the 1920s after the Mexican revolution to produce colorful scores filled with materials drawn from his native culture, including ballets on Aztec subjects.

English Music

Since Henry Purcell in the seventeenth century, England had produced relatively few composers of international standing. Instead, foreign composers enjoyed the greatest success in the island country. In the eighteenth century, Handel, a German, established himself in England. In the nineteenth, Mendelssohn, also German, frequently visited London, where his music was especially popular during the long reign of Queen Victoria.

Dashboard

Read two opposing German and English views on English music.

By the early twentieth century, England was known abroad as the "land without music," although that assessment was soon being challenged. With Sir Edward Elgar (1867–1934), the English once again had a major native composer. Among Elgar's most successful scores were his *Enigma Variations* for orchestra (1899)—a lush, romantic work written as a tribute to his friends. Arguably Elgar's most famous composition was one of his *Pomp and Circumstance* marches, played at the annual London Prom Concerts, but used in the United States for graduation ceremonies. But for all Elgar's accomplishments, a modern English style in music emerged only in the next generations.

One of Edward Elgar's *Pomp and Circumstance* marches is traditionally played at U.S. graduation ceremonies.

The leader of England's musical renaissance was a great-nephew of Charles Darwin, Ralph Vaughan Williams (1872–1958). He unapologetically found his inspiration in English folk music and hymns, and in the English music of the sixteenth and early seventeenth centuries. Vaughan Williams wrote an impressive series of nine symphonies, other orchestral and chamber works, film music, and a wealth of vocal music. An avid collector of English folk songs and hymns, he prepared a new English hymnal in 1906. Vaughan Williams himself contributed several original hymns that became staples of Protestant worship, including "For All the Saints," still in widespread use today.

Even when Vaughan Williams did not cite actual folk melodies, his music betrays an affinity for traditional English music. Vaughan Williams had no qualms about appearing to be unoriginal. What mattered was to make an authentic statement, even if that meant reusing or borrowing from existing material. In his hymn editions and his own music, he did much to preserve native English music, much as Bartók did for native Hungarian music.

Vaughan Williams was less adventurous than Bartók, however, in his approach to tonality, and he never adopted Schoenberg's atonal methods. For him, the traditional tonal triad remained the basis of harmony, even though he often flavored his use of major and minor keys with modal melodies and harmonies. Moreover, Vaughan Williams was an enthusiastic practitioner of counterpoint, which he avidly studied in English Renaissance polyphony. His style owed a debt to this and other forms of early English music.

VAUGHAN WILLIAMS, *FANTASIA ON A THEME BY THOMAS TALLIS* (1910)

Ralph Vaughan Williams (1872–1958).

For the *Fantasia*, Vaughan Williams chose a modal theme from a psalm setting by Thomas Tallis (ca. 1505–1585), one of the leading composers of sacred music in Tudor England. The *Fantasia* is scored for a string orchestra organized in three groups, which sometimes play together, sometimes alternate, and sometimes play separately. The first group (Orchestra I) is divided into six parts, with several players per part. The second group (Orchestra II) is divided into five parts, with only one or two players per part. Smallest and most intimate of all is the third group, a string quartet with four soloists. This unusual organization makes possible a broad range of expression, from the subtle nuances of solo lines and small ensembles to the full-bodied, majestic sound of the entire orchestra.

The Tallis theme describes a long arc, gently rising and falling to end on its opening pitch. Occasionally, the basic $\frac{3}{4}$ meter of the old theme shifts to a lilting $\frac{6}{8}$, disrupting the regular beat and giving the melody a spontaneous flow.

The *Fantasia* opens with the entire ensemble playing *pianissimo* chords (see **Listening Map 63**). Against a sustained high pitch in the violins, the lower strings pluck out the opening motive of the melody (①). Then we hear a series of triads moving in strict parallel motion, giving this section an exotic, modal sound. When the melody enters, the cellos first present it *piano*, answered by the violins *forte*. A transition follows, in which the two orchestras exchange material back and forth. Orchestra I uses a broad dynamic range; Orchestra II plays with mutes applied, producing, an eerie, distant echo.

The central portion of the work shifts to a slightly faster tempo, announced by a graceful viola solo drawn from the Tallis theme but now freely elaborated in the manner of a fantasy (②). Against the backdrop of the two orchestras, the viola yields to a solo violin, and then the solo string quartet engages in free counterpoint. The three groups come together as the music reaches a climax in this free, quasi-development section.

A tempo change to *molto adagio* prepares for the return of the opening. A solo violin accompanied by a solo viola plays the Tallis theme with softly trembling chords from the two orchestras in the background. In the closing measures, the solo violin climbs to its high register, and the orchestra concludes with a swell in volume followed by a diminuendo to a barely audible ***pppp*** on a major chord.

Of the next generation of English composers, Benjamin Britten (1913–1976) emerged as the most influential. He came of age musically during the Second World War. Possessed of enormous musical talent, Britten was already composing impressive works while still in his early twenties. After studying at the Royal College of Music, he wrote music for documentary films in collaboration with the poet W. H. Auden. Britten traveled to the United States in 1939, only to return to England at the outbreak of hostilities, and to defend his status as a conscientious objector. In 1948 he founded a music festival in the small town of Aldeburgh, where many of his compositions were premiered. Like Vaughan Williams, Britten never abandoned tonality, although he supplemented his use of triads with layers of dissonant sonorities. See Part I for a discussion of Britten's *The Young Person's Guide to the Orchestra* (p. 40).

Benjamin Britten (1913–1976).

Britten was comfortable composing in many genres, but his lasting achievements were in opera—specifically, in revitalizing English opera. His choice of libretti favored English and American literature. His first success, *Peter Grimes* (1945), was inspired by the eighteenth-century poetry of George Crabbe, from Britten's native Suffolk. *Billy Budd* (1951) was based on Melville's short novel about man's inhumanity to man. *The Turn of the Screw* (1954) was drawn from a ghost story by Henry James, while *Death in Venice* (1973) was based on a novella by the German novelist Thomas Mann.

Throughout his career, Britten's music showed a strong musical logic and impressive craftsmanship. Although some modernists found his reaffirmation of tonal principles too conservative, Britten demonstrated the viability of English opera as an art form in the twentieth century.

LISTENING MAP 63

VAUGHAN WILLIAMS, *Fantasia on a Theme by Thomas Tallis* {1910}

FORM	Introduction, presentation of the theme by Thomas Tallis, followed by a free fantasy on that theme
METER	Principally $\frac{3}{4}$ and $\frac{6}{8}$, largo sostenuto
SCORING	Two string orchestras in six and five parts and one string quartet for four soloists
OVERVIEW	The piece is based on a theme by the Tudor composer Thomas Tallis, first heard near the beginning in the cellos. The main portion of the work then devolves into a fantasy on this theme, in which the solo instruments of a string quartet emerge, accompanied by different combinations of the two string orchestras, before the theme reappears in the final section.

why to LISTEN

There is much to admire in Vaughan Williams's composition. There is the flexible way in which he introduces and develops Tallis's melody, and his gradual buildup of archaic-sounding harmonies in the orchestra. The use of different string forces, too, ranging from a full orchestra to a string quartet, creates fascinating echo effects that pull the listener in. At times the music softly glows with an almost unearthly sheen as this twentieth-century composer brings us back centuries to the Tudor age. But above all, this is heartfelt music that established an authentic English musical voice and made it relevant for modernity.

first LISTEN

INTRODUCTION	TRANSITION	CENTRAL SECTION	TRANSITION	THEME (RETURN)
0:00	**3:56**	**6:18**	**11:08**	**12:07**
Entire ensemble; statement of theme	Two orchestras exchange parts	Improvisation on theme by viola, violin, and string quartet	Tempo changes to *molto agitato*	Theme returns stated by solo violin accompanied by orchestral chords

Continued

a deeper **LISTEN**

TIME	SECTION	LISTEN FOR THIS
0:00	**Introduction: Largo**	(1) Full ensemble, chords, pizzicato foreshadowing of Tallis theme (***pp***) Cellos (***p***); violins (***f***) **Largo sostenuto** ***mp***
3:56	**Transition**	Orchestra I versus Orchestra II (muted)
6:18	**Central section: More animated**	(2) Free fantasy on Tallis theme; viola solo, then violin solo, string quartet **Poco più animato (A little more animated)** ***p*** *Viola*
8:30		Gradual addition of forces: Orchestra I, Orchestra II, and string quartet
11:08	**Transition: Molto adagio**	Chords, pizzicato
12:07	**Theme**	Solo violin and viola, accompanied by Orchestras I and II, ***p***, ***ff*** diminuendo to ***pppp***

Dmitri Shostakovich and Russian Music

Throughout much of the twentieth century, tonality remained firmly entrenched in the Soviet Union as well. State policy discouraged composers from experimenting with Western modernism (see Chapter 41). Unlike Stravinsky and Prokofiev, who both spent large parts of their careers in the West, Dmitri Shostakovich (1906–1975) matured as a composer in Russia during the 1920s, just as Stalin seized control of the Soviet Union. Even more than Prokofiev, Shostakovich was directly affected by the rise of socialist realism. His career was shaped by the competing pressures of his own need to write music and state censorship.

Dmitri Shostakovich (1906–1975). This portrait was painted by Nadia Khodasevich (Grabowski) Léger, a Russian artist who relocated to Paris.

Shostakovich attended the conservatory in Petrograd (formerly St. Petersburg). His graduation exercise, the First Symphony (1925), was especially well received as the work of a promising young symphonist. It premiered shortly before Joseph Stalin seized power.

As Stalin transformed Russia into a modern totalitarian state, Shostakovich responded by composing his share of music promoting the communist revolution. He wrote symphonies to commemorate the tenth anniversary of the Bolshevik Revolution and the international day celebrated by socialist workers. But then he tried his hand at opera, and premiered *Lady Macbeth of the Mtsensk District* (1934), a sordid tale of nineteenth-century bourgeois life under the tsars. For two years, the opera played in Moscow to acclaim. But after Stalin attended a performance, he had it denounced for its modernist touches—it was dismissed in the state newspaper *Pravda* as "muddle instead of music." The thirty-year-old composer withdrew both the opera and his Fourth Symphony, just placed in rehearsal, in effect turning his back on his creative identity. He lived in mortal fear of being arrested, sent to a Siberian *gulag* (work camp), or worse.

Against all odds—the composer lost several friends and colleagues who were arbitrarily imprisoned or executed—Shostakovich won rehabilitation with his Fifth Symphony (1937). He offered it, as he wrote, in response to the "justified criticism" of his earlier work. The symphony was received as a masterpiece, both in Russia and the West. Cast in a popular style that authorities could tolerate, it featured two weighty outer movements in sonata form, and two contrasting inner movements—a caricature-like scherzo, and a deeply felt, emotionally moving, slow movement. (During the premiere, members of the audience sobbed, then usually a punishable offense in the Soviet Union.) The victorious ending of the symphony was initially taken as a celebration of the human spirit. However, more recent commentators have suggested that beneath the score's surface lay a darker, critical tone, and that the composer actually used his music to protest life in Stalinist Russia. The work's second movement—which seems at times to be wry, farcical, and grotesque—supports this theory.

SHOSTAKOVICH, FIFTH SYMPHONY, SECOND MOVEMENT (1937)

The Symphony's second movement follows the traditional form of a scherzo (see **Listening Map 64**), *ABA*, with *B* representing a contrasting Trio section. The listener follows a parade of themes, now ponderous, now shrill, pompous, and even naïve. It's as if the music turns the symphony on its head, to caricature like a spoof the serious themes of the other movements. In the *A* section, we hear the following in succession:

- A lumbering figure in the low strings (*a*; ①)
- A shrill theme in the winds (*b*; ②)
- A jaunty theme in the winds (*c*; ③)
- A boisterous eruption from the horns (*d*; ④)

In contrast, the Trio (*B*) features a new, simple melody played by a solo violin and then flute (*e*; ⑤), accompanied by "incorrect" harmonies. After the return of *A*, near the end of the movement, Shostakovich briefly flirts with the Trio theme, but it is then cut short by the boisterous ending.

Shostakovich was not the first symphonist to use caricature (one of his models was Gustav Mahler). But we sense in his music a deep tension between his individual voice as an artist and the goals of Stalin's Soviet Union. The Soviet government sought to exploit nationalism in the arts to serve their aims. This often meant stifling artistic creativity in the name of creating "accessible" works. In many of his symphonies, the composer served the state well. The popular Seventh Symphony ("Leningrad," 1941) was written during the horrific German siege of Leningrad during the Second World War. (Shostakovich served as a fire warden during that ordeal.) It was clearly written to celebrate the Russian nation's resilience in the face of these brutal attacks. But only a few years later, in 1948, the authorities again censored Shostakovich for yielding to "formalism"—that is, for subordinating the content of his music to abstract designs coming from the West. Once again, Shostakovich responded by turning to an accessible style.

In his last years, the composer's music grew increasingly somber and contemplative. We can only speculate about what course his music might have taken had he enjoyed the full artistic freedom of the West.

check your **KNOWLEDGE**

1. What is a "national" style? Which composers wrote in this style, and how did their works exemplify it?
2. Which sources did Ralph Vaughan Williams turn to in his pursuit of a modern English musical style?
3. What were Benjamin Britten's contributions to English music?
4. How did Dmitri Shostakovich test and respond to the Soviet policy of socialist realism?

LISTENING MAP 64

SHOSTAKOVICH, Fifth Symphony, Second Movement {1937}

FORM	Scherzo, ABA form
METER	$\frac{3}{4}$, Allegretto
SCORING	Orchestra (one piccolo, two flutes, two oboes, one piccolo clarinet, two clarinets, two bassoons, one contrabassoon, four French horns, three trumpets, three trombones, one tuba, timpani, cymbals, bass drum, two harps, and strings)
OVERVIEW	The form is a simple ABA, typical of scherzos, in which the A section is loaded with a parade of different themes, while the B section uses one simple theme.

why to LISTEN

We take it for granted that a composer completely controls the music he or she chooses to write. But what if the composer were alive in the Soviet Union during the repressive rule of Joseph Stalin? What choices did the composer have, and how did the composer find a voice? Totalitarian regimes can be ruthless in sacrificing individual expression for the supposed collective good of the state. For Shostakovich, whenever he composed a piece that pushed the boundaries of socialist realism—acts that brought condemnation (and nearly worse)—he had to "rehabilitate" himself by writing music in a more accessible style that toed the party line.

How is it that the Fifth Symphony heard in the Soviet Union during one of Stalin's purges as an act of repentance could eventually be heard elsewhere as a masterpiece that could stand on its own? The answer probably has to do with music's awesome power to communicate multiple levels of meaning: in this case, an official, party-sanctioned message on the surface, veiling but not obscuring deeper levels of individual expression and yearning for freedom. The complexity of Shostakovich's intentions encourages us to listen.

first LISTEN

A	B (TRIO)	A
0:00	**1:40**	**3:13**
A succession of themes (*a–d*) stated by various instruments	(*e*) theme by violin, then flute, accompanied by "incorrect" harmonies	Return to opening themes, with the last theme (*e*) abruptly cut off by a surprise ending

Continued

a deeper LISTEN

TIME	SECTION	LISTEN FOR THIS
0:00	A	① (*a*): lumbering theme in low strings 
0:14		② (*b*): shrill theme in woodwinds 
0:51		③ (*c*): jaunty theme in winds 
1:03		④ (*d*): ***ff*** outburst in brass 
1:40	B (Trio)	⑤ (*e*): simple tune in solo violin, then solo flute, accompanied by "incorrect" harmonies 
2:26		Outburst from orchestra
3:13–3:23	A	(*a*) in bassoon (*b*) in pizzicato strings
4:03		(*c*) in woodwinds
4:16		(*d*) in brass
4:25		(*c*)
4:38		(*d*)
4:52		Hint of (*e*) in oboe, interrupted by final cadence

CHAPTER 45
American Music: Beginnings to Aaron Copland

Starting late in the nineteenth century, some prominent composers began visiting the United States—Tchaikovsky, Dvořák, and Prokofiev, for example—followed by three who emigrated and became American citizens: Schoenberg, Stravinsky, and Bartók. But what were the main currents of American music before they arrived, and how did these currents develop? In the 1890s, Dvořák had raised an important question: what was an "American" musical style? During much of the twentieth century, the United States would wrestle with the answer. This history actually begins before the start of the century, and includes the emergence of several prominent composers of art music. It also includes the American phenomenon of jazz (see Chapter 46), along with film music, musical theater, rock, and other forms of popular music (see Chapter 47).

Through much of its history, American music has maintained ties to the European classical tradition, even while celebrating its independence from that tradition. Arguably the defining feature of American music has been its sheer diversity, as it has tapped the rich continuum connecting classical and popular music.

The English settlers who colonized America during the seventeenth and eighteenth centuries brought music, mostly sacred, from their homeland. The first book published in America, the *Bay Psalm Book* of 1640, was a translation of the psalms for singing during worship. There were few well-trained musicians among the early colonists, but by 1698, the volume was being printed with musical notation for several tunes. In the eighteenth century, reform-minded ministers set up singing schools to promote musical literacy. They devised new methods of notation, including **shape-note notation**, in which differently shaped notes—triangles, squares, and so on—represented specific pitches. By learning the shapes, choir members could sing the hymns correctly without having to read standard notation. By the early nineteenth century,

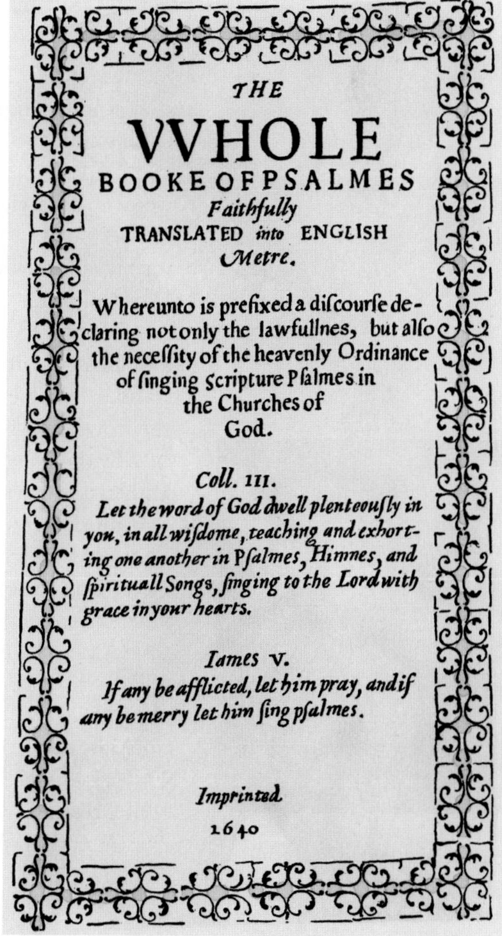

THE
VVHOLE
BOOKE OF PSALMES
Faithfully
TRANSLATED into ENGLISH
Metre.

Whereunto is prefixed a diſcourſe declaring not only the lawfullnes, but alſo the neceſſity of the heavenly Ordinance of ſinging Scripture Pſalmes in the Churches of God.

Coll. III.
Let the word of God dwell plenteouſly in you, in all wiſdome, teaching and exhorting one another in Pſalmes, Himnes, and ſpirituall Songs, ſinging to the Lord with grace in your hearts.

Iames V.
If any be afflicted, let him pray, and if any be merry let him ſing pſalmes.

Imprinted
1640

The first book published in the American colonies was the *Bay Psalm Book* of 1640, a translation of church songs.

A page from *Southern Harmony*, 1854, in shape-note notation.

shape-note singing had spread through rural areas and was well established throughout the country.

To European taste, American music was rough and unsophisticated. There were no American musical centers to rival the renowned musical institutions of Paris, Vienna, or London. One institution that developed a vibrant musical culture was the Moravian Church, which traced its origins to the mid-fifteenth century. Followers of the Czech martyr Jan Hus (ca. 1369–1415), the Moravians had been displaced by persecution. In the eighteenth century, they settled in America, and formed communities in Pennsylvania and North Carolina. Upholding rigorous standards of performance in their services, they performed European music and their own, newly composed works.

Stephen Foster (1826–1864).

By the nineteenth century, popular music of every description—including hymns, anthems, dances, marches ("Yankee Doodle Dandy" was one favorite), ballad operas, and music brought from Africa by slaves—was flourishing throughout the United States. At revivalist meetings, hymns and spirituals (American folk songs with religious texts) were the standard fare. Minstrel shows, which blended theater, music, and vaudeville—at first performed by whites in blackface—gained currency in the 1840s. One American composer who wrote for the minstrel shows was Stephen Foster (1826–1864), who produced the music and lyrics for some 150 songs. Among his most famous songs are "Oh! Susanna, Camptown Races," and "My Old Kentucky Home," sung annually at the Kentucky Derby. Besides the songs he wrote for minstrel performers, Foster is especially remembered for "Jeannie with the Light Brown Hair" and "Beautiful Dreamer," love songs that combine sentiment and nostalgia.

The Civil War established military bands as a familiar musical institution. During the war, bands were used to raise morale and rally the troops. After it ended, many soldier/musicians returned home to play in town bands. The most celebrated American bandmaster later in the century was John Philip Sousa (1854–1932), who directed the Marine Corps Band from 1880 to 1892, before leading his own band on international tours. Sousa composed well over 100 marches. "The Stars and Stripes Forever" of 1897 (see p. 54) remains his most famous composition.

Throughout the nineteenth century, the United States responded to European trends in arts and letters. Romanticism influenced the novels of James Fenimore Cooper, stories of Nathaniel Hawthorne and Edgar Allan Poe, and writings of the transcendentalists Emerson and Thoreau, who promoted a belief in nature and the power of the individual through self-reliance. Although no Romantic composer of the first rank emerged, one American musician did win international acclaim as a virtuoso. The pianist Louis Moreau Gottschalk (1829–1869) combined the spicy flavors of Creole and African-American music in his extravagant piano compositions. He performed in Europe, where his music drew praise from Berlioz and Chopin. Gottschalk gave his works evocative titles: for example, *The Banjo: An American Sketch*, in which the piano simulated the banjo's plucking techniques; *Bamboula*, subtitled *Dance of the Negroes*; and *The Union*, a piece of battle music dedicated to General George McClellan, President Lincoln's first choice to lead the Army of the Potomac against the Confederacy.

Louis Moreau Gottschalk (1829–1869).

Other Americans traveled abroad to study classical music at European conservatories. By the closing decades of the century, a group of New England composers was writing respectable orchestral and chamber music, much of it influenced by Brahms, Wagner, and Liszt. For a while the most successful American composer was Edward MacDowell (1860–1908), who used American-Indian melodies in his music yet was comfortable composing piano music in the grand manner of Liszt. Other distinguished Americans included Amy Beach (1867–1944), a child prodigy who was the first American woman to write a symphony, the "Gaelic" Symphony of 1896.

Dashboard

Read more about the American pianist Louis Moreau Gottschalk.

Amy Beach

Few American musicians were more gifted than Amy Cheney (Beach). She was humming melodies when she was just a one-year-old, beginning to compose piano pieces at the age of four, and playing Bach fugues when she was seven. She demonstrated perfect pitch early on, and experienced synesthesia, associating musical keys with colors. She came from a prominent New England family, and her parents could have sent her to Europe to study music. But the expectations of upper-class women at the time meant a career as a professional musician was out of the question for Amy Cheney. While she did study piano and composition with some local Boston musicians, she mostly taught herself.

In 1885 she married a Boston surgeon twenty-five years her senior. Though highly regarded as a pianist (she performed her own piano concerto with the Boston Symphony), she agreed to limit her public concerts to two a year, and to give any proceeds to charity. In exchange, her husband supported her career as a composer, and she produced hundreds of works, including songs, piano and chamber pieces, but also large-scale compositions. Most of her works were published with her authorship identified as Mrs. H. H. A. Beach. In the years leading up to the First World War, she toured Europe, where her music was well received. Beach never abandoned tonality, and typically employed lush triadic harmonies and washes of sound

Amy Beach (1867–1944).

reminiscent of Brahms and Liszt. In her later music, she did incorporate harmonies that were more daringly modern, suggesting the coming atonal world.

BEACH, ROMANCE FOR VIOLIN AND PIANO, OP. 23 (1893)

Beach's Romance falls into a three-part, *ABA′* form (**Listening Map 65**). After a brief piano introduction, the violin quietly introduces a romantic, yearning theme against a gently rocking accompaniment (①). The theme grows more impassioned as the violin part continues to climb, but then subsides and reaches a quiet cadence. The contrasting *B* section (②) has some dramatic moments, and its harmonies are now bathed in a chromatic language that takes Beach further and further from the tonic key of the beginning. In the final section, *A′*, the main theme returns in the low register of the violin, as the piano accompanies it with softly pulsating chords in its high register (③). The usual positions of the two instruments are thus reversed, until the violin once again climbs into its uppermost stretches, bringing this work to a tranquil close.

Charles Ives

Charles Ives (1874–1954).

Among the most innovative twentieth-century American modernists was Charles Ives (1874–1954), a stubborn musical nonconformist. For much of his life, Ives worked in isolation. After his death his genius was finally fully recognized, although historians are still assessing his achievement.

Ives's father was a Union bandmaster during the Civil War. He enjoyed experimenting with odd combinations of instruments and microtones (intervals smaller than a half step). In 1894, his son entered Yale, where he received musical instruction based on the European tradition. But when Ives was assigned to compose fugues, he wrote some in four different keys simultaneously in a brash display of polytonality. In other works, he interposed quotations from hymns and familiar tunes. He titled one chamber work "An Old Song Deranged," showing his unique sense of humor. In another short piano piece, "Song without (Good) Words," he poked fun at Mendelssohn's lyrical compositions.

Early on, Ives decided not to pursue a career in music. That was probably a wise decision, for few took his eccentric compositions seriously. Instead he sold life insurance and cofounded a profitable business. On evenings and weekends, however, he continued to compose. Toward the end of the First World War, he suffered a heart attack, the first of several; by 1920, he had more or less given up composition, except for writing songs. Ten years later, he retired from business.

Although most of Ives's music was composed between 1906 and 1916, very little was publicly performed before the late 1930s. Eventually, more of his work began to be performed publically, and his Third Symphony won the Pulitzer Prize in 1947. He shared half of the award money with the conductor of the symphony that premiered it, who was hospitalized and in need, suffering from schizophrenia.

LISTENING MAP 65

AMY BEACH, Romance for Violin and Piano, Op. 23 {1893}

FORM	ABA′
METER	$\frac{4}{4}$
SCORING	Violin and piano
OVERVIEW	A lyrical chamber piece written for the American violinist Maud Powell, Amy Beach's Romance is in a ternary ABA′ form, with the theme introduced in the A section, developed in the B section, and revisited and transformed in the A′ section.

why to LISTEN

For many years, the contributions of women to the history of music—as composers, performers, and patrons—were mostly overlooked. Beach's Romance for Violin and Piano is a piece that demands notice. It is particularly noteworthy, not only as the work of a female composer, but also for where it was performed and for whom it was written. The Romance was performed in 1893 at the Columbia World Exposition in Chicago. Like the "Exposition universelle" held in Paris just a few years earlier (see p. 436), the World Exposition was a showcase of new technological marvels, including electric lights, which illuminated the fair at night. Among the Exposition's displays was the Women's Building, which celebrated female contributions to American culture; Amy Beach performed several of her chamber works there, including the Romance. She wrote the piece for Maud Powell (1867–1920), the first American woman to have a distinguished international career as a concert violinist.

first LISTEN

BRIEF INTRODUCTION	A	B	A′
0:00	**0:16**	**1:31**	**3:29**
Piano	*A* theme stated by violin; repeated by violin and piano	*A* developed and explored through various keys	Return of *A* in tonic key, explored in different registers of the violin

Continued

 *a deeper* **LISTEN**

TIME	SECTION	LISTEN FOR THIS
0:00	Brief Introduction	In piano, ***pp***
0:16	A	① Theme stated quietly by violin
0:40		Theme repeated by violin and piano, and extended
1:21		Brief piano interlude
1:31	B	② *A* animated and led through a variety of keys, wider range of dynamics
3:29	A′	③ Return of main theme in the tonic in low register of violin, against soft high chords in piano
3:52		Theme repeated by violin and piano, shift to triplets in piano leading to a ***ff*** climax
4:38		A gradual diminuendo, ending with the violin in its high register

Although Ives subscribed to no particular style of composition, his music is decidedly modern. The question of when it was created has generated controversy. There is some evidence (which has been disputed) that the composer backdated his works to make them appear more pioneering than they actually were. Ives knew little of Schoenberg's music, yet he devised his own powerful atonal language. He used speech-like recitation that resembled Schoenberg's *Sprechstimme*, and employed sets of twelve pitches similar to tone rows. He also knew little of Bartók's music, yet he created chromatic clusters of pitches (to be played by the pianist's forearm, or even by a heavy wooden board depressed on the keys). Ives's music is a mixture of clashing rhythms, spiky harmonies, and scraps of familiar melodic bits and tunes, whether a Stephen Foster melody, a standard American hymn, or a short motive from Beethoven. The complex interplay of elements in Ives's music suggests the collage techniques of later American artists. Somehow, Ives makes all the elements come together into a unified work of art.

Ives pursued a philosophy of music that was as radical as his compositions. Above all, he wanted to extend the scope of music beyond the limits of "correct" sounds. He filled his scores with "wrong" notes and allusions to other music. He sought music that would transcend the ordinary and familiar. He demanded that music be strong and multifaceted and rejected what he labeled "arm-chair" music softened by "pretty little sounds" or "niceties." And he believed in the potential of American music. Spending one day in a Kansas wheat field, he claimed, was worth more than three years in Rome (a reference to the prestigious Prix de Rome, which had sent French composers, Berlioz and Debussy among them, to Rome for study).

Among Ives's works are four symphonies, band pieces, choral pieces, string quartets, violin and piano sonatas, and some 200 songs. One of his most significant creations is his second piano sonata, subtitled "Concord, Mass., 1840–60." Although finished in 1915, its premiere came only in 1939, on the eve of the Second World War. The title refers to the center of New England transcendentalism in the nineteenth century. Concord was the meeting ground of Emerson, Hawthorne, the Alcotts, and Thoreau, and the four movements of the sonata present their musical portraits.

Walden Pond (top) and the Alcotts' residence in Concord, Massachusetts, the meeting ground of nineteenth-century transcendentalist thinkers (bottom), who inspired Ives's second piano sonata (1939). Transcendentalism held that divinity pervades all nature and humanity.

IVES, *GENERAL WILLIAM BOOTH ENTERS INTO HEAVEN* (1914)

In 1914, after the outbreak of the First World War, Ives composed a setting of Vachel Lindsay's poem about the first director of the Salvation Army, William Booth (1829–1912). Booth was an English religious revivalist who dedicated his new organization to saving the down and out. The poem contains cues for musical instruments: bass drums to accompany the procession of Booth's tattered followers, trumpets for militant fanfares, and banjos played by "big-voiced lassies."

Ives's song (see **Listening Map 66**) contains optional cues for a chorus and shouts of "Hallelujah!" to create the effect of a revivalist meeting. He gives the piano strumming, banjo-like textures and rousing fanfares. Dull, thumping chords are played to suggest the bass drum at the very beginning of the song (①), where we encounter Booth leading his ragtag followers. The line "Are you washed in the blood of the Lamb?" from a nineteenth-century hymn recurs throughout the poem (②).

For the refrain, Ives quotes the hymn "Cleansing Fountain," which appears intermittently. As Booth rouses his troops, the music reaches a frenzied climax. Then, in a dignified Adagio, Ives sets the lines "Jesus came from the courthouse door, / Stretched his hands above the passing poor. / Booth saw not, but led his queer ones, / Round and round, round and round and round. . . ." Here the music circles round and round, with a mesmerizing, calming effect, suggesting the blessing of Jesus. As the procession passes on, the piano strikes up its percussive chords once again, and we hear a complete statement of "Cleansing Fountain" (③). The music ends with the distant sound of the drum, as Booth enters heaven with his enraptured followers, "spotless, clad in raiment new," in the words of Lindsay's poem.

IVES, *General William Booth Enters into Heaven* {1914}

FORM	Through-composed song
METER	March tempo
SCORING	Singer and piano
OVERVIEW	The piano frames the song by suggesting the approach and passing of a procession. Woven throughout the music are recurring hymn-like refrains, "Are you washed in the blood of the Lamb," and, near the end, a quotation of the hymn "Cleansing Fountain."

why to LISTEN

Ives's song suggests the sights and sounds of a revivalist meeting. The music is dramatic, and uses sound to imitate the movement of Booth and his followers across space. It audibly suggests the approach of Booth's ragtag followers, who appear, take center stage, and then move on into a distant, muffled din. As listeners we are bystanders, watching and hearing the colorful throng approach and pass by. The song also offers music *about* music: how, for instance, the piano can be made to sound like booming drums or mimic the twang of the banjo; or how, from this noisy event, punctuated by spirited exclamations of "Hallelujah," the traditional hymn "Cleansing Fountain" can emerge. The simple chordal accompaniment suggests the spiritual state of Booth's followers. Ives seems to be saying that music can offer a healing power that can transform the ordinary into the sublime.

first LISTEN

INTRODUCTION	VERSES	BRIEF INTERLUDE	VERSES	VERSES; ADAGIO	VERSES	CONCLUSION
0:00	**0:09**	**1:33**	**1:38**	**3:19**	**4:15**	**5:31**
Piano imitating drum; voice enters: *"Booth led boldly . . ."*; reference to hymn	Lyrics sung to march-like accompaniment: *"The Saints smiled gravely . . ."*	Piano imitating banjos	Reference to hymn	Gentler strains imitating a flute: *"Jesus came from out . . ."*	Return to military-like march: *"Yet in an instant . . ."*	Piano part fades out

a deeper **LISTEN**

TIME	SECTION	LISTEN FOR THIS	TEXT
0:00	**Introduction**	① Piano introduction imitating bass drum and suggesting an unruly procession	
0:09	**Verses**	② First reference to nineteenth-century hymn Are you washed in the blood of the Lamb?	*Booth led boldly with his big bass drum—* *(Are you washed in the blood of the Lamb?)* *Hallelujah.*
0:31			*The Saints smiled gravely and they said: "He's come."* *(Are you washed in the blood of the Lamb?)* *Walking lepers followed, rank on rank,* *Lurching bravoes from the ditches dank,* *Drabs from the alleyways and drug fiends pale—* *Minds still passion-ridden, soul-powers frail:—* *Vermin-eaten saints with mouldy breath,* *Unwashed legions with the ways of Death—* *(Are you washed in the blood of the Lamb?)*
1:33	**Brief Interlude**	Piano imitating banjos	
1:38	**Verses**	Reference to nineteenth-century hymn	*Every slum had sent its half-a-score* *The round world over. (Booth had groaned for more.)* *Every banner that the wide world flies* *Bloomed with glory and transcendent dyes.* *Big-voiced lasses made their banjos bang,* *Tranced, fanatical, they shrieked and sang:—* *"Are you washed in the blood of the Lamb?"* *Hallelujah! It was queer to see* *Bull-necked convicts with that land make free.* *Loons with trumpets blowed a blare, blare, blare,* *On, on upward thro' the golden air!* *(Are you washed in the blood of the Lamb?)*

Continued

TIME	SECTION	LISTEN FOR THIS	TEXT
3:19	Verse; Adagio	Calming tempo *(Sweet flute music)*	*Jesus came from out the court-house door* *Stretched his hands above the passing poor.* *Booth saw not, but led his queer ones there* *Round and round the mighty court-house square.*
4:15	Verse	Return to initial march tempo; ③ quotation of hymn "Cleansing Fountain"	*Yet in an instant all that blear review* *Marched on spotless, clad in raiment new.*
5:08		Final reference to nineteenth-century hymn	*The lame were straightened, withered limbs uncurled* *And blind eyes opened on a new, sweet world.* *Are you washed in the blood of the Lamb?*
5:31	Conclusion	Piano postlude, diminuendo to ***pppp***, as procession disappears	

William Grant Still

Ives's challenging, wide-ranging music brought into sharp focus the dilemma of American composers of modern classical music. If they aimed too high and imitated European models too closely, their music risked being *too* superior and *not* American enough. If they aimed too low, by drawing extensively on popular tunes, their music was viewed as *not* serious enough, and was unable to compete with masterpieces of the European tradition. Ives met the challenge head-on. He freely combined American popular music with elements of the classical tradition to create a unique American music.

In the case of William Grant Still (1895–1978), the first African-American composer to write symphonies and operas performed by major institutions in the United States and abroad, the way forward took a different course. Born in Mississippi, Still lived in Arkansas before attending college in Ohio. An oboist, he was hired as an arranger for W. C. Handy (the "father of the blues") and also worked with jazz musicians such as Eubie Blake and Paul Whiteman (see Chapter 45). Still had extensive training in the classical tradition. His training included two years of study in New York with the French modernist Edgard Varèse (see p. 532), who briefly inspired Still to create music influenced by the ultra-dissonant experiments of the 1920s. But Still's ambition as a composer was to introduce music "representative of the American Negro" into the concert hall, so he turned back on the advancing musical avant-garde. For Still, that meant drawing instead on the blues—the "secular folk music" of African Americans—and bringing it into the hallowed domain of the symphony. Still's approach was as American as Ives's or Copland's; and his breakthrough came in 1930, the year the Great Depression began in earnest.

William Grant Still (1895–1978).

STILL, "AFRO-AMERICAN" SYMPHONY, THIRD MOVEMENT ("HUMOR") (1930)

Still's "Afro-American" Symphony was written as the Great Depression took hold, when Still, along with millions of other Americans, was jobless. It is in four movements according to the classical tradition, but infused throughout with the spirit of the blues. The symphony traces the composer's parallel influences, drawing from his classical training and his African-American musical heritage. Still's symphony represents his own answer to Dvořák's question about the identity of American music.

The third movement (**Listening Map 67**) is an upbeat scherzo subtitled "Humor" that observes a traditional *ABA* form, although it takes some liberties as it responds to the pull of blues-oriented melodic lines and harmonies.

The movement begins with a short introduction, including a timpani roll that introduces the main theme (1). It is in syncopated rhythm, and set in a major key. Its characteristic four-note motive led Still to identify it as the "Hallelujah" theme, and he later prefaced the score with two lines from a poem by the African-American poet Paul Laurence Dunbar, "An' we'll shout ouah hallelujahs / On dat mighty reck'nin day." If you listen carefully, set against the "Hallelujah" theme are short bursts of the opening of a George Gershwin song that took the United States by storm in 1930, "I Got Rhythm" (2). After extending the "Hallelujah" theme (3), Still repeats it at a softer dynamic level.

The *B* section begins suddenly with the brass interjecting a new theme (4). This theme features pitches that are "bent" chromatically, moving the music closer to the world of the blues (see p. 499). In the final section (*A'*), Still varies and draws on his two principal themes, mixing the major key with blues harmonies, before this jubilant movement ends with a final chord and cymbal crash.

After the success of the "Afro-American" Symphony, Still moved to Los Angeles, where he produced music for films and television (including background music for the series *Gunsmoke* and *Perry Mason*). He conducted the Los Angeles Philharmonic at the Hollywood Bowl, and collaborated with leading figures of the Harlem Renaissance, such as Langston Hughes and Zora Neale Hurston. The recipient of many honorary doctorates, he is remembered as the "dean" of African-American composers.

LISTENING MAP 67

WILLIAM GRANT STILL, "Afro-American" Symphony, Third Movement ("Humor")

{1930}

FORM	Scherzo (ABA)
METER	$\frac{4}{4}$
SCORING	Orchestra (piccolo, two flutes, two oboes, English horn, two clarinets, bass clarinet, two bassoons, four French horns, three trumpets, three trombones, tuba, timpani, small cymbal, large suspended cymbal, tenor banjo, and strings)
OVERVIEW	A three-part scherzo with adjustments, so that the overall form is ABA′. Still fills what is essentially a classical form with motives, themes, and harmonies that imitate African-American music, in particular elements of the blues.

why to LISTEN

Still's "Afro-American" Symphony brings together two worlds that had been apart—classical European concert hall music, and the music of African Americans—and joins them in a convincing balance. The two support each other: Still uses a classical orchestra, but doesn't hesitate to add a banjo from the world of popular music. And while his themes and harmonies originate in the blues, Still fits them within an *ABA* form, the basic form found in Haydn and Mozart's minuets and Beethoven's scherzos. Finally, this brief movement, like the symphony's other three, is programmatic, and carries a non-musical message. It celebrates the emancipation of the slaves in 1863 and their continuing struggle for equality, and it welcomes the "New Negro" of the so-called Harlem Renaissance of the 1920s and 1930s. The movement lasts only three minutes, but communicates with humor, force, and honesty much about the American experience.

first LISTEN

A	B	A′
0:00	**1:01**	**2:09**
Opening "Hallelujah" theme (*a*) contrasted with countersubject (similar to "I Got Rhythm"), then extended (*b*), before (*a*) returns	New theme (*c*), featuring bent, "blue" notes	Return of (*a*) and (*c*) themes

 *a deeper* **LISTEN**

TIME	SECTION	LISTEN FOR THIS
0:00	A	Brief flourish-like introduction ① First theme (*a*), syncopated ("Hallelujah")
0:00		② Countersubject, similar to Gershwin's "I Got Rhythm"
0:29		③ Extension of first theme (*b*)
0:44		Quiet repetition of first theme (*a*)
1:01	B	④ New theme in brass (*c*, loud) *ff*
2:09	A′	Return of first theme (*a*)
2:24		Return of new theme (*b*)
2:46		*ff* statement of *a* and triumphant close

MAKING CONNECTIONS *The Harlem Renaissance and the "New Negro"*

The downtown branch of New York's Cotton Club in the 1930s.

In the 1920s and 1930s the neighborhood of Harlem in New York City became the center of a new flowering of African-American arts. Sometimes called the "Harlem Renaissance," this development included African-American writers, poets, musicians, fashion designers, painters and sculptors, and intellectuals. The intellectual spokesman for the Harlem Renaissance was Alain Locke, the first African-American Rhodes Scholar and a professor of philosophy at Howard University. In 1925 Locke published *The New Negro*, an anthology of writings and poetry that included the work of Langston Hughes, Zora Neale Hurston, and W. E. B. Du Bois. Locke himself contributed several essays to the volume, and argued eloquently for the cultural significance of African-American spirituals: "Through their immediate and compelling universality of appeal, through their untarnishable beauty, they seem assured of the immortality of those great folk expressions that survive not so much through being typical of a group or representative of a period as by virtue of being fundamentally and everlastingly human." Musicians associated with the Harlem Renaissance included Duke Ellington (see p. 505) and the bandleader and singer Cab Calloway, among many others who appeared regularly at the Cotton Club, the most famous Harlem nightclub.

George Gershwin

George Gershwin (1898–1937).

Another American composer who explored intersections between jazz, popular music, and classical music was George Gershwin (1898–1937). Gershwin got his start on Tin Pan Alley, the center of the music publishing trade in New York City. There he worked as a "song plugger," someone who played current songs to promote them in department and music stores. While working for various publishers, Gershwin played popular tunes by songsmiths such as George M. Cohan ("You're a Grand Old Flag," "Give My Regards to Broadway"), and Irving Berlin ("Alexander's Ragtime Band").

But soon enough Gershwin was writing his own songs, and he scored an international hit with "Swanee" (1919), which sold millions of copies. "Swanee" was named after a Southern river (actually the Suwannee) that Gershwin had never seen; its lyrics celebrated the "happy life" in the old South. The song was popularized by the entertainer Al Jolson, who later starred in the first full-length film with sound, *The Jazz Singer* (1927). Great songs flowed from Gershwin's pen—among them "Embraceable You" and "I Got Rhythm"—with infectious lyrics often provided by his older brother, Ira. By the advent of the Great Depression in 1929, Gershwin was concentrating on Broadway musicals, a uniquely American art form influenced by the light operettas of Europe. *Funny Face* (1927), *Girl Crazy* (1930), and *Of Thee I Sing* (1931) were among his most successful shows.

For Gershwin, no line divided popular from classical music. Besides popular songs, he aspired to create music in the concert tradition that would draw liberally on jazz. An initial opportunity came in 1924, when he wrote *Rhapsody in Blue*, for solo piano and jazz ensemble. Conceived as an "experiment in modern music" for Paul Whiteman's jazz band, *Rhapsody in Blue* blended materials from jazz, blues, and the symphonic tradition. Gershwin produced two more major works: the Concerto in F, a full-fledged concerto for piano and orchestra (1925), and *An American in Paris* (1928). The latter is a charming orchestral piece that combines the street sounds of Paris, blues music for the homesick traveler, and a frolicking Charleston. He relied on arrangers like Ferde Grofé, who wrote the orchestral parts for Gershwin's *Rhapsody in Blue*.

When Gershwin turned to the French composer Maurice Ravel for advice in composition, Ravel gently declined, fearing that he would turn a "first-rate" Gershwin into a "second-rate" Ravel. In his spare time, Gershwin painted portraits and played tennis with Arnold Schoenberg in Los Angeles, an odd meeting of two creative spirits. In 1937, Gershwin died from a brain tumor. He was only thirty-eight years old, but he left clear evidence of his great genius in his music.

MAKING CONNECTIONS Rhapsody in Blue: *An Icon of American Music*

Gershwin's most famous composition, *Rhapsody in Blue*, was hurriedly created in a few short weeks before its premiere in New York in 1924. It was commissioned by Paul Whiteman, an American bandleader and arranger, who asked Gershwin to write a "jazz concerto" for piano and orchestra as part of a concert touted to explore modern American music. With little time to spare, Gershwin began gathering ideas for the composition, but he found his true inspiration during a train ride to Boston. As he later explained,

> It was on the train, with its steely rhythms, its rattle-ty bang, that is so often so stimulating to a composer—I frequently hear music in the very heart of the noise. . . . And there I suddenly heard, and even saw on paper—the complete construction of the *Rhapsody*, from beginning to end . . . I heard it as a sort of musical kaleidoscope of America, of our vast melting pot, of our unduplicated national pep, of our metropolitan madness. By the time I reached Boston I had a definite plot of the piece.

Through-composed, Gershwin's composition falls into several sections of different tempos, rather like condensed movements of a classical composition. But the style is undeniably American, and draws unstintingly on jazz, ragtime, and blues. The very opening, a low clarinet trill rising rapidly through a scale, was transformed at the premiere by the clarinetist, who played the solo as a sliding glissando extending to a wailing high note that then introduced a blues-inflected melody. Gershwin left some of the piano part unfinished, so that he could improvise at the keyboard at the premiere, nodding to Paul Whiteman when he should cue in the orchestra. These improvised features, plus the use of blue notes and syncopated rhythms, successfully brought jazz into the concert hall, and changed American music.

GERSHWIN, "SUMMERTIME," FROM *PORGY AND BESS* (1935)

Gershwin's masterpiece is the three-act "folk opera" *Porgy and Bess*, set in Catfish Row (a fictitious African-American tenement in Charleston, South Carolina) and written for a company of African-American singers and actors. Based on a novel by Du Bose Heyward, it tells the story of the disabled beggar Porgy, who tries to rescue Bess from Crown, her abusive lover, and Sportin' Life, a drug dealer who tries to seduce her with "happy dust." To prepare for writing the opera, Gershwin traveled to the Low Country region of South Carolina, where he observed the Gullah culture of former African-American slaves living on James Island near Charleston. The opera draws on a wealth of Southern African-American music, including blues, jubilees, work songs, and spirituals. At the same time, it incorporates elements of the pop songs and jazz of Gershwin's early career. But Gershwin also uses techniques from traditional European opera: passages designed as recitatives and arias, thematic development, and a series of motives threaded throughout the score. The opera includes the classic American songs "Summertime," "It Ain't Necessarily So," and "Bess, You Is My Woman Now," thoroughly embedded in our musical consciousness by thousands of recorded versions.

Jazz musicians Ella Fitzgerald and Louis Armstrong in 1954 in the studio recording *Porgy and Bess*.

Listening Map 68 offers a brief synopsis of one celebrated rendition of "Summertime" by noted jazz musicians Ella Fitzgerald and Louis Armstrong. In Gershwin's original 1935 opera, "Summertime" arrives early in Act 1 when Clara, a fisherman's wife and young mother, sings it as a tender lullaby for her baby. Artlessly simple, the music suggests folk music, perhaps a spiritual. Its melody is based on a form of a pentatonic (five-note) scale. Only the gently rocking harmonies beneath betray the song's origins in jazz. In the version presented here, recorded in 1957, Fitzgerald joins Armstrong and a supporting orchestra that effortlessly transport the song from the opera house to the realm of jazz. The haunting melody is heard four times. First, Armstrong takes the lead in a trumpet solo (①). Then Fitzgerald and Armstrong sing in turn the first and second verses. Finally, the two together reprise the first verse (②), with Armstrong improvising a melody using nonsense words (a technique known as **scat singing**), which offers a counterpoint to Fitzgerald's rich lyrical voice.

LISTENING MAP 68

GERSHWIN, "Summertime," from *Porgy and Bess*, as performed by Ella Fitzgerald and Louis Armstrong {1957}

FORM	Song, first heard in the opera as a lullaby
METER	$\frac{2}{2}$
SCORING	In Gershwin's opera, for soprano and orchestra; in this arrangement from 1957, Louis Armstrong (trumpet and voice) and Ella Fitzgerald (voice), accompanied by a studio orchestra
OVERVIEW	Four statements of the famous melody, first as a trumpet solo for Armstrong, then vocal solos for Fitzgerald and Armstrong, and a final statement for both, with Armstrong singing in scat.

why to LISTEN

"Summertime" is just one of many classic songs by Gershwin, one of the greatest songwriters within the scope of the classical and popular traditions. "Summertime" impresses as a traditional folk song that draws on the inflections of spirituals. But Gershwin tinged the accompanying harmonies with the quality of the blues, adding another layer of complexity. Lullaby, spiritual, jazz—they all come together in "Summertime." Although Gershwin conceived the song for an opera, it found ready acceptance from jazz musicians, and the result was undeniably compelling, spawning thousands of renditions and recordings of the tune.

first LISTEN

BRIEF INTRODUCTION	TRUMPET SOLO	FIRST VERSE	SECOND VERSE	REPEAT OF FIRST VERSE
0:00	**0:26**	**1:31**	**2:37**	**3:40**
	Trumpet solo by Armstrong	Vocal by Fitzgerald: *"Summertime, and the livin' . . ."*	Vocal by Armstrong: *"One of these mornings . . ."*	Repeat of first stanza sung by Fitzgerald while Armstrong scats an accompaniment

Continued

 *a deeper* **LISTEN**

TIME	SECTION/VERSE	LISTEN FOR THIS	TEXT
0:00	Brief orchestral introduction		
0:26	① Trumpet solo	By Armstrong	
1:31	First verse	Sung by Fitzgerald	Summertime and the livin' is easy, Fish are jumpin' and the cotton is high. Oh, your daddy's rich and your ma is good lookin' So hush, little baby, don't you cry.
2:37	Second verse	Sung by Armstrong	One of these mornings you're goin' to rise up singing, And you'll spread your wings and you'll take the sky. But till that morning there ain't nothing can harm you With Daddy and Mammy standin' by.
3:40	② Reprise of first verse	By Fitzgerald, with Armstrong singing in scat Sum-mer-time and the li-vin' is ea - sy	

Aaron Copland

Born in New York in 1900, Aaron Copland (1900–1990) came of musical age in the 1920s and 1930s. Traveling to Paris in 1921, he studied with Nadia Boulanger, a French composer, conductor, and teacher who taught many important modern composers. Copland's early compositions incorporated jazz and other American musical idioms. The clashing rhythms and polytonal sonorities of his first efforts reflect the influence of Stravinsky, whom Copland greatly admired.

With the beginning of the Great Depression in 1929, experimentation in the arts declined as the United States retreated from international affairs. Reflecting the mood of the times, Copland turned to American subjects and produced scores with broad popular appeal. He is perhaps best known for three ballet scores, *Billy the Kid*

(1938), *Rodeo* (1942), and *Appalachian Spring* (1944). During the 1930s and 1940s, Copland wrote music for radio and several film scores. In keeping with the patriotic mood of the 1940s, he composed *Lincoln Portrait*, for orchestra and speaker (1942), and *Fanfare for the Common Man*, for brass and percussion (1942).

In later compositions, the composer flirted with twelve-tone techniques. But he never strayed far from his earlier mission: to write American music in a style accessible to a wide audience. Copland's populism came with a price: because of his leftist political leanings (he attended some Communist Party meetings during the 1930s, although never joined the party), he was investigated for being a Communist sympathizer during the early 1950s, and was briefly blacklisted. But the honest, straightforward appeal of Copland's music outlasted his critics. He died at age ninety, greatly revered as the "dean" of American composers.

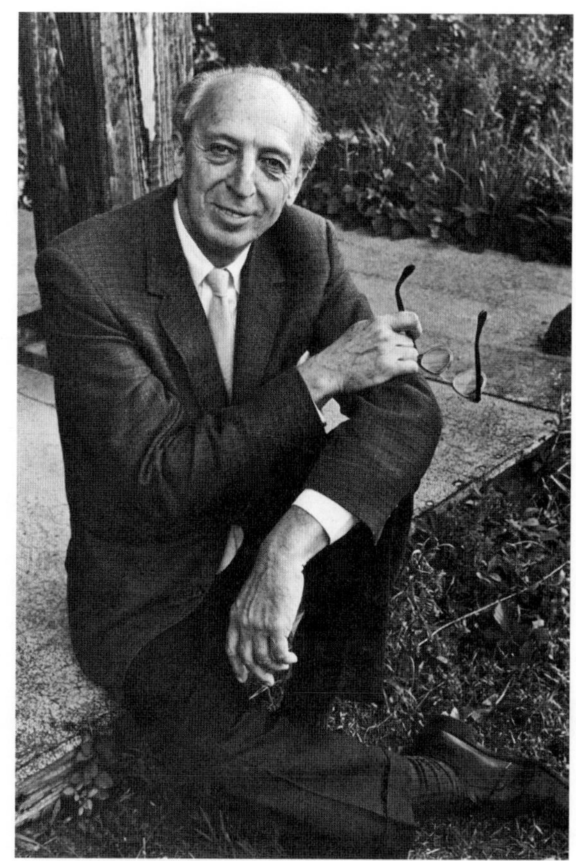

Aaron Copland (1900–1990).

COPLAND, *APPALACHIAN SPRING* (1944)

Copland composed *Appalachian Spring* to fulfill a commission from Martha Graham, the foremost American choreographer of contemporary dance. He wrote the music as a "ballet for Martha," without a fixed idea of its subject matter. It became associated with a setting in rural Pennsylvania in the early nineteenth century, and was understood to celebrate simple American values as seen through the eyes of a newlywed couple.

The original score employed only thirteen instruments. Copland later arranged the work as a concert suite for full orchestra, the version that is usually performed, in eight sections. In the first, Copland slowly blends triads to create tranquil polytonal textures as the principals of the ballet—the bride, the groom, a neighbor, and a revivalist minister and his congregation—are introduced. The second section is an Allegro with wide leaps and forceful accents reminiscent of Stravinsky.

The third section, in moderate tempo, is a duo danced by the couple. In the fourth section, the revivalist and his followers dance a square dance, with prominent interruptions by the violins. The fifth section is a fast dance for the bride, who reflects on motherhood. The sixth section returns to the restrained music of the opening. The seventh section, which depicts the couple's daily life, is based on the Shaker melody "Simple Gifts," heard first in the clarinet. Copland then subjects the melody to five variations, outlined in **Listening Map 69**, before ending the section with a broad statement for full orchestra. The last section depicts the couple in their new house. Hushed and reverent, the closing music recalls the opening strains of this classic American work.

LISTENING MAP 69

COPLAND, *Appalachian Spring*, Section 7: Variations on the Shaker melody "Simple Gifts" {1944}

FORM	Theme and variations
METER	$\frac{2}{4}$
SCORING	Orchestra (two flutes, two oboes, two clarinets, two bassoons, two horns, two trumpets, two trombones, timpani, percussion, harp, piano, and strings)
OVERVIEW	A theme and five variations on the Shaker melody "Simple Gifts," first heard in the clarinet (1) and then varied by different orchestral treatments. Copland's use of a traditional American melody was part of his attempt to create an "American" classical music that would have a wide appeal.

why to LISTEN

For many listeners, *Appalachian Spring* provided a satisfying answer to the "problem" of modern American music. It used classical techniques from the European tradition, as in the theme and variations of the final, seventh section. It paid homage to the modernisms of Igor Stravinsky, by adapting a flexible approach to meter and blending polytonal harmonies. But—most important of all—it made an authentic American statement, by using the Shaker melody "Simple Gifts" as its source material, and by incorporating an accessible style. Like William Grant Still, Copland found a worthy answer to the nagging question that confronted twentieth-century composers: "What is American music?" Copland's answer was to embrace a broad-based musical populism.

first LISTEN

THEME	VARIATION 1	VARIATION 2	VARIATION 3	VARIATION 4	VARIATION 5
0:00	**0:33**	**1:00**	**1:45**	**2:07**	**2:23**
Clarinet, softly	Oboe and bassoon, faster	Strings, half as fast	Strings, twice as fast	Woodwinds, slower	Full orchestra

a deeper LISTEN

TIME	SECTION	LISTEN FOR THIS
0:00	Theme	① Shaker theme performed by the clarinet, ***p***
0:33	Variation 1	Faster tempo, with melody exchanged between oboe and bassoon
1:00	Variation 2	Theme played half as fast in strings
1:45	Variation 3	Theme played twice as fast in trumpets and trombones, ***f***
2:07	Variation 4	Second part of theme played more slowly by woodwinds, ***mf***
2:23	Variation 5	Majestic final presentation of theme by full orchestra, ***ff***

check your KNOWLEDGE

1. Describe several musical styles that evolved during the nineteenth century in America. How did these styles reflect the influence of European music and yet assert a new musical identity?
2. Why is Charles Ives's music still controversial today? How did he wed the influence of American music with modern compositional techniques?
3. Why do you think Amy Beach limited her performances after her marriage? What does this tell you about nineteenth-century attitudes toward women in music?
4. How did William Grant Still lead a double life as a composer?
5. How did George Gershwin combine elements of jazz, popular song, and even opera into his musical compositions? Give specific examples.
6. How did Aaron Copland's music reflect its American roots while at the same time show the influence of modernism?

CHAPTER

46 Jazz

If American music preserved some links to classical European traditions, it also celebrated wave after wave of new popular musical styles, which continue to form. One of the most enduring and influential of these celebrations is **jazz**. Sometimes called America's classical music, jazz arose from African-American music, became established in New Orleans, and then spread to other American cities. Within a few decades, the popularity of jazz was worldwide, and it played an increasingly vital role in the modern musical experience.

Many classical composers drew freely on jazz idioms, yet jazz became a powerful art form in its own right. It experienced a vibrant history all its own, over a century of astonishing experimentation. Just like classical music, jazz has undergone changes in style over its lifespan, including its emergence from blues and ragtime to swing, bebop, and jazz rock. It has become one of the most important world musical styles of our time, playing a key role as both a musical and social force.

Louis Armstrong (1901–1971) plays the trumpet in 1937.

The Rise of Jazz: Ragtime and Blues

The source of the word *jazz* is unclear, but the music's origins were unmistakably in the largely un-notated rhythms and melodies of late nineteenth-century African-American music. During the nineteenth century, the music brought to America by slaves was transformed into a dynamic music that found expression in spirituals, field hollers, and rhythmic patterns, all passed down orally from generation to generation. Because African slaves used complex drumming patterns to communicate, as they had in Africa, drums were outlawed in much of the South, which meant that the rhythms found other outlets—in hand clapping and foot stomping, for instance (often regarded as the origins of tap dancing). When this music came into contact with the rhythms and sounds of marching bands—a musical tradition commonplace since the Civil War—the beginnings of jazz occurred.

Early jazz musicians based their performances on popular tunes. But they excelled in improvising variations on them, elaborating the familiar melodies, adding rhapsodic ornaments and stretches of new material, and changing their rhythms. The lifeblood of emerging jazz was improvisation, and each performance was unique, because there was no authoritative, notated score. Jazz, in short, was constantly reinventing itself. Nevertheless, in time, jazz developed its own traditions and specialized techniques. By the end of the nineteenth century, two distinct types of African-American music had emerged: ragtime and blues. They would combine in the great musical flowering of the 1920s, the Jazz Age.

RAGTIME

Scott Joplin (1868–1917).

Ragtime featured a regular, strong, march-like bass accompanying a treble melody animated with syncopations against the beat. Songs performed in this style, or "rags," were commonly played in the parlors of bordellos to entertain the customers before the music achieved general popularity at the beginning of the twentieth century. Rags were generally performed on the piano, an instrument versatile enough to imitate the sounds and rhythms of a small band. The "King of Ragtime" was Scott Joplin (1868–1917), who first achieved fame in St. Louis and then moved to New York after the turn of the century. Joplin was well versed in composition, and the structure and melodic flair of his music show his skill. He aspired to become a recognized classical composer and completed two operas, including *Treemonisha*, about a freed, educated African-American slave (1911, but not staged until 1970). *Treemonisha* has an overture, arias, and recitatives; it leans on classical traditions, because Joplin aspired to write a "serious" American opera worthy of European examples. Joplin's principal fame, however, rested with his published rags. His most famous example was the Maple Leaf Rag, which appeared in 1899 and sold well enough to provide him with a steady income. (It is considered to be the first piece of sheet music to sell over one million copies, although sales figures were not kept at the time.) Built on a sturdy, march-like bass line and chords, Joplin placed a distinctive melody in the treble, peppered with syncopations off the beat.

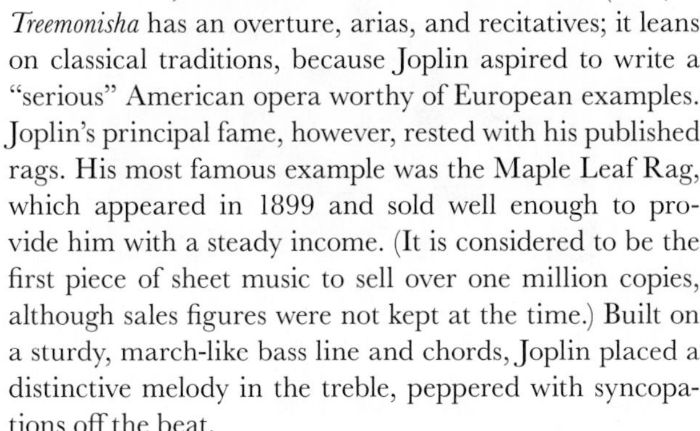

Ragtime was highly popular in the United States and Europe until about 1915, when it was displaced by jazz, a livelier music that depended upon a free, improvisational style. A key figure in the transition from ragtime to jazz was the New Orleans pianist "Jelly Roll" Morton (1890–1941), one of the first jazz composers and arrangers of distinction. By the late 1920s, Morton's ensemble, the Red Hot Peppers, was recording music in this new style.

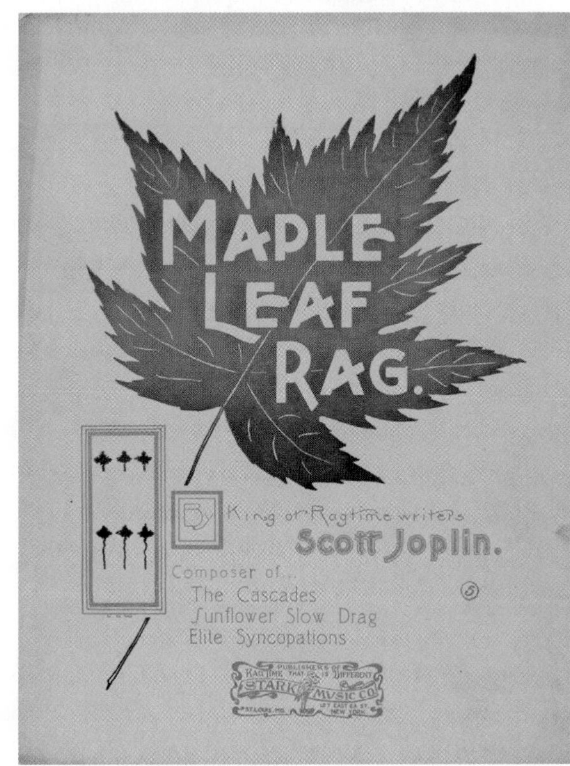

Joplin's Maple Leaf Rag (1899). It is said that this was the first piece of music to sell over 1 million copies.

THE BLUES

The origins of the **blues** are no less obscure than those of ragtime. The blues are songs of misery and oppression. They chronicle every sort of misfortune, from infidelity to unemployment to depression. The so-called country blues were performed by musicians living and working as sharecroppers on the large rural farms in the South that descended from the older, pre–Civil War plantations. Performers like Mississippi-born Charley Patton (d. 1934) and Robert Johnson (1911–1938) gained enough fame to make records in the '20s and '30s. During the 1920s, vaudeville singers such as the "Mother of the Blues" "Ma" Rainey (1886–1939) and "Empress of the Blues" Bessie Smith (1894–1937) popularized the blues for urban audiences. And musicians such as "Jelly Roll" Morton and the

MAKING CONNECTIONS *Robert Johnson and the Blues as Literature*

When musicians approach the blues, they think about the bedrock plan of repeating harmonies that support the lyrics, and how they might add their own melodic comments between the phrases of sung text. But the blues is also literature, and it has made a profound impact as an art form where poetry and music seamlessly interact in subtle ways. Blues lyrics are rightly celebrated for their compelling poetic imagery. They trace narratives of sorrow and suffering, and in the closing verses shed some light on its cause. Here are the opening verses of one classic blues, "Hellhound on My Trail":

> I got to keep moving, got to keep moving,
> Blues falling down like hail, blues falling down like hail.
> Mmm, blues falling down like hail, blues falling down like hail,
> And the day keeps on remindin' me, there's a hellhound on my trail,
> Hellhound on my trail, hellhound on my trail.

This gripping example was the creation of Robert Johnson (1911–1938), who recorded it in 1937, not long before his own death at age twenty-seven. Born in Mississippi, Johnson was later remembered as a young master of the Delta blues style. Life was not easy for him—a wandering musician who worked largely in the South, he played on street corners and in bars and juke joints, before making a few recordings in the last two years of his life. Legends grew up around his memory: that he had made a compact at a crossroads with the devil in order to master his guitar, and that he died from

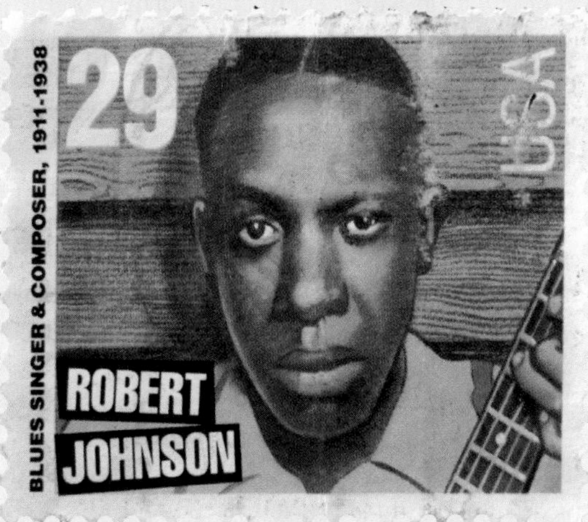

Robert Johnson (1911–1938). Johnson became so well known thanks to artists like Eric Clapton that he was featured on a U.S. postage stamp in the 1990s.

drinking alcohol laced with strychnine by his girlfriend's jealous husband.

Johnson excelled at bending his voice and using microtones (intervals smaller than a half step) to inflect the images of the lyrics and give them increased poignancy. "Hellhound on My Trail" begins with an unexplained sense of restlessness that drives the music. Then the feeling of blues is likened to an unrelenting hailstorm, before we get closer to the cause. Pursuing the singer is some sinister force—a hellhound on his trail. Is the singer a persecuted victim? Has he committed some unspeakable sin? We do not know for sure, but we feel the rootlessness of the music, a powerful marker of the African-American experience.

trumpeter-cornetist Louis "Satchmo" Armstrong (1900–1971) developed instrumental styles for the art form.

Many blues are built on a standard harmonic plan that fills out twelve measures divided into three phrases. These phrases deliver three lines of text, of which the first and second are the same. Generally, each line of text is answered by an improvised instrumental response, a basic call-and-response pattern familiar in African-American music. This give-and-take creates a tension in the music that builds toward the third line, which reveals the reason for the singer's woes.

The characteristic sound of the blues comes from the use of **blue notes**, pitches of the scale that are stretched to sound off-pitch. Not always notated, their spontaneous use by the performers is a distinguishing feature of the blues.

BESSIE SMITH, "LOST YOUR HEAD BLUES" (1926)

Bessie Smith (1894–1937), "Empress of the Blues."

Later known as the "Empress of the Blues," Bessie Smith came from poverty in Chattanooga, Tennessee. By the age of nine, she had lost both parents and was raised by an elder sister. By the age of eighteen, she was performing as a dancer and singer, and joined a traveling minstrel show. But her powerful voice and intensive expression destined her for stardom, and her break came in 1923 when she began recording her blues. Success and fame followed her, and she toured with a band of about forty, traveling on a railroad car she purchased. Tragically, she died in a car crash in 1937. Over ten thousand mourners attended her funeral, but she was buried without a headstone. Rumors spread at the time that a local hospital refused to admit Smith following her accident because she was black. While those rumors were later disproved, they added to Smith's legends as a pioneering black performer. When a tombstone was finally set in 1970—owing in part to the efforts of the rock singer Janis Joplin—the epitaph read, "The greatest blues singer in the world will never stop singing."

"Lost Your Head Blues" (**Listening Map 70**) features Bessie Smith with Joe Smith on cornet and Fletcher Henderson on piano. After a short introduction, in which the cornet slides and bends notes, including its third note (①) she begins the first of five three-line stanzas, with brief comments from the cornet between her lines, while the piano keeps the beat and plays a succession of tonic, subdominant, and dominant harmonies typical of the blues. She uses expressive slides (as on ②, "I" in the first stanza, ④, "tried" in the third stanza, and ⑤, "leave" in the fourth), changes in register as in ③, the swooping descent of "gal" in the second stanza, and embellishments of individual words, as in ⑥, "long" in the fifth stanza to convey the message of the text. These are all imitated in the same range by the sliding, swooping gestures of the cornet.

Listen to a brief biography of Bessie Smith.

LISTENING MAP 70

BESSIE SMITH, "Lost Your Head Blues" {1926}

FORM	Blues
METER	$\frac{2}{4}$
SCORING	Solo voice (Bessie Smith), cornet (Joe Smith) and piano (Fletcher Henderson)
OVERVIEW	A standard 12-bar blues, with 5 three-line stanzas, with cornet comments between lines. Smith's powerful vocal delivery and expressive interpretation of the lyrics make her performance stand out from the many other blues women of the era.

why to LISTEN

The blues is authentic American music closely tied to the African-American experience that followed slavery. After the Civil War, the freed slaves began a collective journey that led from the farms of former Southern plantations to the cities, to the North and other regions of the United States, and to a long struggle for their civil rights. In a sense the blues chronicle this epic social history, in a way that only honest, heartfelt music can. To feel the power of Bessie Smith's performance and to trace the emotional contours of her voice is to grapple with this history, and to understand how a popular means of expression became an art form.

first LISTEN

INTRO	VERSE 1	VERSE 2	VERSE 3	VERSE 4	VERSE 5	CONCLUSION
0:00	0:12	0:44	1:16	1:49	2:20	2:49
Cornet and Piano	*"I was with you . . ."*	*"Once ain't for always . . ."*	*"When you were lonesome . . ."*	*"I'm going to leave . . ."*	*"Days are lonesome . . ."*	Cornet and piano

 *a deeper* **LISTEN**

TIME	SECTION	LISTEN FOR THIS	TEXT
0:00	Brief introduction by cornet and piano	① Third note of cornet bent down	
0:12	Verse 1	② Slide up on "I"	I was with you baby when you did not have a dime. I was with you baby when you did not have a dime. Now since you got plenty money, you have throw'd your good gal down.
0:44	Verse 2	③ Voice swoops down on "gal"	Once ain't for always, two ain't for twice. (2×) When you get a good gal you better treat her nice.
1:16	Verse 3	④ Slide up on "tried"	When you were lonesome I tried to treat you kind. (2×) But since you've got money, it's done changed your mind.
1:49	Verse 4	⑤ Slide on "leave"	I'm going to leave baby, ain't going to say goodbye. (2×) But I'll write you and tell you the reason why.
2:20	Verse 5	⑥ Vocal flourish on "long"	Days are lonesome, nights are long. (2×) I'm a good old gal, but I've just been treated wrong.
2:49	Short conclusion by cornet and piano		

Early Jazz: New Orleans and Beyond

Early jazz was a synthesis of ragtime and blues. Its first center was Storyville, the red-light district of New Orleans, where Dixieland jazz emerged. Storyville was originally established as an area of the city where prostitution was legal, as a means of limiting it to a confined area within the city limits. However, with the beginning of World War I—and a flood of Navy men coming into the city—the local government was pressured to close down the Storyville establishments, which it did in 1917. No longer able to work in bordellos of Storyville, local musicians relocated north to Memphis, Kansas City, and Chicago; west to Los Angeles; and east to

New York. The typical New Orleans jazz band included a cornet, clarinet, trombone, banjo, and drum, an adaptation of the instrumentation of popular marching bands that could perform outdoors and indoors. These groups played for funerals and other outdoor processions, and in taverns and brothels, where they were often joined by a piano.

Early jazz bands were organized into two sections. The melodic section, or **front line**, played the theme. Leading the front line was a cornet (eventually replaced by the louder, more brassy-sounding trumpet), supported by a clarinet and trombone. When not playing a solo, the clarinetist generally played improvised melodic lines that complemented the cornet part. The trombone played in a lower range, performing short solos, working against the main melodic line, and occasionally erupting in colorful glissandos. The second section was the **rhythm section**, made up of a piano, banjo, and drums. This section provided a steady beat and gave the melodic section a firm harmonic foundation. Typically, a performance began with the entire ensemble, continued with improvised solos for the front line, and concluded with the ensemble.

During the 1920s and 1930s, the small Dixieland jazz combos expanded. In Chicago, which attracted such musicians as King Oliver, Louis Armstrong, Bix Beiderbecke, and Earl Hines, the larger ensembles attained the size of big bands. New instruments such as the saxophone were added, and louder, more versatile instruments were substituted for some of the original parts—for example, guitar for banjo, trumpet for cornet. Louis Armstrong recorded with two small combos, the Hot Five and the Hot Seven, and Jelly Roll Morton recorded with his Red Hot Peppers, which counted seven or eight musicians. In the classic "Black Bottom

Jelly Roll Morton and the Red Hot Peppers, circa late 1920s.

Stomp" (1926), Morton used a front line of a trumpet, clarinet, and trombone, and rhythm section of a piano, banjo, double bass, and drum set. He shaped his composition to balance the entire ensemble with virtuosic solos for individual instruments. Impeccably rehearsed, Morton's early recordings gave a clear sense of how jazz could retain its improvisatory spontaneity and yet achieve a formal structure and unity. The need to experiment meant that jazz grew more adventurous and complex.

The Birth of Swing Music

The limitations of early technology made recordings of larger bands at first difficult. Technology improved, and bands, both in and out of the recording studio, increased in size. By the mid-1930s, jazz bands were expanding to thirteen musicians, organized into distinct sections: five brass (trumpets and trombones), four saxophones, and four members of the rhythm section (piano, drums, guitar, and string bass). And some big bands expanded even further. The era of big band music, or **swing**, had arrived.

The new, larger bands could not rely on the individual musician's improvisational skills. To avoid total chaos, the players in each section had to work from written scores. Compositions for larger bands were set down in arrangements known as "charts," which summarized the harmonic and rhythmic shape of the music. These charts still allowed for solo improvisations to be played within the composed frameworks.

Duke Ellington

The most brilliant of the new composers writing for these larger bands was Edward Kennedy "Duke" Ellington (1899–1974). Ellington built ever bigger bands and excelled in new effects, such as blending colors of different instruments. His early bands specialized in unusual timbres, including using mutes for the brass instruments. His total output extends to thousands of compositions. In his early days, Ellington was limited to composing works about three minutes in length, the standard running time of 78-rpm phonograph recordings. Later in his career, Ellington went beyond this short time frame to create ambitious works that used complex forms and adventurous harmonies. For example, his *Black, Brown, and Beige* (1933–1943), is a five-part composition portraying the history of African Americans.

Duke Ellington (1899–1974).

The son of a White House butler, Ellington was born and raised in Washington, D.C. His refined style of dressing earned him early on the nickname "Duke," and he began playing in and organizing bands before moving to New York in 1923. At the Cotton Club in Harlem, an upscale establishment catering to white patrons, Ellington led an ensemble that grew to twelve musicians. He carefully crafted his compositions to showcase his musicians' talents and achieve what became known as the "Ellington effect." He treated his orchestra as a musical laboratory, in which he could explore novel blends of sounds and special effects.

In later years, Ellington continued to appear with his band, including several international tours. He shaped his compositions according to the playing styles of several of his soloists—musicians such as the clarinetist Barney Bigard, trumpeter Cootie Williams, and saxophonist Johnny Hodges. In a sense, the music was a collaborative effort, but Ellington was the master engineer of this music. He understood how to extract a wealth of colors and effects from his band, and how to shape the details into a coordinated and pleasing whole.

Active as a composer until his death from lung cancer in 1974, Ellington spent much of his later years composing what he called "Sacred Concerts." These were extended collections of short religious pieces that were premiered in churches in San Francisco and New York, and in Westminster Abbey in London. They featured the Swedish soprano Alice Babs, a choir, and, of course, the Duke Ellington Band, eighteen members strong.

Ellington's catalogue contains any number of now classic compositions—"It Don't Mean a Thing (If It Ain't Got That Swing)" (1931), "Sophisticated Lady" (1932), and "Caravan" (1937), for instance. Two other signature pieces, "Take the A Train" (1941) and "Satin Doll" (1953) were collaborative efforts with Billy Strayhorn, who joined the band in 1939. Strayhorn served as second pianist in Ellington's band and was a talented arranger and composer in his own right.

ELLINGTON, "MOOD INDIGO" (1930)

Among the enduring favorites of Ellington's Cotton Club band was "Mood Indigo," recorded for radio broadcast in 1930. Barney Bigard, the clarinetist in Ellington's band, provided the main tune. What made this music so unusual was Ellington's particular blend of the three front-line instruments. He turned their normal roles upside down: a muted trombone carried the tune in its high register, played by Arthur Whetsol, supported below by a muted trumpet and a clarinet in its low register. The eerily subdued, wailing sounds of the instruments were so distinctive that they called out for words, later added by Mitchell Parish (although Parish sold his lyrics outright to publisher Irving Mills, who took credit for the authorship). The text describes that sinking feeling of having the blues that "goes stealin' down to my shoes," and captures perfectly the inverted timbres of the original music.

There have been countless recordings of "Mood Indigo"; **Listening Map 71** summarizes one of Duke Ellington's original instrumental recordings from 1930. We hear four statements of the theme, the first with the inverted timbres. Then we hear two freer solos, one for the clarinetist Barney Bigard and one for the trumpet player Cootie Williams. After the solos, a brief piano interlude is played by Ellington, before a final statement for the full ensemble.

Ellington celebrated jazz as a "serious" art form by insisting that his music remained "beyond category." Though hailed as the first great jazz composer, he acknowledged the influence of William Grant Still on the development of his style, and his favorite composers included Debussy and Stravinsky. Not averse

LISTENING MAP 71

DUKE ELLINGTON, "Mood Indigo"

{1930}

FORM	Theme and improvised variations
METER	$\frac{4}{4}$
SCORING	Trombone, trumpet, clarinet, piano, banjo, string bass, and drums
OVERVIEW	Framing the composition are two "inverted" statements of the theme in a high muted trombone supported by trumpet and clarinet. Separating them are two varied solo presentations of the theme by the clarinet and trumpet, and a brief piano interlude. The unusual voicing of the melody gives this piece its characteristic "mood."

why to LISTEN

"Mood Indigo" is a classic jazz composition that can be enjoyed in purely musical terms. But when Mitchell Parish later added words to it, he revisited an issue that we have touched on before. Can pure music express ideas and emotions faithfully, or does it need words to explain its meaning? In Ellington's classic, the music and title came first, the words later. Just as Ellington made many recordings of the music with his band, so too were many recordings made of the piece sung with lyrics. (A classic in its own right is Ella Fitzgerald's recording for Verve Records in 1957.) As you listen to "Mood Indigo," imagine how the music might affect you if you did not know the title. Then, find a recording of the piece with the sung text, and imagine how that text might affect you if the music were different.

first LISTEN

THEME	SECOND STATEMENT	THIRD STATEMENT	INTERLUDE	FOURTH STATEMENT
0:00	**0:41**	**1:21**	**2:00**	**2:10**
Full band; trombone voiced in high register, supported by clarinet and muted trumpet	Clarinet solo	Trumpet solo	Piano chords	Repeat of opening

Continued

a deeper **LISTEN**

TIME	SECTION	LISTEN FOR THIS
0:00	First statement of theme	Full band; theme played by a high muted trombone, harmonized by muted trumpet and clarinet in its low register, and supported in the background by piano, banjo, string bass, and drums
0:41	Second statement	Clarinet solo accompanied by strummed banjo; freely improvised on the main theme, with many bent notes and slurs. Reaches a dramatic height as the accompaniment briefly drops out
1:21	Third statement	Trumpet solo, with strummed banjo and soft trombone counterline
2:00	Brief interlude	Piano: Ellington plays break around chords; regular rhythm drops out
2:10	Fourth statement	Returns to inverted arrangement of opening

Clarinetist Benny Goodman (1909–1986), the "King of Swing."

to exploring connections between jazz and classical music, he arranged for his ensemble classical works such as Tchaikovsky's *Nutcracker Suite*. Above all, Ellington was concerned with the quality of the musical experience—for performers and listeners alike. Central to his mission was the idea that music, for all its entertaining value, conveyed serious messages. After all, it was the Duke who said, "If it sounds good, it *is* good."

During the 1930s era of swing that produced highly polished, arranged music played by carefully rehearsed dance bands, several white musicians joined Ellington in promoting the new style. Among the most gifted was the clarinetist Benny Goodman (1909–1986), the "King of Swing." In 1938 Goodman's band appeared at Carnegie Hall in New York, an event that helped "legitimatize" the position of jazz in American music. Superb bands led by black and white bandleaders like Glenn Miller, Tommy Dorsey, and "Count" Basie spread swing throughout the country with concert tours, recordings, and radio broadcasts. The period also produced such influential musicians as the saxophonist Coleman Hawkins and the singer Billie Holiday. The popularity of swing waned only with the Second World War (1939–1945), when the enthusiasm for the suave big band sound was dampened by the harsh realities of worldwide death and fiery destruction.

The Birth of Bebop

With the war's end, a younger generation of independently minded jazz musicians eager to experiment came to the fore. Some rejected the smooth big band sound in favor of a dynamic new style called **bebop**, or **bop**. Among the great practitioners of this volatile jazz style were the saxophonist Charlie Parker, pianist Thelonious Monk, and trumpeter Dizzy Gillespie. Bop first took hold in late-night "jam" sessions in Harlem nightclubs. Played by small, elite groups of musicians, it featured irregular, improvised lines that soared above the harmonic progressions of familiar tunes of earlier jazz and popular music, often performed at extremely fast tempos.

CHARLIE PARKER, "CONSTELLATION" (1948)

The musician who tested the expressive limits of bebop was Charlie Parker (1920–1955), known as "Bird" or "Yardbird." Born in Kansas City, Parker lived a brilliant life that was tragically shortened by his addictions to heroin and alcohol. In Kansas City he frequented the dance halls and nightclubs where Count Basie's band played, but Parker's maturation as an artist came after he moved to New York in 1938. There, in the 1940s, he excelled at creating astounding melodic improvisations accompanied by small ensembles. The musicians would choose a familiar, popular tune, keep its chord changes and basic form, but replace its melody with newly composed riffs and flourishes, usually executed at breakneck speed. Several of Parker's compositions were in fact based on Gershwin's "I Got Rhythm." However, most listeners were unaware of the source, unless they were well versed in the harmonies or belonged to the growing circle of connoisseurs who frequented Parker's appearances in New York clubs.

In his last years, Parker began to expand his musical horizons beyond the aggressive bebop style. He recorded the album *Charlie Parker with Strings* (released in 1950) in which he was featured with a small rhythm section set against a classical string orchestra, and he expressed a desire to study classical music. He was fascinated with the music of Béla Bartók, and regretted not being able to meet the Hungarian composer before his death in 1945. Parker lived only ten years more, plagued by poor health, but he left behind a rich legacy that indelibly altered the course of jazz.

Bebop musician Charlie Parker (1920–1955) on saxophone, circa 1945.

Among Parker's classic compositions based on Gershwin's "I Got Rhythm" is "Constellation", recorded in 1948 as a quintet, with Parker on alto saxophone, the young Miles Davis on trumpet, John Lewis on piano, Curley Russell on string bass, and Max Roach on drums (**Listening Map 72**). Packed into its explosive two and a half minutes is a dizzying display of virtuosity. After a brief introduction from the rhythm section, Parker and Davis begin together with a syncopated unison figure to which each briefly responds. Next, Parker breaks in with his breathless solo, clusters of rapid notes yielding only occasionally to short breaths. Parker is followed in turn by more compact solos from the trumpet and piano. Then the opening unison figure returns, interrupted by a brief drum solo, and resumed until the abrupt end.

LISTENING MAP 72

CHARLIE PARKER, "Constellation" {1948}

FORM	Popular song
SOURCE	Based on Gershwin's "I Got Rhythm"
METER	$\frac{4}{4}$
SCORING	Alto saxophone, trumpet, piano, string bass, and drums
OVERVIEW	A rapid-fire improvisation on Gershwin's "I Got Rhythm" framed by a short unison figure and featuring solos for the saxophone, trumpet, piano, and drums.

why to LISTEN

The lifeblood of jazz is improvisation, and bebop is nothing if it is not a pure celebration of improvisation. But for Parker's generation, improvisation, however free, still relied on an underlying foundation, even if well hidden from the ears of most listeners. So behind the constellations of exploding notes are predetermined harmonic changes, in this case patterns borrowed from a classic Gershwin song. Parker's "Constellation" could be likened to theme and variations. The critical difference here is that the theme is apparently missing, represented only by the harmonies that support it—more precisely, by harmonies speeded up so as to cover almost all traces of their origins. To test this idea, find a recording of Gershwin's "I Got Rhythm," and listen for the syncopated figures of its memorable tune and the harmonies below it. Now listen to Parker's "Constellation" and see if you can detect any similarities between the two compositions. In the vast space between Gershwin's tune and Parker's free-flung riffs that seem to float into outer space, bebop was born and improvisation was pushed toward unregulated artistic freedom.

first LISTEN

BRIEF INTRO	MAIN MELODIC FIGURE	SAXOPHONE	TRUMPET	PIANO	UNISON THEME	DRUM SOLO	CONCLUSION
0:00	0:06	0:19	1:16	1:40	2:03	2:14	2:21

 *a deeper* **LISTEN**

TIME	SECTION	LISTEN FOR THIS
0:00	Brief intro	Rhythm section, with light beat on ride cymbal
0:06	Main melodic figure	Unison figure shared by saxophone and trumpet, to which each responds briefly
0:19	Saxophone	Extended saxophone solo; short, disjointed bursts of melody, with periods of silence, accompanied by muted piano chords with rhythm on ride cymbal
1:16	Trumpet	Shorter trumpet solo; similar in style to sax solo, with slightly more flowing lines; same accompaniment
1:40	Piano	Shorter piano solo: similar disjointed figures on piano; ride cymbal picks up in intensity and adds accents
2:03	Unison theme	Sax and trumpet; return of unison figure
2:14	Drum solo	Brief drum solo: cymbals drop out
2:21	Conclusion	Brief statement of theme; resumption of unison figure and abrupt end by drums

Cool and Free Jazz

As the edgy qualities of bebop moved to new extremes, other styles arose in reaction. **Cool jazz**, practiced by musicians such as the trumpeter Miles Davis and saxophonist Gerry Mulligan, featured a transparent sound from the brass and reed instruments, which were played with little or no vibrato, and tended to favor relatively relaxed tempos. By the 1960s, the limits of jazz had broadened considerably. In *Kind of Blue* (1959), Miles Davis produced an album based on pitches drawn from scale-like modes rather than on pre-chosen triadic harmonies. In **free jazz**, musicians departed even further from the traditions that had served the art form for half a century. During the 1960s, Ornette Coleman and John Coltrane engaged in more radical improvisations, pushing jazz into the realm of free atonality and giving up preselected chord changes and forms.

MILES DAVIS

Miles Davis (1926–1991) playing the trumpet, 1950s.

Among the most innovative jazz musicians of the twentieth century was the trumpeter Miles Davis (1926–1991). Davis made important contributions to bebop and cool jazz, before pursuing in the late 1960s a new direction that fused elements of jazz and rock, **jazz rock**.

Davis grew up in East St. Louis, and was a professional musician by age fifteen. In 1944 he moved to New York, and studied for a while at Juilliard, but soon sought out his idol, Charlie Parker, and began playing with him in nightclubs. Like Parker, Davis fell victim to heroin addiction for a while during the early 1950s. Nevertheless he formed a series of ensembles—quintets, septets, and a nonet, featured in the recording *Birth of the Cool* (eventually released in 1957)—that showcased some of the greatest jazz musicians of the time. The classic recording *Kind of Blue* (1959), with Davis's signature composition, "So What," continues to be one of the top-selling jazz albums even after becoming a platinum success many times over. But arguably Davis's most remarkable, if provocative, artistic vision was displayed in the recording *Bitches Brew* (1969). This album brought together strains of jazz and rock during a tumultuous period of American history. We will listen to the opening section of a track titled "Miles Runs the Voodoo Down."

Miles Davis, **Bitches Brew,** *"Miles Runs the Voodoo Down" (1969)*

Cover of Davis's *Bitches Brew* (1969).

Like the other tracks on *Bitches Brew*, "Miles Runs the Voodoo Down" (**Listening Map, 73**) uses a rock-influenced band, but with some unusual combinations of instruments to provide a great variety of tone colors. The expanded rhythm section includes a bass clarinet, which occasionally growls in its low register, two electric pianos, an electric guitar, two electric basses, and two drum sets (with congos). The main solos are taken by Miles Davis on trumpet and Wayne Shorter on soprano sax (there are also moments that feature Chick Corea on the electric piano). When the piece was recorded, the musicians were given just a few sketch-like ideas from Davis of what might go into the composition, but nothing structured, allowing them more or less free reign to improvise. The extended track (it runs to over fourteen minutes) was then assembled in the studio, with extensive editing that included adding special reverb and looping effects, so that the post-recording process became a critical aspect of the final product.

The track begins quietly, with the drums and bass establishing the beat and a repeated, ostinato-like figure. When Miles Davis announces his solo (0:35), he enters with a held note in his middle range, with a brief comment or two. Then the music begins to climb, as he reaches his high register (1:29) and very high register (1:48) before falling. At 2:04 he experiments with flutter effects on the instrument, before returning to the high register for rapid bursts of notes (2:28), like distant memories of bebop riffs. The music grows in intensity here before settling down. The trumpet drops out (4:08), leaving the ensemble to carry on its improvisation a few minutes before more solo work in the soprano saxophone and trumpet.

MILES DAVIS, *Bitches Brew* ("Miles Runs the Voodoo Down," opening section)

{1969}

FORM	Freely improvised, then edited in the studio
METER	$\frac{4}{4}$
SCORING	Trumpet, soprano saxophone, bass clarinet, two electric pianos, electric guitar, two electric bass, two drum sets (congos)
OVERVIEW	An improvised fusion of elements of jazz (trumpet solo by Miles Davis) and rock (heavily emphasized rhythm section, chiefly electric instruments). Davis was not content to continue playing in the same style; throughout his career he stretched himself to incorporate new sounds and accompaniments. This track represents one of his most controversial changes, when he embraced rock instrumentation and rhythms.

why to LISTEN

At the time of its release, *Bitches Brew* polarized critical opinion. For some, it was neither jazz nor rock, but something that fell oddly between the two. For others, it was both jazz and rock, a visionary melding of two genres that explored a possible way forward. It was produced at a time of great social upheaval in the United States, at the height of the Vietnam War and student protests, and not long after the assassinations of Martin Luther King and Robert Kennedy (both in 1968). Perhaps the determined freedom of expression in this music—the musicians were playing spontaneously whatever they felt, largely by instinct, with only occasional cues from Davis—reflected the escapist counterculture of the times. In many ways this music was innovative—nothing like it had been heard before, and not every critic was ready to embrace it, although eventually it became a classic in jazz history. Like all great music, it challenged listeners, and continues to challenge us today.

a deeper LISTEN

TIME	SECTION	LISTEN FOR THIS
0:00	Intro	Drums, then bass establish the beat and a repeating, ostinato figure
0:35	Solo	Trumpet solo begins with held note, brief gestures in mid- and low range

Continued

TIME	SECTION	LISTEN FOR THIS
1:29		Trumpet moves to high register; background texture thickens
1:48		Trumpet reaches very high register before falling
2:04		Flutter effects in trumpet
2:28		Dramatic reach to higher register with rapid bursts of notes in trumpet, with prominent distorted guitar chords in the background
2:59		Held note in trumpet
3:32		Rapid bursts; electric piano chords more prominent in background
4:07		Trumpet drops out

check your **KNOWLEDGE**

1. How did jazz evolve in America? What impact did it have on other musical styles?
2. How did ragtime and blues influence the development of jazz?
3. Why is Duke Ellington so important in the history of jazz? Which musical elements did he introduce to the art form?
4. Who were the innovators of bebop? What characterized this new musical style?
5. What was the importance of Miles Davis's music to jazz history? Which innovations did he introduce on his albums *Kind of Blue* and *Bitches Brew*?

CHAPTER 47

Film Music, Musicals, and Contemporary Popular Styles

In addition to jazz, American popular music of the twentieth century has included several other distinctive styles that have had a lasting impact on music around the world. **Film music** was a new genre that developed in the capital of the movie industry, Hollywood. Several classical and popular composers contributed to this new style, bringing twentieth-century composition techniques to a mass audience. Aaron Copland and William Grant Still (see Chapter 45) were two of many American and foreign musicians drawn to Hollywood during the golden era of the 1930s and 1940s to compose music for the newest form of mass entertainment.

American **musicals** developed from loosely assembled revues in the early decades of the twentieth century to plot-driven productions featuring complex musical scores. While jazz was exported to Europe and elsewhere, twentieth-century American musical theater traced its roots to lighter forms of English and European opera. But the American musicals that emerged in the twentieth century were homegrown productions, unique blends of dialogue, songs, and dance that, like jazz, indelibly altered the soundscape of American culture before being embraced worldwide.

Another wave of new popular styles arose in the 1950s and 1960s, as rock and roll evolved into rock. It, too, became an international phenomenon, though it originally grew out of a blending of American country music and rhythm and blues. Rock and several other twentieth-century popular styles effectively offered a synthesis of white and African-American forms of popular music.

The Rise of Film Music

Beginning around 1895, the film industry had emerged first slowly in the early years of silent film, but then grew rapidly as nickelodeons and movie theaters began changing the face of urban American landscapes. Music played a role in silent film for a variety of reasons. From one perspective, silent films were *not* silent: the mechanical noise of the projector disturbed the audience's enjoyment of the film, and music could help mask the unwanted noise. But music also provided an aural thread that could better connect different scenes than could the caption-like title cards, and it could humanize the film by rendering the silent figures on the screen less ghostlike. Then, too, music could provide a kind of emotional backdrop and commentary about the film. And so theaters were built with spaces to accommodate

An early movie theater in Seattle, Washington, ca. 1905.

Charlie Chaplin in *Modern Times,* 1936. This was Chaplin's first sound film (although there was little spoken dialogue). Instead, he used music effectively to accompany the on-screen action.

a piano or theater organ, and musicians were hired who could improvise music appropriate for the film, whether for newsreels or comic features of Charlie Chaplin and Buster Keaton. The most elaborate theaters had pits to accommodate an orchestra that could play during films, in effect, a twentieth-century adaptation of nineteenth-century opera houses. Scores were published with specific cues for musicians to use so they could quickly accompany whatever scene appeared on screen.

Poster for *The Jazz Singer* (1927), the first sound film.

With the introduction of sound in the late 1920s, the film industry was revolutionized. The first film to use sound, *The Jazz Singer* with Al Jolson (1927), had about two minutes of spoken dialogue. The main novelty was hearing the actor singing several songs, including "Toot, Toot, Tootsie, Goodbye." More sophisticated uses of musical sound had to await new recording and mixing technologies. These advances arrived in the early 1930s and permitted music to be more easily synchronized with dialogue in the film. The landmark film associated with that development was *King Kong*, released in 1933 with a film score by Max Steiner. The film featured special sound effects for the mythical ape. Another impressive innovation was Steiner's orchestral score, which helped establish the practice of using music to underscore the dramatic continuity of the story.

During the Great Depression of the 1930s, Hollywood had entered a boom period as Americans flocked to the theaters to escape from the hard realities of their lives. During this Golden Era of Hollywood, which lasted roughly from the 1930s to 1950s, music was meant to be a backdrop to the film, playing a supporting role. The music arose from an invisible source—filmgoers could not see the orchestra producing the music, so it often worked its effect in a seemingly subconscious way. Whether the music was prominent or subtle, filmgoers were of course aware of it, but their primary attention was riveted to the action on the screen. Still, a great film score could enhance the experience of going to the theater. As the craft of writing film music became more sophisticated, it turned into a twentieth-century art form. Steiner was one of several composers who led the way in the new medium. Others included Eric Korngold (*The Adventures of Robin Hood*, 1938) and Bernard Herrmann (*Citizen Kane*, 1941).

Dashboard

Watch a short clip from *Psycho* to hear how Hermann's music built tension in that film.

Film production had remained robust during the Second World War as well, but by the late 1940s and 1950s, the industry experienced a downturn, in part owing to competition from a new medium—television. Once again questions were raised about the role of music, and the genre of film music entered a new phase of experimentation. Film composers still might use lush symphonic orchestras, as Elmer Bernstein did for the theme music of *The Magnificent Seven* (1960), but there was also a push to introduce other kinds of music into film. In *High Noon* (1952) Dimitri Tiomkin composed a cowboy song as the main musical number, and in *Man with the Golden Arm* (1955) Elmer Bernstein turned to jazz idioms. Duke Ellington wrote a jazz film score for *Anatomy of a Murder* (1959). Other trends included substantially reducing music in film, so that it appeared sparingly, and using music in a counter-intuitive ways so that it deliberately seemed out of place with the action (for example, playing a popular waltz during a scene of horrific violence). In lieu of orchestral music, electronic music and effects (see p. 532) were used in the science fiction film *Forbidden Planet* (1956). During the '50s, the whirring sound of the theremin—capable of producing unearthly glissandos—was commonplace in science fiction films. In the epic *2001: A Space Odyssey* (1968), Stanley Kubrick used *Atmosphères*—a modernist orchestral work of the Hungarian composer Gyorgi Ligeti from 1961 with dense, slowly evolving masses of sound—to accompany scenes of deep space.

The film music of the last forty years is quite diverse. It may draw on genres of popular music such as rock (*Pulp Fiction*, 1994) or rap (*The Great Gatsby*, 2013). Or it may freely draw on masterpieces of classical music. Ravel's *Bolero* was used in the film *10* (1979), because of its long history of being associated with sexual attraction and desire. Mendelssohn's "Italian" Symphony in *Breaking Away* (1979) added a touch of "class" to this story of town versus gown; Chopin's keyboard works in *The Pianist* (2002) provide a fitting background to the rarified world of the central character that is disrupted by the rise of Nazism; and a J. S. Bach keyboard suite in *Schindler's List* (1993) plays a similar role in underscoring the horrors of the Holocaust. Sometimes classical music appears in a film score because it actually *is* part of the dramatic narrative, the technical term for which is **diegetic music** or **source music**. Two noteworthy uses of diegetic music appear in *Clockwork Orange* (1971), in which the lead character Alex is obsessed by Beethoven's music; and *Amadeus* (1984), about the life and death of Mozart, which understandably borrows heavily from his music.

JOHN WILLIAMS

With the digitization of sound and sampling techniques, film music can be efficiently generated without engaging an orchestra to record the music. Still, some film composers prefer to write for a classical orchestra. One who has had a distinguished career in reviving the grand orchestral film score is John Williams (b. 1932). Williams worked as a jazz pianist and composer for television in the 1950s before shifting to film music and establishing himself in Hollywood. His impressive film credits include music for nearly 100 movies, among them several classics: *Jaws* (1975), *Close Encounters of the Third Kind* (1977), *Superman* (1978), *Raiders of the Lost Ark* (1981), *E. T. the Extra-Terrestrial* (1982), *Schindler's List* and *Jurassic Park* (1993), and *Harry Potter and the Sorcerer's Stone* (2001). Apart from film, Williams composed the familiar music heard at the end of *NBC Nightly News*, and made an arrangement for piano trio of

John Williams's scores appear in many classic movies, such as *E. T. the Extra-Terrestrial* (1982).

Williams's "Imperial March" from *The Empire Strikes Back* (1980) represents Darth Vader and the force of evil.

Copland's setting of "Simple Gifts" in *Appalachian Spring* (see p. 495) for the first inauguration of President Barack Obama. He also served for many years as the conductor of the Boston Pops Orchestra.

The 1977 launch of the movie *Star Wars,* and with it, the multibillion-dollar *Star Wars* franchise, marked a milestone in film history. The film and its various episodes have provided Williams with a broad canvas on which to paint colorful music of epic proportions. From a musical perspective, Williams's score traces its roots to Wagner's sprawling epic vision of *The Ring of the Nibelung,* which premiered in Germany in 1876, exactly 100 years before the release of *Star Wars* (see p. 371). Like Williams, Wagner composed music for a series of dramas, and developed techniques to ensure that the music supported the dramatic coherence of the whole. Chief among these was the use of recurring leitmotivs, with each associated with either a principal character or a dramatic idea central to the plot. Like Wagner, Williams uses Leitmotivs, and they are instantly recognizable to anyone who has watched the films. There is the opening fanfare music associated with the hero, Luke Skywalker, the "force" theme linked to the Jedi and Obi-Wan Kenobi, and a romantic melody for Princess Leia, among many others. These themes circulate throughout the music, and, like the motives in Wagner's *Ring,* they can be adapted and transformed to accommodate shifts in the dramatic narrative. Like Wagner as well, Williams uses a full orchestra, and writes in a lush, full style that has been described as neo-Romantic.

John Williams, "Imperial March," The Empire Strikes Back *(1980)*

One of the most celebrated musical numbers crafted by Williams for the *Star Wars* saga is the "Imperial March" (**Listening Map 74**). This music is heard in the sequel *The Empire Strikes Back* to introduce the character Darth Vader. Vader leads an imperial star fleet against the rebels, in an effort to defeat them, capture Luke, and turn him to the dark side of the Force.

The march begins with a percussive rhythmic pattern, repeated several times to set the militaristic mood. The theme is first boldly stated by the trumpets (1). It falls into three four-bar phrases driven forward by a steady, march-like pattern. As the theme drops out, the accompaniment resumes, joined by a new rhythmic pattern, with short motives in the flutes and strings. The march theme reappears, now stated in the French horns, with each phrase lengthened (2). Another interlude using the percussive rhythmic pattern follows, before we hear two more statements of the theme, first in the trumpets and immediately again in the horns. The accompaniment then leads to the coda, with a now increasingly dissonant presentation of the march theme, before a final flourish and climactic finish.

LISTENING MAP 74

JOHN WILLIAMS, "Imperial March" from *The Empire Strikes Back*

{1980}

FORM	March
METER	$\frac{4}{4}$
SCORING	One piccolo, two flutes, two oboes, one English horn, two clarinets, one bass clarinet, two bassoons, four French horns, three trumpets, three trombones, one tuba, timpani, percussion, harp, and strings.
OVERVIEW	A militaristic march driven by percussive rhythmic patterns and built around a central theme. The theme is circulated in various instrumentations throughout the orchestra, then interrupted by an interlude, which heightens the effect of the theme's climactic return.

why to LISTEN

Imagine, for a moment, listening to the "Imperial March" without knowing its title and without having seen or even heard of *The Empire Strikes Back*. Would the music mean anything? There is a good chance that we would hear the heavy-footed beats of this rousing music as a march. But understanding that the march represents Darth Vader and the force of evil heightens our experience of the film. It enhances our appreciation of how music can illustrate a dramatic moment and help tie together dramatic threads. The effect is so powerful that the film would seem barren without the music.

first LISTEN

INTRO	MARCH THEME	INTERLUDE	MARCH THEME	INTERLUDE	MARCH THEME	MARCH THEME	INTERLUDE	CODA
0:00	0:09	0:46	1:05	1:37	1:46	2:13	2:32	2:41

Continued

a deeper **LISTEN**

TIME	SECTION	LISTEN FOR THIS
0:00	Introduction	Repetitions of a basic rhythmic pattern
0:09	March theme	① In trumpets: falling in three phrases
0:46	Interlude	Rhythmic pattern resumes, joined by new soft motive in flutes and strings
1:05	March theme	② Second statement, in French horns, with each phrase prolonged
1:37	Interlude	
1:46	March theme	Third statement, in trumpets
2:13	March theme	Fourth statement, in French horns, and full orchestra
2:32	Interlude	
2:41	Coda	March theme becomes more dissonant, climactic ending

Musicals

Just as jazz evolved throughout the twentieth century, another genre of American music traced its own colorful history. Usually in two acts, **musicals** offered a blend of spoken dialogue, popular songs, and dances, drawing on nineteenth-century American and European traditions. One influence from the popular American tradition was **vaudeville**, a form of entertainment featuring songs, comic skits, and perhaps even acrobats and jugglers. Another was the **revue**, a light entertainment featuring songs and dances. Neither vaudevilles nor revues featured unified plots. Instead, that tradition came from European and English operettas, light forms of operas. Leading nineteenth-century composers of operettas had included the Viennese "Waltz King," Johann Strauss (*Die Fledermaus* [*The Bat*], 1874), and Sir Arthur Sullivan, a classically trained composer who collaborated with satirical poet W. S. Gilbert to produce popular English operettas such as *HMS Pinafore* (1878) and *The Mikado* (1885).

One of the first successful American musicals was *Babes in Toyland* (1903), composed by Victor Herbert, an Irish-born, German-raised cellist, conductor, and composer who arrived in the United States in 1886. While *Babes in Toyland* drew

Scene from a 1910 revue.

on characters from nursery rhymes, a new direction was taken by Jerome Kern in *Showboat* (1927), which became a smash hit on Broadway and then played throughout the United States to sold-out audiences. Unlike the much lighter fare of typical musicals, *Showboat* treated the serious American theme of race relations. It focused on a Mississippi River showboat, its white captain and actors, among them a character of mixed descent, and the African-American members of the crew who toiled beneath the deck. Its sobering song *Ol' Man River*, sung by the black stevedore Joe, became an American classic.

Other leading composers of musicals included George Gershwin (see p. 490); Cole Porter (*Kiss Me, Kate*, 1948); Richard Rodgers, who collaborated with the librettist Oscar Hammerstein on *Oklahoma!* (1943), *South Pacific* (1949; film version, 1958), and *The King and I* (1951); and Frederick Loewe (*My Fair Lady*, 1956, with lyricist Alan J. Lerner). All of these works produced their share of hit songs, and entered the repertory of theaters specializing in musicals, in much the same way as opera houses focused on a canon of acknowledged favorite operas. But the genre of the musical was open to innovation, and change came in the form of one of the most successful musicals of all time, a recasting of Shakespeare's *Romeo and Juliet*: Leonard Bernstein's *West Side Story*, which debuted in 1957.

LEONARD BERNSTEIN

A remarkably gifted and versatile musician, Leonard Bernstein (1918–1990) excelled as the first American conductor of the New York Philharmonic, and as

Leonard Bernstein (1918–1990).

a composer, pianist, and author. His works include three symphonies (the Third, the *Kaddish*, was dedicated to the memory of John F. Kennedy in 1963), a Mass, the choral work *Chichester Psalms*, ballets, film scores, and the operetta *Candide* (1956). Bernstein easily traversed classical, jazz, and popular traditions and brought all of them to bear on *West Side Story*. It became an iconic American work by virtue of its compelling combination of drama, dance, and music; its memorable numbers such as "Maria" and "Tonight"; and its unqualified success as a musical and Oscar-winning film adaptation (1961).

West Side Story treated a serious American subject: the violent encounters of rival teenage white and Puerto Rican gangs in New York. It universalized the story by offering it as a modern-day retelling of Shakespeare's *Romeo and Juliet*. Bernstein's genius was to forge an American synthesis of various musical elements. Popular music, jazz, and Latin-American rhythms take their place alongside recurring motives, fugal counterpoint, and an overarching symphonic sweep.

Bernstein, Balcony Scene from West Side Story, *"Tonight" (1957)*

The counterparts to Shakespeare's Romeo and Juliet are Tony, former leader of the Jets, and Maria, sister of Bernardo, leader of the Sharks. They meet at a high school dance, fall in love, and then, in the balcony scene (another nod to Shakespeare), sing the love duet "Tonight" on the fire escape outside Maria's apartment. In the end Tony falls victim to gang violence, and dies in Maria's embrace.

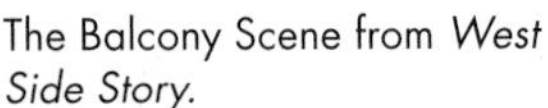

The Balcony Scene from *West Side Story*.

MAKING CONNECTIONS *The Many Roles of Leonard Bernstein*

Harvard educated, Bernstein rose as a young man to join the elite of American classical musicians. He played many different roles: he was a conductor, composer, pianist, author, lecturer, and ambassador of musical education. Steeped in the classical tradition, he also embraced jazz and popular music. He composed tonal music during the age of high modernism, when the avant-garde had little use for traditional harmony, and presented a decidedly American approach to the art of making and disseminating music.

In 1943, Bernstein became the assistant conductor of the New York Philharmonic, and within two months was put to the test when the guest conductor, Bruno Walter, became ill the day of his concert. With just hours to prepare and no time to rehearse, Bernstein at age twenty-five made his unexpected conducting debut, which was broadcast nationally and hailed in the press. He went on to lead the New York Philharmonic for many years and to make hundreds of recordings with the orchestra. Bernstein paid homage to one of its earlier conductors, Gustav Mahler (see p. 402), by recording Mahler's complete symphonies. Bernstein also conceived the Young People's Concerts, a series of lectures and performances with the orchestra. These concerts explored a range of musical topics and were broadcast live (for three years these programs were aired on television in the evenings during prime time).

But perhaps Bernstein's most memorable performance came in 1989, as the Berlin Wall that had divided two Germanys for decades was being dismantled. On Christmas Day, Bernstein led a jubilant concert not far from the wall, with an orchestra that included East and West Berliners, culminating in Beethoven's Ninth Symphony. For the event, the "Ode to Joy" finale became an "Ode to Freedom," as Bernstein substituted the word "Freiheit" (freedom) for "Freude" (joy). Only months later, he would die of cancer.

Fall of the Berlin Wall, 1989.

The Balcony Scene (**Listening Map 75**) begins with quiet music for the strings, including a brief recall of Tony's "Maria," sung in the previous scene. After some dialogue between the lovers, they break into recitative-like exchanges, as a cha-cha rhythmic pulse is established, carrying forward to the opening verses of "Tonight," sung by Maria. Tony answers, and then, as the tempo pulls back, the two sing together, suddenly resuming the faster tempo. When an offstage voice interrupts Maria, the lovers resume their dialogue, briefly breaking into singing for the final bars of the melody, "Good night, good night, sleep well and when you dream, dream of me tonight."

LISTENING MAP 75

LEONARD BERNSTEIN, *West Side Story*, Balcony Scene, "Tonight"

{1957}

FORM	Strophic song
METER	4/4
SCORING	Tony, Maria, and orchestra
OVERVIEW	The scene begins with spoken dialogue between Tony and Maria, shifts to recitative-like singing, before the orchestra introduces the "Tonight" melody, sung by Maria and then by Maria and Tony.

why to LISTEN

When *West Side Story* opened on Broadway in 1957, it surprised theatergoers. Many members of the audience did not imagine that they would be seeing a musical about gang violence on the Upper West Side, at the time an ethnic working-class neighborhood not far from the theater. How could a musical successfully treat such a subject? It had the perfect combination of lyrics by the young Stephen Sondheim (who went on to compose musicals of his own), expertly choreographed dances by Jerome Robbins, and captivating music by Bernstein that drew on a rich musical vocabulary—jazz and Latin-American rhythms, and recurring musical themes to help tie the whole together. The result used universal Shakespearean themes to take on a subject close to home, and it earned an immediate American relevance.

a deeper LISTEN

TIME	SECTION	TEXT
0:00	**Dialogue between the lovers**	
1:43	**Recitative-like exchanges between Maria and Tony**	
2:33	**Introduction of "Tonight" melody in strings** *mf* To - night, to - night, It all be - gan to - night,	

TIME	SECTION	TEXT
2:40	First strophe (Maria)	Tonight, tonight, it all began tonight, I saw you and the world went away. Tonight, tonight, there's only you tonight, What you are what you do what you say.
3:11	Tony	Today I had the feeling, A miracle would happen. I know now I was right. For here you are, and what was just a world is a star, Tonight.
3:50	Second strophe (Maria and Tony), slower tempo, then resuming faster tempo	Tonight, tonight, the world is full of light, With suns and moons all over the place. Tonight, tonight, the world is wild and bright, Going mad, shooting sparks into space. Today the world is just an address A place for me to live in, no better than all right. But here you are, and what was just a world is a star, Tonight.
5:35	Music continues with dialogue	
6:32	Repeat of end of melody	Good night, good night, sleep well and when you dream, dream of me Tonight.

Since *West Side Story*, musicals have continued to thrive. There have been "rock" musicals, such as Galt MacDermot's *Hair* (1967), which explored the hippie movement and shocked audiences with its use of nudity; and Andrew Lloyd Webber's *Jesus Christ Superstar* (1971), conceived as a "rock opera." Stephen Sondheim offered a musical thriller in his *Sweeney Todd: The Demon Barber of Fleet Street* (1979), and Lloyd Webber explored the macabre in *Phantom of the Opera* (1986), which became the longest-running Broadway show. And, in a cross-genre twist, there have been musicals based on animated films, including *The Lion King* (1994), with songs by Elton John and score by Hans Zimmer. Musicals became an international phenomenon as composers, American and non-American alike, explored and expanded the genre.

Contemporary Popular Styles

The twentieth century produced many other streams of popular music, and by mid-century, several were rivaling jazz. Appealing largely to white, working-class Americans, **country music** emerged in the 1940s and developed into a powerful new music industry ultimately centered in Nashville, Tennessee. Derived from rural "hillbilly" music, country music favored string bands (banjo, guitar, violin, and string bass) and spawned subgenres, including **honky-tonk** (featuring the electric steel guitar) and (inspired by the music of Appalachia). **Gospel music**, with origins in nineteenth-century revivalist movements, began by offering consoling spiritual messages drawn from the Bible. Within African-American churches, gospel songs absorbed the syncopations, blue notes, and call-and-response patterns of blues and jazz. This cross-pollination in turn spread gospel music outside church sanctuaries. By the 1960s and 1970s, gospel influenced the emergence of a new secular style, **soul music**. It was tied to the civil rights movement and to singers such as Ray Charles and Aretha Franklin. Another new style, **funk**, associated with James Brown, also carried forward some of the elements of gospel music, particularly in the intensity of Brown's singing. Brown's music featured a strong bass line, interlocked rhythmic patterns, and interjections from the band.

Aretha Franklin performs in a gospel show at the White House in 2015.

Almost inevitably, different strains of American popular music began to influence one another, spawning new genres that transformed popular culture. By far the most powerful synthesis came around the mid-1950s, with the explosive emergence of **rock and roll**. In this music, country music combined with a forceful, African-American urban style known as **rhythm and blues**. With chordal harmonies modeled on blues patterns, rock and roll was performed at fast tempos and with an earthy, guttural vocal quality. In 1954 Bill Haley (1925–1981) recorded "Rock around the Clock," which sold twenty million copies. In 1956 Elvis Presley (1935–1977), the first superstar of rock and roll, took the country by storm with "Heartbreak Hotel" and "Hound Dog." "Elvis the Pelvis"—as he was nicknamed by disapproving mainstream press—captivated audiences with his gyrating stage gestures, and became a film star and idol of American youth.

Elvis Presley (1935–1977), the first rock and roll superstar, in 1957 dancing in the film *Jailhouse Rock*.

Following the relative prosperity of the 1950s, the 1960s brought social upheaval. President Kennedy's "New Frontier," President Johnson's "Great Society," the civil rights movement, the women's liberation movement, and the protest against the Vietnam War shaped the culture of the decade. The popular music of the time, now known simply as **rock**, reflected the social unrest. Rock bands featured heavily amplified electric guitars capable of great volume, and new timbres such as fuzz tone and wah-wah. Usually in $\frac{4}{4}$ time, rock songs typically had accents on the second and fourth beats, rather than the first and third, as in a traditional $\frac{4}{4}$ meter. Emphasizing the second and fourth beats (the "backbeats") generated great rhythmic energy. Singers matched the power of their instrumental bandmates, often pushing their voice (through using falsetto or adding nonsense syllables) to reflect the intensity of rock's message.

Rock reached its greatest popularity with the music of the Beatles. This quartet of English musicians started out playing in the taverns of Liverpool and then the red-light district of Hamburg, Germany, before achieving international stardom with their first American tour in 1964. The Beatles synthesized the blues, rhythm and blues, rock and roll, and other forms of American popular music. Their leaders were the guitarists John Lennon and Paul McCartney, who wrote the words and music of most of their songs. George Harrison played lead guitar, and Ringo Starr played the drums.

MAKING CONNECTIONS *The '60s: Music of Protest*

There is a rich tradition in American popular culture of using music as a means of social protest. The second half of the twentieth century brought this trend to a new intensity. The folk singer Pete Seeger, a political activist, wrote many songs in the 1950s ("Where Have All the Flowers Gone," "Turn, Turn, Turn"). His songs were revived and covered in the 1960s, when their message of peace struck a chord with civil rights activists and antiwar protestors. Bob Dylan followed with his own protest songs in the 1960s such as "Blowin' in the Wind" and "The Times, They Are a-Changin'." Both Seeger and Dylan used acoustic instruments (banjo or guitar for Seeger, guitar and harmonica for Dylan), but in 1965 Dylan turned to rock-inflected amplification in "Like a Rolling Stone." It was the year of Vietnam War escalation and the deployment of 200,000 American troops to Southeast Asia.

Folk singers Bob Dylan and Pete Seeger in 1963 performing at the Newport Folk Festival.

By 1969, four years later, the antiwar movement had galvanized the American public, and the government began looking for ways to de-escalate the conflict. In August, some 400,000 rock fans converged on a farm in rural New York for what was billed as "three days of peace and music." The Woodstock Festival, as it became known, attracted many of the leading performers and bands of the time, among them the folk singers Arlo Guthrie and Joan Baez, the Indian sitarist Ravi Shankar, Latin rock band Santana, and several other rock bands, including Janis Joplin; the Who; Jefferson Airplane; Blood, Sweat & Tears; and Crosby, Stills and Nash. The last performer was Jimi Hendrix, who gave a peace sign and then launched into a booming, distorted version of "The Star Spangled Banner," interpreted as an antiwar statement. For the faithful fans, the event offered an unforgettable experience of the power of music to provoke and soothe, and to suggest a vision of a better world.

Cover of the Beatles' *Sergeant Pepper's Lonely Hearts Club Band* (1967).

The Beatles continued touring for a few more years and enjoyed international acclaim. "Norwegian Wood" (1965), "Yesterday" (1965), "Eleanor Rigby" (1966), and many other songs became classics of popular music. Then, in 1966, the Beatles retired from public performance and produced a series of full-length albums. In *Sergeant Pepper's Lonely Hearts Club Band* (1967), appealing to counterculture youth, they brought together various styles, including blues, jazz, and Indian music, and employed various instruments, among them the Indian sitar and tabla, harpsichord, and orchestral ensembles. Experiments with tape delays, sound collage, and overlapping sounds were incorporated into the album's rich textures. It was one of the first **concept albums**, an album where all the music was unified by an idea or concept rather than existing as a set of separate and unrelated songs. In the case of *Sergeant Pepper*, the songs were imagined as a performance by a band from Edwardian England. The Beatles stood in as members of this imaginary band, and the album created a fictional concert experience, complete with audience noises. The lead music was heard as a kind of overture in the first track and then brought back near the end, giving the album a circular unity. The album redefined the nature and scope of the rock experience and sold eight million copies.

For a few short years, the Beatles continued to experiment in recording albums, producing several mega hits ("Hey Jude," "Let It Be," among many others). Their music ranged from psychedelic rock ("Across the Universe") to lyrical ballads ("Blackbird"). But the band members began to drift apart, and the group finally broke up in 1970. In contrast, a second English rock band, the Rolling Stones, continue to tour and age together decades after their formation in the 1960s. They specialize in a hard-driving blues style, led by lead vocalist Mick Jagger and guitarist Keith Richards, also the group's songwriting team.

As rock became more complex, it sometimes moved closer to the classical tradition. In a movement of the 1970s known as **progressive rock**, several bands (Pink Floyd; Emerson, Lake & Palmer) drew on classical techniques to produce music that tested the boundaries of popular and art music. But by the 1980s new types of rock, characterized by louder music and theatrical gestures, were in vogue. **Heavy metal**, **punk rock**, and **grunge** were a few, all sharing a determined rejection of mainstream rock. Heavy metal used heavily distorted and amplified sound. Punk rock turned against mainstream rock by using an aggressively raw sound and promoting independent "garage bands." Grunge, which arose in Seattle, Washington, in the early '80s, drew on elements from both heavy metal and punk.

During the 1970s, 1980s, and 1990s a bewildering variety of alternatives to rock further enriched the diversity of popular music. In the '70s, **disco** took hold in dance clubs until its heyday passed after a decade or so. Singer-songwriters grew out of **folk rock**, first promoted in the mid-1960s by artists such as Bob Dylan and Simon & Garfunkel, and bringing the style of folk music into the world of rock. **Reggae** offered an alternative in the calypso-infused music of Jamaica. In the early '80s, at African-American dance parties in New York, Detroit, and other cities, disc jockeys played songs on multiple turntables, occasionally interrupting the music by manually slowing down or speeding up the records. In the process they created scratching sounds and other distortions, so that the turntables became a new form of musical instrument, giving rise to **turntablism**. When DJs began improvising rhyming patterns over the music, the seeds were planted for a new art form, **rap**, which would eventually form part of a larger cultural movement known as **hip-hop**. Soon enough, rappers were creating rhyming texts that were spoken rhythmically over a background beat. Rap quickly proved its commercial viability and began spinning off sub-genres. The most controversial was **gangsta rap**, which featured provocative, racially charged texts about inner-city life, crime, and violence.

Tupac Shakur (1971–1996) was an emblem of American gangsta rap.

Finally, the explosion of popular music late in the twentieth century was aided by the extraordinary rise of personal computers, which were introduced in the 1980s. By using **sampling** technology (and synthesizers, sequencers, and drum machines), composers could digitally record and access sounds and beat patterns. Without needing live bands or recording studios, they could then manipulate recorded materials to create a new musical style, now loosely described as **electronica**. This development was not uncontroversial—for one thing, it raised copyright issues. But the result was to set free new, rapidly evolving genres of popular music, which have continued to blend into the mainstream.

The future trajectory of popular music is impossible to predict. But its ever-changing diversity will no doubt continue to mark not only American, but also worldwide musical experiences.

check your **KNOWLEDGE**

1. How was music used during the silent film era? Which challenges did composers face when sound came to the motion picture industry?
2. How do John Williams's film scores draw on traditions of classical music?
3. How did Leonard Bernstein's score for *West Side Story* combine different popular styles? Why was this appropriate music for the libretto of this musical?
4. How do recent musicals draw on traditions developed over the past decades? How do they innovate?
5. Why are the Beatles considered to be among the greatest of all rock bands?
6. How has American popular music been used as protest music?
7. What other styles of popular music have developed since the 1970s?

CHAPTER

48 The Eclipse of Modernism: New Frontiers

Jackson Pollock's work, such as *Number 3, 1949: Tiger* incorporates elements of chance, as did some music of the post-WWII era.

Some of the leading developments of classical music since 1950 have included the extension of twelve-tone music to non-pitch elements, the use of electronic media to explore unconventional musical sounds, the introduction of random choices in the compositional process to produce chance music, and the revival of tonality. Along with these trends, this period witnessed a dramatic increase in the number of women composers; the development of a new musical style known as minimalism; quotation and collage techniques; and, finally, the breaking up of high modernism in music, so that by the 1980s critics were describing a new period known as postmodernism.

The end of the Second World War in 1945 unleashed new experimentation in the arts. In the postwar economy, America was experiencing unprecedented growth and prosperity. Many artists rejected the conformity of 1950s America, and put their efforts into creating new modernist styles. During the 1950s, '60s, and '70s, audiences might hear traditional works intended for concert hall performances but also compositions meant to capture random, everyday sounds, including the lack of sound, silence. Indeed, at no point in the history of Western classical music was music as diverse as in the second half of the century. In the twentieth century's waning decades, probing questions arose about the nature and purpose of music. And yet, while this second revolution in sound attracted avant-garde modernists who wanted to make radical innovations, older musical traditions somehow managed to survive. Music of the last sixty or so years—what used to be known as "contemporary music"—has offered a bewildering juxtaposition of the old and new, the familiar and unimaginable.

Technology helped fuel this second revolution. Joining the earlier development of radio, film, and sound recording, the postwar years saw the introduction of television and the tape recorder. Television brought the arts into the home; the tape recorder gave composers a flexible way to create and preserve their musical works. Mass audiences were easier to reach than ever before, and music of every sort, from art music to jazz and every form of popular music, were more easily distributed. Early experiments were also being made with the potential of computers to create music during the late 1950s, 1960s, and 1970s. These gave way to a boom that began in the 1980s, with the introduction of digital synthesizers, personal computers, sampling devices, and other sound-creating equipment. These technologies enabled composers to explore uncharted musical territory and to generate sounds with unprecedented precision. They gave composers the utmost control over their work, but also raised new issues about composers' relations to their sonic environments and audiences.

The New Order: Total Serialism

Arnold Schoenberg (see p. 446) developed his twelve-tone, or serial system of composition, in the 1920s. His new way of organizing the twelve pitches of the chromatic scale into tone rows was a dominant force in much of the modernist music in the first half of the twentieth century. The logical next step was for composers to serialize, or organize, other aspects of music, such as rhythm, dynamics, and register, to achieve "totally" serialized music. One of the early experimenters in **serialism** was the French composer Olivier Messiaen (1908–1992), who in the late 1940s began structuring non-pitch elements in his compositions. Messiaen found inspiration in a variety of sources, including ancient Greek meters, Hindu rhythmic patterns, Peruvian folk song, and especially birdcalls. An avid ornithologist, he based several works on birdcalls meticulously notated during field expeditions. He explored "non-retrogradable" rhythmic patterns—those with the same sequence of rhythms forward and backward—that invest his compositions with a timeless, spiritual quality.

Two younger composers, the Frenchman Pierre Boulez (1925–2016) and German Karlheinz Stockhausen (1928–2007), pursued further Messiaen's attempt to control non-pitch elements. The serialization of elements in their works, including pitch, rhythm, dynamics, and register, was so complete that it was termed **total serialism**. Boulez's major work in this style was *Structures I* for two pianos, first performed in 1952. To create this unprecedented work, Boulez borrowed a twelve-tone row from Messiaen, and then constructed "rows" of twelve different rhythms, twelve different dynamic levels, and twelve different types of articulations. Next, he aligned his non-pitch rows with rows of pitches. In this way, Boulez was able to predetermine exactly the particular sounds and events of his composition.

Karlheinz Stockhausen was equally fascinated by Messiaen's experiments, describing them as the "fantastic music of the stars." Stockhausen's first major effort in total serialism was *Kreuzspiel* (*Cross-Play*, 1951), for piano, oboe, bass clarinet, and percussion, in which he worked with points of sound. He organized the composition as a series of intersections of different musical components such as pitch, rhythm, and register.

To many, the strict control exercised by Stockhausen and Boulez in their new music marked the final milestone in serialism. Ultimately, total serialism ran its course, and composers searched for other alternatives. The modernist styles that so captured the imagination of young, avant-garde composers failed to appeal to mainstream musical taste, but that did not discourage the leading edge of the avant-garde from discovering new resources in sound.

New Resources in Sound

After the Second World War, the advancing technologies of the electronic age opened up new sonic worlds. Mild tremors of what was to come had already been felt earlier in the century. In 1920, the Russian physicist Léon Theremin invented an instrument that used oscillators to generate audible frequencies. Known as the theremin, the instrument featured two steel wands, one of which controlled pitch and the other volume. A player could move his hands to disrupt the electrical field around each wand, which would raise and lower pitch and volume. In 1928 the French scientist Maurice Martenot produced the *ondes martenot*, a keyboard instrument controlling an oscillator that, in turn, produced sound amplified and projected through a loudspeaker. The 1920s also marked the appearance of the first electric organs.

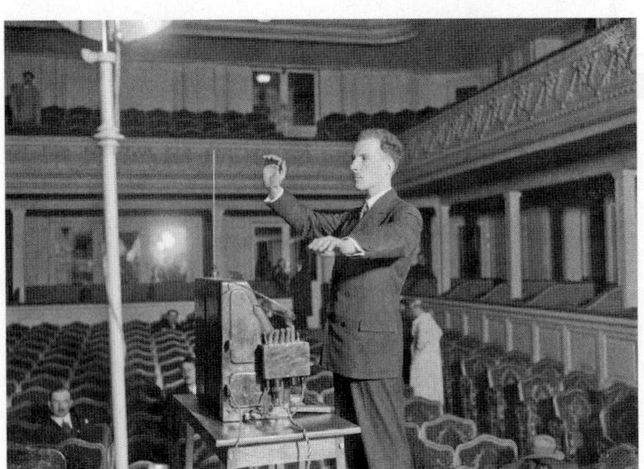

· Léon Theremin playing the instrument he invented.

More advances in manipulating electronic sounds were made in the late 1940s by composers working in a French sound laboratory. They used phonograph discs and later magnetic tape to record sounds of everyday life, including locomotives, musical instruments, cries, and laughter. They then dissected, reassembled, played backward, accelerated, or otherwise manipulated these sounds to produce **musique concrète**, or "concrete music." By the early 1950s, the advent of tape recorders greatly facilitated the collecting, storing, and editing of material.

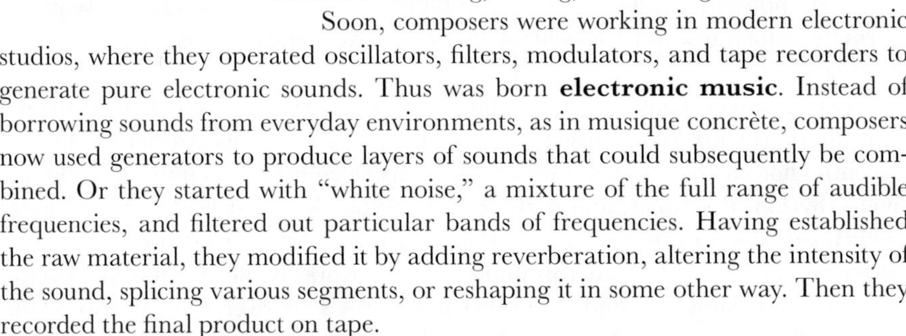

Soon, composers were working in modern electronic studios, where they operated oscillators, filters, modulators, and tape recorders to generate pure electronic sounds. Thus was born **electronic music**. Instead of borrowing sounds from everyday environments, as in musique concrète, composers now used generators to produce layers of sounds that could subsequently be combined. Or they started with "white noise," a mixture of the full range of audible frequencies, and filtered out particular bands of frequencies. Having established the raw material, they modified it by adding reverberation, altering the intensity of the sound, splicing various segments, or reshaping it in some other way. Then they recorded the final product on tape.

The advantage of electronic music was that composers could control with absolute precision the end product. There was no need for musicians or rehearsals. Composers encoded their intentions on magnetic tape. They left nothing to chance; every detail of the music was clinically controlled in the sound laboratory.

EDGARD VARÈSE

One musician who exploited these new musical resources was the Frenchman Edgard Varèse (1883–1965). His goal was nothing less than the "liberation of sound." Although Varèse wrote most of his music before the Second World War, his work was most influential after the war. Varèse arrived in the United States in 1915, having destroyed his early compositions. He followed no trend, and, comparing twelve-tone music to

MAKING CONNECTIONS *An Early Electronic Studio*

After the Second World War, musical modernism took another turn with the exploration of electronic music, as composers sought to expand the sound worlds in which they created music well beyond conventional instruments. In 1957 the RCA Mark II Sound Synthesizer was installed at Columbia University in New York. For the next ten years or so, leading experimental composers worked there to generate examples of electronic music, culminating in Charles Wuorinen's *Time Encomium*, which won a Pulitzer Prize in 1970. The RCA Mark II filled an entire room with sound synthesizing devices, tone oscillators, and a primitive music sequencer, all connected and capable of producing a phonograph record. Bulky, unwieldy, and filled with vacuum tubes, the Mark II was soon enough obsolete, but it counted as the first electronic synthesizer that could be programmed. For the first time, composers could use electronic sounds to determine precisely pitches and rhythms. This development led to increasingly complex textures of sounds well beyond what musicians could achieve in playing a score.

The RCA Mark II at Columbia University (1957) was the first programmable electronic synthesizer. Shown in the photo are composers (l to r): Mario Davidovsky, Milton Babbitt, and Vladimir Ussacheskvy

"hardening of the arteries," dismissed Schoenberg's approach. A militant experimenter, Varèse brought unconventional sounds into his modernist scores and used traditional instruments in unusual ways, all in an effort to create what he called "organized noise."

Rejecting traditional notions of thematic and harmonic development, Varèse described his music as colliding sound masses that repelled each other. He compared his music to crystals, with their infinite variety of shapes. Each composition by Varèse had its own, unique form, the result of his rigorous control of its sound masses. To describe his innovative creations, he turned to scientific titles: *Hyperprism* and *Ionisation*, for example.

Edgard Varèse (1883–1965).

The requirements of Varèse's scores vary from *Amériques* for large orchestra (1921) to *Density 21.5* (1936), written for a single flute made of platinum, whose density is 21.5. He also produced a group of compositions for relatively small chamber ensembles. *Ionisation* (1931) is for percussion instruments alone, mostly unpitched, so that pitch is essentially eliminated as a structural component. Varèse employed a variety of familiar instruments, including drums, castanets, triangle, tambourine, and cymbals. But he also introduced a group of sirens, which produced arching crescendos of sound. In addition, there are distinctive touches of cowbells, sleigh bells, anvils, woodblocks, slapstick, and a "lion's roar," a tub-shaped drum with a rope drawn through its membrane to produce a dull, roaring sound. Reportedly, scientists at Los Alamos, New Mexico, during the 1940s listened to a recording of *Ionisation* as they worked on the first atomic bomb. (The term *ionization* refers to the process by which atomic particles acquire negative or positive charges by adding or losing electrons.)

From 1936 to 1947, Varèse largely withdrew from composition. He was discouraged by what he could achieve with conventional instruments. He yearned for new musical resources, a wish answered after the war by the arrival of electronic music.

Varèse, Poème électronique *(1958)*

In 1954, Varèse composed *Déserts*, a hybrid work in which sections for orchestra alternate with portions of musique concrète. *Déserts* was the first work to combine electronic sounds with an orchestra, and the first work to bring electronically manipulated sounds into the concert hall. In choosing the title, Varèse meant to suggest both barren landscapes of sound and the loneliness of the modern individual.

Four years later, in 1958, the aging composer finished *Poème électronique*, a watershed eight-minute electronic work created for the Philips Radio Corporation pavilion at the Brussels World's Fair, the first world fair since the Second World War. Designed by the French architect Le Corbusier and his Greek assistant Iannis Xenakis, who was also a composer, the pavilion was constructed of prestressed concrete formed into swooping clusters of hyperbolic paraboloids in the shape of a stomach. Upon entering the pavilion, some two million visitors heard Varèse's music broadcast into a central chamber through hundreds of speakers embedded in the walls. The walls displayed projected montages of images: a bull and matador, skeletons, masks, a reclining woman, images of the Holocaust, and atomic explosions. The montages, meant to trace mankind's development and striving toward a new, futuristic harmony, were designed by Xenakis. The final image showed a mother holding an infant, as if to suggest that the unpredictable cycle of modern life would begin anew.

Le Corbusier's Philips Pavilion at the Brussels World's Fair in 1958.

Against these images Varèse offered his own musical montage of electronic sounds, including bits of musique concrète (recordings of bells, machines, trains, etc.) and freely created and manipulated electronic gestures. On first hearing, the composition bombards the listener with seemingly random noise. There are siren-like sequences, various squawks, peeps, low thudding noises, wailing, and drum-like sounds. But this music is not random music, as a few rehearings of the first two and a half minutes reveal (see **Listening Map 76**). Framing this segment of the composition is the tolling of low bells, and a further unifying element is a recurring, slowly sliding series of three ascending pitches. Between these events are arcing sirens, tapping sounds, machine noise, and other events, as if confirming Varèse's desire to "make music out of any and all sounds."

LISTENING MAP 76

EDGARD VARÈSE, *Poème électronique (Electronic Poem)*, opening 2′36″

{1958}

MEDIUM	Electronic music
OVERVIEW	This opening segment begins and ends with tolling bells. Over the course of the 2′36″ we hear a variety of electronically produced sounds, unified by a recurring three-note ascending motive.

why to LISTEN

Varèse's *Poème électronique* concentrated electronically produced sounds emitted through hundreds of speakers to engulf visitors for eight minutes as they informally strolled through a futuristic pavilion in 1958. The visitors also saw a montage of images chosen by Xenakis as a kind of visual counterpoint to the music. We can no longer recreate the original experience of this multimedia artwork, and without Xenakis's images it is difficult to imagine the full effect of this collaborative effort. Today we listen blindly, as it were, to Varèse's succession of careening sounds, mostly unpitched but offering some pitched sounds as well, like a few lifelines to a more familiar musical world. In 1958, these electronic swoops, sirens, taps, and grating sounds announced a brave new world of music that opened up a new horizon of a seemingly infinite variety of sounds. They challenged and pushed listeners' expectations. Moving us out of our comfort zone is one thing that experimental music can do. Whether we embrace the music or not, coming to terms with its ability to provoke and shock, whether through conventional or electronic means, is an important reason to listen.

a deeper LISTEN

TIME	LISTEN FOR THIS
0:00	Tolling of low bells, tapping, sirens, high shrill sounds, pause
0:43	Drum-like sounds and grating noises and squawks
0:56	Rising, three-note motive heard three times

Continued

TIME	LISTEN FOR THIS
1:10	Low sounds with added grating noises, sirens, squawks
1:34	Rising, three-note motive heard once, pause
1:38	Short bursts of squawks, chirping sounds, machine noises, sirens and taps
2:34	Tolling of low bells

Further Developments in Electronic Music

Electronic music celebrated the modernity of the postwar years, and yet reconnected its listeners to their past. In 1956, the new medium inspired the avant-garde German composer Karlheinz Stockhausen to create an ambitious work, *Gesang der Jünglinge* (*Song of the Youths*). Created completely in an electronic studio, this composition combined meandering mixtures of electronic sounds with bits of spoken, if distorted, German text, almost as if to humanize the music. The composition relates the biblical story of Nebuchadnezzar's fiery furnace (Book of Daniel 3), into which three Jews are thrown, but survive unscathed. In 1956, the image of a fiery furnace was all too vivid to a Europe still recovering from the horrors of the Second World War. The whole composition was channeled through five sets of speakers surrounding the audience, transforming the space into an engulfing labyrinth of sound.

Early electronic music was created as tape compositions. No live performers took part in "performances" of the music. The interaction of live performers and taped elements, the next stage in the genre's history, was explored during the 1960s and 1970s. Beginning in the '80s, another development, **live electronic music**, was made possible by new electronic equipment that was portable and could be played in "real time." Electronic music could be performed in the concert hall and combined with live music-making in a new synthesis.

A modern synthesizer.

In recent decades, the equipment composers have used to produce electronic music has become vastly more sophisticated and easier to use than the awkward tape recorders and room-sized synthesizers available at mid-century. Modern synthesizers, increasingly powerful personal computers, and the emergence of sampling techniques facilitated the creation of new electronic music, affording composers far more accuracy in exploring the limits of quantifiable sound.

CHANCE IN MUSIC

Although electronic music offered an ideal way to achieve totally controlled music, some composers moved in the opposite direction: they began introducing spontaneity into their music. For example, Stockhausen's *Klavierstück XI* (*Piano Piece XI*, 1956) has nineteen sections of music that may be played in any order, yielding an ever-changing musical landscape. These experiments were responses to the radically new musical philosophy of the American composer John Cage (1912–1992), who during the early 1950s pioneered the use of chance elements to redefine the very meaning of music.

JOHN CAGE

John Cage (1912–1992).

As early as 1937, Cage was exploring the idea that music should use "any and all sounds that can be heard." He studied composition with Henry Cowell in New York before requesting lessons from Arnold Schoenberg in Los Angeles. Schoenberg agreed to teach him without charge if Cage would devote his life to composition, but ultimately, Cage could not subscribe to the twelve-tone method. Instead, he began pursuing his own path. That meant shattering the traditional mold of classical music, and viewing its themes, harmonies, and rhythms as outworn clichés. Among other influences, Cage admired the work of Marcel Duchamp, who had radically altered perceptions of what might constitute visual art with his "readymades" (found everyday objects that he labeled as artworks) and by painting a mustache on a reproduction of the *Mona Lisa* (see p. 423).

By the 1940s, Cage demonstrated his unorthodox style in a series of works composed for "prepared piano." He altered the piano by attaching various objects, such as screws, bolts, and wedges, to its strings, producing unfamiliar, metallic sounds. The composer could never be sure what sounds would be produced, because the preparation itself could vary from performance to performance. Later on, Cage studied Eastern philosophy and Zen Buddhism. Rejecting Western notions of musical order, he began producing in the early 1950s works whose components were determined by random sequences drawn from the *I Ching*, the ancient Chinese book of changes.

John Cage, **4'33"** *(1952)*

In his early efforts, Cage used random procedures to generate a fixed result. In time, he sought even greater freedom by progressively eliminating evidence of the composer's decision-making process. These attempts culminated in what became his most notorious composition, *4'33"* (**Listening Map 77**), which premiered in 1952 by the pianist David Tudor. At the first performance, Tudor did not play the instrument at all during the "performance" but merely signified the beginning and ending of its three movements by closing and opening the keyboard lid. Filling the silence were the random noises of the surroundings, which of course varied with each "performance." Comparing himself to a "sound tourist," Cage was captivated by the active but random world of *ambient sounds*—the actual sounds that occur all around us at all times—many of which were contributed by the audience itself. For Cage, sounds did not have to mean anything at all, but could simply exist. And silence was the preferred medium, because inevitably external sounds would encroach upon its domain, in purely spontaneous sequences.

LISTENING MAP 77

JOHN CAGE, *4′33″* {1951}

OVERVIEW	Just listen, taking note of ambient, random sounds during the duration of the piece.

why to LISTEN

Why listen to *4′33″*? The title is often given as *4′33″ of Silence*, but that is a misnomer and misses Cage's basic point: there is no silence. The piece was inspired by an experience Cage had after entering a heavily soundproofed room designed to block all external noise. He fully expected to hear nothing at all. Instead, he could perceive high and low sounds, the sounds of his nervous system and blood circulation. At the 1951 premiere of *4′33″*, the pianist David Tudor did not play a single note. Yet the "silence" was filled with ambient sounds—the wind outside the hall, rain on the roof, noises among the audience. Because our normal environment is filled with constantly changing sounds, those sounds can constitute a random type of music. And listening to a piece in which the performer does nothing at all connects us to the greater sound world. It reminds us that music, broadly speaking, is all around us.

first LISTEN

FIRST MOVEMENT*	SECOND MOVEMENT*	THIRD MOVEMENT*
0:00	0:33	3:13

*total duration of the three movements at the premiere in 1952 was 4′33″.

a deeper LISTEN

For this deeper listen, try to be attentive to all the sounds occurring around you. You can create your own "sound map," noting the exact timings for when you hear each individual sound. In this way, you will have a score for your individual performance of this work.

TIME	SECTION	LISTEN FOR THIS
0:00	First Movement	
0:33	Second Movement	
3:13	Third Movement	

MAKING CONNECTIONS *Across the Arts: John Cage, Robert Rauschenberg, and Merce Cunningham*

In conceiving *4′33″*, Cage admitted the influence of the American painter Robert Rauschenberg, who in 1953 began exhibiting his controversial series of *White Paintings*. These were canvases painted white, and, like Cage's *4′33″*, seemingly devoid of content. But they responded to small changes in ambient light, the number of visitors viewing the paintings, and so forth. The paintings became, in Cage's words, "airports of lights, shadows and particles."

Rauschenberg became one of Cage's closest collaborators when both were employed by Merce Cunningham's dance company. Cunningham—Cage's life and creative partner—created dances for which Cage oversaw and wrote much of the music and Rauschenberg oversaw the sets and costumes. This collaboration resulted in several classics of modern dance, including *Summerspace* (1958), with costumes and sets by Rauschenberg and music by Cage's close friend, Morton Feldman.

During the 1950s and 1960s Cage continued to broaden the domain of "music" even further. In 1952 came the first "happening," at Black Mountain College near Asheville, North Carolina, where Cage was teaching. The event was held in a dining hall, where the line between audience and performers blurred. Cage apparently lectured while standing on a ladder, the choreographer Merce Cunningham improvised a dance, and the artist Robert Rauschenberg exhibited his paintings, as the audience freely circulated through the room and coffee cups were filled. Next, Cage conceived of works using what he called the "circus principle," in which several different actions occurred simultaneously, as in *Theatre Piece* (1960, a fifty-minute multimedia show with simultaneous, unrelated live performances), *Musicircus* (1967), and *HPSCHD* (1969, for as many as seven harpsichords, electronic tapes, and various entertainments). The point of such **performance art**, as it became known, was to discover and celebrate the work of art in the actual performance itself.

Not surprisingly, traditional musical notation was irrelevant for Cage's random creations. Instead, he turned to startling graphic designs that the performers interpreted for themselves. Finally, he reduced his music to mere verbal descriptions to suggest the general limits within which random sounds could be generated and experienced.

Dashboard

Follow the link to experiment with the 4′33″ app from the John Cage website.

Music with chance elements came to be known as **chance music** or **aleatoric music** (from *aleae*, Latin for "dice"). By the 1960s, aleatoric music was established as an innovative movement to be reckoned with. Cage and his adherents pursued total freedom just as doggedly as serial composers had sought total control in their music.

Women and Contemporary Music

During the twentieth century, a growing number of women composers pursued active careers and received recognition for their music. Here's a brief survey of a small sampling of these pioneers.

Ethel Smyth (1858–1944).

Lili Boulanger (1893–1918), a French child prodigy, was the first woman composer to win the Prix de Rome. Her exquisitely nuanced scores, such as *Vieille prière Bouddhique* (*Old Buddhist Prayer*) for chorus and orchestra, uses whole-tone scales and modes, in a style somewhat resembling Debussy but with an individuality all her own. Tragically, Boulanger died in her twenties from Crohn's disease. Her elder sister, Nadia (1887–1979), a conductor and composer whose many students included Aaron Copland, lived into her nineties.

Ethel Smyth (1858–1944) composed operas and helped lead the suffragette movement in England. A formidable spirit, Smyth studied in Germany, where she met Clara Schumann and Brahms, and produced a series of powerfully expressive works in a late Romantic idiom. Her opera *The Wreckers*, about Cornish pirates who plundered shipwrecks, had its English premiere in 1909. Not long after, Smyth joined the suffragette movement and composed its rousing anthem, "March of the Women." One verse begins, "Long, long, we in the past, cowered in dread from the light of heaven. / Strong, strong, stand we at last, fearless in faith and with light new-given." Smyth's political activism led to a brief imprisonment. By the time English women received the full right to vote in 1928, she had gone deaf. Unable to continue composing, she turned to writing, and produced a number of autobiographical books.

Ruth Crawford Seeger (1901–1953).

Ruth Crawford Seeger (1901–1953), an American composer, was among the most modern of the 1920s and '30s. Her atonal String Quartet of 1931 is now widely viewed as a masterpiece, and one of the first twentieth-century compositions to extend Schoenberg's twelve-tone system to non-pitch elements. She was awarded a Guggenheim Fellowship for study in Berlin, but during the later 1930s she turned her attention from composition to collecting American folk songs with her husband, Charles Seeger. Her stepson was the folk singer and political activist Pete Seeger (see p. 527).

Florence Price (1887–1953) was an African American who wrote four symphonies, among hundreds of other works, many of which remain unpublished. During the silent film era, she worked as a theater organist. Price became highly regarded for her art songs, including *Songs to the Dark Virgin*, on a poem by Langston Hughes, and transcriptions of spirituals. Her Symphony in E minor was premiered in 1933 by the Chicago Symphony, making her the first African-American composer to have a symphonic work performed by a major American orchestra. Price's music is tonal and has strong ties to classical traditions, but also reflects her African-American heritage by simulating spirituals and invoking the *juba*, an African-American round dance.

Joan Tower (b. 1938) is a Grammy Award–winning American composer who spent several years of her youth in Bolivia. A concert pianist and conductor, Tower was a member for several years of the Da Capo Chamber Players, who devoted themselves to contemporary music. She then served as composer in residence for the St. Louis Symphony before assuming a professorship at Bard College. Among Tower's most striking works is a five-part series titled *Fanfares for an Uncommon Woman*, composed between 1987 and 1993, and written for "women who are adventurous and take risks." In 2004 she completed the orchestral work *Made in America*, which had the unusual distinction of being played by sixty-five community orchestras in all fifty states. Lush and constantly shifting textures support melodic gestures drawn from the familiar anthem "America the Beautiful."

Responding to societal changes and the improving status of women, these and many other composers shattered traditional molds of women's musicality by creating ambitious, full-scale compositions in every genre.

Ellen Taaffe Zwilich (b. 1939).

ELLEN TAAFFE ZWILICH

In 1983 Ellen Taaffe Zwilich (b. 1939) became the first woman to win the Pulitzer Prize in music, for her Symphony No. 1. She held the first Composer's Chair at Carnegie Hall in New York from 1995 to 1999, and has been nominated four times for Grammy Awards. Among her works are chamber compositions, several concertos for various brass and wind instruments, and symphonies, including Nos. 2 and 3 for the New York Philharmonic (1985 and 1992), No. 4 (1997), and No. 5 (2008). Zwilich's early style was centered in a modernist, atonal idiom. But, beginning in the 1980s, she turned her efforts toward music that could communicate in a forceful, direct way. In the process she began integrating into her style direct references to tonality and classical forms. Her music possesses expressive warmth that has caused some critics to label her a neo-Romantic.

Ellen Taaffe Zwilich, Concerto grosso, *First Movement (1985)*

Among Zwilich's most imaginative works is the *Concerto grosso* of 1985, commissioned to celebrate the 300th anniversary of the birth of Handel. In five movements, the concerto is based on, and sometimes quotes directly from, a violin sonata by Handel. Zwilich uses a symmetrical scheme: the two outer movements, and the second and fourth, are paired, leaving the slow third movement as the expressive core of the work. The outer movements employ extensive direct quotations from Handel's sonata, as if Zwilich momentarily leaps across the centuries to embrace Handel's time. The second and fourth movements, on the other hand, unfold briskly in a distinctly modernist vein. Here Zwilich borrows the first four notes of Handel's theme, but uncoils them in rapid bursts of atonal energy that resonate with her own time. It is as if Handel's dignified baroque gestures suddenly accommodate the tastes of the 1980s.

The *Concerto grosso* is scored for one flute, two oboes, one bassoon, two horns, strings, and harpsichord, a small chamber orchestra that approximates the world of Handel's music. The harpsichord, which occasionally plays a figured bass, is a distinctive link to the baroque. In this way and throughout the piece, the music functions like a time machine, mediating between the present and past.

Listening Map 78 outlines the first movement, which begins with all of the instruments playing in unison the pitch D, heard three times. This stately opening reflects the piece's historical roots. It could almost announce the beginning of a symphony by Haydn or Mozart, or perhaps something from the Baroque—at first, we do not know for sure. While the bass prolongs the D, the violins execute an energetic phrase with wide leaps, a late twentieth-century flourish that transports us back to the 1980s (①). Now the composer thins out the texture and we return to the past as we hear the beginning of Handel's sonata (②), the first of several direct quotations that alternate with vigorous interjections of the violins' flourish. The second quotation from Handel appears in the oboe (③), while the third is heard *forte* in the full orchestra (④). Toward the end the angular flourish returns a last time, and then a series of dissonant chords brings the movement to a close.

LISTENING MAP 78

ELLEN TAAFFE ZWILICH, *Concerto grosso*, First Movement {1985}

FORM	Concerto grosso
METER	$\frac{4}{4}$ (maestoso, majestically)
SCORING	Chamber orchestra (one flute, two oboes, one bassoon, two French horns, strings, and harpsichord)
OVERVIEW	A mixture of modernist passages alternating with quotations from Handel's stately Violin Sonata in D major, as the musical present (1985) confronts the eighteenth-century past of Handel's Baroque.

why to LISTEN

Zwilich's *Concerto grosso* marks a decided turn against the high modernism of the 1960s and 1970s by re-exploring connections to the past, in this case through quoting from the Baroque period of Handel. The reintroduction of triads—even the triads associated with the Baroque finery of the eighteenth century—gives parts of this music a familiarity, while its excursions into more jarring, non-triadic harmonies elsewhere brings the listener back to the 1980s. In a sense, there are two musical tenses at play here—the musical past and present—and sometimes it almost seems as if the distinctions between the two become blurred. Music can play on our memories of the past and experiences of the present. Zwilich takes full advantage of that mysterious power.

a deeper LISTEN

TIME	LISTEN FOR THIS
0:00	Orchestral unison on D (three statements)
0:19	① Energetic, angular phrases in the violins  Maestoso *f*

TIME	LISTEN FOR THIS
0:37	② First quotation from Handel's Violin Sonata in D major, with thinned out orchestra, and harpsichord playing figured bass *mp*
0:57	Energetic phrases in strings and woodwinds
1:17	③ Resumption of Handel quotation, this time featuring the oboe
1:33	Energetic phrases in violins
1:53	④ Final quotation from Handel, for full orchestra
2:05	Energetic phrases in strings that dissipate against sustained chords in the winds and harpsichord

Postmodernism

The use of quotations from Handel's work is one conspicuous way in which Zwilich distinguished her concerto from the high modernism of the 1960s and '70s, and made her music more accessible to audiences. She followed a path previously explored by the Italian composer Luciano Berio (1925–2003). Berio had used the Scherzo of Mahler's Second Symphony as scaffolding for a movement of his own *Sinfonia* (1969), which is studded with quotations from Beethoven, Debussy, Stravinsky, and many others. Other late twentieth-century composers, too, began introducing quotations into their music. For instance, the American George Crumb's *Black Angels* for electric string quartet, written in 1970 at the height of the Vietnam War, quotes Schubert's famous song, "Death and the Maiden," among other pieces.

But some composers went beyond literal quotation techniques to embrace the past more directly, in particular by reaffirming the validity of tonal music. In a series of sacred works from the 1960s and 1970s, the Polish composer Krzysztof Penderecki (b. 1933) began displacing atonal clusters of sound in his scores with tonal passages. The American George Rochberg (1918–2005) turned to tonality in the 1960s and '70s to protest what he viewed as the dehumanizing tendencies of modern technology and science. All these developments suggested that by the closing decades of the twentieth century, high modernism had run its course, and that music had entered a new phase, **postmodernism**.

MINIMALISM

A particularly powerful new movement associated with postmodernism is **minimalism**, developed in the 1960s in the visual arts and then pursued by a group of

American composers. Minimalists work with scraps of material—a short motive, triad, or turn of phrase—repeated with a regular pulse to build up an entire composition. *In C* by Terry Riley (b. 1935) is one of the earliest examples of minimalist composition (1964). Intended for any number of instruments, *In C* consists of fifty-three short motives, mostly bits of triads or scales, with each repeated as often as the performers wish. Each performer decides when to move on to the next motive. When they have played all the motives, the composition is finished. Supporting the performance is a piano pulse, which repeats the top two C's of the keyboard with metronomic regularity.

Philip Glass (b. 1937) has explored complex minimalist techniques.

Other American composers have explored especially complex minimalist techniques. One is Philip Glass (b. 1937), who studied with Nadia Boulanger in Paris, and absorbed the intricate rhythmic patterns of Indian music into his early scores. In 1967 he formed an ensemble to perform his work, a series of mesmerizing instrumental compositions. Then, he turned to the theater and opera. One of his major works is *Einstein on the Beach* (1976), created with theatrical director Robert Wilson. It is an extravagant opera in four acts set off by five shorter sections that serve to introduce the essential bits of melodic and harmonic material on which the opera is based. An essential image of the work, an accelerating train, is suitably captured in the repetitive, shifting patterns of the music. Throughout the opera, the character Einstein appears as a violinist, placed midway between the actors onstage and a small chamber orchestra.

An especially prolific composer, Glass went on to compose several more operas, including *Satyagraha* (1980, on the life of Mahatma Gandhi) and *Appomattox* (2007, on the closing days of the Civil War), nine symphonies, many film scores (he has received three Academy Award nominations), chamber music, and music for a video game.

Another famous minimalist, Steve Reich (b. 1936), who, like Philip Glass, has performed with his own ensemble, has investigated the rhythms of African drumming. He has written compositions for multiple numbers of a single instrument. In his early music of the 1960s (*Come Out*, 1966; *Piano Phase*, 1967), he developed a technique known as **phasing**, in which several instruments play the same material that

MAKING CONNECTIONS *Minimalism in the Visual Arts*

In the visual arts, minimalism arose in the 1960s and 1970s as painters and sculptors embraced a reductive, simple style of art that avoided dramatic gestures or suggestions of emotional content. Simple geometric shapes and planes of color replaced the more involved displays of abstract expressionism that had dominated earlier decades. Frank Stella's *Die Fahne hoch!* of 1959, which resembles a black rectangle, is one early example of minimalist art. To produce the painting, Stella generated simple geometric designs by applying bands of black enamel paint separated by thin lines of unpainted canvas. The title, "The Flag on High," was a reference to an anthem used by the Nazi Party in the 1930s and '40s. But this controversial allusion seems to have little bearing on the painting, which, in typical minimalist fashion, is devoid of emotional content, and reduced to one color and repeating patterns.

gradually moves out of phase, producing hypnotic, free blends of sound. *Music for 18 Musicians* (1974) extended these techniques to a larger ensemble, consisting of a cello, violin, two clarinets, four pianos, three marimbas, two xylophones, a vibraphone, and four women's voices singing syllables. Reich structured the work on a cycle of eleven chords, presented in an introduction, then individually explored through his minimalist lens, and recapitulated in a final section.

By the 1980s, Reich had moved on to compositions with pronounced extra-musical content. *Different Trains*, for string quartet and electronic tape (1988), contrasted the composer's childhood experiences of traveling between New York and California with the experiences of the victims of the Holocaust. The multimedia opera *The Cave* (1993), for voices, percussion, strings, and video, examines connections between Judaism, Christianity, and Islam. And more recently, *WTC 9/11*, for string quartet and tape, takes one of the most established genres of classical music—the string quartet—and introduces taped recordings of air traffic controllers, firefighters, and residents who responded to the horrific terrorist attack on the World Trade Center. The event is especially personal for Reich because at the time he lived only four blocks away. Premiered in 2011, nearly a decade after the event, *WTC 9/11* unfolds with the firm conviction of a documentary, as portions of authentic text from the time of the tragedy interact with live musicians.

JOHN ADAMS

Another leading American composer with roots in minimalism is John Adams (b. 1947). As a student, Adams reacted against the drudgery of "chasing" twelve-tone rows in serial compositions, and embraced minimalist techniques in his early works. But by the mid-1980s, his work began to embody **post-minimalism**, a style that has employed some techniques of minimalism, but seeks as well other alternatives to questions of musical form and structure. His pulsating scores began to include lush, expressive melodies, as in his *Harmonielehre* (1985), a post-minimalist reflection on Western harmony. A series of highly praised operas followed, including *Nixon in China* (1987, on President Nixon's historic diplomatic opening to China in 1972) and *Dr. Atomic* (2005, on the physicist J. Robert Oppenheimer, who worked on developing the atomic bomb). *On the Transmigration of Souls* (2002), which commemorated the victims of the terrorist attack on the World Trade Center, received a Pulitzer Prize. Twenty-five minutes in duration, it requires an orchestra, chorus, children's chorus, and prerecorded tape.

John Adams (b. 1947).

Adams, Short Ride in a Fast Machine *(1986)*

One of Adams's most popular pieces is *Short Ride in a Fast Machine*, commissioned by the Pittsburgh Symphony in 1986 (**Listening Map 74**). Scored for a large orchestra with expanded percussion and keyboard synthesizers, this compact work throbs with rhythmic energy. Launched by the regular pulse of a woodblock (①), the music teems with repeated chords that slowly change, short ostinato figures, and fanfare-like gestures (②). The work unfolds as a series of crescendos and contains three broad sections. It culminates in a brassy display of the fanfare theme in the trumpets, as Adams's musical machine propels itself forward with delirious excitement and abandon to its sudden end.

LISTENING MAP 79

JOHN ADAMS, *Short Ride in a Fast Machine* {1986}

METER	Beginning in $\frac{3}{2}$, then various meters
SCORING	Large orchestra (two piccolos, two flutes, two oboes, one English horn, two clarinets, three bassoons, one contrabassoon, four French horns, four trumpets, three trombones, one tuba, timpani, wood blocks, bass drum, snare drum, large bass drum, cymbal, sizzle cymbal, tam-tam, tambourine, triangle, Glockenspiel, xylophone, crotales (small, tuned cymbals), two synthesizers, and strings)
OVERVIEW	Frenzied music driven by a constant pulse announced in the woodblocks. The composition divides into three main sections: (1) rhythmic figures and shrill flourishes featuring woodwinds, brass, and synthesizers; (2) a lumbering, dance-like passage featuring low strings and tuba, with cross accents from the trumpets leading to deafening strokes of the tam-tam, and (3) the introduction of the fanfare theme in the trumpets, with a countersubject in the French horns.

why to LISTEN

The title *Short Ride in a Fast Machine* suggests some kind of musical journey, and that, in turn, suggests an origination point and final destination. Most of the Western music we have examined depends on the idea of a theme that is developed toward some goal. There is a goal in Adams's composition, and that is the delayed emergence of the bright trumpet fanfare (the "theme") near the end. However, where we start, and how we eventually arrive at the theme, is anything but clear. Instead, we are swept up in the delirious excitement of this music, which seems static at first, but then evolves through slowly changing units and harmonies. Music is about time, and this piece throbs with the pulse of the woodblocks, which is like the ticking seconds of a clock. Like a sweeping second hand, these constant repetitions of temporal units ultimately lead nowhere. When the music abruptly stops, its trance-like power encourages us to continue the beating pulse ourselves for a few more repetitions, before we leave the delirium of this journey into musical space, and return to real time.

first LISTEN

INTRODUCTION	SECTION 1	SECTION 2	SECTION 3
0:00	**0:03**	**1:41**	**3:04**
Woodblock pulse	Rhythmic figures and shrill flourishes; becomes increasingly dissonant	"Lumbering" theme in low-voiced instruments	Fanfare-like melody in trumpets; sudden ending

 *a deeper* **LISTEN**

TIME	SECTION	LISTEN FOR THIS
0:00	Introduction	(1) Woodblock establishes regular pulse ♩ ♩ ♩ ♩ | ♩ ♩ ♩ ♩ |
0:03	Section 1	Woodwinds, synthesizer, repeated chords in trumpets, shrill flourishes in piccolo
1:01		Cross-cutting accents in bass drum, rising chords, music becomes more dissonant
1:41	Section 2	Sudden drop in dynamics, rumbling figure in tuba, cellos, and double bass
1:48		Two-note descending leap in bass, cross-accents, deafening strokes of the tam-tam
2:46		Sudden drop in dynamics
3:04	Section 3	(2) Fanfare-like melody in trumpets, with contrapuntal lines added in French horns
4:02		Series of consonant major triads in brass, sudden end

THE FUTURE BECKONS

Minimalism and post-minimalism have offered compelling alternatives to the high modernism of the avant-garde that many believe climaxed in the 1970s. But the recent results of classical music's struggle to find a new identity have proven rather murky. Some commentators have used the term **polystylism**, which is the mixture of different styles and approaches in composition, to describe the music of the 1990s and beyond, whether it re-embraces tonality in some form, perseveres with atonality, or uses minimalist or other techniques. But polystylism is at best a catch-all term to denote a kind of holding pattern until the next revolution in the classical tradition takes place and is recognized.

Into the Twenty-First Century

So, now that we have a foothold in the twenty-first century, where is classical music going? Does it remain relevant today? Some will say that classical music is dying. For years orchestras have struggled mightily to balance their budgets, and some have indeed ceased to exist. (In 1988 the New Orleans Symphony, having run out of funds, closed its season ten weeks early; appropriately, the last work performed was Haydn's *Farewell* Symphony, which ends with the musicians leaving one by one as they finish their staggered parts.) Fewer and fewer classical radio stations broadcast today, and the recording industry continues to be transformed. Classical music claims a diminishing share of the market, and if the trend continues, the doomsayers say, there will be no audience for classical works.

And yet, classical music continues to survive, like some indelible part of our culture, even if its footprint, when measured by the numbers, is smaller than before. It is not just the familiar masterworks that have survived: New composers are still attempting to extend into the future the long traditions of classical music. Whether or how they will be embraced is unclear. However, their works continue the same drive to create new and engaging music relevant to the twenty-first century.

SOFIA GUBAIDULINA

The Russian composer Sofia Gubaidulina (b. 1931) has experienced a remarkable career that began in the waning years of the Soviet Union and now continues to look confidently to the future. She studied at the Moscow Conservatory, but in 1979 was reprimanded for writing music too experimental to be acceptable to the Soviet state. She found an early champion in Shostakovich (see Chapter 44), who advocated for her music and advised her to continue on her "mistaken path." Gubaidulina's music is influenced by Christian mysticism, and filled with images of transfiguration and the Apocalypse. Powerfully emotional, the music is nevertheless cerebral and carefully calculated. It is often based on mathematical sequences such as the Fibonacci series (1, 2, 3, 5, 8 . . .) and Lucas series (2, 1, 3, 4, 7 . . .), sequences of numbers generated by adding the two previous numbers in the series. In the hands of a composer, these numbers can be translated into rhythmic durations or metronome markings. Gubaidulina has made a detailed study of numerology in the music of J. S. Bach, and, not surprisingly, his music has deeply influenced the evolution of her style. But her music defies ready classification. She has resisted the idea that she is an avant-garde composer, and yet, as she puts it, she prefers to "swim against the stream."

Sofia Gubaidulina (b. 1931).

With the collapse of the Soviet Union, Gubaidulina moved to Germany in 1992, and now resides in Hamburg. Her recent major works include the St. John Passion, premiered in 2000 in Stuttgart, and her second violin concerto, titled *In tempus praesans* (*In the Present Time*), written in 2007 for the German virtuoso Anne-Sophie Mutter, an eloquent advocate for contemporary music.

Sofia Gubaidulina, Violin Concerto No. 2 ("In tempus praesens") (2007)

Violin Concerto No. 2 lasts about half an hour and divides into five sections. It pits the solo violinist, who represents the individual but also wisdom (*sophia*, the Greek word for "wisdom," is a name the composer shares with Anne-Sophie Mutter) against the orchestra, who represents society. The violin tends to favor or climb toward its high register, as if reaching for some clairvoyant light. In contrast, the orchestra, which does not have violins in the string section, tends to remain in the lower registers. It produces dark textures with low brass harmonies and heavy percussion that resist the soaring flights of the violin. Periodically the shattering blow of a gong marks off one section and announces the next.

Listening Map 80 offers a diagram of the opening section of the concerto. It opens quietly with a solo for the violin, rather like a recitative with its text removed (①). The violin begins to ascend until it encounters a shimmering, metallic sound from the orchestra, a distinctive blend of the piccolo, antique cymbals, celesta, and other percussion (②). For the next three minutes, the music essentially alternates between the soloist and orchestra: the soloist moves again and again to its high register with striking chromatic lines and abrupt shifts, only to be weighed down by brief orchestral commentaries. The pattern is broken by a brief silence at 2:53. After a series of pronounced brass chords, the opening section concludes with the deafening stroke of the gong (③).

The Future

This book has discussed a thousand years and more of the Western classical tradition. It began with the monophonic chants of the Roman Catholic Church, and closed in the musical present, situated somewhere around the early twenty-first century. It has not been a "short ride in a fast machine," but an epic journey, with many stops along the way. It has shown the various patterns within Western art music of change, consolidation, more experimentation, and renewal. Now, less than two decades into its second millennium, we are hard pressed to predict the future of classical music. No one style definitively points the way ahead; no single method of composition seems to offer the greatest potential for young composers. Classical music survives today, if tenuously, alongside innumerable types of popular music. Music is becoming increasingly international as the Internet shrinks and connects the world, for better or worse. Though separated by physical space, different cultures continue to come closer together, occasionally colliding to generate new ways of hearing, listening to, and thinking about music. Perhaps the future of Western classical music lies in the still only partially tapped potential for different musical cultures, Western and non-Western, to cross fertilize, to generate new, so far unimagined types of music.

Whatever that future will bring, music will remain a common element of our humanity, and will bind people together. In the West, classical music, in all its diversity, has amused, pleased, annoyed, comforted, and profoundly moved us for centuries. Something that durable will probably last in some shape or form, so that future generations, beginning with yours, will continue to listen.

LISTENING MAP 80

SOFIA GUBAIDULINA, Violin Concerto No. 2 ("In tempus praesens"), opening section

{2007}

METER	Frequent changes
SCORING	Solo violin and large orchestra (one piccolo, three flutes, three oboes, three clarinets, one bass clarinet, three bassoons, one contrabassoon, three French horns, three trumpets, four trombones, three Wagner tubas, one tuba, timpani, triangle, chimes, whip, snare drum, tom-tom, bass drum, six cymbals, two tam-tams, crotales, bells, xylophone, vibraphone, marimba, two harps, celesta, harpsichord, piano, violas, cellos, and double basses)
OVERVIEW	The opening section pits the solo violin against the orchestra, with climbing violin statements being answered by the orchestra in lower registers. A stroke of the gong marks the end of the section.

why to LISTEN

Gubaidulina's work could be interpreted as an autobiographical commentary about her early experiences in the Soviet Union. We might see this work as the struggle between the individual and society, between individual freedom and totalitarian rule. But there is also a prominent spiritual element in the music, and an uplifting quality that transcends the here and now. Gubaidulina has actually written that instead of living in the present, we tend to shuttle constantly between the past and future, without grasping the present. Her music is an attempt to grasp the present, and to find a spiritual relevance in it.

a deeper **LISTEN**

TIME	LISTEN FOR THIS
0:00	① Solo violin melody, recitative-like *f espr.* *mf* *f*
0:33	Violin begins to climb
0:42	② Metallic, shimmering sound from orchestra
0:51	Alternating passages with violin passages stretching into the high register answered by darker orchestral commentaries in lower registers
2:55	Brief silence, followed by the continunation of the violin-orchestra interchange
3:39	③ Gong stroke

check your **KNOWLEDGE**

1. What role did new technologies play in the emergence of new musical styles after the Second World War?
2. How did total serialism develop from the work of Arnold Schoenberg?
3. What is musique concrète? How did the composer Edgard Varèse use musique concrète and electronic sounds in his music?
4. What is aleatoric music? What role did composer John Cage play in its development?
5. How did women composers contribute to twentieth-century music?
6. What is postmodernism? How does it relate to minimalism? What role did composers such as Philip Glass play in its development?
7. How did composer John Adams develop minimalism to create a unique musical style?
8. How would you describe the music of Sofia Gubaidulina?

PART VII SUMMARY: THE MODERN ERA

- Twentieth-century modernism was a decisive break from nineteenth-century arts and culture.
  - Several new movements—among them impressionism, symbolism, Futurism, cubism, and expressionism—explored radical new ways of relating the arts to the modern world.
  - Composers began developing alternatives to traditional tonality, by using new scales such as the whole-tone scale, and new harmonies not based on triads, or by rejecting tonality altogether.

- In the first decade of the twentieth century Arnold Schoenberg began exploring atonality. It abandoned traditional triads and key signatures and treated all twelve pitches of the chromatic scale as equally significant.
  - During the 1920s Schoenberg developed a type of atonality known as twelve-tone music, based on tone rows—atonal orderings of the twelve pitches of the chromatic scale.
  - Modernist composers also turned their attention to freer treatments of rhythm, meter, and timbre. For instance, they varied their choice of meters to break away from the traditional Western approach of dividing musical time into equal portions separated by bar lines.

- The pioneers of musical modernism included Claude Debussy, Igor Stravinsky, Arnold Schoenberg, and Schoenberg's students Alban Berg and Anton Webern.
  - Inspired by symbolist poets, Debussy developed a nuanced French style that drew upon whole-tone and non-Western scales and harmonies.
  - The cosmopolitan Stravinsky experimented with flexible rhythms and frequent meter changes.
  - After making a decisive break from tonality in 1908, Schoenberg explored the new world of atonality, as did his students Berg and Webern, before introducing twelve-tone music in the 1920s.

- Neoclassicism was a broad-based movement in the arts that found new inspiration in classical subjects, themes, and techniques. Reacting against nineteenth-century Romanticism, neoclassical composers such as Stravinsky and Bartók found models in earlier music, especially of the eighteenth century.

- Twentieth-century composers continued to develop national styles as alternatives to the traditionally dominant German, French, and Italian styles.
  - In England, Ralph Vaughan Williams and Benjamin Britten led an English musical renaissance.
  - In Hungary, Béla Bartók based his compositions on folk music that he recorded and transcribed.
  - In Russia, Sergei Prokofiev and Dmitri Shostakovich struggled to find their musical voice while responding to the artistic dictates of the Stalinist state.

- Characterized by a rich diversity of influences, American music has at times drawn on the European classical tradition even while declaring its independence from that tradition by celebrating ever changing popular styles.

- An important twentieth-century American modernist was Charles Ives, who experimented with atonality, and quotation and collage techniques, and incorporated American hymns and popular song into his music.
- Amy Beach was a pioneering woman composer and pianist whose later music moved toward the harmonic innovations of modernism.
- William Grant Still brought elements of African-American music, in particular the blues, into the domain of the classical concert hall.
- George Gershwin, who composed songs, musicals, and other compositions, tried to bridge the classical tradition and jazz.
- Aaron Copland began as a modernist steeped in European music but then adopted a populist American idiom for his music.

- Meanwhile, different forms of popular music developed next to the classical tradition. Early in the century, jazz arose out of ragtime and blues. It established a distinctly American style of music that evolved into an art form heavily dependent on improvisation.
    - Early jazz arose in New Orleans and then spread throughout the United States and abroad, aided by the advent of the recording industry.
    - In the 1930s the relatively small jazz bands grew in size to accommodate the new style of swing, and the big band sound.
    - Jazz depended largely on improvisation, but swing bands required a careful coordination of the musicians, and that, in turn, required more specific compositional decisions.
    - Among the most important jazz composers and arrangers was Duke Ellington, who produced thousands of compositions.
    - The late 1940s witnessed the emergence of bebop, an aggressive style of jazz that reacted against the suave, elegant sound of the big bands.
    - The second half of the twentieth century saw many new forms of jazz, including cool jazz, free jazz, and jazz rock.
    - Miles Davis was a highly influential performer/composer/bandleader whose album *Bitches Brew* helped launch the jazz-rock revolution.

- The new Hollywood film industry helped promote a new art form: film music.

- The American musical featured a mixture of songs, spoken dialogue, and dancing.
    - *West Side Story*, with music by Leonard Bernstein and lyrics by Stephen Sondheim, brought a new level of realism to the Broadway stage. Bernstein's music combined elements of pop, jazz, and Latin rhythms to depict young gangs fighting over their turf in New York City.

- In the 1950s, popular music found a new impulse in rock and roll, predecessor to rock, which featured small bands with amplified guitars and drums.
    - Rock and roll in the 1950s wed country and rhythm and blues styles.

Continued

- Among the most important rock groups was the Beatles. They brought a new level of sophistication to their music, and helped pioneer the idea of a creating a unified sequence of songs known as a "concept album."
- From the late '60s on, several new styles of rock evolved, including progressive rock, heavy metal, punk, and grunge.

- Popular music continued evolving through many new styles. Among the most important was rap, in which a rapper recited rhyming verses against a rhythmic soundtrack.

- In the second half of the twentieth century, musical modernism splintered into several directions, including:
  - extending twelve-tone music to non-pitch elements such as rhythm, dynamics, and register;
  - using electronic media to generate unconventional musical sounds; and
  - injecting random, chance elements into music.

- By the 1970s, composers were beginning to return to tonality, either by quoting tonal music in their scores or by writing music based on triads.

- The twentieth century witnessed a dramatic rise in the number of successful women composers.

- In the 1970s and 1980s the minimalists developed a viable new style based on repetitive treatments of simple musical elements. Leading minimalist composers included Terry Riley, Steve Reich, and Philip Glass.

- By the 1980s, some critics asserted that high modernism had run its course, and had yielded to a new period known as postmodern.

- Today composers draw on a variety of styles and techniques, of which none seems to be dominant.

KEY TERMS

aleatoric music 539
atonality 432
bebop (bop) 509
blue note 501
blues 499
chance music 539
cool jazz 511
concept album 528
country music 526
cubism 423, 424
Dadaism 425
diegetic music 517
disco 528
double fugue 458
electronic music 532
electronica 529
expressionism 425
false recapitulation 455
film music 515
folk music 452
folk rock 528
free jazz 511
front line 504
funk 526

KEY COMPOSERS

Claude Debussy (1862–1918)
Sir Edward Elgar (1867–1934)
Amy Beach (1867–1944)
Scott Joplin (1868–1917)
Ralph Vaughan Williams (1872–1958)
Charles Ives (1874–1954)
Arnold Schoenberg (1874–1951)
Maurice Ravel (1875–1937)
Béla Bartók (1881–1945)
Igor Stravinsky (1882–1971)
Edgard Varèse (1883–1965)
Anton von Webern (1883–1945)
Alban Berg (1885–1935)
Sergei Prokofiev (1891–1953)
Bessie Smith (1894–1937)
William Grant Still (1895–1978)
George Gershwin (1898–1937)
Duke Ellington (1899–1974)
Louis Armstrong (1900–1971)
Aaron Copland (1900–1990)
Dmitri Shostakovich (1906–1975)
John Cage (1912–1992)
Benjamin Britten (1913–1976)
Leonard Bernstein (1918–1990)
Charlie Parker (1920–1955)
Miles Davis (1926–1991)
Karlheinz Stockhausen (1928–2007)
Sofia Gubaidulina (b. 1931)
John Williams (b. 1932)
Steve Reich (b. 1936)
Philip Glass (b. 1937)
Ellen Taaffe Zwilich (b. 1939)
John Adams (b. 1947)

MUSICAL JOURNEYS
African-American Lined Hymn

Congregational singing in eighteenth-century America was based on a style called "lining out." Because much of the congregation could not read music, church leaders had to develop a way to teach them hymns to be sung as part of the religious services. They came up with the idea of having a lead singer first sing a line of the hymn, which the congregation could then repeat. The congregational melody is not necessarily identical with that sung by the leader. This "lining out" of the song allowed non-musically literate singers to participate in the choirs. The custom began in England about 1645 and had disappeared by 1800. However, it remained popular in the American colonies. More broadly, the practice existed since the Middle Ages in European churches, where it is known as *antiphonal singing.*

Portrait of Rev. Richard Allen, who founded the African Methodist Episcopal Church in 1794.

Although the underlying song structure and lyrics came from the European hymn tradition, "lining out" is similar to the African musical tradition of "call-and-response." In that form, one singer or group sings one part of a song, and a second singer or group responds with another part. "Lining out" also incorporated African-American musical elements, including vocal embellishments, rhythmic syncopation, and improvisation.

The 1794 founding of the African Methodist Episcopal (AME) church by freed slave Rev. Richard Allen (1760–1831) in Philadelphia formally established a black religious tradition in the United States. Allen's *Collection of Spiritual Songs and Hymns* (1801) was the first hymnbook published by an African American for use by African Americans, and many of the hymns collected in it later became sources for black spirituals. Following the tradition of New England hymnals, Allen's book contains songs by white composer Isaac Watts and others whose forms encourage responses among participants.

Hymns were a powerful tool used to convert African Americans to Christianity. However, most white congregations were not open to having African Americans as members. In 1819, John F. Watson, a black Northern minister, criticized integrated camp meetings in which black musical practices were absorbed into the white church world. Nonetheless, he recognized the contribution of African Americans to creating a new musical style: "In the blacks' quarter, the coloured people get together and sing for hours together, short scraps of disjointed affirmations, pledges, or prayers, lengthened out with long repetition choruses."

"Am I a Solider of the Cross?"

The Anglo-American hymn was thoroughly transformed through the incorporation of African-American vocal, melodic, and rhythmic styles. "Am I a Solider of the Cross?" (**Listening Map I.6**) is a striking performance demonstrating these elements. While the leader quickly states the lyrics and simple melody for each line, the group is unrestrained in how it transforms all elements into a free-wheeling response. Eventually, the leader's part is nearly totally absorbed by the choir, which sings wordless syllables behind the solo and rushes in to respond to it. The simple words and melody give way to an ecstatic statement of religious faith. Although each member of the chorus is singing approximately the same melody, there are many subtle variations, creating a musical texture known as **heterophony**. In this way, both the individual expression of faith and the group experience are brought together as one.

The group heard on this recording was assembled to recreate the eighteenth-century style of singing heard in the AME Church. They were drawn from choir members of the Mother Bethel Church in Philadelphia, the descendants of Rev. Allen's first congregation.

LISTENING MAP *I.6*

"Am I a Soldier of the Cross?," leader THEODORE KING, performed by the RICHARD ALLEN SINGERS: EDWINA WHITE, REBECCA POWELL, GROZELIA STEPNEY, CURLY KING, THEODORE KING, THERESA DAVIS, JUANITA ROLLINS, EVELYN SIMPSON CURRENTON, and BERNICE JOHNSON REAGON

FORM	Lined hymn
METER	Free
TEMPO	Slow
SCORING	Leader and vocal chorus
OVERVIEW	"Am I a Solider of the Cross?" is an example of a lined hymn, a style found in both Anglo- and African-American traditions. Listen for the interplay between the song leader and the congregation: while the leader gives a brief statement of the lyric and melody for each line, the congregation follows with a much longer and highly improvised response. The use of heterophony—slightly different statements of the same melody sung simultaneously—is a hallmark of this performance.

why to **LISTEN**

In this lined hymn, the chorus extends the singing of the line with rich harmonies and melodic embellishments. As the singing progresses, individual choir members are moved to say "Great God!" and "Hallelujah," as the spirit of the music inspires deep religious expression. Here the lyrics give way to a group feeling of euphoria, as if the congregation is being swept by the religious spirit.

first LISTEN

LINE 1		LINE 2		LINE 3	
Am I a soldier of the Cross, a follower of the Lamb?		*And shall I fear to own His cause, or blush to speak His name?*		*Must I be carried to the skies on flow'ry beds of ease,*	
0:00	**0:10**	**0:59**	**1:07**	**1:53**	**2:02**
Leader sings first line; choir in background (beginning 0:04)	Choir responds, extending the verse line	Leader sings; group in background	Choir responds, extending the verse line	Leader sings; group in background	Choir responds, extending the verse line

LINE 4		LINE 5		LINE 6		
When others fought to win the prize, and sailed thro' bloody seas?		*Sure I must fight if I would reign, increase my courage,* Lord		*I'll bear the toil, endure the pain, supported by Thy word.*		
2:46	**2:55**	**3:38**	**3:48**	**4:33**	**4:41**	**5:27**
Leader sings; group in background	Choir responds, extending the verse line	Leader sings; group in background	Choir responds, extending the verse line	Leader sings; group in background	Choir responds, extending the verse line	Group concludes

a deeper LISTEN

TIME	SECTION	LISTEN FOR THIS	TEXT
0:00	**Line 1**		*Am I a soldier of the cross, a follower of the Lamb?*
0:04		Group enters as the leader finishes second phrase of the line.	
0:10		Group repeats the line ("Am I . . .") with a heterophonic rendering (simultaneous ornamented variations) of the main melodic structure.	
0:18			*A sol . . .*
0:26			*. . . dier of the Cross,*
0:41			*A fol . . .*
0:48			*. . . lower of*
0:54			*the lamb?*

Continued

TIME	SECTION	LISTEN FOR THIS	TEXT
0:59	Line 2	Leader sings while group continues.	*And shall I fear to own His cause, or blush to speak His Name?*
1:07		Group repeats the second line. Follow the lyric for each sung phrase, as above, noting that the text setting is two syllables per sung phrase.	
1:53	Line 3	Leader sings.	*Must I be carried to the skies on flow'ry beds of ease*
2:02		Group sings the third line. The sung phrases sometimes end in the middle of a two-syllable word (e.g., "car-*ried*" at 2:15).	
2:46	Line 4	Leader sings.	*When others fought to win the prize, and sailed thro' bloody seas?*
2:55		Group sings the fourth line. Note again the two-syllable text setting per sung phrase.	
3:38	Line 5	Leader sings	*Sure I must fight if I would reign, increase my courage, Lord,*
3:48		Group sings the fifth line.	
4:33	Line 6	Leader sings.	*I'll bear the toil, endure the pain, supported by Thy word.*
4:41		Group sings the sixth line.	
5:27		Group concludes.	

Glossary

absolute music: Instrumental music not based on literary or other extra-musical ideas; also referred to as *pure music.*

a cappella: Choral music without instrumental accompaniment.

accelerando: A gradual increase in tempo.

accent: Emphasis placed on a note or chord, often indicated by a wedge-shaped mark (< or >).

accidental: A sign used to alter a pitch: sharp (♯), flat (♭), natural (♮).

accompanied recitative: A recitative accompanied by an orchestra instead of by a harpsichord or small continuo section.

accordion: A musical instrument of the aerophone class consisting of a small vertical keyboard and metal reeds activated by a pleated bellows when squeezed.

adagio: Slow; a movement in a slow tempo.

aerophone: A class of musical instruments that employ a column of air as the vibrating medium to produce their sound.

aleatory (**aleatoric music**). See **chance music**.

allegretto: Moderately fast.

allegro: Fast.

allemande: A Baroque dance in a slow duple meter.

alto: The low female vocal register (also **contralto**); also, a part that employs that register.

andante: Moderately slow, a "walking" tempo.

answer: A version of a fugal subject that typically follows a statement of the subject.

anthem: An English choral work for use in church services; also, a national patriotic hymn.

antiphony (**antiphonal**)**:** A style of performance with alternating choirs.

arco: A direction for players of string instruments to bow rather than pluck the strings. See also **pizzicato**.

aria: A movement in an opera, oratorio, or cantata for solo voice and orchestra.

arioso: A style of singing less melodic than an aria and more melodic than a recitative.

arpeggio: A "broken" chord, with its notes played successively rather than simultaneously.

Ars nova**:** A term used in the fourteenth century to describe the polyphony of that era.

art song: A composed song, typically for voice and piano, as distinguished from a folk song. See also **lied**.

atonality (**atonal**)**:** Music written without a key center; a musical style developed by Arnold Schoenberg around 1908.

augmentation: The technique of increasing the rhythmic values of a melody, typically by doubling their duration.

avant-garde: The vanguard of radical, advanced movements in the arts.

ballad: A narrative poem in several stanzas, often set to music as a song.

ballade: A type of fourteenth- and fifteenth-century secular music and poetry; in the nineteenth century, a programmatic instrumental composition, typically for piano.

ballet: An art form that uses music to accompany staged dancing of soloists and ensembles, with costumes and scenery.

bar (**bar line**). See **measure**, **measure line**.

baritone: A male vocal register between tenor and bass.

baritone horn: Brass band instrument similar in appearance to the tuba, but with a higher range.

Baroque period: The period of Western music from roughly 1600 to 1750.

bass: The low male vocal register; also, the lowest sounding part in a vocal or instrumental composition (hence, bass line).

bass clarinet: A type of clarinet, curved before its bell, that plays in a low range.

bass clef: A clef (𝄢) used to locate the lower sounding pitches.

bass drum: A large drum of indefinite pitch.

basso continuo. See **continuo**.

bassoon: A double-reed woodwind instrument that plays in a bass range.

basso ostinato: A bass ostinato pattern; an unchanging bass pattern that is repeated.

baton: A thin rod used to beat musical time, indicate changes in tempo and dynamics, and cue musicians.

beam: A horizontal line used to connect a series of eighth notes, sixteenth notes, and so on.

beat: The fundamental pulse in a musical composition; the basic subdivision within the measure lines of a composition.

bebop (**bop**)**:** A style of jazz developed in the 1940s and 1950s that featured explosive rhythmic patterns and small ensembles.

bel canto: A style of singing, common in nineteenth-century Italian opera, that emphasizes the beautiful, lyrical qualities of the voice.

big bands: The jazz bands of the 1930s and 1940s, typically comprising ten to twenty musicians.

binary form: A musical form in two basic parts, often repeated, as in the following design: [𝄆 A 𝄇 𝄆 B 𝄇]

block chord: a chord built directly below the melody to create a four-part harmonized texture.

blue note: In the blues, a pitch that is sung or played slightly below its notated value.

blues: A variety of African-American popular music featuring texts of laments and a standard harmonic pattern.

boogie-woogie: In jazz, a style of piano playing, developed in the 1920s, with short repeated bass patterns.

bop. See **bebop**.

brass instruments: Instruments with bent, straight, or coiled sections of brass and cupped mouthpieces, including the French horn, trumpet, trombone, and tuba.

break: A term used in jazz to describe an instrumental solo.

bridge: In sonata form, a modulating transition that links the first and second thematic sections of the exposition.

cabaletta: A short operatic solo, often preceded in nineteenth-century Italian opera by a slower cavatina.

cadence: A series of notes or chords that suggests a musical pause or point of arrival; in harmony, a series of harmonic progressions that serves to define a key.

cadenza: A virtuosic display passage, often improvised by a soloist, as in an aria or concerto.

call and response: Used in particular to describe a performance style in African, African-American music, and jazz, in which a voice or instrument is answered in turn by another, or by a group.

canon (**canonic**): A high style of counterpoint; a composition in which the pitches of one part are strictly imitated by one or more other parts.

cantabile: In a "singing" manner.

cantata: A chamber composition, often in several movements, developed during the Baroque period for various combinations of soloists, a chorus, and an orchestra, with a sacred or secular text.

cantus firmus: In medieval and Renaissance music, a borrowed melody, such as a plainchant or tune, used as the basis of polyphonic compositions.

canzone: A song in strophic form with Italian text.

castrato: A male singer, castrated during boyhood, who has the range of an alto or soprano.

cavatina: In eighteenth-century opera, a short aria; in nineteenth-century Italian opera, a complex aria that generally includes a slow, lyrical section and a fast, brilliant section (known as a cabaletta).

celesta: Percussion instrument resembling a small upright piano, with a keyboard activating hammers that strike tuned metal bars.

cello (violoncello): A string instrument held upright and played between the legs, with a range between the viola and double bass.

chaconne: A slow Baroque dance in triple meter, often featuring a basso ostinato.

chamber music: Music intended to be performed in an intimate setting or with a small ensemble (e.g., piano trio, string quartet).

chamber orchestra: A small orchestra suitable for performing chamber music.

chamber sonata. See **sonata da camera**.

chance music: Post–World War II music in which elements of chance determine the shape or structure of a composition (also called **aleatoric music**).

chanson: French for "song"; a song with a secular French text.

chant: A monophonic melody. See also **plainchant**.

character piece: A short composition, often for piano solo, with programmatic elements, especially common during the nineteenth century.

chimes: Percussion instrument consisting of several tuned metal tubes that are struck by a hammer.

chivalry: Derived from *chevalier* (French for "knight"), chivalry promoted the virtues of honor, valor, and fidelity during the Middle Ages.

choir: A vocal or an instrumental ensemble, with more than one musician per part.

chorale: A German (Lutheran) hymn.

chorale cantata: A church cantata in which one or more movements employ a chorale melody.

chorale prelude: An organ composition based on a chorale.

chord: Two or more notes sounded simultaneously.
chordophone: A class of musical instruments that use strings as the vibrating medium to produce their sound.
chord progression: The progression from one chord to a second chord.
chorus: A vocal choir.
chromatic (**chromaticism**)**:** Tonal music that draws on the pitches of the chromatic scale rather than on a **diatonic** scale.
chromatic scale: The Western scale in which the octave is divided into twelve half steps.
church modes: In medieval and Renaissance music, diatonic scales based on D, E, F, and G.
church sonata. See **sonata da chiesa**.
circle of fifths: A circular representation of the keys arranged in ascending order of flats and sharps.
clarinet: A single-reed woodwind instrument ending in a bell.
classical music: General term used to describe Western art music, from the Middle Ages to the present (compare **Classical period**).
Classical period: In Western music history the period from roughly 1750 to 1810.
clavichord: A Baroque keyboard instrument of relatively narrow range in dynamics in which metal tangents strike strings.
clef: A musical symbol placed at the beginning of the staff that indicates which pitches are represented on the staff. See also **bass clef**; **treble clef**.
climax: The highest note or most intense emotional point of a composition.
closing passage: The closing section of the exposition and recapitulation in sonata form.
coda: The closing section of a movement.
coloratura: A highly ornate style of singing, often employed by sopranos.
comic opera: A type of opera, originating in the eighteenth century, that featured comic characters as opposed to characters drawn from tragedy. See also **opera buffa**.
common time: A meter with four quarter-note beats per measure, indicated by $\frac{4}{4}$ or **C**.
compound meter: Meter with subdivisions of the main beats into groups of three, as in (*1* 2 3 *4* 5 6) or (*1* 2 3 *4* 5 6 *7* 8 9 *10* 11 12).
computer music: Music that uses a computer to generate and manipulate sounds.
con brio: With energy.
concept album: An album in which all the music is unified by an idea or concept rather than comprising separate, unrelated songs.
concertino: The group of solo instrumentalists in a concerto grosso.
concerto: An instrumental composition for a soloist and an orchestra.
concerto grosso: A type of Baroque concerto featuring a group of soloists (concertino) set off from an orchestra (ripieno).
concert overture: A one-movement work for orchestra, often with programmatic elements, developed during the nineteenth century.
conductor: A musician who directs an ensemble of musicians, such as an orchestra or chorus.
conjunct motion: Melodic motion by half step or whole step.

consonance (**consonant**)**:** An interval or a chord that sounds stable and harmonious, as opposed to **dissonance**. See also **imperfect consonance**; **perfect consonance**.

continuo: A practice of musical accompaniment developed during the Baroque period in which a bass line is provided with figures (hence, figured bass) that indicate a series of chords to be performed or realized above the bass line; the term also applied to the instrumental ensemble entrusted with this task.

contrabassoon: A double-reed woodwind instrument of the bassoon family that plays one octave below the bassoon.

contralto: The low female vocal register (also called **alto**).

contrapuntal. See **counterpoint**.

contrary motion: Melodic motion in which two parts move in opposite directions.

contrast: The use of different musical means to provide variety (as in a contrasting theme).

cool jazz: Jazz of the 1950s and 1960s that featured a transparent sound from the brass and reed instruments, which were played with little or no vibrato, and tended to favor relatively relaxed tempos.

cornet: Brass instrument similar in appearance to the trumpet but with a less piercing tone.

counterpoint (**contrapuntal**)**:** The art of setting separate musical lines against each other; also, a musical part composed to be set "in counterpoint" against another part. See also **polyphony**.

Counter-Reformation: A movement in the Catholic Church in response to the sixteenth-century Protestant Reformation.

countersubject: In a fugue, a contrapuntal part that continues the subject and is usually heard against the answer.

country music: type of poplar American music originating in the southern United States during the twentieth century.

courante (also **corrente**)**:** A moderately fast Baroque dance in triple meter, often the second dance of a Baroque suite.

courtly love: A medieval tradition of love between a knight and a noblewoman.

crescendo: Growing louder.

cubism: An early twentieth-century movement in the visual arts, centered in Paris, that presented objects from a variety of perspectives instead of from a single perspective.

cut time: Duple meter indicated by $\frac{2}{2}$ (or ¢).

cyclical form: Usually applied to a composition of several movements, in which materials from one movement (such as a theme) are recycled in later movements.

cymbals: Percussion instrument of indefinite pitch, in which two brass plates are struck against each other.

da capo: "From the beginning," an instruction to the performer to return to the beginning of the composition.

da capo aria: A type of aria developed during the Baroque period with the plan *ABA*; the repeat of the *A* section is indicated by the term "da capo" placed at the end of the *B* section.

Dadaism: an early twentieth-century avant-garde movement in the arts that rejected conventional cultural values.

damper pedal: On the piano, the right, foot-activated pedal that raises the dampers, allowing the strings to vibrate freely.
dance suite. See **suite**.
decrescendo: Becoming softer; **diminuendo**.
development: The technique of reworking or developing in some way previously stated themes and motives; the central portion of **ternary sonata form**.
diatonic: Based on the pitches of a major or minor scale, as opposed to chromatic.
diegetic music (source music): in film music, music that is heard that is implied or literally stated in the action of the film.
***Dies irae*:** A chant in the Requiem Mass for the dead concerning the Day of Judgment.
diminished: A class of intervals that have been decreased by a half step.
diminuendo: Becoming softer; **decrescendo**.
diminution: The technique of shortening the rhythmic values of a melody, typically by halving them.
disco: a genre of popular dance music from the mid-1960s and 1970s.
disjunct motion: Melodic motion by skip, as opposed to **conjunct motion**.
dissonance (dissonant): An interval or a chord that sounds harsh, as opposed to **consonance**.
divertimento: An eighteenth-century instrumental composition in a light style, typically consisting of several dance movements.
Divine Office: In the Roman Catholic Church, the daily services apart from the Mass.
dodecaphony. See **twelve-tone system**.
dominant: The fifth degree of a major or minor scale; the triad built upon that degree; the key or tonality based upon that degree.
dot. See **dotted note**.
dotted note: A note with a dot placed after it to increase its rhythmic value by half (e.g., 𝅗𝅥.).
dotted rhythm: A stately rhythmic pattern with a dotted note followed by a short note (e.g., ♪. ♬ ♪. ♬).
double aria: Aria that features two parts: a slow lyrical section followed by a fast, brilliant section.
double bar: Vertical lines placed to denote the end of a section of a composition or of the entire composition.
double bass (also bass viol, contrabass, and string bass)**:** A large string instrument, played standing upright, with a range lower than a cello.
double dots: Dots placed within double bars to indicate music that is to be repeated (𝄆 𝄇).
double exposition: In the first movement of a concerto, the double statement of the main themes, first by the orchestra, and then by the soloist.
double fugue: a fugue that uses two different subjects, typically one at a time, and then in a culminating combination.
double stop: On a string instrument, stopping and bowing two strings simultaneously to produce a chord.
downbeat: The accented beat at the beginning of a measure. See also **upbeat**.
drone: A sustained tone, often in a bass part, typically held for several measures.
duple meter: A meter with two beats per measures: *1* 2 *1* 2 (e.g., $\frac{2}{2}$ or 𝄵).

duration: How long a pitch, chord, or section of music lasts.
dynamics: The levels of loudness and softness in music.
eighth note: ♪, a note one half the value of a quarter note, one quarter the value of a half note, and one eighth the value of a whole note.
electronica: a broad term encompassing a variety of electronic types of popular music.
electronic music: Music that employs electronic means to generate its sounds.
electrophone: A class of musical instruments that use electronic means to produce their sound.
embellishment: See **ornament**.
English horn: Double-reed woodwind instrument with a range lower than the oboe.
English madrigal: A secular vocal work with English text popular in the late sixteenth and early seventeenth centuries.
Enlightenment: A movement in the history of ideas, culminating in the eighteenth century, that emphasized mankind's power of reason and self-improvement.
ensemble: A small group of instrumental or vocal musicians.
episode: In a fugue, a passage between statements of the fugal subject; in a rondo, a passage between statements of the refrain.
erhu: A Chinese two-string fiddle.
espressivo: With expression.
estampie: A medieval instrumental dance.
etude: A work for a solo instrument intended as a technical exercise.
euphonium: A brass instrument, resembling the tuba, that plays in a tenor range.
exit aria: Aria in which a soloist appeals to the audience for applause before abruptly exiting.
exoticism: The use of musical materials (themes, harmonies, rhythms, orchestration, etc.) in European music to evoke distant, non-Western regions.
exposition: The first main section of sonata form; in a fugue, the opening and subsequent passages that present the fugal subject successively in all the voices.
expressionism: An early twentieth-century movement in German and Austrian art and music that attempted to capture the depth of subjective emotions.
false recapitulation: in sonata form, the entrance of the recapitulation in the wrong key (i.e., not the tonic).
fanfare: A short, ceremonial flourish typically played by brass instruments.
fantasia (**fantasy**)**:** A contrapuntal instrumental composition of the Renaissance; a composition in free form.
fermata: A sign (𝄐) placed above or below a note indicating that it should be held beyond its rhythmic value.
figured bass (or **thoroughbass**)**:** The technique employed in the Baroque basso continuo in which a bass line is provided with figures to indicate the chords to be realized above the bass line. See also **continuo**.
film music: Music written and coordinated to be heard during a screening of a film.
finale: The movement that concludes an instrumental composition (e.g., symphony, concerto); the ensemble that concludes an act of an opera.
first theme (**first theme group**)**:** The first theme or group of themes in the exposition of sonata form.

flag: In musical notation, a flag-like symbol that indicates the duration of a note.

flat: An accidental sign before a note (♭) indicating that the note should be lowered one half step.

flute: Woodwind instrument held horizontally and capable of playing in a high range.

folk music: Music of particular ethnic groups that is handed down from generation to generation orally rather than through notation.

folk rock: a genre of popular music blending elements of folk and rock music.

form: The structural organization of a composition (e.g., sonata form, theme and variation form).

forte (***f***): Loud.

fortepiano: The original term for the piano, invented early in the eighteenth century (literally, "loud-soft"); subsequently known as the pianoforte, and now, piano.

fortissimo (***ff***): Very loud.

four-part harmony: Harmony in four parts, referred to as the soprano, alto, tenor, and bass parts. In four-part harmony, one part typically doubles a pitch of the basic triads used.

free imitation: In counterpoint, a type of imitation in which one part is freely imitated by other parts.

free jazz: a type of jazz developed in the 1950s and 1960s that disregarded the established conventions of the art form to promote free exchanges of material between the musicians.

French horn: A brass instrument with coiled tubing and valves.

French overture: A Baroque instrumental movement with a slow opening section, often featuring dotted rhythms, followed by a faster section in fugal style.

frequencies: The vibrations produced by a particular pitch, calculated in the number of frequencies per second.

front line: In Dixieland and other early jazz the section of instruments that improvise on the melody, as opposed to the supporting rhythm section.

fugal exposition. See **exposition**.

fugato: Small-scale fugue.

fugue (**fugal**): A composition in a high style of counterpoint in which a subject is introduced and elaborated in various combinations by two or more parts. In highly complex fugues, more than one subject may be employed (hence double fugue, triple fugue, etc.).

fundamental pitch: A basic pitch that generates a series of harmonics.

funk: A genre of African-American music of the 1960s that deemphasizes melody and harmony in favor of a strong rhythmic groove.

fusion: A style of music developed in the 1970s that joins jazz improvisation with the rhythms and timbres of rock.

Futurism: A movement in early twentieth-century art originating in Italy that celebrated the dynamic sights and sounds of the modernist age.

galant music: A style of music from the middle decades of the eighteenth century that featured a tuneful simplicity.

galliard: A Renaissance dance in triple meter, in a lively tempo, frequently performed with a pavan.

gamelan: A musical ensemble from Java or Bali that uses gongs, drums, chimes, and metallophones.

gangsta: A type of rap with lyrics centered on gang culture and violence.
genre: A category or type of composition; for example, concerto, opera, symphony.
***Gesamtkunstwerk*:** "Total art work," applied to the music dramas of Richard Wagner.
gigue (jig): A fast Baroque dance in compound meter, often the last movement of a suite.
glissando: Sliding through a range of pitches to produce a continuum of sound.
gong (tam-tam): A circular percussion instrument suspended from a frame and struck with a mallet.
gospel music: A style of twentieth-century popular sacred music associated with African-American Protestant churches.
gradual: A Proper chant sung or recited between the Epistle and Gospel readings in the Mass.
grand opera: A type of nineteenth-century French opera characterized by spectacular stage effects and scenery, ballets, and pageantry.
grave: Slow, gravely.
Gregorian chant: Monophonic chant used in the early Roman Catholic Church, named after Pope Gregory I (r. 590–604).
ground bass (or **basso ostinato**): The technique of grounding music over an unchanging bass pattern; see also **ostinato**.
grunge: Music that arose in Seattle, Washington, in the early 1980s that drew on elements from both heavy metal and punk.
guitar: A plucked string instrument, typically with six strings over a fingerboard with frets.
habanera: a dance popularized in Cuba during the nineteenth century.
half note: 𝅗𝅥, a note half the value of a whole note, twice the value of a quarter note, and four times the value of an eighth note.
half step (or **semitone**): The interval between successive pitches of the chromatic scale; the smallest interval in conventional Western music.
harmonic: A term in acoustics used to describe the various "partial" sounds generated by a vibrating medium in addition to the fundamental pitch; the frequencies of the partial are multiples of the fundamental pitch.
harmonic progression: A progression from one chord to another.
harmony (**harmonic**): The vertical combinations of pitches to produce chords; the study of chord relationships.
harp: A plucked string instrument, with the strings running vertically within a triangular frame, and perpendicular to a sounding board at the base.
harpsichord: A keyboard instrument, used widely in the seventeenth and eighteenth centuries, in which strings are plucked by quills instead of being struck by hammers, as in the piano.
heavy metal: A type of rock that uses heavily distorted and amplified sound.
heterophony: A performance practice in which different musicians perform different versions of the same melody simultaneously.
homophony (**homophonic**): A texture characterized by a single melodic line supported by block-like chords, as opposed to polyphony.
honky-tonk: country music of the southern United States played in a bar.
humanism: A Renaissance movement, stimulated in part by a Greek and Roman revival, that centered its attention on human values.

hymn: A stanzaic religious song sung by a congregation.

idée fixe: A "fixed idea," a term used by Berlioz in his *Symphonie fantastique* to describe the recurring melody that represents the beloved in each movement.

idiophone: A class of musical instruments that produce their sound by being struck or rubbed.

imitation: A contrapuntal technique in which one voice is imitated by one or more others.

imitative counterpoint: Counterpoint that makes extensive use of imitation between the voices.

imitative polyphony: Polyphony that makes extensive use of imitation between the voices.

imperfect consonance: A class of consonant intervals that includes thirds with three or four half steps and sixths with eight or nine half steps.

impressionism: A nineteenth-century movement in French visual arts that sought to capture the effect of light on objects, sometimes freely applied to the music of Debussy and Ravel.

impromptu: A character piece, typically for piano, that suggests an improvisation.

improvisation: the act of improvising music.

incidental music: Music composed for the production of a play.

instrumentation. See **orchestration**.

intermezzo: In the nineteenth century, a section of a larger instrumental work, or a short, instrumental: composition.

interval: The distance between two pitches.

inversion: Playing a melody upside-down; also, a reordering of a chord by transposing the bass note so that it is no longer the lowest sounding note.

Janissary music: Military music of the Turkish sultan that uses wind and percussion instruments; Janissary music was imitated by European composers especially in the eighteenth and early nineteenth centuries.

jazz: Twentieth-century African-American music characterized by an improvisatory melodic style, with strong rhythmic and harmonic organization.

jazz rock (jazz fusion): a musical genre of the 1960s that combined elements of jazz and rock.

kettledrum. See **timpani**.

key: The major or minor mode of a composition (G major, F major, D minor, etc.).

keyboard instrument: An instrument in which sound is produced by depressing keys in order to strike strings through various means. See also **celesta**; **clavichord**; **harpsichord**; and **piano**).

key signature: The collections of sharps and flats at the beginning of a staff to indicate the key of a composition.

***Klangfarbenmelodie*:** "Sound-color-melody," a term coined by Arnold Schoenberg in 1911 to identify tone color as an element of composition.

largo (**larghetto**)**:** "Slow"; a slow movement.

ledger lines: Small parts of imaginary horizontal lines above and below the staff to accommodate extra pitches.

legato: A smooth manner of performance, as opposed to **staccato**.

leitmotif: In Wagner's music dramas, a "leading" motive associated with a character or dramatic element.

lento: Slow.
libretto: Italian for "little book"; the text of an opera or oratorio.
lied (**pl. lieder**)**:** German for "art song."
linear perspective: A method of creating the illusion of space and distance on a flat surface.
liturgy: The official ritual in a church service.
live electronic music: music that uses electronic sound-generating devices and computers, usually in an improvisational way.
lute: A plucked string instrument of Middle Eastern descent that appeared in Europe during the Middle Ages.
lyre: Plucked string instrument of antiquity used to accompany singing.
madrigal: A secular vocal work cultivated during the Renaissance in Italy and then transplanted to England.
madrigalism. See **word painting**.
major intervals: Seconds, thirds, sixths, and sevenths with two, four, nine and eleven half steps, respectively.
major mode: Applied to music in a key based on a major scale and using primarily major triads.
major scale: A diatonic scale with half steps between scale degrees 3 and 4 and 7 and 8 and characterized by a major third between degrees 1 and 3. See also **minor scale**.
major triad: A triad consisting of a major third and a minor third; the two together constitute a perfect fifth (e.g., C major triad: C-E-G)
masque: A staged dramatic entertainment of the sixteenth and seventeenth centuries, popular especially in England.
Mass: The principal service of the Roman Catholic Church; in music, the **Ordinary** of the Mass is frequently set to music.
mazurka: A Polish dance in a moderate or lively triple meter.
measure (or **bar**)**:** The basic temporal division of Western music, periodically indicated by vertical measure lines.
measure line (or **bar line**)**:** A vertical line across a staff to indicate the division of the music into measures.
mediant: The third scale degree; the triad built on the third scale degree.
medieval period. See **Middle Ages**.
melisma (**melismatic**)**:** Several notes sung to one syllable of text.
melody (**melodic**)**:** A succession of pitches with a memorable shape.
membranophone: A class of musical instruments that use a stretched membrane to produce their sound.
meno: Less.
metallophone: a class of musical instruments with metal bars struck by a mallet.
meter (**metrical**)**:** A regular arrangement of stressed and unstressed beats.
metronome: A mechanical device that emits regular beats according to an adjustable scale.
mezzo: "Half"; hence, mezzo forte (half loud).
mezzo-soprano: A female voice range between alto and soprano.
microtone: An interval smaller than a half step.
Middle Ages: a long period in Western history of about one thousand years spanning roughly the fall of Rome in 476 to 1450.

minimalism: A musical style that developed in the closing decades of the twentieth century from a related movement in the visual arts, and that uses repetitions of short musical figures to construct compositions.

Minnesinger: German poet-musician of the late Middle Ages.

minor intervals: Seconds, thirds, sixths, and sevenths with one, three, eight, and ten half steps, respectively.

minor mode: Applied to music in a key based on a minor scale and using primarily minor triads.

minor scale: A diatonic scale with half steps between scale degrees 2 and 3 and usually 5 and 6, and characterized by a minor third between degrees 1 and 3.

minor triad: A triad consisting of a minor third and a major third; the two together constitute a perfect fifth (e.g., A minor triad: A-C-E).

minuet and trio: A Baroque dance in a moderate triple meter; often used as a movement in such classical instrumental works as the symphony, string quartet, and sonata.

mirror inversion. See **inversion**.

mode (**modal**, **modality**)**:** Applied to music based on scales in Western music through roughly the sixteenth century. Modal is typically used to describe music based on the church modes; since roughly the seventeenth century, *mode* refers to the major or minor mode.

moderato: Moderately.

modernism: A broad movement of striking experimentation in the arts, originating early in the twentieth century and reacting against the late nineteenth century.

modified strophic song: A strophic song in which the recurring music for each strophe is somewhat modified.

modulation (**modulate**)**:** The technique of changing keys within a composition.

molto: Much.

monody (**monodic**)**:** A style of music developed in Italy about 1600 in which a solo singer is accompanied, typically by a basso continuo.

monophony (**monophonic**)**:** A type of music with a single melodic line, as opposed to polyphony.

motet: A sacred polyphonic vocal composition, usually with a Latin text, first developed in the thirteenth century.

motive: A short musical gesture, such as a melodic fragment or rhythmic pattern.

movement: A separate portion of a larger composition, such as a movement of a symphony, sonata, etc.

musical: A type of twentieth-century American theatrical entertainment derived from operetta and featuring spoken dialogue, songs, and dancing.

music drama: A term used by Wagner to describe his later operas.

musique concrète: A type of music developed about 1950 in which natural sounds are recorded and manipulated electronically.

mute (**muted**)**:** An object applied to an instrument to soften its sound.

nationalism: A nineteenth-century movement in the arts to promote the cultural identity of specific countries or ethnic regions; in music, nationalism featured folk music, folk dances, and subjects drawn from folklore.

natural sign: A sign (♮) used in notation to cancel a previous sharp or flat.

neoclassicism: Music of roughly the 1920s, '30s, and '40s that makes use in some way of eighteenth-century musical techniques; more broadly, neoclassicism is used in the arts to describe the idea of a revival of classical antiquity.

neume: In the early Middle Ages, a dash, dot, or curved, hook-like figure that could be used to represent a musical tone.

New Orleans jazz: Early improvised jazz centered in New Orleans that typically used an ensemble consisting of a cornet (or trumpet), clarinet (or saxophone), trombone, piano, double bass, banjo (or guitar), and drums.

nocturne: "Night piece"; a lyrical instrumental composition of the nineteenth century, typically for piano.

Noh: A type of Japanese music drama that employs singing, stylized acting, flute, and percussion.

noise: Sound with no discernible pitch.

non-imitative counterpoint: Counterpoint in which the different parts are relatively independent and do not imitate one another.

non troppo: Not too much.

notation: The system of symbols used in writing down music.

note: The notational symbol for a pitch.

oboe: Double-reed woodwind instrument with a soprano range.

occasional music: Music for a specific occasion.

octave: The interval between the first and last pitches of a scale. The ratio of frequencies in an octave is 2:1, with the high pitch vibrating twice as fast as the lower.

Office. See **Divine Office**.

opera: A staged dramatic work that employs solo singers, ensembles and choruses, an orchestra, costumes, sets, and scenery, and occasionally dance.

opera buffa: Italian comic opera of the eighteenth and early nineteenth centuries.

opera seria: Italian serious opera of the eighteenth century.

operetta: A light opera, usually on a comic subject.

opus (abbr. **op.**)**:** Latin for "work"; opus numbers are used to catalogue the works of composers.

oratorio: A dramatic work on a religious subject similar to an opera but without staged action.

orchestra (**orchestral**)**:** A large ensemble of instrumental performers; a contemporary orchestra typically has about one hundred performers.

orchestration: The technique of choosing different instrumental combinations for an orchestral work or a large ensemble; also called *instrumentation*.

Ordinary: The chants of the Mass whose texts remain the same from day to day in the liturgical calendar. See also **Proper**.

organ (pipe organ): a musical instrument, typically with one or more keyboards and a row of foot pedals, in which wind produced by bellows moves through ranks of pipes to produce pitches.

organum: Early medieval polyphony in which a freely composed part or parts are added to a preexistent plainchant.

ornament: Patterns of pitches, such as a trill, used to decorate a melodic line; also known as an embellishment.

ostinato: A relatively short figure repeated over and over; such a figure in the bass is known as a basso ostinato.

overtone. See **harmonic**.

overture: An instrumental (often orchestral) composition that prefaces a larger work such as an opera or oratorio; an independent overture is known as a concert overture.

palindrome: A sequence that occurs in the same order forward and backward.

pandiatonicism: The addition to triads of pitches drawn from their underlying diatonic scales, a technique developed in the twentieth century.

pantonality: Music that relies on all pitches of the chromatic scale.

parallel motion: Two musical parts that move in the same direction while preserving the same distance between them.

parallel organum: Organum in which the parts move in parallel motion.

paraphrase technique: In Renaissance music, an elaboration of a plainchant melody.

parody technique: In Renaissance music, a composition that borrows heavily from a preexistent composition so that it is, in effect, a reworking of its model.

part: One of the lines in a musical composition; also, the music played by a musician, as in "oboe part."

partial. See **harmonic**.

partita: A Baroque suite of dance movements, originally variations of one another.

passacaglia: A type of composition developed during the Baroque period, usually instrumental, comprising a series of variations based on an ostinato figure.

Passion: A sacred musical work relating the events of the suffering and crucifixion of Christ.

pavan (also **pavanne**): A slow dance in duple meter of the sixteenth and early seventeenth centuries, often paired with a galliard.

pedal point: A pitch, usually in the bass, that is sustained while other parts move more rapidly; pedal points are frequently encountered in fugues.

pentatonic scale: A five-pitch scale common in folk music and non-Western music; on the piano, a pentatonic scale may be produced by playing the black keys.

percussion: A classification of instruments played by various means of striking or shaking. Some percussion instruments, such as some drums, triangle, cymbals, and castanets, produce no definite pitch; others, such as the timpani, xylophone, and tubular bells, produce definite pitches.

perfect consonance: A class of intervals including the unison, fourths with five half steps, fifths with seven half steps, and octaves with twelve half steps.

perfect fifth: An interval of a fifth with seven half steps.

performance art: a type of performance, either random or coordinated in some way, that involves a performer or performers and an audience, and that might combine visual, spoken, and musical elements.

phasing: A technique in which several instruments play the same material that gradually moves out of phase, producing hypnotic, free blends of sound.

phrase: A self-contained portion of a melody.

pianissimo (***pp***): Very softly.

piano (***p***): Softly.

piano: A keyboard instrument in which strings are struck by felt-covered hammers; when engaged, a damper pedal raises dampers to allow the strings to vibrate freely.

piano trio: A piece of chamber music for piano, violin, and cello.
piccolo: A small flute that plays one octave above the flute.
pitch: The relative height of sound in music.
***più*:** More.
pizzicato: Plucking the strings of a string instrument rather than bowing them. See also **arco**.
plainchant (also **plainsong** or **chant**): The official monophonic texted music of the Roman Catholic liturgy.
plainsong. See **plainchant**.
***poco*:** Somewhat.
point of imitation: In polyphonic music, a texture in which the various voices enter in imitation with the same musical figure.
polonaise: A Polish dance in triple meter.
polychoral: Music for two or more choirs.
polyphony (**polyphonic**)**:** A texture in which two or more independent musical lines are contraposed, as opposed to homophony.
polyrhythm: The juxtaposition of distinct rhythmic layers.
polystylism: The mixture of different styles and approaches in composition.
polytonality (**polytonal**)**:** A twentieth-century technique in which music is written in two or more keys simultaneously.
postmodernism: a broad movement in the arts during the late twentieth century that departed from modernism and freely mixed different styles.
prelude (**prélude**)**:** A short instrumental piece intended as an introduction; in the nineteenth century, a short instrumental piece, typically for piano.
prepared piano: A piano, developed by John Cage, that alters the sound of the instrument by inserting various metal, rubber, and other objects between the strings.
presto: Very fast.
program music (**programmatic**)**:** Instrumental music with some extramusical element or idea, often drawn from literature or the other arts.
progression. See **harmonic progression**.
progressive rock: a genre of rock of the 1960s and 1970s in the United Kingdom and United States that attempted to invest rock with a new artistic stature by borrowing compositional techniques from jazz and classical music.
Proper: The chant of the Mass whose texts change from day to day in the liturgical calendar.
psalmody: The singing of psalms.
punk rock: A loud and aggressive style of rock music from the late 1970s and 1980s.
quadruple meter: A basic meter with four beats per measure.
quadruple stop: Playing four notes simultaneously on a bowed string instrument (such as a violin or cello).
quartal harmony: Harmony constructed of fourths.
quarter note: ♩, a note one fourth the value of a whole note, one half the value of a half note, and twice the value of an eighth note.
quartet: A work for four musicians, as in string quartet.
ragtime: A type of African-American music, popular from roughly 1890 through the 1920s, that was one of the precursors of jazz. Ragtime featured a syncopated treble line and a regular chordal accompaniment.

***rallentando*:** Becoming slower.
range: The range of pitches in a composition, from the lowest to the highest note.
rap: Style of African-American popular music from the 1980s and 1990s that features spoken rhymed lyrics accompanied by a rhythmic track.
realism: a broadly based movement in nineteenth-century arts that reacted against Romanticism by attempting to treat subjects as realistically as possible.
recapitulation (reprise): The third principal section of a movement in sonata form in which the events and materials of the exposition are brought back in the tonic key.
recitative: A type of vocal style intended to approximate the natural inflections of speech, used especially in operas, oratorios, and cantatas.
recorder: End-blown woodwind instrument commonly used in medieval and Renaissance music, and similar to a flute but with a whistle mouthpiece.
reed: A pliable strip of cane (or in some instruments metal) that vibrates when activated by a column of air.
refrain: A passage that periodically returns throughout a composition.
reggae: popular music originating in Jamaica in the 1960s with strong off-beats.
register: The relative height of the pitches played by an instrument, as in "high register," "low register."
Renaissance: In music history the period from roughly 1450 to 1600.
repeat marks: A sign (𝄆 𝄇) indicating that a passage is to be repeated.
repeat sign: See **repeat marks**.
repetition: A compositional technique that creates a sense of musical unity by repeating a motive, theme, or larger section of a work.
requiem: In the Roman Catholic liturgy, the Mass for the dead.
resolution: A progression from a dissonant chord to a consonant chord, releasing or "resolving" the tension of the dissonance.
responsorial: A type of performance, as in a plainchant, in which a soloist is answered by a choir.
rest: Silence in music; a notational sign, for example, 𝅀, 𝄿, 𝄾, 𝄽, 𝄼, 𝄻, specifying a momentary pause.
retransition: In sonata form, a passage toward the end of the development that prepares for the return of the tonic key in the recapitulation.
retrograde: The performance of a given musical line backward.
retrograde inversion: The performance of a musical line backwards and in mirror inversion.
revue: A light entertainment featuring songs and dances.
rhapsody: A free fantasy, typically for piano solo, often with a nationalistic character.
rhythm (rhythmic): A fundamental aspect of music that concerns the organization of sounds into temporal relationships, also applied to a particular rhythmic pattern.
rhythm and blues: A style of popular African-American music from the 1950s, commonly regarded as the forerunner of rock.
rhythm section: The instruments in a jazz ensemble whose primary function is to establish and reinforce the beat (typically piano, double pass, and drums).
ripieno: In a concerto grosso, the orchestra that accompanies the concertino.
ritard: A slowing down of the tempo.

ritornello: In Baroque music, a kind of musical refrain, especially the opening section of a concerto or an aria.

ritornello form: A form structured around a recurring ritornello; especially common in Baroque music.

rock: Popular music developed in the 1960s characterized by heavy electronic amplification.

rock and roll: Genre of popular American music that developed during the 1950s and is often viewed as the precursor to rock.

rococo: A term borrowed from the visual arts to describe a light, playful style of music in fashion during the mid-eighteenth century.

Romanticism: A broad concept that concerns the ability of art to express emotions and subjective states; in music, Romanticism is commonly applied to much of the nineteenth century.

rondeau: French form of secular song and poetry of the fourteenth and fifteenth centuries.

rondo: An instrumental form cultivated from the seventeenth century on in which a refrain alternates with contrasting episodes (for example, *ABACA*, *ABACABA*, *ABCA*).

root: In harmony, a pitch on which a triad or chord is constructed.

round: A vocal polyphonic work in canonic style with strict imitation between the voices.

rounded binary: A musical form with two sections, each repeated, in which the second concludes by reusing material from the first.

row. See **tone row**.

rubato: "Robbed" time; in performance, a technique in which the available time within a measure is stretched or distorted in some way.

sackbut: A medieval and Renaissance brass instrument, forerunner to the trombone.

sacred music: Music that uses a sacred text or is intended for use in church or private devotion.

saltarello: A lively Italian folk dance in a fast triple meter, native to Naples.

sampling: the technique of choosing a portion, or sample, of music and reusing it in another composition.

sarabande: A slow Baroque dance in triple meter encountered in suites, often with an emphasis on the second beat of the measure.

saxophone: A single-reed woodwind instrument used particularly in wind bands or jazz ensembles.

scale: A group of consecutive pitches filling out an octave, as in major scale, minor scale, or chromatic scale.

scat singing: A style of jazz singing that uses nonsense syllables to improvise a vocal line.

scherzo: Italian for "joke"; an instrumental movement of humorous character in rapid triple meter developed in the eighteenth and nineteenth centuries; in the nineteenth century, the scherzo and trio replaced the minuet and trio.

score: The complete musical notation for a composition, usually involving several aligned parts for different performers, for use by the conductor.

secco recitative: "Dry" recitative; recitative accompanied only by a continuo section, as opposed to accompanied recitative.

second theme (second thematic group): The second theme or group of themes in the exposition of sonata form.

semitone: Half step.

sequence: The repetition of a melodic portion or harmonic progression at higher or lower pitch levels; in medieval plainchant, a texted melody added after the Alleluia in the Mass.

serenade: "Evening music"; a light instrumental composition cultivated in the eighteenth and nineteenth centuries.

serial (serial music, serialism): A twentieth-century technique in which a composition is based on a series or ordering of pitches, most commonly a twelve-tone row.

series: An ordering of pitches, as in a twelve-tone row.

***sforzando* (*sf*):** A sharp accent.

shape-note notation: A type of notation in which differently shaped notes—triangles, squares, and so on—represented specific pitches; used in American congregational singing from the eighteenth and nineteenth centuries.

sharp: An accidental sign before a note (♯) indicating that the note should be raised one half step.

siciliano: A Baroque dance in compound meter.

simple meter: Basic meters in which the beats are subdivided into two.

sinfonia: Italian for "symphony."

Singspiel: German opera of the eighteenth and nineteenth centuries with spoken dialogue replacing recitative.

sitar: A chordophone from north India that has a long neck with movable frets, plucked strings and freely resonating strings.

sixteenth note: 𝅘𝅥𝅯, a note one sixteenth the value of a whole note, one eighth the value of a half note, one fourth the value of a quarter note, and one half the value of an eighth note.

slow introduction: An introductory passage in a slow tempo that precedes the exposition of sonata form.

slur: A curved figure over two or more notes directing the performer to play them in a smooth, legato fashion.

snare drum (side drum): a double-headed drum with a set of wires (snares) stretched across the bottom.

Socialist realism: in the Soviet Union the official theory of the arts sanctioned by the state to promote the ideals of socialism.

solo: For performance by one performer.

sonata: An instrumental composition in several movements, usually three or four. In the Baroque period, sonatas were typically performed by one or two treble melody instruments and a basso continuo; since the Classical period, sonatas are generally written for one or two instruments.

sonata da camera: In the Baroque period, a "chamber sonata," often consisting of various dances, as in a suite.

sonata da chiesa: In the Baroque period, a "church sonata," more serious in mood than a sonata da camera, and often in four movements in the succession slow-fast-slow-fast.

sonata form (sonata-allegro form): A form most often used in the first movements of sonatas, string quartets, symphonies, and so on, with three principal sections: exposition, development, and recapitulation.

sonata-rondo form: A form that uses elements of sonata form and rondo, most often found in the finales of sonatas, string quartets, and symphonies.
song: A musical setting of a poem or other text for one or more voices and accompaniment.
song cycle: A collection of songs unified by a narrative or poetic idea or by musical means.
sonority: A term used to describe the general sound quality of a composition or musical passage, sometimes used to refer to a chord.
soprano: The highest female vocal register; a high musical part.
soul music: a type of popular American music originating in the 1950s and blending African-American gospel music, rhythm and blues, and jazz.
spiritual: A type of religious folk song cultivated by African Americans in the nineteenth century; also, a type of religious folk song cultivated in American revivalist meetings during the eighteenth and nineteenth centuries.
Sprechstimme: A style of singing, developed by Arnold Schoenberg, halfway between speech and song; "spoken song."
staccato: A detached manner of performance indicated by dots above or below note heads, as opposed to **legato**.
staff (stave): A series of five lines and four spaces used to notate music: ═══.
stanza: A group of lines in a poem, typically with recurring rhymes and meters.
stepwise motion: motion in which a pitch moves to its neighboring pitch either above or below.
stretto: In a fugue, a passage in which entries of the subject overlap; also, an increase in tempo.
strict imitation: Canonic imitation.
string instruments: Instruments that produce sounds by means of vibrating strings; in the modern orchestra, the string section includes the violin, viola, cello, and double bass.
string quartet: A composition for a chamber group, consisting of two violins, a viola, and a cello, developed during the eighteenth century, principally by Haydn and Mozart.
strophic song: Applied to songs in which the various stanzas of text are set to the same music, as opposed to **through-composed songs**.
style: In music a broad term to describe the general sound qualities of a composition, determined by elements such as melody, rhythm, harmony, dynamics, and timbre.
subdominant: The fourth degree of a scale; the triad built on that degree.
subject: In a fugue, the initial theme; also, a musical idea.
suite: An instrumental composition consisting of a series of stylized dance movements.
surrealism: an avant-garde movement in twentieth-century arts that sought to liberate the irrational forces of the unconscious and dream states.
swing: A type of jazz practice by big bands during the 1930s and 1940s.
syllabic: A type of text setting in which each syllable is set to one note. See also **melismatic**.
symphonic poem: A genre of program music in one movement for orchestra developed in the nineteenth century by Franz Liszt.
symphony: A work for orchestra, usually in three or four movements, originating in the eighteenth century.

syncopation: A rhythmic device in which normally unaccented beats are accented (e.g., 1 *2*, 1 *2*, instead of *1* 2, *1* 2).
synesthesia: A phenomenon in which one sense—such as hearing the sounds produced by instruments—stimulates a second sense, particularly vision.
tabla: A pair of tuned drums common in music of north India.
tala: Repeated series of beats in Indian classical music.
tambourine: Percussion instrument of indefinite pitch resembling a small drum with small metal plates around the rim that jangle which the tambourine is struck.
tempo: The speed of a musical composition.
tenor: The high male vocal register; also a part that uses that register; in medieval church polyphony, the tenor is the voice entrusted with the plainchant or other melody on which the composition is based.
tenuto: Held.
ternary form: Three-part form, ABA.
ternary sonata form: Sonata form that emphasizes a division into three parts, the exposition, development, and recapitulation.
terraced dynamics: Shifts in dynamic levels, typically between *forte* and *piano*, common in Baroque music.
tetrachord: A succession of four consecutive pitches.
texture: A general term used to describe the blending of melodic lines and harmonies in a composition.
theme (**thematic**)**:** A melody or musical idea on which a composition is based.
theme and variations: A composition in which a theme is presented and varied, modified, or altered in some way in a series of variations.
thoroughbass. See **figured bass**.
three-part form (**ABA**)**:** A three-part form that has an opening section repeated after a contrasting middle section.
through-composed song: A song in which each stanza of text is set to different music, as opposed to a **strophic song**.
tie: In notation, a curved figure connecting two pitches to indicate that they should be held as one continuous sound.
timbre. See **tone color**.
time signature: In notation, a ratio at the beginning of the staff to indicate the meter of a composition, for example, $\frac{4}{4}$.
timpani: Tuned drums played with mallets and consisting of a skin stretched over a copper bowl.
toccata: An instrumental composition, often for a keyboard instrument, in a free, virtuoso style.
tonality (**tonal**)**:** The principal musical system in Western music from the Baroque period to the twentieth century. Tonal music conveys a feeling of gravitational pull toward a tonic pitch, a tonic triad constructed on that pitch, and a hierarchy of triads around the tonic triad; also, a key of a tonal composition.
tone: A pitch of definite height.
tone cluster: A chord made up of several closely adjacent notes.
tone color: The quality of sound of a musical instrument; also called *timbre*.
tone poem: A programmatic composition for orchestra, developed by Richard Strauss, similar to a symphonic poem.

tone row: A fixed sequence of all twelve chromatic pitches that can be transposed, inverted and/or performed in retrograde, and used as the basis for a twelve-tone composition.
tonic: In tonal music, the central or "home" pitch or triad; the first degree of a diatonic scale.
total serialism: A type of serial music developed around 1950 in which pitch and non-pitch elements such as rhythm, dynamics, and register are controlled according to a series or some ordering.
transition: A passage leading from one section of a composition to another.
transposition (transpose): A repetition of a musical line or idea so that it begins on a different pitch; for example, C-D-E-F-G may be transposed to G-A-B-C-D or to F-G-A-B♭-C.
treble: A high voice or part, as opposed to bass.
treble clef: A clef (𝄞) used to locate the higher sounding pitches.
tremolo: On string instruments, the rapid reiteration of a single pitch, produced by short up-and-down bow strokes.
triad: A chord consisting of three pitches, constructed by adding pitches a third and a fifth above a fundamental pitch (e.g., C-E-G, D-F-A).
triangle: Percussion instrument consisting of a metal rod bent into the shape of a triangle that is suspended and struck by a beater.
trill: An embellishment in which two adjacent pitches are alternated rapidly, indicated by the sign ***tr*** placed above a note.
trio: A work for three instruments or voices; the middle section of a minuet, scherzo, and so on.
trio sonata: In Baroque music, a sonata for two treble instruments and a basso continuo.
triple meter: A meter with three beats per measure, the first of which is accented: *1* 2 3 *1* 2 3.
triple stop: Playing three notes simultaneously on a bowed string instrument (such as a violin or cello).
triplet: A rhythmic grouping of three notes (e.g., ♩♩♩ with 3) with the same duration as two similar notes.
tritone: The interval of three whole steps.
trombone: A brass instrument of medium to low range equipped with a sliding mechanism to produce its sounds.
troubadour, trouvère: In the Middle Ages, aristocratic French poet-musicians who composed courtly love songs.
trumpet: A brass instrument with valves that plays in the highest range.
tuba: A valved brass instrument that plays in the lowest range.
tune: A simple melody easy to sing.
tutti: Italian for "all"; in a Baroque concerto grosso, the entire ensemble, including the concertino and the ripieno.
twelve-tone system: A technique in twentieth-century music that employs twelve-tone rows. See also **serial**.
two-part form (*AB*). See **binary form**.
unison: The interval formed when two voices or instruments perform the same pitch.
upbeat: A weak beat that precedes a downbeat.
valse: French for "waltz."

variation: A varied or elaborated statement of a previously stated theme. In a variation, certain aspects of the theme remain the same while others are altered.
vaudeville: A form of entertainment featuring songs, comic skits, and perhaps even acrobats and jugglers.
verismo: Applied to late nineteenth-century Italian opera, which was distinguished by its realism.
vespers: A service of the Roman Catholic Office held during the early evening.
vibrato: An expressive shaking effect caused by rapid, minute variations in a pitch during its production.
viol: A family of bowed string instruments common in the Renaissance and Baroque, usually with six strings and a fretted keyboard.
viola: Bowed string instrument with a range between the violin and cello.
violin: Bowed string instrument that plays in a high range.
virelai: A French form of secular song and poetry of the fourteenth and fifteenth centuries.
virginal: English name for the harpsichord.
virtuoso: A highly skilled performer.
***vivace*:** Lively.
vocable: A nonsense syllable used in singing.
vocal: Having to do with the human voice; hence, music with text.
voice: The human voice; a musical part or line in a composition.
walking bass: A bass part moving largely in stepwise motion and imitating walking.
waltz: A nineteenth-century dance in triple meter; also *valse*.
whole note: 𝅝, a note twice the value of a half note, four times the value of a quarter note, and eight times the value of an eighth note.
whole step (or **whole tone**)**:** The interval of a second consisting of two half steps.
whole-tone scale: A scale consisting of whole steps, used especially by Liszt, and by Debussy and other twentieth-century composers.
wind instruments: Instruments in which sound is produced by means of a column of air.
woodwind (**wind**)**:** A section of the modern orchestra that includes the flute, oboe, clarinet, and bassoon and their families of instruments.
word painting: A musical illustration of a word or phrase by means of a rhythmic, melodic, or harmonic motive or figure.
xylophone: Percussion instrument with tuned wooden bars arranged in the order of a keyboard and struck with hard mallets.

Credits

p. 2: MR. INTERIOR/Shutterstock
p. 3: bpk, Berlin / Art Resource, NY
p. 4: Jorgeinthewater/iStockphoto
p. 7: imagestock/iStockphoto
p. 12: © Pictorial Press Ltd / Alamy Stock Photo
p. 20: Alim/Shutterstock
p. 25: © Vibrant Pictures / Alamy Stock Photo
p. 26: Bartosz Hadyniak/iStockphoto
p. 30: Image copyright © The Metropolitan Museum of Art. Image source: Art Resource, NY
p. 34: Alenavlad/Shutterstock
p. 34: 3drenderings/iStockphoto
p. 34: Susan Trigg/iStockphoto
p. 34: Dennis Guillaume/iStockphoto
p. 34: RodrigoBlanco/iStockphoto
p. 34: venusphoto/iStockphoto
p. 34: ayzek/iStockphoto
p. 34: 3drenderings/iStockphoto
p. 34: perets/iStockphoto
p. 34: nuiiko/iStockphoto
p. 34: CagriOner/iStockphoto
p. 34: Tan Wei Ming/iStockphoto
p. 34: wbgorex/iStockphoto
p. 34: mladn61/iStockphoto
p. 34: Oktay Ortakcioglu/iStockphoto
p. 34: furtseff/Shutterstock
p. 34: Marek Walica/iStockphoto
p. 34: ?/iStockphoto
p. 34: uatp2/iStockphoto
p. 34: daseaford/Shutterstock
p. 34: DNY59/iStockphoto
p. 34: Veniamin Kraskov/iStockphoto
p. 34: Hogie/iStockphoto
p. 34: EdnaM/iStockphoto
p. 36: Photo by Hiroyuki Ito/Getty Images
p. 37: Pavel L Photo and Video/Shutterstock
p. 38: © WENN Ltd / Alamy Stock Photo
p. 39: Album / Album
p. 39: © Tracksimages.com / Alamy Stock Photo
p. 44: John Warburton Lee / John Warburton Lee
p. 44: The Philadelphia Museum of Art / Art Resource, NY. © 2016 Artists Rights Society (ARS), New York / ADAGP, Paris
p.46; M. Unal Ozmen/Shutterstock
p. 47: PARAMOUNT PICTURES / Album / Album
p. 50: Erich Lessing / Art Resource, NY
p. 50: The Art Archive at Art Resource, NY
p. 50: Bridgeman Images
p. 50: Museum of Fine Arts, Boston, Massachusetts, USA / From the George Alfred Cluett Collection / given by Florence Cluett Chambers / Bridgeman Images
p. 50: INTERFOTO / Alamy Stock Photo
p. 50: V&A Images, London / Art Resource, NY. © 2016 ADAGP, Paris / Avec l'aimable autorisation de M. Pierre Bergé, président du Comité Jean Cocteau
p. 50: The Solomon R. Guggenheim Foundation / Art Resource, NY. © 2016 Frank Stella / Artists Rights Society (ARS), New York
p. 52: Everett Historical/Shutterstock
p. 60: Erich Lessing / Art Resource, NY
p. 61: HUANG Zheng/Shutterstock
p. 61: AnLe/Shutterstock
p. 66: DeAgostini / DeAgostini
p. 68: © RMN-Grand Palais / Art Resource, NY
p. 71: Erich Lessing / Art Resource, NY
p. 75: Viacheslav Lopatin/Shutterstock
p. 75: pawel.gaul/iStockphoto
p. 76: AnkNet/iStockphoto
p. 80: Gianni Dagli Orti / The Art Archive at Art Resource, NY
p. 83: © BnF, Dist. RMN-Grand Palais / Art Resource, NY
p. 89: Travel Pictures Ltd / Travel Pictures Ltd
p. 92: Cameraphoto Arte, Venice / Art Resource, NY
p. 93: Reeed/Shutterstock
p. 94: DeAgostini / DeAgostini
p. 95: Everett Historical/Shutterstock
p. 99: Borisb17/Shutterstock
p. 100: The Art Archive at Art Resource, NY
p. 101: Peter Zaharov/Shutterstock
p. 104: Fine Art Images / Fine Art Images
p. 105: Everett - Art/Shutterstock
p. 105: DeAgostini / DeAgostini
p. 109: Oratorio dei Filippini, Rome, Italy / Bridgeman Images
p. 109: © Rufus Crosby / Alamy Stock Photo
p. 110: © PRISMA ARCHIVO / Alamy Stock Photo
p. 111: SuperStock / SuperStock
p. 115: SuperStock / SuperStock
p. 115: CBCK-Christine/iStockphoto
p. 119: Image copyright © The Metropolitan Museum of Art. Image source: Art Resource, NY
p. 120: © "Fine Art Images" / Fine Art Images
p. 126: Photo by Tony Russell/Redferns
p. 130: Album / Prisma / Album / Superstock
p. 131: DeAgostini / DeAgostini / Superstock
p. 132: Ilona5555/Shutterstock
p. 132: Album / Joseph Martin / Album / SuperStock
p. 133: SuperStock / SuperStock

p. 133: Pecold/Shutterstock
p. 136 © RMN-Grand Palais / Art Resource, NY
p. 140: Art Archive, The / Art Archive, The / Superstock
p. 142: SuperStock / SuperStock
p. 143: Philip Bird LRPS CPAGB/Shutterstock
p. 144: Museo Correr, Venice, Italy / Bridgeman Images
p. 145: De Agostini Picture Library / G. Nimatallah / Bridgeman Images
p. 145: Scala / Art Resource, NY
p. 149: © "Fine Art Images" / Fine Art Images / Superstock
p. 149: © Heritage Image Partnership Ltd / Alamy Stock Photo
p. 150: Iberfoto / Iberfoto / SuperStock
p. 151: © Peter Horree / Alamy Stock Photo
p. 154: bpk, Berlin / Art Resource, NY
p. 155: Ham House, Surrey, UK / Bridgeman Images
p. 155: wrangel/iStockphoto
p. 157: Art Archive, The / Art Archive, The / Superstock
p. 160: SuperStock / SuperStock
p. 161: DeAgostini / DeAgostini / Superstock
p. 164: Art Archive, The / Art Archive, The / Superstock
p. 166: Collection Christophel / Alamy Stock Photo
p. 167: TommL/iStockphoto
p. 169: Alfredo Dagli Orti / The Art Archive at Art Resource, NY
p. 171; Fondation Beyeler
p. 171: Gianni Dagli Orti / The Art Archive at Art Resource, NY. © 2016 The Josef and Anni Albers Foundation / Artists Rights Society (ARS), New York
p. 174: Staatsbibliothek, Berlin, Germany / Bridgeman Images
p. 180: Christian Draghici/Shutterstock
p. 180: claudiodivizia/iStockphoto
p. 186: Art Archive, The / Art Archive, The / Superstock
p. 187: National Portrait Gallery
p. 187: © Clive Collie / Alamy Stock Photo
p. 188: Photo by The Print Collector/Print Collector/Getty Images
p. 188: © Lebrecht Music and Arts Photo Library / Alamy Stock Photo
p. 189: Lobkowicz Palace, Prague Castle, Czech Republic / Bridgeman Images
p. 194: Archivart / Alamy Stock Photo
p. 194: © Ricardo Rafael Alvarez / Alamy Stock Photo
p. 195: POM POM/Shutterstock
p. 201: © Bildarchiv Monheim GmbH / Alamy Stock Photo
p. 205: sadikgulec/iStockphoto
p. 208: Fine Art Images / Fine Art Images / Superstock
p. 209: Everett - Art/Shutterstock
p. 209: miflippo/iStockphoto
p. 210: Fine Art Images / Fine Art Images / Superstock
p. 211: Nikitin Mikhail/Shutterstock
p. 211: Daniel M. Silva/Shutterstock
p. 214: SuperStock / SuperStock
p. 214: Fine Art Images / Fine Art Images / Superstock
p. 216: kevinhung/Shutterstock
p. 216: Premysl/Shutterstock
p. 217: © Lebrecht Music and Arts Photo Library / Alamy Stock Photo
p. 219: DeAgostini / DeAgostini / Superstock
p. 221: PARAMOUNT/Allstar Picture Library
p. 228: Art Archive, The / Art Archive, The / Superstock
p. 234: Art Archive, The / Art Archive, The
p. 235: nimu1956/iStockphoto
p. 235: cmfotoworks/iStockphoto
p. 236: © The Metropolitan Museum of Art. Image source: Art Resource, NY
p. 237: Private Collection / Bridgeman Images
p. 242: Fine Art Images / Fine Art Images
p. 246: Art Archive, The / Art Archive, The
p. 246: Art Archive, The / Art Archive, The
p. 247: Erich Lessing / Art Resource, NY
p. 248: Godong / robertharding / Superstock
p. 249: ORION/Allstar Picture Library
p. 251: ÖNB/Wien, Mus.Hs. 17559 fol. 11v.
p. 251: SuperStock / SuperStock
p. 255: Sara Krulwich/The New York Times/Redux
p. 263: akg-images / Superstock
p. 264: Fine Art Images / Fine Art Images / SuperStock
p. 265: Erich Lessing / Art Resource, NY
p. 266: Gianni Dagli Orti / The Art Archive at Art Resource, NY
p. 270: Fine Art Images / Fine Art Images
p. 285: Erich Lessing / Art Resource, NY
p. 286: Erich Lessing / Art Resource, NY
p. 290: Steve Vidler / Steve Vidler
p. 291: Design Pics / Design Pics
p. 294: MATTES Ren / Hemis.fr / SuperStock
p. 295: Everett - Art/Shutterstock
p. 296: Album / Joseph Martin / Album
p. 297: © The Trustees of the British Museum / Art Resource, NY
p. 301: Everett Historical/Shutterstock
p. 302: © Look and Learn / Illustrated Papers Collection / Bridgeman Images
p. 304: Tate, London / Art Resource, NY
p. 305: Alfredo Dagli Orti / Art Resource, NY
p. 307: DeAgostini / DeAgostini
p. 310: Everett Historical/Shutterstock
p. 311: Art Archive, The / Art Archive, The / SuperStock
p. 312: INTERFOTO / Alamy Stock Photo
p. 314: SuperStock / SuperStock
p. 318: Art Archive, The / Art Archive, The / SuperStock
p. 319: © RMN-Grand Palais / Art Resource, NY
p. 320: Fine Art Images / Fine Art Images / SuperStock
p. 327: The Museum of the City of New York / Art Resource, NY
p. 328: Bridgeman-Giraudon / Art Resource, NY
p. 329: © Photo Researchers / Alamy Stock Photo
p. 330: Bridgeman Art Library / Bridgeman Art Library / SuperStock
p. 330: SuperStock / SuperStock
p. 335: Fine Art Images / Fine Art Images
p. 335: Fine Art Images / Fine Art Images / SuperStock
p. 336: Alfredo Dagli Orti / The Art Archive at Art Resource, NY
p. 337: Pictorial Press Ltd / Alamy Stock Photo
p. 342: Private Collection / Bridgeman Images
p. 343: DeAgostini / DeAgostini

p. 344: bpk, Berlin/Art Resource, NY
p. 345: bpk, Berlin/Art Resource, NY
p. 346: SuperStock / SuperStock
p. 352: Fine Art Images / Fine Art Images / SuperStock
p. 352: Alfredo Dagli Orti / The Art Archive at Art Resource, NY
p. 353: Bridgeman-Giraudon / Art Resource, NY
p. 356: Private Collection / © Look and Learn / Bridgeman Images
p. 362: The Art Archive at Art Resource, NY
p. 363: DeAgostini / DeAgostini
p. 363: Art Archive, The / Art Archive, The / SuperStock
p. 364: Art Archive, The / Art Archive, The / SuperStock
p. 365: Alfredo Dagli Orti / The Art Archive at Art Resource, NY
p. 368: France, Paris, cover for William Tell play / De Agostini Picture Library / J. L. Charmet / Bridgeman Images
p. 369: Art Archive, The / Art Archive, The / SuperStock
p. 370: DeAgostini / DeAgostini / SuperStock
p. 372: Heller Joachim/Shutterstock
p. 374: © AF Fotografie / Alamy Stock Photo
p. 381: British Library / The Art Archive at Art Resource, NY
p. 381: Art Archive, The / Art Archive, The / SuperStock
p. 382: Art Archive, The / Art Archive, The / SuperStock
p. 383: © Heritage Image Partnership Ltd / Alamy Stock Photo
p. 386: Christie's Images / Christie's Images / SuperStock
p. 386: Art Archive, The / Art Archive, The / SuperStock
p. 387: The Museum of the City of New York / Art Resource, NY
p. 391: bpk, Berlin/Art Resource, NY
p. 392: Fine Art Images / Fine Art Images / SuperStock
p. 392: Fine Art Images / Fine Art Images / SuperStock
p. 394: © SPUTNIK / Alamy Stock Photo
p. 396: Culver Pictures, Inc. / Culver Pictures, Inc. / SuperStock
p. 397: Fine Art Images / Fine Art Images / SuperStock
p. 398: DeAgostini / DeAgostini
p. 402: Fine Art Images / Fine Art Images / SuperStock
p. 406: © DeA Picture Library / Art Resource, NY
p. 410: Buyenlarge / Buyenlarge
p. 416: agf photo / agf photo
p. 416: Wolfgang Kaehler / Wolfgang Kaehler
p. 420: ACME Imagery / ACME Imagery. © 2016 Estate of Pablo Picasso / Artists Rights Society (ARS), New York
p. 421: SuperStock / SuperStock
p. 422: Bridgeman Art Library, London / Bridgeman Art Library, London
p. 423: Scala/White Images / Art Resource, NY. © Succession Marcel Duchamp / ADAGP, Paris / Artists Rights Society (ARS), New York 2016
p. 423: Album / Joseph Martin / Album. © Salvador Dalí, Fundació Gala-Salvador Dalí, Artists Rights Society (ARS), New York 2016
p. 431: Fine Art Images / Fine Art Images
p. 432: Art Archive, The / Art Archive, The
p. 435: © "Fine Art Images" / Fine Art Images
p. 436: majeczka/Shutterstock
p. 437: Fine Art Images / Fine Art Images
p. 440: Fine Art Images / Fine Art Images
p. 441: Fine Art Images / Fine Art Images
p. 442: Art Resource, NY. © 2016 Succession H. Matisse / Artists Rights Society (ARS), New York
p. 443: V&A Images, London / Art Resource, NY. © 2016 ADAGP, Paris / Avec l'aimable autorisation de M. Pierre Bergé, président du Comité Jean Cocteau
p. 446: Art Archive, The / Art Archive, The
p. 447: Album / Art Resource, NY
p. 448: Iberfoto / Iberfoto. © 2016 Artists Rights Society (ARS), New York / ADAGP, Paris
p. 451: DeAgostini / DeAgostini
p. 452: Alfredo Dagli Orti / The Art Archive at Art Resource, NY
p. 453: Album / Documenta / Album
p. 454: Fine Art Images / Fine Art Images
p. 463: DeAgostini / DeAgostini
p. 467: robertharding / robertharding
p. 468: Gianni Dagli Orti / The Art Archive at Art Resource, NY
p. 469: hxdbzxy/Shutterstock
p. 469: Pantheon / Pantheon
p. 470: Album / Documenta / Album
p. 473: Fine Art Images / Fine Art Images
p. 477: © North Wind Picture Archives / Alamy Stock Photo
p. 478: National Portrait Gallery, Smithsonian Institution / Art Resource, NY
p. 479: Granger Historical Picture Archve / Alamy Stock Photo
p. 479: Library of Congress Prints and Photographs Division Washington, D.C. 20540 USA
p. 480: National Portrait Gallery, Smithsonian Institution / Art Resource, NY
p. 483: From The New York Public Library
p. 483: From The New York Public Library
p. 487: Music Division, The New York Public Library for the Performing Arts, Astor, Lenox and Tilden Foundations
p. 490: Culver Pictures, Inc. / Culver Pictures, Inc.
p. 490: Fine Art Images / Fine Art Images
p. 492: AF archive / Alamy Stock Photo
p. 495: Library of Congress Prints and Photographs Division Washington, D.C. 20540 USA
p. 498: Library of Congress Prints and Photographs Division Washington, D.C. 20540 USA
p. 499: Photographs and Prints Division, Schomburg Center for Research in Black Culture, The New York Public Library, Astor, Lenox and Tilden Foundations
p. 499: From The New York Public Library
p. 500: neftali/Shutterstock
p. 501: Library of Congress Prints and Photographs Division Washington, D.C. 20540 USA
p. 504: Granamour Weems Collection / Alamy Stock Photo
p. 505: Library of Congress Prints and Photographs Division Washington, D.C. 20540 USA
p. 508: Library of Congress Prints and Photographs Division Washington, D.C. 20540 USA
p. 509: William P. Gottlieb Collection (Library of Congress).
p. 512: New York World-Telegram and the Sun Newspaper Photograph Collection (Library of Congress)

p. 512: © EyeBrowz / Alamy Stock Photo
p. 516: Library of Congress Prints and Photographs Division Washington, D.C. 20540 USA
p. 516: Culver Pictures, Inc. / Culver Pictures, Inc.
p. 516: AF archive / Alamy Stock Photo
p. 518: Photononstop / Photononstop
p. 518: LUCASFILM/Allstar Picture Library
p. 521: Museum of the City of New York / The Art Archive at Art Resource, NY
p. 522: Library of Congress, Photographer: Victor Kraft. (Music Division)
p. 522: MIRISCH-7 ARTS/UNITED ARTISTS / Album / Album
p. 523: SuperStock / SuperStock
p. 526: White House Photo / Alamy Stock Photo
p. 527: AF archive / Alamy Stock Photo
p. 528: © CBW / Alamy Stock Photo
p. 529: AP
p. 530: Album / Oronoz / Album. © 2016 The Pollock-Krasner Foundation / Artists Rights Society (ARS), New York
p. 532: Bettman/Getty Images
p. 533: ZUMA Press, Inc. / Alamy Stock Photo
p. 533: Bettman/Getty Images
p. 536: Albert Veress/Shutterstock
p. 540: National Portrait Gallery
p. 540: By permission of the Family of Ruth Crawford and Charles Louis Seeger
p. 541: Photo by Mark Kauffman/The LIFE Images Collection/Getty Images
p. 544: CTK via AP Images
p. 545: AP Photo/Jessica Hill
p. 548: © SPUTNIK / Alamy Stock Photo
p. 556: Photographs and Prints Division, Schomburg Center for Research in Black Culture, The New York Public Library, Astor, Lenox and Tilden Foundations

Index

Numbers in italics indicate an illustration; numbers with a *t* indicate a table and with an *f* indicate a figure.